Principles of Microeconomics
Version 9.0

John B. Taylor and Akila Weerapana

978-1-4533-3496-6

Principles of Microeconomics
Version 9.0

John B. Taylor and Akila Weerapana

Published by:

FlatWorld
292 Newbury Street
Suite #282
Boston, MA 02115-2832

Gen: 202010071831

Brief Contents

Contents

About the Authors

John B. Taylor

John B. Taylor is one of the field's most inspiring teachers. As the Raymond Professor of Economics at Stanford University, his distinctive instructional methods have made him a legend among introductory economics students and have won him both the Hoagland and Rhodes prizes for teaching excellence.

Professor Taylor is also widely recognized for his research on the foundations of modern monetary theory and policy. One of his well-known research contributions is a rule—now widely called the Taylor Rule—used at central banks around the world.

Taylor has had an active career in public service, including a four-year stint as the head of the International Affairs division at the United States Treasury, where he had responsibility for currency policy, international debt, and oversight of the International Monetary Fund and the World Bank and worked closely with leaders and policymakers from countries throughout the world. He has also served as economic adviser to the governor of California, to the U.S. Congressional Budget Office, and to the President of the United States and has served on several boards and as a consultant to private industry.

Professor Taylor began his career at Princeton, where he graduated with highest honors in economics. He then received his Ph.D. from Stanford and taught at Columbia, Yale, and Princeton before returning to Stanford.

Akila Weerapana

Akila Weerapana is an Associate Professor of Economics at Wellesley College. He was born and raised in Sri Lanka and came to the United States to do his undergraduate work at Oberlin College, where he earned a B.A. with highest honors in Economics and Computer Science in 1994. He received his Ph.D. in Economics from Stanford in 1999, writing his dissertation on monetary economics under the mentorship of John Taylor.

Since then, Professor Weerapana has taught in the Economics Department at Wellesley College. His teaching interests span all levels of the department's curriculum, including introductory and intermediate macroeconomics, international finance, monetary economics, and mathematical economics. He was awarded Wellesley's Pinanski Prize for Excellence in Teaching in 2002.

He also enjoys working with thesis students. In addition to teaching, Professor Weerapana has research interests in macroeconomics, specifically in the areas of monetary economics, international finance, and political economy.

Acknowledgments

Completing a project like this is a team effort, and we both have been blessed with good students and colleagues who have given us advice and encouragement.

John B. Taylor

I am grateful to many colleagues and students, whom I have consulted over the years, including Don Brown, Tim Breshanan, Marcelo Clerici-Arias, Anne Kreuger, Tom McCurdy, Paul Milgrom, Roger Noll, John Pencavel, Paul Romer, Nate Rosenberg, Mark Tendell and Frank Wolak. I must acknowledge with very special gratitude Akila's partnership in this project. Akila first demonstrated his extraordinary teaching and writing skills even before completing his PhD at Stanford. After receiving his PhD, Akila joined the faculty at Wellesley College, where he has taught the Principles course for many semesters and further established his reputation for teaching excellence, and in 2002, received the Anna and Samuel Pinanski Teaching Award. His ability to get complex topics across to his students and his enthusiasm for bringing policy implications alive is clearly reflected in our new coauthored book.

Akila Weerapana

I am exceedingly grateful to John for giving me the opportunity to communicate my enthusiasm for teaching economics to a broader audience than the students in my classes at Wellesley. My passion for economics stems from the inspiration I received from my economics professors: Barbara Craig and Peter Montiel at the undergraduate level, and John Taylor, Frank Wolak, and Chad Jones at the graduate level. I too have benefited immensely from working with my colleagues. The faculty members in the Economics Department at Wellesley live up to the liberal arts ideal that I aspire to, combining excellent teaching with active research. Special thanks are owed to the late Chip Case, Courtney Coile and David Lindauer for the time they spent helping me understand how best to pitch topics in microeconomics that I am less familiar with teaching than they are. The real inspirations for this book, however, are the students that I have taught over the past two decades—two years at Stanford, but especially, the last seventeen years at Wellesley. Without their enthusiasm for economics, their willingness to be continually challenged, and their need to better understand an ever-changing world, none of this would be possible. My contributions to this book are shaped by countless hours spent talking economics with my students.

Together

Together, we would also like to thank William B. Stronge of Florida Atlantic University, who provided wonderful end-of-chapter problems that are conceptually challenging and require students to think more deeply about the concepts. Bill's efforts helped us meet an incredibly demanding schedule, and we are grateful for his contributions. Numerous reviewers provided insights, suggestions, and feedback along the way—often at critical points in product and supplement development. These individuals include Mohsen Bahmani-Oskooee, University of Wisconsin, Milwaukee; Erik Craft, University of Richmond; David H. Eaton, Murray State University; Lewis Freiberg, Northeastern Illinois University; Wang Fuzhong, Beijing University of Aeronautics & Astronautics; Janet Gerson, University of Michigan; Lisa Grobar, California State University, Long Beach; Ritika Gugnani, Jaipuria Institute of Management (Noida); Gautam Hazarika, University of Texas, Brownsville; Aaron Johnson, Missouri State University; Jacob Kurien, Rockhurst University; Babu Nahata, University of Louisville; Soloman Namala, Cerritos College; Sebastien Oleas, University of Minnesota, Duluth; Greg Pratt, Mesa Community College; Virginia Reilly, Ocean County College; Brian Rosario, University of California, Davis; William B. Stronge, Florida Atlantic University; Della Lee Sue, Marist College; J. S. Uppal, State University of New York, Albany; Michele T. Villinski, DePauw University; and Laura Wolff, Southern Illinois University, Edwardsville. We are grateful to Sarah L. Stafford of the College of William and Mary and Robert J. Rossana of Wayne State University for their detailed and timely accuracy checks of the main texts and several key supplements. We are especially appreciative of the contributions of the Sixth Edition supplements authors for their creativity, dedication, and careful coordination of content; this group includes Sarah E. Culver, University of Alabama, Birmingham; David H. Eaton, Murray State University; John Kane, State University of New York, Oswego; Jim Lee, Texas A&M University, Corpus Christi; John S.Min, Northern Virginia Community College; Wm. Stewart Mounts, Jr., Mercer University; David H. Papell, University of Houston; Virginia Reilly, Ocean County College Center for Economic Education; Brian Rosario, University of California, Davis; John Solow, University of Iowa; William B. Stronge, Florida Atlantic University; Eugenio D. Suarez, Trinity University; and Laura Wolff, Southern Illinois University, Edwardsville. We would also like to thank Edward Gullason of Dowling College for reviewing many of these supplements and Matthew Berg and Julia Ong for copyediting them.

Reviewers

- Matthew Alford, Southeastern Louisiana University
- Charles Anderson, Kean University
- Len Anyanwu, Union County College
- Kenneth Ardon, Salem State College
- Sukhwinder Bagi, Bloomsburg University
- Gaurango Banerjee, University of Texas at Brownsville
- Kevin Beckwith, Salem State College
- Charles A. Bennett, Gannon University
- Derek Berry, Calhoun Community College
- Charles Bondi, Morgan State University
- Joyce Bremer, Oakton Community College
- Amy Chataginer, MS Gulf Coast Community College

- Paul Clement, Fashion Institute of Technology-SUNY
- Marcelo Clerici-Arias, Stanford University
- Barbara Collister-Priestley, Concordia University Ann Arbor
- Mitchell Dudley, The College of William & Mary
- Dr. J. Pat Fuller, Brevard CC
- Cynthia Gamez, The University of Texas at El Paso
- Lara Gardner, Southeastern Louisiana University
- Dale Garrett, Evangel University
- Satyajit Ghosh, University of Scranton
- Sarah Ghosh, University of Scranton
- Alan Gin, University of San Diego
- Judith Grenkowicz, Kirtland Community College
- Curry Hilton, Guilford Technical Community College
- James Holcomb, University of Texas at El Paso
- Gokhan Karahan, Delta State University
- Ghebre Keleta, Grambling State University
- Deborah Kelly, University of San Diego
- Tori Knight, Carson-Newman College
- Viju Kulkarni, Mesa College
- Sonja Langley, Prairie View A&M University
- Sang Lee, Southeastern Louisiana University
- Charles Link, University of Delaware
- Linda Loubert, Morgan State University
- Farzin Madjidi, Pepperdine University/GSEP
- Tim McCabe, Tompkins Cortland Community College
- Todd McFall, Wake Forest University
- Daniel Morvey, Piedmont Technical College
- Shahriar Mostashari, Campbell University
- Francis Mummery, Fullerton College
- Pattabiraman Neelakantan, East Stroudsburg University
- Ogbonnaya Nwoha, Grambling State University
- Olugbenga Onafowora, Susquehanna University
- Chuck Parker, Wayne State College
- Van Pham, Salem State College
- Roxana Postolache, Capital University
- Rahim Quazi, Prairie View A&M University
- MG Quibria, Morgan State University
- David Rodgers, Northwestern Connecticut Community College
- S. Scanlon Romer, Delta College
- Daniel Saros, Valparaiso University
- Mark Scanlan, Stephen F. Austin State University
- Ted Scheinman, Mt. Hood Community College
- Virginia Shingleton, Valparaiso University
- Noel Smith, Palm Beach State College

- Donald Sparks, The Citadel
- Mark Steckbeck, Campbell University
- TaMika Steward, Tarrant County College
- Chin-Chyuan Tai, Averett University
- Robert Tansky, St. Clair Community College
- Jill Trask, Tarrant County College
- Margie Vance, North Arkansas College
- Lisa Verdon, College of Wooster
- Ann Wimmer, Iowa Lakes Community College
- Benaiah YongoBure, Kettering University
- Ildiko Roth, North Idaho College

Preface

Our goal in this book is to present modern economics in a form that is intuitive, relevant, and memorable to students who have had no prior exposure to the subject. We both teach introductory economics—Taylor at Stanford, Weerapana at Wellesley—and we enjoy teaching greatly. We especially enjoy interacting with students in the classroom as we endeavor to make the basic economic ideas as clear and understandable as possible. In this book we aim for that same clarity and teacher-student interaction, often imagining that we are talking with students or responding to their questions as we write.

The New Economics from Generation to Generation

We remember what it was like when we first took introductory economics—Taylor in the 1960s, Weerapana in the 1990s. People called 1960s-vintage economics the "new economics," because many new ideas, including those put forth by John Maynard Keynes, were being applied to public policy for the first time. By the 1990s there was a "new" new economics, stressing incentives, expectations, long-run fundamentals, institutions, and the importance of stable, predictable economic policies. In the 1980s and 1990s, the United States experienced far fewer recessions than in the 1960s and 1970s and the recessions were relatively short and mild.

But instability returned with the crisis and recession of 2007–2009—one of the longest and deepest in American history. The recession, and the long drawn-out recovery from the recession, caused a great deal of harm to millions of people. In the first decade of the twenty-first century, the global financial crisis, the great recessions in the United States and Europe, and explosive growth in emerging markets required a re-examination of whether the traditional frameworks needed to be augmented to explain this new reality, presenting new challenges and opportunities for instructors of introductory economics.

Economists engaged in a vigorous debate about what caused the crisis and how best to prevent future crises. After the recession ended, they grappled with whether the slow growth in the United States was in fact "the new normal." The concerns were not restricted to the United States, China's economy showed signs of slowing from the torrid pace it has sustained for much of the past two decades. The move towards closer economic integration in Europe suffered a devastating blow in 2016 from the Brexit vote, adding to the strains that had been placed on the Eurozone by the Greek debt crisis which neared the end of its 7th year with little relief in sight for the people of Greece, experiencing a downturn that resembled the Great Depression in terms of the depth and length of economic impact.

In this edition, we give these and other recent developments a prominent, clearly explained place within the basic tradition of economics. We emphasize the central idea of economics: that people make purposeful choices with scarce resources and interact with other people when they make these choices. We explain this idea using examples of choices that students actually face. We give real-world examples of how markets work, and we explain why markets are efficient when the incentives are right and inefficient when the incentives are wrong. We stress long-run fundamentals, but we also discuss current public policy issues relating to the crisis where the short run matters. The big policy questions about the role of government being debated by economists and others today receive special attention. We know from our teaching experience that examples of how economic ideas are used in practice make economics more interesting to students, thereby making learning economics easier.

A Brief Tour

Recognizing that teachers use a wide variety of sequences and syllabi, *Principles of Economics* allows for alternative plans of coverage. Furthermore, the text is also available in two self-contained volumes, *Principles of Microeconomics* and *Principles of Macroeconomics*. The following is a description of the *Principles of Economics* volume.

The basic workings of markets and the reasons they improve people's lives are the subjects of the first seven chapters. Chapter 1 outlines the unifying themes of economics: scarcity, choice, and economic interaction. The role of prices, the inherent international aspect of economics, the importance of property rights and incentives, and the difference between central planning and markets are some of the key ideas in this chapter. Chapter 2 introduces the field of economics through a case study showing how economists observe and explain economic puzzles. Chapters 3 and 4 cover the basic supply and demand model and elasticity. Here, the goal is to show how to use the supply and demand model to make sense of the world—and to learn how to "think like an economist." A trio of chapters—5, 6, and 7—explains why competitive markets are efficient, perhaps the most important idea in economics. The parallel exposition of utility maximization (Chapter 5) and profit maximization (Chapter 6) culminates in a detailed description of why competitive markets are efficient (Chapter 7). The inclusion of interesting results from experimental economics plays a dual role: to illustrate how well models work, and to make the discussion of these important topics less abstract.

A modern market economy is not static; rather, it grows and changes over time as firms add new and better machines and as people add to their skills and training. Chapters 8 and 9 describe how firms and markets grow and change over time. Chapters 10 and 11 demonstrate how economists model the behavior of firms that are not perfectly competitive, such as monopolies. The models of dynamic behavior and imperfect competition developed here are used to explain the rise and fall of real-world firms and industries. Chapter 12 reviews the policy implications. Chapter 13 considers labor markets. Chapters 14 and 15 are devoted to the role of government in the economy. Tax policy, welfare reform, environmental policy, and the role of government in producing public goods are analyzed. Different countries have taken widely different approaches to the economy. The policy of some countries has been to intervene directly in virtually every economic decision; other countries have followed more hands-off policies. The problem of government failure is analyzed using models of government behavior. Chapter 16 discusses capital markets.

The study of macroeconomics begins with Chapter 17. This chapter gives an overview of the facts, emphasizing that macroeconomics is concerned with the growth and fluctuations in the economy as a whole. The overall structure of the book is to begin by introducing students to key macroeconomic variables, how they are measured and what their limitations are, then discuss economic growth, followed by economic fluctuations before moving on to discussing financial markets and economic interconnections between countries.

Chapter 18 shows how GDP and other variables are measured. Chapter 19 starts with the first macro model to determine the long run shares of GDP, illustrating how saving and investment are interrelated in the economy. Chapter 20 gives an analysis of how the level of unemployment in the economy as a whole is determined, concluding the discussion of key macroeconomic variables.

Labor, capital, and technology are then presented in Chapter 21 as the fundamental determinants of the economy's growth path. One clear advantage of this approach is that it allows students to focus first on issues about which there is general agreement among economists. Moreover, this ordering helps students better understand short-term economic fluctuations. Similarly, the long-run treatment of money, presented in Chapter 22, sets the stage for the discussion of economic fluctuations.

Chapters 23–25 focus on how the economy fluctuates even as it grows over time. Declines in production and increases in unemployment (characteristics of recessions) have not vanished from the landscape as long-term growth issues have come to the fore. These chapters delve into the causes of these fluctuations and propose an analysis of why they end. Chapters 26 and 27 take a deep dive into the world of macroeconomic policy, first fiscal policy and then monetary policy. These chapters discuss how policy can be used to minimize the impact of economic fluctuations but also point out some of the debates that economists engage in as they assess whether policy has been successful at achieving the overall goal of smoothing out fluctuations.

The last decade and a half have taught us that financial markets and global economic linkages are key elements of the world that today's students of economics will grow up to live in. Chapter 28 discusses economic growth, development and convergence around the world while Chapters 29 and 30 aim to equip students with a better understanding of how and why goods and money are traded among countries. When issues about which there are many differing opinions arise, the text tries to explain these opinions as clearly and as objectively as possible; it also stresses the areas of agreement.

We hope you enjoy learning economics from this textbook. We are always receptive to feedback and eager to hear from users of the text (instructors and students) about their experience and welcome feedback about how to present material in a way that is more instructive to the reader.

Pedagogical Features

Examples within the text. Illustrations of real-world situations help explain economic ideas and models. We have attempted to include a wide variety of brief examples and case studies throughout the text.

Examples to give real-life perspectives. Stimulating vignettes appear at the beginning of each chapter. Examples of opening vignettes include explanation of economic events such as the price of Super Bowl tickets and discussions on how the United Nations evaluated the Millennium Development Goals it established at the dawn of the new millennium. Complete captions and small conversation boxes in graphs are also included. The captions and shaded conversation boxes make many of the figures completely self-contained. In some graphs, sequential numbering of these conversation boxes stresses the dynamic nature of the curves.

Use of photos to illustrate abstract ideas. Special care has gone into the search for and selection of photos to illustrate difficult economic ideas, such as inelastic supply curves or opportunity costs. Many text photos or photo spreads have short titles and captions to explain their relevance to the text discussion.

Key term definitions. Definitions of key terms appear in the margins next to where the key term is presented in the text and are listed in the index, complete with page references.

Brief reviews appear at the end of each major section. These reviews summarize the key points in abbreviated form as the chapter evolves; they are useful for preliminary skim reading as well as for review.

Questions for review appear at the end of every chapter. These are tests of recall and require only short answers; they can be used for oral review or as a quick self-check.

Problems. An essential tool in learning economics, the problems have been carefully selected, revised, and tested for this edition. An ample supply of these problems appears at the end of every chapter and appendix. Some of the problems ask the reader to work out examples that are slightly different from the ones given in the text; others require a more critical thinking approach.

What's New in Version 9.0?

- Many graphs are now hyperlinked to the underlying Federal Reserve Economic Data (FRED) source. Students can become familiar with manipulating FRED data and easily link to the most updated FRED data for each graph.
- Key updates to this version include:
  - Can AI and machine learning improve resource allocations? (Chapter 1)
  - Netflix pricing and demand elasticity. (Chapter 4)
  - Google as a monopoly. (Chapter 10)
  - Antitrust developments (RiteAid/Walgreens, Amazon, Apple, Google, and Facebook). (Chapter 12)
  - Net neutrality and differential rate pricing. (Chapter 12)
  - Tax discussions updated to align with Tax Cut and Jobs Act of 2017. (Chapter 14)
  - Updates specific to the COVID-19 pandemic throughout include:
    - New boxed feature on "The Price System During National Disasters." (Chapter 1 Section 3)
    - Clear illustration of differences between correlation and causation using impact of the pandemic on gas prices and miles traveled. (Chapter 2 Section 2)
    - Ventilators and impact of demand on pricing. (Chapter 3)
    - Price elasticity of supply for scarce goods in a crisis. (Chapter 4 Section 4)
    - Profile of the company that produces Purell hand sanitizer. (Chapter 6)
    - Business challenges resulting from the initial shutdown response to the pandemic. (Chapter 8)
    - Expanded discussion of long-run equilibrium to encompass firms impacted by the pandemic. (Chapter 9 Section 2)
    - Hazard pay considerations and compensating differentials. (Chapter 13 Section 5)
    - Unemployment insurance during the pandemic. (Chapter 14 Section 2)
    - Social distancing and mask wearing as positive externalities. Subsidies for encouraging use of masks and sanitizers. (Chapter 15 Section 2 and Chapter 15 Section 3)
    - Impact of pandemic responses on early 2020 stock returns. (Chapter 16)

CHAPTER 1
The Central Idea

At the center of **economics** is the idea that people make *purposeful choices* with *scarce resources* and interact with others when they make these choices. Sometimes those choices that people make have substantial impacts on the global economy. Consider Mark Zuckerberg, the founder and CEO of Facebook. He faced a big choice when he was in college in 2004: that is, whether to finish his degree or to drop out and devote all his time to transforming a novel idea into a start-up firm. Completing college while pursuing the start-up was not an option, because time is scarce, only 24 hours in a day. He did not have enough time to do both activities and sleep a bit, so he had to make a choice. In choosing one activity, he would have to incur the cost of giving up the other activity. Dropping out of college would mean passing up a degree that would help him get a good job, but staying in college would mean he could not start up a new firm.

> **economics**
>
> The study of how people deal with scarcity.

Zuckerberg chose to drop out of college, and it looks like he made the right choice: His firm, Facebook, is now worth billions of dollars and provides a social media platform that connects hundreds of millions of people all over the world. Or consider the story of Elon Musk, the founder and CEO of Tesla and SpaceX among other companies. Musk chose to stay in college and earned not one but two degrees—one in economics and one in physics—at the University of Pennsylvania, choosing to extend his time spent in college to five years. He joined the PhD program in Physics at Stanford University, but then decided to leave the program in a matter of days, choosing instead to join the entrepreneurial start-up culture of neighboring Silicon Valley. The resulting companies that Elon Musk founded have expanded the technological frontier of the economy over the past decade.

Of course, not every successful choice involves dropping out of college! In most cases, the choice to stay in school and pursue an education is what pays off. Consider the story of the late Maryam Mirzakhani. She was a mathematical prodigy growing up in Iran, where she won two gold medals at the International Mathematical Olympiad. After completing her undergraduate education in Iran, Mirzakhani had to make a choice about whether to continue her mathematical studies and also about where to pursue those further studies. She chose to pursue her PhD at Harvard, became a professor at Stanford, and in 2014 was the first woman to win the prestigious Fields Medal in Mathematics, considered by some to be an achievement harder than winning a Nobel Prize in an academic discipline.

FIGURE 1.1 A Man Who Made a Purposeful Choice

Mark Zuckerberg, founder and CEO of Facebook, had a great idea. However, bringing this idea to fruition would require so much of his time that he had to make a choice about how to allocate his scarce time resources. Should he finish his degree at Harvard? Or drop out to grow his new start-up company?

Source: catwalker/Shutterstock.com

The purposeful choices that these remarkable people made were magnified by the opportunities they had to interact with people. Hundreds of millions of people around the world interact through Facebook. Facebook benefits from this interaction, too, in part because people pay to advertise products on their site. Mirzakhani's discoveries have inspired other mathematicians and researchers in other areas like physics and engineering to make more discoveries. The electric cars produced by Tesla and the positive experiences of Tesla drivers has inspired many other manufacturers to pursue the use of electric motors in cars and to pursue other forms of technological advances such as driverless cars.

scarcity

The situation in which the quantity of resources is insufficient to meet all wants.

choice

A selection among alternative goods, services, or actions.

economic interactions

Exchanges of goods and services between people.

market

An arrangement by which economic exchanges between people take place.

Scarcity is a situation in which people's resources are limited. People always face a scarcity of some sort. Scarcity implies that people must make a **choice** to forgo, or give up, one thing in favor of another. The successes of Mirzakhani, Musk and Zuckerberg also reflect purposeful choices that other individuals, organizations, firms and governments made with scarce resources. Harvard University had to decide who received admission to the select few openings in their PhD program, venture capitalists in Silicon Valley had to decide which of the many hundreds of entrepreneurs asking for their financial investments were the most worthy recipients, thousands of college students had to decide that they needed to take a study break on a regular basis to connect with their friends, the government of Iran had to decide how much funding to allocate to their universities to allow young talented students like Maryam Mirzakhani to achieve their full potential, and the government of the United States had to decide how many immigrants—like the South African–born Musk and the Iranian-born Mirzakhani—should be granted the opportunity to become American citizens and make contributions to the economy and the country. As you read this text, you may find yourself reflecting on decisions that you have to make—whether to major in economics or biology, whether to take all your classes after 10:00 A.M. or to schedule them all before noon, whether to search the Internet or to study.

Economic interactions between people occur every time they trade or exchange goods with each other. A college student buys education services from a university in exchange for tuition. A teenager sells labor services to Taco Bell in exchange for cash. Within a household, one member may agree to cook dinner in exchange for the other person agreeing to wash the dishes. Economic interactions typically take place in a **market**. A market is simply an arrangement by which buyers and sellers can interact and exchange goods and services with each other. There are many types of markets, ranging from the New York stock market to a local flea market. Interactions do not have to take place with the buyer and seller in physical proximity to each other; the Internet, for example, greatly enhances the opportunities for economic interaction.

 ### Scarce versus Free Resources

Economics is the study of the allocation of scarce resources.

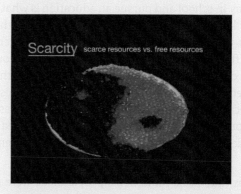

View the video online at: http://www.youtube.com/embed/iy-fhpbTH9E?rel=0

The purpose of this book is to introduce you to the field of economics, to provide you with the knowledge that will help you understand how so much of what happens in the world is shaped by the actions of people who had to make choices when confronted by scarcity. A better understanding of economics will equip you to handle the opportunities and challenges you face—should you continue with schooling if the economy is weak and it is hard to find a job? It also will leave you better informed about the challenges that the nation faces—should the government intervene in the economy to regulate businesses, or should it provide economic stimulus packages to help the economy? Soon you will find yourself viewing the world through the lens of economics. Your friends may tell you that you are "thinking like an economist." You should take that as a compliment. The first step on this path is to understand the enormous power of the central ideas of scarcity, choice, and economic interactions. That's the purpose of this chapter.

1.1 Scarcity and Choice for Individuals

It is easy to find everyday examples of how people make purposeful choices when they are confronted with a scarcity of time or resources. A choice that may be on your mind when you study economics is how much time to spend on these studies versus other activities. If you spend all your time on economics, you may get a 100 percent on the final exam, but a 0 percent in biology. If you spend all your time on biology, then you may get a 100 percent in biology and a 0 percent in economics. Most people resolve the choice by balancing out their time to get a decent grade in both subjects. If you are pre-med, then you probably will devote more time to biology. If you are interested in business, then devoting more time to economics might be appropriate.

Now let us apply this basic principle to two fundamental economic problems: individual choices about what to *consume* and what to *produce*. For each type of economic problem, we first show how scarcity forces one to make a choice, and then we show how people gain from interacting with other people.

Consumer Decisions

Consider Maria, who is going for a walk in a park on a sunny day. Maria would love to wear a hat (baseball style with her school logo) and sunglasses on the walk, but she forgot them at home. Maria has brought $20 with her, however, and there is a store in the park that is having a "two-for-one" sale. She can buy two hats for $20 or two pairs of sunglasses for $20. She would prefer to buy one hat and pair of sunglasses, but that is not possible. Her scarcity of funds causes her to make a choice. The $20 limit on her spending is an example of a *budget constraint*, a scarcity of funds that limits her to spending no more than this amount. Her choice will depend on her tastes. Let us assume that when she is forced by scarcity to make a choice, she will choose the sunglasses.

Opportunity Cost

Maria's decision is an example of an economic problem that all people face: A budget constraint forces them to make a choice between different items that they want. Choosing one item means that you have to give up other items. The **opportunity cost** of a choice is the value of the next-best forgone alternative that was not chosen. The opportunity cost of the hats is the loss from not being able to wear the sunglasses. An opportunity cost occurs every time there is a choice. For example, the opportunity cost of waking up to attend an 8:00 A.M. class rather than sleeping in is the hours of sleep you lose when you get up early. The opportunity cost of Mark Zuckerberg's staying in college versus pursuing his start-up would have been the money he earned from Facebook. In many cases involving choice and scarcity, you have to choose from among many more than two options. If you choose vanilla ice cream out of a list of many possible flavors, then the opportunity cost is the loss from not being able to consume the *next-best* flavor, perhaps strawberry.

opportunity cost

The value of the next-best forgone alternative that was not chosen because something else was chosen.

Now, suppose Maria is not the only hiker. Also in the park is Adam, who also has $20 to spend. Adam also loves both hats and sunglasses, but he likes hats more than sunglasses. When forced to make a choice, he buys the hats. His decision is shaped by scarcity just as Maria's is: Scarcity comes from the budget constraint. He must make a choice, and each choice has an opportunity cost.

Gains from Trade: A Better Allocation

gains from trade

Improvements in income, production, or satisfaction owing to the exchange of goods or services.

Now suppose that Adam and Maria meet each other in the park. Let's consider the possibility of economic interaction between them. Maria has two pairs of sunglasses and Adam has two hats, so Maria and Adam can trade with each other. Maria can trade one of her pairs of sunglasses for one of Adam's hats, as shown in Figure 1.2. Through such a trade, both Maria and Adam can improve their situation. There are **gains from trade** because the trade reallocates goods between the two individuals in a way that they both prefer. Trade occurs because Maria is willing to exchange one pair of sunglasses for one hat, and Adam is willing to exchange one hat for one pair of sunglasses. Because trade is mutually advantageous for both Maria and Adam, they will voluntarily engage in it if they are able to. In fact, if they do not gain from the trade, then neither will bother to make the trade.

This trade is an example of an economic interaction in which a reallocation of goods through trade makes both people better off. The total quantity of goods produced does not change. The number of hats and sunglasses has remained the same. Trade simply reallocates existing goods.

The trade between Maria and Adam is typical of many economic interactions that we will study in this book. Thinking like an economist in this example means recognizing that a voluntary exchange of goods between people must make them better off. Many economic exchanges are like this, even though they are more complicated than the exchange of hats and sunglasses.

FIGURE 1.2 Gains from Trade through a Better Allocation of Goods
Without trade, Maria has more pairs of sunglasses than she would like, and Adam has more hats than he would like. By trading a hat for a pair of sunglasses, they both gain.

Producer Decisions

Now consider two producers—Emily, a poet, and Johann, a printer. Both face scarcity and must make choices. Because of differences in training, abilities, or inclination, Emily is much better at writing poetry than Johann is, but Johann is much better at printing greeting cards than Emily is.

If Emily writes poetry full time, she can produce 10 poems in a day; but if she wants to make and sell greeting cards with her poems in them, she must spend some time printing cards and thereby spend less time writing poems. However, Emily is not very good at printing cards; it takes her so much time to do so that if she prints one card, she has time to write only one poem rather than 10 poems during the day.

If Johann prints full time, he can produce 10 different greeting cards in a day. However, if he wants to sell greeting cards, he must write poems to put inside them. Johann is so bad at writing poems that if he writes only one poem a day, his production of greeting cards drops from 10 to one per day.

The following is a summary of the choices Emily and Johann face because of a scarcity of time and resources.

	Emily, the Poet		Johann, the Printer	
	Write Full Time	Write and Print	Print Full Time	Write and Print
Cards	0	1	10	1
Poems	10	1	0	1

If Emily and Johann cannot interact, then each can produce only one greeting card with a poem on the inside in a day. Alternatively, Emily could produce 10 poems without the cards and Johann could produce 10 cards without the poems, but then neither would earn anything. We therefore assume that when confronted with this choice, both Emily and Johann will each choose to produce, by themselves, one greeting card with a poem inside. In total, they produce two greeting cards.

Gains from Trade: Greater Production

Now consider the possibility of economic interaction. Suppose that Emily and Johann can trade. Johann could sell his printing services to Emily, agreeing to print her poems on nice greeting cards. Then Emily could sell the greeting cards to people. Under this arrangement, Emily could spend all day writing poetry, and Johann could spend all day printing. In total, they could produce 10 different greeting cards together, expending the same time and effort it took to produce two greeting cards when they could not trade.

Note that in this example the interaction took place in a market: Johann sold his print jobs to Emily. Another approach would be for Emily and Johann to go into business together, forming a firm, Dickinson and Gutenberg Greetings, Inc. Then their economic interaction would occur within the firm, without buying or selling in the market. Whether in a market or within a firm, the gains from trade in this example are huge. By trading, Emily and Johann can increase their production of greeting cards five fold, from two cards to 10 cards.

Specialization, Division of Labor, and Comparative Advantage

specialization

A concentration of production effort on a single specific task.

division of labor

The division of production into various parts in which different groups of workers specialize.

comparative advantage

A situation in which a person or group can produce one good at a lower opportunity cost than another person or group.

This example illustrates another way in which economic interaction improves people's lives. Economic interaction allows for **specialization**: people concentrating their production efforts on what they are good at. Emily specializes in poetry, and Johann specializes in printing. The specialization creates a **division of labor**. A division of labor occurs when some workers specialize in one task while others specialize in another task. They divide the overall production into parts, with some workers concentrating on one part (printing cards) and other workers concentrating on another part (writing poetry).

The writing-printing example of Emily and Johann also illustrates another economic concept, comparative advantage. In general, a person or group of people has a **comparative advantage** in producing one good relative to another good if that person or group can produce that good at a lower opportunity cost (in terms of the other good) than another person or group can produce that good. For example, compared with Johann, Emily has a comparative advantage in writing relative to printing because for her, writing 10 poems requires giving up only 1 print (Johann would have to give up 100 prints to write 10 poems). And compared with Emily, Johann has a comparative advantage in printing relative to writing because for him, printing 10 cards only requires giving up 1 poem (Emily would have to give up 100 poems to print 10 cards). As this example shows, production can be increased if people specialize in the skill in which they have a comparative advantage—that is, if Emily specializes in writing and Johann in printing.

 Opportunity Cost

The opportunity cost for consumers and producers is the value of the choice not taken.

View the video online at: http://www.youtube.com/embed/hR5E7Y4Dxuc?rel=0

International Trade

international trade

The exchange of goods and services between people or firms in different nations.

Thus far, we have said nothing about where Emily and Johann live or work. They could reside in the same country, but they also could reside in different countries. Emily could live in the United States; Johann, in Germany. If this is so, when Emily purchases Johann's printing service, **international trade** will take place because the trade is between people in two different countries.

The gains from international trade are thus of the same kind as the gains from trade within a country. By trading, people can better satisfy their preferences for goods (as in the case of Maria and Adam), or they can better utilize their comparative advantage (as in the case of Emily and Johann). In either situation, both participants can gain from trade.

Review

- All individuals face scarcity in one form or another. Scarcity forces people to make choices. For every choice that is made, there is also an opportunity cost of not doing one thing because another thing has been chosen.
- People benefit from economic interactions—trading goods and services—with other people.
- Gains from trade occur because goods and services can be allocated in ways that are more satisfactory to people.
- Gains from trade also occur because trade permits specialization through the division of labor. People should specialize in the production of goods in which they have a comparative advantage.

1.2 Scarcity and Choice for the Economy as a Whole

Just as individuals face scarcity and choice, so too does the economy as a whole. The total amount of resources in an economy—workers, land, machinery, and factories—is limited. Thus, the economy cannot produce all the health care, crime prevention, education, or entertainment that people want. A choice must be made. Let us first consider how to represent scarcity and choice in the whole economy and then consider alternative ways to make those choices.

Production Possibilities

To simplify things, let us suppose that production in the economy can be divided into two broad categories. Suppose the economy can produce either computers (laptops, desktops, servers) or movies (thrillers, love stories, mysteries, musicals). The choice between computers and movies is symbolic of one of the most fundamental choices individuals in any society must face: how much to invest to produce more or better goods in the future versus how much to consume in the present. Computers help people produce more or better goods. Movies are a form of consumption. Other pairs of goods also could be used in our example. Another popular example is guns versus butter, representing defense goods versus nondefense goods.

With a scarcity of resources, such as labor and capital, a choice exists between producing some goods, such as computers, versus other goods, such as movies. If the economy produces more of one, then it must produce less of the other. Table 1.1 gives an example of the alternative choices, or the **production possibilities**, for computers and movies. Observe that six different choices could be made, some with more computers and fewer movies, others with fewer computers and more movies.

Table 1.1 tells us what happens as available resources in the economy are moved from movie production to computer production or vice versa. If resources move from producing movies to producing computers, then fewer movies are produced. For example, if all of the resources are used to produce computers, then 25,000 computers and zero movies can be produced, according to the

production possibilities

Alternative combinations of production of various goods that are possible, given the economy's resources.

table. If all resources are used to produce movies, then no computers can be produced. These are two extremes, of course. If 100 movies are produced, then we can produce 24,000 computers rather than 25,000 computers. If 200 movies are produced, then computer production must fall to 22,000.

TABLE 1.1 Production Possibilities

	Movies	Computers
A	0	25,000
B	100	24,000
C	200	22,000
D	300	18,000
E	400	13,000
F	500	0

Increasing Opportunity Costs

The production possibilities in Table 1.1 illustrate the concept of opportunity cost for the economy as a whole. The opportunity cost of producing more movies is the value of the forgone computers. For example, the opportunity cost of producing 200 movies rather than 100 movies is 2,000 computers.

increasing opportunity costs

A situation in which producing more of one good requires giving up an increasing amount of production of another good.

An important economic idea about opportunity costs is demonstrated in Table 1.1. Observe that movie production increases as we move down the table. As we move from row to row, movie production increases by the same number: 100 movies. The decline in computer production between the first and second rows—from 25,000 to 24,000 computers—is 1,000 computers. The decline between the second and third rows—from 24,000 to 22,000 computers—is 2,000 computers. Thus, the decline in computer production gets greater as we produce more movies. As we move from 400 movies to 500 movies, we lose 13,000 computers. In other words, the opportunity cost, in terms of computers, of producing more movies increases as we produce more movies. Each extra movie requires a loss of more and more computers. What we have just described is called **increasing opportunity costs**, with an emphasis on the word *increasing*.

Why do opportunity costs increase? You can think about it in the following way. Some of the available resources are better suited for movie production than for computer production, and vice versa. Workers who are good at building computers might not be so good at acting, for example, or moviemaking may require an area with a dry, sunny climate. As more and more resources go into making movies, we are forced to take resources that are much better at computer making and use them for movie making. Adding specialized computer designers to a movie cast would be quite costly in terms of lost computers, and it might add little to movie production. Thus, more and more computer production must be lost to increase movie production by a given amount.

The Production Possibilities Curve

Figure 1.3 is a graphical representation of the production possibilities in Table 1.1 that nicely illustrates increasing opportunity costs. We put movies on the horizontal axis and computers on the vertical axis of the figure. Each pair of numbers in a row of the table becomes a point on the graph. For example, point *A* on the graph is from row A of the table. Point *B* is from row B, and so on.

When we connect the points in Figure 1.3, we obtain the **production possibilities curve**. This curve shows the maximum number of computers that can be produced for each quantity of movies produced. Note that the curve in Figure 1.3 slopes downward and is bowed out from the origin. That the curve is bowed out indicates that the opportunity cost of producing movies increases as more movies are produced. As resources move from computer making to movie making, each additional movie means a greater loss of computer production.

production possibilities curve

A curve showing the maximum combinations of production of two goods that are possible, given the economy's resources.

FIGURE 1.3 The Production Possibilities Curve
Each point on the curve shows the maximum number of computers that can be produced when a given amount of movies is produced. The points with letters are the same as those in Table 1.1 and are connected by smooth lines. Points in the shaded area inside the curve are inefficient. Points outside the curve are impossible. For the efficient points on the curve, the more movies that are produced, the fewer computers that are produced. The curve is bowed out because of increasing opportunity costs.

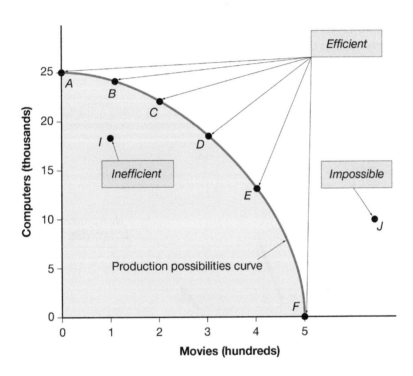

Inefficient, Efficient, or Impossible?

The production possibilities curve shows the effects of scarcity and choice in the economy as a whole. Three situations can be distinguished in Figure 1.3, depending on whether production is in the shaded area, on the curve, or outside the curve.

First, imagine production at point *I*. This point, with 100 movies and 18,000 computers, is inside the curve. But the production possibilities curve tells us that it is possible to produce more computers, more movies, or both with the same amount of resources. For some reason, the economy is not working well at point *I*. For example, a talented movie director may be working on a computer assembly line because her short film has not yet been seen by studio executives, or perhaps a financial crisis has prevented computer companies from getting loans and thus disrupted all production of computer chips. Points inside the curve, like point *I*, are *inefficient* because the economy could produce a larger number of movies, as at point *D*, or a larger number of computers, as at point *B*. Points inside the production possibilities curve are possible, but they are inefficient.

Second, consider points on the production possibilities curve. These points are *efficient*. They represent the maximum amount that can be produced with available resources. The only way to raise production of one good is to lower production of the other good. Thus, points on the curve show a *trade-off* between one good and another.

Third, consider points to the right and above the production possibilities curve, like point *J* in Figure 1.3. These points are *impossible*. The economy does not have the resources to produce those quantities.

Shifts in the Production Possibilities Curve

The production possibilities curve is not immovable. It can *shift* out or in. For example, the curve is shown to shift out in Figure 1.4. More resources—more workers, for example, or more cameras, lights, and studios—would shift the production possibilities curve out. A technological innovation that allowed one to edit movies faster also would shift the curve outward. When the production possibilities curve shifts out, the economy grows because more goods and services can be produced. The production possibilities curve need not shift outward by the same amount in all directions. The curve could move up more than it moves to the right, for example.

FIGURE 1.4 Shifts in the Production Possibilities Curve
The production possibilities curve shifts out as the economy grows. The maximum numbers of movies and computers that can be produced increase. Improvements in technology, more machines, or more labor permits the economy to produce more.

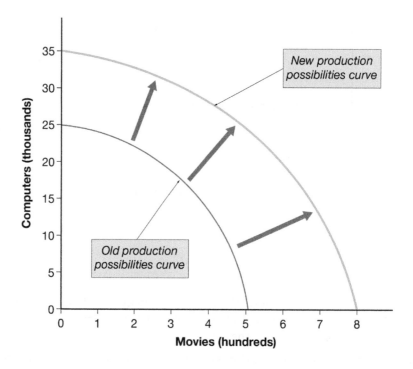

As the production possibilities curve shifts out, impossibilities are converted into possibilities. Some of what was impossible for the U.S. economy in 1975 is possible now. Some of what is impossible now will be possible in 2035. Hence, the economists' notion of possibilities is a temporary one. When we say that a certain combination of computers and movies is impossible, we do not mean "forever impossible," we mean only "currently impossible."

Scarcity, Choice, and Economic Progress

However, the conversion of impossibilities into possibilities is also an economic problem of choice and scarcity: If we invest less now—in machines, in education, in children, in technology—and consume more now, then we will have less available in the future. If we take computers and movies as symbolic of investment and consumption, then choosing more investment will result in a larger outward shift of the production possibilities curve, as illustrated in Figure 1.5. More investment enables the economy to produce more in the future.

The production possibilities curve represents a *trade-off*, but it does not mean that some people win only if others lose. First, it is not necessary for someone to lose in order for the production possibilities curve to shift out. When the curve shifts out, the production of both items increases. Although some people may fare better than others as the production possibilities curve is pushed out, no one necessarily loses. In principle, everyone can gain. Second, if the economy is at an inefficient point (like point *I* in Figure 1.3), then production of both goods can be increased with no trade-off. In general, therefore, the economy is more like a win-win situation, where everyone can achieve a gain.

FIGURE 1.5 Shifts in the Production Possibilities Curve Depend on Choices
On the left, few resources are devoted to investment for the future; hence, the production possibilities curve shifts only a little over time. On the right, more resources are devoted to investment and less to consumption; hence, the production possibilities curve shifts out by a larger amount over time.

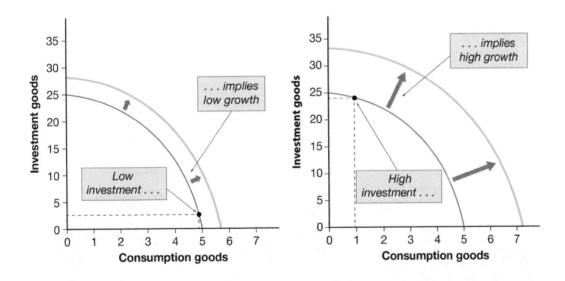

Review

- The production possibilities curve represents the choices open to a whole economy when it is confronted with a scarcity of resources. As more of one item is produced, less of another item must be produced. The opportunity cost of producing more of one item is the reduced production of another item.
- The production possibilities curve is bowed out because of increasing opportunity costs.
- Points inside the curve are inefficient. Points on the curve are efficient. Points outside the curve are impossible.

- The production possibilities curve shifts out as resources increase.
- Outward shifts of the production possibilities curve or moves from inefficient to efficient points are the reasons why the economy is not a zero-sum game, despite the existence of scarcity and choice.

1.3 Market Economies and the Price System

Every economy, whether it is a small island economy or a large economy like the United States, must find a way to solve three essential questions or problems.

- *What* is to be produced: movies, computers, guns, butter, greeting cards, Rollerblades, health care, or something else? In other words, where on the production possibilities curve should an economy be?

- *How* are these goods to be produced? In other words, how can an economy use the available resources so that it is not at an inefficient point inside the production possibilities curve?

- *For whom* are the goods to be produced? We know from the hat versus sunglasses example that the allocation of goods in an economy affects people's well-being. An economy in which Maria could not trade her sunglasses for a hat would not work as well as one in which such trades and reallocations are possible. Moreover, an economy in which some people get everything and others get virtually nothing also is not working well.

FIGURE 1.6 Three Fundamental Questions for Any Economic System
Any economic system has to answer three questions: What goods and services should be produced—cars, movies, or something else? How should these goods or services be produced—in what type of factory, and with how much equipment and labor? And for whom should these goods be produced?

What?   **How?**   **For whom?**

Source: MikeDotta/Shutterstock.com

Broadly speaking, the **market economy** and the **command economy** are two alternative approaches to answering these questions. In a market economy, most decisions about what, how, and for whom to produce are made by individual consumers, firms, governments, and other organizations interacting in markets. In a command, or centrally planned, economy, most decisions about what, how, and for whom to produce are made by those who control the government, which, through a central plan, commands and controls what people do.

Command economies are much less common in the twenty-first century than they were in the mid-twentieth century, when nearly half the world's population, including the residents of Eastern Europe, the Soviet Union, and China, lived in centrally planned economies. After many decades of struggling to make this system work, leaders of the command economies gradually grew disillusioned with the high degree of inefficiency resulting from the planned approach, which required that the state, or central planners, make critical detailed production decisions; this often resulted in shortages or surplus of products and, as a by-product, in political unrest. Since 1990, most command economies have, with varying degrees of success, tried to convert from a command to a market system. The difficulties with converting these systems are partly due to the fact that these economies have none or few of the social, legal, or political fixtures critical to the market system. China has been by far the most successful of these economies at making the transition, developing a model that the Chinese term "socialism with Chinese characteristics." Beginning in the 1970s, elements of both the command and market economies coexisted in China; in the mid-1990s, market mechanisms grew more dominant. In the twenty-first century, while its political system is still highly centralized, China's economy is much more decentralized. Many people credit China's rapid economic growth in recent years to its successful transition away from a centralized economic system.

market economy
An economy characterized by freely determined prices and the free exchange of goods and services in markets.
command economy
An economy in which the government determines prices and production also called a centrally planned economy.

Key Elements of a Market Economy

Let's take a closer look at some of the ingredients critical to a market economy.

Freely Determined Prices

In a market economy, most prices—such as the price of computers—are freely determined by individuals and firms interacting in markets. These **freely determined prices** are an essential characteristic of a market economy. In a command economy, most prices are set by government, and this leads to inefficiencies in the economy. For example, in the former Soviet Union, the price of bread was set so low that farmers fed bread to the cows. Feeding bread to livestock is an enormous waste of resources. Livestock could eat plain grain. By feeding the cows bread, farmers added the cost of the labor to bake the bread and the fuel to heat the bread ovens to the cost of livestock feed. This is inefficient, like point *I* in Figure 1.3.

freely determined prices
Prices that are determined by the individuals and firms interacting in markets.

In practice, not all prices in market economies are freely determined. For example, some cities control the price of rental apartments. We will look at these exceptions later. But the vast majority of prices are free to vary.

Property Rights and Incentives

Property rights are another key element of a market economy. **Property rights** give individuals the legal authority to keep or sell property, whether land or other resources. Property rights are needed for a market economy because they give people the ability to buy and sell goods. Without property rights, people could take whatever they wanted without paying. People would have to devote time and resources to protecting their earnings or goods.

property rights
Rights over the use, sale, and proceeds from a good or resource.

incentive

A device that motivates people to take action, usually to increase economic efficiency.

Moreover, by giving people the rights to the earnings from their work, as well as letting them suffer some of the consequences or losses from their mistakes, property rights provide an **incentive**. For example, if an inventor could not get the property rights to an invention, then the incentive to produce the invention would be low or even nonexistent. Hence, there would be few inventions, and we all would be worse off. If property rights did not exist, people would not have incentives to specialize and reap the gains from the division of labor. Any extra earnings from specialization could be taken away.

Freedom to Trade at Home and Abroad

Economic interaction is a way to improve economic outcomes, as the examples in this chapter indicate. Allowing people to interact freely is thus another necessary ingredient of a market economy. Freedom to trade can be extended beyond national borders to other economies.

International trade increases the opportunities to gain from trade. This is especially important in small countries, where it is impossible to produce everything. But the gains from exchange and comparative advantage also exist for larger countries.

A Role For Government

market failure

Any situation in which the market does not lead to an efficient economic outcome and in which the government has a potential role.

government failure

A situation in which the government fails to improve on the market or even makes things worse.

Just because prices are freely determined and people are free to trade in a market economy does not mean that there is no role for government. For example, in virtually all market economies, the government provides defense and police protection. The government also helps establish property rights. But how far beyond that should it go? Should the government also address the "for whom" question by providing a safety net—a mechanism to deal with the individuals in the economy who are poor, who go bankrupt, who remain unemployed? Most would say yes, but what should the government's role be? Economics provides an analytical framework to answer such questions. In certain circumstances—called **market failure**—the market economy does not provide good enough answers to the "what, how, and for whom" questions, and the government has a role to play in improving on the market. However, the government, even in the case of market failure, may do worse than the market, in which case economists say there is **government failure**.

The Role of Private Organizations

It is an interesting feature of market economies that many economic interactions between people take place in organizations—firms, families, charitable organizations—rather than in markets. Some economic interactions that take place in an organization also take place in a market. For example, many large firms employ lawyers as part of their permanent staff. Other firms simply purchase the services of such lawyers in the market; if the firm wants to sue someone or is being sued by someone, it hires an outside lawyer to represent it.

Economic interactions in firms differ from those in the market. Staff lawyers inside large firms are usually paid annual salaries that do not depend directly on the number of hours worked or their success in the lawsuits. In contrast, outside lawyers are paid an hourly fee and a contingency fee based on the number of hours worked and how successful they are.

Incentives within an organization are as important as incentives in markets. If the lawyers on a firm's legal staff get to keep some of the damages the firm wins in a lawsuit, they will have more incentive to do a good job. Some firms even try to create market-like competition between departments or workers in order to give more incentives.

Why do some economic interactions occur in markets and others in organizations? Ronald Coase of the University of Chicago won the Nobel Prize for showing that organizations such as firms are created to reduce market *transaction costs*, the costs of buying and selling, which include finding a buyer or a seller and reaching agreement on a price. When market transaction costs are high, we see more transactions taking place within organizations. For example, a firm might have a legal staff rather than outside lawyers because searching for a good lawyer every time there is a lawsuit is too costly. In a crisis, a good lawyer may not be available.

The Price System

The previous discussion indicates that in market economies, freely determined prices are essential for determining what is produced, how, and for whom. For this reason, a market economy is said to use *the price system* to solve these problems. In this section, we show that prices do a surprising amount of work: (1) Prices serve as *signals* about what should be produced and consumed when there are changes in tastes or changes in technology, (2) prices provide *incentives* to people to alter their production or consumption, and (3) prices affect the *distribution of income*, or who gets what in the economy.

Let's use an example. Suppose that there is a sudden new trend for college students to ride bicycles more and drive cars less. How do prices help people in the economy decide what to do in response to this new trend?

 ### The Information in Prices

Crop prices incentivize farmers to adjust their production by signaling which crops are in need.

View the video online at: http://www.youtube.com/embed/WPy-QKXofQs?rel=0

Signals

First, consider how the information about the change in tastes is signaled to the producers of bicycles and cars. As students buy more bicycles, the price of bicycles rises. A higher price will signal that it is more profitable for firms to produce more bicycles. In addition, some bicycle components, like lightweight metal, will also increase in price. Increased lightweight metal prices signal that production of lightweight metal should increase. As the price of metal rises, wages for metalworkers may increase. Thus, prices are a signal all the way from the consumer to the metalworkers that more bicycles should be produced. This is what is meant by the expression "prices are a signal."

It is important to note that no single individual knows the information that is transmitted by prices. Any economy is characterized by limited information, where people cannot know the exact reasons why prices for certain goods rise or fall. Hence, it is rather amazing that prices can signal this information.

Incentives

Now let's use this example to consider how prices provide incentives. A higher price for bicycles will increase the incentives for firms to produce bicycles. Because they receive more for each bicycle, they produce more. If there is a large price increase that is not merely temporary, new firms may enter the bicycle business. In contrast, the reduced prices for cars signal to car producers that production should decrease.

Distribution

How do prices affect the distribution of income? On the one hand, workers who find the production of the good they make increasing because of the higher demand for bicycles will earn more. On the other hand, income will be reduced for those who make cars or who have to pay more for bicycles. Local delivery services that use bicycles will see their costs increase.

Financial Crises and Recessions

financial crises

Disruptions to financial markets that make it difficult for people and business firms to borrow and obtain loans.

recession

A decline in production and employment that lasts for six months or more.

Economies are sometimes hit by **financial crises**. When the World Trade Center was destroyed by terrorists in September 2001, the financial markets in New York had to close down because trading rooms and electronic networks for making trades were destroyed. However, backup facilities were soon made operational and the markets reopened after only a few days. Fortunately, the financial crisis was over soon after it began.

In August 2007 another financial crisis began, but this one lasted much longer. A fall in home prices in 2006 and 2007 following a prior rapid rise caused people to stop making payments on their home loans; banks and other financial institutions then became reluctant to lend. As a result people throughout the economy had trouble getting loans, and they reduced their purchases of goods and services. This meant that firms had to cut production of these goods and services and they laid off people who were employed producing them. A **recession**—a period of declining production and employment—thus began in December 2007 and ended in June 2009.

Economies have been subject to financial crises and recessions for hundreds of years. By far the worst in the United States was the Great Depression of the 1930s, but comparably serious financial crises have occurred in other regions and countries, most recently in Latin America, Asia, and Russia in the 1990s. The 1980s and 1990s in the United States was a period of unusual financial calm with few recessions. There is a great debate about whether financial crises are inevitable—a kind of market failure where the market economy does not work well—and government has a role to play in trying to prevent them and mitigate them, or whether the crises are due to government actions which make things worse—a kind of government failure.

The Price System during National Disasters

Periodically, regions of the country are hit by natural disasters such as hurricanes, earthquakes, fires, or blizzards. In the aftermath of a disaster, or sometimes even during the buildup (for a foreseeable event), certain goods become scarce in the economy. Examples of genuine shortages of necessary goods include fuel, food, medicine, or water in a hurricane-zone or hand sanitizers, masks, and gloves during the COVID-19 crisis. Another reason for scarcity of goods is speculative buying, sometimes in anticipation of future shortages but other times just out of overreaction. Good examples of the latter include the panicked buying of toilet paper, bottled water, and canned food during the COVID-19 crisis when there was little reason to believe that the supply of these goods would be disrupted. Even when there was a potential explanation for increased purchases of some goods—for instance more people were using toilet paper at home because they were not going to work—the increase in purchases dwarfed the actual need for use of those goods.

When such a scarcity occurs, the price system has a critical role to play in allocating resources. Prices of scarce goods will rise, often quite substantially. As you will soon learn, this increase in price plays an important role in allocating the now-scarce resources but the resulting outcomes often lead to disgruntlement with the price system. When prices of essentials rise, those who are most willing and able to pay will have access to those goods whereas those who need the goods but are unable to pay the high prices will have to do without. When consumers see firms selling bottled water at prices that are ten times higher than prices during normal times, or see sellers on Amazon charging $50 for a bottle of hand sanitizer that usually sells for $4, they feel that they are being taken advantage of. Calls for investigations of price gouging behavior and the imposition of limits on price rises typically increase along with calls for suspending the use of the price system as a method of allocation and using an alternative method of allocation such as rationing.

By the time you finish this course in Economics, you will be able to better understand the complexity of this topic. For now, you should know that the price system has both advantages and disadvantages in allocating resources in the aftermath of a national disaster. For certain goods, higher prices can act as a signal that encourages firms to supply more to the affected region or for stores to stock up their inventories, for example adding more sandbags, bottled water, and camping stoves before a hurricane arrives. Price increases can also discourage hoarding and speculative buying by consumers, so for example, the people who bought what effectively will be 8 months-worth of toilet paper supply for their household may not have done so in the face of a price increase, leaving more available for others to buy. On the other hand, for goods where the production lags are long or supply chains complicated, there will be a limited supply response in response to price increases. This means that under-resourced buyers who genuinely need goods will not be able to access them. Examples of this include ventilators, N95 masks, and personal protective equipment (PPE) during the COVID-19 crisis. Worldwide demand for these goods spiked, prices rose sharply (news reports suggested that mask prices increased six-fold), and well-resourced, well-connected hospitals in rich areas were able to access these goods much more easily than poorer, rural hospitals were able to. Another example would be rationing of staple foods during World War II where people with no access to land for growing food or jobs for earning money were not able to pay the higher prices for food to meet their basic nourishment needs, but were able to do so with ration cards.

Artificial Intelligence, Economics, and the Price System

Artificial intelligence is a branch of computer science that focuses on building and using machines that react like humans, and often react much better than humans do in recognizing, for example, speech or faces. With machine learning, computers can also adapt automatically and change as circumstances change; for example, as people develop different speaking accents within the same language. Amazing improvements in artificial intelligence and machine learning have been made in recent years. Computers can quickly identify people, and they match them in giant data sets based only on photos. These advancements raise questions about economics—the study of people making purposeful choices with scarcity and interacting with other people when they make such choices. Students ask, perhaps after taking some computer science courses, "Do we really need economics anymore? Can't fast artificial intelligence examine preferences and allocate resources and people more efficiently than markets can and thus determine what, how, and for whom to produce?"

No. It's the opposite. Economics is more important now than ever as the world becomes more computerized and quantified. The price system itself becomes more valuable because prices of goods and services incorporate enormous amounts of relevant information that no one person, no one computer, can possibly incorporate. Prices convey information about what is happening throughout the world, they provide incentives to millions of people to act in various ways, and they affect the distribution of income. A central computer cannot possibly allocate people or resources efficiently without this information, certainly not in a way that takes account of the shifting preferences of millions of consumers and a technology that moves forward every day. Ignoring economics as we apply the latest in artificial intelligence and machine learning is a recipe for disaster.

At the same time, it's possible—as never before in history—to make economic ideas work better in practice to improve people's lives by using the latest advances in computer science. One way to understand this idea is to distinguish between prediction and causation or the question "what happens if something else happens?" Artificial intelligence is very good at predicting whether a picture is a cat or a dog or a person, or at predicting whether a person with certain characteristics will "click" on an advertisement on the computer screen. But the computer—without the aid of economics and the decentralized price system—is not good at answering such causal "what if" questions, such as "What will happen to sales of an item if the price is increased or decreased?" Nor is it good at developing or dealing with entirely new products that will exist tomorrow or next year that do not exist today. These same issues came up years ago when central planning was still used around much of the world, including in Russia and China. That experience helped people learn about the magic of the price system, and so central planning was abandoned in much of the world. Currently there is a renewed interest in alternatives to market economics, whether you call it socialism or more simply highly interventionist government economic policy. With the demise of the Soviet Union, old case studies that showed the harms of central planning are forgotten, and they do not seem so relevant. It was helpful then to discuss how Soviet production plants could fulfill centrally imposed plans by producing, for example, one 500-pound nail rather that 500 one-pound nails, even though the giant nail was useless. The examples are different today when more modern examples of clicking or using search engines are relevant and we can deal with huge quantities of data. But they are as relevant as ever and you will see such examples throughout this text.

 ## Benefits of Understanding Economic Principles

Watch this video for an explanation of the importance of following basic economic principles for everyone.

View the video online at: http://www.youtube.com/embed/uk6HwKZAEs4?rel=0

Review

- The market economy and the command economy are two alternative systems for addressing the questions any economy must face: what to produce, how to produce, and for whom to produce.
- A market economy is characterized by several key elements, such as freely determined prices, property rights, and freedom to trade at home and abroad.
- For a market economy to work well, markets should be competitive and the government should play a role when there is a market failure.
- Prices are signals, they provide incentives, and they affect the distribution of income.
- Market economies are sometimes hit by financial crises and recessions, creating another role for government in preventing or alleviating them.

1.4 End-of-Chapter Material

Conclusion

One basic idea lies at the center of economics: People make purposeful choices with scarce resources, and interact with other people when they make these choices.

This introductory chapter illustrates this idea, starting with decisions by Elon Musk and Mark Zuckerberg about whether to leave school and continuing with simple examples of people making choices about what to consume or produce.

From this central idea, many other powerful ideas follow, as summarized visually in Figure 1.7. An *opportunity cost* exists every time a choice is made. People *gain from trade*, both through a *better allocation* of goods and through *comparative advantage*. Every society faces trade-offs described by *production possibilities curves*. Every society faces three fundamental questions: *what, how,* and *for whom* to produce. Market economies—characterized by *freely determined prices, property rights, freedom to trade,* and a *role for both government and private organizations*—provide answers to these three questions. The price system helps a market economy work by providing *incentives*, sending *signals*, and affecting the *distribution* of income.

FIGURE 1.7 From One Central Idea, Many Powerful Ideas Follow

As you study economics, you will see the same central idea again and again. This figure illustrates how many powerful economic ideas are connected to the one in the center.

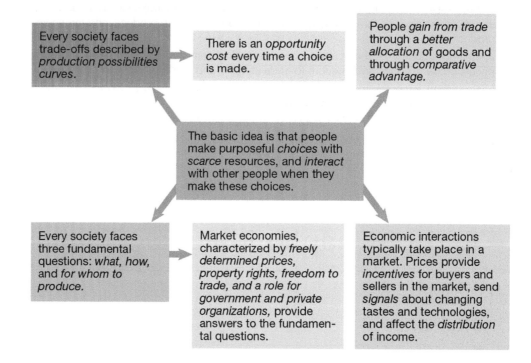

You will see this central idea again and again as you continue to study economics.

Key Points

1. Everyone faces a scarcity of something, usually time or resources.

2. Scarcity leads to choice, and choice leads to opportunity costs.

3. Trade leads to gains because it allows goods and services to be reallocated in a way that improves people's well-being.

4. Trade also leads to gains because it permits people to specialize in what they are relatively good at.

5. The production possibilities curve summarizes the trade-offs in the whole economy because of scarcity.

6. Economic production is efficient if the economy is on the production possibilities curve. Production is inefficient if the economy is inside the production possibilities curve.

7. Points outside the production possibilities curve currently are impossible. More investment, more workers, or better technology can shift the production possibilities curve out and make the impossible possible.

8. The three basic questions that any economy must face are what, how, and for whom production should take place.

9. A well-functioning market system, involving freely determined prices, property rights, freedom to trade, and a role for government and private organizations, can answer these basic questions.

10. Prices transmit signals, provide incentives, and affect the distribution of income in a market economy. If prices are set at incorrect levels by government, waste and inefficiency—such as feeding bread to livestock—will result.

Questions for Review

1. What is the basic idea at the center of economics?
2. Why does scarcity imply a choice among alternatives?
3. What is the opportunity cost of making a choice?
4. How can gains be achieved from trade even when total production of goods and services does not change?
5. How can specialization lead to gains from trade?
6. What is the principle of increasing opportunity costs?
7. Why is the production of a combination of goods that is located inside the production possibilities curve considered to be inefficient?
8. How can financial crises cause inefficiencies?
9. What are the key ingredients of a market economy?
10. What are the three basic questions that any economic system must address?
11. What roles do prices play in a market economy?
12. What role does the price system play during a national disaster?

Problems

1. Suppose that you are president of the student government, and you have to decide how to allocate a $20,000 fund for guest speakers for the year. Conan O'Brien and Will Ferrell each cost $10,000 per appearance, Stephen Colbert costs $20,000 per appearance, and former economic advisers to the government charge $1,000 per lecture. Explain the economic problem of choice and scarcity in this case. What issues would you consider in arriving at a decision?

2. Michelle Wie, a teenage golf prodigy who earned $16 million in endorsements and $4 million in prize money and appearance fees in 2006, announced that she would enroll as a student at Stanford University in the fall of 2007. What was her opportunity cost of a year of college? How does it compare to your opportunity cost of a year of college?

3. Allison will graduate from high school next June. She has ranked her three possible postgraduation plans in the following order: (1) work for two years at a consulting job in her hometown paying $20,000 per year, (2) attend a local community college for two years, spending $5,000 per year on tuition and expenses, and (3) travel around the world tutoring a rock star's child for pay of $5,000 per year. What is the opportunity cost of her choice?

4. Suppose you have two boxes of chocolate chip cookies and a friend of yours has 2 gallons of milk. Explain how you can both gain from trade. Is this a gain from trade through *better allocation* or *greater production*?

5. Suppose Tina and Julia can produce brownies and romantic poems (which can be combined to make a lovely gift) in the following combinations in a given week:

Tina		Julia	
Brownies	Poems	Brownies	Poems
50	0	25	0
40	1	20	1
30	2	15	2
20	3	10	3
10	4	5	4
0	5	0	5

a. If Tina and Julia are each currently producing two poems per week, how many brownies are they producing? What is the total production of brownies and poems between them?

b. Is there a possibility for increasing production? Why or why not?

c. Suppose Julia completely specializes in producing poems and Tina completely specializes in producing brownies. What will be their total production of brownies and poems?

6. Suppose you must divide your time between studying for your math final and writing a final paper for your English class. The fraction of time that you spend studying math and its relation to your grade in the two classes given in the table below.

Fraction of Time Spent on Math	Math Grade	English Grade
0	0	97
20	45	92
40	65	85
60	75	70
80	82	50
100	88	0

a. Draw a trade-off curve for the math grade versus the English grade.

b. What is the opportunity cost of increasing the time spent on math from 80 to 100 percent? What is the opportunity cost of increasing the time spent on math from 60 to 80 percent?

c. Are there increasing opportunity costs from spending more time on math? Explain.

d. Suppose your parents want you to get a 92 percent in both subjects. What would you tell them?

7. A small country produces only two goods, cars and cakes. Given its limited resources, this country has the following production possibilities:

Cars	Cakes
0	200
25	180
50	130
75	70
100	0

a. Draw the production possibilities curve.

b. Suppose car production uses mainly machines and cake production uses mainly labor. Show what happens to the curve when the number of machines increases, but the amount of labor remains unchanged.

8. Tracy tells Huey that he can improve his economics grade without sacrificing fun activities or his grades in other courses. Can you imagine ways in which this might be possible? What does that imply about the initial situation? If Huey is taking just two courses and he can improve his economics grade without hurting his math grade, how could you represent this situation graphically?

9. Suppose decreased production of oil in the Middle East causes the price of oil to rise around the world. Explain how this change in the price signals information to U.S. producers of various goods, provides incentives to U.S. producers of various goods, and affects the distribution of income.

10. When you look at the economies of the United States, Europe, or Japan, you see most of the ingredients of a market economy. For example, consider bicycles. Prices in the bicycle market are free to vary; people have property rights to the bicycles they buy; many people sell bicycles; many bicycles sold in the United States, Europe, and Japan come from other countries; the government regulates bicycle use (no bicycles on the freeways, for example); and bicycle production takes place within firms with many workers. Replace bicycles with another good or service of your choosing and comment on whether the statement is still true.

CHAPTER 2
Observing and Explaining the Economy

Economics is a way of thinking. It entails accurately *describing* economic events, *explaining* why the events occur, *predicting* under what circumstances such events might take place in the future, and *recommending* appropriate courses of action. To make use of economics, you will want to learn to do the describing, the explaining, and even the predicting and recommending yourself—that is, to reason and think like an economist. By making use of economics in this way, you can better understand the economic challenges and opportunities you face, and thereby make improvements in your own life or the lives of those around you. Just as physicists try to explain the existence of black holes in outer space and biologists try to explain why dinosaurs became extinct, economists try to explain interesting observations and facts about the economy. One reason is pure intellectual excitement: It can be fun to solve economic puzzles. But understanding economic events or trends is also essential for making sound policy recommendations, whether in business or in government. An incorrect explanation for the financial crisis in 2008, for example, could bring about harmful policy responses in the future with unintended consequences despite the best of intentions.

FIGURE 2.1 Observing and Explaining the World
Economics is a way of thinking about how the world works. Economists learn how to describe and explain economic events, and then draw on that understanding to recommend how to best respond to economic events and also to predict when certain events may occur.

Source: Sergey Nivens/Shutterstock.com

Are there some economic observations—from your own experience, from recent news stories, or from your history or political science courses—that you find puzzling? Some of your questions might be like these: Why is college tuition so high? Why have the wages of college graduates increased much more rapidly than the wages of high school dropouts since the 1970s? Why are there seventeen different types of toothpaste? Why is the average income of people in the United States about 35 times higher than that of people in India? Why did the U.S. economy go into a recession in 2008? What is the best way to assist workers and families impacted by the economic disruptions caused by the COVID-19 pandemic?

All these questions are based on observations about the economy. Some, like the question about college tuition, are fairly obvious and are based on casual observation. Others, like the question about the historical trends in the wages of high school and college graduates, would become evident in the course of reading a book or talking to a parent or a relative. In order to answer such questions, economists, like physicists or biologists, need to systematically document and quantify their observations and look for patterns. Learning to apply economic ideas to such real-world questions is an important part of learning economics, but it also is one of the most challenging parts because the real world is never quite as tidy as we would like and usually the explanation has several factors. In this chapter, we explain some of the ways that economists explain the facts in practice, and we point out some of the key pitfalls. We start by using a practical example to show how economists document and quantify their observations. As we will see, even documenting the facts can be tricky.

2.1 Why Has Driving Shifted into Reverse?

The Federal Highway Administration provides data on how many miles Americans drive in a year. A year–by–year analysis of this data shows that Americans have been driving less in recent years. Graphs are a helpful way to document and pinpoint such trends. Figure 2.2 plots the total miles traveled by all the vehicles—cars, trucks, and motorcycles—on all the streets, roads, and highways in the United States from 1993 to 2019. The vertical axis is measured in billions of miles; the horizontal axis is measured in years. Observe that after rising for many years, "vehicle miles traveled" reached a temporary peak around 3,000 billion, or 3 trillion miles, driven in 2007 and then declined in 2008. The number of miles driven did not change very much for the next six years between 2008 and 2014. It was only in 2015 and 2016 that the number of miles driven increased again, moving past the previous peak of around 3 trillion miles driven. Why did the driving trend reverse after moving up for many years? If the reversal was connected to the recession, why did it take so long after the recession ended for the driving trend to recover?

The first thing to investigate is whether changes in the number of people in the United States may have been a factor in changes in the miles traveled. You would expect that more people would lead to more total driving and fewer people to less total driving. To test this possibility, one can simply divide vehicle miles traveled by the population of the United States. If total miles traveled were 3,000 billion and approximately 300 million people lived in the United States; this implies that the average miles traveled per person were about 10,000, which probably is a more understandable number than 3 trillion. Vehicle miles traveled per person for the other years from 1993 to 2019 are plotted in Figure 2.3. Now note something important about Figure 2.3; compared with Figure 2.2, it reaches a peak in 2005, a few years before the recession. Thus, miles traveled started growing more slowly than the population in that year. So we should think of 2005 rather than 2007 as the turning point to try to explain the change in miles traveled. Another difference between Figure 2.2 and Figure 2.3 is that the line graph in Figure 2.3 shows a continued fall until around 2011, illustrating that, relative to the population, driving continued to decline in 2011. Finally, even though total miles driven in 2015 and 2016 exceeded the pre-recession peak, Figure 2.3 shows that adjusted for the increase in population, even by 2019, vehicle miles traveled per person still has not recovered to pre-recession levels.

FIGURE 2.2 "Vehicle Miles Traveled" in the United States, 1993–2019

For each year from 1993 through 2019, the total amount of miles traveled in vehicles on U.S. roads and streets is plotted; a line then connects the points to better visualize the trends and turning points.

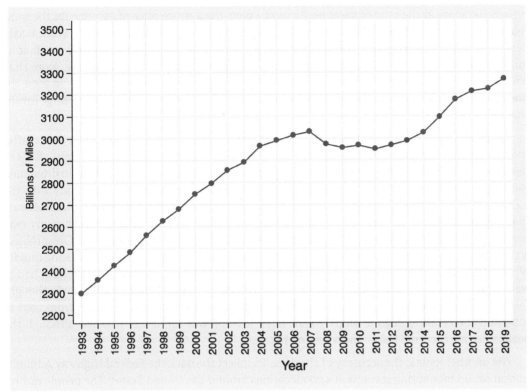

Source: Federal Highway Administration.

FIGURE 2.3 Vehicle Miles Traveled Per Person

For each year, vehicle miles traveled from Figure 2.2 is divided by the population of the United States and plotted in the graph.

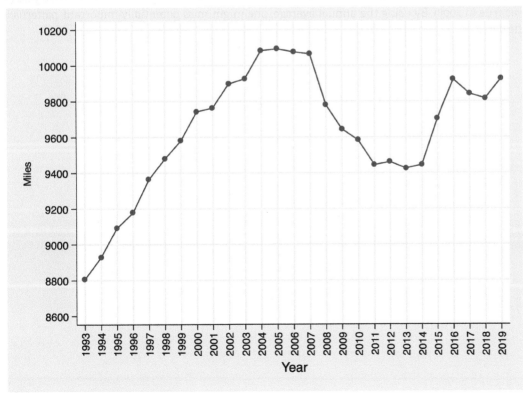

Sources: Figure 2.2 and Bureau of the Census.

We can look in many places for an explanation of the reversal in this trend, but the first obvious place is the price of gasoline. If the price of gasoline increases, then people will have a greater incentive to walk or ride a bike or take a train or plane rather than drive their car, truck or motorcycle. So let's look at the price of gasoline. Figure 2.4 plots the average price of gasoline for the same years as Figure 2.2 and Figure 2.3 in the United States; dollars per gallon are now on the vertical axis. Look carefully at the pattern of the price of gasoline. Note that the price did not rise much at all for nearly ten years from 1993 to 2002, but then it took off at a much more rapid rate, more than doubling. Recall that the data plotted in Figure 2.4 are the average prices for each year. In 2008, the price during the summer months reached more than $4 per gallon, even though the average for the year was $3.30.

By comparing Figure 2.3 and Figure 2.4 one can see that the peak in driving occurred soon after the price of gasoline started to rise rapidly. Furthermore, gasoline prices rose again right after the recession ended, which could have ended up making it more expensive for Americans to drive their cars. Only after 2016, did gasoline prices fall back to the post-recession lows, coinciding with the increase in miles driven. Based on the data in these figures, one can begin to make a plausible case that higher gasoline prices are the explanation for the decline in driving. But, as with many real-world economic events, the explanation is not as clear and obvious as one might hope. One problem is that the turning point in driving occurred in 2005, several years after prices started rising rapidly. What could cause such a lag? Perhaps people took a while to adjust; commuters may have had to wait until they could find a place to live closer to the train station. Perhaps some people thought the high price of gasoline was temporary. Another possibility is that the recession from 2007 to 2009, and the resulting high unemployment rates, led to fewer commutes to work, although the peak in driving occurred before the recession began.

Yet another issue is the accuracy of the data. To collect the data, the Federal Highway Administration set up monitoring stations at 4,000 locations around the United States. The people recording the traffic flows could have made reporting errors or missed key intersections. In general, economic data collected via survey methods can be inaccurate; people sometimes do not understand the questions, or they do not have the correct information. Sometimes, data may be more aggregated than you would like them to be; for example, the average price of a gallon of gasoline during a given year conceals the substantial variation in gasoline prices that occur within a year (as was true in 2008). By using the annual average, one might miss potentially important patterns in the data.

FIGURE 2.4 Average Retail Price of Gasoline in the United States, 1993–2019
For each year, the price of a gallon of gasoline is averaged across the year and across all grades and plotted in the graph.

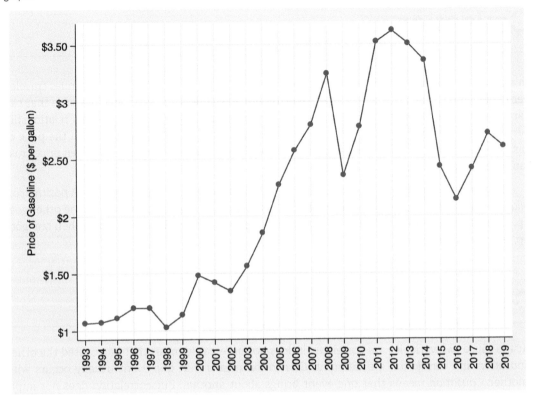

Source: Department of Energy.

It is also important to check the difference between the price of gasoline and the *relative* price of gasoline compared with other goods. If you find that the price of other forms of transportation—trains, planes, or bicycles—rose just as fast as gasoline, then the rising price of gasoline would not be a good explanation for the decline in driving. In sum, although it seems quite reasonable that an explanation for the reversal in driving trends was the rise in the price of gasoline, as always in economics, there are other possible competing views to discuss and assess.

Review

- Explaining real-world economic trends and events is both interesting in its own right and essential for sound policymaking. The first step is to find good data to describe the trend or event, then to identify what factors may have caused the trend, and finally to assess how changes elsewhere in the economy could affect the explanation.

- When applying economic ideas to explain real-world trends and events, it is best to recognize the limitations of the analysis and think critically about all possible causal factors. For example, when studying changes over time, it is important to take account of changes in the population which have large effects.

2.2 Variables, Correlation, and Causation

economic variable

Any economic measure that can vary over a range of values.

In examining U.S. driving trends, we focused on two economic variables: (1) vehicle miles traveled per person and (2) the price of gasoline. An **economic variable** is any economic measure that can vary over a range of values. In explaining the reversal in driving trends, we noted a relationship between these two variables. In other words, we considered the correlation between the price of gasoline and the subsequent number of miles driven; in particular, we noted that, when prices rose rapidly, driving declined.

Two variables are said to be *correlated* if they tend to move up or down together. A *positive correlation* exists if the two variables move in the same direction—when one goes up, the other goes up. A *negative correlation* exists if the two variables move in opposite directions—when one goes up, the other goes down.

Correlation versus Causation

Just because two variables are correlated it does not necessarily mean that one caused the other. *Causation* and *correlation* are different. *Correlation* means that one event usually occurs with another. *Causation* means that one event brings about another. But correlation does not imply causation. For example, high readings on a thermometer are correlated with hot weather: high readings occur when it is hot. But the thermometer readings do not cause the hot weather. Causation is the other way around: hot weather causes the reading on the thermometer to be high.

In many instances, determining causation is difficult. In the example of miles driven, you can see how causation can run both ways. If the oil exporting nations cut back on production, then gas prices will rise and the higher gas prices can discourage road trips, resulting in fewer miles driven. Conversely, if people are concerned about the safety of air travel following a well-publicized aviation tragedy, they may be more likely to travel by road and the resulting increased demand for gasoline can cause gas prices to rise. Sometimes, we can look at the timing of changes—did gasoline prices lead or lag the change in miles traveled—to determine the causation, but this is not easy to do.

In some cases, a third factor could be the causal one. For example, the COVID-19 crisis brought about a dramatic decline in miles driven—between 25–40 percent decline in March and April of 2020—but also resulted in a global decline in oil prices as economic activity across the globe slowed down along with air travel. This is why a favorite phrase among economists is "correlation does not mean causation."

The Lack of Controlled Experiments in Economics

In many sciences—psychology, physics, and biology—investigators perform **controlled experiments** to determine whether one event causes another event. An example of a controlled experiment is the clinical trial of a new drug. New drugs are tested by trying them out on two groups of individuals. One group gets the new drug; the other group, the control group, gets a placebo (a pill without the drug). If the experiment results in a significantly greater number of people being cured among the group taking the drug than among the group taking the placebo, investigators conclude that the drug causes the cure.

Controlled experiments are rare in economics. When faced with a situation with limited data (say, data for one country over a particular time period), causation is hard to determine. In these circumstances, we can try to look at other countries' experiences, or we can look at the experiences of different states within the United States. But, unfortunately, no two countries or states are alike in all respects. Thus, attempting to control for other factors is not as easy as in the case of clinical trials.

In recent years, economists have adapted some of the methods of experimental science and have begun to conduct economic experiments in laboratory settings that are similar to the real world. These experiments can be repeated, and various effects can be controlled for. **Experimental economics** is a growing area of economics. The findings of experimental economics have affected economists' understanding of how the economy works. Experiments in economics also provide an excellent way to *learn* how the economy works, much as experiments in science courses can help one learn about gravity or the structure of plant cells. But because it is difficult to replicate real-world settings as precisely as in such experiments, they have yet to be applied as widely as the clinical or laboratory experiments in other sciences.

> **controlled experiments**
>
> Empirical tests of theories in a controlled setting in which particular effects can be isolated.

> **experimental economics**
>
> A branch of economics that uses laboratory experiments to analyze economic behavior.

Economic Models

To explain economic facts and observations, one needs an economic theory, or *model*. An **economic model** is an explanation of how the economy or a part of the economy works. In practice, most economists use the terms *theory* and *model* interchangeably, although sometimes the term *theory* suggests a general explanation and the term *model* suggests a more specific explanation. The term *law* also is used interchangeably with the terms *model* and *theory* in economics.

Economic models are always abstractions, or simplifications, of the real world. They take complicated phenomena, such as the behavior of people, firms, and governments, and simplify them. Economists like to draw an analogy between a model and a road map—both are abstractions of a much more complex reality. Some maps (like some models) can be detailed; others are just broad abstractions. No single model is "correct," just like no single map is "correct." If you wanted to drive from New York to California, you would need an interstate map, one that ignores the details of individual streets within a city to show the main highways. In contrast, if you were headed from one neighborhood of Chicago to another, an interstate map would be of no use; instead, you would need a map that showed city streets in greater detail.

> **economic model**
>
> An explanation of how the economy or a part of the economy works.

Microeconomics versus Macroeconomics

Microeconomics looks at individual firms, individuals, households, or markets while macroeconomics focuses on the national or global economy.

View the video online at: http://www.youtube.com/embed/DJG-liA19eY?rel=0

Microeconomic versus Macroeconomic Models

There are two types of models corresponding to the two main branches of economics: microeconomics and macroeconomics. They each have their purpose.

microeconomics

The branch of economics that examines individual decision making at firms and households and the way they interact in specific industries and markets.

Microeconomics studies the behavior of individual firms and households or specific markets like the health care market or the college graduate market. It looks at variables such as the price of a college education or the reason for increased wages of college graduates. Microeconomic models explain why the price of gasoline varies from station to station and why airfares are discounted. The analogy in the map world is to the city street map.

macroeconomics

The branch of economics that examines the workings and problems of the economy as a whole—GDP growth and unemployment.

Macroeconomics focuses on the whole economy—the whole national economy or even the whole world economy. The most comprehensive measure of the size of an economy is the **gross domestic product (GDP)**. GDP is the total value of all goods and services made in the country during a specific period of time, such as a year. GDP includes all newly made goods, such as cars, shoes, gasoline, airplanes, and houses; it also includes services like health care, education, and auto repair. Macroeconomics tries to explain the changes in GDP over time rather than the changes in a part of the GDP, like health care spending. It looks at questions such as, what causes the GDP to grow and why many more workers are unemployed in Europe than in the United States? The analogy in the map world is to the interstate map.

gross domestic product (GDP)

A measure of the value of all the goods and services newly produced in an economy during a specified period of time.

Do not be critical of economic models just because they are simplifications. In every science, models are simplifications of reality. Models are successful if they explain reality reasonably well. In fact, if they were not simplifications, models would be hard to use effectively. Economic models differ from those in the physical sciences because they endeavor to explain human behavior, which is complex and often unpredictable. It is for this reason that the brilliant physicist Max Planck said that economics was harder than physics.

Economic models can be described with words, numerical tables, graphs, or algebra. To use economics, it is important to be able to work with these different descriptions. Figure 2.5 and Figure 2.6 show how models can be illustrated with graphs. By looking at a graph, we can see quickly whether the model has an inverse or a direct relationship. If a model says that one variable varies inversely with the other, this means that if the first variable rises, then the second falls. If a model says that one variable varies directly with another, this means that if one variable rises, the other also rises. In economics, the expression "is positively related to" is frequently used in place of the phrase "varies directly with," which is more common in other sciences. Similarly, the expression "is negatively related to" is frequently used in place of "varies inversely with."

FIGURE 2.5 A Model with Two Positively Related Variables
The upward-sloping line shows how the variables are related. When one variable increases from *A* to *B*, the other variable increases from *C* to *D*. If one variable declines from *B* to *A*, the other variable declines from *D* to *C*. We say that Variable 1 is positively related to Variable 2, or that Variable 1 varies directly with Variable 2.

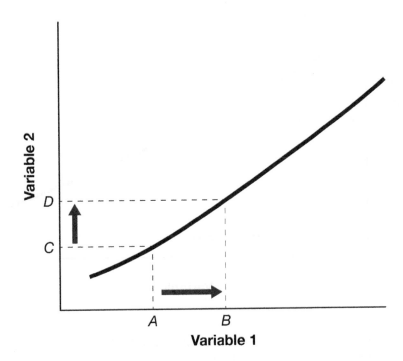

FIGURE 2.6 A Model with Two Negatively Related Variables

When one variable increases from *A* to *B*, the other variable decreases from *D* to *C*. Likewise, when one variable decreases from *B* to *A*, the other variable increases from *C* to *D*. We say that Variable 1 is negatively related to Variable 2, or that Variable 1 varies inversely with Variable 2.

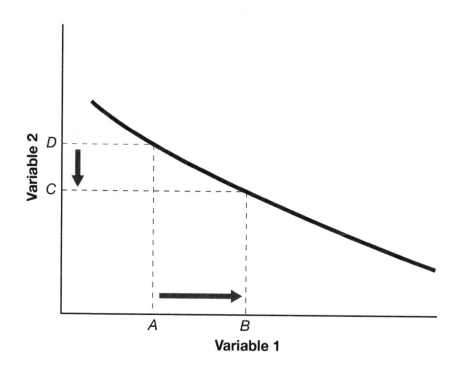

positively related

A situation in which an increase in one variable is associated with an increase in another variable; also called *directly related*.

negatively related

A situation in which an increase in one variable is associated with a decrease in another variable; also called *inversely related*.

In Figure 2.5, two variables are shown to be **positively related**. In other words, when Variable 1 increases from *A* to *B*, Variable 2 increases from *C* to *D* by the specific amount given by the curve. Likewise, when Variable 1 decreases from *B* to *A*, Variable 2 decreases from *D* to *C*. In Figure 2.6, a model with two variables that are **negatively related** is shown. Here, when Variable 1 increases from *A* to *B*, Variable 2 decreases from *D* to *C*. Likewise, when Variable 1 decreases from *B* to *A*, Variable 2 increases from *C* to *D*. Models have *constants* as well as variables. The constants in the models in Figure 2.5 and Figure 2.6 are the positions and shapes of the curves.

An Example: A Model with Two Variables

Figure 2.7 shows a model describing how doctors employed in a health maintenance organization (HMO) provide physical examinations. The model illustrates that the more doctors who are employed at the HMO, the more physical exams can be given. The model is represented in four different ways: (1) words, (2) a numerical table, (3) a graph, and (4) algebra.

A verbal description appears on the lower right of Figure 2.7: More doctors mean more physical exams, but additional doctors increase the number of exams by smaller amounts, presumably because the diagnostic facilities at the HMO are limited; for example, only so many rooms are available for physical exams.

FIGURE 2.7 Economic Models in Four Ways

Each model has advantages and disadvantages; this book focuses mostly on verbal descriptions, graphs, and numerical tables, but occasionally some algebra will be used to help explain things.

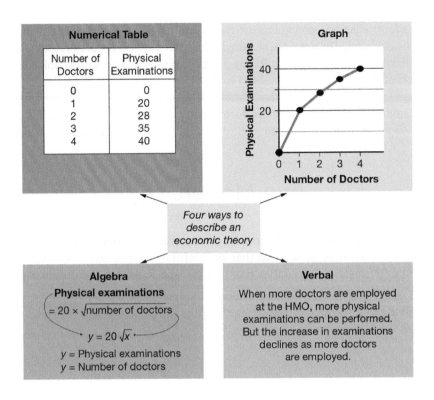

On the upper left, a table with numbers shows how the number of examinations depends on the number of doctors. Exactly how many examinations can be given by each number of doctors is shown in the table. Clearly, this table is much more specific than the verbal description. Be sure to distinguish between the meaning of a table that presents a model and a table that presents data. They look similar, but one is a model of the real world and the other represents observations about the real world.

On the upper right, a curve shows the relationship between doctors and physical examinations. The curve shows how many exams each number of doctors can perform.

The points on the curve are plotted from the information in the table. The vertical axis has the number of examinations; the horizontal axis has the number of doctors. The points are connected with a line to help visualize the curve.

Finally, the lower left shows the doctor-examination relationship in algebraic form. In this case, the number of exams can be approximated by the square root of the number of doctors times 20. If we use the symbol y for the number of exams and x for the number of doctors, the model looks a lot like the equations in an algebra course.

All four ways of representing models have advantages and disadvantages. The advantage of the verbal representation is that we usually communicate with people in words, and if we want our economic models to have any use, we need to communicate with people who have not studied economics. The verbal representation, however, is not as precise as the other three models. In addition to verbal analysis, in this book we focus on tabular and graphical representations and, when appropriate, algebraic descriptions as well.

The *Ceteris Paribus* Assumption

ceteris paribus

"All other things being equal"; refers to holding all other variables constant or keeping all other things the same when one variable is changed.

To use models for prediction, economists use the assumption of **ceteris paribus**, which means "all other things being equal." For example, the prediction that Variable 2 will fall from *D* to *C* assumes that the curve in Figure 2.6 does not shift: The position of the curve when Variable 1 is at *A* is *equal* to the position of the curve when Variable 1 is at *B*. If other things were not equal—if the curve shifted—then we could not predict that Variable 2 would fall from *D* to *C* when Variable 1 rose from *A* to *B*. Similarly, predicting that more doctors can produce more physical exams assumes that there is no power outage that would cause the diagnostic equipment to stop operating.

The Use of Existing Models

Because economics has been around for a long time, many existing models can be applied to explain observations or make predictions that are useful to decision makers. In practice, whether in government or business or universities, economists use models that are already in existence.

The models are used in many different types of applications, from determining the effects of discrimination in the workplace to evaluating the gains from lower health care prices. Frequently, the models are applied in new and clever ways.

The Development of Models

Like models in other sciences, economic models change and new models are developed. Many of the models in this book are different from the models in books published 40 years ago. New economic models evolve because some new observations cannot be explained by existing models.

The process of the development of new models or theories in economics proceeds much like that in any other science. First one develops a *hypothesis*, or a hunch, to explain a puzzling observation. Then one tests the hypothesis by seeing if its predictions of other observations are good. If the hypothesis passes this test, then it becomes accepted. In practice, however, this is at best a rough description of the process of scientific discovery in economics. Existing models are constantly reexamined and tested. Some economists specialize in testing models; others specialize in developing them. The process of creating and testing of models in economics is ongoing.

Review

- One of the most significant challenges for an economist is to identify whether one variable has a causal impact on another. Even though two variables may be strongly correlated, correlation does not imply causation.
- In the natural sciences, controlled experiments are used to establish causation. Because controlled experiments are rare in economics, establishing causation is more difficult in this field. Fortunately, experimental economics is now beginning to have a greater impact on research.
- Economists use models to describe economic phenomena and to understand how changes in some variables affect the variable of interest. Economic models are abstractions, or simplifications, of a more complex reality. They can be extremely detailed or rather abstract, depending on the purpose or use.

- Economic models are different from models in the physical sciences because they must deal with human behavior. Models can be represented with words, numerical tables, graphs, and algebra.
- Economists also have a long-standing interest in improving the economic policy of governments. Economics can be used in a positive sense, to understand why government policies are the way they are, or in a normative sense, to identify what government policies should be enacted.

2.3 Recommending Appropriate Policies

Ever since the birth of economics as a field—around 1776, when Adam Smith published the *Wealth of Nations*—economists have been concerned about and motivated by a desire to improve the economic policy of governments. In fact, economics originally was called *political economy*. Much of the *Wealth of Nations* is about what the government should or should not do to affect the domestic and international economy.

Adam Smith argued for a system of *laissez faire*—little government control—in which the role of the government is mainly to promote competition, provide for national defense, and reduce restrictions on the exchange of goods and services. More than one hundred years later, Karl Marx brought an alternative perspective to Smith's (and other classical economists') view of political economy, arguing against the laissez-faire approach. His analysis of market economies, or **capitalism**, centered on the contradictions that he saw arising out of such a system, particularly the conflict between the owners of production and the laborers. He argued that these contradictions would result in the inevitable collapse of capitalism and the emergence of a new economic system, called **socialism,** in which government essentially would own and control all production. Although Marx actually wrote little about what a Socialist or Communist economy would look like, the centrally planned economies that arose in the Soviet Union, Eastern Europe, and China in the twentieth century can be traced to Marx's ideas.

In the twenty-first century, most countries have rejected the command economy and have moved toward market economies, but the debate about the role of government continues. In many modern market economies, the government plays a large role, and for this reason, such economies are sometimes called **mixed economies**. How great should the role of government be in a market economy? Should the government provide health care services? Should it try to break up large firms? The answers to these questions are difficult to comprehend and have been debated for years.

capitalism

An economic system based on a market economy in which capital is individually owned, and production and employment decisions are decentralized.

socialism

An economic system in which the government owns and controls all the capital and makes decisions about prices and quantities as part of a central plan.

mixed economies

A market economy in which the government plays a very large role.

Capitalism, Socialism, and Communism

Today most economies are mixed, as the government plays a role to varying degrees in several sectors of the economy, such as banking and health care services.

View the video online at: http://www.youtube.com/embed/JpVv49v8BLQ?rel=0

Positive versus Normative Economics

positive economics

Economic analysis that explains what happens in the economy and why, without making recommendations about economic policy.

normative economics

Economic analysis that makes recommendations about economic policy.

Council of Economic Advisers

A three–member group of economists appointed by the president of the United States to analyze the economy and make recommendations about economic policy.

In debating the role of government in the economy, economists distinguish between positive and normative economics. **Positive economics** is about what *is*; **normative economics** is about what *should be*. For example, positive economics endeavors to explain why driving declined in 2008. Normative economics aims to develop and recommend policies that might prevent driving from increasing in the future, perhaps with the aim of improving the environment. In general, normative economics is concerned with making recommendations about what the government should do—whether it should control the price of gasoline or health care, for example. Economists who advise governments spend much of their time doing normative economics. In the United States, the president's **Council of Economic Advisers** has legal responsibility for advising the president about which economic policies are beneficial and which policies are detrimental to the economy.

Positive economics also can be used to explain *why* governments do what they do. Why were tax rates cut in the 1980s, increased in the 1990s, and then cut again in the 2000s? Positive analysis of government policy requires a mixture of both political science and economic science, with a focus on what motivates voters and the politicians they elect.

Economics as a Science versus Partisan Policy Tool

Although economics, like any other science, is based on facts and theories, it is not always used in a purely scientific way.

In political campaigns, economists put forth arguments in favor of one candidate, emphasizing the good side of their candidate's ideas and de-emphasizing the bad side. In a court of law, one economist may help a defendant—making the best case possible—and another economist may help the plaintiff—again, making the best case possible. In other words, economics is not always used objectively. A good reason to learn economics for yourself is to see through fallacious arguments.

But economics is not the only science that is used in these two entirely different modes. For example, there is currently a great controversy about the use of biology and chemistry to make estimates of the costs and benefits of different environmental policies. This is a politically controversial subject, and some on both sides of the controversy have been accused of using science in nonobjective ways.

Economics Is Not the Only Factor in Policy Issues

Although economics can be useful in policy decisions, it frequently is not the only factor. For example, national security sometimes calls for a recommendation on a policy issue different from one based on a purely economic point of view. Although most economists recommend free exchange of goods between countries, the U.S. government restricted exports of high-technology goods such as computers during the Cold War because defense specialists worried that the technology could help the military in the Soviet Union, and this was viewed as more important than the economic argument. The government still places heavy restrictions on trade in nuclear fuels for fear of the proliferation of nuclear weapons. More recently, the U.S. government banned Federal agencies from awarding telecommunication contracts to the Chinese company Huawei for national security reasons.

 ### Balancing Economic and Public Health Concerns during the COVID-19 Pandemic

Governments were forced to drastically slow economic activity to address public health concerns during the 2020 pandemic.

View the video online at: http://www.youtube.com/embed/UHLUyD_OpaA?rel=0

Observing Different Economic Conditions over Time and across Countries

Watch this video for observations on changes in government policy and the economy of the U.S. and other nations in recent decades.

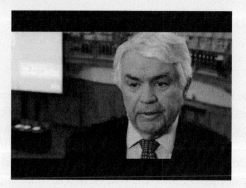

View the video online at: http://www.youtube.com/embed/U5Kgen5c-x8?rel=0

Disagreement between Economists

Watching economists debate issues on television or reading their opinions in a newspaper or magazine certainly gives the impression that they rarely agree. There are major controversies in economics, and we will examine them in this book. But when people survey economists' beliefs, they find a surprising amount of agreement.

Why, then, is there the popular impression of disagreement? Because there are many economists, and one can always find an economist with a different viewpoint. When people sue other people in court and economics is an issue, it is always possible to find economists who will testify for each side, even if 99 percent of economists would agree with one side. Similarly, television interviews or news shows want to give both sides of public policy issues. Thus, even if 99 percent of economists agree with one side, the producers are able to find at least one who holds the opposing view.

Economists are human beings with varying moral beliefs and different backgrounds and political views that frequently are unrelated to economic models. For example, an economist who is concerned about the importation of drugs into the United States might appear to be more willing to condone a restriction on coffee exports from Brazil and other coffee-exporting countries to give Colombia a higher price for its coffee to offset a loss in revenue from cocaine. Another economist, who felt less strongly about drug imports, might argue forcefully against such a restriction on coffee. But if they were asked about restrictions on trade in the abstract, both economists probably would argue for government policies that prevent such restrictions.

2.4 End-of-Chapter Material

Conclusion: A Reader's Guide

In Chapter 1, we explored the central idea of economics: scarcity, choice, and economic interaction. In this chapter, we discussed how economists observe economic events and use economic models to explain these phenomena. It is now time to move on and learn more about the models and application of the central idea. As you study economic models in the following chapters, it will be useful to keep three points in mind, which are implied by the ideas raised in this chapter.

First, *economics—more than other subjects—requires a mixture of verbal and quantitative skills*. Frequently, those who come to economics with a good background in physical science and algebra find the mix of formal models with more informal verbal descriptions of markets and institutions unusual and perhaps a little difficult. If you are one of these people, you might wish for a more cut-and-dry, or algebraic, approach.

In contrast, those who are good at history or philosophy may find the emphasis on formal models and graphs difficult and might even prefer a more historical approach that looked more at watershed events and famous individuals and less at formal models of how many individuals behave. If you are one of these people, you might wish that economic models were less abstract.

In reality, however, economics is a mixture of formal modeling, historical analysis, and philosophy. If you are good at algebra and you think the symbols and graphs of elementary economics are too simple, think of Max Planck's comment about economics and focus on the complexity of the economic phenomena that these simple models and graphs are explaining. Then when you are asked an open-ended question about government policy that does not have a simple yes or no answer, you will not be caught off guard. Or if your advantage is in history or philosophy, you should spend more time honing your skills at using models and graphs. Then when you are asked to solve a cut-and-dry economic problem with an exact answer requiring graphic analysis, you will not be caught off guard.

Second, *economics is a wide-ranging discipline*. When your friends or relatives hear that you are taking economics, they may ask you for advice about what stock to buy. Economists' friends and relatives are always asking for such advice. Some topics that you study in economics will help you answer questions about whether to invest in the stock market or put your money in a bank or how many stocks to buy. But even these areas of economics will not offer any predictions about the success of particular companies. Rather, what economics gives you is a set of tools that you can use to obtain information about companies, industries, or countries and to analyze them yourself. Furthermore, the scope of economics is vast. Even among the faculty in a small college, you will find economists who study childhood obesity, trade barriers, real estate markets, abortion policy, the formation of American corporations, economic growth, international lending agencies, social security, agricultural pollution, and school choice.

Third, and perhaps most important, *the study of economics is an intellectually fascinating adventure in its own right*. Yes, economics is highly relevant, and it affects people's lives. But once you learn how economic models work, you will find that they actually are fun to use. Every now and then, just after you have learned about a new economic model, put the book down and think of the economic model independent of its message or relevance to society—try to enjoy it the way you would a good movie. In this way, too, you will be learning to think like an economist.

Key Points

1. Economics is a way of thinking that requires observation (describing economic events), explanation (identifying variables that are potential explanatory variables of the event), prediction (building and using economic models to predict future events), and policy recommendations (courses of action for government—and business—to follow, based on these observations and models).

2. Finding the appropriate data series to explain economic events is a challenge because data often can be hard to find or incomplete, or can be misleading if they are not appropriately transformed.

3. Finding explanations for why an economic event occurred is challenging because even if you can find variables that are correlated with the variable in which you are interested, correlation does not imply causation. The inability to run controlled experiments also makes it difficult for economists to definitively establish a causal explanation for an economic event.

4. Economists have to explain the complex behavior of humans in economic situations. They often use models that are abstractions, or simplifications, of reality in their work. Economic models, like models in other sciences, can be described with words, tables, graphs, or algebra. All four ways are important and complement each other.

5. Economists use the tools of economic analysis to come up with policy insights concerning what the government is doing, or what the government should be doing, with regard to the economist's area of interest. Improving economic policy has been a goal of economists since the time of Adam Smith.

6. Economics is a discipline that requires a combination of analytical, algebraic, and verbal skills. You can apply the tools of economics to almost any problem that involves decision making by individuals. Many students are interested in studying economics because they find it relevant to events that occur in the world, but the study of economics can be an intellectually stimulating exercise in its own right.

Questions for Review

1. How do economists typically approach an economics-related problem?

2. What are the challenges that economists face in trying to describe an economic event?

3. What is meant by a relative price, and why is it important in certain situations to look at the relative price of a good instead of the actual price of that good?

4. What does it mean for two variables to be correlated? What is the difference between positive and negative correlation?

5. Why doesn't correlation imply causation? Can you come up with your own example of why correlation does not imply causation?

6. Why do economists use economic models? Can you come up with some reasons why economists should be careful in using models?

7. What is the *ceteris paribus* assumption? Why is it so important in economics?

8. What is the difference between macroeconomics and microeconomics? Between positive and normative economics?

9. What academic disciplines do you think of as being more scientific than economics? Why do you think so? Which disciplines do you consider to be less scientific, and why?

10. Look through the research and teaching interests of the economics faculty members in your department. Collectively, how wide-ranging are those interests? Were you surprised to find that the tools of economics could be applied to a particular area?

Problems

1. Which of the following variables are studied as part of microeconomics, and which are studied as part of macroeconomics?

   a. The U.S. unemployment rate.

   b. The amount of tips earned by a waiter.

   c. The national rate of inflation.

   d. The number of hours worked by a student.

   e. The price paid to obtain this economics textbook.

2. Consider the following table, which provides the price of chicken and the price of all foods from 1996 to 2006.

Year	Price of All Foods ($)	Price of Chicken ($)	Relative Price ($)
1996	92	95	
1997	93	98	
1998	96	98	
1999	97	99	
2000	100	100	
2001	103	103	
2002	104	105	
2003	108	106	
2004	111	114	
2005	113	116	
2006	116	114	

   a. Calculate the relative price of chicken for each year using the formula below.

   b. Plot the relative price of chicken.

   c. What can you say about how the price of chicken has varied in comparison to the price of all foods in the decade from 1996 to 2006.

$$\text{relative price of chicken} = \left(\frac{\text{price of chicken}}{\text{price of all foods}} \right) * 100$$

3. A change in the relative price of a good matters more than the change in the price of a good in analyzing the change in spending on that good. Show that the relative price of a good can fall on occasions when the price of that good is rising, falling, or remaining unchanged, using numerical examples from the table in Problem 2.

4. Indicate whether you expect positive or negative correlation for the following pairs of variables, labeled X and Y. For each pair, state whether X causes Y, Y causes X, or both.

   a. Sunrise (X) and crowing roosters (Y).

   b. The use of umbrellas (X) and a thunderstorm (Y).

   c. The price of theater tickets (X) and the number of theatergoers (Y).

   d. Weekly earnings of a worker (X) and the number of hours a week she works at her job (Y).

   e. The number of children who were vaccinated against a disease (X) and the number of children who currently suffer from that disease (Y).

5. Consider an economic model of donut production. Show how to represent this model graphically, algebraically, and verbally, as in Figure 2.7.

Number of Workers	Number of Donuts Produced
0	0
1	100
4	200
9	300
16	400

6. Suppose you decide to build a model to explain why the average worker in a particular occupation works more hours during some weeks than during others.

   a. What data would you collect to describe this phenomenon?

   b. What variable do you believe would supply the major part of the explanation of the variation in hours worked?

   c. If you graph the data with hours worked on the vertical axis and your explanatory variable on the horizontal axis, will the relationship be upward-sloping or downward-sloping?

   d. What does your answer to part c imply for whether the data on hours worked and the data on your explanatory variable are positively or negatively correlated?

7. Why is it typical for economists to make the *ceteris paribus* assumption when making predictions? Now consider the statement: "If the local McDonald's reduces the price of a Big Mac hamburger, it will sell a lot more hamburgers." What other variables are most likely being held fixed under the *ceteris paribus* assumption when this statement is being made?

8. Suppose you wanted to modify the Bertrand and Mullainathan study to focus on gender discrimination. Describe the "experiment" that you would run. Also be sure to explain how the *ceteris paribus* assumption is involved in terms of the names you would choose for the men and for the women.

9. Identify whether the following policy statements are positive or normative. Explain.

   a. The price of gasoline is too high.

   b. The average price of gasoline rose to a record high of $4.02 in June 2008.

   c. Forty-four million Americans lack access to health insurance.

   d. The government needs to provide basic health care to the uninsured.

   e. A collapse in the stock market will affect many Americans.

10. Suppose an economic study shows that increasing the tax rate on cigarettes will reduce the amount of smoking. Which of the following statements can be validly made on the basis of the study because they are positive statements, and which cannot be validly made because they are normative statements?

   a. Increasing the cigarette tax rate is a method of reducing smoking.

   b. If the government wishes to reduce smoking, it should raise the cigarette tax.

   c. If the government wishes to reduce smoking, it can raise the cigarette tax.

   d. The government should reduce smoking by raising the cigarette tax.

   e. The government should not raise the cigarette tax on low-income smokers.

2.5 Appendix: Reading, Understanding, and Creating Graphs

Whether you follow the stock market, the health care market, or the whole economy, graphs are needed to understand what is going on. That is why the financial pages of newspapers contain so many graphs. Knowing how to read, understand, and even create your own graphs is part of learning to "think like an economist." Graphs help us see correlations, or patterns, in economic observations. Graphs also are useful for understanding economic models. They help us see how variables in the model behave. They help us describe assumptions about what firms and consumers do.

Computer software to create graphs is now widely available. To understand how helpful graphs can be, you might want to create a few of your own graphs. Here we provide a short review of elementary graphing techniques.

Visualizing Observations with Graphs

Most economic graphs are drawn in two dimensions, like the surface of this page, and are constructed using a **Cartesian coordinate system**. The idea of Cartesian coordinates is that pairs of observations on variables can be represented in a plane by designating one axis for one variable and the other axis for the other variable. Each point, or coordinate, on the plane corresponds to a pair of observations.

Cartesian coordinate system

A graphing system in which ordered pairs of numbers are represented on a plane by the distances from a point to two perpendicular lines, called axes.

Time-Series Graph

In many instances, we want to see how a variable changes over time. Consider the federal debt held by the public—all the outstanding borrowing of the federal government that has not yet been paid back. Table 2.1 shows observations of the U.S. federal debt. The observations are for every ten years. The observations in Table 2.1 are graphed in Figure 2.8. The graph in Figure 2.8 is called a **time-series graph** because it plots a series—that is, several values of the variable—over time.

time-series graph

A graph that plots a variable over time, usually with time on the horizontal axis.

TABLE 2.1 U.S. Federal Government Debt (Illustrative Example)

Year	Debt (billions of dollars) ($)
1960	237
1970	283
1980	712
1990	2,412
2000	3,410
2010	9,018
2020 (Projected)	16,845

FIGURE 2.8 U.S. Federal Debt

Each point corresponds to a pair of observations—the year and the debt—from Table 2.1.

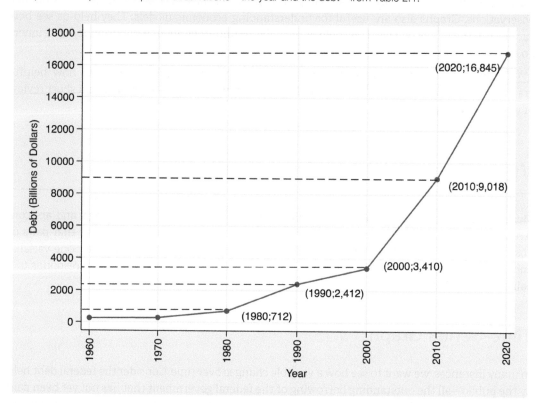

Observe the scales on the horizontal and vertical axes in Figure 2.8. The seven years are put on the horizontal axis, spread evenly from the year 1960 to the year 2020. The last year is a forecast. For the vertical axis, one needs to decide on a scale. The range of variation for the debt in Table 2.1 is wide—from a minimum of $237 billion to a maximum of $16,845 billion. Thus, the range on the vertical axis—from $0 to $18,000 billion in Figure 2.8—must be wide enough to contain all these points.

Now observe how each pair of points from Table 2.1 is plotted in Figure 2.8. The point for the pair of observations for the year 1960 and the debt of $237 billion is found by going over to 1960 on the horizontal axis, then going up to $237 billion and putting a dot there. The point for 1970 and $283 billion and all the other points are found in the same way. To better visualize the points, they can be connected with lines. These lines are not part of the observations; they are only a convenience to help in eyeballing the observations. The points for 1980, 1990, and 2000 are labeled with the pairs of observations corresponding to Table 2.1, but in general, such labels are not needed.

One could choose scales different from those in Figure 2.8, and if you plotted your own graph from the data in Table 2.1 without looking at Figure 2.8, your scales probably would be different. The scales determine the amount of movement in a time-series graph. For example, Figure 2.9 shows two ways to stretch the scales to make the increase in the debt look more or less dramatic. So as not to be fooled by graphs, it is important to look at the scales and think about what they mean.

FIGURE 2.9 Stretching the Debt Story in Two Ways
The points in both graphs are identical to those in Figure 2.8, but by stretching or shrinking the scales, the problem can be made to look either less dramatic or more dramatic.

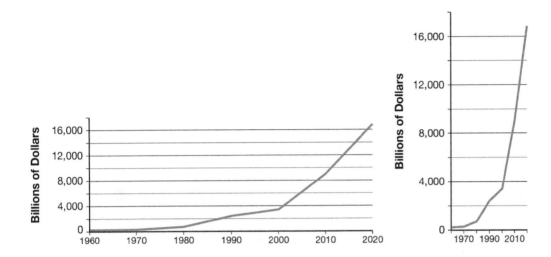

As an alternative to time-series graphs with dots connected by a line, the observations can be shown on a bar graph, as in Figure 2.10. Some people prefer the visual look of a bar graph, but, as is clear from a comparison of Figure 2.8 and Figure 2.10, they provide the same information as time-series graphs.

FIGURE 2.10 U.S. Federal Debt in Bars
The observations are identical to those in Figure 2.8.

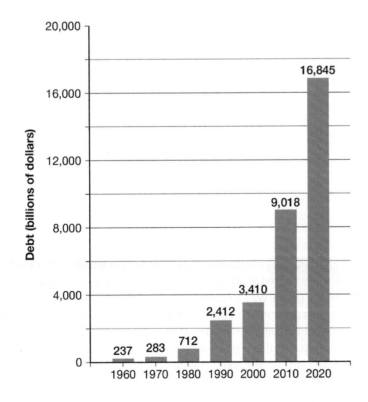

The debt as a percentage of GDP is given in Table 2.2 and graphed in Figure 2.11. Note that this figure makes the debt look different from the way it looks in the first one. As a percentage of GDP, the debt fell from the end of World War II (when it was large because of the war debt) until around 1980. It increased during the 1980s and declined in the 1990s, but started to increase again in the 2000s.

FIGURE 2.11 U.S. Federal Debt as a Percentage of GDP
Each point corresponds to a pair of observations from Table 2.2.

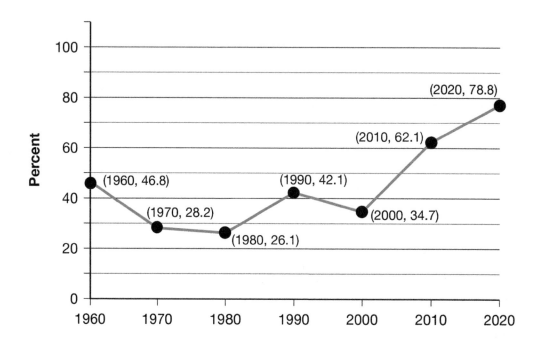

TABLE 2.2 U.S. Federal Debt as a Percentage of GDP (Illustrative Example)

Year	Debt (percent of GDP)
1960	46.8
1970	28.2
1980	26.1
1990	42.1
2000	34.7
2010	62.1
2020 (Projected)	78.8

Source: Congressional Budget Office.

Some data to be graphed have no observations close to 0, in which case including 0 on the vertical axis would leave some wasted space at the bottom of the graph. To eliminate this space and have more room to see the graph, we can start the range near the minimum value and end it near the maximum value. This is done in Figure 2.12, where the debt as a percentage of GDP is shown up to 1990. Note, however, that cutting off the bottom of the scale could be misleading to people who do not look at the axis. In particular, 0 percent is no longer at the point where the horizontal and vertical axes intersect. To warn people about the missing part of the scale, a little cut is sometimes put on the axis, as is done in Figure 2.12, but you have to look carefully at the scale.

FIGURE 2.12 A Look at Debt as a Percentage of GDP from 1960 to 1990
(*Note:* To alert the reader that the bottom part of the axis is not shown, a break point is sometimes used, as shown here.)

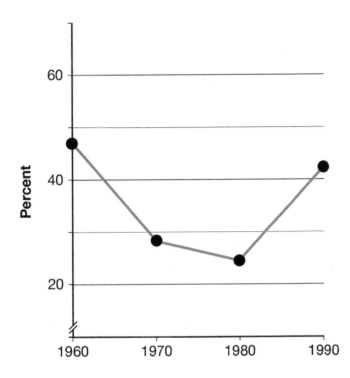

Time-Series Graphs Showing Two or More Variables

So far, we have shown how a graph can be used to show observations on one variable over time. What if we want to see how two or more variables change over time together? Suppose, for example, we want to look at how observations on debt as a percentage of GDP compare with the interest rate the government must pay on its debt. (The interest rate for 2020 is, of course, a forecast.) The two variables are shown in Table 2.3.

TABLE 2.3 Interest Rate and Federal Debt as a Percentage of GDP (Illustrative Example)

Year	Debt (percent of GDP)	Interest Rate (percent)
1960	46.8	4.1
1970	28.2	7.3
1980	26.1	11.5
1990	42.1	8.6
2000	34.7	6.0
2010	62.1	3.2
2020 (Projected)	78.8	2.3

dual scale

A graph that uses time on the horizontal axis and different scales on the left and right vertical axes to compare the movements of two variables over time.

The two sets of observations can easily be placed on the same time-series graph. In other words, we can plot the observations on the debt percentage and connect the dots and then plot the interest rate observations and connect the dots. If the scales of measurement of the two variables are much different, however, it may be hard to see both. For example, the interest rate ranges between 1 and 12 percent; it would not be visible on a graph going all the way from 0 to 100 percent, a range that is fine for the debt percentage. In this situation, a **dual scale** can be used, as shown in Figure 2.13. One scale is put on the left-hand vertical axis, and the other scale is put on the right-hand vertical axis. With a dual-scale diagram, it is essential to be aware of the two scales. In Figure 2.13, we emphasize the different axes by the color line segment at the top of each vertical axis. The color line segment corresponds to the color of the curve plotted using that scale.

FIGURE 2.13 Comparing Two Time Series with a Dual Scale
When two variables have different scales, a dual scale is useful. Here the interest rate and the debt as a percentage of GDP are plotted from Table 2.3.

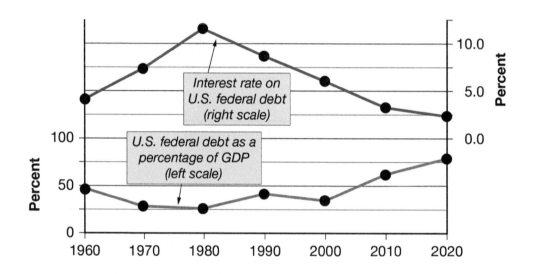

Scatter Plots

scatter plot

A graph in which points in a Cartesian coordinate system represent the values of two variables.

Finally, two variables can be usefully compared with a **scatter plot**. The Cartesian coordinate method is used, as in the time-series graph; however, we do not put the year on one of the axes. Instead, the horizontal axis is used for one of the variables and the vertical axis for the other variable. We do this for the debt percentage and the interest rate in Figure 2.14. The interest rate is on the vertical axis, and the debt percentage is on the horizontal axis. For example, the point at the upper left is 26.1 percent for the debt as a percentage of GDP and 11.5 percent for the interest rate.

FIGURE 2.14 Scatter Plot
Interest rate and debt as a percentage of GDP are shown using data from Table 2.3.

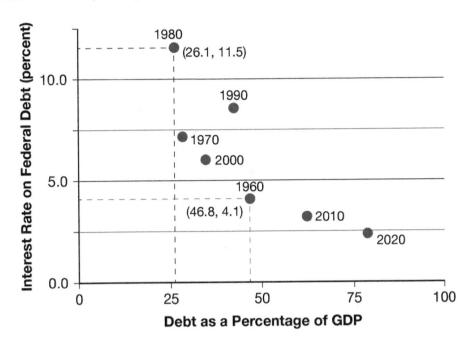

Visualizing Models with Graphs

Graphs can also represent models. Like graphs showing observations, graphs showing models usually are restricted to curves in two dimensions.

Slopes of Curves

Does a curve slope up or down? How steep is it? These questions are important to economics, as in other sciences. The **slope** of a curve tells us how much the variable on the vertical axis changes when we change the variable on the horizontal axis by one unit.

The slope is computed as follows:

$$\text{slope} = \frac{\text{change in variable on vertical axis}}{\text{change in variable on horizontal axis}}$$

In most algebra courses, the vertical axis is usually called the y-axis and the horizontal axis is called the x-axis. Thus, the slope is sometime described as

$$\text{slope} = \frac{\text{change in } y}{\text{change in } x} = \frac{\Delta y}{\Delta x}$$

where the Greek letter Δ means "change in." In other words, the slope is the ratio of the "rise" (vertical change) to the run (horizontal change).

Figure 2.15 shows how to compute the slope. In this case, the slope declines as the variable on the x-axis increases.

slope

A characteristic of a curve that is defined as the change in the variable on the vertical axis divided by the change in the variable on the horizontal axis.

FIGURE 2.15 Measuring the Slope

The slope between two points is given by the change along the vertical axis divided by the change along the horizontal axis. In this example, the slope declines as *x* increases. Because the curve slopes up from left to right, it has a positive slope.

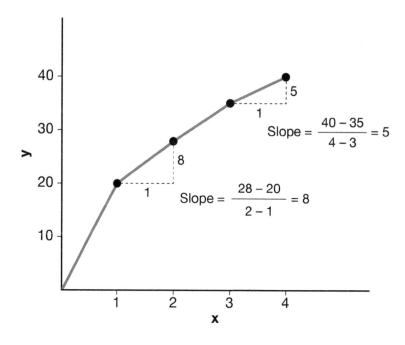

positive slope

A slope of a curve that is greater than zero, representing a positive or direct relationship between two variables.

negative slope

A slope of a curve that is less than zero, representing a negative or inverse relationship between two variables.

Observe that *the steeper the curve, the larger the slope*. When the curve gets very flat, the slope gets close to zero. Curves can either be upward-sloping or downward-sloping. If the curve slopes up from left to right, as in Figure 2.15, it has a **positive slope**, and we say that the two variables are positively related. If the curve slopes down from left to right, it has a **negative slope**, and we say that the two variables are negatively related. Figure 2.16 shows a case where the slope is negative. When *x* increases by 1 unit ($\Delta x = 1$), *y* declines by 2 units ($\Delta y = -2$). Thus, the slope equals –2; it is negative. Observe how the curve slopes down from left to right.

FIGURE 2.16 A Relationship with a Negative Slope
Here the slope is negative: as *x* increases, *y* falls. The line slopes down from left to right. In this case, *y* and *x* are inversely, or negatively, related.

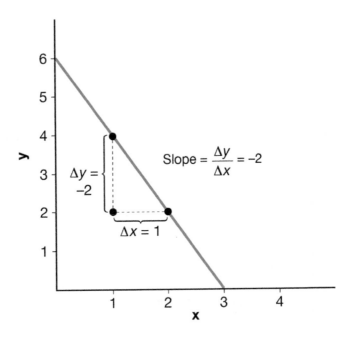

If the curve is a straight line, then the slope is a constant. Curves that are straight lines—like that in Figure 2.16—are called **linear**. But economic relationships do not need to be linear, as the example in Figure 2.15 makes clear. Figure 2.17 shows six different examples of curves and indicates how they are described.

linear

A situation in which a curve is straight, with a constant slope.

FIGURE 2.17 Six Types of Relationships
In the top row, the variables are positively related. In the bottom row, they are negatively related.

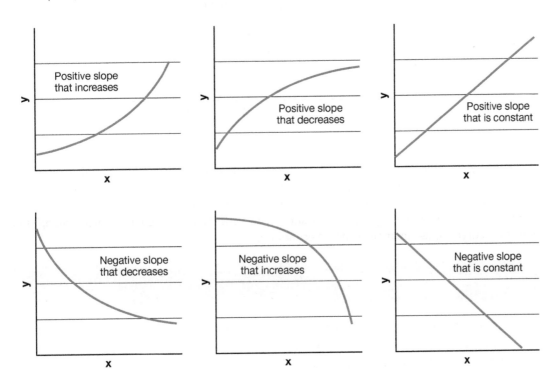

Graphs of Models with More Than Two Variables

In most cases, economic models involve more than two variables. For example, the number of physical examinations could depend on the number of nurses as well as the number of doctors. Or the amount of lemonade demanded might depend on the weather as well as on the price.

Economists have devised several methods for representing models with more than two variables with two-dimensional graphs. Suppose, for example, that the relationship between y and x in Figure 2.16 depends on a third variable z. For a given value of x, larger values of z lead to larger values of y. This example is graphed in Figure 2.18. As in Figure 2.16, when x increases, y falls. This is a **movement along the curve**. But what if z changes? We represent this as a **shift of the curve**. An increase in z shifts the curve up; a decrease in z shifts the curve down.

movement along the curve

A situation in which a change in the variable on one axis causes a change in the variable on the other axis, but the position of the curve is maintained.

shift of the curve

A change in the position of a curve, usually caused by a change in a variable not represented on either axis.

FIGURE 2.18 A Third Variable Shifts the Curve
To represent models with three variables (x, y, and z) on a two-dimensional graph, economists distinguish between movements along the curve (when x and y change, holding z unchanged) and shifts of the curve (when z changes).

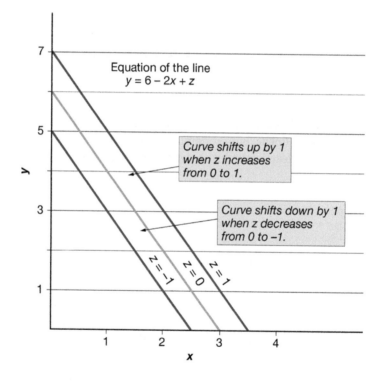

Thus, by distinguishing between shifts of and movements along a curve, economists represent models with more than two variables in only two dimensions. Only two variables (x and y) are shown explicitly on the graph, and when the third (z) is fixed, changes in x and y are movements along the curve. When z changes, the curve shifts. The distinction between "movements along" and "shifts of" curves comes up many times in economics.

Questions for Review

1. What is the difference between a scatter plot and a time-series graph?
2. Why are dual scales sometimes necessary?
3. What is the advantage of graphs over verbal representations of models?

4. What does a curve with a negative slope look like?
5. What is the difference between a shift in a curve and a movement along a curve?

Problems

1. Suppose the following table presents data on the debt (in billions of dollars), the debt to GDP ratio, and the interest rate predicted by the Congressional Budget Office for the United States for each year through 2021.

Year	Debt ($)	Debt to GDP Ratio (percent)	Interest Rate
2010	9,018	62.1%	3.2
2011	10,439	69.4%	3.4
2012	11,598	73.9%	3.8
2013	12,386	75.5%	4.2
2014	12,996	75.3%	4.6
2015	13,625	74.9%	5.0
2016	14,358	75.0%	5.3
2017	15,064	75.2%	5.4
2018	15,767	75.3%	5.4
2019	16,557	75.8%	5.4
2020	17,392	76.2%	5.4
2021	18,253	76.7%	5.4

   a. Construct a time-series plot of the ratio of government debt to GDP.
   b. Construct a time-series plot of the debt.
   c. Construct a scatter plot of the debt ratio and the interest rate.

2. The following table shows the number of physical examinations given by doctors at health maintenance organizations with three different-size clinics: small, medium, and large. The larger the clinic, the more patients the doctors can handle.

Exams per Small Clinic	Exams per Medium Clinic	Exams per Large Clinic	Number of Doctors
0	0	0	0
20	30	35	1
28	42	49	2
35	53	62	3
40	60	70	4

   a. Show the relationship between doctors and physical exams given with three curves, where the number of doctors is on the horizontal axis and the number of examinations is on the vertical axis.
   b. Describe how the three relationships compare with one another.
   c. Is a change in the number of doctors a shift of or a movement along the curve?
   d. Is a change in the size of the clinic a shift of or a movement along the curve?

CHAPTER 3
The Supply and Demand Model

In February of 2020, as the COVID-19 crisis began spreading across the world, doctors and hospitals began emphasizing that patients who were severely impacted by the virus needed access to a specialized piece of medical equipment known as a ventilator. The coronavirus, which causes COVID-19, led to serious damage to the lungs of elderly patients in particular but also to those with health complications, resulting in a drop of oxygen levels in the body. Ventilators are devices that push more oxygen directly into the patient's lungs, preventing major organ failure and effectively taking over the most essential function of life, breathing. But ventilators were scarce and COVID-19 patients often occupied a ventilator for weeks on end. This meant that in hard-hit areas, the number of patients were already exceeding the number of ventilators and in areas where an uptick of cases was expected, there simply were not enough ventilators to handle anticipated needs. As a result, hospitals and governments all over the world scrambled to purchase as many ventilators as possible.

FIGURE 3.1 Why Did Ventilator Prices Rise So Much?
The supply and demand model can help us understand why the COVID-19 crisis led to a sharp increase in the price of ventilators, a medical device that can help patients get more oxygen into their lungs.

Source: Dan Race/Shutterstock.com

In a late March press conference, New York Governor Andrew Cuomo said that New York needed to buy 30,000 ventilators but that the price that the state had to pay for the ventilators had risen to $45,000 per ventilator (about a 50 percent increase from pre-COVID prices). Why did the price of a ventilator rise by so much? Who decides what price to charge for a piece of medical equipment that is essential for saving lives? Should hospitals have to compete against one another in a time of national emergency to buy equipment or should state governments or the Federal government step in, buy ventilators at the higher prices, and resell them at pre-crisis prices to hospitals?

Similar concerns arise in situations where the stakes are not as high as in a pandemic. For instance, every January we see the appearance of news stories marveling at the costs of a Super Bowl ticket (thousands of dollars for one ticket) or the cost of a television commercial (millions of dollars to get 30 seconds of attention from viewers) to be aired during the Super Bowl. Why are fans willing to pay so much money for one football game? Why do the NFL and the participating teams use a lottery system to select fans who are then permitted to buy tickets at a much lower price than that charged by a street seller or by an online ticket broker? Who ends up going to the Super Bowl, and who ends up selling their ticket and watching the game and the commercials on television? Why do firms pay such a premium to have their commercials aired during the Super Bowl rather than during primetime network television shows? The purpose of this chapter is to show how to find the answers to such questions using the supply and demand model.

Recall from Chapter 2 that a model is a simplified description of a more complex reality. The supply and demand model is what economists use to explain how prices are determined in a market. We can use this model to understand the market for ventilators, hand sanitizer, or Super Bowl tickets, as well as in a variety of other settings. What causes the price of gasoline to fluctuate? What causes the price of desktop computers to fall over time, even though the prices of most other goods seem to rise over time? Why do roses cost more on Valentine's Day? Once you understand how the model works, you will find yourself using it over and over again to understand the markets that you come across in your everyday life.

The supply and demand model consists of three elements: *demand*, describing the behavior of consumers in the market; *supply*, describing the behavior of firms in the market; and *market equi-*

librium, connecting supply and demand and describing how consumers and firms interact in the market. Economists like to compare the supply and demand model to a pair of scissors. Demand is one blade of the scissors, and supply is the other. Either blade alone is incomplete and virtually useless; however, when the two blades of a pair of scissors are connected to form the scissors, they become an amazingly useful, yet simple, tool. So it is with the supply and demand model.

3.1 Demand

demand

A relationship between *price* and *quantity demanded*.

price

The amount of money or other goods that one must pay to obtain a particular good.

quantity demanded

The quantity of a good that people want to buy at a given price during a specific time period.

To an economist, the term *demand*—whether the demand for tickets or the demand for roses—has a very specific meaning. **Demand** is a relationship between two economic variables: (1) *the price of a particular good* and (2) *the quantity of that good that consumers are willing to buy at that price during a specific time period*, all other things being equal. For short, we call the first variable the **price** and the second variable the **quantity demanded**. The phrase *all other things being equal*, or *ceteris paribus*, is appended to the definition of demand because the quantity that consumers are willing to buy depends on many other things besides the price of the good; we want to hold these other things constant, or equal, while we examine the relationship between price and quantity demanded.

Demand can be represented by a numerical table or by a graph. In either case, demand describes how much of a good consumers will purchase at each price. Consider the demand for bicycles in a particular country, as presented in Table 3.1. Of course, because of the many kinds of bicycles—mountain bikes, racing bikes, children's bikes, and inexpensive one-speed bikes with cruiser brakes—you need to simplify and think about this table as describing demand for an average, or typical, bike.

TABLE 3.1 Demand Schedule for Bicycles (millions of bicycles per year)

Price ($)	Quantity Demanded	Price ($)	Quantity Demanded
140	18	240	5
160	14	260	3
180	11	280	2
200	9	300	1
220	7		

Observe that, as the price rises, the quantity demanded by consumers goes down. If the price goes up from $180 to $200 per bicycle, for example, the quantity demanded goes down from 11 million to 9 million bicycles. On the other hand, if the price goes down, the quantity demanded goes up. If the price falls from $180 to $160, for example, the quantity demanded rises from 11 million to 14 million bicycles.

demand schedule

A tabular presentation of demand showing the price and quantity demanded for a particular good, all else being equal.

law of demand

The tendency for the quantity demanded of a good in a market to decline as its price rises.

The relationship between price and quantity demanded in Table 3.1 is called a **demand schedule**. The relationship shows price and quantity demanded moving in opposite directions, and this is an example of the **law of demand**. The law of demand says that the higher the price, the lower the quantity demanded in the market; and the lower the price, the higher the quantity demanded in the market. In other words, the law of demand says that the price and the quantity demanded are negatively related, all other things being equal.

The Demand Curve

Figure 3.2 represents demand graphically. The price of the good appears on the vertical axis and the quantity demanded of the good appears on the horizontal axis. It shows the demand for bicycles given in Table 3.1. Each of the nine rows in Table 3.1 corresponds to one of the nine points in Figure 3.2. For example, the point at the lower right part of the graph corresponds to the first row of the table, where the price is $140 and the quantity demanded is 18 million bicycles. The resulting curve showing all the combinations of price and quantity demanded is the **demand curve**. It slopes downward from left to right because the quantity demanded is negatively related to the price.

demand curve

A graph of demand showing the downward-sloping relationship between price and quantity demanded.

FIGURE 3.2 The Demand Curve
The demand curve shows that the price of a good and the quantity demanded by consumers are negatively related—the curve slopes down. For each price, the demand curve gives the quantity demanded, or the quantity that consumers are willing to buy at that price. The points along the demand curve for bicycles shown here are the same as the pairs of numbers in Table 3.1.

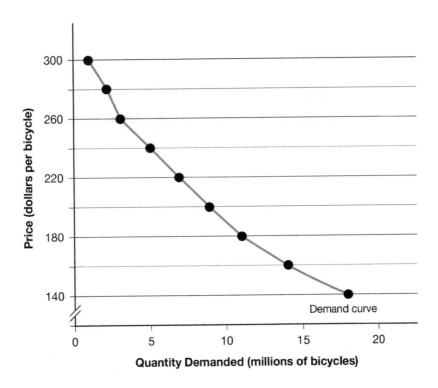

Why does the demand curve slope downward? When economists draw a demand curve, they hold constant the price of other goods: running shoes, in-line skates, motor scooters, and so on. Consumers have scarce resources and need to choose between bicycles and other goods. If the price of bicycles falls, then bicycles become more attractive to people in comparison with these other goods—some consumers who previously found the price of bicycles too high may decide to buy a bicycle rather than buy other goods. Conversely, when the price of bicycles increases, then bicycles become less attractive to people in comparison with other goods—some consumers may decide to buy in-line skates or motor scooters instead of bicycles. As a result, quantity demanded declines when the price rises and vice versa.

Plenty of real-world evidence indicates that demand curves are downward sloping. In 2016, the ride sharing firm Uber announced a cut in the per-mile travel charge in over a hundred cities that Uber had a presence in. News reports speculated that this price cut was aimed at putting pressure on their rival ride sharing firm Lyft. You might (correctly) speculate that this reduction in the price of ride sharing was intended to increase the number of potential customers switching from using Lyft vehicles to using Uber vehicles for their rides.

Similarly, policies designed to reduce smoking by teenagers or to cut down on drinking on college campuses often aim to do this by raising the price of cigarettes and alcohol. The idea, of course, is that teens would buy fewer cigarettes and students would buy less alcohol if these goods were more expensive.

 The Demand Curve

In general, the price and demand for a good are negatively related. Thus, the demand curve is downward sloping.

View the video online at: http://www.youtube.com/embed/kUPm2tMCbGE?rel=0

Shifts in Demand

Price is not the only thing that affects the quantity of a good that people buy. Weather conditions, concerns about the environment, or the availability of bike lanes on roads can influence people's decisions to purchase bicycles, for example. If climate change brought on an extended period of warm weather, people would have more opportunities to ride their bicycles. As a result, more bicycles would be purchased at any given price. Or perhaps increased awareness of the health benefits of exercise might lead people to ride their bicycles to work rather than drive their cars. This also would lead to more purchases of bicycles at any given price. Alternatively, if bike lanes are taken away to allow for an extra lane of cars on the road, fewer bicycles would be purchased at any given price.

The demand curve is drawn assuming that all other things are equal, except the price of the good. A change in any one of these other things, therefore, will shift the demand curve. An increase in demand shifts the demand curve to the right—at every price, quantity demanded will increase. A decrease in demand shifts the demand curve to the left—at every price, quantity demanded will decrease.

An increase in demand is illustrated in Figure 3.3. The lightly shaded curve labeled "old demand curve" is the same as the demand curve in Figure 3.2. An extended period of warm weather will increase demand and shift the demand curve to the right. The arrow shows how this curve has shifted to the right to the more darkly shaded curve labeled "new demand curve." When the demand curve shifts to the right, more bicycles are purchased than before at any given price. For example, before the shift in demand, a $200 price led to 9 million bicycles being purchased. But when the demand curve shifts to the right because of warmer weather, that same price leads to 13 million bicycles being purchased. On the other hand, if bicycle lanes were taken away from roads, then the demand curve would shift to the left because people's purchases of bicycles would now be less at any given price.

FIGURE 3.3 A Shift in the Demand Curve
The demand curve shows how the quantity demanded of a good is related to the price of the good, all other things being equal. A change in one of these other things—the weather or people's tastes, for example—will shift the demand curve, as shown in the graph. In this case, the demand for bicycles increases; the demand curve for bicycles shifts to the right.

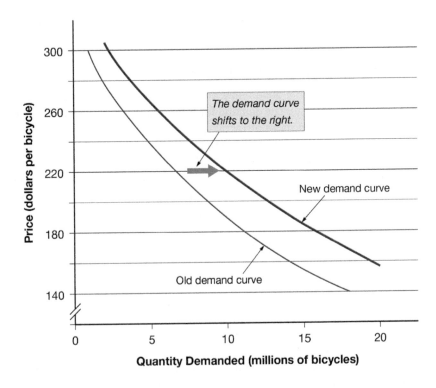

The demand curve may shift for many reasons. Most of these reasons can be attributed to one of several sources: *consumers' preferences, consumers' information, consumers' incomes, the number of consumers in the market, consumers' expectations of future prices,* and *the price of related goods.* Let us briefly consider each source of shifts in demand.

Consumers' Preferences

In general, a change in people's tastes or preferences for a product compared with other products will change the amount of the product they purchase at any given price. On many college campuses, demand for clothing that is certified as not having been produced in "sweatshops" has increased. Also, over the last couple of decades, consumers have shown a great deal of interest in buying "organically grown" fruits and vegetables, which are produced without using artificial pesticides or fertilizers.

Consumers' Information

A change in information relating to a product can also cause the demand curve to shift. For example, when people learned about the dangers of smoking, the demand for cigarettes declined. Shortly after an outbreak of *E. coli* in parts of the United States was linked to contaminated spinach, demand for spinach at grocery stores decreased. In 2015, the Environmental Protection Agency ruled that the German car-manufacturing giant Volkswagen had intentionally programmed their diesel cars to make it seem like they were emitting less pollution than they actually were. This scandal eventually led to a $4 billion fine and a recall of over 11 million cars. The fallout from this episode led to a sharp fall in the demand for diesel-engine automobiles made by Volkswagen.

Consumers' Incomes

normal goods

A good for which demand increases when income rises and decreases when income falls.

If people's incomes change, then their purchases of goods usually change. An increase in income increases the demand for most goods, while a decline in income reduces the demand for these goods. Goods for which demand increases when income rises and decreases when income falls are called **normal goods** by economists. Many of the goods that people typically purchase—shoes, clothing, jewelry—fall into the category of normal goods.

inferior goods

A good for which demand decreases when income rises and increases when income falls.

However, the demand for some goods may decline when income increases. Such goods are called **inferior goods** by economists. The demand for inferior goods declines when people's income increases because they can afford more attractive goods. For example, instant noodles form the basis of many college students' diets. After these students leave college and start working and earning a salary, however, many will switch over to eating microwavable meals or to eating out in restaurants. Thus, the demand for instant noodles will fall as income rises. Another example of an inferior good that is familiar to many college students in Boston and New York is the cheap bus service that runs between the Chinatowns in the two cities; a bus ticket may cost as little as $10, whereas a plane ticket between the two cities may cost $150. As students graduate and start earning money, however, they often buy more of the $150 plane tickets and fewer of the $10 bus tickets. In this case, the plane ticket is categorized as a normal good, and the bus ticket is categorized as an inferior good.

Number of Consumers in the Market

Demand is a relationship between price and the quantity demanded by *all* consumers in the market. If the number of consumers increases, then demand will increase. If the number of consumers falls, then demand will decrease. For example, the number of teenagers in the U.S. population expanded sharply in the late 1990s. This increased the demand for *Seventeen* magazine, Rollerblades, Clearasil, and other goods that teenagers tend to buy. As the baby boom generation in the United States ages, the demand for health care, hair coloring kits, and luxury skin care products is increasing.

Consumers' Expectations of Future Prices

If people expect the price of a good to increase, they will want to buy it before the price increases. Conversely, if people expect the price of goods to decline, they will purchase fewer items and wait for the decline. One often sees this effect of expectations of future price changes. "We'd better buy before the price goes up" is a common reason for purchasing items during a clearance sale. Or, "Let's put off buying that flat-screen television until the post-holiday sales."

In general, it is difficult to forecast the future, but consumers sometimes know quite a bit about whether the price of a good will rise or fall, and they react accordingly. Thus, demand increases if people expect the *future* price of the good to rise. And demand decreases if people expect the *future* price of the good to fall.

In 2009, Congress created a program that aimed to provide incentives for U.S. consumers to buy new, more fuel-efficient cars by trading in their older, less fuel-efficient vehicles. This program, popularly known as "Cash for Clunkers," offered customers about a $4,000 discount for buying a new car. Many people moved up their planned car purchases to take advantage of the "Cash for Clunkers" program. The program, which was planned to run for five months, exhausted all the available funds allocated to it, and $2 billion more in additional allocations, in less than two months.

Prices of Closely Related Goods

A change in the price of a closely related good can increase or decrease demand for another good, depending on whether the good is a substitute or a complement. A **substitute** is a good that provides some of the same uses or enjoyment as another good. Butter and margarine are substitutes. In general, the demand for a good will increase if the price of a substitute for the good rises, and the demand for a good will decrease if the price of a substitute falls. Binge watching shows on streaming services like Hulu and Netflix are substitutes for watching weekly episodes of shows on cable television. In recent years, there has been a sharp decline in cable subscriptions as more people "cut the cord" and move to streaming services. College students of today do not even know what a music CD looks like, as the price of music streaming services like Spotify has decreased to the point where virtually any song is available at their fingertips.

A **complement** is a good that tends to be consumed together with another good. Gasoline and sport utility vehicles (SUVs) are complements. The rapid increase in gasoline prices in 2007 and the early part of 2008 led to a decrease in demand for SUVs. Charging stations and electric vehicles (EVs) are complements. As the availability of charging stations increases and the price of charging a vehicle at a station falls, there is an increase in the demand for EVs.

substitute

A good that has many of the same characteristics as, and can be used in place of, another good.

complement

A good that usually is consumed or used together with another good.

Movements Along versus Shifts of the Demand Curve

We have shown that the demand curve can shift, and we have given many possible reasons for such shifts. As you begin to use demand curves, it is important that you be able to distinguish *shifts* of the demand curve from *movements along* the demand curve. This distinction is illustrated in Figure 3.4.

A *movement along* the demand curve occurs when the quantity demanded changes as a result of a *change in the price of the good*. For example, if the price of bicycles rises, causing the quantity demanded by consumers to fall, then there is a movement along the demand curve. You can see in Figure 3.4 that at point *A*, the price is $200 and the quantity demanded is 9 million. Now suppose the price rises to $220. The quantity demanded then falls from 9 million to 7 million. This can be shown as a movement along the demand curve for bicycles from point *A* to point *B*. Conversely, if the price of a bicycle falls to $180, then the quantity demanded will increase to 11 million bicycles.

This can be shown as an increase from point *A* to point *C* in Figure 3.4. Economists refer to a movement along the demand curve as a *change in the quantity demanded*.

FIGURE 3.4 Shifts of versus Movements Along the Demand Curve

A *shift* of the demand curve occurs when a change in something (other than the good's own price) affects the quantity of a good that consumers are willing to buy. An increase in demand is a shift to the right of the demand curve. A decrease in demand is a shift to the left of the demand curve. A *movement along* the demand curve occurs when the price of the good changes, causing the quantity demanded to change, as, for example, from point *A* to point *B* or *C*.

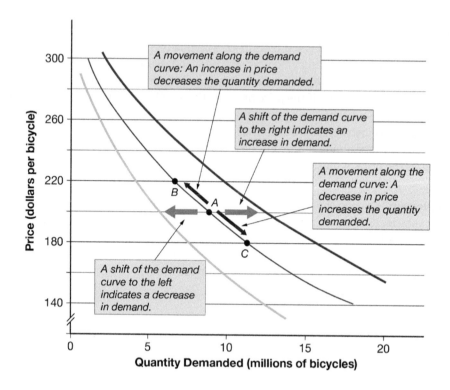

A *shift* of the demand curve, on the other hand, occurs when a change is caused by *any source except the price*. Remember, the term *demand* refers to the entire curve or schedule relating price and quantity demanded, whereas the term *quantity demanded* refers to a single point on the demand curve. As we discussed, if warm weather increases, people would be more likely to buy bicycles at any given price. This means that the entire demand curve would shift to the right. On the other hand, if bicycle lanes are eliminated, people would be less likely to buy bicycles at any given price. The entire demand curve would shift to the left. Economists refer to a shift in the demand curve as a *change in demand*.

You should be able to tell whether an economic event causes (1) a change in demand or (2) a change in the quantity demanded; or, equivalently, whether an event causes (1) a shift in the demand curve or (2) a movement along the demand curve. Use the following example to test your understanding of demand shifts and movement along the demand curve. Suppose that Disney's theme park attendance was lower in a recession year than in previous years because of a weak economy. Because of the fall in attendance, suppose Disney lowered the adult admission price at its California Adventure park, which helped increase attendance. Which of these was a *change in demand* and which was a *change in the quantity demanded* in the market for theme parks?

The decrease in attendance caused by the weak economy was a decrease in demand—fewer people were going to theme parks in a recession year than in prior years for any given ticket price. The demand curve for theme park visits thus shifted to the left. When Disney lowered its admission price, it hoped to entice more people to spend their money on a trip to its California Adventure park instead of on other goods. This is an increase in the quantity demanded—the park management anticipated more attendance at a lower price. This was a movement along the demand curve for theme park visits.

The Impact of COVID-19 on Consumers and Businesses

Focus on minutes 2:00 to 4:30 of this video for a discussion on how the COVID-19 pandemic affected consumer spending and business revenues.

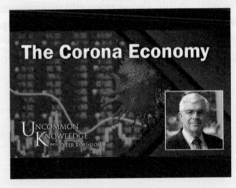

View the video online at: http://www.youtube.com/embed/TAYWWzD9c9E?rel=0

Review

- Demand is a negative relationship between the price of a good and the quantity demanded, all other things being equal.

- The demand curve slopes down because when the price of a good rises, consumers are less likely to use their scarce resources to buy that good. Conversely, when the price of a good falls, some consumers who previously had not chosen to buy the good because the price was too high may decide to buy the good.

- It is important to distinguish shifts of the demand curve from movements along the demand curve. When the quantity demanded changes as a result of a price change, we have a movement along the demand curve. When a change in demand is brought about by something other than a price change, we have a shift of the demand curve.

3.2 Supply

Whereas demand refers to the behavior of consumers, supply refers to the behavior of firms. The term *supply*—whether it is the supply of tickets or the supply of computers—has a specific meaning for economists. **Supply** is a relationship between two variables: (1) *the price of a particular good* and (2) *the quantity of the good that firms are willing to sell at that price*, all other things being the same. We call the first variable the price and the second variable the **quantity supplied**.

supply

A relationship between price and quantity supplied.

quantity supplied

The quantity of a good that firms are willing to sell at a given price.

supply schedule

A tabular presentation of supply showing the price and quantity supplied of a particular good, all else being equal.

law of supply

The tendency for the quantity supplied of a good in a market to increase as its price rises.

Supply can be represented by a numerical table or by a graph. An example of the quantity supplied (in millions of bicycles) in the entire market by bicycle-producing firms at each price is shown in Table 3.2. For example, at a price of $180, the quantity supplied is 7 million bicycles. Observe that as the price increases, the quantity supplied increases, and that as the price decreases, the quantity supplied decreases. For example, if the price rises from $180 to $200, the quantity supplied increases from 7 to 9 million bicycles. The relationship between price and quantity supplied in Table 3.2 is called a **supply schedule**. The relationship shows price and quantity supplied moving in the same direction, and this is an example of the law of supply. The **law of supply** says that the higher the price, the higher the quantity supplied; and the lower the price, the lower the quantity supplied. In other words, the law of supply says that the price and the quantity supplied are positively related, all other things being equal.

TABLE 3.2 Supply Schedule for Bicycles (millions of bicycles per year)

Price ($)	Quantity Supplied
140	1
160	4
180	7
200	9
220	11
240	13
260	15
280	16
300	17

The Supply Curve

supply curve

A graph of supply showing the upward-sloping relationship between price and quantity supplied.

We can represent the supply schedule in Table 3.2 graphically by plotting the price and quantity supplied on a graph, as shown in Figure 3.5. The scales of each axis in Figure 3.5 are exactly the same as those in Figure 3.2, except that Figure 3.5 shows the quantity supplied, whereas Figure 3.2 shows the quantity demanded. Each pair of numbers in Table 3.2 is plotted as a point in Figure 3.5. The resulting curve showing all the combinations of prices and quantities supplied is the **supply curve**. Note that the curve slopes upward: At a price of $280, the quantity supplied is high—16 million bicycles. If the price were $160 a bicycle, then firms would be willing to sell only 4 million bicycles.

FIGURE 3.5 The Supply Curve
The supply curve shows that the price and the quantity supplied by firms in the market are positively related. The curve slopes up. For each price on the vertical axis, the supply curve shows the quantity that firms are willing to sell along the horizontal axis. The points along the supply curve for bicycles match the pairs of numbers in Table 3.2.

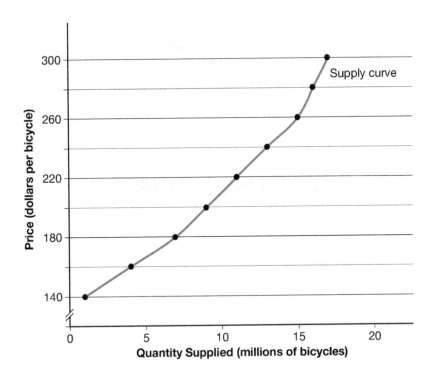

Why does the supply curve slope upward? Imagine yourself running a firm that produces and sells bicycles. If the price of the bicycles goes up from $180 to $280, then you can earn $100 more for each bicycle you produce and sell. Given your production costs, if you earn more from each bicycle, you will have a greater incentive to produce and sell more bicycles. If producing more bicycles increases the costs of producing each bicycle, perhaps because you must pay the bike assembly workers a higher wage for working overtime, the higher price will give you the incentive to incur these costs. Other bicycle firms will be thinking the same way. Thus, firms are willing to sell more bicycles as the price rises. Conversely, the incentive for firms to sell bicycles will decline as the price falls. Basically, that is why a positive relationship exists between price and quantity supplied.

When formulating economic policy, it is important to remember this supply relationship. When the price of a good increases, it leads to an increase in the quantity supplied. If U.S. agricultural policy results in the U.S. government offering to pay farmers a higher price for their corn, then the farmers will respond by increasing their production of corn. If coffee prices on the world market collapse, some coffee farmers in developing countries will switch to producing other crops instead of coffee.

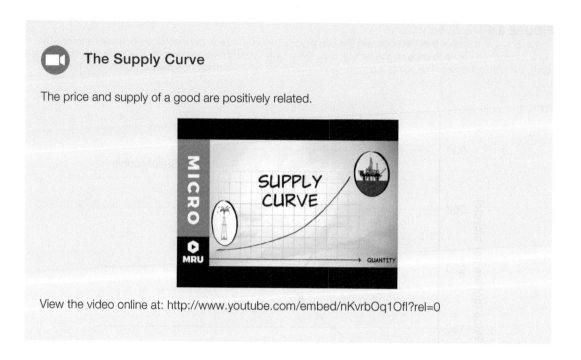

The Supply Curve

The price and supply of a good are positively related.

View the video online at: http://www.youtube.com/embed/nKvrbOq1Ofl?rel=0

Shifts in Supply

The supply curve is a relationship between price and the quantity supplied drawn on the assumption that all other things are held constant. If any one of these other things changes, then the supply curve shifts. For example, suppose a new machine is invented that makes it possible to produce bicycle frames at less cost; then firms would have more incentive at any given price to produce and sell more bicycles. Supply would increase, and the supply curve would shift to the right.

Figure 3.6 shows that the supply curve for bicycles would shift to the right because of a new cost-reducing machine. The supply curve would shift to the left if supply decreased. Supply would decrease, for example, if bicycle-producing firms suddenly found that their existing machines would break down unless they were oiled with an expensive lubricant each time a bicycle was produced. This would raise costs, lower supply, and shift the supply curve to the left.

Many things can cause the supply curve to shift. Most of these can be categorized by the source of the change in supply: *technology, weather conditions, the price of inputs used in production, the number of firms in the market, expectations of future prices,* and *government taxes, subsidies, and regulations.* Let us briefly consider the sources of shifts in supply.

FIGURE 3.6 A Shift in the Supply Curve
The supply curve is a relationship between the quantity supplied of a good and the price of the good, all other things being equal. A change in one of these other things (other than the good's price) will shift the supply curve, as shown in the graph. In this case, the supply of bicycles increases; the supply curve for bicycles shifts to the right.

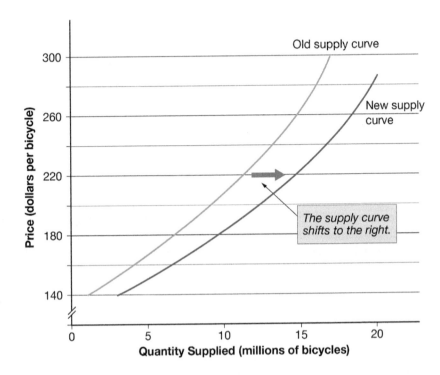

Technology

Anything that changes the amount a firm can produce with a given amount of inputs to production can be considered a change in technology. The Harbour Report, a study that examines the number of labor hours needed to produce an automobile, calculated that in 2005, General Motors needed 34 hours per vehicle, while Toyota needed only 28 hours per vehicle. Suppose an improvement in technology enabled General Motors to reduce the time it took to produce a car by six hours per vehicle. This improvement in technology would correspond to an increase in supply, a shift in the supply curve to the right. Another way of viewing an increase in supply is that producers are willing to sell any given quantity at a lower price than before. This makes sense, because production costs are lower with the improvement in technology.

Weather Conditions

Droughts, earthquakes, and hurricanes also affect how much of certain types of goods can be produced with given inputs. A drought can reduce the amount of wheat that can be produced on a farm in the Midwest. The floods that devastated some regions in Australia in early 2011 resulted in a fall in cotton supplies on the world market, for which Australia is a leading producer and exporter. Hurricanes Katrina and Rita disrupted oil drilling and refining activities in Texas and Louisiana. Because such events change the amount that can be produced with a given amount of inputs, they are similar to changes in technology. In the examples just given, the supply curve shifted to the left, although you could have favorable weather conditions that would shift the supply curve for a particular good to the right.

The Price of Inputs Used in Production

If the prices of the inputs to production—raw materials, labor, and capital—increase, then it becomes more costly to produce goods, and firms will produce less at any given price. In this case, the supply curve will shift to the left. When the U.S. government imposed trade restrictions that caused the price of imported aluminum and steel to rise in 2018, firms that used imported steel and aluminum to produce household appliances were unwilling to produce the same quantity of appliances at existing price levels. So an increase in production costs causes the supply curve to shift to the left, and a decrease in production costs causes the supply curve to shift to the right.

The Number of Firms in the Market

Remember that the supply curve refers to *all* the firms producing the product. If the number of firms increases, then more goods will be produced at each price: supply increases, and the supply curve shifts to the right. A decline in the number of firms, on the other hand, would shift the supply curve to the left. For example, if a country removes barriers that prevent foreign car manufacturers from selling cars to the domestic market, then the number of firms producing cars for that country's domestic market will increase, and the supply curve for cars in that economy will shift to the right.

Expectations of Future Prices

If firms expect the price of the good they produce to rise in the future, then they will hold off selling at least part of their production until the price rises. For example, farmers in the United States who anticipate an increase in wheat prices because of political unrest in the Russian Federation may decide to store more wheat in silos and sell it later, after the price rises. Thus, expectations of *future* price increases tend to reduce supply. Conversely, expectations of *future* price decreases tend to increase supply.

Government Taxes, Subsidies, and Regulations

The government has the ability to affect the supply of particular goods produced by firms. For example, the government imposes taxes on firms to pay for such government services as education, police, and national defense. These taxes increase firms' costs and reduce supply. The supply curve shifts to the left when a tax on what firms sell in the market increases.

The government also makes payments—subsidies—to firms to encourage those firms to produce certain goods. Such subsidies have the opposite effect of taxes on supply. An increase in subsidies reduces firms' costs and increases the supply. If the U.S. government provided subsidies for corn production to encourage the use of ethanol, an alternative fuel for cars that is produced from corn, this would increase the production of corn. On the other hand, when the U.S. government imposes a tax on cigarettes, the supply of cigarettes will decrease.

Governments also regulate firms. In some cases, such regulations can change the firms' costs of production or their ability to produce goods and thereby affect supply. For example, if a city government decides that only vendors who successfully pass a health and sanitation inspection are allowed to sell food from street carts, the supply curve for street-vendor food will shift to the left.

Movements Along versus Shifts of the Supply Curve

As with the demand curve, it is important that you understand how to distinguish between *shifts* of the supply curve and *movements along* the supply curve. This distinction is illustrated in Figure 3.7.

A *movement along* the supply curve occurs when the quantity supplied changes as a result of a *change in the price of the good*. For example, if a copper mine in Zambia increases its production because the price of copper has increased on the world market, then that indicates a movement along the supply curve. In our bicycle example, an increase in the price of bicycles from $200 to $220 would increase the quantity supplied from 9 million bicycles to 11 million bicycles. This can be shown as a movement along the supply curve for bicycles from point *D* to point *F*. Conversely, if the price of a bicycle were to fall from $200 to $180, then the quantity supplied would decrease to 7 million bicycles. This can be shown as movement from point *D* to point *E* in Figure 3.7. Economists refer to a movement along the supply curve as a *change in the quantity supplied*.

FIGURE 3.7 Shifts of versus Movements Along the Supply Curve
A shift of the supply curve occurs when a change in something (other than the price) affects the amount of a good that firms are willing to supply. An increase in supply is a shift to the right of the supply curve. A decrease in supply is a shift to the left of the supply curve. A movement along the supply curve occurs when the price of the good changes, causing the quantity supplied by firms to change—for example, from point *D* to point *E* or *F*.

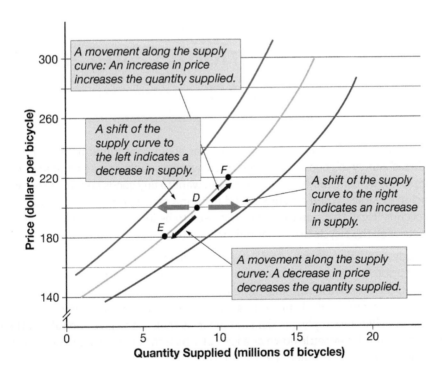

A *shift* of the supply curve, on the other hand, occurs if a change is caused by *any source except the price*. An unexpected winter freeze in California will mean that farmers will be able to produce fewer oranges at any given price. This means that the supply curve of oranges will shift to the left. When the supply curve shifts, economists call that a *change in supply*.

You should be able to tell whether a change in something causes (1) a change in supply or (2) a change in the quantity supplied; or, equivalently, if a change causes (1) a shift in the supply curve or (2) a movement along the supply curve. The following example will test your ability to distinguish between movement along a supply curve and a shift in the supply curve. Suppose that U.S. agricultural policy guarantees farmers a specific price on certain crops. An economist suggested that the government instead should pay farmers to not plant some of their fields. Which policy is describing a *change in supply* and which is describing a *change in the quantity supplied* in the market for corn?

A policy that pays farmers to leave cornfields unplanted describes a decrease in supply. The amount of corn supplied will be lower at any price. When the U.S. government guarantees the price of corn, this describes an increase in the quantity supplied—more corn will be grown in anticipation of the higher price. The increase in price leading to an increase in quantity supplied corresponds to movement along the supply curve.

Review

- Supply is a positive relationship between the price of a good and the quantity supplied of the good by firms.
- The supply curve slopes upward because, all else equal, a higher price offers greater incentive for a firm to produce and sell more goods.
- It is important to distinguish shifts of the supply curve from movements along the supply curve. When the quantity supplied changes because of a change in price, we have a movement along the supply curve. Other factors—such as technology, weather, the number of firms, and expectations—can lead to a shift in the supply curve.

3.3 Market Equilibrium: Combining Supply and Demand

Figure 3.8 summarizes what you have learned thus far about consumers' demand for goods in a market and firms' supply of goods in a market. Now, we put supply and demand together to complete the supply and demand model. Consumers who want to buy goods and firms that want to sell goods interact in a market. When consumers and firms interact, a price is determined at which the transaction occurs. Recall that a market does not need to be located at one place; the U.S. bicycle market consists of all the bicycle firms that sell bicycles and all the consumers who buy bicycles.

Fascinatingly, no single person or firm determines the price in the market. Instead, the market determines the price. As buyers and sellers interact, prices may go up for a while and then go down. Alfred Marshall, the economist who did the most to develop the supply and demand model in the late nineteenth century, called this process the "higgling and bargaining" of the market. The assumption underlying the supply and demand model is that, in the give and take of the marketplace, prices adjust until they settle down at a level at which the quantity supplied by firms equals the quantity demanded by consumers. Let's see how.

FIGURE 3.8 Overview of Supply and Demand

This figure summarizes why the demand curve and supply curve are shaped the way they are, what factors cause a movement along one of the curves, and what factors cause the curves to shift.

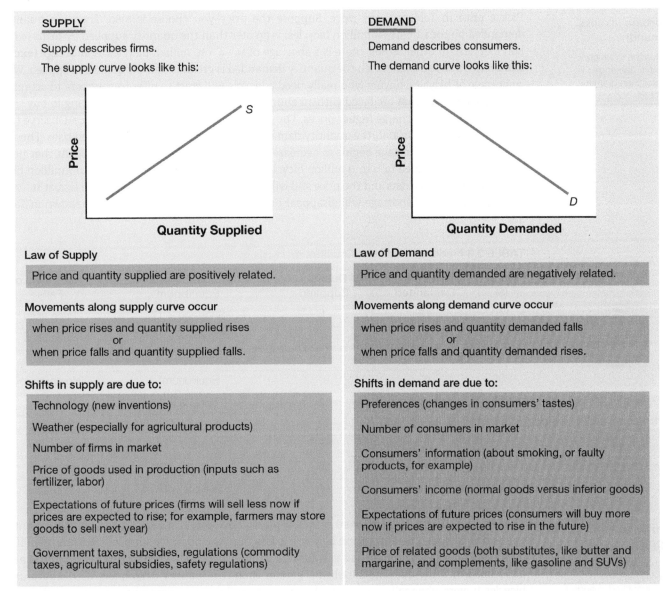

SUPPLY

Supply describes firms.

The supply curve looks like this:

(Graph: Price on vertical axis, Quantity Supplied on horizontal axis, upward-sloping curve labeled S)

Law of Supply

Price and quantity supplied are positively related.

Movements along supply curve occur

when price rises and quantity supplied rises
or
when price falls and quantity supplied falls.

Shifts in supply are due to:

Technology (new inventions)

Weather (especially for agricultural products)

Number of firms in market

Price of goods used in production (inputs such as fertilizer, labor)

Expectations of future prices (firms will sell less now if prices are expected to rise; for example, farmers may store goods to sell next year)

Government taxes, subsidies, regulations (commodity taxes, agricultural subsidies, safety regulations)

DEMAND

Demand describes consumers.

The demand curve looks like this:

(Graph: Price on vertical axis, Quantity Demanded on horizontal axis, downward-sloping curve labeled D)

Law of Demand

Price and quantity demanded are negatively related.

Movements along demand curve occur

when price rises and quantity demanded falls
or
when price falls and quantity demanded rises.

Shifts in demand are due to:

Preferences (changes in consumers' tastes)

Number of consumers in market

Consumers' information (about smoking, or faulty products, for example)

Consumers' income (normal goods versus inferior goods)

Expectations of future prices (consumers will buy more now if prices are expected to rise in the future)

Price of related goods (both substitutes, like butter and margarine, and complements, like gasoline and SUVs)

Determination of the Market Price

To determine the market price, we combine the demand relationship with the supply relationship. We can do this using either a table or a diagram. First consider Table 3.3, which combines the demand schedule from Table 3.1 with the supply schedule from Table 3.2. The price is in the first column, the quantity demanded by consumers is in the second column, and the quantity supplied by firms is in the third column. Observe that the quantity that consumers are willing to buy is shown to decline with the price, whereas the quantity that firms are willing to sell is shown to increase with the price.

Finding the Market Price

shortage (excess demand)

A situation in which quantity demanded is greater than quantity supplied.

Pick a price in Table 3.3, any price. Suppose the price you choose is $160. Then the quantity demanded by consumers (14 million bicycles) is greater than the quantity supplied by firms (4 million bicycles). In other words, there is a shortage of 14 - 4 = 10 million bicycles. A **shortage (excess demand)** is a situation in which the quantity demanded is greater than the quantity supplied. With a shortage of bicycles, buyers who really need a bicycle will start to offer to pay more to acquire a bicycle, while firms that are faced with an abundance of potential customers wanting to buy their bicycles will begin to charge higher prices. Thus, $160 cannot last as the market price. Observe that as the price rises above $160, the quantity demanded falls and the quantity supplied rises. Thus, as the price rises, the shortage begins to decrease. Suppose the price increases to $180. At that price, the quantity demanded falls to 11 million bicycles and the quantity supplied rises to 7 million bicycles. A shortage still exists and the price still will rise, but the shortage is now much less, at 11 − 7 = 4 million bicycles. The shortage will disappear only when the price rises to $200, as shown in Table 3.3.

TABLE 3.3 Finding the Market Equilibrium

Price ($)	Quantity Demanded	Quantity Supplied	Shortage, Surplus, or Equilibrium	Price Rises or Falls
140	18	1	Shortage = 17	Price rises
160	14	4	Shortage = 10	Price rises
180	11	7	Shortage = 4	Price rises
200	9*	9*	Equilibrium*	No change*
220	7	11	Surplus = 4	Price falls
240	5	13	Surplus = 8	Price falls
260	3	15	Surplus = 12	Price falls
280	2	16	Surplus = 14	Price falls
300	1	17	Surplus = 16	Price falls

surplus (excess supply)

A situation in which quantity supplied is greater than quantity demanded.

Suppose instead that you had picked a price above $200, let's say $260. Then the quantity demanded by consumers (3 million bicycles) is less than the quantity supplied by firms (15 million bicycles). In other words, there is a surplus of 12 million bicycles. A **surplus (excess supply)** is a situation in which the quantity supplied is greater than the quantity demanded. With a surplus of bicycles, buyers who really need a bicycle have an abundance of sellers who are eager to sell them a bicycle, while firms have to compete with one another to entice buyers for their products. Therefore, the price of bicycles will fall: Firms that are willing to sell bicycles for less than $260 will offer to sell to consumers at lower prices. Thus, $260 cannot be the market price either. Observe that as the price falls below $260, the quantity demanded rises and the quantity supplied falls. Thus, the surplus decreases. If you choose any price above $200, the same thing will happen: A surplus will exist, and the price will fall. The surplus disappears only when the price falls to $200.

equilibrium price

The price at which quantity supplied equals quantity demanded.

Thus, we have shown that for any price below $200, a shortage exists, and the price rises, while for any price above $200, a surplus exists, and the price falls. What if the market price is $200? Then the quantity supplied equals the quantity demanded; there is not a shortage or a surplus, and there is no reason for the price to rise or fall. This price of $200 is called the **equilibrium price** because, at this price, the quantity supplied equals the quantity demanded, and the price has no tendency to change. There is no other price for which quantity supplied equals quantity demanded. If you look at all the other prices, you will see either a shortage or a surplus, and thus the price has a tendency to either rise or fall.

The quantity bought and sold at the equilibrium price is 9 million bicycles. This is the **equilibrium quantity**. When the price equals the equilibrium price and the quantity bought and sold equals the equilibrium quantity, economists call this a **market equilibrium**.

Our discussion of the determination of the equilibrium price shows how the market price coordinates the buying and selling decisions of many firms and consumers. We see that the price serves a *rationing function*. When a shortage exists, a higher price reduces the quantity demanded and increases the quantity supplied to eliminate the shortage. Similarly, when a surplus exists, a lower price increases the quantity demanded and decreases the quantity supplied to eliminate the surplus. Thus, both shortages and surpluses are eliminated by the forces of supply and demand.

equilibrium quantity

The quantity traded at the equilibrium price.

market equilibrium

The situation in which the price is equal to the equilibrium price and the quantity traded equals the equilibrium quantity.

Two Predictions

By combining supply and demand, we have completed the supply and demand model. The model can be applied to many markets, not just the example of the bicycle market. One prediction of the supply and demand model is that *the equilibrium price in the market will be the price for which the quantity supplied equals the quantity demanded*. Thus, the model provides an answer to the question of what determines the price in the market. Another prediction of the model is that *the equilibrium quantity bought and sold in the market is the quantity for which the quantity supplied equals the quantity demanded*.

Finding the Equilibrium with a Supply and Demand Diagram

The equilibrium price and quantity in a market can also be found with the help of a graph. Figure 3.9 combines the demand curve from Figure 3.2 and the supply curve from Figure 3.5 in the same diagram. Observe that the downward-sloping demand curve intersects the upward-sloping supply curve at a single point. At that point of intersection, the quantity supplied equals the quantity demanded. Hence, the *equilibrium price is at the intersection of the supply curve and the demand curve*. The equilibrium price of $200 is shown in Figure 3.9. At that price, the quantity demanded is 9 million bicycles, and the quantity supplied is 9 million bicycles. This is the equilibrium quantity.

If the price were lower than this equilibrium price, say, $160, then the quantity demanded would be greater than the quantity supplied. A shortage would exist, and demand would pressure the price to increase, as shown in the graph. The increase in gasoline prices in 2007 and the early part of 2008 led to an increase in demand for hybrid automobiles. With a shortage of hybrid vehicles and long waiting lists, some automobile sellers increased the price of the hybrids.

On the other hand, if the price were above the equilibrium price, say, $260, then the quantity supplied would be greater than the quantity demanded. A surplus would exist, and excess quantity would pressure the price to fall. After September 11, 2001, a large number of vacationers canceled vacation plans that involved air travel. Caribbean hotels, with a surplus of vacant hotel rooms following this decrease in demand, began to offer big discounts.

Thus, the market price will tend to move toward the equilibrium price at the intersection of the supply curve and the demand curve. We can calculate exactly what the equilibrium price is in Figure 3.9 by drawing a line over to the vertical axis. And we can calculate the equilibrium quantity by drawing a line down to the horizontal axis.

FIGURE 3.9 Equilibrium Price and Equilibrium Quantity

When buyers and sellers interact in the market, the equilibrium price is at the point of intersection of the supply curve and the demand curve. At this point, the quantity supplied equals the quantity demanded. The equilibrium quantity also is determined at that point. At a higher price, the quantity demanded will be less than the quantity supplied; a surplus will exist. At a lower price, the quantity demanded will be greater than the quantity supplied; a shortage will exist.

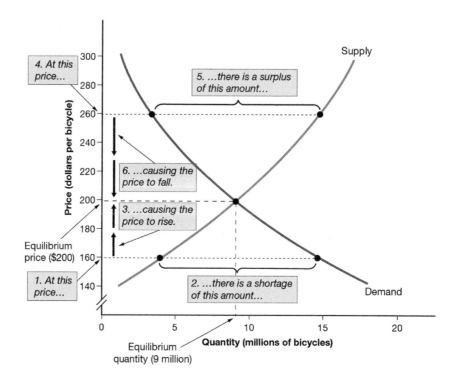

Market Outcomes When Supply or Demand Changes

Now that you know how to find the equilibrium price and quantity in a market, we can use the supply and demand model to analyze the impact of factors that change supply or demand on equilibrium price and quantity. We first consider a change in demand and then a change in supply.

Effects of a Change in Demand

Figure 3.10 shows the effects of a shift in the demand curve for bicycles. Suppose that a shift occurs because of a fitness craze that increases the demand for bicycles. The demand curve shifts to the right, as shown in Figure 3.10(a). The demand curve before the shift and the demand curve after the shift are labeled the "old demand curve" and the "new demand curve," respectively.

FIGURE 3.10 Effects of a Shift in Demand
When demand increases, as in graph (a), the demand curve shifts to the right. The equilibrium price rises, and the equilibrium quantity also rises. When demand decreases, as in graph (b), the demand curve shifts to the left. The equilibrium price falls, and the equilibrium quantity also falls.

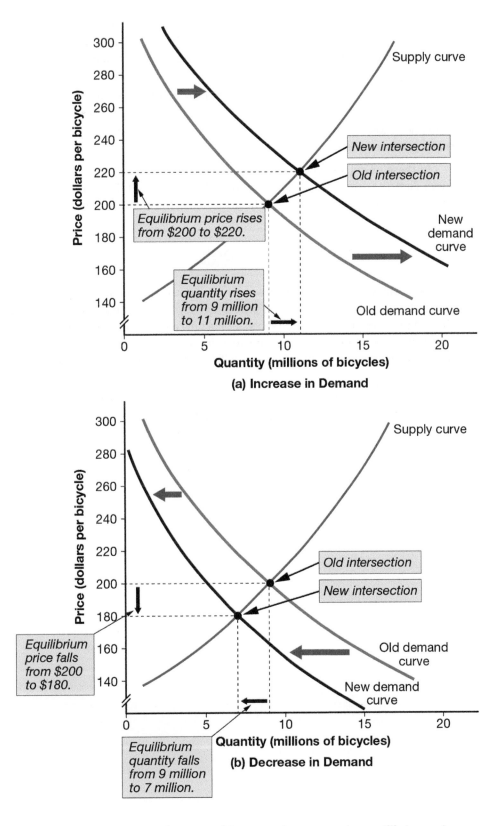

(a) Increase in Demand

(b) Decrease in Demand

If you look at the graph, you can see that something must happen to the equilibrium price when the demand curve shifts. The equilibrium price is determined at the intersection of the supply curve and the demand curve. With the new demand curve, there is a new intersection and, therefore, a new equilibrium price. The equilibrium price is no longer $200 in Figure 3.10(a); it is up to $220 per bicycle. Thus, the supply and demand model predicts that the price in the market will rise if demand increases. Note also that the equilibrium quantity of bicycles changes. The quantity of bicycles sold and bought has increased from 9 million to 11 million. Thus, the equilibrium quantity has increased along with the equilibrium price. The supply and demand model predicts that an increase in demand will raise both the price and the quantity sold in the market.

We can use the same method to find out what happens if demand decreases, as shown in Figure 3.10(b). Suppose that the elimination of dedicated bicycle lanes on roads shifts the demand curve for bicycles to the left. At the new intersection of the supply and demand curves, the equilibrium price is lower, and the quantity sold also is lower. Thus, the supply and demand model predicts that a decrease in demand will both lower the price and lower the quantity sold in the market.

In these examples, when the demand curve shifts, it leads to a movement along the supply curve. First, the demand curve shifts to the right or to the left. Then there is a movement along the supply curve because the change in the price affects the quantity of bicycles that firms will sell.

Effects of a Change in Supply

Figure 3.11 shows what happens when a change in the market shifts the supply curve. Suppose a new technology reduces the cost of producing bicycles, resulting in the supply curve for bicycles shifting to the right. Figure 3.11(a) shows that a new equilibrium price is lower than the old equilibrium price. In addition, the equilibrium quantity rises. Thus, the supply and demand model predicts that an increase in the supply of bicycles will lower the price and raise the quantity of bicycles sold.

Suppose instead that an increase in the cost of bicycle tires increases the cost of producing bicycles, resulting in the supply curve for bicycles shifting to the left. Figure 3.11(b) shows that the equilibrium price rises, and the equilibrium quantity falls. Thus, the model predicts that a decrease in the supply of bicycles will raise the price of bicycles and lower the quantity of bicycles sold.

FIGURE 3.11 Effects of a Shift in Supply

When supply increases, as in graph (a), the supply curve shifts to the right, the equilibrium price falls, and the equilibrium quantity rises. When supply decreases, as in graph (b), the supply curve shifts to the left, the equilibrium price rises, and the equilibrium quantity falls.

(a) Increase in Supply

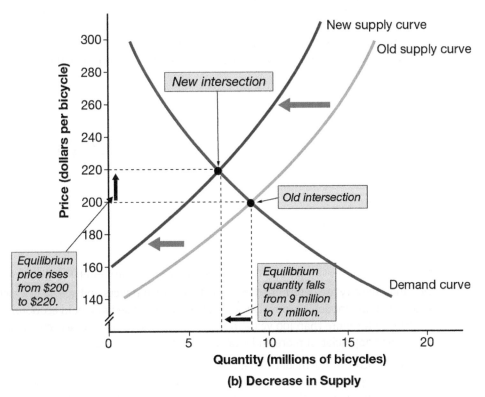

(b) Decrease in Supply

Table 3.4 summarizes the results of this analysis of shifts in the supply and demand curves.

TABLE 3.4 Effects of Shifts in Demand and Supply Curves

Shift	Effect on Equilibrium Price	Effect on Equilibrium Quantity
Increase in demand	Up	Up
Decrease in demand	Down	Down
Increase in supply	Down	Up
Decrease in supply	Up	Down

When Both Curves Shift

The supply and demand model is easiest to use when you are analyzing a factor that shifts either demand or supply, but not both. In reality, however, it is possible for something or several different things to simultaneously shift both supply and demand. To predict whether the price or the quantity rises or falls in such cases, we need to know whether demand or supply shifts by a larger amount.

Review

- The supply and demand model is used to predict the price and the quantity that result from interactions of consumers and producers in a market.
- In a market, the price will adjust upward or downward until the quantity supplied equals the quantity demanded. This price is called the equilibrium price, and the corresponding quantity is called the equilibrium quantity.
- Changes in the economy that cause the demand curve to shift to the right will raise both the equilibrium price and the equilibrium quantity. Changes that cause the demand curve to shift to the left will lower both the equilibrium price and the equilibrium quantity.
- Changes in the economy that cause the supply curve to shift to the right will lower the equilibrium price and raise the equilibrium quantity. Changes that cause the supply curve to shift to the left will raise the equilibrium price and lower the equilibrium quantity.

3.4 End-of-Chapter Material

Conclusion

This chapter has shown how to use the supply and demand model to find out how equilibrium price and quantity are determined in markets in which buyers and sellers interact freely. The supply and demand model is probably the most frequently used model in economics, and it has been in existence for more than 100 years in pretty much the same form as economists use it now. You will come to appreciate it more and more as you study economics.

A key feature of the model is that the equilibrium price and quantity are found at the intersection of the supply and demand curves. We can use the model to analyze how a change in factors that shift either the supply curve or the demand curve (or both) will affect equilibrium price and quantity in the market.

In later chapters, we will take a closer look at the supply and demand model to understand issues like how much equilibrium price or quantity changes when the demand curve or the supply curve shifts. We also can look at whether a market in which buyers and sellers interact freely can deliver the best outcomes for society, or whether their outcomes can be improved.

We also will look at what happens when buyers and sellers are not able to interact freely because of restrictions that limit how much a seller can charge for a good or how much a buyer has to pay for a good. This examination will enable you to better understand policy debates about minimum wages and rent controls.

Key Points

1. Demand is a negative relationship between the price of a good and the quantity demanded by consumers. It can be shown graphically by a downward-sloping demand curve.

2. A movement along the demand curve occurs when a higher price reduces the quantity demanded or a lower price increases the quantity demanded.

3. A shift of the demand curve occurs when something besides a change in price changes the quantity of a good that people are willing to buy.

4. Supply is a positive relationship between the price of a good and the quantity supplied by firms. It can be shown graphically by an upward-sloping supply curve.

5. A movement along the supply curve occurs when a higher price increases the quantity supplied or a lower price decreases the quantity supplied.

6. A shift of the supply curve occurs when something besides a change in price changes the quantity of a good that firms are willing to sell.

7. The equilibrium price and equilibrium quantity are determined by the intersection of the supply curve and the demand curve. At this intersection point, the quantity supplied equals the quantity demanded—no shortages or surpluses exist.

8. The adjustment of prices moves the market into equilibrium. In situations in which a shortage or an excess demand exists for goods, price will rise, increasing the quantity supplied and reducing the quantity demanded. In situations in which a surplus or an excess supply of goods exists, price will fall, decreasing the quantity supplied and increasing the quantity demanded.

9. We can use the supply and demand model to analyze the impact of changes in factors that move the supply curve or the demand curve or both. By shifting either the supply curve or the demand curve, observations of prices can be explained and predictions about prices can be made.

10. When the demand curve shifts to the right (left), both equilibrium price and equilibrium quantity will increase (decrease). When the supply curve shifts to the right (left), the equilibrium price will fall (rise), and the equilibrium quantity will rise (fall).

Questions for Review

1. Why does the demand curve slope downward?
2. Why does the supply curve slope upward?
3. What is the difference between a shift in the demand curve and a movement along the demand curve?
4. What are four things that cause a demand curve to shift?
5. What is the difference between a shift in the supply curve and a movement along the supply curve?
6. What are four things that cause a supply curve to shift?
7. How can one find the equilibrium price and equilibrium quantity?
8. What happens to the equilibrium price if the supply curve shifts to the right?

9. What happens to the equilibrium price if the demand curve shifts to the right?

10. If both the supply curve and the demand curve shift to the right, what happens to the equilibrium quantity? What about the equilibrium price?

Problems

1. For each of the following markets, indicate whether the stated change causes a shift in the supply curve, a shift in the demand curve, a movement along the supply curve, or a movement along the demand curve.

   a. The housing market: Consumers' incomes fall.

   b. The tea market: The price of sugar goes down.

   c. The coffee market: A freeze in Brazil severely damages the coffee crop.

   d. The fast-food market: The number of fast food restaurants in an area decreases.

   e. The peanut market in the U.S. Southeast: A drought lowers supply.

2. Determine which of the following four sentences use the terminology of the supply and demand model correctly.

   a. The price of bicycles rose, and therefore the demand for bicycles went down.

   b. The demand for bicycles increased, and therefore the price went up.

   c. The price of bicycles fell, decreasing the supply of bicycles.

   d. The supply of bicycles increased, and therefore the price of bicycles fell.

3. Use the supply and demand model to explain what happens to the equilibrium price and the equilibrium quantity for frozen yogurt in the following cases:

   a. The number of firms producing frozen yogurt expands significantly.

   b. It is widely publicized in the press that frozen yogurt is not more healthy for you than ice cream.

   c. It is widely publicized in the press that people who eat a cup of frozen yogurt a day live to be much happier in their retirement years.

   d. The price of milk used to produce frozen yogurt suddenly increases.

   e. Frozen yogurt suddenly becomes popular because a movie idol promotes it in television commercials.

4. Suppose a decrease in consumers' incomes causes a decrease in the demand for chicken and an increase in the demand for potatoes. Which good is inferior and which is normal? How will the equilibrium price and quantity change for each good?

5. Consider the following supply and demand model of the world tea market (in billions of pounds):

Price per Pound ($)	Quantity Supplied	Quantity Demanded
0.38	1,500	525
0.37	1,000	600
0.36	700	700
0.35	600	900
0.34	550	1,200

   a. Is there a shortage or a surplus when the price is $0.38? What about $0.34?

   b. What are the equilibrium price and the equilibrium quantity?

   c. Graph the supply curve and the demand curve.

d. Show how the equilibrium price and quantity can be found on the graph.

e. If there is a shortage or surplus at a price of $0.38, calculate its size in billions of pounds and show it on the graph.

6. Consider Problem 5. Suppose that there is a drought in Sri Lanka that reduces the supply of tea by 400 billion pounds at every price. Suppose demand does not change.

a. Write down in a table the new supply schedule for tea.

b. Find the new equilibrium price and the new equilibrium quantity. Explain how the market adjusts to the new equilibrium.

c. Graph the new supply curve along with the old supply curve and the demand curve.

d. Show the change in the equilibrium price and the equilibrium quantity on the graph.

e. Did the equilibrium quantity change by more or less than the change in supply? Show how you arrived at your answer using both the table and the supply and demand diagram that you drew.

7. Suppose you notice that the prices of fresh fish have been rising while the amounts sold have been falling in recent years. Which of the following is the best explanation for this?

a. Consumer preferences have shifted in favor of fish because it is healthier than red meat.

b. Fishermen are prevented from using the most advanced equipment because of concerns about overfishing.

c. Consumers' incomes have risen faster than inflation.

d. Consumers have become worried about mercury levels in fish.

8. Suppose the prices of illegal drugs fall in your community at the same time that police drug seizures increase. Which is the best explanation for this?

a. Fewer drugs are being supplied locally.

b. Police arrests are removing more drug dealers.

c. Police arrests are reducing drug consumption sharply.

d. More drugs are being supplied locally.

9. In the United States, corn often is used as an ingredient in animal feed for livestock. Why does an increase in the use of corn to make ethanol, an additive that is used in gasoline, raise the price of meat? Use supply and demand curves for the corn market and the meat market to explain your answer.

10. Using the demand and supply diagrams (one for each market), show what short-run changes in price and quantity would be expected in the following markets if terrorism-related worries about air safety cause travelers to shy away from air travel. Each graph should contain the original and new demand and supply curves, and the original and new equilibrium prices and quantities. For each market, write one sentence explaining why each curve shifts or does not shift.

a. The market for air travel.

b. The market for rail travel.

c. The market for hotel rooms in Hawaii.

d. The market for gasoline.

CHAPTER 4
Subtleties of the Supply and Demand Model

In April of 2015, the minimum wage for workers in the city of Seattle was increased to $11 per hour. This was the first in a series of increases that would result in the minimum wage reaching $15/hour for most workers by 2018 and rising to $18 an hour by 2025. Supporters of the legislation argued that an increase in the legally mandated minimum wage would boost the incomes of low-wage workers and help improve their lives. They also argued that the increase would be good for businesses in the city because workers who earned higher wages would be able to buy more goods and services for their families, thus helping local businesses. Opponents argued that intervening in the labor market would not help these workers and might even end up hurting them. They pointed out that raising the minimum wage would result in some low-wage workers, losing their jobs either because the business would not be able to survive with the higher costs or because the business owners would resort to automation—using ordering kiosks instead of hiring more cashiers, for example. They also argued that since the minimum wage only applied within the city limits of Seattle, businesses would move to nearby areas outside the city's jurisdiction and avoid paying higher wages.

FIGURE 4.1 Will an Increase in the Minimum Wage Help Poor Workers?
Protestors asking for a $15 minimum hourly wage.

Source: a katz/Shutterstock.com

The debate in Seattle mirrored a debate that was taking place all over the United States as the recovery from the 2008–09 recession gathered steam. Both New York and California passed laws that would gradually raise statewide minimum wages to $15 over the next few years (by 2018 in New York City, 2021 in New York State, and 2023 in California). In 2015, President Barack Obama praised the decisions by New York and California while expressing frustration that the federal minimum wage had not increased from the value of $7.25 that was set all the way back in June of 2009. That increase itself had been the culmination of a legislative process that began in May 2007. President George W. Bush signed a bill that raised the minimum wage to $5.85 in 2007, $6.55 in 2008, and, finally, to $7.25 in 2009. President Obama left office in January of 2017 without succeeding in persuading the Republican-controlled Congress to raise the minimum wage. Only two other presidents had previously failed to raise the minimum wage since it came into existence in the aftermath of the Great Depression. Three years into President Donald Trump's term, even in the face of a strong economy in 2019, the federal minimum wage remained at $7.25, exactly where it was a decade earlier.

Were the supporters of the plan correct in their claim that many poor people's lives could be improved by instituting a higher minimum wage? Or were the opponents correct to claim that a higher minimum wage could end up hurting more people than it helped? In the case of Seattle's minimum wage, a team of economists from the University of Washington closely studied the impact of the minimum wage and concluded that the impact was mixed. Wages increased and hours decreased for workers in the city of Seattle, a combination that would have ambiguous effects on worker earnings. The researchers found that the wage gains outweighed the hours decrease for more experienced workers but that they canceled each other out for less-experienced workers. They also found that workers whose hours may have declined modestly in the city of Seattle following the introduction of the new minimum wage found additional hours of work in surrounding areas.

In this chapter, we look at more sophisticated aspects of the supply and demand model that are helpful in understanding policy debates, like the minimum-wage increase. We first look at how to use the supply and demand model in situations in which government policies do not allow price to be freely determined in a market. These interventions can take the form of a *price ceiling*, a maximum price imposed by the government when it feels that the equilibrium price is "too high," or a *price floor*, a minimum price imposed by the government when it feels that the equilibrium price is "too low," as in the case of the minimum wage. This extension of the supply and demand model also will be helpful in solidifying your understanding of the important role played by prices in the allocation of resources.

We then move on to discussing an elegant, and remarkably useful, economic concept called *elasticity* that economists use when they work with the supply and demand model. In economics, elasticity is a measure of how sensitive one variable is to another. In the case of the supply and demand model, elasticity measures how sensitive the quantity of a good that people demand, or that firms supply, is to the price of the good. In this chapter, we show how the concept of elasticity can be used to answer the question raised earlier about how much unemployment is caused when the minimum wage is raised. You will learn a formula that shows how elasticity is calculated and then learn how to work with and talk about elasticity.

4.1 Interference with Market Prices

Thus far, we have used the supply and demand model in situations in which the price is freely determined without government control. But at many times throughout history, and around the world in the twentieth century, governments have attempted to control market prices. The usual reasons are that government leaders were not happy with the outcome of the market or were pressured by groups who would benefit from price controls.

Price Ceilings and Price Floors

price controls

A government law or regulation that sets or limits the price to be charged for a particular good.

price ceiling

A government price control that sets the maximum allowable price for a good.

price floor

A government price control that sets the minimum allowable price for a good.

rent control

A government price control that sets the maximum allowable rent on a house or apartment.

In general, the government imposes two broad types of **price controls**. Controls can stipulate either a **price ceiling**, a maximum price at which a good can be bought and sold, or a **price floor**, a minimum price at which a good can be bought and sold. Why would a government choose to intervene in the market and put in a price floor or a price ceiling? What happens when such an intervention is made?

Ostensibly, the primary purpose of a price ceiling is to help consumers in situations in which the government thinks that the equilibrium price is "too high" or is inundated with consumer complaints that the equilibrium price is too high. For example, the U.S. government controlled oil prices in the early 1970s, stipulating that firms could not charge more than a stated maximum price of $5.25 per barrel of crude oil at a time when the equilibrium price was well over $10 per barrel. As another example, some cities in the United States place price controls on rental apartments; landlords are not permitted to charge a rent higher than the maximum stipulated by the **rent control** law in these cities. Tenants living in rent-controlled units pay less than the market equilibrium rent that would prevail in the absence of the price ceiling.

Conversely, governments impose price floors to help the suppliers of goods and services in situations in which the government feels that the equilibrium price is "too low" or is influenced by complaints from producers that the equilibrium price is too low. For example, the U.S. government requires that the price of sugar in the United States not fall below a certain amount. Another example can be found in the labor market, in which the U.S. government requires that firms pay workers a wage of at least a given level, called the **minimum wage**.

minimum wage

A wage per hour below which it is illegal to pay workers.

Side Effects of Price Ceilings

Even though price ceilings typically are implemented with the idea of helping consumers, they often end up having harmful side effects that hurt the consumers that the ceiling was put in place to help. If the price ceiling that the government puts in place to prevent firms from charging more than a certain amount for their products is lower than the equilibrium price, then a shortage is likely to result, as illustrated in Figure 4.2. The situation of a persistent shortage, in which sellers are unwilling to supply as much as buyers want to buy, is illustrated for the general case of any good in the top graph in Figure 4.2 and for the specific case of rent control in the bottom graph.

FIGURE 4.2 Effects of a Maximum-Price Law
The top diagram shows the general case when the government prevents the market price from rising above a particular maximum price, or sets a price ceiling below the equilibrium price. The lower diagram shows a particular example of a price ceiling, rent controls on apartment units. The supply and demand model predicts a shortage. The shortage occurs because the quantity supplied is less than consumers are willing to buy at that price. The shortage leads to rationing, black markets, or lower product quality.

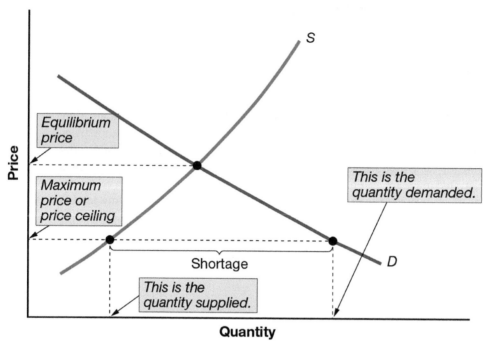

The General Case of a Price Ceiling

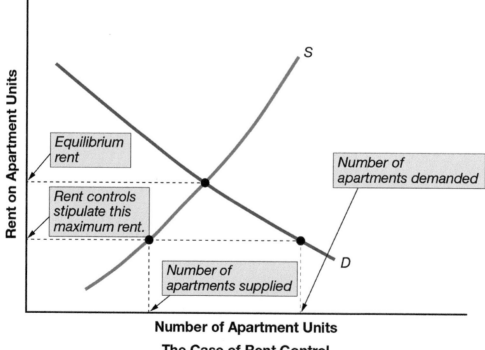

The Case of Rent Control

Dealing with Persistent Shortages

Because higher prices are not allowed, the shortage must be dealt with in other ways. Sometimes the government issues a limited amount of ration coupons, which do not exceed the quantity supplied at the restricted maximum price, to people to alleviate the shortage. This was done in World War II when people had to present these ration coupons at stores to buy certain goods, and only those individuals who had ration coupons could buy those goods. If the price ceiling had not been in place, the shortage would have driven prices higher, and those who were willing and able to pay the higher price would have been able to buy the goods without the need for a ration coupon.

Alternatively, if ration coupons are not issued, then the shortage might result in long waiting lines. In the past, in centrally planned economies, long lines for bread frequently were observed because of price controls on bread. Sometimes black markets develop, in which people buy and sell goods outside the watch of the government and charge whatever price they want. In the past, this was typical in command economies. In the twenty-first century, black markets are common in less-developed countries when the governments in these countries impose price controls.

Another effect of price ceilings is a reduction in the quality of the good sold. By lowering the quality of the good, the producer can reduce the costs of producing it. A frequent criticism of rent control is that it can lower the quality of housing—landlords are more reluctant to paint the walls or to repair the elevator because they are prevented from charging a higher rent.

Making Things Worse

Although the stated purpose of price ceilings is to help people who have to pay high prices, the preceding examples indicate how price ceilings can make things worse. Issuing ration coupons raises difficult problems about who gets the coupons. In the case of a price ceiling on gasoline, for example, should the government give more coupons to those who use a lot of gasoline because they drive vehicles with poor gas mileage than to those who use less gasoline because they drive more fuel-efficient cars or use public transportation for their daily commute? Rationing by waiting in line also is an undesirable outcome. People who are waiting in line could be doing more enjoyable or more useful things. Similarly, black markets, being illegal, encourage people to go outside the law. People transacting in black markets also may be more vulnerable to theft or fraud. Lowering the quality of the good is also a bad way to alleviate the problem of a high price. This simply eliminates the higher-quality good from production; both consumers and producers lose. Price ceilings also are not particularly well targeted. Even though the goal of a price ceiling may be to ensure that someone who cannot afford to pay the equilibrium price still can purchase the good, there is no way to guarantee that only those who cannot afford to pay the equilibrium price end up purchasing the good. For instance, many people who end up living in rent-controlled apartments may not be poor at all.

Side Effects of Price Floors

Price floors typically are enacted with the goal of helping producers who are facing low market equilibrium prices, but, as with price ceilings, they often end up having harmful side effects that hurt the people that the policy was put in place to help. If the price floor that the government imposes exceeds the equilibrium price, then a surplus will occur. The situation of a persistent surplus, in which sellers are willing to supply more output than buyers want to buy, is illustrated for the general case of any good in the top graph of Figure 4.3 and for the specific case of the minimum wage in the bottom graph.

FIGURE 4.3 Effects of Minimum-Price Law

The top diagram shows the general case when the government prevents the market price from falling below a particular minimum price, or sets a price floor above the equilibrium price. The lower diagram shows a particular example when the price of labor—the wage—cannot fall below the minimum wage. The supply and demand model predicts that sellers are willing to sell a greater quantity than buyers are willing to buy at that price. Thus, there is a surplus of the good or, in the case of labor, unemployment for some of those who would be hired only at a lower wage.

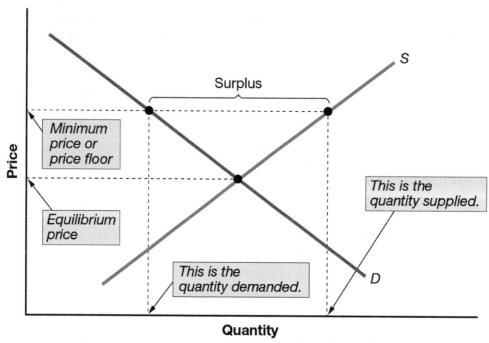

The General Case of a Price Floor

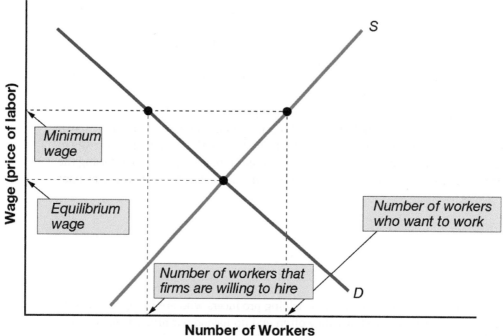

The Case of the Minimum Wage

Dealing with Persistent Surpluses

How is this surplus dealt with in actual markets? In markets for farm products, the government usually has to buy the surplus and, perhaps, put it in storage. Buying farm products above the equilibrium price costs taxpayers money, and the higher price raises costs to consumers. For this reason, economists argue against price floors on agricultural goods. As an alternative, the government sometimes reduces the supply by telling farms to plant fewer acres or to destroy crops. But government requirements that land be kept idle or crops destroyed in exchange for taxpayer's money are particularly repugnant to most people.

When the supply and demand model is applied to labor markets, the price is the price of labor (or the wage) and a minimum wage is a price floor. What does the supply and demand model predict about the effects of a minimum wage? The lower diagram in Figure 4.3 shows that a minimum wage can cause unemployment. If the minimum wage exceeds the equilibrium wage, the number of workers demanded at that wage is less than the number of workers who are willing to work. Even though some workers would be willing to work for less than the minimum wage, employers are not permitted to pay them less than the minimum wage. Therefore, there is a surplus of unemployed workers at the minimum wage.

 Understanding the Effects of Minimum Wages with the Supply and Demand Model

Watch this video for an explanation of the effect of the minimum wage, particularly on people with little education.

View the video online at: http://www.youtube.com/embed/grnqqhvCL0c?rel=0

Making Things Worse

Even though the stated purpose of price floors is to help sellers by paying them a higher price, the preceding examples indicate how price floors can make things worse. The resources allocated to building grain silos to store surplus grain could have been used to hire doctors or teachers or to build low-income houses. The land that farmers are encouraged to keep in an undeveloped yet unfarmed state could have been used for a housing development or as a high school athletic field. Price floors, like price ceilings, also are not particularly well targeted. Even though the goal of a price floor may be to ensure that a poor farmer does not suffer because crop prices are too low, the benefits of the higher price typically will accrue to extremely wealthy farmers and large agricultural businesses with lots of resources. In the case of the minimum wage, teenagers from relatively well-off families may end up earning a higher salary as a result of the minimum wage, but a poor parent may end up losing his or her job and joining the ranks of the unemployed.

 Price Floors and Ceilings

Price floors and ceilings may end up harming the suppliers or consumers they intend to help.

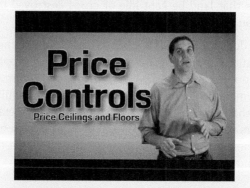

View the video online at: http://www.youtube.com/embed/1EzY4Vl460U?rel=0

Review

- Governments occasionally will intervene in markets because they think that the equilibrium price is too high or too low. In some instances in which the government thinks the price that buyers have to pay is too high, it may impose a price ceiling. In some instances in which the government thinks the price that sellers are receiving is too low, it may impose a price floor.

- Price ceilings cause persistent shortages, which, in turn, cause rationing, black markets, and a reduced quality of goods and services. Price ceilings also may not end up helping the people that the policy was designed to benefit. In the case of rent control, for example, the people who end up in rent-controlled apartments may be more affluent than the individuals who are unable to find an apartment because of the persistent shortages.

- Price floors cause persistent surpluses, which, in turn, result in resources being diverted away from other productive activities. Price floors may not end up helping the people that the policy was designed to benefit. In the case of a minimum wage, for example, the workers who end up in jobs earning the higher minimum wage may be teenagers from relatively well-off families, while a poor worker may be unable to find a job because of the surplus of unemployed workers.

4.2 Elasticity of Demand

Defining the Price Elasticity of Demand

The price elasticity of demand is a measure of the sensitivity of the *quantity demanded* of a good to the *price* of the good. "Price elasticity of demand" is sometimes shortened to "elasticity of demand," the "demand elasticity," or even simply "elasticity" when the meaning is clear from the context. The price elasticity of demand always refers to a particular demand curve or demand schedule, such as the world demand for oil or the U.S. demand for bicycles. The price elasticity of demand is a measure of *how much* the quantity demanded changes when the price changes.

For example, when economists report that the price elasticity of demand for contact lenses is high, they mean that the quantity of contact lenses demanded by people changes by a large amount when the price changes. Or if they report that the price elasticity of demand for bread is low, they mean that the quantity of bread demanded changes by only a small amount when the price of bread changes.

We can define the price elasticity of demand clearly with a formula: **price elasticity of demand** is the percentage change in the quantity demanded divided by the percentage change in the price. That is,

$$\text{price elasticity of demand} = \frac{\text{percentage change in quantity demanded}}{\text{percentage change in price}}$$

We emphasize that the price elasticity of demand refers to a particular demand curve; thus, the numerator of this formula is the percentage change in quantity demanded when the price changes by the percentage amount shown in the denominator. All the other factors that affect demand are held constant when we compute the price elasticity of demand. This expression will have a negative sign because the numerator and denominator are of opposite signs. Because the demand curve slopes downward, as the price increases, the quantity demanded by consumers declines, and as the price decreases, the quantity demanded by consumers increases, all else held equal. The convention is to ignore the negative sign or, alternatively, take the negative sign for granted when we discuss the elasticity of demand.

For example, if the price elasticity of demand for gasoline is said to be about 0.2, that means that if the price of gasoline increases by 10 percent, the quantity of gasoline demanded will fall by 2 percent (0.2 x 10). If the price elasticity of demand for alcoholic beverages is said to be about 1.5, that means that when the price of alcoholic beverages rises by 10 percent, the quantity demanded will fall by 15 percent (1.5 x 10). As you can see from these examples, knowing the elasticity of demand enables us to determine how much the *quantity demanded* changes when the price changes.

> **price elasticity of demand**
>
> The percentage change in the quantity demanded of a good divided by the percentage change in the price of that good.

The Size of the Elasticity: High versus Low

The two graphs in Figure 4.4 each show a different possible demand curve for oil in the world. We want to show why it is important to know which of these two demand curves gives a better description of economic behavior in the oil market. Each graph has the price of oil on the vertical axis (in dollars per barrel) and the quantity of oil demanded on the horizontal axis (in millions of barrels of oil a day).

FIGURE 4.4 Comparing Different Sizes of the Price Elasticity of Demand
Both sets of axes have exactly the same scale. In the top graph, the quantity demanded is sensitive to the price; the elasticity is high. In the bottom graph, the quantity demanded is not sensitive to the price; the elasticity is low. Thus, the same increase in price ($2, or 10 percent) reduces the quantity demanded much more when the elasticity is high (top graph) than when it is low (bottom graph).

Both of the demand curves pass through the same point *A*, where the price of oil is $20 per barrel and the quantity demanded is 60 million barrels per day. But observe that the two curves show different degrees of sensitivity of the quantity demanded to the price. In the top graph, where the demand curve is relatively flat, the quantity demanded of oil is sensitive to the price; in other words, the demand curve has a high elasticity. For example, consider a change from point *A* to point *B*: When the price rises by $2, from $20 to $22, the quantity demanded falls by 12 million, from 60 million to 48 million barrels a day. In percentage terms, when the price rises by 10 percent (2/20 = 0.10, or 10 percent), the quantity demanded falls by 20 percent (12/60 = 0.20, or 20 percent).

On the other hand, in the bottom graph, the quantity demanded is not quite as sensitive to the price; in other words, the demand curve has a low elasticity. It is relatively steep. When the price rises by $2 from point *A* to point *C*, the quantity demanded falls by 3 million barrels. In percentage terms, the same 10 percent increase in price reduces the quantity demanded by only 5 percent (3/60

= 0.05, or 5 percent). Thus, the sensitivity of the quantity to the price, or the size of the elasticity, is what distinguishes these two graphs.

The Impact of a Change in Supply on the Price of Oil

Now consider what happens when there is a decline in supply in the world oil market. In Figure 4.5, we combine the supply curve for oil with the two demand curves for oil from Figure 4.4. Initially the oil market is in equilibrium in Figure 4.5; in both graphs, the quantity demanded equals the quantity supplied. The equilibrium price is $20 per barrel, and the equilibrium quantity is 60 million barrels a day, just like at point A in Figure 4.4. A reduction in the supply of oil—perhaps because of the reduction in Iraqi oil production or the shutdown of refineries following Hurricane Katrina—is also shown. The exact same leftward shift in supply is shown in the top and bottom graphs of Figure 4.5.

Now, observe how the equilibrium price changes in the two graphs. Recall that this change is our prediction—using the supply and demand model—of what would happen to the price of oil if the supply declined. We know that a decrease in supply will lead to an increase in the equilibrium price and a decrease in the equilibrium quantity. As the two graphs show, however, there is a huge difference in the size of the predicted price increase. In the top graph, the oil price increases only a little. If the elasticity is very high, then even a small increase in the price is enough to get people to reduce their use of oil and thereby bring the quantity demanded down to the lower quantity supplied. On the other hand, in the bottom diagram, the price rises by much more. Here the elasticity is very low, and thus a large increase in price is needed to get people to reduce their use of oil and bring the quantity demanded down to the quantity supplied.

Thus, to determine how much the price will rise in response to a shift in oil supply, we need to know how sensitive the quantity demanded is to the price, or the size of the elasticity of demand.

FIGURE 4.5 The Importance of the Size of the Price Elasticity of Demand
The impact on the oil price of a reduction in oil supply is shown for two different demand curves. The reduction in supply is the same for both graphs. When the price elasticity of demand is high (top graph), there is only a small increase in the price. When the price elasticity of demand is low (bottom graph), the price rises by much more.

Review

- We know that an increase in price will lower the quantity demanded, whereas a decrease in price will increase the quantity demanded. The price elasticity of demand is a number that tells us by how much the quantity demanded changes when the price changes.
- The price elasticity of demand, which we also refer to as "elasticity of demand" or just as "elasticity," is defined as the percentage change in the quantity demanded divided by the percentage change in the price.

- A given change in price has a larger impact on quantity demanded when the elasticity of demand is higher.
- A given shift of the supply curve will have a larger impact on equilibrium quantity (and a smaller impact on equilibrium price) when the elasticity of demand is higher.

4.3 Working with Demand Elasticities

Having demonstrated the practical importance of elasticity, let us examine the concept in more detail and show how to use it. Some symbols will be helpful.

If we let the symbol e_d represent the price elasticity of demand, then we can write the definition as

$$e_d = \frac{\Delta Q_d}{Q_d} \div \frac{\Delta P}{P} = \frac{\left(\frac{\Delta Q_d}{Q_d}\right)}{\left(\frac{\Delta P}{P}\right)}$$

where Q_d is the quantity demanded, P is the price, and Δ means "change in." In other words, the elasticity of demand equals the "percentage change in the quantity demanded" divided by the "percentage change in the price." Observe that to compute the percentage change in the numerator and the denominator, we need to divide the change in the variable (or ΔQ_d) by the variable (P or Q_d).

Keep in mind again that because the quantity demanded is negatively related to the price, the elasticity of demand is a negative number: When $\Delta P/P$ is positive, $\Delta Q_d/Q_d$ is negative. But when economists write or talk about elasticity, they usually ignore the negative sign and report the absolute value of the number. Because the demand curve always slopes downward, this nearly universal convention need not cause any confusion, as long as you remember it.

It is easy to do back-of-the-envelope computations of price elasticity of demand. Suppose a study shows that when the price of Australian wine fell by 8 percent, the quantity of Australian wine demanded increased by 12 percent. The price elasticity of demand for Australian wine is

$$e_d = \frac{\left(\frac{\Delta Q_d}{Q_d}\right)}{\left(\frac{\Delta P}{P}\right)} = \frac{12}{8} \equiv 1.5$$

Suppose your university raises student season ticket prices from \$50 to \$60, which results in the quantity of season tickets sold falling from 2,000 to 1,800. The price elasticity of demand for season ticket prices would be

$$e_d = \frac{\left(\frac{\Delta Q_d}{Q_d}\right)}{\left(\frac{\Delta P}{P}\right)} = \frac{\left(\frac{200}{2000}\right)}{\left(\frac{10}{50}\right)} = \frac{0.1}{0.2} = 0.5$$

Notice that measured in percentage changes, the demand for Australian wine is more responsive to changes in its price than the demand for season tickets is to changes in its price.

The Advantage of a Unit-Free Measure

unit-free measure

A measure that does not depend on a unit of measurement.

An attractive feature of the price elasticity of demand is that it does not depend on the units of measurement of the quantity demanded—whether barrels of oil or pounds of peanuts. It is a **unit-free measure** because it uses percentage changes in price and quantity demanded. Thus, it provides a way to compare the price sensitivity of the demand for many different goods. It even allows us to compare the price sensitivity of less expensive goods—like rice—with that of more expensive goods—like steak.

For example, suppose that when the price of rice rises from $0.50 to $0.60 per pound, the quantity demanded falls from 20 tons to 19 tons of rice—that is, a decline of 1 ton for a *$0.10* price increase. In contrast, suppose that when the price of steak rises by $1, from $5 to $6 per pound, the quantity demanded falls by 1 ton, from 20 tons to 19 tons of steak—that is, a decline of 1 ton for a *$1* price increase.

Using these numbers, the price sensitivity of the demand for steak and the demand for rice might appear to be different: $0.10 to get a ton of reduced purchases versus $1 to get a ton of reduced purchases. Yet the elasticities are the same. The percentage change in price is 20 percent in each case ($1/$5 for steak = $0.10/$0.50 for rice = 0.20, or 20 percent), and the percentage change in quantity is 5 percent in each case: 1 ton of rice/20 tons of rice = 1 ton of steak/20 tons of steak = 0.05, or 5 percent. Hence, the elasticity is 5/20 = 1/4 in both cases.

Elasticity allows us to compare the price sensitivity of different goods by looking at ratios of percentage changes regardless of the units for measuring either price or quantity. With millions of different goods and hundreds of different units of measurement, this is indeed a major advantage.

Elasticity versus Slope

After looking at Figure 4.4, you might be tempted to say that demand curves that are steep have a low elasticity, and demand curves that are flat have a high elasticity. That turns out not to be the case, so you have to be careful not to simply look at a flat demand curve and say that it has a high elasticity. You need to understand why the *elasticity of the demand curve* is not the same as the *slope of the demand curve*. Remember that the slope of a curve is the change in the *y* variable over the change in the *x* variable; in the case of the demand curve, the slope is defined as the change in price divided by the change in quantity demanded. The slope is not a unit-free measure—it depends on how the price and quantity are measured. Elasticity, on the other hand, is a unit-free measure.

To illustrate the difference between slope and elasticity, we show in Figure 4.6 a demand curve for rice and a demand curve for steak. The two demand curves have different slopes because the prices are so different. When the price of rice increases by $0.10, the quantity demanded of rice falls by 1 ton, whereas when the price of steak increases by $1 (or 100 cents), the quantity demanded of steak falls by 1 ton. The slope of the steak demand curve is (–$1 a ton), which is 10 times greater than the slope of the rice demand curve (–$0.10 cents a ton). Yet the elasticity is the same for the change from *A* to *B* for both demand curves—the price of rice and the price of steak both increased by 20 percent, while the quantity demanded of rice and the quantity demanded of steak both decreased by 5 percent.

FIGURE 4.6 Different Slopes and Same Elasticities
The slope of the steak demand curve in the bottom graph is greater than the slope of the rice demand curve in the top graph. The price elasticity of demand for rice and steak from point A to point B is the same, however. From point A to point B, the price rises by 20 percent and the quantity demanded decreases by 5 percent. Thus, the elasticity is one fourth for both rice and steak at these points.

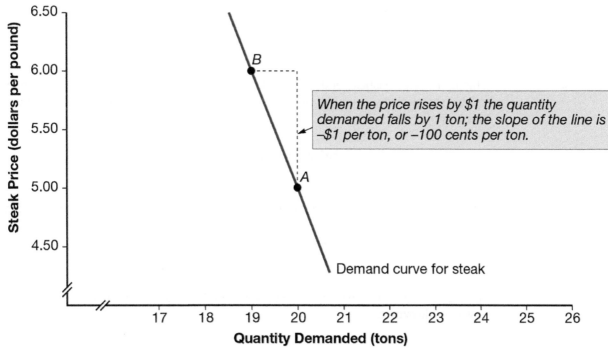

Calculating the Elasticity with a Midpoint Formula

To calculate the elasticity, we need to find the percentage change in the quantity demanded and divide it by the percentage change in the price. As we have illustrated with examples, to get the percentage change in the price or quantity, we need to divide the change in price (ΔP) by the price (P) or the change in quantity demanded (ΔQ_d) by the quantity demanded (Q_d). But when price and quantity demanded change, a question arises about what to use for P and Q_d. Should we use the old price and the old quantity demanded before the change, or should we use the new price and the new quantity demanded after the change?

The most common convention that economists use is a compromise between these two alternatives. They take the *average*, or the *midpoint*, of the old and new quantities demanded and the old and new prices. That is, they compute the elasticity using the following formula, called the *midpoint formula:*

$$\text{price elasticity of demand} = \frac{\dfrac{\text{change in quantity}}{\text{average of old and new quantities}}}{\div \dfrac{\text{change in price}}{\text{average of old and new prices}}}$$

For example, if we use the midpoint formula to calculate the price elasticity of demand for oil when the price changes from \$20 to \$22 and the quantity demanded changes from 60 million to 48 million barrels a day, we get

$$\text{price elasticity of demand} = \frac{12}{(60+48)/2} \div \frac{2}{(22+20)/2}$$
$$= \frac{2}{9} \div \frac{2}{21} = \frac{7}{3}$$

That is, the price elasticity of demand is 2.33 using the midpoint formula. When we originally calculated the elasticity using the old price and the old quantity demanded, we came up with an elasticity of

$$\text{price elasticity of demand} = \frac{12}{60} \div \frac{2}{20}$$
$$= 2$$

If we had used the new price and the new quantity, we would have calculated the elasticity to be

$$\text{price elasticity of demand} = \frac{12}{48} \div \frac{2}{22}$$
$$= 2.75$$

So the elasticity calculated using the midpoint formula turns out to be in between these two values, as you would expect.

Demand Elasticity

Elastic versus inelastic demand: what factors affect demand elasticity?

View the video online at: http://www.youtube.com/embed/Pduf_fpshkU?rel=0

Talking about Elasticities

Economists classify demand curves by the size of the price elasticities of demand, and they have developed a very precise terminology for doing so.

Elastic versus Inelastic Demand

Goods for which the price elasticity is greater than one have an **elastic demand**. For example, the quantity of foreign travel demanded decreases by more than 1 percent when the price rises by 1 percent because many people tend to travel at home rather than abroad when the price of foreign travel rises.

Goods for which the price elasticity of demand is less than one have an **inelastic demand**. For example, the quantity of eggs demanded decreases by less than 1 percent when the price of eggs rises by 1 percent because many people do not want to substitute other things for eggs at breakfast.

elastic demand

Demand for which the price elasticity is greater than one.

inelastic demand

Demand for which the price elasticity is less than one.

Perfectly Elastic versus Perfectly Inelastic Demand

A demand curve that is vertical is called **perfectly inelastic demand**. Figure 4.7 shows a perfectly inelastic demand curve. The elasticity is zero because when the price changes, the quantity demanded does not change at all. No matter what the price, the same quantity is demanded. People who need insulin have a perfectly inelastic demand for insulin. As long as there are no substitutes for insulin, they will pay whatever they have to for the insulin.

perfectly inelastic demand

Demand for which the price elasticity is zero, indicating no response to a change in price and therefore a vertical demand curve.

FIGURE 4.7 Perfectly Elastic and Perfectly Inelastic Demand
A perfectly inelastic demand curve is a vertical line at a certain quantity. The quantity demanded is completely insensitive to the price: Whatever happens to the price, the quantity demanded does not change. A perfectly elastic demand curve is a flat line at a certain price. An increase in price reduces the quantity demanded to zero; a small decrease in price raises the quantity demanded by a huge (literally infinite) amount.

perfectly elastic demand

Demand for which the price elasticity is infinite, indicating an infinite response to a change in price and therefore a horizontal demand curve.

A demand curve that is horizontal is called **perfectly elastic demand**. Figure 4.7 also shows a perfectly elastic demand curve. The elasticity is infinite. The perfectly flat demand curve is sometimes hard to imagine because it entails infinitely large movements of quantity for tiny changes in price. To better visualize this case, you can imagine that the curve is tilted ever so slightly. Goods that have a lot of comparable substitutes are likely to have high elasticities of demand.

Table 4.1 summarizes the terminology about elasticities.

TABLE 4.1 Terminology for Price Elasticity of Demand

Term	Value of Price Elasticity of Demand (e_d)
Perfectly inelastic	0 (vertical demand curve)
Inelastic	Less than 1
Elastic	Greater than 1
Perfectly elastic	Infinity (horizontal demand curve)

Revenue and the Price Elasticity of Demand

When people purchase 60 million barrels of oil at $20 a barrel, they must pay a total of $1,200 million ($20 x 60 million). This is a payment to the oil producers and is the producers' revenue. In general, revenue is the price (*P*) times the quantity (*Q*), or *P* x *Q*. A change in price therefore will affect revenue. Although this seems obvious, it is important that you understand exactly how price affects revenue. In fact, a change in price has two opposite effects on revenue. For instance, when the price increases, people pay more for each item, which increases revenue; but they buy fewer items, which in turn reduces revenue. The price elasticity of demand determines which of these two opposite effects dominates, because elasticity is a measure of how much the quantity demanded changes when price changes.

Figure 4.8, which is a replica of Figure 4.4 with the scales changed, illustrates the effects on revenue. In the top graph, revenue went from $1.2 billion (60 million x $20 = $1,200 million) to $1.056

billion (48 million x $22 = $1,056 million). In other words, revenue declined by $144 million even though price increased. Now compare this to the revenue changes in the bottom graph. There revenue went from $1.2 billion to $1.254 billion (57 million x $22 = $1,254 million), an increase of $54 million. Using the old price and the old quantity demanded, you can show that the elasticity of demand in the top graph is 2 while the elasticity of demand in the bottom graph is 0.5. We can see from this example that, following a price increase, revenue fell in the case where the elasticity was greater than one, and revenue rose when elasticity was less than one.

FIGURE 4.8 Effects of an Increase in the Price of Oil on Revenue

These graphs are replicas of the demand curves for oil shown in Figure 4.4, with the scale changed to show the change in revenue when the price of oil is increased. An increase in the price has two effects on revenue, as shown by the shaded rectangles. The increase in revenue (horizontal rectangle) is due to the higher price. The decrease in revenue (vertical rectangle) is due to the decline in the quantity demanded as the price is increased. In the top graph, where elasticity is greater than one, the net effect is a decline in revenue; in the bottom graph, where elasticity is less than one, the net effect is an increase in revenue.

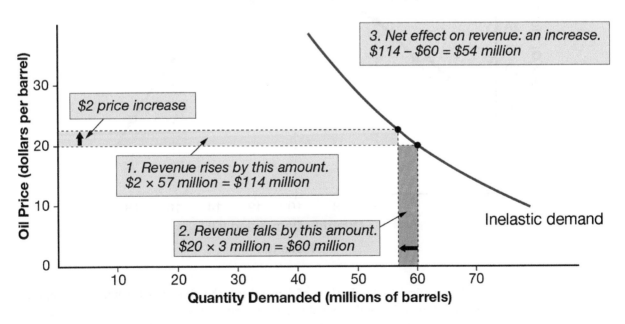

Is this always the case? We can illustrate the relationship between elasticity and revenue better by using a simple straight-line demand curve, as shown in Figure 4.9. Because this is a straight line, the slope is identical at all points on the demand curve—a $1 change in price will change quantity demanded by two units.

FIGURE 4.9 Revenue and Elasticity of a Straight-Line Demand Curve
Along the straight-line demand curve in the top panel, the price elasticity ranges from above 1 (to the left) to below 1 (to the right). When the price elasticity is greater than 1 an increase in the price will reduce revenue, as shown in the lower panel.

Demand

Revenue

If you calculate the elasticity of demand at each point along the line, what you will find is that the elasticity of demand is equal to one at a price of $5 and a quantity demanded of 10. At this point, a $1 change in price (which is equivalent to a 20 percent change in the price) results in a two-unit change in quantity demanded (which is also equivalent to a 20 percent change in the quantity demanded). To the left of this point, the elasticity of demand is greater than one. You can see this by considering what happens at a price of $6 and a quantity demanded of eight. A $1 change in price will continue to bring about a two-unit change in quantity demanded, but the percentage change in price is smaller ($1/$6 = 16.66 percent instead of 20 percent), and the percentage change in quantity is larger (2/8 = 25 percent instead of 20 percent). Thus, the elasticity will now be greater than one. To the right of this point, the elasticity of demand is less than one. You can see this by considering what happens at a price of $4 and a quantity demanded of twelve. A $1 change in price will continue to bring about a two-unit change in quantity demanded, but the percentage change in price is larger ($1/$4 = 25 percent instead of 20 percent), and the percentage change in quantity is smaller (2/12 = 16.67 percent instead of 20 percent). Thus, the elasticity will now be less than one.

For each point along the demand curve, you can calculate revenue by simply multiplying price and quantity. The bottom panel of Figure 4.9 shows how revenue changes as the quantity demanded changes. Revenue begins at $0 (at a price of $10, quantity demanded is zero), increases for a while as quantity demanded increases, starts decreasing again, and ends up at $0 (because quantity demanded of 20 corresponds to a price of zero). Interestingly, you can see that the range over which revenue is rising with quantity demanded corresponds exactly with the range at which the elasticity is greater than one. Similarly, the range over which revenue is falling corresponds with the region of the demand curve at which the elasticity is less than one. Table 4.2 summarizes the relationship between revenue and the price elasticity of demand. An increase in price will raise revenue if the elasticity is less than one and will lower revenue if the elasticity is greater than one.

TABLE 4.2 Revenue and the Price Elasticity of Demand

Elasticity Is	Effect of a Price Increase on Revenue	Effect of a Price Decrease on Revenue
Less than 1 (<1)	Revenue increases	Revenue decreases
Equal to 1 (=1)	No change in revenue	No change in revenue
Greater than 1 (>1)	Revenue decreases	Revenue increases

This relationship between the elasticity of demand and the revenue impact of a price change is important. Businesses need to know the price elasticity of demand for their products to understand the implications of raising or lowering prices. For instance, suppose Amazon.com announces that it would sharply cut the price of its e-book reader, the Kindle, from $259 to $189, a drop of about 30 percent. Would the lower price entice more people to buy a Kindle? If so, would the increase in customers lead to an increase or a decrease in Amazon.com's revenue? The answer depends on the price elasticity of demand for Amazon's e-book readers. Similarly, suppose Netflix announced that it was raising the price for its streaming service from $12.99 to $14.99, an increase of around 14 percent using the midprice formula. Could this increase drive away many Netflix customers to rival streaming sites like Hulu or Amazon Prime? If so, would the decrease in customers be so large as to lower Netflix's revenue? The answer depends on the price elasticity of demand for streaming video on Netflix.

If demand for Amazon's e-book readers is price elastic and the demand for movie downloads on Netflix is price inelastic, then both Amazon and Netflix changed prices to increase revenue—Amazon cut the price of e-book readers to increase revenue, taking advantage of price-elastic demand, and Netflix increased the price of streaming video to increase revenue, taking advantage of price-inelastic demand. How would Amazon or Netflix know whether demand would be elastic or inelastic? The next section discusses the determinants of price elasticity of demand. You should judge as you read this chapter whether demand for business air travel and demand for cellphone service are likely to be price elastic or price inelastic.

What Determines the Size of the Price Elasticity of Demand?

Table 4.3 shows price elasticities of demand for several different goods and services. The price elasticity for jewelry, for example, is 2.6. This means that for each percentage increase in the price of jewelry, the quantity demanded will fall by 2.6 percent. Compared with other elasticities, this is large. On the other hand, the price elasticity of eggs is very small. For each percentage increase in the price of eggs, the quantity of eggs demanded falls by only 0.1 percent.

TABLE 4.3 Estimated Price Elasticities of Demand

Type of Good or Service	Price Elasticity
Jewelry	2.6
Eggs	0.1
Telephone (first line)	0.1
Telephone (second line)	0.4
Foreign travel	1.2
Cigarettes (age 18-24)	0.6
Cigarettes (age 25-39)	0.4
Cigarettes (ages 40-older)	0.1
Gasoline (short run)	0.2
Gasoline (long run)	0.7

Why do these elasticities differ in size? Several factors determine a good's elasticity.

The Degree of Substitutability

A key factor is whether the item in question has good substitutes. Can people easily find a substitute when the price goes up? If the answer is yes, then the price elasticity will be high. Foreign travel has a high elasticity because it has a reasonably good substitute: domestic travel.

On the other hand, the low price elasticity of eggs can be explained by the lack of good substitutes. As many fans of eggs know, these items are unique; synthetic eggs are not good substitutes. Hence, the price elasticity of eggs is small. People will continue to buy them even if the price rises a lot.

The degree of substitutability depends in part on whether a good is a necessity or a luxury. If you want to easily preserve food for more than a few hours, a refrigerator has no good substitute. A fancy refrigerator with an exterior that blends in with the rest of your kitchen, however, is more of a luxury and likely will have a higher price elasticity.

FIGURE 4.10 Price Elasticity of Cell Phone Service in the Desert
There's probably not much of a substitute available for long-distance communication in the desert, which would make the price elasticity of the cell phone used here quite low. Do you think the caller in this picture would be equally insensitive to an increase of $0.10 per minute in the price of his calls if he were seated in his apartment in Chicago?

Source: DimClaire/Shutterstock.com

Big-Ticket versus Little-Ticket Items

If a good represents a large fraction of people's income, then the price elasticity will be high. If the price of foreign travel doubles, many people will not be able to afford to travel abroad. On the other hand, if the good represents a small fraction of income, the elasticity will be low. For example, if the price of eggs doubles, most people still will be able to afford to buy as many eggs as before the price increase.

Temporary versus Permanent Price Changes

If a change in price is known to be temporary, the price elasticity of demand will tend to be high, because many people can easily shift their purchases either later or earlier. For example, suppose a sewing machine store announces a discount price that will last only one day. Then people will shift their sewing machine purchase to the day of the sale. On the other hand, if the price cut is permanent, the price elasticity will be smaller. People who expect the price decrease to be permanent will not find it advantageous to buy sooner rather than later.

Differences in Preferences

Different groups of consumers may have different levels of elasticity. For example, young cigarette smokers, whose habit of smoking may not be entrenched, are more sensitive to changes in prices than older smokers. Table 4.3 shows that the price elasticity of demand for cigarettes for young adults between 18 and 24 years old is much higher than the very low price elasticity for people more than 40 years old.

Long-Run versus Short-Run Elasticity

Frequently the price elasticity of demand is low immediately after a price change, but then it increases after a period of time has passed. To analyze these changes, economists distinguish between the *short run* and the *long run*. The short run is simply a period of time before people have made all their adjustments or changed their habits; the long run is a period of time long enough for people to make such adjustments or change their habits.

Many personal adjustments to a change in prices take a long time. For example, when the price of gas increases, people can reduce the quantity demanded in the short run only by driving less and using other forms of transportation more, or by reducing the heating in their homes. This may be inconvenient or impossible. In the long run, however, when it comes time to buy a new car or a new heating system, they can buy a more fuel-efficient item or one that uses an alternative energy source. Thus, the quantity of gas demanded falls by larger amounts in the long run than in the short run (see Table 4.3).

Habits that are difficult to break also cause differences between short-run and long-run elasticity. Even a large increase in the price of tobacco may have a small effect on the quantity purchased because people cannot break the smoking habit quickly. But after a period of time, the high price of cigarettes may encourage them to break the habit, while discouraging potential new users. Thus, the long-run elasticity for tobacco is higher than the short-run elasticity.

FIGURE 4.11 The Price Elasticity of Video Streaming Services
If Netflix raises its subscription fee, would you still continue to subscribe to the service? How high would the increase have to be before you quit using the service? How would your behavior depend on the availability of alternative streaming services?

Source: sitthiphong/Shutterstock.com

The following examples will test your understanding of the determinants of the price elasticity of demand. Suppose the movie industry reported that its summer revenue was 3 percent higher than the previous year. A closer analysis reveals that ticket sales were down 1 percent. How could ticket revenue increase at the same time that the number of tickets sold decreased? The ticket price must have increased. Demand for movies also must be price inelastic, so that the reduction in ticket sales was more than offset by the increase in the price of the movie tickets. Does this make sense for the movie industry? It is plausible that some people feel that they *must see* the newest release and that the cost of the movie is a little-ticket item for many people who go to the movies. This would make the price elasticity of demand low and plausibly make demand price inelastic.

In January of 2019, Netflix announced that they were raising their subscription rates by around 15 percent. In response to this announcement, analysts predicted that Netflix would earn more revenue because they anticipated that, as with previous rate hikes, this particular rate increase would not result in a reduction in subscribers to the service. Revenue would increase if the price for the service rose by more than the use of the service declined. In other words, Netflix (and the analysts who kept an eye on the company's prospects) were predicting that the demand for Netflix was price inelastic. However, by the end of the year, the introduction of new streaming services like Disney+ and the continued growth of existing services like Amazon Prime Video and Hulu meant that the same analysts were predicting that future price increases for Netflix were very unlikely. In other words, the increased number of services that are close substitutes for Netflix would increase the price elasticity of demand and make the demand for Netflix plausibly price elastic. In that case, an increase in the price would reduce the use of the service by enough to lower Netflix's revenue.

Income Elasticity and Cross-Price Elasticity of Demand

Recall that the price elasticity of demand refers to movements along the demand curve. We emphasized in Chapter 3 the difference between a shift in the demand curve and a movement along the demand curve. A *shift* in the demand curve occurs when the quantity that people are willing to buy changes because of a change in anything except the price—for example, a change in income.

The concept of elasticity also can be applied to measure how changes in the quantity that consumers are willing to buy respond to changes in income. This elasticity must be distinguished from the price elasticity of demand. The **income elasticity of demand** is the percentage change in the quantity of a good demanded at any given price divided by a percentage change in income. That is,

> **income elasticity of demand**
>
> The percentage change in quantity demanded of a good divided by the percentage change in income.

$$\text{income elasticity of demand} = \frac{\text{percentage change in quantity demanded}}{\text{percentage change in income}}$$

For example, if incomes rise by 10 percent and, as a result, people purchase 15 percent more health care at a given price, the income elasticity of health care is 1.5. Table 4.4 lists income elasticities of demand for several different goods and services.

TABLE 4.4 Estimated Income Elasticities of Demand

Type of Good or Service	Income Elasticity
Food	0.58
Clothing/footwear	0.58
Transport	1.18
Medical care	1.35
Recreation	1.42

As discussed in Chapter 3, the demand for most goods increases when people's incomes increase. If you have more income, your demand for movies probably will increase at each price. Recall that a normal good is a good or service whose demand increases as income increases. But not every good is a normal good; if the demand for a good declines when income increases, the good is called an inferior good. The income elasticity of demand for an inferior good is negative and is reported as a negative number by economists.

Another type of elasticity relating to shifts in the demand curve is the **cross-price elasticity of demand**, which is defined as the percentage change in the quantity demanded divided by the percentage change in the price of another good. For example, an increase in the price of Rollerblades would *increase* the quantity demanded of bicycles at every price as people shift away from Rollerblading to bicycle riding. Rollerblades are a substitute for bicycles. A cross-price elasticity also can go in the other direction. An increase in the price of bicycle helmets may *reduce* the demand for bicycles. Bicycle helmets and bicycles are complements. For a complement, the cross-price elasticity of demand is negative.

> **cross-price elasticity of demand**
>
> The percentage change in the quantity demanded of one good divided by the percentage change in the price of another good.

Cross-Price Elasticity of Demand

Changes in the price of a related good can positively or negatively affect demand depending on whether the related good is a substitute or complement.

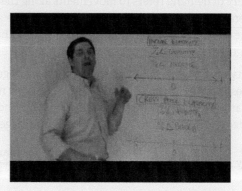

View the video online at: http://www.youtube.com/embed/Ig7igjoGyjM?rel=0

Review

- The price elasticity of demand, or elasticity, is used to measure how much the quantity demanded changes when the price changes. Elasticity also helps determine how large a price increase will occur as a result of a shift in supply, and by how much revenue will change when the price rises.

- Elasticity is a unit-free measure—it is the ratio of the percentage change in quantity demanded to the percentage change in price. In other words, it measures by what percentage quantity demanded changes when the price changes by 1 percent.

- Horizontal demand curves have infinite price elasticity. Vertical demand curves have zero price elasticity. Most products have a price elasticity between these two extremes. We use the term *elastic demand* to refer to an elasticity of demand that is greater than one and *inelastic demand* to refer to an elasticity of demand that is less than one.

- Other than the horizontal and vertical cases, elasticity is different from the slope of the demand curve, however. A demand curve that is a straight line has a different elasticity of demand at each point.

- The size of the price elasticity of demand depends on the availability of substitutes for the item, whether the item represents a large fraction of income, and whether the price change is temporary or permanent.

- Whereas the price elasticity of demand refers to movements along the demand curve, the income elasticity of demand refers to shifts in the demand curve caused by changes in income. Most goods are normal and have a positive income elasticity of demand. Inferior goods have a negative income elasticity of demand.

- The cross-price elasticity of demand also relates to shifts in the demand curve, in this case, a change in the price of a complement or substitute good.

4.4 Elasticity of Supply

Knowing how sensitive the quantity supplied is to a change in price is just as important as knowing how sensitive the quantity demanded is. The price elasticity of supply measures this sensitivity. "Price elasticity of supply" is sometimes shortened to "supply elasticity" or "elasticity of supply." Supply describes the behavior of firms that produce goods. A high price elasticity of supply means that firms raise their production by a large amount if the price increases. A low price elasticity of supply means that firms raise their production only a little if the price increases.

The **price elasticity of supply** is defined as the percentage change in the quantity supplied divided by the percentage change in the price. That is,

$$\text{price elasticity of supply} = \frac{\text{percentage change in quantity supplied}}{\text{percentage change in the price}}$$

price elasticity of supply

The percentage change in quantity supplied divided by the percentage change in price.

The price elasticity of supply refers to a particular supply curve, such as the supply curve for gasoline or video games. All other things that affect supply are held constant when we compute the price elasticity of supply. For example, suppose the price elasticity of supply for video games is 0.5. Then, if the price of video games rises by 10 percent, the quantity of video games supplied will increase by 5 percent (0.5 x 10).

Working with Supply Elasticities

All the attractive features of the price elasticity of demand also apply to the price elasticity of supply. To see this, let us first take a look at the definition of the price elasticity of supply using symbols. If we let the symbol e_s be the price elasticity of supply, then it can be written as

$$e_s = \frac{\Delta Q_s}{Q_s} \div \frac{\Delta P}{P} = \frac{\left(\frac{\Delta Q_s}{Q_s}\right)}{\left(\frac{\Delta P}{P}\right)}$$

where Q_s is the quantity supplied and P is the price. In other words, the price elasticity of supply is the percentage change in the quantity supplied divided by the percentage change in price. Observe the similarity of this expression to the analogous expression for the price elasticity of demand on page 80: The only difference is the use of quantity supplied (Q_s) rather than quantity demanded (Q_d). This means that the concepts and terminology for supply elasticity are very similar to those for demand elasticity. For example, in Table 4.1, if you replace "Demand" with "Supply," you have the terminology for the price elasticity of supply. Moreover, like the price elasticity of demand, the price elasticity of supply is a unit-free measure, and the elasticity of supply and the slope of the supply curve are not the same thing.

Because of this similarity, our discussion of supply elasticity can be brief. It is useful to consider the extreme cases of perfectly elastic supply and perfectly inelastic supply, and then to go through an example illustrating the importance of knowing the size of the price elasticity of supply.

Perfectly Elastic and Perfectly Inelastic Supply

perfectly elastic supply

Supply for which the price elasticity is infinite, indicating an infinite response of quantity supplied to a change in price and therefore a horizontal supply curve.

perfectly inelastic supply

Supply for which the price elasticity is zero, indicating no response of quantity supplied to a change in price and therefor a vertical supply curve.

As in the case of demand, there can be **perfectly elastic supply** or **perfectly inelastic supply**, as shown in Figure 4.12. The vertical supply curve is perfectly inelastic; it has zero elasticity. Such supply curves are not unusual. For example, only one *Mona Lisa* exists. A higher price cannot bring about a higher quantity supplied, not even one more *Mona Lisa*. But the supply curve for most goods is not vertical. Higher prices will encourage coffee producers to use more fertilizer, hire more workers, and eventually plant more coffee trees. Thus, the quantity supplied increases when the price rises.

FIGURE 4.12 Perfectly Elastic and Perfectly Inelastic Supply
When the quantity supplied is completely unresponsive to the price, the supply curve is vertical and the price elasticity of supply is zero; this case is called perfectly inelastic supply. When the quantity supplied responds by large amounts to a price change, the supply curve is horizontal; economists say that supply is perfectly elastic.

The horizontal supply curve is perfectly elastic. In this case, the price does not change at all. It is the same regardless of the quantity supplied. It is easier to understand the horizontal supply curve if you view it as an approximation to a supply curve that is *nearly* horizontal, one with a very high elasticity. Then, only a small increase in price brings forth a huge increase in the quantity supplied by firms.

Why the Size of the Price Elasticity of Supply Is Important

Now let us look at the importance of knowing the size of the supply elasticity even if it is not at one of these two extremes. Figure 4.13 shows two different supply curves for coffee. The horizontal axis shows the quantity of coffee supplied around the world in billions of pounds; the vertical axis shows the price in dollars per pound of coffee. For the supply curve in the top graph, the quantity supplied is very sensitive to the price; the price elasticity of supply is high. For the supply curve in the bottom graph, the price elasticity of supply is much lower.

FIGURE 4.13 Comparing Different Sizes of the Price Elasticities of Supply

In the top graph, the quantity supplied is much more sensitive to price than in the bottom graph. The price elasticity of supply is greater between points *A* and *B* at the top than between points *A* and *C* at the bottom.

FIGURE 4.14 Perfectly Inelastic Supply

The paintings of Leonardo da Vinci provide an example of a good with a perfectly inelastic supply. The supply curve is vertical because no matter how high the price, no more *Mona Lisas* can be produced. However, what about the demand to see the *Mona Lisa* at the Louvre? Is it perfectly inelastic? Will raising the price of admission charged by the Louvre Museum in Paris reduce the number of people coming to see the painting?

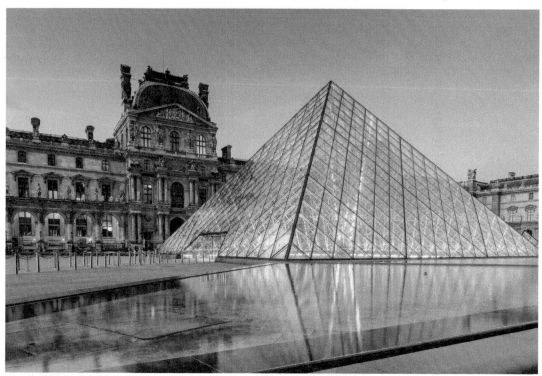

Source: Nattee Chalermtiragool/Shutterstock.com

The price elasticity of supply is important for finding the response of price to shifts in demand. This is shown in Figure 4.15, in which the demand for coffee declines, perhaps because of concerns about the effect of the caffeine in coffee or because of a decrease in the price of caffeine-free substitutes for coffee. In either case, if the price elasticity of supply is high, as in the top graph, the price does not change as much as when the price elasticity of supply is low, as in the bottom graph. With a high price elasticity, a small change in price is enough to get firms to bring the quantity supplied down to the lower quantity demanded.

FIGURE 4.15 Importance of Knowing the Size of the Price Elasticity of Supply
When demand changes, the price also will change. If the price elasticity of supply is high, a small change in price will result. If the price elasticity of supply is low, a large change in price will result.

The ongoing COVID-19 pandemic has provided many examples that show how differences in the magnitude of the price elasticity of supply can explain observed differences in prices. For example, when the demand for ventilators and N95 masks skyrocketed as the virus started spreading across the globe, prices increased sharply because these were specialized goods that only a few firms were capable of producing in the quantities needed by hospitals and nursing homes. You can see the resulting outcome for yourself by redoing the lower panel of Figure 4.15 for an increase in demand—the equilibrium price of the good will rise by a lot. On the other hand, demand for goods like reusable cloth masks, hand sanitizer, toilet paper, and home thermometers also increased as people started stocking up in anticipation of future needs. These goods were much easier to produce and thus would be examples of goods where the supply elasticity was relatively high. You can see the resulting outcome for yourself by redoing the upper panel of Figure 4.15 for an increase in demand—the equilibrium price of the good will rise by much less when the supply curve is more elastic. Keep in mind, though, that even if the price elasticity of supply for the overall product may be high, price elasticity for a particular brand name—Purell sanitizer, Charmin ultra-soft toilet paper—may still be quite low and prices for that particular brand may increase by more than overall prices for the product would.

Review

- The price elasticity of supply is a number that tells us how sensitive the quantity supplied is to the price. It is defined as the percentage change in the quantity supplied divided by the percentage change in the price.
- The attractive features of the price elasticity of demand are also true for the price elasticity of supply. Its size does not depend on the units of measurement of either price or quantity.
- The price elasticity of supply is useful for determining how much prices will change when demand changes.

4.5 End-of-Chapter Material

Conclusion

In this chapter, we have extended our analysis of the supply and demand model in two directions. We first learned about what happens when the government intervenes to put a price ceiling or a price floor into the economy. Understanding how to use the supply and demand model with price floors and ceilings enables us to better understand policy debates such as the one surrounding the increase in the minimum wage.

The second extension was to develop an understanding of *how much* the equilibrium price and quantity change in response to changes in supply or demand. The concept of price elasticity of demand helps us understand what happens to the quantity demanded when price changes or when the supply of a good changes. We also can predict whether revenue will increase or decrease when prices are cut or raised. The related concept of the elasticity of supply is also useful in understanding what happens to the quantity supplied when price changes or when the demand for a good changes. We also discussed the concept of an income elasticity of demand, which can clarify how the quantity demanded for various goods will change as incomes rise, and the cross-price elasticity of demand, which tells us how much the quantity demanded of a good changes as prices for substitute or complementary goods change.

Key Points

1. Governments occasionally will intervene in markets because they think that the equilibrium price is too high or too low. When they act to impose a maximum price on a market, because they think the price that buyers have to pay is too high, they are said to be imposing a price ceiling. When they act to impose a minimum price on a market, because they think the price that sellers are receiving is too low, they are said to be imposing a price floor.

2. Price ceilings cause shortages, with the quantity supplied being less than the quantity demanded. Shortages lead to rationing or black markets. Price floors cause surpluses,

with the quantity supplied being greater than the quantity demanded. Surpluses lead to resources being diverted away from other productive activities to deal with the extra output that needs to be stored or disposed of.

3. Rent controls are a classic application of a price ceiling, and minimum wages are a classic application of a price floor. The supply model helps us understand some basic issues related to these policies, which frequently appear in the news. We will develop the supply and demand model further, which will allow us to do a more sophisticated analysis of minimum-wage laws, for example, than we have done in this chapter.

4. Elasticity is a measure of the sensitivity of one economic variable to another. For example, the price elasticity of demand measures how much the quantity demanded changes when the price changes.

5. Elasticity is a unit-free measure. The price elasticity of demand is the percentage change in the quantity demanded divided by the percentage change in price. It refers to changes in price and quantity demanded along the demand curve, all other things being equal.

6. Demand is said to be elastic if the price elasticity of demand is greater than one and inelastic if the price elasticity of demand is less than one.

7. When the elasticity is greater than one, an increase in the price reduces the quantity demanded by a percentage greater than the percentage increase in the price, thereby reducing revenue. When the elasticity is less than one, an increase in the price reduces the quantity demanded by a percentage less than the percentage increase in the price, thereby increasing revenue.

8. The elasticity of demand for a good depends on whether the good has close substitutes, whether its value is a large or a small fraction of total income, and the time period of the change.

9. Whereas the price elasticity of demand refers to movements along the demand curve, the income elasticity of demand refers to shifts in the demand curve caused by changes in income, and the cross-price elasticity of demand refers to shifts in the demand curve caused by changes in the price of other goods. Most goods are normal and have a positive income elasticity of demand. Inferior goods have a negative income elasticity of demand.

10. The price elasticity of supply is defined as the percentage change in the quantity supplied divided by the percentage change in the price. If a good has a high price elasticity of supply, then a change in price will cause a big change in the quantity supplied. Conversely, if a good has a low price elasticity of supply, then a change in price will have only a small impact on the quantity supplied.

Questions for Review

1. Why is the price elasticity of demand a unit-free measure of the sensitivity of the quantity demanded to a price change?

2. What factors determine whether the price elasticity of demand is high or low?

3. What is the difference between elastic and inelastic demand?

4. Why is the price elasticity of demand useful for finding the size of the price change that occurs when supply shifts?

5. If the price elasticity of demand for textbooks is two and the price of textbooks increases by 10 percent, by how much does the quantity demanded fall?

6. Why is the price elasticity of demand lower in the short run than in the long run?

7. For what values of the price elasticity of demand do increases in the price increase revenue?

8. What is the income elasticity of demand?

9. What is the difference between the price elasticity of demand and the income elasticity of demand?

10. What is the slope of a perfectly elastic supply curve?

Problems

1. Consider the market for automatic teller machine (ATM) services in a city. The price is the fee for a cash withdrawal.

   a. Sketch the demand curve and the supply curve for ATM transactions.

   b. How is the equilibrium price determined?

   c. If the town council imposes a ban on ATM fees— equivalent to a price ceiling in this market—what happens to quantity supplied and quantity demanded?

   d. Economists frequently argue against price controls because of the shortages and associated problems that they create. What are some of the potentially negative side effects of interference in the ATM market?

2. In 1991, the price of milk fell 30 percent. Senator Leahy of Vermont, a big milk-producing state, supported a law in the U.S. Congress to put a floor on the price. The floor was $13.09 per hundred pounds of milk. The market price was $11.47.

   a. Draw a supply and demand diagram for milk and show how the equilibrium price and quantity would be determined in the absence of the price floor.

   b. Using the diagram you just drew, explain the effects of the legislation.

   c. The dairy farmers supported the legislation, while consumer groups opposed it. Why?

   d. Economists frequently argue against price floors because of the surpluses and associated problems that they create. What are some of the potentially negative side effects of interference in the milk market?

3. More than 20 states have laws outlawing price gouging during a state of emergency, which might be declared after a hurricane or an earthquake. These laws prohibit price increases on basic necessities, such as gasoline. Which of the arguments against price ceilings might not be significant during a state of emergency?

4. Donors of organs for transplantation or medical research are prohibited from charging a price for these organs (there is a price ceiling of zero). Will this result in a shortage? How will the market cope with the shortage?

5. Consider the following data for a demand curve:

Price ($)	Quantity
11	10
10	20
9	30
8	40
7	50
6	60
5	70
4	80
3	90

   a. Use the midpoint formula to calculate the elasticity between a price of $10 and $11.

   b. Use the midpoint formula to calculate the elasticity between a price of $3 and $4.

   c. Because this is a linear demand curve, why does the elasticity change?

   d. At what point is price times quantity maximized? What is the elasticity at that point?

6. Consider the following data for a supply curve:

Price ($)	Quantity Supplied
2	10
3	20
4	30
5	40
6	50
7	60
8	70
9	80

a. Use the midpoint formula to calculate the price elasticity of supply between a price of $7 and $8.

b. Use the midpoint formula to calculate the price elasticity of supply between a price of $3 and $4.

c. How does supply elasticity change as you move up the supply curve?

d. Why does the supply elasticity change even though the slope of the supply curve is unchanged as you move up the supply curve?

7. Given the following income elasticities of demand, would you classify the following goods as normal or inferior goods?

a. Potatoes: elasticity = 0.5

b. Pinto beans: elasticity = -0.1

c. Bottled water: elasticity = 1.1

d. Video cameras: elasticity = 1.4

8. Calculate the cross-price elasticity for the following goods. Are they substitutes or complements?

a. The price of movie theater tickets goes up by 10 percent, causing the quantity demanded for video rentals to go up by 4 percent.

b. The price of computers falls by 20 percent, causing the quantity demanded of software to increase by 15 percent.

c. The price of apples falls by 5 percent, causing the quantity demanded of pears to fall by 5 percent.

d. The price of ice cream falls by 6 percent, causing the quantity demanded of frozen yogurt to fall by 1 percent.

9. Food items often have low elasticities of demand. Suppose excellent weather leads to bumper yields of agricultural crops. Why might farmers complain about market conditions?

10. The board of directors of an airline wishes to increase revenue. One group favors cutting airfares, and the other group favors raising airfares. What are the assumptions each group is making about the price elasticity of demand?

11. Compare a market in which supply and demand are very (but not perfectly) inelastic to one in which supply and demand are very (but not perfectly) elastic. Suppose the government decides to impose a price floor $1 above the equilibrium price in each of these markets. Compare, diagrammatically, the surpluses that result. In which market is the surplus larger?

12. In 1992, the federal government placed a tax of 10 percent on goods like luxury automobiles and yachts. The yacht-manufacturing industry had huge declines in orders for yachts and laid off many workers, whereas the reaction in the auto industry was much milder. (The tax on yachts was subsequently removed.) Explain this situation using two supply and demand diagrams. Compare the elasticity of demand for luxury autos with that for yachts based on the experience with the luxury tax.

CHAPTER 5
The Demand Curve and the Behavior of Consumers

This is a true story about a college professor who loves to teach introductory economics.

The professor is younger than most college professors but is hard of hearing and wears hearing aids in both ears. The professor teaches one of those large lecture courses, and most students are not even aware that the professor wears the hearing aids.

In the middle of one of the lectures, the professor simultaneously brings one hand to one ear and the other hand to the other ear and suddenly pulls out both hearing aids, saying, "I can't hear a thing. If it were not for these hearing aids, I wouldn't be here. I couldn't be a teacher. Do you know how much benefit I get from these hearing aids? Certainly more than from my car and maybe even more than from my house. If I had to give you a dollar amount, I would say that the benefit to me is about $60,000. Without the hearing aids, I would probably earn less, and I know my life would not be as enjoyable. Of course, I had to buy these hearing aids, and they are not very cheap. They cost me $500. But, you know, they cost me a lot less than they benefit me. The difference between $60,000 and $500 is $59,500, a huge amount. That difference is a measure of what the hearing aid market delivers to me over and above what I had to pay for the hearing aids. Most people would call that a good deal, but because I am an economics professor, I call it a *consumer surplus*."

In this chapter, we show how and why the demand curve for any good—whether hearing aids, digital music players, grapes, or bananas—can be used to measure the "good deal," or the "consumer surplus," that markets deliver to people.

Figure 5.2 shows a typical demand curve, with price on the vertical axis and quantity demanded on the horizontal axis. The demand curve is for an entire market, which might consist of millions of consumers. But consumers do not go to the market with a demand curve; they go with certain preferences and objectives. In this chapter, we look under the surface of the demand curve and examine how a consumer's preferences and objectives, combined with the constraints that the consumer faces, determine the demand curve for a particular good for an individual.

Then we show how aggregating individual demand curves across millions of consumers generates a demand curve for the entire market for that good.

By the end of this chapter, you should better understand two important concepts. The first is exactly what determines the slope and position of the demand curve—why it slopes downward and why changes in people's preferences or incomes cause it to shift. The second is how to quantify the "good deal," or the "consumer surplus," that the market delivers to consumers. Consumer surplus is extremely important for measuring how well a market economy actually works. One of the most important conclusions of the study of economics is that, under certain circumstances, a market economy works better than alternative systems to produce and allocate goods and resources. To understand that conclusion—to question it, to criticize it, to prove it, to defend it—we must better understand how much benefit consumers are getting from a market.

FIGURE 5.1 The Consumer Surplus Delivered by a Hearing Aid
The consumer surplus delivered by a good to a consumer is the difference between the consumer's willingness to pay for the good and the price of the good. For a person who is hard of hearing, even a $500 hearing aid can deliver substantial consumer surplus.

Source: Oksana Shufrych/Shutterstock.com

FIGURE 5.2 A Typical Demand Curve
Demand curves typically slope downward. In this chapter, we examine the behavior of the consumers who underline the demand curve.

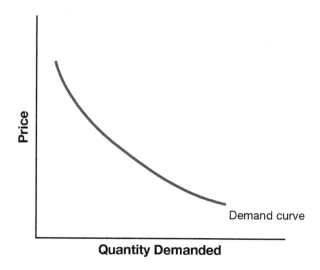

5.1 Utility and Consumer Preferences

Our examination of consumer behavior in this chapter involves constructing a model. The main assumption of the model is that people make purposeful choices with limited resources to increase their satisfaction and better their lives. To make this assumption operational, economists have developed the idea of *utility*, which represents people's preferences for different items (products, jobs, leisure time) among a set of alternatives.

Every person has tastes and preferences for some goods relative to other goods. The millions of people who underlie a typical demand curve do not all have the same tastes and preferences, of course. Some people like brussels sprouts; some people hate brussels sprouts. We first focus on how to derive a demand curve for an individual consumer and then show how the behavior of the millions of individuals adds up to generate a market demand curve.

Utility is a numerical indicator of a person's preference for some goods compared with others. If one prefers some activity, such as eating a pizza and drinking two Cokes, to some other activity, such as eating two pizzas and drinking one Coke, then the utility from "one pizza and two Cokes" is greater than the utility from "two pizzas and one Coke." In general, if activity A is preferred to alternative B, then the utility from A is greater than the utility from B.

Be careful not to confuse the economist's definition of utility with the everyday meaning. If you look up *utility* in the dictionary, you probably will see the word *usefulness*, but to an economist, higher *utility* does not mean greater "usefulness"; it simply means that the item is preferred to another item. Watching *Game of Thrones* or reruns of *The Office* might give you more utility than attending a review session for your economics course, even though it certainly is not as useful for studying for the final.

utility

A numerical indicator of a person's preferences in which higher levels of utility indicate a greater preference.

A Consumer's Utility Depends on the Consumption of Goods

Let us consider an example of utility. Grapes are a product with which we have a lot of experience. They have been around for more than 4,000 years (at least since 2400 B.C. in ancient Egypt), and, in one form or another, they still are consumed around the world. Bananas are another popular fruit, also consumed around the world. Let us use grapes and bananas for our example of utility.

Figure 5.3 shows an example of the utility that one individual might get from consuming different amounts of grapes and bananas. Remember that every person is different, so the utility shown in Figure 5.3 is just an example. You might imagine that the person is you, standing in front of a bin of fresh grapes and bananas in a grocery store and deciding what fruit to buy. Or it could be someone at an open-air market who is deciding how many pounds of grapes and bananas to buy with her money.

FIGURE 5.3 Example of Utility from Grapes and Bananas
The numbers inside the box give the utility from consuming the amounts of grapes and the amounts of bananas shown outside the box. For example, utility from 4 pounds of grapes and 3 pounds of bananas is 36. Combinations of grapes and bananas with higher utility are preferred to combinations with lower utility.

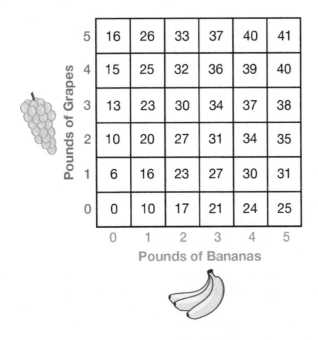

Observe how Figure 5.3 is organized. The number of pounds of grapes is listed vertically on the left outside the box, from 0 up to 5 pounds. The number of pounds of bananas is listed horizontally below the box, from 0 to 5 pounds. The entries inside the box show the utility from consuming different combinations of grapes and bananas. The box at the intersection of a row and a column shows the utility for the consumption of that specific combination of grapes and bananas. For example, if the individual consumes 2 pounds of grapes and 2 pounds of bananas, then the utility is 27.

Remember that utility is an indicator of people's preferences, with higher utility indicating a stronger preference. As you move up a column or across a row, utility increases. This increase in utility is called **marginal utility**. In general, *marginal utility* is the increase in utility from consuming an additional unit of a good.

marginal utility

The increase in utility when consumption of a good increases by one unit.

For example, consider an individual consuming 2 pounds of grapes and 2 pounds of bananas. For this individual, at that level of consumption, consuming 1 additional pound of grapes (making her consumption 3 pounds of grapes and 2 pounds of bananas) increases utility by 3 (from 27 to 30); the marginal utility of a pound of grapes is 3.

Had she instead chosen to consume 1 more pound of bananas (making her consumption 2 pounds of grapes and 3 pounds of bananas), her utility would have increased by 4 (from 27 to 31); the marginal utility of a pound of bananas is 4.

Important Properties of Utility

We can use Figure 5.3 to illustrate some important assumptions that economists often make about utility.

diminishing marginal utility

The tendency for a consumer to derive less additional benefit from adding to the consumption of a good as consumption of that good increases.

1. *Utility can be used to rank alternative consumption combinations.* A consumer's utility describes the consumer's preference for one good compared with another. According to Figure 5.3, the consumer prefers a combination of 4 pounds of grapes and 1 pound of bananas to a combination of 1 pound of grapes and 2 pounds of bananas because the utility of the former (25) is greater than the utility of the latter (23). Other combinations can be ranked similarly. In some cases, utility levels are identical; for example, the consumer is *indifferent* as to 2 pounds of grapes and 3 pounds of bananas versus 1 pound of grapes and 5 pounds of bananas because the utility of both is 31. Of all possible combinations, the one with the highest (maximum) utility is the one that is preferred to all the others. Thus, by maximizing utility, the consumer is making decisions that lead to the most preferred outcome from her viewpoint. In this way, utility maximization implements the assumption that people make purposeful choices to increase their satisfaction.

2. *Having more of a good never makes an individual worse off.* In Figure 5.3, as you move across a row or up a column, utility is increasing, which means that marginal utility is a positive value. This implies that this individual would get more utility from 3 pounds of grapes and 2 pounds of bananas (utility = 30) or from 2 pounds of grapes and 3 pounds of bananas (utility = 31) than she would gain from 2 pounds of grapes and 2 pounds of bananas (utility = 27). This assumption seems reasonable. On occasion, an individual may derive zero marginal utility from a particular good, although that is not the case in the example in Figure 5.3. As long as you can freely dispose of goods, adding more of a good should never reduce utility, in other words, marginal utility should never be negative.

3. A corollary of statement #2. is that having more of both goods is always a more preferred option for a consumer, just as having less of both goods is always a less preferred option. For example, consider the choice of 2 pounds of grapes and 2 pounds of bananas for the individual, highlighted in Figure 5.4. All the bundles that involve the same amount or more of one fruit and more of the other (which are the upper shaded entries to the right and above) are preferred to the combination of 2 pounds each of grapes and bananas. Alternatively, the consumer prefers the 2 pounds of grapes and 2 pounds of bananas combination to all the bundles that involve the same amount or less of one fruit and less of the other (which are the lower shaded entries to the left and below). The consumer would find the remaining combinations (which involve more bananas and fewer grapes or fewer bananas and more grapes) either more preferred or less preferred or would be indifferent between them, depending on what is contained in those combinations.

4. *Marginal utility decreases as the consumption of a good increases.* If you look at Figure 5.3, you can see that marginal utility is decreasing as you consume more bananas or more grapes. For example, the marginal utility of a pound of bananas for a consumer who is consuming 2 pounds of bananas and 2 pounds of grapes is 4 (31 - 27 = 4). But the marginal utility of adding 1 more pound of bananas to her new consumption bundle of 3 pounds of bananas and 2 pounds of grapes is only 3 (34 - 31 = 3). Intuitively, what this is showing is that the more an individual is

consuming of a good, the less additional benefit she will get from adding to her consumption of that good. This is known as **diminishing marginal utility**.

5. *The units that utility is measured in do not matter.* Utility is a numerical indicator of preferences, but the units used to measure it do not matter. For example, suppose we multiply the utilities from grapes and from bananas in Figure 5.3 by 10, and then re-examine what utility implies about preferences. Rather than 27 units of utility, we would have 270 units of utility from 2 pounds of grapes and 2 pounds of bananas. Instead of this combination, the consumer would still prefer 3 pounds of grapes and 3 pounds of bananas, which now would have a utility of 340 instead of 34. In fact, you can multiply utility by any positive number—even a billion or a billionth—and still get the same ordering of one combination compared with another. The fact that the description of people's preferences does not depend on the units we use to measure utility is important, because in reality economists have no way to measure utility. That is why Figure 5.3 does not give units, just a number.

6. *You cannot compare utility levels across people.* Because you can multiply the utility of any individual by any number without changing the description of that individual's preferences, the utilities of different people cannot be compared. In other words, we cannot say that one person's utility is higher or lower than another person's utility. Only the preferences of a particular person are represented by utility.

FIGURE 5.4 Deriving Utility from Grapes and Bananas
Consuming 2 pounds each of grapes and bananas gives a utility level of 27. Combinations that have at least as much of one fruit and more of the other have a higher level of utility (upper shaded region). Combinations that have at least as much of one fruit and less of the other have a lower level of utility (lower shaded region).

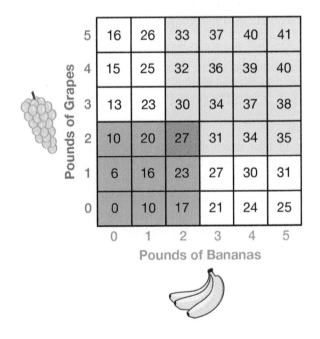

Review

- Utility is a numerical indicator of a person's preferences for different goods.
- Each combination of goods has a numerical value of utility. Combinations of goods with a higher utility are preferred to combinations of goods with a lower utility.
- The change in utility from consuming one additional unit of a good is known as marginal utility. As long as you can freely dispose of goods, marginal utility never will be negative.

- Marginal utility typically will decrease as the consumption of a good increases—additional units of a good will be more valued when the consumer is not already consuming much of that good.
- The units by which utility is measured do not affect the preference for one combination compared with another.
- Utility levels cannot be compared across people. Utility is an indicator of one individual's preferences.

5.2 The Budget Constraint and Utility Maximization

We now know how a consumer's preferences can be described by utility. We also know that the consumer wants to maximize utility—to make a purposeful choice that provides the most satisfaction. Because marginal utility is never negative for a good, you might be wondering how a consumer can ever reach a maximum level of utility. Wouldn't she always want to consume one more unit of a good? Keep in mind that economics is about how people make purposeful choices *using scarce resources*. In other words, the consumer is maximizing utility given some constraints, or limits, on her behavior. Even though she may want one more unit of a good, she may not be able to afford that additional unit. In this section, we will introduce the limits on the consumer's choice and explain how utility maximization works.

The Budget Constraint

budget constraint

An income limitation on a person's expenditure on goods and services.

Consumers are limited in how much they can spend when they choose between grapes and bananas or other goods. For example, suppose the individual choosing between grapes and bananas is limited to spending a total of $8. That is, total spending on grapes plus bananas must be less than or equal to $8. This limit on total spending is called the **budget constraint**. In general, a budget constraint tells us that total expenditures on all goods and services must be less than a certain amount, perhaps the person's income for the year. The budget constraint is what limits the consumer's choices.

How much a consumer can spend and still remain within the budget constraint depends on the prices of the goods. Suppose the price of a pound of grapes is $1 and the price of a pound of bananas is $1. Her expenditure on a combination of 2 pounds of grapes and 2 pounds of bananas would be $4, well within the budget constraint of $8. But the cost of buying 5 pounds of each would be $10, a sum that exceeds the budget constraint and, therefore, is not possible. So even though 5 pounds of bananas and 5 pounds of grapes have a utility level of 41, compared with a utility level of 27 for the combination of 2 pounds of bananas and 2 pounds of grapes, you will not see the consumer buy that bundle because of her constrained budget.

Figure 5.6 shows expenditures on grapes and bananas for two different situations. In the left panel, both the price of bananas and the price of grapes are $1. All the combinations of grapes and bananas from Figure 5.3 are shown in Figure 5.6, but several of the combinations are not within the $8 budget constraint; these are in the upper shaded area. What happens if the price of grapes is $2 instead of $1? The resulting expenditure for each combination is listed in the panel on the right. Because the price of grapes has risen from $1 to $2, each bundle is now more expensive than before. As a result, more combinations are outside the budget constraint and fewer are within the budget constraint. In general, a higher price for a good reduces consumption opportunities for the individual.

FIGURE 5.5 Modeling a Consumer's Choice

This consumer, with a limited amount to spend, makes a choice that maximizes her utility. The combination of grapes and bananas that she prefers to other possible combinations of grapes and bananas must have a higher utility for her than the other combinations have.

Source: Iakov Filimonov/Shutterstock.com

FIGURE 5.6 The Budget Constraint and Expenditures at Two Different Prices
The numbers inside the box give the total dollar expenditures on different combinations of grapes and bananas. For example, in the left panel where the price of both bananas and grapes is $1 per pound, the total dollar expenditure would be $7 for 4 pounds of grapes and 3 pounds of bananas. If the price of grapes was $2 per pound and the price of bananas was $1 per pound, as in the right panel, that same combination would cost $11. The numbers in the shaded area are greater than the $8 budget constraint.

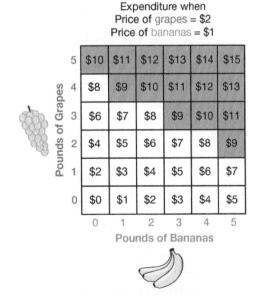

Maximizing Utility Subject to the Budget Constraint

utility maximization

An assumption that people try to achieve the highest level of utility given their budget constraint.

Given the utility in Figure 5.3 and the budget constraint in Figure 5.6, we now can show what happens when the individual maximizes utility subject to the budget constraint. **Utility maximization** means that people choose the highest possible level of utility given their budget constraint. Figure 5.7 shows the utility combinations from Figure 5.3, but now we shade in the combinations for which expenditures are greater than the $8 budget constraint from Figure 5.6. The budget constraint means that your choices are limited to those combinations that are outside the shaded area; these are the combinations that do not violate the budget constraint.

FIGURE 5.7 Maximizing Utility Subject to the Budget Constraint at Two Different Prices
The shaded areas represent combinations for which total expenditures would be greater than the $8 budget constraint. The blue number is the maximum level of utility for which spending is less than or equal to $8. In the left panel, the maximum utility of 39 represents a choice of 4 pounds of grapes and 4 pounds of bananas. In the right panel, with the higher price of grapes, the maximum utility is 34, corresponding to 2 pounds of grapes and 4 pounds of bananas.

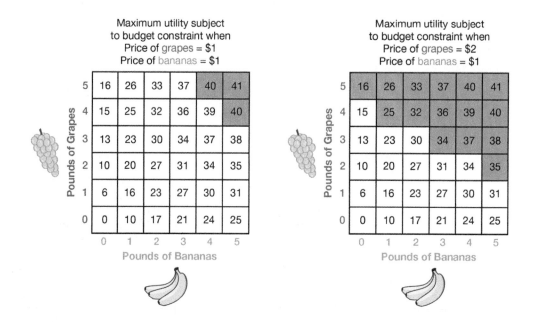

Suppose first that the price of grapes is $1 per pound and the price of bananas is $1 per pound. By looking at the left panel you can find the choice that generates the highest level of utility achievable by the consumer with an $8 budget constraint. That combination is 4 pounds of grapes and 4 pounds of bananas (with a utility level of 39). The utility-maximizing choice, and the resulting level of utility, is shown in blue boldface type. This is the most preferred combination that the individual can buy. Even though utility is higher for some combinations that lie in the shaded areas, those represent combinations for which total expenditures would be greater than the $8 budget constraint, and hence they are not possible choices.

The right panel does a similar exercise; however, as in the right panel of Figure 5.6, it assumes that the price of grapes is now higher at $2, which increases the number of unaffordable combinations. When a price changes, individuals typically will end up choosing a different utility-maximizing combination. But the reason for their switch is not because the level of utility for each combination changed; in fact, you can clearly see that the utility levels of the different combinations did not change when the price changed. Instead, what changed were the combinations that the consumer could or could not afford. For example, at the new higher price of grapes, the previous utility-maximizing choice of 4 pounds of bananas and 4 pounds of grapes is not affordable; it is in a shaded box. Now the utility-maximizing choice is 4 pounds of bananas and 2 pounds of grapes, corresponding to a utility level of 34.

Deriving the Individual's Demand Curve

We can use the results from the utility maximization to derive the individual's demand curve for grapes. When the price of grapes was $1 (and the price of bananas was also $1), the individual would choose to consume 4 pounds of grapes (and 4 pounds of bananas). Another way of saying this is that at a price of $1 per pound of grapes, the quantity demanded of grapes by this individual would be 4 pounds. But what happened when the price of grapes rose to $2 (with the price of bananas still being $1)? The individual chose to consume only 2 pounds of grapes. At a price of $2, therefore the quantity demanded will now be 2.

These two points are plotted in Figure 5.8. Notice that what we have derived are two points on a demand curve for the consumer. When the price goes up, the quantity demanded goes down; when the price goes down, the quantity demanded goes up. Thus, we have shown that the assumption that people maximize utility subject to a budget constraint implies that a higher price leads to a reduced quantity demanded. In other words, we have derived two points that lie along a downward-sloping demand curve. Furthermore, we have shown that changes in price lead to a *movement along* a demand curve.

FIGURE 5.8 An Individual's Demand Curve
The consumer demanded 4 pounds of grapes when the price was $1 and 2 pounds of grapes when the price was $2. We can put these values into a graph and connect them to form a demand curve.

Price of Grapes	Quantity of Grapes Demanded by the Consumer
$1	4 pounds
$2	2 pounds

Effect of a Change in Income: A Shift in the Demand Curve

Now consider the effect of a change in the individual's income on the quantity of grapes that the individual will purchase. Suppose that the individual has only $5 to spend rather than $8; in other words, the individual's income is reduced $3. What will happen to the quantity of grapes demanded by the consumer? At a price of $1 per pound of grapes and $1 per pound of bananas (which means that the boxes on the left of Figure 5.6 and Figure 5.7 apply), the number of unaffordable combinations has increased, or, equivalently, the number of affordable combinations has shrunk. As an exercise, you should see whether you can figure out which combinations need to be shaded because they are no longer affordable, given that expenditure is limited to $5. If expenditures are limited to $5, then the maximum utility occurs when 2 pounds of grapes and 3 pounds of bananas are purchased, resulting in a utility level of 31.

We also can calculate the effects of a similar income change at a different set of prices. If the price is $2 for grapes and $1 for bananas, then the boxes on the right of Figure 5.6 and Figure 5.7 apply. (Again, you might want to shade the additional combinations of grapes and bananas that are not feasible with only $5 to spend.) With a limit of $5 to spend, the maximum utility occurs when 1 pound of grapes and 3 pounds of bananas are purchased, resulting in a utility level of 27.

With $8 to spend, the quantity of grapes demanded was 2 (at a price of $2) and 4 (at a price of $1). Now, with only $5 to spend, the quantity of grapes demanded is 1 (when the price is $2) and 2 (when the price is $1). Thus, as shown in Figure 5.9, we have derived another demand curve corresponding to the decreased amount of income. Observe that the demand curve with the lower amount of income ($5) is shifted to the left compared with the demand curve with the higher amount of income ($8). Thus, we have shown explicitly that a change in income will *shift* the consumer's demand curve.

FIGURE 5.9 A Shift in the Individual's Demand Curve
A fall in income will result in the consumer reducing the quantity demanded at each price level. For example, the figure depicts that at a price of $2, the consumer will now only demand 1 pound of grapes, and at a price of $1, the consumer now only demands 2 pounds of grapes.

Price of Grapes	Quantity of Grapes Demanded by the Consumer
$1	2 pounds
$2	1 pound

Income and Substitution Effects of a Price Change

Using the concepts of utility and the budget constraint, economists distinguish between two separate reasons why an increase in the price leads to a decrease in the quantity demanded. When the price of grapes rises from $1 to $2 per pound, the price increase affects the quantity demanded of grapes in two ways.

First, certain combinations are no longer within the budget constraint at a grape price of $2 per pound, even though they were within the budget constraint at a grape price of $1 per pound.

For instance, a total of 15 options are outside the budget constraint at a grape price of $2 per pound (in the shaded area of the right tables of Figure 5.6 and Figure 5.7), whereas only 3 are outside the budget constraint at a grape price of $1 per pound (in the shaded area of the left tables of Figure 5.6 and Figure 5.7). In other words, the purchasing power of the consumer's income is curtailed even though her income was unchanged.

Second, you can now buy 2 pounds of bananas for the same price as a pound of grapes (whereas before you could buy only 1 pound of bananas for the price of a pound of grapes). Because the relative price of grapes has risen, consumers will be more likely to buy bananas than grapes. These are the two ways in which an increase in price affects quantity demanded. The first is known as the income effect, and the second is known as the substitution effect.

 Income and Substitution Effect

The impact of the change in the price of a good can be decomposed into the income and substitution effect.

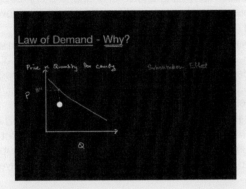

View the video online at: http://www.youtube.com/embed/xGL5mbOvTmQ?rel=0

The Income Effect of a Change in the Price

The **income effect** is the amount by which quantity demanded falls because of the decline in real income from the price increase. When we say that "real income" has decreased, what we mean is that income measured in terms of what goods we can buy with it has decreased. Another way to think about this is that the rise in the price of grapes reduces the number of affordable combinations; for example, the combinations of grapes and bananas that the consumer can buy have decreased *even though her actual income has not decreased*. The income effect is a general phenomenon that applies to many goods; for example, when the price of gasoline rises, people will spend less on gasoline in part because their real income has declined. With less real income, they also will spend less on most goods and services.

income effect

The amount by which the quantity demanded falls because of the decline in real income from a price increase.

The Substitution Effect of a Change in the Price

An increase in the price of grapes with no change in the price of other goods causes an increase in the relative price of grapes. Because grapes become relatively more expensive, people will switch their purchases away from grapes toward bananas, and would do so even if you were to give them additional income to make up for the income effect. A more technical way to think about this is that at the higher price of $2 per pound of grapes, the opportunity cost of consuming a pound of grapes is 2 pounds of bananas (at $1 per pound), whereas at a price of $1 per pound of grapes, the

substitution effect

The amount by which quantity demanded falls when the price rises, exclusive of the income effect.

opportunity cost of consuming a pound of grapes is 1 pound of bananas. Because 2 more pounds of bananas will yield more marginal utility than 1 more pound of bananas, consumers will be more likely to consume less grapes and more bananas *even if you give them additional income to make up for the income effect*. The **substitution effect** is the amount by which the quantity demanded falls when the price rises, exclusive of the income effect.

Review

- Individuals choose the combination of goods that maximizes utility, but the set of options from which to make that choice is constrained by scarce resources.
- The demand curve for an individual can be derived from the assumption that people maximize utility subject to a budget constraint. Given a certain set of prices for goods and a certain level of income, an individual will choose the combination that gives her the most utility from among the affordable combinations.
- A change in the price of a good changes the number of affordable combinations and thus changes the utility-maximizing quantity demanded. We showed that when the price of grapes rises, the utility-maximizing choice changes to a combination that contains fewer grapes. In other words, a higher price of grapes leads to a lower quantity demanded for grapes, indicating a downward-sloping demand curve.
- A change in income also changes the number of affordable combinations, and thus changes the utility-maximizing quantity demanded. We showed that a reduction in income would reduce the quantity demanded of grapes for any given price of grapes. This reduction represents a shift in of the demand curve. An increase in income would, on the other hand, lead to a shift out of the demand curve.
- The total effect of a change in the price on the quantity demanded can be divided into two parts—an income effect and a substitution effect. The income effect captures the change in demand that is brought about by the change in real income. The substitution effect captures the change in demand that is brought about by the change in relative prices, exclusive of the income effect.

5.3 Willingness to Pay and the Demand Curve

The choice between one good (grapes) and another good (bananas) in the previous section is useful for showing how to derive a demand curve from the basic idea that consumers maximize utility subject to a budget constraint. In this section, we extend the analysis to move beyond the simple choice between two goods and consider the choice between one good and all possible other goods.

Measuring Willingness to Pay and Marginal Benefit

Suppose we asked a person who is consuming a zero amount of good X, "How much money would you be willing to pay for one unit of X?" Because the money that the person would pay can be used to buy all goods, not just one good, the question implicitly asks the person to compare X with all other goods. In general, the answer to this question will depend on how much the person's utility would increase with one unit of X and how much the person's utility would decrease because less would be spent on other goods, given the budget constraint. In other words, the answer would depend on the person's preferences for X and all other goods, as represented by utility.

Suppose that the person gives us a truthful answer of $5. Now, we could ask, "How much would you be willing to pay for two units of X?" Suppose the answer is, "I would be willing to pay $8." We could then continue to ask the consumer about more and more units of X. We summarize the hypothetical answers in Figure 5.10. The column labeled "Willingness to Pay for X" tabulates the answers to the question.

FIGURE 5.10 Willingness to Pay (Benefit) and Marginal Benefit
The marginal benefit is calculated as the change in the willingness to pay as an additional unit of the good is consumed.

Quantity of X	Willingness to Pay for X (Benefit from X)	Marginal Benefit from X
0	$ 0.00	
1	$ 5.00	$5.00
2	$ 8.00	$3.00
3	$ 9.50	$1.50
4	$10.50	$1.00
5	$11.00	$0.50

The connecting lines emphasize how marginal benefit is the change in benefit (or willingness to pay) as one more unit of a good is consumed.

Assuming that the answers to the questions are true, willingness to pay measures how much the consumer would *benefit* from different amounts of X. The **marginal benefit** from X is the increase in benefit from one more unit of a good, or the additional willingness to pay. Observe that the marginal benefit in Figure 5.10 diminishes as more is consumed. This implies that as a person consumes more and more of a good, the marginal benefit from additional amounts is likely to diminish.

You intuitively can understand this better if you suppose that X is pizza. Imagine that you are hungry and have no food at home, and you have a craving for pizza. At this point, you might be willing to pay $5 for a big, hot slice of pizza. Now suppose that after you have eaten that slice of pizza, you're still a little hungry. You might be willing to pay $3 for an additional slice. Now your willingness to pay for a third slice of pizza is going to be even less because you are no longer as hungry and your craving has, for the most part, been satisfied. So the more slices of pizza you eat, the less you are willing to pay for another slice of pizza.

marginal benefit

The increase in the benefit from, or the willingness to pay for, one more unit of a good.

Graphical Derivation of the Individual Demand Curve

A demand curve can be derived from the information about willingness to pay (benefit) and marginal benefit of X for the person described in Figure 5.10. Suppose that X is chocolate-covered raisins (pizza, ice cream, orange juice, DVDs, movie tickets, or any other good will serve just as well as an example). Suppose that the person has $10 to spend on chocolate-covered raisins and other goods. We want to ask how many pounds of chocolate-covered raisins the person would buy at different prices. We imagine different hypothetical prices for chocolate-covered raisins, from astronomical levels like $7 a pound to bargain basement levels like $0.50 a pound.

To proceed graphically, we first plot the marginal benefit from Figure 5.10 in Figure 5.11. Focus first on the black dots in Figure 5.11; the associated lines will be explained in the next few paragraphs. The horizontal axis in Figure 5.11 measures the quantity of chocolate-covered raisins. On the vertical axis, we want to indicate the price as well as the marginal benefit, so we measure the scale of the vertical axis in dollars. The black dots in Figure 5.11 represent the marginal benefit that an individual gets from consuming different amounts of chocolate-covered raisins.

FIGURE 5.11 Derivation of the Individual Demand Curve

The dots are exactly the same as the marginal benefit in Figure 5.10. At each dot, price equals marginal benefit. The vertical lines indicate how much is demanded at each price if the consumer is restricted to purchasing whole pounds.

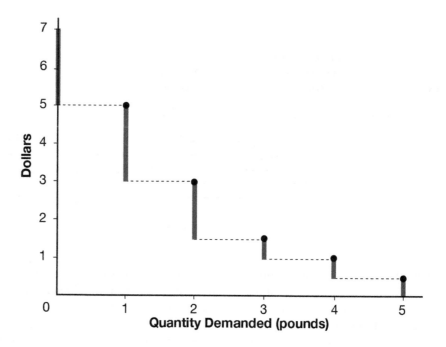

How many pounds of chocolate-covered raisins would this person consume at different prices? First, suppose that the price is very high—$7 a pound. We are going to derive a demand curve for this individual by gradually lowering the price from this high value and asking the same question: How many pounds would the person buy at this price? To make things simple at the start, assume that the person buys only whole pounds of chocolate-covered raisins. You might want to imagine that the chocolate-covered raisins come in 1-pound cellophane packages. We consider fractions of pounds later.

Suppose, then, that the price is $7 a pound. The marginal benefit from 1 pound of chocolate-covered raisins is $5. Thus, the price is greater than the marginal benefit. Would the person buy a pound of chocolate-covered raisins at this price? Because the price the person would have to pay is greater than the marginal benefit, *the answer would be no*; the person would not buy a pound of raisins at a price of $7. We have shown, therefore, that the quantity demanded of raisins is *zero* when the price is $7.

Now start to lower the price. As long as the price is more than $5, the person will not buy any chocolate-covered raisins because the most he is willing to pay for that first pound of chocolate-covered raisins is $5. Hence, the quantity demanded at all prices higher than $5 is 0 pounds. We indicate this by the line on the vertical axis above the $5 mark.

When the price drops to $5, the marginal benefit from a pound of chocolate-covered raisins is $5 and the price is $5, so the marginal benefit of the pound of chocolate-covered raisins is sufficient to cover the price. Because the person is willing to pay the $5 to buy 1 pound of chocolate-covered raisins, the person buys 1 pound rather than 0 pounds when the price is $5. Figure 5.11 shows that the quantity demanded is given by the black dot at 1 pound when the price equals $5.

Continue lowering the price from $5. Consider, for example, a price of $4. The person has already decided that 1 pound will be bought; the question is whether a second pound of chocolate-covered raisins is worthwhile. Another pound has a marginal benefit of $3 (willingness to pay goes from $5 to $8 as the quantity increases from 1 to 2 pounds). The person has to pay $4, which is more than the marginal benefit. Hence, *the quantity demanded stays at 1 pound when the price is $4.* In fact, the quantity demanded will stay at 1 pound as long as the price remains above the marginal benefit of buying another pound of chocolate-covered raisins, which is $3. When the price falls to $3, however, another pound is purchased. That is, when the price is $3, the quantity demanded is 2 pounds, which is shown graphically by the black dot at 2 pounds.

Now suppose the price falls below $3, perhaps to $2. Is a third pound purchased? The marginal benefit of a third pound is $1.50; is it worth it to buy a third pound at $2 per pound? No. The quantity demanded stays at 2 pounds when the price is between $3 and $1.50, which we denote by extending the line downward from the black dot at 2 pounds. This story can be continued. As the price continues to fall, more pounds of chocolate-covered raisins are demanded.

By considering various prices from more than $5 to less than $0.50, we have traced out an **individual demand curve** that slopes downward. As the price is lowered, more chocolate-covered raisins are purchased. The demand curve is downward sloping because of diminishing marginal benefit. At each black dot in the diagram, price equals the marginal benefit.

The jagged shape of the demand curve in Figure 5.11 may look strange. It is due to the assumption that the consumer can consider only 1-pound packages of chocolate-covered raisins. If it is possible to buy fractions of a pound, and if the marginal benefits of the fractions are between the values for the whole pounds, then the demand curve will be a smooth line, as shown in Figure 5.12. The price then will equal marginal benefit not only at the black dots but also on the lines connecting the dots. If you are unsure of this, imagine creating a new Figure 5.10 and Figure 5.11 with *ounces* of raisins. Each ounce will be represented with a point, and with 16 ounces per pound, there will be so many points that the curve will be as smooth as Figure 5.12.

individual demand curve

A curve showing the relationship between quantity demanded of a good by an individual and the price of the good.

FIGURE 5.12 A Smooth Individual Demand Curve
If the consumer can buy fractions of a pound and if the marginal benefits of these fractions are between the whole pound amounts, the demand curve becomes a smooth line, as in the figure, rather than the series of steps in Figure 5.11. In some cases, such as the demand for cars, we cannot consider fractions, and so these individual demand curves will look like steps.

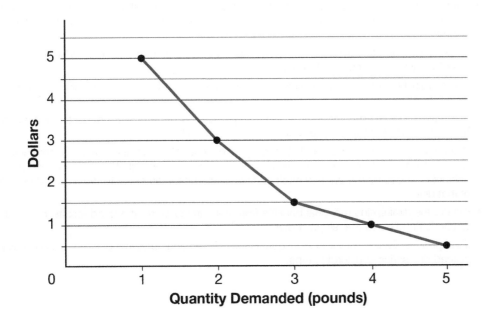

The Price Equals Marginal Benefit Rule

We have discovered an important principle of consumer behavior. If the consumer can adjust consumption of a good in small increments—such as fractions of a pound—then the consumer will buy an amount for which the *price equals marginal benefit*. The price equals marginal benefit rule can explain a number of otherwise puzzling observations. For example, consider Adam Smith's diamond-water paradox. As Smith put it,

> *Nothing is more useful than water: but it will purchase scarce any thing; scarce any thing can be had in exchange for it. A diamond, on the contrary, has scarce any value in use; but a very great quantity of other goods may frequently be had in exchange for it.*[1]

Why then are diamonds expensive and water cheap even though diamonds are less "useful" to the world's population than water?

The price equals marginal benefit rule helps explain the paradox. The price of diamonds will be high if the marginal benefit of diamonds is high. The price of water will be low if the marginal benefit of water is low. As we saw earlier, the marginal benefit of something declines the more people consume of it. Thus, water has relatively low marginal benefit because with water being so plentiful, people consume a lot of it every day. The marginal benefit is low even though the total benefit from water consumption in the world is very high. On the other hand, diamonds have a high marginal benefit because, with diamonds being so scarce, people consume relatively little of them. The marginal benefit of diamonds is high even though the total benefit of diamonds may be low. Thus, the price equals marginal benefit rule explains the diamond-water paradox.

Review

- People's preferences are reflected in their willingness to pay for different amounts of a good. Because dollars can be used to buy any good, willingness to pay compares one good with all other goods.
- The marginal benefit from a good is the increase in the benefit from, or the additional willingness to pay for, one more unit of a good.
- The marginal benefit that an individual derives from a good typically will decline as the individual increases consumption of that good.
- An individual demand curve can be traced by changing the price of a good and looking at how many units consumers are willing to buy at each price.
- When the price of a good exceeds the marginal benefit of the first unit of a good, consumers will not demand any of that good. As the price falls, consumers will demand more and more units of the good as the price of each additional unit becomes equal to the marginal benefit of that unit.
- Hence, the diminishing marginal benefits from consuming more of a good results in an individual demand curve that slopes down.
- If the good is divisible into fractional quantities, the demand curve will become a smooth line instead of a series of discrete steps.

5.4 The Market Demand Curve

Thus far, we have graphically derived the demand curve for an individual. Now we consider the **market demand curve**, which is the sum of the individual demand curves. Figure 5.13 shows how we do the summing up. The figure shows the demand curves for chocolate-covered raisins for two individuals, Jim and Pam. To get the market demand curve, add up, for each given price, the total amount demanded by both Jim and Pam. For example, at a price of $5, Jim's demand is 1 pound and Pam's demand is 1 pound. The market demand is then 2 pounds. When the price is $3 a pound, the demand is 2 pounds for Jim and 2 pounds for Pam, or 4 pounds for the market as a whole. Obviously, the market for chocolate-covered raisins consists of more than just Jim and Pam. To get the whole market, you would have to sum up the demands for millions of people.

market demand curve

The horizontal summation of all the individual demand curves for a good; also simply called the demand curve.

FIGURE 5.13 Derivation of the Market Demand Curve
The market demand curve is the sum of the demand curves of many individuals. The figure shows this for only two individuals with the same preferences. As more individuals with a diversity of tastes are added, the market demand curve becomes smoother and looks more like Figure 5.2.

Different Types of Individuals

In Figure 5.13, Jim's and Pam's demand curves are the same. They do not have to be. In fact, it is most likely that Jim and Pam have different preferences. Jim could be a health food fan and be willing to pay less for chocolate-covered raisins than Pam would. It is incorrect to assume that everyone will be willing to pay the same amount for any good. All kinds of people in the world have different preferences. But you still can add up the demands of all these people at any given price to get the market demand curve. As you add up many individual demand curves for different types of people, the market demand curve gets smoother, even when the product cannot be bought in fractions of a unit. For example, the market demand curve for cars is smooth even though most individuals buy either zero, one, or perhaps two cars. When you add the demand curves for millions of people, the market demand curve for cars looks like the market demand curve (see Figure 5.2) that we typically draw—smooth and downward sloping. To confirm your understanding of the market demand curve, make sure you work through the problems at the end of the chapter.

Changes of Consumer Behavior in the COVID-19 Pandemic

Watch from minute 6:01 to 9:41 of this video for a discussion of how to model and stimulate consumer spending during the coronavirus outbreak.

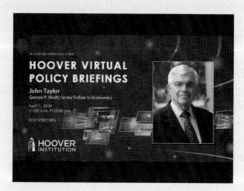

View the video online at: http://www.youtube.com/embed/zM3Rsp3FDnI?rel=0

Review

- The market demand curve is derived from individual demand curves. At each price, we add up how much is demanded by all individuals; the total is the market demand at that price.
- Even if the individual demand curves are not smooth, the market demand curve will be smooth because people have different tastes and preferences and prefer different benefits.

5.5 Consumer Surplus

consumer surplus

The difference between what a person is willing to pay for an additional unit of a good—the marginal benefit—and the market price of the good; for the market as a whole, it is the sum of all the individual consumer surpluses, or the area below the market demand curve and above the market price.

In many cases, people are willing to pay more for an item consumed than they have to pay for it. For example, you might be willing to pay $45 to see your favorite movie star appear in a new blockbuster movie. But like everyone else in line at the movie theater, you pay only $15, even though it is worth $45 to you. In general, **consumer surplus** is the difference between the willingness to pay for an additional item (say, $45 to see the movie)—its marginal benefit—and the price paid for it ($15 to buy a ticket that lets you see the movie). Consumer surplus is $30. The college professor who was willing to pay $60,000 for a $500 hearing aid that enabled him to lecture to a large audience of students would derive a consumer surplus of $59,500 from the hearing aid. If the hearing aid cost $5,000 instead, he still would derive $55,000 in consumer surplus.

A graphic derivation of how to find consumer surplus is shown in Figure 5.14, which shows the individual demand curve for chocolate-covered raisins that we derived in Figure 5.11. At a price of $2, the consumer will demand 2 pounds of chocolate-covered raisins. The first pound produced a marginal benefit of $5 and cost $2 to buy, thus the consumer surplus associated with the first pound would be $3. The second pound has a marginal benefit of $3 and cost $2 to buy, so the consumer surplus associated with the second pound would be $1. Overall consumer surplus is $3 + $1 = $4. Consumer surplus therefore can be defined as the sum of the differences between the marginal benefit of each unit and the price paid for the item. Graphically, consumer surplus is the area between the demand curve and the line indicating the price. In Figure 5.14, the total shaded area is equal to 4, consisting of two rectangular blocks, one with an area of 3 and the other with an area of 1. The area is the extra amount that the consumer is getting because the market price is lower than what the consumer is willing to pay.

FIGURE 5.14 Consumer Surplus for an Individual
The consumer surplus is the difference between the marginal benefit that a person gets from consuming a good and the price. It is given by the area between the demand curve and the price.

Consumer surplus for the entire market is the sum of the consumer surpluses of all individuals who have purchased goods in the market. In Figure 5.15, consumer surplus is the area between the market demand curve and the market price line.

Consumer surplus has many uses in economics. It is a measure of how well off consumers are (because it measures how much they were willing to pay above and beyond the price to acquire the good), and thus it is an important component used to gauge how well the market system works. Consumer surplus also can be used to measure the gains to consumers from an innovation. For example, if a new production technique or a policy change lowers the price of a good and increases the quantity demanded, consumer surplus for the market will increase. Those who had a high willingness to pay now will derive even more consumer surplus as a result of the lower price, and those who had a marginal benefit that was less than the old price now will demand more of the good as well. In short, when the market price of a good falls, the area between the demand curve and the market price line increases. This increase is a measure of how much the new technique or the policy change is worth to society.

FIGURE 5.15 Consumer Surplus for the Market

The sum of the consumer surplus for all individuals in the market is the area between the demand curve and the price.

Consumer Surplus

Consumer surplus is the gain to consumers from trade.

View the video online at: http://www.youtube.com/embed/oL20S7c0ZJE?rel=0

Review

- Consumer surplus is the area between the individual demand curve and the market price line. It is a measure of how much the consumer gains from buying goods in the market.
- The consumer surplus for the market is the sum of the individual consumer surpluses. It can be calculated as the area between the market demand curve and the market price line. It is

a measure of how much all the consumers in the economy gain from buying goods in the market.

- Consumer surplus is an important tool for measuring the performance of an economic system. Changes in consumer surplus can be used to measure the beneficial impact of a technology change or a policy change that changes the market price of a good.

5.6 End-of-Chapter Materials

Conclusion

This chapter is the first of three that looks at the individual behavior that underlies the economist's demand and supply curves. This chapter focused on consumers, Chapter 6 looks at firms, and Chapter 7 looks at the interaction of consumers and firms in markets. The payoffs in terms of understanding how and how well markets work will not be fully realized until we have completed all three chapters, but we already have derived a number of useful results.

We showed that the idea that people make purposeful choices with limited resources can be made operational with utility. In a two-good setting, we showed that utility maximization can be used to derive an individual demand curve that is downward sloping, and that individual demand curves can be aggregated to obtain a market demand curve.

In a more general setting, we showed how to derive an individual demand curve from the idea that consumers would buy an additional unit of a good only when the marginal benefit was not less than the price of the good. Because marginal benefit declines as you buy more units of a good, a lower price leads to a higher quantity demanded. Aggregating the individual demand curves would generate a market demand curve.

Finally, we derived the concept of consumer surplus for an individual, the difference between the individual's marginal benefit and the market price. Adding up individual consumer surplus generates the consumer surplus for the entire market, an important measure of how much gain people receive from the market.

Key Points

1. The idea of utility maximization subject to a budget constraint implements the assumption that people make purposeful choices with limited resources.

2. Utility indicates the preferences people have for one activity compared with other activities. The units used to measure utility do not matter, and the utility level of one person cannot be compared with the utility level of another person.

3. Economists assume—at least as an approximation—that people maximize their utility subject to a budget constraint that limits how much they can spend. This implies that they choose the feasible combination of goods that delivers the most utility.

4. An individual's demand curve can be derived from utility maximization subject to a budget constraint. Utility maximization implies that a higher price reduces the quantity demanded.

5. A higher price can reduce the quantity demanded in two ways: by reducing the purchasing power of an individual's income (income effect), and by making the relative price of that good more expensive (the substitution effect).

6. In general, the demand curve for an individual can be derived by applying the principle that the individual will demand to buy the number of units for which marginal benefit is equal to price.

7. Market demand curves are derived by adding up the quantity demanded by all individuals at each price.

8. An individual's consumer surplus is the sum of the differences between the marginal benefit the individual receives from each unit and the market price of that unit.

9. An individual's consumer surplus can be calculated as the area between the individual's demand curve and the market price line. Consumer surplus for an individual is a measure of how much benefit an individual gains from buying a product.

10. Overall consumer surplus is the sum of consumer surplus across individuals. It can be calculated as the area between the market demand curve and the market price line. Consumer surplus for a market is a measure of how much all consumers in that market gain from buying a product.

Questions for Review

1. What is the relationship between utility and preferences?
2. Why don't the units by which utility is measured matter?
3. Why are economists typically interested in utility maximization subject to constraints?
4. Why does an increase in the price of a good typically reduce the quantity demanded by a utility maximizing consumer?
5. Why does a reduction in income typically lead to a reduction in the quantity demanded at each price?
6. Why are market demand curves usually smoother than individual demand curves?
7. What is the relationship between willingness to pay and marginal benefit?
8. Why does marginal benefit decrease as the number of units consumed of a good increases?
9. What does an individual's "consumer surplus" measure? How can you find what the individual's consumer surplus is from the demand curve?
10. What is the relationship between individual consumer surplus and consumer surplus for the market? How can you find what the consumer surplus for the market is from the demand curve?

Problems

1. Using the example of utility in Figure 5.3, find the quantity of each good the consumer will purchase in the cases shown in the table below.

Case	Budget ($)	Price of Grapes ($)	Price of Bananas ($)
A	7	1	1
B	6	2	1
C	8	1	2

2. Analyze the following data for Mara's utility from consumption of books and coffee.

Quantity of Books	4	50	75	81	83	84
	3	46	70	76	78	79

2	40	60	66	68	69
1	30	40	46	48	49
0	0	10	16	18	19
	0	**1**	**2**	**3**	**4**

Quantity of Coffee

a. Determine how much of each good Mara will consume if she has $20 and if the price of books is $10 and the price of coffee is $3.

b. Suppose the price of coffee goes up to $5. How much coffee will Mara consume now? Why does the amount change?

c. Multiply the utility received from books and coffee by 10. Will your answers to parts (a) and (b) change? Explain.

3. Which of the following statements are true? The income effect of a reduction in the price of gasoline refers to

   a. the reduction of income incurred by gas stations.

   b. the increase in the demand for other products as gasoline buyers experience increased real incomes.

   c. the increase in the quantity demanded of gasoline as gasoline buyers experience increased real incomes.

   d. the increase in the quantity demanded of gasoline as gasoline buyers experience increased nominal incomes.

4. Which of the following statements are true? The substitution effect of a decrease in the price of beef, with no changes in the prices of other goods, refers to

   a. the decrease in the quantity demanded of beef and the increase in the quantity demanded of substitutes such as chicken.

   b. the increase in the quantity demanded of beef and the decrease in the quantity demanded of substitutes such as chicken.

   c. the increase in the quantity demanded of beef and the increase in the quantity demanded of substitutes such as chicken.

   d. the decrease in the quantity demanded of beef and the decrease in the quantity demand for substitutes such as chicken.

5. Consider the example of willingness to pay for X (chocolate-covered raisins) in Figure 5.10. Assume that the price is $0.75 and that the person has $10 to spend.

   a. Compute what it costs to pay for different amounts of chocolate-covered raisins from 0 to 5 pounds.

   b. For each of the above amounts, calculate how much is left over from the $10 the person started out with.

   c. Using the information from Figure 5.10 and your answers above, calculate the sum of the benefit plus the dollars left over for different amounts of chocolate-covered raisins from 0 to 5 pounds.

   d. How many pounds of raisins will maximize the sum of the benefit plus the dollars left over? How does the answer compare with that using the price equals marginal benefit condition?

6. Individuals receive diminishing marginal benefits from consuming more of a particular good. Do you think this means that individuals receive diminishing marginal benefits from each extra dollar that they earn? Explain your answer.

7. The following table shows Carl's willingness to pay for clothing.

Quantity of Clothing	Willingness to Pay ($)
1	35
2	60
3	80
4	97
5	112
6	126

a. Calculate Carl's marginal benefit from clothing.

b. Draw Carl's individual demand curve for clothing.

c. Suppose the price of one item of clothing is $17. How much would Carl consume, and what is his consumer surplus? Show your answer graphically as well as numerically.

8. Suppose that the willingness to pay for hearing aids by the economics professor mentioned in the introduction to this chapter was $60,000 for one pair, $60,400 for two pairs, $60,600 for three pairs, and $60,700 for four pairs.

a. Draw the professor's demand curve for hearing aids.

b. If the price of a pair of hearing aids is $500, how many pairs would the professor buy?

c. Now suppose that a technological breakthrough reduces the price of hearing aids to $150 a pair. How many pairs would the professor buy now?

9. The following table shows Margaret's and Dennis's willingness to pay for cookies.

Quantity of Cookies	Margaret	Dennis
1	$7	$15
2	$13	$25
3	$18	$34
4	$21	$42
5	$23	$45

a. Calculate the marginal benefits for both people.

b. Derive Margaret's and Dennis's individual demand curves for cookies. Derive the market demand curve if only Margaret and Dennis are in the market.

c. Suppose that the price of cookies is $4.50. How many cookies will Margaret and Dennis buy? Calculate their consumer surplus. Draw a diagram to show the area representing consumer surplus.

d. Use a diagram to show the consumer surplus for the whole market using the market demand curve.

10. Economics professors like to ask their students about the diamond-water paradox: Why is it that a good that is as essential to human existence as water costs so much less than a good like a diamond that is far less useful? Show that if we use consumer surplus, rather than price, as our measure of how "valuable" a good is to human existence, then no paradox exists—water is valued much more highly than diamonds.

5.7 Appendix: Consumer Theory with Indifference Curves

Chapter 5 derives the demand curve from the assumption that consumers maximize utility subject to a budget constraint. Here we give a graphic illustration of that derivation.

Consider a single consumer deciding how much of two items to buy. Let one of the items be X and the other be Y. We first show that the consumer's budget constraint can be represented by a budget line, and then we show that the consumer's preferences can be represented by indifference curves.

The Budget Line

Suppose that the consumer has $20 to spend on X and Y, and suppose that the price of X is $2 per unit and the price of Y is $4 per unit. How much of X and Y can the consumer buy? If the consumer spends all $20 on Y, then 5 units of Y and no units of X are consumed. If the consumer buys 4 units of Y at $4 per unit, then $16 will be spent on Y and the remaining $4 can be spent buying 2 units of X. These and several other amounts of X and Y that can be bought with $20 are shown in the following table.

Units of Y	Units of X	Expenditures
5	0	$(5 \times \$4) + (0 \times \$2) = \$20$
4	2	$(4 \times \$4) + (2 \times \$2) = \$20$
3	4	$(3 \times \$4) + (4 \times \$2) = \$20$
2	6	$(2 \times \$4) + (6 \times \$2) = \$20$
1	8	$(1 \times \$4) + (8 \times \$2) = \$20$
0	10	$(0 \times \$4) + (10 \times \$2) = \$20$

These combinations represent the maximum amounts that can be purchased with $20. Note that the amounts are inversely related; as more is spent on X, less must be spent on Y. This inverse relationship is shown graphically in Figure 5.16. We put units of Y on the vertical axis and units of X on the horizontal axis, and then plot the pairs of points from the table. The points are then connected. The points trace a downward-sloping line starting at the upper left at $X = 0$ and $Y = 5$ and ending on the right with $X = 10$ and $Y = 0$. All the other combinations of X and Y in the table, such as $X = 4$ and $Y = 3$, are shown on the line. If it is possible to consume fractions of X and Y, then all the points on the line between the plotted points also can be purchased with the $20. (For example, 2.5 units of Y and 5 units of X would cost $20: $2.5 \times \$4 + 5 \times \$2 = \$20$.) Because all these pairs of X and Y on this line can be purchased with a $20 budget, we call it the **budget line**. The consumer is constrained to buy combinations of X and Y that are either on or below the budget line. Amounts of X and Y consumed below the budget line cost less than $20. Points above the line require more than $20 and are not feasible.

budget line

A line showing the maximum combinations of two goods that it is possible for a consumer to buy, given a budget constraint and the market prices of the two goods.

FIGURE 5.16 Budget Line for a Consumer
The line shows how much a consumer with $20 can consume of quantity X at a price of $2 per unit and quantity Y at $4 per unit. If $20 is spent on Y and nothing on X, then 5 units of Y can be purchased, as shown on the vertical axis. If $20 is spent on X and nothing on Y, then 10 units of X can be purchased. Other combinations are shown on the line.

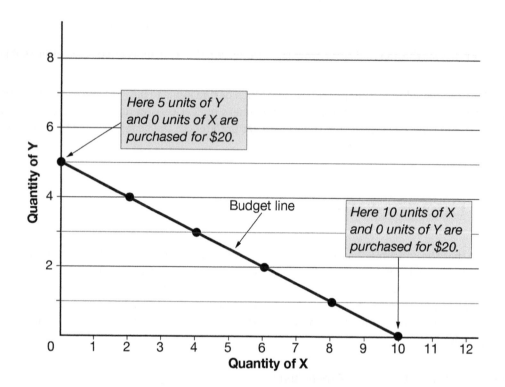

The budget line will shift out if the consumer has more to spend, as shown in Figure 5.17. For example, if the consumer has $24 rather than $20, then the budget line will shift up by 1 unit because the extra $4 permits the consumer to buy 1 more unit of Y. Alternatively, we could say that the budget line shifts to the right by 2 units in this case because the consumer can buy 2 more units of X with $4 more.

FIGURE 5.17 Effect of a Change in Income on the Budget Line
If the consumer has more to spend, then the budget line is farther out. If the consumer has less to spend, then the budget line is closer in. Here a higher and a lower budget line are compared with the $20 budget line in Figure 5.16.

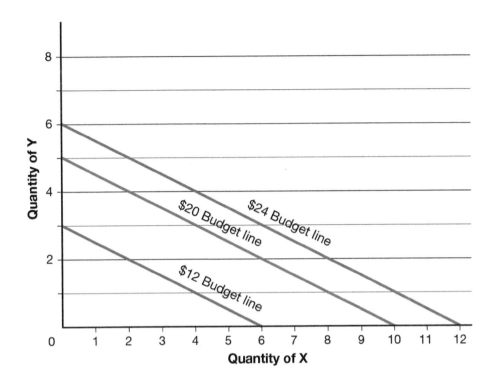

The steepness of the budget line depends on the prices of X and Y. In particular, the slope of the budget line is equal to –1 times the ratio of the price of X to the price of Y. That is, slope $= -\dfrac{P_x}{P_y}$, which is –1/2 in this example. Why is the slope determined by the price ratio? Recall that the slope is the change in Y divided by the change in X. Along the budget line, as X is increased by 1 unit, Y must fall by 1/2 unit: Buying 1 more unit of X costs $2 and requires buying 1/2 unit less of Y. Thus, the slope is –1/2.

To derive the demand curve for X, we need to find out what happens when the price of X changes. What happens to the budget line when the price of X increases from $2 to $4, for example? The budget line twists down, as shown in Figure 5.18. The intuitive rationale for the twist is that the slope steepens to $-\dfrac{P_x}{P_y} = -\dfrac{4}{4} = -1$, and the position of X = 0 and Y = 5 on the vertical axis does not change, because 5 units of Y can still be purchased. You can show this by creating a new table with pairs of X and Y that can be purchased with $20 at the new price and then plotting the points.

FIGURE 5.18 Effect of a Higher Price of *X* on the Budget Line

The budget line pivots if the price of *X* changes. Here the price of *X* rises from $2 to $4 and the budget line twists down.

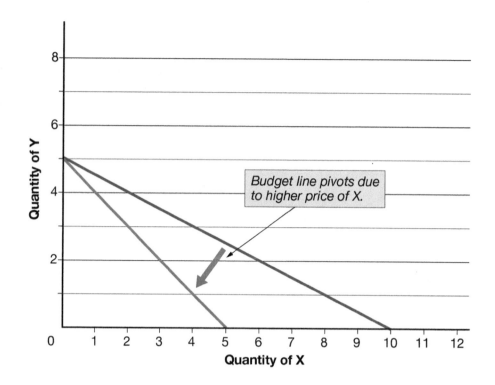

To summarize, we have shown how a budget line represents the budget constraint for the consumer; now we show how to represent the consumer's preferences.

The Indifference Curve

Utility is an indicator of how a consumer prefers one combination of items in comparison with another. If the level of utility is the same for two combinations of X and Y, then the consumer is *indifferent* between the two combinations. Suppose that the utility is the same for the combinations of X and Y that appear below.

Units of *Y*	Units of *X*
6	1
4	2
2	6
1	12

The consumer is indifferent among these combinations. Observe that these amounts are inversely related. As consumption of Y declines, the consumer must be compensated with more X if the level of utility is not to decline.

We can plot these different amounts on the same type of graph we used for the budget line, as shown in Figure 5.19. The consumer is indifferent among all four points. We have connected the points with a curve to represent other combinations of X and Y about which the consumer is indifferent. The curve is called an **indifference curve** because the consumer is indifferent among all points on the curve. The indifference curve slopes downward from left to right.

FIGURE 5.19 An Indifference Curve for a Consumer
The consumer is indifferent between A and B or any other point on an indifference curve. For example, the consumer is indifferent between consuming 4 units of Y and 2 of X or 2 units of Y and 6 of X.

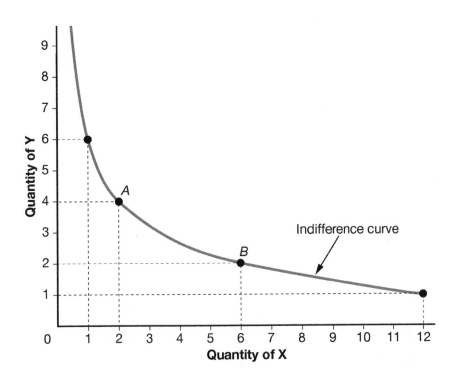

The slope of the indifference curve can be found from the marginal utilities of X and Y. Marginal utility is *the increase in utility from consuming an additional unit of a good*. For example, look back at Figure 5.3 and consider the marginal utility of increasing consumption of grapes by 1 additional pound, from 3 pounds to 4 pounds. You will see that utility increases by 2. Thus, the marginal utility of grapes is 2 at the amount of consumption. Let MU_X be the marginal utility of X, and let MU_Y be the marginal utility of Y.

The slope of the indifference curve is equal to the ratio of the marginal utility of X to the marginal utility of Y; that is, slope = $(-MU_X/MU_Y)$. The reason is that utility is the same for all points on an indifference curve. In other words, the decline in utility as X falls $(-MU_X \times \Delta X)$ must equal the increase in utility as Y rises $(MU_Y \times \Delta Y)$. Thus,

$$MU_X \times \Delta X = MU_Y \times \Delta Y,$$

or,

$$-\frac{MU_X}{MU_Y} = \frac{\Delta Y}{\Delta X},$$

which is the slope of the indifference curve.

marginal rate of substitution

The amount of one good for which the consumer is willing to trade one unit of another good and still have the same utility.

The ratio of marginal utilities MU_X/MU_Y is called the **marginal rate of substitution**; it gives the number of units of one good (Y) for which the consumer is willing to trade 1 unit of the other good (X) and have the same amount of utility—or be indifferent. For example, if the marginal rate of substitution is 4, then the consumer is willing to trade 4 units of Y for 1 unit of X with utility remaining the same.

Note that the indifference curve is bowed in toward the origin. That is, the indifference curve is steep when a small amount of X is consumed and flat when a large amount of X is consumed. This curvature is due to the declining marginal rate of substitution. When the consumer is consuming only a little bit of X, a large amount of Y is required as compensation for a reduction in X. As X increases, less of Y is required as compensation.

We can represent higher levels of utility or more preferred combinations of X and Y by higher indifference curves, as shown in Figure 5.20. Any point on a higher indifference curve is preferred to any point on a lower indifference curve.

FIGURE 5.20 Higher and Lower Indifference Curves
Amounts of X and Y on indifference curves that are higher are preferred to amounts on indifference curves that are lower. Of the three combinations C, D, and E, the combination at D is the least preferred and the combination at C is the most preferred.

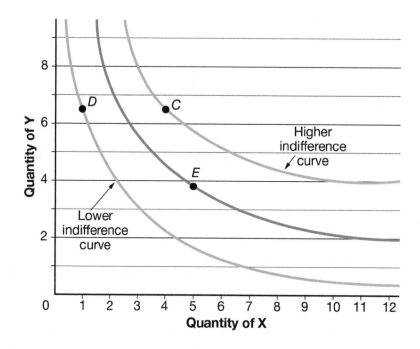

Getting to the Highest Indifference Curve Given the Budget Line

tangency point

The only point in common for two curves; the point at which the two curves just touch.

Now we can combine the budget line and the indifference curves on the same diagram to illustrate the model of consumer behavior. Utility maximization subject to the budget constraint means getting to the highest possible indifference curve without going above the budget line. The process is shown in Figure 5.21. The budget line from Figure 5.16 and the indifference curves from Figure 5.20 are shown in the diagram. The consumer cannot go beyond the budget line, and any point inside the budget line is inferior to points on the budget line. Thus, the combination of X and Y with the highest utility must be on the budget line. The highest indifference curve with points on the budget line is the one that just touches—is tangent to—the budget line. This occurs at point T in

Figure 5.21. The **tangency point** is the highest level of utility the consumer can achieve subject to the budget constraint. It is the combination of X and Y that the consumer chooses. Figure 5.21 shows that, in this example, the consumer buys 2 1/4 units of Y and 5 1/2 units of X.

FIGURE 5.21 The Best Choice for the Consumer
When the budget line is tangent to the indifference curve, the consumer cannot do any better. The point of tangency is at point T. Compare this with the other points. Point U is not the best point because it is inside the budget line. Point V is not the best point because other points on the budget line are preferred. Point W is preferred to point T, but it is not feasible.

The Utility-Maximizing Rule

Observe that, at the tangency point, the slope of the budget line is equal to the slope of the indifference curve. That is, $P_X/P_Y = MU_X/MU_Y$. In other words, the ratio of the price of two goods equals the ratio of the marginal utility of the two goods as long as the consumer is maximizing utility. This equality between the price ratio and the ratio of the marginal utilities, or the marginal rate of substitution, is called the *utility-maximizing rule*.

Effect of a Price Change on the Quantity Demanded

Now suppose that the price of X increases; then the budget line twists down, as shown in the lower panel of Figure 5.22. With the new budget line, the old consumer choice of 2 1/4 units of Y and 5 1/2 units of X is no longer feasible: Point S is outside the new budget line. The highest level of utility the consumer can now achieve is at point T in the lower panel of Figure 5.22. At point T, the quantity of X has declined. Thus, a higher price of X has reduced the quantity demanded of X.

In the top graph in Figure 5.22, we show the relationship between the price of X and the quantity demanded of X. The price of X is put on the vertical axis, and the quantity demanded of X is put on the horizontal axis. The lower quantity demanded at the higher price shows the negative slope of the demand curve.

FIGURE 5.22 An Increase in the Price of X

If the price of X rises, the budget line pivots down and the consumer's choice changes from point S to point T in the lower panel. The quantity of X consumed goes down. The price of X and the quantity of X are plotted in the top panel, showing the negative relationship between price and quantity demanded.

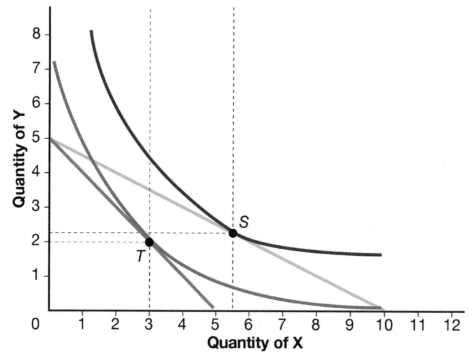

Effect of an Income Change on Demand

We also can examine what happens when the consumer's income changes but the price remains constant. This is illustrated in Figure 5.23, where income declines. The lower income leads to less consumption of both X and Y. In this case, both X and Y are normal goods because consumption goes down when income goes down. If the consumption of X increased as the budget curve shifted in, then X would be an inferior good.

FIGURE 5.23 A Decrease in Income
If the consumer's income falls, utility is maximized at a new point: The consumer moves from point M to point N. In this case, consumption of both X and Y declines. Neither good is an inferior good in this example.

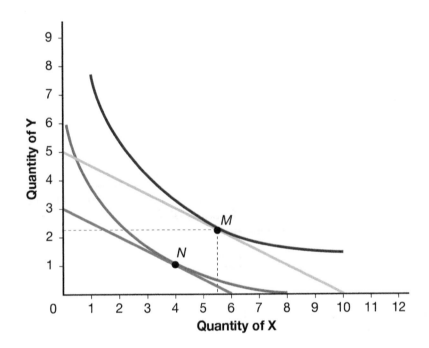

Graphic Illustration of the Income Effect and the Substitution Effect

The effect of a change in the price on the quantity demanded can be divided into an income effect and a substitution effect. These two effects can be represented graphically as shown in Figure 5.24.

As in Figure 5.22, the budget line twists down due to the higher price of X. But now we draw in another budget line—the dashed line in Figure 5.24. This budget line has the same slope as the new budget line, but it allows the consumer to stay on the same indifference curve as she originally was. The dashed line can be used to find the substitution effect without the income effect because it has the same slope as the new budget line—the move from the dashed line to the new budget line is purely an income change rather than a relative price change.

FIGURE 5.24 Illustration of Income Effect and Substitution Effect of Price Change
The dashed budget line has the same slope as the new budget line but allows the consumer to stay on the same indifference curve. This isolates the substitution effect. The rest of the decline is the income effect.

The decline of consumption from S to S' is the substitution effect. Intuitively, you can think of this as the point that the consumer would choose if she were to (hypothetically) receive a sum of money that would compensate her for the utility loss she suffered as a result of the price increase. The remaining decline from S' to T is the income effect. Because that hypothetical sum of money never transpires, this shift clearly reflects the purchasing power that the consumer suffered as a result of the price increase.

Key Points

1. The budget line represents the consumer's budget constraint in a diagram with the quantity consumed of each of two goods on the axes.

2. The budget line is downward sloping, with the slope equal to –1 times the ratio of the price of the good on the horizontal axis to the price of the good on the vertical axis.

3. A higher price of the good on the horizontal axis twists the budget line down.

4. An indifference curve shows the combinations of goods among which the consumer is indifferent.

5. Combinations of goods on higher indifference curves are preferred to combinations of goods on lower indifference curves.

6. The model of consumer behavior assumes that the consumer tries to get to the highest possible indifference curve without going beyond the budget line.

7. The consumer chooses the combination at the tangency of the budget line and the indifference curve.

8. A higher price of a good lowers the quantity demanded, according to the indifference curve and budget line diagram.

Questions for Review

1. Why does the budget line slope downward?
2. What determines the slope of the budget line?
3. Why does the indifference curve slope downward?
4. Why does the consumer choose a point at which the indifference curve is tangent to the budget line?

Problems

1. Darnell has $30 to spend on either muffins, which cost $3 each, or cartons of orange juice, which cost$1.50 each.

   a. Graph Darnell's budget line for muffins and orange juice.

   b. What is the maximum quantity of orange juice that Darnell can buy with $30?

   c. Suppose the price of orange juice increases to $2 per carton. Show the change in the budget line.

2. Suppose you are having a party in half an hour and you have two 6-packs of beer in your refrigerator. One is an imported premium beer, and the other is a standard domestic beer. A neighbor comes to you and asks you to trade some imported premium beer for the standard domestic beer, because he is also having a party. You agree to trade two premium bottles for three standard bottles. Twenty minutes later, the neighbor comes back and asks for two more premium bottles. Will you still trade on a two premium bottles for three standard bottles basis? Suppose you demand four standard bottles for two premium bottles. What property of indifference curves is illustrated by this example?

3. Suppose that the prices of two goods consumed by an individual are reduced by the same percentage. What change will happen to the budget line? What change will happen to the consumer's indifference curves? What will happen to the consumption of the two goods? Show each of the above graphically.

4. Sarah has $20 to spend on slices of pizza and cans of diet cola. Pizza costs $1 per slice, and diet cola costs $0.50 per can.

   a. Graph Sarah's budget line for pizza and diet cola.

   b. Suppose Sarah's total budget for pizza and diet cola increases to $25. How does her budget line shift?

   c. Draw a set of indifference curves for the situation in which pizza is a normal good, and one for the situation in which pizza is an inferior good.

Endnotes

1. Adam Smith, *Wealth of Nations* (New York: Modern Library Edition, 1994), 31–32.

CHAPTER 6
The Supply Curve and the Behavior of Firms

Thousands of budding entrepreneurs, innovators, and inventors dream of the day that millions of people will clamor to buy their creations. For Gojo Industries, a family-owned business in Ohio that has been around for about 75 years, the old adage "be careful what you wish for" has been particularly relevant in 2020. A profile of the company that appeared in *Forbes* in 2020 describes what the company, the manufacturer of Purell hand sanitizer, experienced during the COVID-19 pandemic.[1] Even prior to the crisis, Purell was the most widely used brand of hand sanitizer in the United States. Purell pump bottles and wall dispensers were a ubiquitous sight and people became accustomed to the ritual of squirting some sanitizer on to their hands as they left a doctor's office or entered a daycare facility. But as the virus began to spread and demand for Purell skyrocketed, it became increasingly difficult to find Purell as store shelves emptied out as soon as they were restocked and refills for wall-mounted dispensers were redirected from office buildings to health care providers.

As the Forbes story and other news stories highlighted in their profile, Gojo had to scramble to ramp up production to keep up with the increased demand. They had to hire more workers to run more shifts in existing factories and looked for new facilities in which they could manufacture enough hand sanitizer to meet the sharply increased demand. Purell, a product that had already brought in billions for the company, was now fueling even greater sales for the company because of a global pandemic.

In this chapter, we examine how a firm like Gojo Industries decides how much Purell to produce and how it responds to changing market conditions. The behavior of firms like Gojo can be described by supply curves like the one in Figure 6.2, which shows a typical supply curve, with price on the vertical axis and quantity supplied on the horizontal axis. The supply curve is for an entire market; it tells us how much all the firms in the market—not just a single firm like Gojo but also other established sanitizer manufacturers as well as new entrants into the sanitizer production business—would produce at each price. In this chapter, we look under the surface of the supply curve and examine how the profit-maximizing behavior of a firm determines how much of a good that firm will choose to produce at a given market price. Then we show how aggregating individual firms' supply curves generates a supply curve for the entire market for that good.

FIGURE 6.1 A Surge in Demand
Purell is the most widely used brand of hand sanitizer in the United States. Purell pump bottles and wall dispensers were a ubiquitous sight prior to the COVID-19 crisis. But as the virus began to spread and demand for Purell skyrocketed, the company had to sharply increase their productive capacity to keep up with the increased need from health care providers and consumers.

Source: Debbie Ann Powell/Shutterstock.com

FIGURE 6.2 A Typical Supply Curve for a Market

Supply curves typically slope upward. In this chapter, we look at the factors that motivate firms in the market to increase the quantity supplied as the price rises.

FIGURE 6.3 Applying the Central Idea of Economics

People make purposeful choices with scarce resources and interact with other people when they make these choices. In Chapter 5, the people were the consumers. In this chapter, they are the firms. In Chapter 7, the consumers and the firms interact with each other.

Basic Economic Principle	When Applied to the Behavior of Consumers	When Applied to the Behavior of Firms
People...	*Consumers...*	*Firms...*
make purposeful choices...	maximize utility...	maximize profits...
with scarce resources.	subject to a budget constraint relating expenditure to income.	subject to a production function relating output to input.

As with our study of the consumers who underlie the demand curve in Chapter 5, we have two important reasons to study the firms that underlie the supply curve. First, we want to show why the supply curve has the slope and position it does. Such information enables us to assess how a change in technology or societal trends or a new government policy affects the supply curve. Second, we want to show how and why a supply curve can be used to measure the "producer surplus" of firms. Producer surplus is a measure of how much a producer gains from participating in the market. In conjunction with consumer surplus, producer surplus is extremely useful for measuring how well a market economy actually works, and in explaining why a market economy works better than alternative systems to produce and allocate goods and resources.

6.1 Definition of a Firm

We start by looking at the behavior of a single firm. A **firm**, by definition, is an organization that produces goods or services. Just as no two consumers are exactly alike, no two firms are exactly alike. A firm can be a small family farm in the country or a grocery store in the city. Bakeries, restaurants, auto dealers, and bicycle shops are all examples of firms that are usually relatively small. Other firms—such as Coca-Cola—are very large, producing many different products in large volume.

The terms *firm*, *company*, and *business* are used interchangeably. A firm may include several *establishments*, which are separate physical locations, such as an office, a factory, or a store, where work is done. For example, the U.S.-based grocery chain Kroger is a firm with more than 2,500 supermarkets (most operating under the Kroger or Ralph's labels), almost 800 convenience stores (including Turkey Hill and Kwik Shop), and more than 400 jewelry stores (including Fred Meyer jewelers). Of course, not all firms are like Kroger; most small firms have only one establishment.

In the United States, about 80 percent of all firms are *sole proprietorships*, with one owner, or *partnerships*, with only a few owners, who usually manage the firm. Most of these are very small when compared with corporations like Kroger or Coca-Cola. A *corporation* is unlike a sole proprietorship or partnership in that the managers are usually somewhat removed from the owners. For example, most people who own shares of General Motors never even meet the managers of the firm. This separation of managers and owners means that the managers must be given an incentive to keep the owners' interests in mind. A common incentive is to have managers share in the profits of the firm.

You might expect that the decisions made by the managers of a firm would be more complicated—and consequently more difficult to understand—than the decisions made by consumers. Of course, many more people have had the experience of being a consumer than have had the experience of managing a firm. But if you can picture yourself as the owner or manager of your own firm, you will see that the economics of a firm's decision about how much to sell is analogous to the economics of a consumer's decision about how much to buy. The following example places you in that position.

firm

An organization that produces goods or services.

Your Own Firm: A Pumpkin Patch

Imagine that you are the owner and manager of a firm that grows pumpkins on a pumpkin patch; the patch has good soil and gets plenty of rain. Your firm is one of many specializing in growing and selling pumpkins—in other words, you must compete with many other firms. During the spring and summer you grow the pumpkins, and in the fall you sell them. As owner and manager of the firm, you must pay rent at the start of each growing season to the landlord who owns the pumpkin patch. During the season, you hire workers to tend the patch. The more workers you have tending the pumpkins, the more pumpkins you can grow on the patch.

Your firm is typical of many small firms and has features that apply to larger firms as well. Your firm is one with a single product (pumpkins) and two factors of production—land (the patch) and labor (the workers). One of the factors of production, land, cannot be changed during the season because the rent was paid in advance; this makes land a *fixed factor*. The other factor, labor, can be varied during the season, because you can choose to hire more or fewer workers; this makes labor a *variable factor*.

Your Firm as a Price-Taker in a Competitive Market

FIGURE 6.4
A Small Firm's Supply Curve
Imagine you own a small pumpkin farm. The supply curve for your firm describes how many pumpkins your firm will bring to market at various given prices.

Source: Andy Dean Photography/ Shutterstock.com

price-taker

Any firm that takes the market price as given; this firm cannot affect the market price because the market is competitive.

FIGURE 6.5
A Small Firm as a Price Taker
Many people buy pumpkins in the fall to use as Halloween decorations or to make delicious foods like pumpkin pie or pumpkin soup. As the owner of a small pumpkin firm, you are a price-taker because your pumpkins are like everyone else's pumpkins.

Source: Alita Xander/Shutterstock. com

competitive market

A market in which no firm has the power to affect the market price of a good.

The first task is to derive the supply curve for your pumpkin firm. *A supply curve for a single firm tells us the quantity of a good that that firm will produce at different prices.* To find the supply curve, we imagine that the firm looks at the price of the good it is selling and then decides how much to produce. For example, a baker considers the price of a loaf of bread prevailing in the market when deciding how many loaves of bread to produce. So in this case you must decide how much to produce and sell after looking at the price of pumpkins in the market. In a competitive market, any individual firm will be a **price-taker**; this means that the firm cannot influence the market price but instead has to decide how much to produce and sell at the given market price of the goods. In the case of your pumpkin firm, what this implies is that you cannot affect the price of pumpkins in the market through your decision to produce more or fewer pumpkins.

This description of a firm as a price-taker may seem odd to you. After all, if the firm does not set the price, then who does? Of course, in some sense, each firm does. If you go to a bakery for a loaf of bread, a price tag states the price of the loaf, so the baker is clearly determining the price. But this is not the way economists look at it; economists describe the market in a more subtle way. When many bakers are selling bread, in an important sense, the individual bakers do not have the ability to affect the price by much. If one baker charges $3 for a loaf of bread, and all the other bakers in the community charge $1.50 for the same loaf, no one will buy bread from the first baker. People will not even go to the store if they know the price is that high. They will go to other bakeries, where bread sells for $1.50 a loaf. Although in principle an individual firm has the ability to set any price it wants, in reality, a firm cannot charge a price far from the price that prevails in the market without soon losing all its customers.

A market in which a single firm cannot affect the market price is called a **competitive market**. Because many firms are producing pumpkins along with your pumpkin firm, the pumpkin market is competitive. A competitive market requires that there be at least several firms competing with one another. Exactly how many firms are required to make a market competitive is difficult to say without studying the market carefully—as we do in later chapters. If a market is competitive, so that firms are price takers, then we can derive a supply curve for the individual firm by asking, "How many pumpkins would the pumpkin firm produce if the price of pumpkins were $35 a crate? $70 a crate?" and so on.

Other Types of Markets

Not all markets are as competitive as the fresh bread market or the pumpkin market, and part of our job later in the book is to study these markets. The exact opposite of a competitive market is a market that has only one firm, in which case the firm is called a *monopoly*. Strictly speaking, the question "How much does the monopoly produce at a given price?" has no meaning because the monopoly is not a price-taker that has to take the price as given. Instead, it is a price-maker who can dictate the price. We consider monopolies in Chapter 10. For now we focus on the price-taking firms in a competitive market.

In deriving the demand curve in Chapter 5, we assumed that the individual consumer could not affect the price. This assumption seems natural, because we usually do not see buyers setting the price for bread or other commodities. As long as the market has at least several buyers and several sellers, we can assume that the price is taken as given by both buyers and sellers. In Chapter 7, when we study the interaction of buyers and sellers in markets, we will show how the market price is determined.

6.2 The Firm's Profits

Profits for any firm—a bakery producing bread or a farm producing pumpkins—are defined as the *total revenue* received from selling the product minus the *total costs* of producing the product. That is,

$$\text{profits} = \text{total revenue} - \text{total costs}$$

When profits are negative—total revenue is less than total costs—the firm runs a loss. When profits are zero—total revenue is equal to total costs—the firm is *breaking even*.

> **profits**
>
> Total revenue received from selling the product minus the total costs of producing the product.

We assume that the firm *maximizes profits*. That is, the firm decides on the quantity of production that will make profits as high as possible. To see how this is done, we must examine how profits depend on the quantity produced. To do this, we must consider how total revenue and total costs—the two determinants of profits—depend on the quantity produced. We consider first total revenue and then total costs.

Total Revenue

Total revenue is the total number of dollars the firm receives from people who buy its product. Total revenue can be computed by multiplying the price of each unit sold by the quantity sold. That is,

$$\begin{aligned} \text{total revenue} &= \text{price} \times \text{quantity} \\ &= P \times Q \end{aligned}$$

> **total revenue**
>
> The price per unit times the quantity the firm sells.

where we use the letter P to stand for price and Q to stand for quantity. Because we are looking at an individual firm and a particular product, P is the price of the particular product the individual firm is selling, and Q is the number of items the firm sells. We can measure the quantity sold in a variety of ways: number of pumpkins, crates of pumpkins, or pounds of pumpkins. Any of these measures will suffice for our analysis.

Table 6.1 uses crates of pumpkins as the measure of quantity. Note that total revenue depends both on the price of a crate of pumpkin and on the number of crates of pumpkins sold. Each row of the table shows the total revenue the firm receives from selling a specific amount of pumpkins: zero crates, one crate, and so on. Each column showing total revenue corresponds to a different price: $35 per crate, $70 per crate, and $100 per crate. For example, when the firm can get $70 per crate, it receives $280 for selling four crates.

From Table 6.1, you can see that the more items that are sold at a given price, the higher total revenue is. Thus, the firm can increase total revenue by producing and selling more goods. Total revenue therefore increases with the quantity produced for your pumpkin-producing firm.

TABLE 6.1 Total Revenue from Pumpkin Production at Three Prices

Quantity Produced (crates)	Total Revenue		
	Price = $35/crate	*Price = $70/crate*	*Price = $100/crate*
0	0	0	0
1	35	70	100
2	70	140	200
3	105	210	300
4	140	280	400
5	175	350	500

Production and Costs

total costs

The sum of all costs incurred in producing goods or services.

Now that we have seen how total revenue depends on the quantity produced, let's examine how total costs depend on the quantity produced. **Total costs** are what the firm has to incur to produce the product. For your pumpkin firm, total costs include the workers' salaries and the rent on the land. To see how total costs depend on the quantity produced, we must look at what happens to the quantity of labor and land used by the firm when the quantity produced increases or decreases.

The Time Period

Here, we are looking at the pumpkin firm's production decisions over a short period of time—such as one growing season—rather than over a long period of time—such as several growing seasons. Because we are focusing on the short run, we assume that only the labor input to production can be varied. Our analysis of the firm in this chapter is called a *short-run* analysis because the time is too short to change the other factors of production, such as land; only labor can be changed. We make this assumption simply because it is easier to examine the firm's decisions when only one factor of production can be changed. It is a simplifying assumption that we will modify. In Chapter 8 we take up the *long run*, in which other factors of production—such as the size of the pumpkin patch—can change as well as labor.

Reminder: *In Chapter 1, we saw that costs include opportunity costs. Thus, total costs for your pumpkin firm would include the opportunity cost of any time you spent operating the firm rather than doing something else, like studying for an exam. To emphasize that opportunity costs are included in total costs when computing profits, economists sometimes use the term "economic profits" rather than simply "profits".*

The Production Function

Figure 6.6 plots the relationship between pumpkin production and labor input for a given size of pumpkin patch. The number of hours of work is on the horizontal axis, and the quantity produced is on the vertical axis. Each point in Figure 6.6 shows the number of hours of work and the quantity of pumpkins produced: To produce three crates requires 10 hours of work; to produce five crates requires 30 hours of work. Clearly, more pumpkin production requires more labor input. The graph in Figure 6.6 is called the firm's **production function** because it tells us how much is produced for each amount of labor input, given a fixed amount of land input.

> **production function**
>
> A relationship that shows the quantity of output for any given amount of input.

FIGURE 6.6 A Production Function Relating Output to Labor Input
As more workers are employed, production increases. But the increase in production added by each additional hour of work declines as more workers are hired because the land the workers have to work with does not increase. Thus, there is a decreasing marginal product of labor, or diminishing returns to labor.

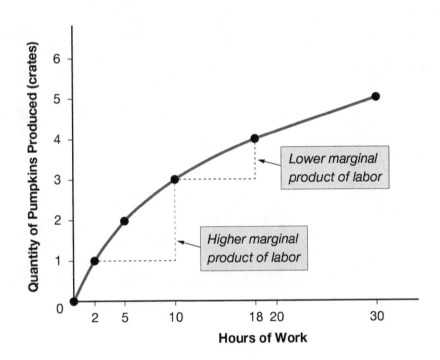

The **marginal product of labor** is defined as the increase in production that comes from an additional unit of labor. Figure 6.6 shows that, because of the curvature of the production function, the marginal product of labor *declines* as labor input increases. In other words, the same increase in hours of work leads to a smaller increase in production when labor input is large than when labor input is small. In Figure 6.6, when the hours of work increase from 2 to 10, the quantity of pumpkin crates produced increases by two crates, from one to three crates. However, an increase of labor input of the identical magnitude from 10 to 18 will increase the quantity of pumpkins by only one crate, from three to four crates.

> **marginal product of labor**
>
> The change in production due to a one-unit increase in labor input.

Another term for the phenomenon of declining marginal product of labor is **diminishing returns to labor**. In your pumpkin firm, diminishing returns to labor occur as additional workers are employed. For a given amount of land, hiring more workers initially is helpful in terms of increasing output, as the workers can water the pumpkins, pull out weeds, and harvest the pumpkins at the appropriate time. But as more and more workers are employed on a given amount of land, each worker has fewer tasks to do, and each additional worker adds less and less additional output. Diminishing returns is a general phenomenon that occurs when some inputs to production—such as land or machines—are fixed. Because the size of your pumpkin patch is fixed,

> **diminishing returns to labor**
>
> A situation in which the increase in output due to a unit increase in labor declines with increasing labor input; a decreasing marginal product of labor.

additional workers must eventually add less to production. Otherwise, a single plot of land could produce all the world's pumpkins by employing huge numbers of workers. Diminishing returns to labor occur in nonagricultural examples as well. Employing more and more workers in an automobile factory without increasing the size of the factory or adding more machines will increase the amount of cars produced by the factory by less and less.

FIGURE 6.7 Diminishing Returns to Labor

Adding the second worker to this machine in a French vineyard increased the quantity of grapes produced by much less than the first worker did. Adding a third worker to the machine would increase the quantity of grapes produced by even less than adding the second worker did. Thus, this is an example of a decreasing marginal product of labor, or diminishing returns to labor.

Source: robert paul van beets/Shutterstock.com

 Diminishing Returns to Labor

Each additional employee increases the firm's output by less than the previous employee did.

View the video online at: http://www.youtube.com/embed/lt6LpwBNSIM?rel=0

Costs

Table 6.2 shows how total costs depend on the quantity of pumpkins produced at your pumpkin firm. The first column shows the quantity of pumpkins produced. The second column shows the labor input required to produce that quantity of pumpkins, using the production function from Figure 6.6. The third column shows the costs of hiring the labor input at a rate of $10 per hour of work. These costs are called **variable costs** because they vary according to how much is produced; more workers are hired and more wages paid as more pumpkins are produced. We also assume that you have to pay $50 in advance for rent on the patch. The fourth column shows the cost of the land. The $50 payment for the land is considered to be a *fixed cost* because it must be paid no matter how many pumpkins are produced or even if you produce no pumpkins at all. By definition, **fixed costs** are the part of total costs that do not depend on how much is produced. Variable costs and fixed costs together constitute all the costs of producing the product. Hence, *the sum of fixed costs and variable costs equals total costs*, as shown in the last column of Table 6.2.

variable costs

Costs of production that vary with the quantity of production.

fixed costs

Costs of production that do not depend on the quantity of production.

TABLE 6.2 Example of Costs for a Single Firm

Quantity Produced (crates)	Hours of Labor Input	Variable Costs at $10 Wage ($)	Fixed Costs ($)	Total Costs ($)
0	0	0	50	50
1	2	20	50	70
2	5	50	50	100
3	10	100	50	150
4	18	180	50	230
5	30	300	50	350

Each row of Table 6.2 shows the costs of producing a particular quantity of pumpkins. The first row indicates that even if no pumpkins are produced, the firm will incur the fixed costs of $50. The second row shows the cost of producing one crate of pumpkins. Since two units of labor are needed for the production of this one crate, the total cost of producing one crate of pumpkins is $70, the $50 fixed costs plus the $20 in variable costs. The third row of Table 6.2 shows the costs of producing two crates of pumpkins. Because five units of labor (at a cost of $10 each) are needed for the production of these two crates, the total cost of producing two crates of pumpkins is $100, the $50 fixed costs plus the $50 in variable costs.

As more pumpkins are harvested, more workers must be hired, and the total costs increase. The remaining rows of Table 6.2 show what happens to costs as the quantity produced increases further.

Marginal cost is defined as the increase in total costs associated with an additional unit of production. Figure 6.8 shows how marginal cost is calculated for the example in Table 6.2. For example, the marginal cost of increasing production from one crate to two crates is $30 ($100 − $70 = $30), and the marginal cost of increasing production from two crates to three crates is $50 ($150 − $100 = $50).

Notice how marginal cost increases as production increases. Marginal cost is greater when we go from two crates to three crates ($50) than when we go from one crate to two crates ($30). The pattern of *increasing marginal* cost is apparent throughout the range of production in Figure 6.8.

marginal cost

The change in total costs due to a one-unit change in quantity produced.

FIGURE 6.8 Total Costs and Marginal Cost
Marginal cost is the change (increase) in total costs for an additional unit of output produced.

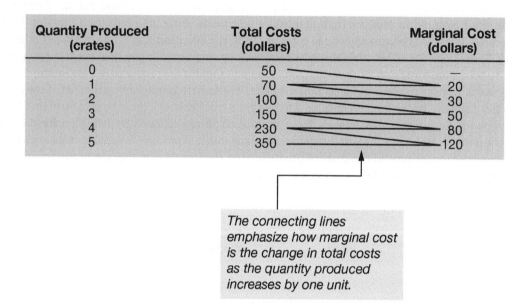

Quantity Produced (crates)	Total Costs (dollars)	Marginal Cost (dollars)
0	50	—
1	70	20
2	100	30
3	150	50
4	230	80
5	350	120

The connecting lines emphasize how marginal cost is the change in total costs as the quantity produced increases by one unit.

Observe that *increasing marginal cost is due to the diminishing marginal product of labor*: The marginal cost of going from two crates to three crates is greater than that of going from one crate to two crates because more worker hours are required to raise production from two crates to three crates (five additional hours of labor) than are required to raise production from one crate to two crates (three additional hours of labor).

Increasing marginal cost is a general phenomenon that occurs in many production processes. It is essential for deriving the supply curve. In fact, as we will soon see, increasing marginal cost is the whole reason that the supply curve for an individual firm slopes upward.

The principle of increasing marginal cost has important exceptions. One of these exceptions is that marginal cost need not be increasing over the entire range of production. For example, a decrease in marginal cost may occur at very low levels of production. If a team of at least two workers is needed to harvest pumpkins, for example, then the marginal product of a second worker might be greater than the marginal product of a first worker. One worker might add very little, whereas the second might add a lot. But diminishing returns to labor and increasing marginal cost eventually set in as more workers are hired and more pumpkins are produced.

In this chapter, we assume that marginal cost increases over the whole range of production. This is a common assumption used by economists and is a good approximation except for very low levels of production.

Graphical Representation of Total Costs and Marginal Cost

A better understanding of how a firm's total costs depend on production can be obtained by representing the total costs graphically. Figure 6.9 plots the pairs of numbers for total costs and quantity produced from the first two columns of Figure 6.8. Dollars are on the vertical axis, and the quantity of pumpkins produced is on the horizontal axis. Note how the total costs curve bends up: As the quantity of pumpkins produced increases, the curve gets steeper, or the slope increases. The marginal cost is the slope of the total costs curve. The increasing slope is a visual way to show the increasing marginal cost.

FIGURE 6.9 Total Costs
To produce goods, a firm incurs costs. For example, more workers must be paid to produce more goods. As more goods are produced, the firm's total costs rise, as shown here. At higher levels of production, costs increase by larger amounts for each additional item produced.

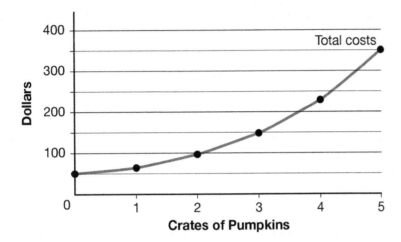

Figure 6.10 shows the relationship between marginal cost and the number of crates of pumpkins produced. The points in Figure 6.10 correspond to the pairs of numbers in the first and third columns of Figure 6.8. Note that the marginal cost curve slopes upward, illustrating how marginal cost increases as the quantity of pumpkins produced increases.

FIGURE 6.10 Marginal Cost
The change in total costs as more units of the good are produced is called marginal cost. Marginal cost increases as more units are produced, as illustrated here.

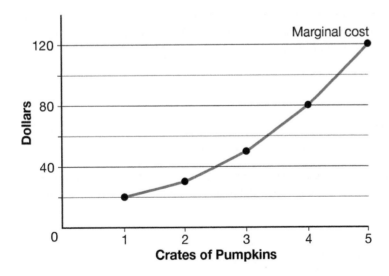

Review

- Profits are defined as the difference between total revenue and total costs. Profits depend on the quantity produced because both total revenue and total costs depend on the quantity produced.

- Total revenue is defined as the price (P) times the quantity (Q) produced and sold. Total revenue increases as the quantity produced increases.
- Total costs are all the costs that the firm has to incur to produce its product. The costs that a firm incurs include opportunity costs.
- In this chapter, we look at the firm's production decisions over a short period of time. One factor of production, land, has to be held fixed whereas the other factor of production, labor, can be varied as the quantity produced varies.
- The production function describes how much output can be produced as the quantity of inputs (in this case hours of labor) varies. Typically, the marginal product of labor declines as more and more labor is employed. This phenomenon also is described as diminishing returns to labor.
- Total costs are the sum of fixed costs (which do not vary with the quantity produced) and variable costs (which vary according to how much is produced). In the pumpkin firm example, fixed costs are the cost of renting the pumpkin patch, and variable costs are the costs of hiring workers.
- Variable costs increase with the quantity produced because it takes more inputs—such as workers—to produce more output. As a result, total costs also increase with the quantity produced.
- Marginal cost is defined as the change in total costs associated with an additional unit of production. Marginal cost increases as more is produced because of diminishing returns to labor.

6.3 Profit Maximization and the Individual Firm

profit maximization

An assumption that firms try to achieve the highest possible level of profits—total revenue minus total costs given their production function.

To derive the firm's supply curve, we assume that the firm chooses a quantity of production that maximizes profits. This is the assumption of **profit maximization**. Now that we have seen how profits depend on the quantity produced, we can show how the firm chooses a quantity to maximize profits.

An Initial Approach to Derive the Supply Curve

Continuing with our pumpkin firm, we create a table that uses total revenue and total costs to calculate profits. Because total revenue depends on the price, we need a separate panel for each of three possible prices.

A Profit Table

TABLE 6.3 Profit Tables Showing Total Costs and Total Revenue at Different Prices

PANEL I			
If price equals $35 per crate, then production equals two crates.			
Crates	Total Revenue	Total Costs	Profits
0	0	50	-50
1	35	70	-35
2	**70**	**100**	**-30**
3	105	150	-45
4	140	230	-90
5	175	350	-175

PANEL II			
If price equals $70 per crate, then production equals three crates.			
Crates	Total Revenue	Total Costs	Profits
0	0	50	-50
1	70	70	0
2	140	100	40
3	**210**	**150**	**60**
4	280	230	50
5	350	350	0

PANEL III			
If price equals $100 per crate, then production equals four crates.			
Crates	Total Revenue	Total Costs	Profits
0	0	50	-50
1	100	70	30
2	200	100	100
3	300	150	150
4	**400**	**230**	**170**
5	500	350	150

Table 6.3 shows profits for your pumpkin firm. It has three panels, one for each of three possible prices. (The prices are the same as in Table 6.1.) Each panel reports total revenue and total costs for quantities ranging from zero to five crates. The last column of each panel reports profits, which are defined as total revenue less total costs.

Total revenue, shown in the second column, increases with the number of pumpkins sold. Because total revenue depends on the price, we need a separate panel showing total revenue for each price. The third column of Table 6.3 shows how total costs increase with production. This information is the same as that presented in Table 6.2. We repeat it here so that total costs can be compared easily with total revenue to calculate profits. The range of total costs is the same for all three panels because total costs do not depend on the price.

Consider Panel I, in which the price of pumpkins is $35 a crate. Total revenue equals the price ($35) times the number of crates sold. If you sell one crate, the revenue is $35; if you sell two crates, the revenue is $70, and so on. Clearly, if no pumpkins are sold, the total revenue will be zero. Panels II and III show total revenue for two higher prices—$70 per crate and $100 per crate.

The last column of Table 6.3 shows profits, which equal total revenue minus total costs. Consider the $35 per crate price in Panel I first. When no pumpkins are produced, total costs are $50 because $50 is paid for the land. Total revenue is zero. Profits, therefore, are –$50, which implies that the firm loses $50. If you produce one crate, the loss is $35; the revenue from one crate ($35) minus the total cost of producing one crate ($70) equals a profit of –$35. For two crates, profits are still negative, at –$30. Total revenue is $70; total costs are $100, leaving a loss of $30. Three crates of pumpkins yield an even greater loss of $45.

A glance down the last column in Panel I shows that profits are negative at all production levels. In this case, any production at all may seem fruitless. But remember that you already paid $50 for the use of the pumpkin patch. Hence, it is best to produce two crates and cut your losses to $30. You still lose, but not as much as by producing only zero or one crate. Even though it may seem strange because profits are negative, the profit-maximizing level of production is two crates. The maximum of profits would be –$30. Stated differently, the minimum loss would be $30.

The same type of profit-maximizing exercise with a different price is illustrated in Panel II of Table 6.3. Here the price of pumpkins is $70 per crate, and so the total revenue is higher. If you sell nothing, then total revenue is zero and the loss is $50. If you sell one crate, total revenue is $70 and profits are zero. But if you sell two crates, total costs are $100 and total revenue is $140. Finally, some positive profit can be seen. Profits can be increased further: The profit-maximizing level of production is three crates.

Panel III shows profits for a still higher price, $100 a crate. At this price, you would produce four crates. Profits would be $170. More or less production than four crates would lower profits.

In these three cases, you maximize profits by adjusting the quantity supplied. As the price rises from $35 to $70 to $100, the profit-maximizing quantity of pumpkins supplied goes from two crates to three crates to four crates. Thus, the price and the quantity supplied are positively related. This is the positively sloped supply curve.

A Profit Graph

The relationship between profits and production for your pumpkin firm given in Table 6.3 can be illustrated with a graph that compares total costs and total revenue. This comparison is shown in Figure 6.11. The curved line in the top graph of Figure 6.11 is the total costs curve. It corresponds to the total costs listed in Table 6.3 and is the same as the total costs curve in Figure 6.9. The upward-sloping straight line shows what total revenue would be for a price of $70 per crate. This line corresponds to the total revenue column in Panel II of Table 6.3.

FIGURE 6.11 An Initial Approach to Profit Maximization
The top panel shows total costs and total revenue for a price of $70 per crate of pumpkins. Profits are the gap between total revenue and total costs. The bottom panel shows explicitly how profits first increase and then decrease as production increases.

Profits are given by the gap between the total revenue line and the total costs curve. The gap—profits—is plotted in the lower panel of Figure 6.11. Note how profits first increase and then decrease as more is produced. The profit-maximizing firm chooses the quantity to produce that leads to the biggest gap, or the biggest level of profits. That quantity is three crates of pumpkins.

The Marginal Approach to Deriving the Supply Curve

The above approach to deriving the supply curve can be involved because of the need to calculate a separate profit table for each price level. Economists use a different approach to analyzing profit maximization and deriving the supply curve. Once you know this approach, you will find that it is an easier and faster way to derive the individual firm's supply curve than using total revenue, total costs, and total profits.

Continuing with our pumpkin firm, we first plot the marginal cost from Figure 6.8 in Figure 6.12. Focus for now on the black dots in Figure 6.12; we derive the lines in the next few paragraphs. Each dot in Figure 6.12 represents the marginal cost of producing a crate of pumpkins at a different level of production (the marginal cost when production is one crate is $20, the marginal cost when production is two crates is $30, and so on).

FIGURE 6.12 Derivation of the Individual Firm's Supply Curve
The dots represent the marginal cost from Figure 6.10. At each dot, price equals marginal cost. These dots and the thick vertical lines indicate the quantity the firm is willing to supply at each price. Along the vertical lines, the firm produces the quantity that keeps marginal cost closest to price without exceeding it.

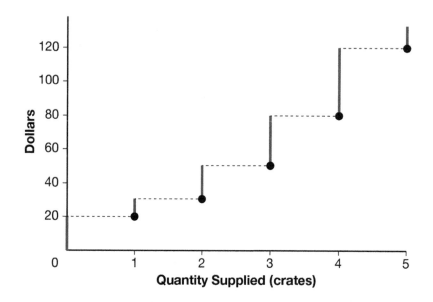

Finding the Quantity Supplied at Different Prices

Suppose the price of pumpkins is $10 a crate. At $10, the price is less than the marginal cost of producing one unit, which is $20, according to Figure 6.12. Would it make sense to produce pumpkins at this price? No, because the *additional* revenue that comes from producing one more crate, the price of a crate of pumpkins, is $10. Because laying out $20 and getting back $10 reduces profits, you would not bother to produce any pumpkins.

marginal revenue

The change in total revenue due to a one-unit increase in quantity sold.

The additional, or extra, revenue that results from producing and selling one more unit of output is called **marginal revenue**. We can summarize the above conclusion by saying that we do not increase production from zero to one crate because the marginal cost of increasing production would be greater than the marginal revenue. Therefore, producing nothing would be the profit-maximizing thing to do.

Suppose the price of pumpkins rises. As long as the price is below $20, there is no production because marginal costs exceed marginal revenue (which is the price). Thus, the amount supplied at prices from $0 to $20 is given by the thick line at the bottom of the vertical axis, indicating that quantity supplied equals zero.

Suppose the price rises to $20. Now the price equals the marginal cost, and the marginal revenue from selling a crate of pumpkins will just cover the marginal cost of producing the crate. You now have sufficient incentive to produce some pumpkins. Strictly speaking, the price would have to be a little bit greater than $20 (say, $20.01) for you to earn more by producing one crate rather than zero crates. At a price of exactly $20, you might be indifferent between producing zero crates and one crate. At a price of $19.99, you definitely would produce nothing. At a price of $20.01, you would produce one crate. The price of $20 is right between, but let's assume that you produce one crate rather than zero crates at a price of $20. We indicate this in Figure 6.12 by showing that the quantity supplied is given by the black dot at one crate and $20.

Now consider further increases in the price. At prices above $20 up to $30, you would produce one crate because the marginal revenue received for producing an extra crate (which again is the price of a crate of pumpkins) is less than the marginal cost of $30. At a price of $30, however, the quantity supplied increases to two crates because price just equals the marginal cost of increasing production from one to two crates. A supply curve is now beginning to take shape. You can complete the curve by continuing to raise the price and watching what happens.

To shorten the story, let us move toward the other end of the scale. Suppose the price of pumpkins is $100 and you are producing four crates of pumpkins. Would it make sense to produce another crate? No, because increasing production from four crates to five crates has a marginal cost of $120. The marginal revenue that comes from producing one more crate is $100. Because laying out $120 and getting back $100 is a losing proposition, you would not do it. Production would stay at four crates. If production went up to five crates, profits would go down because the marginal cost of producing the fifth crate is greater than the marginal revenue.

We have traced out the complete *individual* supply curve for your firm using Figure 6.12 with the assumption of profit maximization and the concept of marginal cost. The supply curve in Figure 6.12 is step-like; it consists of small vertical segments shooting up from the dots. At the dots, price equals marginal cost; on the vertical segments above the dots, the price is greater than the marginal cost of production, but the price is not great enough to move on to a higher level of production. What the vertical lines show is that as the price rises, the quantity supplied of pumpkins increases as well.

In reality, for most products, it is possible to divide production into smaller units—half crates, quarter crates, even a single pumpkin. As we do so, the jaggedness of the diagram disappears, as shown in Figure 6.13. In reality, the diagram would consist of hundreds of dots rather than five dots. With hundreds of dots, the vertical segments would be too small to see and the firm's supply curve would be a smooth line. Price would equal marginal cost at every single point.

FIGURE 6.13 A Smooth Individual Supply Curve
If the firm can adjust its production by small amounts, the supply curve becomes a smooth line, as in this figure, rather than a series of steps. In some cases, such as the building of an airport, a dam, or a suspension bridge, fractions are not possible, and the supply curves will still have steps.

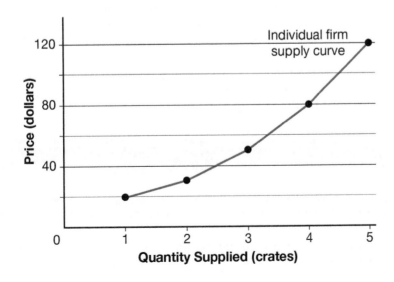

The Price Equals Marginal Cost Rule

In deriving the supply curve with Figure 6.12, we have discovered the key condition for profit maximization for a firm: *The firm will choose a quantity to produce so that marginal revenue equals marginal cost.* This general rule makes intuitive sense for any profit-maximizing firm, whether it is a competitive firm or a monopoly. If the marginal revenue from producing an additional quantity of output is greater than the marginal cost, then the firm should produce that quantity; by doing so, it will increase total revenue by more than it increases total costs, and therefore it will increase profits. If the marginal revenue from an additional quantity is less than the marginal cost, however, then the firm should not produce that quantity. Thus, the firm maximizes profits by choosing the quantity of production for which marginal revenue equals marginal cost.

In a competitive market, we can come up with a special case of this rule that makes finding the profit-maximizing quantity even easier. *The firm will choose its quantity such that price equals marginal cost.* You can see that from Figure 6.12. When the price is $80, the firm chooses a level of production for which the marginal cost equals $80 and produces four crates. Why is the price-equals-marginal-cost rule for a competitive firm a special case of the marginal-revenue-equals-marginal-cost rule? Because *for the case of a price-taking firm in a competitive market, the marginal revenue is equal to the price.* Changes in the quantity of goods that the firm supplies do not affect the market price, so each additional unit sold brings in the same additional revenue, namely, the market price of the good. For example, as we showed above, if the price of pumpkins is $10 per crate, then the marginal, or additional, revenue from producing one crate of pumpkins is $10. Later, in Chapter 10, we will show that for a monopoly, the marginal revenue does not equal the price, so that even though marginal revenue equals marginal cost, the price does not equal marginal cost.

A Comparison of the Two Approaches to Profit Maximization

We have considered two different approaches to profit maximization. One approach looks at the explicit relationship between profits and production. The other compares the price to the marginal cost. Both give the same answer. How do the approaches compare?

In Table 6.3 we looked at several prices, and we derived the profit-maximizing level of production by looking at profits for different levels of production at these prices. To do so, we had to create a new table for each price. This process is quite time-consuming. In contrast, with the marginal cost approach, we only had to look at marginal cost for each unit of production and compare it with the price. Thus, the price-equals-marginal cost approach is considerably easier. Moreover, because marginal-cost increases as the number of items produced increases, the price-equals-marginal-cost approach tells us why the supply curve slopes upward. It is for these two reasons that economists usually use the price-equals-marginal-cost approach.

Review

- The supply curve for a firm is derived by assuming that the firm chooses the quantity of production that maximizes profits. Profits are the difference between total revenue and total costs.
- As price changes, the profit-maximizing quantity changes as well. The relationship between price and the profit-maximizing quantity is the firm's supply curve.

- A profit table is an accurate if long-winded way of determining the profit-maximizing quantity produced by a firm for a given price. As the price changes, the profits calculated in the table change, providing a different profit-maximizing quantity.

- For the pumpkin-producing firm, the profit-maximizing quantity increased with price, resulting in an upward sloping supply curve.

- A less work-intensive way of calculating the profit maximizing quantity is to consider the marginal revenue and the marginal cost of an additional unit of production. If marginal revenue exceeds marginal cost, then profits would go up with the additional unit of production. If marginal revenue is less than marginal cost, then profits would go down with the additional unit of production.

- A profit-maximizing firm therefore would produce at a quantity such that marginal revenue equaled marginal cost.

- For a competitive firm, marginal revenue equals the price of the good, because the firm's production decisions do not affect the market price. Therefore, the profit-maximizing quantity easily can be found as the quantity that equates the marginal cost with the price of the good.

- Marginal cost increases as the quantity produced increases. Therefore, as price rises, the profit maximizing firm will respond by increasing the quantity it produces. In other words, the upward sloping marginal cost curve implies an upward-sloping supply curve.

6.4 The Market Supply Curve

The *market* supply curve can be obtained by adding up the supply curves of all the *individual* firms in the market. Figure 6.14 gives an example of two individual firm supply curves for pumpkins: One curve corresponds to your pumpkin firm, and the other, which is identical to yours, corresponds to the firm of your competitor, Fred, who is growing pumpkins on the other side of town. You and Fred have the same marginal cost for pumpkin growing, so your supply curves are exactly the same. You both will choose to produce the same number of pumpkins if the price is the same.

If only you and Fred are in the market, the market supply curve is the sum of just your two supplies. You get the market curve by adding in the horizontal direction, as shown in Figure 6.14. For example, if the price is $30, the quantity supplied by Fred will be two crates, and the quantity you supply will be two crates; thus, the quantity supplied in the market at $30 is four crates. If the price rises to $50, Fred will produce three crates and you also will produce three crates; thus, the quantity supplied in the market rises to six crates.

FIGURE 6.14 Derivation of the Market Supply Curve
The market supply curve is the sum of the individual firms' supply curves for all the firms in the market. The figure shows how the supply curves of two firms—Fred's and yours—sum to a market supply curve.

In reality, of course, a competitive market has more than two firms, and the individual supply curves for different firms in the market usually are different. But the concept of deriving the market supply curve is the same whether there are only 2 firms or 2,000 firms, and whether they are all the same or are all different. After adding up the individual supply curves for all the firms in the market, we arrive at a market supply curve like Figure 6.2. Thus, we have fulfilled one of the objectives of this chapter—deriving the market supply curve.

If a market has many different firms, the market supply curve can be much smoother than the individual supply curves. For example, a general contractor may be able to build only one house a year. But the market for new houses in any one year consists of many contractors with many different marginal costs. As the price of new houses rises, more and more contractors will build houses, and the market supply curve for houses will look smooth.

 Solving for the Market Supply Curve

The market supply curve in a perfectly competitive market is the sum of each firm's supply curve.

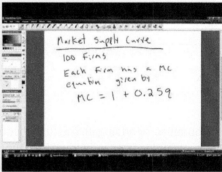

View the video online at: http://www.youtube.com/embed/bvfhn_djYrl?rel=0

The Slope of the Supply Curve

We have shown that the slope and position of the individual firms' supply curves depend on the marginal cost at the different firms. If marginal cost rises very sharply with more production, then the supply curve will be very steep. If marginal cost increases more gradually, then the supply curve will be flatter.

Because the market supply curve is the sum of the individual firms' supply curves, its slope also will depend on marginal cost. The market supply curve can get steep at high levels of production because marginal cost gets high when production is high.

Shifts in the Supply Curve

Because the supply curve for the individual firm is given by its marginal cost, anything that changes marginal cost will shift the individual supply curves and therefore the market supply curve. For example, a new technology might reduce the marginal cost at every level of production. If this happens, then the marginal cost curve will shift down and the profit-maximizing quantity for each price level will increase. Observe that a downward shift of the marginal cost curve is equivalent to a rightward shift of the supply curve. Similarly, an increase in marginal cost—perhaps because of a disease affecting the pumpkins, so that more labor is required for each crate of pumpkins—would shift the supply curve upward or to the left (see Figure 6.15).

FIGURE 6.15 Shifts in the Market Supply Curve
An increase in marginal cost would shift the supply curve upward or to the left.

Review

- The market supply curve is derived by adding up the individual supply curves of all the firms in the market.
- When the price rises, the individual firms in the market increase the quantity supplied. Hence, the market supply curve is upward sloping.
- The slope of the supply curve depends on how sharply marginal cost increases. If marginal cost rises sharply with more production, then the supply curve will be steep. If marginal cost does not change much as production increases, the supply curve will be flat.
- Anything that raises marginal cost will shift the market supply curve upward or to the left. Conversely, anything that lowers marginal cost will shift the market supply curve downward or to the right.

6.5 Producer Surplus

In Chapter 5, we learned about consumer surplus, the difference between the marginal benefit derived from consuming an additional item and the price paid for it, as a measure of how well off consumers are. We can derive a similar concept for measuring how well off producers are by engaging in the production of goods for the market. **Producer surplus** is defined as the difference between the marginal cost of an item and the price received for it. For example, suppose that the price of pumpkins is $25, at which price you produce one crate of pumpkins costing you $20. Then you get $25 for producing one crate and incur $20 in marginal cost. The difference, $5, is your producer surplus for producing that first crate of pumpkins. If the price of pumpkins is $35, you produce two crates with the marginal cost for the second crate being $30. Then your producer surplus is $15 ($35 – $20) for the first crate plus $5 ($35 – $30) for the second crate, for a total producer surplus of $20.

A Graphic Representation of Producer Surplus

Producer surplus can be represented graphically as the area above the individual firm supply curve and below the price line, as illustrated in Figure 6.16. Producer surplus in the whole market can be obtained by adding up producer surplus for all producers or by looking at the area above the market supply curve and below the price. This is illustrated in Figure 6.17. Producer surplus provides a measure of how much a producer gains from the market. The sum of producer surplus plus consumer surplus is a comprehensive measure of how well a market economy works, as we will see in Chapter 7.

FIGURE 6.16 Producer Surplus for an Individual Firm
As shown here, for an individual firm, the producer surplus is the area between the price line and the supply curve.

FIGURE 6.17 Producer Surplus for the Market
If we add up producer surplus for every firm, we get the producer surplus for the whole market. This surplus is given by the area between the price and the market supply curve.

Producer Surplus

Producer surplus is the difference between revenue and marginal cost for all goods produced.

View the video online at: http://www.youtube.com/embed/ECz2hEbEagw?rel=0

The Difference between Profits and Producer Surplus

Profits and producer surplus are not the same thing. Profits are the difference between total revenue and total costs, while the producer surplus measures the difference between the price and the marginal cost of every unit. How can we compare these two measures?

Suppose the price of pumpkins is $70 per crate; then you are willing to produce three crates of pumpkins. Total revenue is $210 and total costs are $150; thus, you are making a $60 profit. (See Panel II of Table 6.3.) How much is your producer surplus when three crates are sold at $70? As just defined,

$$\text{producer surplus} = (P - MC_1) + (P - MC_2) + (P - MC_3)$$

$$(\$70 - \$20) + (\$70 - \$30) + (\$70 - \$50) = \$110$$

where MC_1 is the marginal cost of the first crate, MC_2 is the marginal cost of the second crate, and MC_3 is the marginal cost of the third crate. Thus, profits are $60 and producer surplus is $110.

Notice the $50 difference between producer surplus and profits. Try doing the same calculation for a price of $100. Panel III of Table 6.3 tells us that profits are $170, and you can calculate producer surplus to be equal to ($80 + $70 + $50 + $20) or $220. Once again producer surplus and profits have a difference of $50. If you try using this method for different prices and quantities sold, you will arrive at the same result. Note that $50 is equal to the fixed costs of the firm. Producer surplus equals profit plus fixed costs. We now show that this is not a coincidence.

When the producer sells a quantity Q, we can say that

$$\text{producer surplus} = (P - MC_1) + (P - MC_2) + (P - MC_3) + \cdots + (P - MC_Q)$$

The number of terms in this sum is Q. For the example above, $Q = 3$ and three terms were included in the sum. Thus, we can translate this definition of producer surplus into the price (P) of the good times the quantity (Q) sold minus the sum of the marginal costs of all units. That is,

$$\text{producer surplus} = P \times Q - \text{sum of marginal costs}$$

Because $P \times Q$ is total revenue, we can write the above equation as

$$\text{producer surplus} = \text{total revenue} - \text{sum of marginal costs}$$

The marginal cost of an additional unit is the additional costs incurred in producing that unit of output. Thus, as we sum up marginal costs for any quantity Q produced, we count all costs associated with increasing production from zero units to Q units. To obtain total costs, we would need to add fixed costs, the cost of producing zero units, to the above sum. In other words,

$$\text{total costs} = \text{sum of marginal costs} + \text{fixed costs}$$

This can be rearranged to show that

$$\text{sum of marginal costs} = \text{total costs} - \text{fixed costs}$$

Substituting into the definition of producer surplus, we can see therefore that

$$\text{producer surplus} = \text{total revenue} - (\text{total costs} - \text{fixed costs})$$

This implies that

$$\text{producer surplus} = \text{total revenue} - \text{total costs} + \text{fixed costs}$$

which gives us the result we want to understand—the difference between profits and producer surplus, namely that

$$\text{producer surplus} = \text{total profits} + \text{fixed costs}$$

Review

- Producer surplus associated with an item is the difference between the price a firm receives for selling that item and the marginal cost of producing that item. It is a measure of how well off producers are as a result of their decision to produce that item.
- Graphically, producer surplus for a firm is the area below the price line and above the firm's supply curve.

- For all the firms in a market, the producer surplus is the area below the price line and above the market supply curve.
- Producer surplus is different from profits. Producer surplus is greater than profits by the amount of fixed costs.

6.6 End-of-Chapter Materials

Conclusion

In this chapter, we derived the supply curve in a competitive market by looking at the behavior of firms. We assumed that a firm decides how much to produce at a given market price by choosing the quantity that maximizes profits. The firm makes this decision taking prices as given and considering its production function, which relates the number of hours of work at the firm to the output of the firm. The production function enters the firm's profit calculations through its effects on the firm's costs. Because the production function has diminishing returns to labor, the firm faces increasing marginal cost.

Profit maximization implies that the firm will produce the quantity for which marginal revenue equals marginal cost. In a competitive market, the marginal revenue from selling an additional unit always equals the price. Therefore the profit-maximizing quantity is the amount at which price equals marginal cost.

As the price rises, the firm will respond by increasing production until marginal cost and price are equal again. As a result, the supply curve for an individual firm will be upward sloping. The slope of the supply curve will be steep when marginal cost increases rapidly as more units are produced, and it will be flat when marginal cost does not rise by very much as more units are produced. The supply curve will shift out when marginal cost falls because of some event like a change in technology and shift in when marginal cost rises.

The connection between marginal cost and the supply curve is fundamental to understanding how markets work. We will make use of this connection many times throughout this book, especially when we consider public policy issues, such as the efficiency of markets, taxation, and regulation of firms. When economists see or draw a supply curve, they usually are thinking about the marginal cost of the firms that underlie the supply curve. The supply curve and the marginal cost curve are virtually synonymous for economists.

We have examined firm behavior in this chapter and consumer behavior in Chapter 5. In Chapter 7, we will examine the interactions of these firms and consumers. In Chapter 5 and Chapter 6, we derived two rules for characterizing individual and firm behavior: Profit maximizing firms will produce according to the price equals marginal cost rule, while utility-maximizing consumers will consume according to the price equals marginal benefit rule. In Chapter 7, we will combine these two concepts to point out an attractive feature of competitive markets.

Key Points

1. A firm is an organization that uses inputs to produce goods or services.
2. In a competitive market, no single firm can affect the price.

3. The foundations of supply are found in the profit maximizing behavior of firms, with each firm's supply curve being derived as the profit maximizing quantity that corresponds to various possible market prices.

4. Profits are defined as total revenue minus total costs. Total revenue increases as the quantity sold increases. Total costs, which are the sum of fixed costs and variable costs, also increase with production.

5. The change in total costs when production is increased is called marginal cost. How large marginal cost is depends on the production function, which shows how many inputs are needed for producing different quantities of output. Marginal cost increases as more is produced because of diminishing returns to inputs.

6. A firm produces up to the point at which marginal revenue equals marginal cost, which is the key rule for profit maximization. In a competitive market, marginal revenue always equals the price of the good. Therefore, the profit-maximizing quantity for a price-taking firm easily can be found as the quantity such that price equals marginal cost.

7. The reason the supply curve slopes upward is that marginal cost is increasing. A higher price enables the firm to produce at higher levels of marginal cost. The marginal cost curve and the supply curve are virtually synonymous.

8. The market supply curve is obtained by adding up the individual supply curves. The market supply curve can be smooth even if the individual supply curves are not.

9. Producer surplus is the difference between the price of a good and its marginal cost of production. Graphically, producer surplus for an individual firm is the area above the individual supply curve and below the price line. The producer surplus for all firms in the market is the area above the market supply curve and below the price line.

10. Producer surplus and profit are not the same thing. Producer surplus equals profits plus fixed costs.

Questions for Review

1. What is a firm?
2. What is the definition of a competitive market?
3. Describe the relationships that exist among total costs, fixed costs, variable costs, and marginal cost.
4. Why does marginal cost increase as more is produced?
5. Why does profit maximization imply that marginal revenue equals marginal cost? Why is it that in a competitive market only, profit maximization implies that price equals marginal cost?
6. What is the relationship between an individual firm's supply curve and its marginal cost curve?
7. How is the market supply curve derived from individual supply curves?
8. Why might the market supply curve be smoother than the individual supply curves?
9. What is producer surplus and how is it calculated?
10. How does producer surplus differ from profits?

Problems

1. Name three businesses in which firms are price takers. Name three businesses in which firms are not price-takers. Suppose you set up a business through which you tutor students on campus. Would you be a price-taker or a price-maker?

2. Does the assumption that firms are price-takers in a market seem less valid than the assumption that consumers are price-takers in that market? Explain why. Would your answer change if you were told that the market included 50 firms and 50 consumers? Explain.

3. Before the Industrial Revolution, people lived in agricultural societies. What are the two primary inputs to production in an agricultural society? Which one of these inputs is variable and which one is fixed? Why is there reason to believe that the rate of growth of the food supply will slow down as the population increases?

4. Consider the example of the cost of pumpkins in Table 6.3. Compute the total revenue, total costs, and profits when the price of a crate of pumpkins is $60. How many crates of pumpkins will maximize profits? Now find the profit-maximizing quantity by using the marginal cost approach. How do your answers compare? Which approach did you find easier?

5. The following table shows the total costs of producing strawberries on a small plot of land.

Pounds of Strawberries	Total Costs ($)
0	10
1	11
2	14
3	18
4	25
5	34

   a. Calculate the marginal cost schedule.

   b. Draw the farmer's supply curve.

   c. Suppose the price of 1 pound of strawberries is $4. How much would this farmer produce? What are profits?

   d. Suppose the price of strawberries goes up to $7 per pound. How much will the farmer produce now? What are profits now?

6. Suppose a price-taking producer of barrels for storing wine has the following total costs schedule:

Quantity	Total Costs ($)
0	20
1	30
2	42
3	55
4	75
5	100
6	130

   a. Calculate marginal cost. If the price of a barrel in the market is $20, how many barrels will the firm produce?

   b. Suppose the price in the market falls to $12 per barrel. How many barrels will this firm produce in order to maximize profits?

   c. Suppose an improvement in technology shifts total costs down by $8 at every level of production. How much will the firm produce and what will profits be at a price of $20 and at a price of $12?

7. Consider the following information:

Daily Production and Costs at Jill's Bread Bakers	
Quantity Produced (dozens of loaves)	Total Cost ($)
0	20
1	22
2	26
3	32
4	40
5	50
6	62
7	76

a. Calculate the marginal cost for Jill's bread production.

b. Draw the supply curve for this firm.

c. Jill can sell as many loaves as she wants in the market at a price of $12 for a dozen loaves. How many loaves will she sell each day? What are her profits?

d. Use your diagram to show how much producer surplus Jill receives.

8. Suppose you are able to mow lawns at $12 per hour. The only cost to you is the opportunity cost of your time. For the first three hours, the opportunity cost of your time is $9 per hour. But after three hours, the opportunity cost of your time rises to $15 per hour because of other commitments. Draw the marginal cost to you of mowing lawns. On that diagram, draw in the price you receive for mowing loans, indicate for how long you will mow lawns, and graphically indicate the area of your producer surplus in addition to calculating the magnitude of your producer surplus.

9. Consider the following information about a firm that sells ice cream–making machines:

Quantity	Total Costs ($)	Total Revenue ($)
0	500	0
1	700	500
2	1,100	1,000
3	1,500	1,500
4	2,300	2,000
5	3,500	2,500

a. On a single diagram, plot the total revenues and total costs curves for this firm.

b. What are the maximum profits that this firm can earn?

c. Show this level of profits in the diagram.

d. What is the relationship between the slopes of the two curves at the quantity that maximizes profits?

10. What is the relationship between producer surplus, profits, and fixed costs? In what types of industries would you expect producer surplus to be high while profits are low? Provide one or two examples of such industries.

Endnotes

1. Will Yakowicz, "Meet The Billion-Dollar Family Company That Makes Purell," *Forbes*, March 10, 2020.

CHAPTER 7
The Efficiency of Markets

This is an old but true story, going back to before the field of economics even existed. It is about an absent-minded philosophy professor who was interested in understanding human interaction. He was particularly fascinated by how the economy, consisting of the interaction of millions of people pursuing their own interests, worked. He did not have much to go on; his school, or any other school, did not have economics professors. So, although he was a gifted teacher, he quit his teaching job at the university and traveled; he interviewed business people; he visited factories; he talked to workers; he watched ships come and go; he studied the economies of other countries and of other times. Amazingly, he not only was able to pull all this material together into a coherent view, but also managed to get it down on paper for other people to read, learn, and enjoy. By doing so, he invented the field of economics and presented a view of the economy that is still the dominant view in the twenty-first century.

The professor's name was Adam Smith, and the book he wrote, called Wealth of Nations, was first published in 1776. His deepest insight, among many deep insights, is called the **invisible hand** theorem, best stated using his own words: "It is not from the benevolence of the butcher, the brewer, or the baker that we expect our dinner, but from their regard to their own interest." And whether it is the butcher, the brewer, or the baker, he is "led by an invisible hand to promote an end which was no part of his intention. . . . By pursuing his own interest he frequently promotes that of the society more effectually than when he really intends to promote it."[1] In other words, without any formal coordination, firms (butchers, brewers, bakers, and many others) that are pursuing their own interests interact with consumers who also are pursuing their own interests, and somehow everyone ends up producing and consuming a quantity that is efficient.

The main goal of this chapter is to state clearly and prove the invisible hand theorem. The theorem is not always true, and we want to be clear about the circumstances in which it is true. We first need to explain what is meant by efficient (the modern term for Smith's "effectual"), and then show why, and under what circumstances, the quantity produced and consumed is efficient. We also show how to measure the economic loss from producing more or less than the efficient quantity.

Chapter 5 and Chapter 6 have paved the way for our goal in this chapter. In Chapter 5, we studied the behavior of consumers. We can say that consumers who maximize their utility are pursuing their own interests. In Chapter 6, we studied the behavior of firms. We can say that firms that maximize profits also are pursuing their own interests. Now we study the interactions of firms and consumers in competitive markets. Figure 7.2 is a schematic illustration of the model we use to explain this interaction and thereby explain the invisible hand theorem. The model, called the **competitive equilibrium model**, is the supply and demand model discussed in Chapter 3, now with the behavior of consumers and firms explicit.

FIGURE 7.1 Adam Smith, Author of *Wealth of Nations*
Adam Smith had many deep insights into how the economy worked, none more profound than the invisible-hand theorem.

Source: Heartland Arts/Shutterstock.com

invisible hand

The idea that the free interaction of people in a market economy leads to a desirable social outcome; the term was coined by Adam Smith.

competitive equilibrium model

A model that assumes utility maximization on the part of consumers and profit maximization on the part of firms, along with competitive markets and freely determined prices.

FIGURE 7.2 The Interaction of Buyers and Sellers in the Marketplace

In this chapter, we explain how individual buyers and sellers interact in a market by combining the behavior of consumers (Chapter 5) with the behavior of firms (Chapter 6) to get a model of competitive equilibrium (Chapter 7).

The Invisible Hand

Under the invisible hand theorem, efficiency is reached by firms and consumers acting in their own self-interest.

View the video online at: http://www.youtube.com/embed/ulyVXa-u4wE?rel=0

7.1 Individual Consumers and Firms in a Market

In our analysis of economic interaction, it is important to think about what individual consumers and firms are doing. Consider an example of consumers and producers of the same commodity: long-stemmed roses. Maria and Ken are two of many potential rose consumers who are deciding how many roses to buy. Both are willing to pay a certain amount for roses, but not necessarily the same amount. Hugo and Mimi are two of many rose producers who are deciding how many roses to produce in their gardens. They both are willing to sell roses provided the price is right, but they have different marginal costs for producing roses.

The Hard Way to Process Information, Coordinate, and Motivate

The actions of Maria, Ken, Hugo, Mimi, and all the others in the market clearly have an effect on one another. For example, an increase in Hugo's marginal costs—perhaps because of the need to use a new pesticide to ward off an insect infestation—probably will reduce the number of roses he decides to produce; either this means less rose consumption for Ken, Maria, and other consumers, or it means more rose production for Mimi and other producers. Similarly, if Ken finds a new romantic interest and decides to purchase more roses on a weekly basis, someone else must decide to decrease consumption or to increase production.

How are all these decisions worked out? What *information* is needed to determine that an increase in rose production is needed to meet the additional demand coming from Ken or to cover the shortfall in production coming from Hugo? Who *coordinates* whether the production increases needed to meet Ken's demand comes from Hugo's garden or Mimi's garden? Who decides whether

Maria should cut back her consumption or Mimi should increase her production in response to Hugo's production cutbacks? What *motivates* Hugo, Mimi, and others to produce more if consumption rises, or motivates Ken, Maria, and other consumers to consume less if production falls?

Suppose you had to work out all these issues. To make your job easier, suppose that Maria, Ken, Hugo, and Mimi were the whole world as far as roses go. If you and they were all in one place together, you might imagine providing information so that they could adjust their consumption and production activities to respond to changing market conditions. When more production was needed, you would inform Mimi of the problems that Hugo was having and ask her to increase the number of roses she produces to make up for the shortfall. When Ken started buying more roses, you would have to explain to Maria about Ken's new romantic interest and ask her to cut back on her consumption, or you would have to inform Hugo and Mimi that they need to increase production to meet Ken's insatiable demand for roses.

But simply providing information is not enough. You also would have to coordinate the responses of the various consumers and firms. In response to Ken's increased purchases of roses, for example, you would have to determine how much of the extra output was being produced by Mimi and how much was being produced by Hugo. You also would have to ensure that Maria's consumption plans had not changed in the meantime. Coordinating the actions of even two consumers and two firms can be a challenge.

Even if you provided sufficient information, and in spite of your best attempts at coordinating everyone's responses, there would be no guarantee that either the consumers or the producers would change their behavior unless they had a reason for doing so. To provide motivation, you might reason with Mimi that she could sell more now that Hugo had production problems, or plead with Maria to cut back on her rose purchases until Ken's romantic fervor cools, or cajole Hugo and Mimi to increase production.

If this is not already beginning to sound ridiculously impossible, remember that if you had this job in the real world, you would have to coordinate, motivate, and know intimately millions of consumers and producers. This is an amazingly complex job even for this single, relatively simple commodity.

The Easy Way to Process Information, Coordinate, and Motivate

Fortunately, you do not need to worry about being called on to perform such an impossible task. What Adam Smith showed was that a remarkable device does the information processing, coordinating, and motivating for us. No one person invented this device; it evolved slowly over thousands of years and probably is still evolving. It is called the *market*. Of course, like many markets, the rose market does not take place in any one location. It consists of all the florists, street carts, and farmers' markets where roses are sold and all the gardens and greenhouses where roses are grown, whether in the United States, Europe, Latin America, Africa, Australia, or Asia. Fortunately, a market can serve as an information-processing, coordinating, and motivating device even if it does not take place at any one location. In fact, buyers and sellers never even have to see one another.

How does the market work? What will be the total quantity of roses consumed? Who will consume what amount? What will be the total quantity of roses produced? Which firm will produce what amount? Let us see how economists answer these questions about how people interact in a market.

FIGURE 7.3 One-Stop Shopping for Processing Information, Coordinating, and Motivating: The Market
This flower vendor in Barcelona, Spain, represents just one piece of the huge and multifaceted market for flowers that exists throughout the world.

Source: © Gordana Sermek/Shutterstock, Inc.

The Competitive Equilibrium Model

Economists use the *individual* demand curves and the *individual* supply curves derived in Chapter 5 and Chapter 6 to describe what happens to consumers and firms when they interact in a market.

Recall that each of the individual demand curves depends on the marginal benefit—the willingness to pay for additional consumption—the individual gets from consuming a good. Together, these marginal benefits create a market demand curve for roses. The demand curve shows how much consumers in total are willing to buy at each price.

Recall also that individual supply curves depend on the marginal costs of the firms. Together, their marginal costs create a market supply curve for roses. The supply curve shows the total quantity supplied by all firms at each price.

The resulting market demand and supply curves are shown in the center of Figure 7.4, flanked by Maria's and Ken's individual demand curves and by Hugo's and Mimi's individual supply curves. We continue to assume that Maria, Ken, Hugo, and Mimi are the whole market so that we can show the market in one diagram. A competitive market typically would require more buyers and sellers. The price (*P*, measured in dollars per rose) is on the vertical axis, and the quantity (*Q*, the number of roses) is on the horizontal axis.

We have seen supply and demand curves like those in the center of Figure 7.4 before in Chapter 3. But now—after Chapter 5 and Chapter 6—we know much more about what the demand and supply curves mean. Individual consumer behavior and individual firm behavior now are seen as underlying the supply and demand model. To emphasize that the supply and demand model incorporates utility-maximizing consumers and profit-maximizing firms in competitive markets, we refer to it as the *competitive equilibrium model*. Making the behavior of consumers and firms more explicit implies that we can do more analysis with the competitive equilibrium model than we previously were able to do with the supply and demand model.

FIGURE 7.4 Price and Quantity Determination
The market demand curve is the sum of the individual demand curves of the consumers in the market. The market supply curve is the sum of the individual supply curves for the producers. When quantity demanded equals quantity supplied, the two curves intersect. The equilibrium price and quantity will be given by this intersection. The individual firm and consumer decisions then can be read off the individual supply and demand curves at those prices.

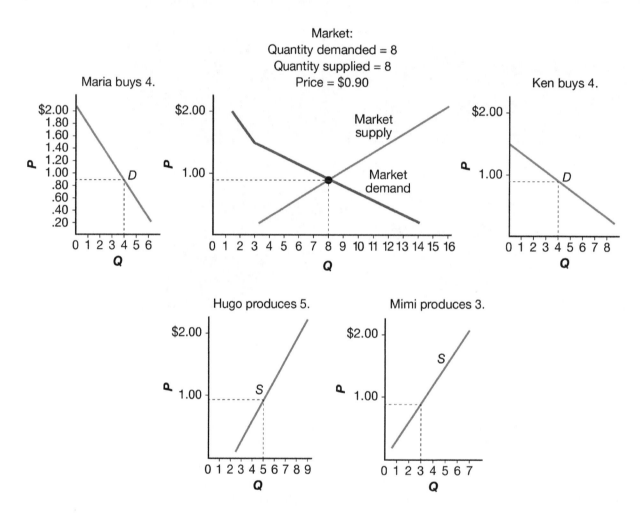

Individual Production and Consumption Decisions

equilibrium price

The price at which quantity supplied equals quantity demanded.

A key prediction of the competitive equilibrium model is that a price will emerge from the interaction of people in the market such that the quantity supplied *equals* the quantity demanded. This is the **equilibrium price**. Graphically, the price is given at the point of intersection of the market supply curve and the market demand curve; here, the quantity supplied in the market equals the quantity demanded in the market. For the example shown in Figure 7.4, the equilibrium price is $0.90 a rose.

Once we have determined the price in this way, the supply and demand curves tell us how much in total will be consumed and produced at that price. We look at the market demand curve and see how much is demanded at that price, and we look at the market supply curve and see how much is supplied at that price. Because the curves intersect at the market price, the quantity demanded and the quantity supplied are the same. They are at the point on the horizontal axis directly below the intersection. In Figure 7.4, the quantity bought and sold is eight roses.

Thus far, we have not done anything more with the competitive equilibrium model than we did with the supply and demand model. But now, armed with the price, we can go to the individual demand curves to see how much Maria and Ken will buy. Look to the left in Figure 7.4 to find the quantity demanded by Maria and by Ken when the price is $0.90 a rose. They each buy four roses. Maria and Ken are motivated to buy this amount—without any central coordinator—because, at $0.90 a rose, they maximize their respective utilities by consuming this amount. Observe that Maria and Ken do not have the same individual demand curves. Nevertheless, the quantity demanded by each still can be determined from their demand curves, as shown in Figure 7.4.

The individual supply curves tell us how much Hugo and Mimi will produce. Look to the bottom in Figure 7.4 to see how much Hugo and Mimi produce when the price is $0.90 a rose. Hugo produces five roses, and Mimi produces three roses. Hugo and Mimi are motivated to produce this amount—again without any central coordinator—because, at $0.90 a rose, they maximize their profits by producing this amount. In sum, the competitive equilibrium model, which includes the behavior of the consumers and the firms, not only predicts the equilibrium price and quantity in the market, but also predicts the quantity consumed by each person and the quantity produced by each firm.

Adjustment to the Equilibrium Price

In Figure 7.4, consider what would happen if the price were higher than the price at the intersection of the supply curve and the demand curve, say $1.20. At that price, utility-maximizing consumers like Ken and Maria would decrease their consumption to three units (Maria) and two units (Ken), so the quantity demanded would be five units. However, at the higher price, profit maximizers like Hugo and Mimi would increase their production, with Hugo producing six units and Mimi producing four units. The quantity supplied would exceed the quantity demanded; there would be a **surplus** in the market. When surplus appears, the price will fall, resulting in the quantity demanded increasing and the quantity supplied decreasing until the surplus disappears.

Conversely, suppose the price were lower than the predicted market price, say $0.60. At that price, utility maximizers like Ken and Maria would increase consumption to six units (Ken) and five units (Maria), so the quantity demanded would be 11 units. However, at the lower price, profit maximizers like Hugo and Mimi would decrease their production, with Hugo producing four units and Mimi producing two units. The quantity supplied would be much less than the quantity demanded; there would be a **shortage** in the market. When a shortage appears, the price will rise, resulting in the quantity demanded decreasing and the quantity supplied increasing until the shortage disappears. Thus, if the price falls when there is a surplus and rises when there is a shortage, the actions of profit-maximizing firms and utility-maximizing consumers will ensure that the price will converge to the equilibrium price.

surplus

A situation in which quantity supplied is greater than quantity demanded.

shortage

A situation in which quantity demanded is greater than quantity supplied.

Review

- Centrally coordinating and motivating the thousands of consumers and producers of any good would be an amazingly complex task requiring a vast amount of information.
- The market is a device that provides information and coordinates and motivates consumers and producers in a decentralized way. The market does this job in a way that no one individual can.
- Economists describe the interactions of people in the market through the competitive equilibrium model, which is the supply and demand model with consumer and firm behavior made more explicit.
- According to the model, the equilibrium price and quantity are given by the intersection of the market supply and demand curves. At the equilibrium price, we can use the individual

demand curves to find out each individual's decisions about consumption and use the individual firms' supply curves to figure out each firm's production decisions.

7.2 Are Competitive Markets Efficient?

We have shown how to use the competitive equilibrium model to explain *how* a market works. Now let's use the competitive equilibrium model to see *how well* the market works. Are the quantities produced and consumed in the market efficient?

The Meaning of Efficient

In general, an inefficient outcome is one that wastes scarce resources, and an efficient outcome is one that does not waste scarce resources. Extremely inefficient economic outcomes are easy to spot. Constructing 300 million new coffeehouses each year in the United States (or approximately one store per person) obviously would be wasteful. The workers building the new stores could be building other things that people wanted. If the U.S. economy produced such an outcome, everyone would say it was inefficient; shifting production to fewer coffeehouses clearly would make many people better off.

An equally inefficient situation would occur if only one new coffeehouse a year were built; at that rate, it would take more than 7,000 years to match the number of Starbucks stores that now exist in the United States. In such a situation, shifting production toward more coffeehouses clearly would make many people better off.

Both of these situations are inefficient because a change in production could make people better off. We might, therefore, define an efficient outcome as one that is so good that no change would make people better off.

The Need for a More Precise Definition

Because the economy consists of many different people, however, we need to be more careful in defining efficiency. For every economic outcome, it is possible to make someone better off at the expense of someone else. If someone takes a long-stemmed rose from Maria and gives it to Ken, then Ken is better off, but Maria is worse off. More generally, the possibility of transferring a good from one person to another, thereby making someone better off at the expense of someone else, is not an indication that an economic situation is inefficient or wasteful.

However, if a situation existed in which it was possible to change consumption or production in a way that would make someone better off without hurting someone else, then that situation would be inefficient. In such a situation, resources are being wasted, because someone, perhaps many people, could have a better life without someone else being harmed.

Based on such considerations, economists have developed the following definition of efficiency: An outcome is **Pareto efficient** if it is not possible to make someone better off without hurting someone else. The Italian economist Vilfredo Pareto is the person who developed this concept of efficiency. Economists use the term *Pareto* to distinguish this definition of efficiency from other meanings, but unless we say otherwise, when we use the term *efficient* in this chapter, we mean efficient in the sense of Pareto. If a market is not efficient in the sense of Pareto, then something is wrong with the market.

Three Conditions for Efficient Outcomes

Three conditions must hold if a market outcome is to be efficient in the sense of Pareto efficiency.

First, the marginal benefit (MB) must equal the marginal cost (MC) of the last item produced. Why is this condition needed for efficiency? Suppose it did not hold. If the marginal cost of the last item produced is greater than the marginal benefit, then too much is being produced. In the example of producing 300 million coffeehouses a year, the marginal cost of producing the 300 millionth coffeehouse is much greater than the marginal benefit. Reducing production (by a lot) would be appropriate. If the marginal cost of the last item produced is less than the marginal benefit, then too little is being produced. In the example of producing only one coffeehouse a year, the marginal cost is certainly much less than the marginal benefit; more production would be appropriate. Only when marginal benefit is equal to marginal cost is the economic outcome efficient.

One way to better appreciate this condition is to imagine that you grow your own roses in your own garden. Clearly you would never produce more roses if the marginal cost to you was greater than the marginal benefit to you. But you would produce more roses if your marginal benefit from more roses was greater than your marginal cost. Only when marginal benefit equals marginal cost would you stop producing and consuming more.

The second condition for efficiency relates to the production of goods at different firms. It is that *the marginal cost of a good should be equal for every producer*. Again, if this were not the case, then production could be increased without increasing costs. For example, if Hugo's rose garden could produce an extra dozen roses at a marginal cost of $10 and Mimi's rose garden could produce an extra dozen roses at a marginal cost of $50, then it would make sense for Mimi to reduce her production of roses by a dozen, saving her $50, and use that money to pay Hugo to produce two dozen roses that she could then sell on the market. Both Hugo and Mimi would be better off as a result. Only when the marginal costs are the same can production increase without cost. It is not necessary for Hugo and Mimi or any other producer to be the same or even to have the same total costs; all that we require for efficiency is that the *marginal* costs be the same.

The third condition for efficiency relates to the allocation of goods to different consumers. It is that *the marginal benefit of consuming the same good should be equal for all consumers*. If the marginal benefits were not equal, then there could be a gain for some people with no loss for anyone else. For example, suppose Ken's marginal benefit from a rose was $3 and Maria's was $1; then if Maria sold a rose to Ken for $2, both would be better off. But if their marginal benefits were the same, then no improvement for one without harming the other would be possible.

In sum, three conditions are needed for efficiency: (1) the marginal benefit equals the marginal cost for the last item produced; (2) the marginal cost of producing each good is equal for all producers; and (3) the marginal benefit from consuming each good is equal for all consumers.

First efficiency condition: MB = MC for last item produced.

Second efficiency condition: Every producer's MC is the same.

Third efficiency condition: Every consumer's MB is the same.

Pareto efficient

A situation in which it is not possible to make someone better off without making someone else worse off.

Is the Market Efficient?

Now that we know the three conditions for efficiency, can we say that the market is efficient? The competitive equilibrium model provides us with a quick answer to that question.

According to the model of consumer behavior in Chapter 5, an individual consumer chooses a quantity of a good such that *price equals marginal benefit*—that is, $P = MB$. This equality holds for every consumer at every point on the market demand curve. According to the model of firm behavior in Chapter 6, a firm produces a quantity of a good such that *price equals marginal cost*. That is, $P = MC$. This equality holds for every firm at every point on the market supply curve. At a point of intersection of the supply curve and the demand curve, both of these conditions must hold because the point of intersection is on both the supply curve and the demand curve and the price P is the same. That is, $P = MB$ and $P = MC$ simultaneously. This implies that at the quantity produced by the market, *marginal benefit equals marginal cost*. That is, $MB = MC$. This is true of every good.

Thus we have proved that a competitive market satisfies the first condition of efficiency. The marginal cost of producing roses, grapes, bread, peanuts, or automobiles is equal to the marginal benefit that people get from consuming them. This occurs without any person coordinating consumers and producers.

The result is illustrated in Figure 7.5. At the market equilibrium quantity (point E), the marginal cost (the point on the supply curve) is equal to the marginal benefit (the point on the demand curve). At any other point, either marginal benefit will be greater than marginal cost or marginal benefit will be less than marginal cost.

FIGURE 7.5 The Efficiency of the Market: Marginal Benefit Equals Marginal Cost
Only at quantity E is the marginal benefit of an extra unit equal to the marginal cost of an extra unit. Point D is not efficient because the marginal benefit of an extra unit is greater than the marginal cost of producing it. Point F is also not efficient because the marginal cost of producing an extra unit is greater than the marginal benefit.

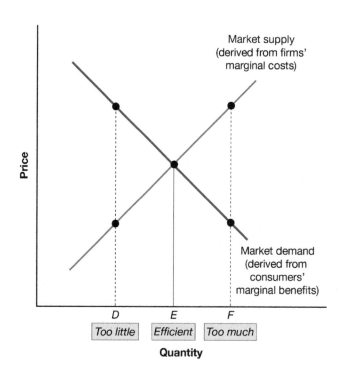

The other two criteria for efficiency also hold in a competitive market. To see this, it will help to look back at Figure 7.4. Observe that, in a market equilibrium, the marginal cost for the producers is the same, because *they all face the same price*. Along each of their individual supply curves, all producers—Hugo, Mimi, and others—set marginal cost equal to the price. Similarly, in a market equilibrium, *all consumers*—Maria, Ken, and others—*face the same market price*. Hence, their marginal benefits are all equal, because on each of their individual demand curves the marginal benefit equals the price.

Here's the reason in a nutshell why the first condition is satisfied: P = MB and P = MC. Thus since P = P, we must have MC = MB.

Here's the reason in a nutshell why the second condition is satisfied: Hugo's MC = P. Mimi's MC = P. Thus, Hugo's MC = Mimi's MC.

Here's the reason in a nutshell why the third condition is satisfied: Maria's MB = P. Ken's MB = P. Thus, Maria's MB = Ken's MB.

In sum, for each good produced in a competitive market, (1) the marginal benefit equals the marginal cost of the last item produced, (2) the marginal cost is equal for all producers in the market, and (3) the marginal benefit is equal for all consumers in the market. Thus, we can say that the competitive market is Pareto efficient. In a competitive market, it is not possible to make one person better off without hurting someone else.

The proposition that competitive markets are efficient is one of the most important in economics, so much so that when it is proven with the mathematics necessary to keep track of many different goods and time periods, it is called the **first theorem of welfare economics**. The word *welfare* means that the theorem is about the overall well-being of people in the economy (the word *welfare* is synonymous with "well-being," not with a transfer payment to a poor person). The word *first* is used to distinguish this theorem from the second theorem of welfare economics, which states the converse of the first: Any Pareto efficient outcome can be obtained via a competitive market.

first theorem of welfare economics

The conclusion that a competitive market results in an efficient outcome; sometimes called the "invisible hand theorem"; the definition of efficiency used in the theorem is Pareto efficiency.

Efficiency and Income Inequality

Efficiency is an important goal of an economic system, but it is not the only goal. Another goal is to avoid outcomes in which a few people earn most of the income and do most of the consumption in the economy, while the rest of the population falls into dire economic circumstances. Thus, reducing **income inequality** is another desirable goal in most economic systems.

income inequality

Disparity in levels of income among individuals in the economy.

It is important to emphasize that efficiency and income equality are not the same thing. An allocation of bread between Hugo and Mimi is efficient if their marginal benefit of bread is the same and if the marginal benefits equal the marginal cost of bread. Then no mutually advantageous trade of bread between Hugo and Mimi will make one better off without hurting the other.

However, suppose that Hugo has a low income, earning only $7,000 per year, and that Mimi has a high income, earning $70,000 per year. Suppose a severe drought raises the price of wheat and thus the price of bread. If the price of bread in the market gets very high, say, $3 a loaf, then Hugo will be able to buy few loaves of bread and may go hungry, especially if he has a family. In this case, the economy gets good marks on efficiency grounds but fails on income inequality grounds.

To remedy the situation, a common suggestion is to put price controls on bread. For example, to help Hugo and others like him, a law might be passed requiring that bread prices not exceed $0.50 a loaf. Although this may help the income inequality problem, it will cause inefficiency because it interferes with the market. At $0.50 a loaf, bread producers will not produce much, and Mimi probably will start buying bread to feed the birds, wasting scarce resources.

The temptation to deal with income inequality problems in ways that interfere with the efficiency of the market is great in all societies. Price ceilings (rent controls) on rental apartments in some U.S. cities, which we examined in Chapter 4, are one example. A better solution to the income inequality problem is to transfer income to Hugo and other low-income people from Mimi and other high-income people. With a transfer of income—say, through an income-support payment to the poor—the market would be able to function and the inefficiencies caused by price controls on bread would not occur. Even at the high price of bread, Hugo will be able to eat, perhaps buying some rice or a bread substitute, and the bread, which is so expensive to produce, will not be wasted on the birds. We will see that such transfers have advantages and disadvantages. Compared with price controls, their main advantage is that they allow the market to operate efficiently. On the other hand, such transfer programs typically will have to be financed through taxes, which often are going to create inefficiencies, as you will see in one of the sections that follows.

 ### Market Efficiency as One of the "First Principles"

Watch this video on a conversation of the importance of economic freedom and free markets for economic prosperity.

View the video online at: http://www.youtube.com/embed/uk6HwKZAEs4?rel=0

Review

- Economic inefficiency implies a waste of resources. A Pareto efficient outcome is one in which no person's situation can be improved without hurting someone else.
- Three conditions must hold if an outcome is to be Pareto efficient. These conditions are that (1) the marginal benefit of the last item produced must equal its marginal cost, (2) the marginal cost of production for all producers must be identical, and (3) the marginal benefit for all consumers must be identical.
- If marginal benefit exceeds marginal cost, then too little of the good is being produced, whereas if marginal cost exceeds marginal benefit, too much of the good is being produced. In both cases, adjusting the quantity being produced would enhance efficiency.
- If the marginal costs of producers were not identical, then it would be possible to increase production without increasing costs, simply by making the producer with the high marginal cost produce less and the producer with the low marginal cost produce more.
- Finally, if marginal benefits are not identical, then having the person with the high marginal benefit buy the item from the person with the low marginal benefit for a price that is in between the two marginal benefits would enhance efficiency by making both parties better off.
- One of the most desirable features of competitive markets is that at the equilibrium level of production, on the demand curve, marginal benefit equals the market price, while on the supply curve, marginal cost equals the market price. Together, these imply that marginal benefit equals marginal cost.

- Similarly, because all consumers and all firms face the same market price, the marginal benefits of each consumer will be identical (and equal to the market price), as will the marginal costs of each individual producer.
- Thus, competitive markets are efficient. Any change in consumption or production that makes one person better off must make someone else worse off.
- Efficiency is not the same thing as equality. An efficient outcome can coexist with an unequal outcome.
- Attempts to remedy an unequal situation by the use of price ceilings or by rationing lead to inefficiencies in production and consumption. It may be better to redistribute resources from the more affluent to the less well off.

7.3 Measuring Waste from Inefficiency

We know from Chapter 5 and Chapter 6 that consumer surplus and producer surplus are measures of how much consumers and producers gain from buying and selling in a market. The larger these two surpluses are, the better off people are.

Maximizing the Sum of Producer Plus Consumer Surplus

An attractive feature of competitive markets is that they maximize the sum of consumer and producer surplus. Producer and consumer surplus are shown in the market supply and market demand diagram in Figure 7.6. Recall that the producer surplus for all producers is the area above the supply curve and below the market price line, and that the consumer surplus for all consumers is the area below the demand curve and above the market price line. Both the consumer surplus and the producer surplus are shown in Figure 7.6. The lightly shaded area is the sum of consumer surplus plus producer surplus. The equilibrium quantity is at the intersection of the two curves.

FIGURE 7.6 Measuring Economic Loss

When production is less or more than the market equilibrium amount, the economic loss is measured by the loss of consumer surplus plus producer surplus. In the top diagram, the quantity produced is too small. In the bottom diagram, it is too large. In the middle diagram, it is efficient.

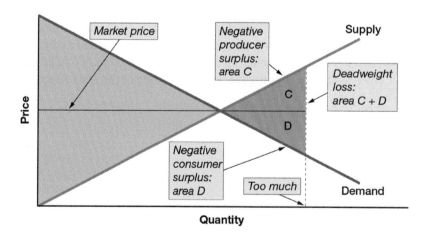

Deadweight Loss

We can show that at the equilibrium price and quantity, consumer surplus plus producer surplus is maximized. Figure 7.6 also shows what happens to consumer surplus plus producer surplus when the efficient level of production does not occur. The middle panel of Figure 7.6 shows what the sum of consumer surplus and producer surplus is at market equilibrium. The top panel of Figure 7.6 shows a situation in which the quantity produced is lower than the market equilibrium quantity. Clearly, the sum of consumer and producer surplus is lower. By producing a smaller quantity, we lose the amount of the consumer and producer surplus in the darkly shaded triangular area $A + B$. The bottom panel of Figure 7.6 shows the opposite situation, in which the quantity produced is too high. In this case, we have to subtract the triangular area $C + D$ from the lightly shaded area on the left because price is greater than marginal benefit and lower than marginal cost, which means that consumer surplus and producer surplus are negative in the area $C + D$. In both the top and bottom panels of the figure, these darkly shaded triangles are a loss to society from producing more or less than the efficient amount. Economists call the loss in this darkly shaded area the **deadweight loss**. It is a measure of the waste from inefficient production.

Deadweight loss is not simply a theoretical curiosity with a morbid name; it is used by economists to measure the size of the waste to society of deviations from the competitive equilibrium. By calculating deadweight loss, economists can estimate the benefits and costs of many government programs. When you hear or read that the cost of U.S. agricultural programs is billions of dollars or that the benefit of a world-trade agreement is trillions of dollars, it is the increase or decrease in deadweight loss that is being referred to. To compute the deadweight loss, all we need is the demand curve and the supply curve.

Another way to think about the lightly shaded areas in the graphs: The sum of consumer surplus plus producer surplus is the triangular area between the demand curve and the supply curve—shown by the lightly shaded area in the middle graph of Figure 7.6. The graph shows another way to think about this sum: The sum of consumer surplus plus producer surplus equals the marginal benefit minus the marginal cost of all the items produced.

 Deadweight Loss

Deadweight loss is the economic loss which occurs when the market is not operating efficiently.

View the video online at: http://www.youtube.com/embed/-mEn9zxQ0Q0?rel=0

deadweight loss

The loss in producer and consumer surplus because of an inefficient level of production.

7.4 The Deadweight Loss from Price Floors and Ceilings

In Chapter 4, we used the supply and demand model to examine situations in which governments have attempted to control market prices because they were unhappy with the outcome of the market, or because they were pressured by groups who would benefit from price controls. We examined two broad types of price controls: price ceilings, which specify a maximum price at which a good can be bought or sold, and price floors, which specify a minimum price at which a good can be bought or sold. An example of a price floor was the minimum wage, and an example of a price ceiling was a rent control policy.

Using the supply and demand model, we were able to illustrate some of the problems that stemmed from the imposition of price floors or ceilings. When a price floor that is higher than the equilibrium price is imposed, the result will be persistent surpluses of the good. This situation is illustrated by Figure 7.7. The surpluses imply that an inefficient allocation of resources is going toward the good whose price has been inflated artificially. Frequently, costly government programs will be created to buy up surplus production. When a price ceiling that is lower than the equilibrium price is imposed on a market, then the result will be persistent shortages of the good. These shortages mean that mechanisms like rationing, waiting lines, or black markets will be used to allocate the now scarce good. This situation is illustrated by Figure 7.8. Now that we understand the concepts of consumer and producer surplus as well as the idea of deadweight loss, we can use these tools to quantify the negative impacts of price ceilings and price floors.

FIGURE 7.7 Price and Quantity Effects of a Price Floor
If the price floor is set higher than the competitive market price, the quantity demanded by consumers decreases and the quantity supplied by firms increases, creating excess supply.

FIGURE 7.8 Price and Quantity Effects of a Price Ceiling
If the price ceiling is set below the competitive market price, the quantity demanded by consumers increases and the quantity supplied by firms decreases, creating excess demand.

The Deadweight Loss from a Price Floor

Figure 7.9 shows how consumer and producer surplus are affected by the imposition of a price floor. Before the imposition of the price floor, the sum of consumer and producer surplus is given by the area of the triangle *ABC*, of which the area *BCD* denotes consumer surplus and the area *ACD* denotes producer surplus.

Now consider what happens to consumer surplus and producer surplus when a price floor is imposed. The impact on producer surplus is ambiguous. On the one hand, those producers who are fortunate enough to sell at a higher price will obtain more producer surplus. But because the quantity demanded is lower at the higher price, there will be a loss of producer surplus for those producers who previously were able to sell the good but now have no buyers. Producer surplus would be given by the area *AEFG*, which reflects an increase of *DEFI* (shown in the vertical striped area) and a decrease of *CGI* (shown in the shaded area) from the previous level of producer surplus. Consumer surplus is reduced unambiguously by the amount *CDEF* (shown in cross-hatched lines). Overall, when we add up the lost consumer and producer surplus and the gained producer surplus, a deadweight loss is equivalent to the area *CFG* in Figure 7.9.

FIGURE 7.9 The Deadweight Loss from a Price Floor
The price floor creates an excess supply of goods at the new higher price. Consumers are unambiguously worse off. Producers may be better off or worse off depending on whether they are able to sell at the higher price. The sum of consumer and producer surplus is lower, indicating a deadweight loss associated with the floor.

The Deadweight Loss from a Price Ceiling

Figure 7.10 shows how consumer and producer surplus are affected by the imposition of a price ceiling. As before, before the imposition of the price ceiling, the sum of consumer and producer surplus is given by the area of the triangle *ABC*, of which the area *BCD* denotes consumer surplus and the area *ACD* denotes producer surplus.

FIGURE 7.10 The Deadweight Loss from a Price Ceiling
The price ceiling creates an excess demand for goods at the new lower price. Producers are unambiguously worse off. Consumers may be better or worse off depending on whether they are able to buy at the lower price. The sum of consumer and producer surplus is lower, indicating a deadweight loss associated with the ceiling.

Now consider what happens to consumer surplus and producer surplus when a price ceiling is imposed. The impact on consumer surplus is ambiguous: Those consumers who are able to acquire the good at the lower price will obtain more consumer surplus. Because only a smaller quantity of goods is available for purchase, however, there will be a loss of consumer surplus for those who previously were able to buy the good but now cannot. Consumer surplus would be given by the area *BFGH*, which reflects an increase of *DHGI* (shown in the vertically striped area) and a decrease of *CFI* (shown in cross-hatched area) from the previous level of consumer surplus. Producer surplus is reduced unambiguously by the amount *CDHG* (shown by the shaded area). Overall, when we combine the lost consumer and producer surplus with the gained consumer surplus, a deadweight loss is equivalent to the area *CFG* in Figure 7.10.

Review

- Both price floors and price ceilings bring about deadweight loss. Some parties clearly lose; other parties may gain, but overall, the losses exceed the gains.

- In the case of a price floor, consumers unambiguously lose because they buy fewer units at a higher price. Some producers gain because they are able to sell at a higher price than before. Others lose because they are no longer able to sell the good because the government does not allow them to lower the price to attract buyers.

- In the case of a price ceiling, producers unambiguously lose because they sell fewer units at a lower price. Some consumers gain because they are able to buy the good at a lower price than before. Others lose because they are no longer able to buy the good, even though they are willing to pay more, because the government does not allow firms to raise the price.

7.5 The Deadweight Loss From Taxation

Another important application of deadweight loss is in estimating the impact of a tax. To see how, let's examine the impact of a tax on a good. We will see that the tax shifts the supply curve, leads to a reduction in the quantity produced, and reduces the sum of producer surplus plus consumer surplus.

Figure 7.11 shows a supply and demand diagram for a particular good. In the absence of the tax, the sum of producer and consumer surplus is given by the area of the triangle *ABC*, of which the area *BCD* denotes consumer surplus and the area *ACD* denotes producer surplus.

A Tax Paid by a Producer Shifts the Supply Curve

A tax on sales is a payment that must be made to the government by the seller of a product. The tax may be a percentage of the dollar value spent on the products sold, in which case it is called an ad valorem tax. A 6 percent state tax on retail purchases is an *ad valorem tax*. Or it may be proportional to the number of items sold, in which case the tax is called a *specific tax*. A tax on gasoline of $0.50 per gallon is an example of a specific tax.

Because the tax payment is made by the producer or the seller to the government, the immediate impact of the tax is to add to the marginal cost of producing the product. Hence, the immediate impact of the tax will be to shift the supply curve. For example, suppose each producer has to send a certain amount, say, $0.50 per gallon of gasoline produced and sold, to the government. Then $0.50 must be added to the marginal cost per gallon for each producer.

The resulting shift of the supply curve is shown in Figure 7.11. The vertical distance between the old and the new supply curves is the size of the sales tax in dollars. The supply curve shifts up by this amount because this is how much is added to the marginal costs of the producer. (Observe that this upward shift can just as accurately be called a leftward shift because the new supply curve is above and to the left of the old curve. Saying that the supply curve shifts up may seem confusing because when we say "up," we seem to mean "more supply." But the "up" is along the vertical axis, which has the price on it. The upward, or leftward, movement of the supply curve is in the direction of less supply, not more supply.)

FIGURE 7.11 Deadweight Loss from a Tax

In this graph, the lightly shaded triangle represents the deadweight loss and the shaded rectangle the amount of tax revenue that goes to the government. The sales tax, which is collected and paid to the government by the seller, adds to the marginal cost of each item the producer sells. Hence, the supply curve shifts up. The price rises, but by less than the tax increase.

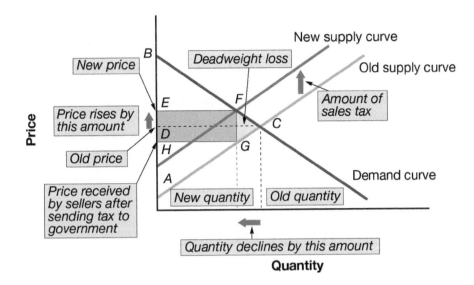

A New Equilibrium Price and Quantity

What does the competitive equilibrium model imply about the change in the price and the quantity produced? Observe the new intersection of the supply curve and the demand curve. Thus, the price rises to a new, higher level, and the quantity produced declines.

The price increase, as shown in Figure 7.11, is not as large as the increase in the tax. The vertical distance between the old and the new supply curves is the amount of the tax, but the price increases by less than this distance. Thus, the producers are not able to "pass on" the entire tax to the consumers in the form of higher prices. If the tax increase is $0.50, then the price increase is less than $0.50, perhaps $0.40. The producers have been forced by the market—by the movement along the demand curve—to reduce their production, and by doing so they have absorbed some of the impact of the tax increase.

Deadweight Loss and Tax Revenue

Now consider what happens to consumer surplus and producer surplus with the sales tax. Because the total quantity produced is lower, there is a loss in consumer surplus and producer surplus. The right part of the triangle of consumer plus producer surplus, corresponding to the area *CFG*, has been cut off, and this is the deadweight loss to society, as shown in Figure 7.11.

Consumer surplus is now given by the triangle *BEF*, while producer surplus is given by the triangle *AGH* (keep in mind that producers do not receive the new price; they only get the new price less the tax). The tax generates revenue for the government that can be used to finance government activity. Some of what was producer surplus and consumer surplus thus goes to the government. If the tax is $1 and 100 items are sold, the tax revenue is $100. This amount is shown by the shaded rectangle *EFGH* on the diagram. Adding up consumer and producer surplus plus the government revenue gives us an area corresponding to *ABFG*, which differs from the original sum of consumer and producer surplus (*ABC*) by the magnitude of the deadweight loss (*CFG*). So even though taxes may be necessary to finance the government, they cause a deadweight loss to society in the form of lost consumer surplus and producer surplus that are no longer available to anyone in the economy.

Review

- The impact of a tax on the economy can be analyzed using consumer surplus and producer surplus.
- Taxes are necessary to finance government expenditures, but they lower the production of the item being taxed.
- The loss to society from the decline in production is measured by the reduction in consumer surplus and producer surplus, the deadweight loss due to the tax.

7.6 Informational Efficiency

FIGURE 7.12 Coordination Without a Market
Although prices provide a valuable coordination role in a market economy, some activities are better coordinated without the market. It would not be efficient to coordinate each of the hand and foot movements of these skydivers with prices.

Source: Mauricio Graiki/Shutterstock.com

We have shown that a competitive market works well in that the outcome is Pareto efficient. For every good, the sum of consumer surplus and producer surplus is maximized. These are important and attractive characteristics of a competitive market.

Another important and attractive characteristic of a competitive market is that the market processes information efficiently. For example, in a competitive market, the price reflects the marginal benefit for every buyer and the marginal cost for every seller. If a government official were asked to set the price in a real market, there would be no way that such information could be obtained, especially with millions of buyers and sellers. In other words, the market seems to be informationally efficient. Pareto efficiency is different from this *informational efficiency*.

In the 1930s and 1940s, as the government of the former Soviet Union tried to centrally plan production in the entire economy, economists became more interested in the informational efficiency of markets. One of the most outspoken critics of central planning, and a strong advocate of the market system, was Friedrich Hayek, who emphasized the importance of the informational efficiencies of the market. In Hayek's view, a major disadvantage of central planning—in which the government sets all the prices and all the quantities—is that it is informationally inefficient.

If you had all the information about all the buyers and sellers in the market, you could set the price to achieve a Pareto efficient outcome. To see Hayek's point, it is perhaps enough to observe that, without private information about every one of the millions of buyers and sellers, you or any government official would not know where to set the price. However, economists do not have results as neat as the first theorem of welfare economics to prove Hayek's point. In some situations, the market would be unwieldy, and it is difficult to describe these situations with any generality.

Difficulties arise in using a market system in situations in which prices will not bring about a sufficiently precise or speedy response. For example, if demand for furniture made out of mahogany timber rises, it is difficult for producers to meet that demand immediately, because it takes several dozen years for a mahogany tree to reach maturity. In such a situation, unscrupulous producers may chop down mahogany trees in a public forest to meet the demand. This result implies that we should not rely solely on the competitive market system to motivate producers to increase production in situations in which property rights are weak or communal resources need to be managed. Nevertheless, a competitive market system offers considerable informational advantages over other systems.

Review

- The market has the ability to process information efficiently. The lack of informational efficiency is a key reason why central planning does not work well in complex and changing environments.
- For some activities, however, the market has few informational advantages. A production process in situations in which property rights are weak or in which communal resources need to be managed will be poorly coordinated through prices.

7.7 End-of-Chapter Materials

Conclusion

Adam Smith's idea of the "invisible hand" is perhaps the most important discovery in economics: Individuals, by freely pursuing their own interests in a market economy, are led as if by an invisible hand to an outcome that is best overall. The first theorem of welfare economics is the modern statement of Adam Smith's famous principle; in tribute to Smith's seminal idea, we call it the "invisible hand theorem." Understanding why, and under what circumstances, the invisible hand theorem is true is an important part of thinking like an economist.

Understanding the theorem has required an investment in economic model building: The behavior of consumers and the behavior of firms were combined into a competitive equilibrium model describing how consumers and firms interact in markets. This model is an extension of the supply and demand model we used in Chapter 3 and Chapter 4.

Building the competitive equilibrium model has had payoffs beyond understanding this most important theorem in economics. We can use individual demand curves and individual firm supply curves to determine the actions of each individual consumer and each individual producer at the market equilibrium price. Armed with the ideas of consumer surplus and producer surplus, we can measure the costs of deviations from the competitive market equilibrium. Such measures are used by economists to assess the costs and benefits of government programs that interfere, for better or worse, with the market outcomes. Starting with Chapter 10, we will see that deviations from the competitive market equilibrium are caused by monopolies and other factors. But first, in Chapter 8 and Chapter 9, we will look more closely at how costs and production within individual firms and competitive industries change over time.

Key Points

1. Processing information and coordinating and motivating millions of consumption and production decisions is difficult, but the market is a device that can do the job remarkably well.

2. The interaction of producers and consumers in a market can be explained by the competitive equilibrium model, which is the supply and demand model with consumer and firm behavior made more explicit.

3. Using the competitive equilibrium model, we not only can find the equilibrium price and quantity, but also can use each individual's demand curve to find that individual's consumption decision and use each individual firm's supply curve to figure out its production decision.

4. An outcome is Pareto efficient if it is not possible to change production or consumption in a way that will make one person better off without hurting someone else.

5. Pareto efficiency requires three criteria to hold: Marginal benefit must equal marginal cost for the last item produced, all producers must have identical marginal costs, and all consumers must have identical marginal benefits.

6. A competitive market is Pareto efficient. In a competitive market, the sum of producer surplus and consumer surplus is maximized.

7. Efficiency is not the same thing as equality. An efficient outcome can coexist with an unequal outcome.

8. Attempts to remedy an unequal situation by the use of price ceilings or floors lead to inefficiencies in production and consumption. Using transfers to redistribute resources from the more affluent to the less well off may be better than imposing price or quantity controls.

9. Such transfers often need to be financed by tax revenue. The imposition of a tax that reduces the quantity produced creates deadweight loss for society. The competitive equilibrium model can be used to calculate the magnitude of this deadweight loss.

10. The market also has the ability to process information much more efficiently than a central planner could do. However, no general theorems prove the informational efficiency of the market.

Questions for Review

1. What are the information-processing, coordination, and motivation functions that arise when buyers and sellers interact?

2. Why is it difficult for one person or group of persons to perform the functions listed in Question 1? How does the market perform these functions?

3. What is the relationship between the competitive equilibrium model and the supply and demand model?

4. How does the competitive equilibrium model explain the decisions of individual consumers and producers?

5. What is the meaning of Pareto efficiency?

6. What are the conditions that are needed for Pareto efficiency to hold? Why would the violation of any one of those conditions bring about a situation that is not Pareto efficient?

7. How does a competitive market satisfy the conditions that are needed for Pareto efficiency to hold?

8. Why is the sum of consumer surplus and producer surplus maximized in the competitive market?

9. How does the imposition of a price floor create deadweight loss for the economy?

10. How does the imposition of a tax create deadweight loss for the economy?

Problems

1. Suppose that in a competitive market for ukuleles, three buyers (Peter, Paul, and Mary) have the marginal benefit (*MB*) schedules below.

Quantity	MB – Peter ($)	MB – Paul ($)	MB – Mary ($)
1	150	140	130
2	120	110	100
3	90	80	70
4	60	50	40
5	30	20	10

If the equilibrium price is $80, calculate the following:

a. The quantity purchased by each buyer.

b. The consumer surplus for each buyer.

c. The consumer surplus for the market as a whole.

2. In the same market, three sellers (John, George, and Ringo) have the marginal cost (*MC*) schedules shown below.

Quantity	MC – John ($)	MC – George ($)	MC – Ringo ($)
1	30	20	10
2	60	50	40
3	90	80	70
4	120	110	100
5	150	140	130

If the equilibrium price is $80, calculate the following:

a. The quantity produced by each seller.

b. The producer surplus for each seller.

c. The producer surplus for the market as a whole.

3. Using the answers you provided above for Problems 1 and 2, verify that the three efficiency conditions are satisfied for the ukulele market.

4. Firm A and firm B both produce the same product with the following total costs:

Firm A		Firm B	
Quantity Produced	Total Costs ($)	Quantity Produced	Total Costs ($)
1	5	0	2
2	6	1	5
3	8	2	9
4	11	3	14
5	15	4	20

Consider a situation in which the market price is $3 and four units are produced in total: Firm A produces two units, and firm B produces two units.

a. Explain why this situation is not Pareto efficient.

b. Come up with two different production allocations for the two firms that allow the four items to be produced at a lower overall total cost.

c. Which of these two allocations would be the outcome in a competitive market in which both firms maximized profits?

d. How would the actions of the two firms be coordinated in a competitive market to achieve this outcome?

5. Suppose that in the ukulele market described in Problem 2, the government imposes a $40 sales tax, which causes the equilibrium price to go up to $100. Calculate the following:

a. The quantity purchased by each buyer, the consumer surplus for each buyer, and the consumer surplus for the market as a whole.

b. The quantity produced by each seller, the producer surplus for each seller, and the producer surplus for the market as a whole.

c. The amount of revenue collected by the government.

d. The deadweight loss for the economy resulting from the tax.

6. Consider the following supply and demand schedule for candy bars:

Price ($)	Supply (millions of candy bars)	Demand (millions of candy bars)
0.25	2	14
0.50	6	12
0.75	10	10
1.00	14	8
1.25	18	6
1.50	22	4
1.75	26	2

a. Sketch the market supply and demand curves. Show the equilibrium quantity and price.

b. Graphically show the producer surplus and consumer surplus in the market for candy bars.

c. What would happen to the price of this product if a tax of $0.75 per candy bar sold were enacted by the government? Show your answer graphically.

d. Show the deadweight loss due to the tax on your diagram.

7. Suppose that an unanticipated bout of good weather results in almost ideal growing conditions, leading to a substantial increase in the supply of wheat in the United States.

a. Draw a supply and demand diagram to show what will happen to the equilibrium price and quantity of wheat in the United States, assuming that the demand curve does not shift.

b. Suppose the U.S. government observes that the price of wheat is likely to fall rapidly and imposes a price floor equal to the original equilibrium price. What effect does the price floor have on the quantity supplied and demanded of wheat?

c. How are consumer and producer surplus affected by the price floor?

d. Graphically show the deadweight loss created by the price floor.

8. High international prices for soybeans in recent years led many Argentinean farmers to switch land that had been used as pasture to raise cattle to soybean production. This resulted in a shortfall in the supply of beef.

a. Draw a supply and demand diagram to show what will happen to the equilibrium price and quantity of beef in Argentina, assuming that the demand curve does not shift.

b. In March 2007, the Argentinean government, concerned about the rising price of beef, imposed a price ceiling on beef. Assuming that the price ceiling was equal to the original equilibrium price before the supply decreased, what effect does the price ceiling have on the quantity supplied and demanded of beef?

c. How are consumer and producer surplus affected by the price ceiling?

d. Graphically show the deadweight loss created by the price ceiling.

Endnotes

1. T. Nelson and P. Brown, eds. (1827). Smith, Adam. An Inquiry Into the Nature and Causes of the Wealth of Nations. Edinburgh: The University Press, pp.6-7 and p.84. Retrieved from: https://books.google.com/books?id=rpMuAAAAYAAJ&ppis=_e&source=gbs_navlinks_s.

CHAPTER 8

Costs and the Changes at Firms Over Time

On the night before I laid off all 30 of my employees, I dreamed that my two children had perished, buried alive in dirt, while I dug in the wrong place, just five feet away from where they were actually smothered.... For 10 days, everyone in my orbit had been tilting one way one hour, the other the next ... With no clear directive from any authority—public schools were still open—I spent those 10 days sorting through the conflicting chatter, trying to decide what to do. And now I understood abruptly: I would lay everybody off, even my wife. Prune, my Manhattan restaurant, would close at 11:59 p.m. on March 15.[1]

This evocative news story was one example of an unfortunately widespread COVID-19 phenomenon—a restaurant, impacted by the stay-at-home orders, the need for social distancing, and reluctance of consumers to gather in crowded places, being forced to shut its doors forever. Restaurants are an ephemeral business. Even in a boom year, many restaurants shut down and a majority of new restaurants don't make it past the first year. For instance, the arrival of a new Italian restaurant headlined by a celebrity chef may lead to a shutting down of a beloved family run trattoria in a city or lead to a decision by a large chain to choose another city for expanding their franchise. But the COVID-19 crisis has been particularly damaging to the restaurant industry given that it has led to an unprecedented, across the board reduction in restaurant patronage. Even though restaurants have been able to keep going for a few months by providing takeout and delivery meals, in the long-run the money they earn through those sales will not cover the costs of staying in business in the form of bills that need to be paid for rent, salaries, liquor licenses, and utilities. By the end of 2020, thousands of restaurants that existed at the end of 2019 would likely not be in business anymore, many more than would shut down in a typical year.

Outside of a pandemic, more firms start up each year in the United States—some 700,000—than shut down so that the number of firms in existence continues to increase year after year. Many of these firms are successful and will expand, but others may have to downsize and eventually shut down. The purpose of this chapter is to develop a model for analyzing the changes at firms over time. To do so, we will extend the model of firm behavior developed in Chapter 6.

FIGURE 8.1 The Rise and Fall of Businesses
Small businesses make up the largest share of businesses in the United States, employing, on average, half of all private-sector employees. Nearly 23 million small businesses operate in the United States, and they open and close at a fairly steady rate. At least two-thirds of small businesses survive the first two years; about 50 percent are still open after four years. Small businesses close for a variety of reasons, including lack of adequate capital, but some businesses simply run their course.

Source: Carolyn Franks/Shutterstock.com

What we will find in this chapter is that costs are of vital importance to a firm's decision to start up or shut down. Some of the most successful new firms in the United States, as well as some of the most rapidly growing older firms, have prospered because of their ability to use innovative management techniques and new technologies that cut costs. For example, Jeffrey Bezos founded Amazon.com, which was able to become one of the largest bookstores in the world by conducting its entire business online on the Web, thus avoiding the "brick and mortar" costs of building or renting space in which to sell books. Walmart—a firm that expanded rapidly in the past two decades—developed a system whereby sales clerks electronically scan a barcode on each item and automatically transmit the information back to the manufacturer, who can then begin producing more of that item. This process enabled Walmart to reduce costs by minimizing its need to hold lots of unsold goods in inventory.

In addition to determining which firms grow and which firms shrink, costs determine how large a firm should be. Differences in the costs of the equipment needed for manufacturing cement and the equipment needed to set up a hair salon, for example, mean that cement firms are usually large and hair salons are usually small.

Costs also determine where firms should expand. For example, firms take into account the costs of labor and transportation as well as the effects of government policy when they choose between expanding their manufacturing facilities in the United States or establishing facilities abroad. In recent years, many call centers—places that handle telephone calls and provide customer service—have relocated to India, where educated English-speaking workers can be hired for less money than in the U.S. Similarly, car manufacturers in Germany have set up plants in countries like Slovakia because the cost of hiring workers there is considerably cheaper than in Western Europe.

In this chapter, we will show how costs are a crucial determinant of firm behavior. You will learn how economists can capture the whole essence of a firm with a graph of its costs. By looking at such a graph, economists can determine the profitability of a firm and whether it should shut down or expand. This chapter shows how.

8.1 Costs for an Individual Firm

In this section, we show how to find different types of cost measures for a hypothetical firm. These measures include total costs, average costs, fixed costs, variable costs, and marginal costs. It is important to have a clear and intuitive understanding of each of these concepts and how they relate to one another. We also will look at how the costs of a firm are related to the firm's production function. This will illuminate how changes in the technology used by firms to produce output affect the firm's cost function.

Total Costs, Fixed Costs, Variable Costs, and Marginal Cost

total costs

The sum of all costs incurred in producing goods or services.

fixed costs

Costs of production that do not depend on the quantity of production.

variable costs

Costs of production that vary with the quantity of production.

Total costs (*TC*) are the sum of all costs incurred by a firm in producing goods or services. The more that is produced, the larger the total costs. Recall from Chapter 6 that **fixed costs (*FC*)** and **variable costs (*VC*)** are the two key components of total costs.

Fixed costs are the part of total costs that do not vary with the amount produced in the short run; they include the cost of the factories, land, machines, and all other things that do not change when production changes in the short run. Variable costs are the part of total costs that vary in the short run as production changes. *Variable costs* include wage payments for workers, gasoline for trucks, fertilizer for crops, and all other things that change when the amount produced changes. By definition, total costs equal fixed costs plus variable costs; or, in symbols, $TC = FC + VC$.

The Short Run and the Long Run

Distinguishing the short run from the long run is the key to distinguishing fixed costs from variable costs. The *short run* and the *long run* are two broad categories into which economists parcel time. The **short run** is the period of time during which it is not possible to change all the inputs to production; only some inputs, such as labor, can be changed in the short run. The short run is too short, for example, to build a new factory or apartment building, to lay a fiber-optic cable, to launch a new communications satellite, or to get out of a lease on a storefront. The **long run** is a period of time long enough that all inputs, including capital, can be changed. The cost of each of the items that cannot be changed in the short run—factories, buildings, satellites—can be changed in the long run.

Economists frequently use *capital* as an example of a factor that does not change in the short run and use labor as an example of a factor that can change in the short run. In the examples in this chapter, we refer to the cost of labor as the main variable cost and the cost of capital as the main fixed cost.

Figure 8.2 illustrates these definitions with cost data for a hypothetical firm called Melodic Movements. The firm, located in Houston, Texas, specializes in the strenuous but delicate job of moving pianos from one part of Houston to another. We use these hypothetical data rather than actual data to keep the example simple, but Roadway Express, an actual moving firm that started in Houston with sixteen trucks and has since gone nationwide, is a more complex example illustrating the same point. Figure 8.2 lists the total costs, fixed costs, and variable costs for different levels of output at Melodic Movements. Observe that, consistent with the definition, fixed costs do not change as output changes, but variable costs do increase with output.

FIGURE 8.2 Finding Average and Marginal Cost for Melodic Movements (costs measured in dollars per day)
This table shows the total costs, and the breakdown between fixed and variable costs, associated with various levels of production. It also shows what marginal and average costs are for each level of production.

Quantity (pianos moved per day) (Q)	Total Costs (TC)	Fixed Costs (FC)	Variable Costs (VC)	Marginal Cost (MC)	Average Total Cost (ATC)	Average Fixed Cost (AFC)	Average Variable Cost (AVC)
0	300	300	0	—	—	—	—
1	450	300	150	150	450	300	150
2	570	300	270	120	285	150	135
3	670	300	370	100	223	100	123
4	780	300	480	110	195	75	120
5	900	300	600	120	180	60	120
6	1,040	300	740	140	173	50	123
7	1,200	300	900	160	171	43	128
8	1,390	300	1,090	190	174	38	136
9	1,640	300	1,340	250	182	33	149
10	1,960	300	1,660	320	196	30	166
11	2,460	300	2,160	500	223	27	196

$TC = FC + VC$ $\dfrac{\text{Change in } TC}{\text{Change in } Q}$ $ATC = \dfrac{TC}{Q}$ $AFC = \dfrac{FC}{Q}$ $AVC = \dfrac{VC}{Q}$

The pictographs in Figure 8.3 show that fixed costs do not change in the short run at Melodic Movements. Fixed costs, or the cost for four trucks and two terminals where the trucks are parked, are $300 per day regardless of how many pianos are moved during the day. Figure 8.3 also shows that variable costs increase with the amount produced.

FIGURE 8.3 Fixed Costs versus Variable Costs

Fixed costs remain constant as the output of the firm increases in the short run. In the example of Melodic Movements, fixed costs are the daily rental or interest costs for trucks and terminals under long-term lease or owned by the firm. Variable costs change with the level of output. In the case of MelodicMovements, more workers must be hired to move more pianos.

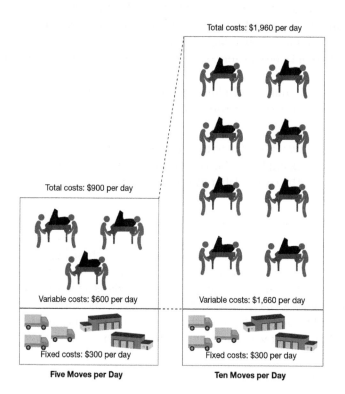

Total costs: $1,960 per day

Total costs: $900 per day

Variable costs: $600 per day

Variable costs: $1,660 per day

Fixed costs: $300 per day

Fixed costs: $300 per day

Five Moves per Day

Ten Moves per Day

They increase from $600 to $1,660 as the number of pianos delivered per day rises from 5 to 10. Variable costs are shown in Figure 8.3 to rise because additional workers are hired to carry the goods and to drive and service the trucks. Thus, total costs rise from $900 to $1,960 as the number of pianos delivered rises from 5 to 10.

Figure 8.4 shows the same type of information as Figure 8.3 in graph form. Pairs of numbers on total costs and quantity from Figure 8.2 are plotted in Figure 8.4. Connecting these dots results in the total costs curve. You can see how the total costs of moving the pianos steadily increase with the number of pianos moved. Fixed costs are shown to be unchanged at all levels of output. Figure 8.4 shows variable costs by the distance between the total costs curve and the fixed costs curve.

FIGURE 8.4 Total Costs Minus Fixed Costs Equal Variable Costs

The two lines on the diagram show total costs and fixed costs for Melodic Movements. Variable costs are the difference between the two lines. Variable costs rise with production, but fixed costs are constant.

Marginal Cost

Figure 8.2 also shows how the **marginal cost** of Melodic Movements depends on the quantity of services produced (the number of pianos moved). Recall from Chapter 6 that marginal cost is the change in total costs resulting from a one-unit change in the quantity produced. For example, the marginal cost of increasing production from five piano moves to six piano moves a day is the change in total costs ($1,040 – $900 = $140) when we increase the number of piano moves from five to six. The fifth column of Figure 8.2 shows the marginal cost for each additional piano moved by Melodic Movements, from the first to the 11th piano.

Observe that in Figure 8.2, marginal cost declines at low levels of production and then begins to increase again. Marginal cost reaches a minimum of $100 when production increases from two to three units of output. Recall that in the examples in Chapter 6 (see Figure 6.10), marginal cost increased throughout the whole range of production. In the example of Melodic Movements, marginal cost declines over part of the range of production. We will explain the reason for the difference later in this chapter.

marginal cost

The change in total costs resulting from a one-unit change in quantity produced.

Average Cost

average total cost

Total costs of production divided by the quantity produced (also called cost per unit).

average variable cost

Variable costs divided by the quantity produced.

average fixed cost

Fixed costs divided by the quantity produced.

Average total cost (ATC) is defined as total costs (TC) of production divided by the quantity (Q) produced; in other words, it is the cost per unit of production. In symbols, $ATC = TC/Q$. For example, if the total costs of producing four items are $3,000, then the average total cost is $750 ($3,000/4). We also can define average cost for fixed and variable costs. Thus, **average variable cost (AVC)** is defined as variable costs divided by the quantity produced: $AVC = VC/Q$. **Average fixed cost (AFC)** is defined as fixed costs divided by the quantity produced: $AFC = FC/Q$. Of the three averages, we will use average total cost most frequently. However, the other two averages are important for knowing whether to shut down a firm or keep it open when it is losing money.

Average total cost for Melodic Movements is shown in Figure 8.2. For example, total costs for two pianos moved (Q = 2) are $570; dividing $570 by two gives an average total cost of $285. For three pianos moved (Q = 3), total costs are $670; dividing by three gives $223 for average total cost. Notice that, in this example, average total cost initially declines as production increases from low levels. Then average total cost starts to increase once the output level reaches eight units. That average total cost first decreases and then increases as production rises is a common pattern for most firms.

Average variable cost is also illustrated in Figure 8.2. For two pianos moved (Q = 2), for example, average variable cost is $270 divided by two, or $135. You can see that average variable cost, in this example, first declines and then increases throughout the rest of the range of production. Finally, observe in Figure 8.2 that average fixed cost gets smaller as production rises. Because average fixed cost is calculated by dividing fixed costs (which are by definition fixed) by the quantity produced, average fixed cost must decline as the quantity produced rises.

 Charting Costs

Learn more about building a cost table.

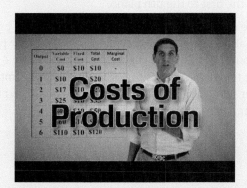

View the video online at: http://www.youtube.com/embed/ucJBO9UTmwo?rel=0

The Relationship between a Firm's Costs and the Firm's Production Function

The cost information in Figure 8.2 is determined by how much input of labor and capital it takes to produce a given quantity of output and by the price of capital and labor. First consider some illustrative calculations of costs as the firm increases production. According to Figure 8.2, it costs

Melodic Movements $300 a day for capital, which is four trucks and two terminals (suppose trucks cost $25 per day and a terminal costs $100 per day). If the trucks and terminals were leased for one year, then the fixed costs would include the rental payment on the lease. If the trucks and the terminals were purchased on credit by Melodic Movements, then the fixed costs would include interest payments on the loans. If the trucks and the terminals were bought outright, then the fixed costs would include the opportunity cost—the forgone interest payments—of the funds used to buy the trucks and the terminals. These fixed costs will be incurred even if zero pianos are moved.

To move pianos, however, Melodic Movements needs labor. To move one piano, it might be enough to have one driver, one mechanic to service the truck, and one worker to help carry and load the piano. As production increases from Q = 0 to Q = 1, variable costs increase from zero to $150 and total costs increase from $300 to $450. Thus, the marginal cost of moving one piano rather than zero pianos is $150. If wages are $10 an hour, this implies that 15 hours of work are needed collectively from the three employees to move that first piano.

FIGURE 8.5 Inputs and the Production Function

Labor (the two workers) and capital (the truck) are inputs to production (moving the piano).

Source: XiXinXing/Shutterstock.com

To move to a higher level of production, Melodic Movements requires more hours of work. According to Figure 8.2, if production rises from one piano moved to two pianos moved, then total costs increase from $450 to $570; marginal cost is $120. With wages of $10 an hour, this marginal cost is the cost of 12 more hours of work. Notice that marginal cost declines as production increases from one to two units of output. Why? Because it takes less additional labor input to move from one piano move to two piano moves than it did to move from zero piano moves to one piano move. For instance, you may need to hire a second driver and a second loader, but the same mechanic may be able to service two trucks in less than twice the time it takes to service one truck. A full picture of how costs depend on the inputs to production becomes evident from the firm's production function.

The Production Function

Table 8.1 shows the number of hours of work required to move different numbers of pianos at Melodic Movements. Melodic Movements' short-run **production function** shows how much output can be produced for each amount of labor input. You can calculate the variable costs at Melodic Movements, assuming a wage of $10 per hour, using the information in Table 8.1. To move one piano takes 15 hours of work; at $10 per hour, variable costs are $150. To move 10 pianos takes 166 hours of work; at $10 per hour, variable costs are $1,660. Similar calculations for all levels of output are shown in the third column of Table 8.1. Note that the variable costs in Table 8.1 are the same as those in Figure 8.2. Thus, we have shown explicitly how the firm's costs depend on its production function.

production function

A relationship that shows the quantity of output for any given amount of input.

TABLE 8.1 Using the Production Function to Compute Variable Costs

Observe that increasing marginal product of labor exists at low levels of production; for example, it takes only 10 hours of labor to increase production [by one unit] from two to three units, whereas it takes 12 hours of labor to increase production [by one unit] from one to two units. At higher levels of production, decreasing marginal product of labor exists.

Quantity (pianos moved)	Hours of Work	Labor Costs at $10 Wage (variable costs)
0	0	0
1	15	150
2	27	270
3	37	370
4	48	480
5	60	600
6	74	740
7	90	900
8	109	1,090
9	134	1,340
10	166	1,660
11	216	2,160

average product of labor

The quantity produced divided by the amount of labor input.

Recall from Chapter 6 that the *marginal product of labor* is the change in production that can be obtained with an additional unit of labor. Decreasing marginal product of labor is called *diminishing returns to labor*. Increasing marginal product of labor is called *increasing returns to labor*. The marginal product of labor is illustrated in Figure 8.6, which shows a graph of the production function from Table 8.1. Be sure to distinguish between the marginal product of labor and the average product of labor. The **average product of labor** is the quantity produced, or *total product*, divided by the amount of labor input. Thus, the average product of labor is Q/L, where Q is total product and L is labor input. The marginal product of labor is $\Delta Q/\Delta L$, where ΔQ is the change in the quantity produced and ΔL is the change in labor input.

You can see in Figure 8.6 that, for low levels of labor input, the marginal product of labor increases as labor input increases. This relationship is akin to the previous example in which you needed one driver, one loader, and one mechanic to move that first piano, but you needed only another driver and another loader (but not a second mechanic) to increase production to two piano moves. But you also can see that, at high levels of labor input, the marginal product starts to decline as labor input increases: Diminishing returns set in. Adding a third loader or a third driver will not help the firm move more pianos unless it can expand its capital stock. In the short run, with a fixed capital stock, the marginal product while falling initially) is likely to rise as production increases.

FIGURE 8.6 Melodic Movements' Production Function
The curve shows the production function in which more labor input gives more output. Capital (trucks and terminals) is not changed. Observe that the marginal product of labor first increases and then decreases with more labor input.

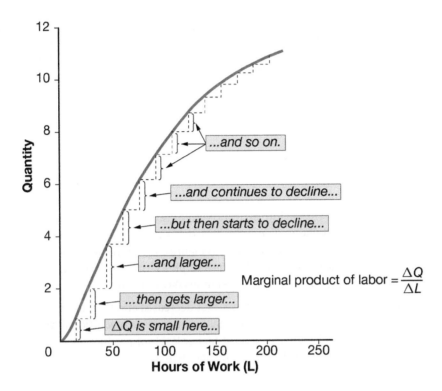

What this means is that initially, when the marginal product of labor is *increasing*, the marginal cost will be *decreasing*: Each additional unit of output requires fewer additional units of labor, and hence has a smaller additional cost. Subsequently, when the marginal product of labor is decreasing, the marginal cost will be increasing: Each additional unit of output requires more additional units of labor, and hence has a larger additional cost. To summarize:

Increasing marginal product of labor —> Decreasing marginal cost

Decreasing marginal product of labor —> Increasing marginal cost

Review

- The short run is the period of time in which it is not possible to change all inputs to production; only some inputs, such as labor, can be changed.
- The long run is the period of time in which the firm can vary all inputs to production, including capital.
- Total costs are the sum of all costs incurred by the firm in producing goods and services. Total costs can be written as the sum of fixed costs plus variable costs. Fixed costs are constant in the short run for all levels of production. Variable costs increase as more is produced.
- The marginal cost is the change in total costs as a result of producing one more unit of output. Marginal cost may rise or fall as production increases.
- The total cost per unit produced is called the average total cost. It can be separated into two parts: average variable cost, defined as variable costs divided by quantity, and average fixed cost, defined as fixed costs divided by quantity.

- A firm's cost function depends on its production function. In the simple example we study, the firm's production function shows how many hours of labor are needed to produce a particular quantity of output, given a certain fixed level of capital.

- When the marginal product of labor is increasing, it takes fewer workers to produce an additional unit of output; hence the additional cost of producing that unit of output (marginal cost) is decreasing. Conversely, when the marginal product of labor is decreasing, it takes more workers to produce an additional unit of output; hence the additional cost of producing that unit of output (marginal cost) is increasing.

8.2 Cost Curves

A portion of Figure 8.2 can be turned into an informative graph, as shown in Figure 8.7. The vertical axis of Figure 8.7 shows the dollar cost, and the horizontal axis shows the quantity produced. The pairs of points from Figure 8.2 are plotted as dots in Figure 8.7, and the dots have been connected to help visualize the curves. The curves are called the *marginal cost curve*, the *average total cost curve*, and the *average variable cost curve*. We label the curves *MC*, *ATC*, and *AVC*, respectively.

It is clear from Figure 8.7 that marginal cost first decreases and then increases, as observed in Figure 8.2. We now know the reason: The marginal product of each additional worker increases at lower levels of production and then decreases at higher levels of production. Figure 8.7 also makes it clear that average total cost first declines and then increases. In other words, the average total cost curve is *U-shaped*.

FIGURE 8.7 Average Cost and Marginal Cost from a Numerical Example

Average total cost first declines and then increases as more is produced. Marginal cost is below average total cost when average total cost is falling and above average total cost when average total cost is rising. This relationship also holds between average variable cost and marginal cost. These cost curves are plotted from the data given in Figure 8.2.

The relative positions of the average total cost curve and the marginal cost curve in Figure 8.7 are important and will come up repeatedly. Observe that whenever the marginal cost curve is below the average total cost curve, average total cost is declining. Whenever the marginal cost curve is above the average total cost curve, however, average total cost is increasing. This result also holds for average variable cost: If marginal cost is greater than average variable cost, then average variable cost is increasing; if marginal cost is less than average variable cost, then average variable cost is decreasing.

This relationship implies a general and important result: *Marginal cost intersects average total cost at the lowest point of the average total cost curve. This has to be the case because whenever marginal cost is less than average total cost (to the left of the intersection point), average total cost is falling. Whenever marginal cost is more than average total cost (to the right of the intersection point), average total cost is rising.*

The same result holds between marginal cost and average variable cost. These relationships between the two average cost curves and the marginal cost curve are essential to the analysis that follows.

Marginal versus Average in the Classroom

The reason for the relationship between marginal cost and average total cost or average variable cost can be seen with an analogy. Consider another example of averages, say, your average grades on the weekly homework assignments in your economics class. Suppose that the average grade you have received on your first two assignments is 75. Now suppose that you get a 100 on your third homework assignment. The 100 you received on the third assignment was greater than the average grade of 75 you had on the first two; in other words, your marginal grade of 100 is greater than your average grade of 75. What happens to your average homework grade? It will rise to 83.33. Now suppose that you had scored only a 60 on your third assignment. Then your marginal grade of 60 is less than the average grade of 75; hence, your average grade declines from 75 to 70.

This is a property of averaging, and it applies to grades, heights, weights, and so on, as well as to costs. When you add something into a group, an above-average contribution from the new addition increases the group average, whereas a below-average contribution decreases it.

Generic Cost Curves

The relationship between marginal and average allows us to sketch a *generic* cost curve diagram, the general properties of which characterize virtually all firms, not just Melodic Movements. Such a diagram is shown in Figure 8.8. Again, the vertical axis is the dollar cost and the horizontal axis is the quantity, but in a generic picture, we do not scale the axes because they apply to any firm, whether in textiles, moving, or electronics. Note that the marginal cost curve cuts both the average total cost curve and the average variable cost curve at the minimum point. If the marginal cost curve does not go through the lowest point of both the average total cost curve and the average variable cost curve, you have made an error in drawing a cost function.

Reminder: *It is helpful to use the following checklist when you draw this graph:*

1. *Ensure that the marginal cost curve cuts through the average total cost curve and the average variable cost curve at their minimum points, and understand the reason for this.*

2. *Ensure that the distance between average total cost and average variable cost gets smaller as you increase the amount of production.*

3. *Put a small dip on the left-hand side of the marginal cost curve before the upward slope begins. This allows for the possibility of decreasing marginal cost at very low levels of production.*

Another important relationship is evident in Figure 8.8. The distance between the average total cost curve and the average variable cost curve gets smaller as production increases because fixed costs are an increasingly smaller proportion of total costs as production increases. Recall that fixed costs do not change as Q increases. The distance between the average total cost curve and the average variable cost curve is *FC/Q*, which declines as quantity increases. Hence, the distance between the *ATC* curve and the *AVC* curve grows smaller as you move to the right in the diagram. Any picture you draw should show this relationship.

FIGURE 8.8 Generic Sketch of Average Cost and Marginal Cost
Every firm can be described by cost curves of the type drawn here. Compare these generic curves with the specific curves in Figure 8.7. Check these curves against the checklist in the Reminder paragraph.

Finally, observe that the marginal cost curve in the generic picture of Figure 8.8 has a region of declining marginal cost at low production levels. The graph allows for the possibility that at low production levels, the marginal product of labor increases and, therefore, marginal cost declines. This was true for Melodic Movements, which had increasing marginal product of labor initially, and we allow for it in the generic case.

For the cost curves for Melodic Movements in Figure 8.7, the marginal cost curve and the average variable cost curve touch at one unit of output. This occurs because the marginal cost of producing one rather than zero units of output must equal the variable cost of producing one unit, and hence the average variable cost of producing one unit, as shown in Figure 8.2. Thus, if the generic cost curve were drawn all the way over to one unit of output on the left of Figure 8.8 then the marginal cost curve and the average variable cost curve would start at the same point. Because we usually do not draw generic cost curves that go all the way over to the vertical axis, we do not show them starting at the same point.

Cost Curves

Learn more about graphing the marginal, average total, average variable, and average fixed cost curves.

View the video online at: http://www.youtube.com/embed/C3m9FC3T3vw?rel=0

Review

- The marginal cost curve, the average total cost curve, and the average variable cost curve are closely related. In the region in which the marginal cost is higher than the average total (or variable) cost, average total (or variable) cost is increasing, and vice versa.

- We can apply the lessons learned in the example of Melodic Movements to derive the generic shapes of a firm's cost curves. These curves should have the following attributes:

  - The marginal cost (MC) curve should cut through both the average total cost (ATC) curve and the average variable cost (AVC) curve at their lowest points.

  - The average fixed cost becomes very small as output increases. Therefore, the gap between average total cost and average variable cost gets smaller as more is produced.

  - The marginal cost curve typically slopes downward at very low levels of output before sloping upward. The marginal cost and the average variable cost are also identical at one unit of output.

8.3 The Production Decision in the Short Run

As we saw in Chapter 6, a competitive firm takes the market price as given. If it is maximizing profits, it will choose a quantity to produce in the short run such that its marginal cost equals the market price ($P = MC$). But when the firm produces this quantity, are its profits positive? Or is the firm running a loss? If it is running a loss, should it shut down in the short run? To answer these questions, we need to use the cost curves to find the firm's profits.

The Profit or Loss Rectangle

The level of production for a competitive firm with the cost curves in Figure 8.8 is shown in Figure 8.9. The quantity produced is determined by the intersection of the marginal cost (*MC*) curve and the market price line (*P*). We draw a dashed vertical line to mark the quantity (*Q*) produced. Because profits equal total revenue minus total costs, we need to represent total revenue and total costs on the average cost diagram.

FIGURE 8.9 Price Equals Marginal Cost

If a firm is maximizing profits, then it chooses a quantity (*Q*) such that price equals marginal cost. Thus, the quantity is determined by the intersection of the market price line and the marginal cost curve, as shown on the diagram. In this picture, the *ATC* and *AVC* curves are a sideshow, but they enter the main act in Figure 8.10, when we look at the firm's level of profits.

The Total Revenue Area

Figure 8.9 shows a particular market price *P* and the corresponding level of production *Q* chosen by the firm. The total revenue that the firm gets is price *P* times quantity *Q*. Figure 8.10 shows that this total revenue can be represented by the area of a rectangle with width *Q* and height *P*. The shaded area in Figure 8.10 illustrates this rectangle. The area of this rectangle, $P \times Q$, is total revenue.

FIGURE 8.10 Showing Profits on the Cost Curve Diagram

The price and quantity produced are the same as those in Figure 8.9. The area of the shaded rectangle is total revenue. We use the *ATC* curve to find total costs to compute profits. First, we mark where the *ATC* curve intersects the dashed vertical line showing the quantity produced. The area of the rectangle with the hash marks is total costs because the total costs (*TC*) equal average total cost (*ATC*) times quantity produced, *TC = ATC x Q*. The part of the shaded rectangle rising above the hash-marked area is profits.

The Total Costs Area

Total costs also can be represented in Figure 8.10. First, observe the dashed vertical line in Figure 8.10 marking the profit-maximizing quantity produced. Next, observe the point at which the average total cost curve intersects this dashed vertical line. This point tells us what the firm's average total cost is when it produces the profit-maximizing quantity. The area of the rectangle with the hash marks shows the firm's total costs. Why? Remember that average total cost is defined as total costs divided by quantity. If we take average total cost and multiply by quantity, we get total costs: $ATC \times Q = TC$. The quantity produced (Q) is the width of the rectangle, and average total cost (ATC) is the height of the rectangle. Hence, total costs are given by the area of the rectangle with the hash marks.

Profits or Losses

Because profits are total revenue less total costs, we compute profits by looking at the difference between the two rectangles. The difference is a rectangle, shown by the part of the revenue rectangle that rises above the total costs rectangle. *Profits are positive* in Figure 8.10 because total revenue is greater than total costs. But profits can also be negative, as shown in Figure 8.11.

FIGURE 8.11 Showing a Loss on the Cost Curve Diagram
In this figure, the market price is lower than in Figure 8.10. The market price line intersects the marginal cost curve at a point below the average total cost curve. Thus, the area of the total costs rectangle is larger than the area of the total revenue rectangle. Profits are less than zero, and the loss is shown in the diagram.

Suppose that the market price is at a point at which the intersection of the marginal cost curve and the market price line gives a quantity of production for which average total cost is *above* the price. This situation is shown in Figure 8.11. At this lower price, we still have the necessary condition for profit maximization. The firm will produce the quantity that equates to price and marginal cost, as shown by the intersection of the price line and the marginal cost curve.

The amount of total revenue at this price is again price times quantity ($P \times Q$), or the shaded rectangle. Total costs are average total cost times the quantity produced, that is, $ATC \times Q$, or the area of the rectangle with the hash marks.

The difference between total revenue and total costs is profit, but in this case *profits are negative*, that is, at a loss. Total revenue is less than total costs, as shown by the cost rectangle's extending above the revenue rectangle. The extent of cost overhang is the loss.

The Breakeven Point

If the intersection of price and marginal cost is at a quantity at which price exceeds average total cost, the firm makes profits. If, on the other hand, the intersection of price and marginal cost is at a quantity at which price is less than the average total cost, the firm loses money. Therefore, if the intersection of price and marginal cost is at a quantity at which price is equal to average total cost, the firm is breaking even, neither making nor losing money.

breakeven point

The point at which price equals the minimum of average total cost.

Breaking even is shown in the middle panel of Figure 8.12. The market price is drawn through the point at which the marginal cost curve intersects the average total cost curve, which is the minimum point on the average total cost curve. At that price, average total cost equals the price, so that the total revenue rectangle and the total cost rectangle are exactly the same. Thus, the difference between their areas is zero. At P = minimum ATC, the firm is at a **breakeven point** and economic profits are zero. The firm earns positive profits if the price is greater than the breakeven point ($P >$ minimum ATC), as shown in the left panel. The firm has negative profits (a loss) if the price is lower than the breakeven point ($P <$ minimum ATC), as shown in the right panel of Figure 8.12.

FIGURE 8.12 The Breakeven Point
When profits are zero, we are at the breakeven point, as shown in the middle panel. In this case, the market price line intersects the marginal cost curve exactly where it crosses the average total cost curve. The left panel shows a higher market price, and profits are greater than zero. The right panel shows a lower market price, and profits are less than zero—there is a loss. The cost curves are exactly the same in each diagram.

The Shutdown Point

The situation illustrated in the right panel of Figure 8.12 is not uncommon; every day we hear of businesses losing money. But many of these money-losing firms continue to stay in business. In 1993, Adidas, the running shoe company, lost $100 million. In 2001, Amazon.com lost more than $1 billion, but the money-losing firm did not shut down in either case. Why does a firm with negative profits stay in business? At what point does it decide to shut down? Let's examine this more carefully.

The key concept is that, in the short run, the fixed costs have to be paid even if the firm is shut down. So the firm should keep operating if it can minimize its losses by doing so, in other words, if the losses from shutting down exceed the losses from continuing to operate. Using our example of the piano-moving firm, Melodic Movements should keep producing as long as its revenue from moving pianos exceeds the cost of paying its workers to move the pianos, even if its revenue is insufficient to cover total costs, which include paying for the trucks and terminals in addition to paying the workers. If the firm shuts down, it will end up losing more because it will lose the entire fixed costs, whereas if it keeps operating, it will earn enough to cover at least part of the fixed costs. Conversely, if the price of moving pianos is so low that the revenue from moving the pianos is less than the workers are paid to move the pianos, it is best to shut down production and not move any pianos. The firm will lose the fixed costs for the trucks and the garage, but at least it will not lose any additional money.

We can make this analysis more formal by presenting it in terms of the cost curves shown in Figure 8.13. If the price is above minimum average variable cost (P > minimum AVC), as shown in the left panel of Figure 8.13, the firm should not shut down, even if the price is below average total cost and profits are negative. Because total revenue is greater than variable costs, shutting down would eliminate this extra revenue. By continuing operations, the firm can minimize its losses, so it is better to keep producing in the short run. For example, Adidas did not shut down in 1993 because it had to pay fixed costs in the short run; with the price of running shoes greater than the average variable cost of producing them, the losses were less than if it had shut down.

FIGURE 8.13 The Shutdown Point

When price is above average variable cost, the firm should keep producing even if profits are negative. But if price is less than average variable cost, losses will be smaller if the firm shuts down and stops producing. Hence, the shutdown point is the point at which price equals average variable cost.

The firm should shut down if the price falls below minimum average variable cost ($P <$ minimum AVC) and is not expected to rise again, as shown in the right panel of Figure 8.13. Because total revenue is less than variable costs, shutting down would eliminate the extra costs. By shutting down, the firm will have to pay its fixed costs in the short run but will not have the burden of additional losses. Economists have developed the concept of sunk cost, which may help you understand and remember why a firm like Adidas would have continued to operate in the short run even though it was reporting losses. A sunk cost is a cost that you have committed to pay and that you cannot recover. For example, if a firm signs a year's lease for factory space, it must make rental payments until the lease is up, whether the space is used or not. The important thing about a sunk cost is that once you commit to it, you cannot do anything about it, so you might as well ignore it in your decisions. The firm cannot recover these costs by shutting down. All Adidas could do in the short run was reduce its losses, and it did so by continuing to produce shoes (assuming that the revenue from each pair of shoes was greater than the variable cost of producing them).

shutdown point

The point at which price equals the minimum of average variable cost.

Now, observe that the middle panel of Figure 8.13 shows the case in which price exactly equals the minimum point of the average variable cost curve ($P =$ minimum AVC). This is called the **shutdown point**: It is the price at which total revenue exactly equals the firm's variable costs. If the price falls below the shutdown point, the firm should shut down. If the price is above the shutdown point, the firm should continue producing.

In thinking about the shutdown point, the time period is important. We are looking at the firm during the short run, when it is obligated to pay its fixed costs and cannot alter its capital. The question for Melodic Movements is what to do when it already has committed to paying for the trucks and terminals, but the price of moving pianos falls to such a low level that it does not cover variable costs. The shutdown rule says to stop producing in that situation. However, if profits are negative, but the price is greater than average variable cost, then it is best to keep producing.

The shutdown point can be incorporated into the firm's supply curve. Recall that the supply curve of a single firm tells us the quantity of a good that the firm will produce at different prices. As long as the price is above minimum average variable cost, the firm will produce a quantity such that marginal cost equals the price. Thus, for prices above minimum average variable cost, the marginal cost curve is the firm's supply curve, as shown in Figure 8.14. If the price falls below minimum average variable cost, however, then the firm will shut down; in other words, the quantity produced will equal zero (Q = 0). Thus, for prices below minimum average variable cost, the supply curve jumps over to the vertical axis, where Q = 0, as shown in the marginal figure.

FIGURE 8.14 Finding the Shutdown Point on the Supply Curve
The firm will keep producing as long as price is above average variable cost. Since price is equal to marginal cost when the firm is producing, the shutdown point is where the marginal cost (MC) curve intersects the average variable cost curve (AVC) at the minimum of AVC.

Ensure that you understand the difference between the shutdown point and the breakeven point. The shutdown point is the point at which price equals the minimum average variable cost (Figure 8.13). The breakeven point is the point at which price equals the minimum average total cost (Figure 8.12). If the price is between the minimum average total cost and the minimum average variable cost, then the firm is not breaking even; it is losing money. It does not make sense to shut down in the short run, however, unless the price falls below the shutdown point.

Two different points:

Shutdown point: P = minimum AVC

Breakeven point: P = minimum ATC

Reminder: *You can use some algebra to check the result that a firm should stop producing when the price is less than average variable cost:*

$$P < AVC$$

Note that Profits = total revenue – total costs

Because total costs equal variable costs plus fixed costs, we can replace total costs to get

$$\text{profits} = P \times Q - \text{VC} - \text{FC}$$

Now, since $VC = AVC \times Q$, we have

$$\text{profits} = P \times Q - \text{AVC} \times Q - \text{FC}$$

Rearranging this gives

$$\text{profits} = (P - AVC) \times Q - \text{FC}$$

If P < AVC, the first term in this expression is negative unless Q = 0. Thus, if P < AVC, the best your firm can do is set Q = 0. This eliminates the negative drain on profits in the first term in the last expression. You minimize your loss by setting Q = 0.

Review

- Total revenue for a firm for a given price is represented by the area of the rectangle whose height is the price and whose width is the profit-maximizing quantity corresponding to that price. Total costs for a firm producing that quantity are represented by the area of the rectangle whose width is the quantity and whose height is the average total cost corresponding to that quantity.
- Profits also can be represented as a rectangle on the cost curve diagram. The profit or loss rectangle is the difference between the revenue rectangle and the loss rectangle.
- When P > minimum ATC, total revenue exceeds total costs, so the firm is making profits. When P < minimum ATC, total costs exceed total revenue, so the firm is losing money. When P = minimum ATC, the firm is making zero profits; this is called the breakeven point.
- A firm that is losing money may continue to operate, or it may choose to shut down. That decision depends on the relationship between price and average variable cost, keeping in mind that fixed costs already have been incurred in the short run.
- If P > minimum AVC, then the firm will continue to operate in the short run because it is earning enough to cover its variable costs and some, but not all, of its fixed costs. When P < minimum AVC, profits are maximized by shutting down because continuing to operate will result in the firm losing even more than its fixed costs.
- The point at which P = minimum AVC is called the shutdown point. When price is in between the breakeven point and the shutdown point, the firm is losing money, but it is minimizing its losses in the short run by continuing to operate.
- The shutdown point can be incorporated into the supply curve. Because the firm will choose to stay in business only when P > minimum AVC, the supply curve will be zero for prices below minimum AVC. Above minimum AVC, the marginal cost curve will be the supply curve.

8.4 Cost and Production: The Long Run

Thus far, we have focused our analysis on the short run. By definition, the short run is the period of time during which it is not possible for firms to adjust certain inputs to production. But what happens in the long run, when it *is* possible for firms to make such adjustments? For example, what happens to Melodic Movements when it opens new terminals or takes out a lease on a fleet of new trucks? To answer this question, we need to show how the firm can adjust its costs in the long run. All costs, fixed costs as well as variable costs, can be adjusted in the long run.

The Effect of Capital Expansion on Costs

First, consider what happens to fixed costs when the firm increases its capital. Suppose Melodic Movements increases the size of its fleet from four trucks to eight trucks and raises the number of terminals from two to four. Then its fixed costs would increase because more rent would have to be paid for four terminals and eight trucks than for two terminals and four trucks. To obtain the increase in fixed costs, we need to use the price of capital. Suppose trucks cost $25 per day and a terminal costs $100 per day. Then four trucks and two terminals would cost $300 and eight trucks and four terminals would cost $600. Fixed costs would rise from $300 to $600.

Second, consider what happens to variable costs when the firm increases its capital. An increase in capital increases the amount that each additional worker can produce. For example, according to Table 8.1, 166 worker-hours were required for Melodic Movements to move 10 pianos when it had four trucks and two terminals. With more capital (eight trucks and four terminals), it will take fewer hours of work to move the pianos. Assume, for example, that it takes only 120 worker-hours to deliver 10 pianos. In this scenario, with the wage equal to $10 per hour, the variable cost of moving 10 pianos falls from $1,660 to $1,200. In other words, variable costs decline as the firm expands its capital.

Now consider total costs. With fixed costs larger and variable costs smaller as a result of the increase in capital, what is the effect on total costs, which are the sum of fixed costs and variable costs? After the expansion, total costs will be higher at very low levels of output, in which case fixed costs dominate, but they will be lower at high levels of output, in which case variable costs dominate.

Figure 8.15 illustrates this using the total cost curve. Figure 8.15 is essentially the same as Figure 8.4 except that the curves show the old costs before the expansion of capital and the new costs with the additional capital. The diagram shows that the new fixed costs are higher and the new variable costs are lower. The new total cost curve (TC_2) is twisted relative to the old total cost curve (TC_1). The new total cost curve is above the old total cost curve at low levels of output and below the old total cost curve at high levels of output.

FIGURE 8.15 Shifts in Total Costs as a Firm Increases Its Capital in the Long Run
When a firm increases its capital, its fixed costs increase; as shown in the diagram, fixed costs rise from FC_1 to FC_2. Its variable costs decrease, however, which also is shown. Thus, the new total costs curve (TC_2) will be above the old total costs curve (TC_1) for low-level output and below the old total costs curve (TC_1) for high-level output.

Table 8.2 provides the numerical information about the costs that appear in Figure 8.15. To see the effect of the firm's expansion on its costs, compare the fixed costs, variable costs, and total costs in Table 8.2 with those in Figure 8.2. Observe that fixed costs are higher: $600 rather than $300. Variable costs are lower throughout the range of production. As a result, total costs are higher in Table 8.2 than in Figure 8.2 for production of less than eight units, and total costs are lower in Table 8.2 than in Figure 8.2 for production of eight units or more.

TABLE 8.2 Costs with More Capital
(Compared with the table in Figure 8.2, fixed costs are higher and variable costs are lower in this table because capital is higher than in Figure 8.2. Costs are measured in dollars.)

Quantity	Total Costs ($)	Fixed Costs ($)	Variable Costs ($)	Average Total Cost ($)
0	600	600	0	—
1	690	600	90	690
2	770	600	170	385
3	840	600	240	280
4	920	600	320	230
5	1,010	600	410	202
6	1,110	600	510	185
7	1,220	600	620	174
8	1,340	600	740	168
9	1,470	600	870	163
10	1,610	600	1,010	161
11	1,880	600	1,280	171
12	2,300	600	1,700	192

Our analysis of the effects of the firm's capital expansion on total costs can be used to derive the effects on average total cost. Remember, average total cost (ATC) is total costs (TC) divided by the quantity (Q). Thus, if total costs increase at a given quantity of output, so too will average total cost. And if total costs decrease at a given level of output, so too will average total cost.

This scenario is illustrated in Figure 8.16. An average total cost curve, labeled ATC_1, corresponding to average total cost in Figure 8.2 is plotted. Another average total cost curve, labeled ATC_2, corresponding to average total cost in Table 8.2 also is plotted. The new average total cost curve (ATC_2) is above the old average total cost curve (ATC_1) at low levels of output and below the old average total cost curve (ATC_1) at higher levels of output. Average total cost is higher for production of less than eight units and lower for production of eight units or more. This is precisely what is shown for total costs in Figure 8.15.

FIGURE 8.16 Shifts in Average Total Cost Curves When a Firm Expands Its Capital
The effects on average total cost follow directly from the effects on total costs in Figure 8.15. Here ATC_1 is the average total cost curve with a lower amount of capital, and ATC_2 is the average total cost curve with a higher amount of capital. To the left, at lower levels of output, higher fixed costs raise average total cost; to the right, at higher levels of output, lower variable costs tend to lower average total cost.

The Long-Run *ATC* Curve

Now that we have seen what happens at Melodic Movements when capital is expanded by a certain amount, we can see what happens when capital increases by even larger amounts. For example, suppose Melodic Movements expands throughout Houston, and even beyond Houston, by expanding the size of its fleet of trucks and the number of terminals to park and service the trucks.

Figure 8.17 shows four different average total cost curves. Each of the average total cost curves corresponds to increased capital expansion at Melodic Movements. The first two of these, ATC_1 and ATC_2, are the average total cost curves from Figure 8.16. Note that the second curve (ATC_2) is above the first (ATC_1) at low levels of output and below the first at high levels of output. The third and fourth curves are for even more trucks and terminals. The third average total cost curve (ATC_3) is above the second (ATC_2) at lower levels of output and below the second (ATC_2) at higher levels of output. The same is true of the fourth curve compared with the third.

FIGURE 8.17 Long-Run versus Short-Run Average Total Cost
In the short run, it is not possible to change certain inputs, like the size of the factory or the number of machines. In the long run, these inputs can be changed. For example, in the long run, Melodic Movements can build more terminals around town. This means that the *ATC* curve shifts. The diagram shows four different *ATC* curves for Melodic Movements; each new *ATC* curve represents more terminals, buildings, and machines than the *ATC* curve to its left. The long run average total cost curve is shown by the thicker orange line.

long-run average total cost curve

The curve that traces out the short-run average total cost curves, showing the lowest average total cost for each quantity produced as the firm expands in the long run.

The thick light-orange curve tracing out the bottoms of the four average total cost curves gives the lowest average total cost at any quantity produced. This thick line tells us what average total cost is when the firm can expand (or contract) its capital; in other words, this is the average total cost curve for the long run. For this reason, we call the curve that traces out the points on the lowest average total cost curves the **long-run average total cost curve**. The other average total cost curve that we have been discussing is called the *short-run average total cost curve*, or simply the average total cost curve.

The lack of smoothness in the long-run average total cost curve may seem strange. It occurs in Figure 8.17 because we have drawn only four short-run average total cost curves. If it is possible to expand capital in smaller amounts, then the curve will look smoother. For example, between the first and second short-run average total cost curves (ATC_1 and ATC_2) in Figure 8.17, there might be an average total cost curve for six trucks and three terminals. When we put in more and more short-run average total cost curves, the long-run average total cost curve gets smoother and smoother. But it simply traces out the points of lowest cost for each level of output.

Capital Expansion and Production in the Long Run

How does a firm like Melodic Movements decide whether to expand or contract its capital in the long run? How much does it produce in the long run? The decision is similar to the short-run decision about whether to hire more workers to move more pianos. Again, the firm sets the quantity produced to maximize profits. But now the quantity produced and profits can be affected by changes in capital as well as labor. At any level of capital and labor input, we can compute profits.

If the firm can increase its profits by expanding its capital and its output, then we predict that it will do so. If we find that the firm can increase its profits by reducing its capital and its output, then we predict that it will do so. In other words, the firm adjusts the amount of capital to maximize profits.

Furthermore, in the long run, the firm adjusts both its capital and its labor. What determines the mix of labor and capital when both are variable? The relative price of labor compared with capital will be the deciding factor.

In deriving the cost curves for Melodic Movements, we assumed that the cost of labor was $10 per hour and that the cost of capital, consisting of trucks and terminals, was $25 a day for trucks and $100 a day for terminals. If the cost of labor was higher, say, $20 per hour, then Melodic Movements would have the incentive to rent more trucks rather than hire more workers, at least to the extent that this was feasible.

If the cost of capital rose relative to that of labor, however, then the firm would have the incentive to hire more workers. In general, the firm will use more capital relative to labor if the cost of capital declines relative to that of labor. Conversely, the firm will use less capital relative to labor if the cost of capital rises relative to that of labor.

Review

- In the long run, the firm can expand by increasing its capital. Fixed costs increase and variable costs decline at each level of production as the firm expands its capital.
- Thus, total costs, and average total cost, are higher at low levels of production and lower at high levels of production.
- The average total cost in the long run can be found by tracing out the lowest points of the short-run average total cost curves.
- In the long run, the firm adjusts the amount of capital to maximize profits. It also will choose the mix of labor and capital that maximizes profits, so that when the price of labor rises relative to capital, the firm will switch away from labor toward capital, and vice versa.

8.5 Economies of Scale

The long-run average total cost curve is one way in which economists study the behavior of a firm over time. Whether the long-run average total cost curve slopes up or down, and over what range, is crucial for understanding the nature of a firm, the industry in which it operates, and the role of government.

The long-run average total cost curve describes a situation in which the firm can expand all its inputs. When all inputs increase, we say that the scale of the firm increases. For example, if the number of workers at the firm doubles, the number of trucks doubles, the number of terminals doubles, and so on, then we say that the scale of the firm doubles. Thus, the long-run average total cost curve describes what happens to a firm's average total cost when its scale increases. We use specialized terminology to describe different shapes of the long-run average total cost curve.

economies of scale

A situation in which long-run average total cost declines as the output of a firm increases.

diseconomies of scale

A situation in which long-run average total cost increases as the output of a firm increases.

constant returns to scale

A situation in which long-run average total cost is constant as the output of a firm changes.

We say that there are **economies of scale**, or *increasing returns to scale*, if long run average total cost falls as the scale of the firm increases. We say that there are **diseconomies of scale**, or *decreasing returns to scale*, if long-run average total cost rises as the scale of the firm increases. The situation in the middle, in which case long run average total cost neither rises nor falls, is called **constant returns to scale**. Figure 8.18 illustrates these three possible shapes for the long-run average total cost curve.

FIGURE 8.18 Economies and Diseconomies of Scale

If the long-run average total cost curve slopes downward, we say that there are economies of scale. If the long-run average total cost curve slopes upward, we say that there are diseconomies of scale. If the long-run average total cost curve is flat, we say that there are constant returns to scale, as shown in the middle panel.

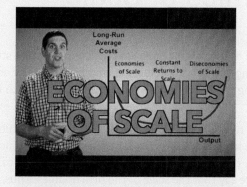

Economies of Scale

Long run average cost curves can tell us about growth prospects for a firm in a particular market.

View the video online at: http://www.youtube.com/embed/JdCgu1sOPDo?rel=0

Determining Whether a Firm Has Economies or Diseconomies of Scale

Whether a firm has increasing, decreasing, or constant returns to scale depends on the type of firm and the type of product. Consider a firm like Melodic Movements. One can imagine that economies of scale would result as the firm expanded the number of terminals around the city of Houston;

with more terminals, trucks could be serviced at many different locations and would not have to be driven so far at the end of the day or towed so far in the event of a breakdown. With a larger work-force, Melodic Movements could have workers who specialize in moving different types of pianos or who specialize in servicing different parts of the trucks. Some might specialize in moves to high-rise buildings. In other words, as the scale of a firm increases, the work can be divided into different tasks, and some members of the labor force can specialize in each task.

Is there a limit to economies of scale? What about expanding beyond Houston to Galveston, Dallas, Tulsa, Mexico City, or even Lima, Peru? In the case of piano moving, returns to scale probably would decline at some point. The extra administrative costs of organizing a large interstate or worldwide piano-moving firm probably would raise average total cost. Thus, one could imagine that the long-run average total cost curve for Melodic Movements would first decline and then increase as the firm grows in size.

Although no two firms are alike, the long-run average total cost curve for most firms probably declines at low levels of output, then remains flat, and finally begins to increase at high levels of output. As a firm gets very large, administrative expenses, as well as coordination and incentive problems, will begin to raise average total cost. The smallest scale of production for which long-run average total cost is at a minimum is called the **minimum efficient scale**. A typical long-run average cost curve and its minimum efficient scale are shown in Figure 8.19.

FIGURE 8.19 Typical Shape of the Long-Run Average Total Cost Curve
For many types of firms, the long-run *ATC* curve slopes down at low levels of output, then reaches a flat area, and finally begins to slope up at high levels. The minimum efficient scale is shown.

Mergers and Economies of Scope

An increase or decrease in the scale of a firm through capital expansion or contraction—as described in the previous two sections—is one kind of change in the firm over time. Firms can also change over time in other ways. They can grow through mergers between one firm and another firm. If the product lines of the two firms are similar, then such mergers may be a way to reduce costs, for example, by consolidating the number of executives or by reducing inefficient duplication of resources. That is one reason why large oil companies, such as Exxon and Mobil, merged in the 1990s.

Mergers are also a common way for firms to combine different skills or resources to develop new products. For example, America Online (AOL), an Internet firm, and Time Warner, a large firm producing movies, magazines, and compact discs, merged in 2001. By bringing together distribution resources with content resources, this merger was intended to widen the scope of both firms and help them develop new products. The results did not turn out as expected, however, and in 2003 Time Warner dropped AOL from its corporate name in an effort to demonstrate that the company still valued its "core" assets—magazines, books, cable channels (HBO, CNN), and movies. Combining different types of firms to reduce costs or create new products is sometimes called *economies of scope*. Table 8.3 lists some of the big mergers of recent years. Observe that most of the companies listed involve similar products.

TABLE 8.3 Recent Big Mergers

Names before Merger		Name after Merger	Primary Industry
Exxon	Mobil	ExxonMobil	Oil
BP	Amoco	BP Amoco (now BP)	Oil
J.P. Morgan	Chase Manhattan	JP Morgan Chase	Banking
Bank of America	Fleet Boston Financial	Bank of America Corp.	Banking
Chrysler	Daimler-Benz	DaimlerChrysler	Motor Vehicles
WorldCom	MCI Communications	MCI WorldCom (now WorldCom)	Telecommunications
Walt Disney	Capital Cities/ABC	Walt Disney	Entertainment
Bank of America	Merrill Lynch	Bank of America	Banking
America Online	Time Warner	AOL Time Warner (now Time Warner)	Internet and Entertainment
Travelers	Citicorp	Citigroup	Financial Services
Walt Disney	21st Century Fox	Walt Disney	Entertainment
Bristol-Myers Squibb	Celgene	Bristol-Myers Squibb	Pharmaceuticals

When two firms merge into one firm, each of the original firms may become a division within the new firm. A merger of one firm with another means that the coordination of production moves from the market to within the organization. For example, the merger of the U.S. firm Chrysler with the German firm Daimler-Benz meant that the different makes of cars were produced in two divisions of the same firm. As with the AOL–Time Warner merger, Daimler and Chrysler found out that the merger did not bring the anticipated gains; they parted ways in 2007.

Reminder: *Most of these mergers are in the same industry and illustrate economies of scale. A few mergers (J.P. Morgan/Chase Manhattan, America Online/Time Warner and Travelers/Citicorp), are the result of expected economies of scope.*

Review

- Economies of scale are said to exist for a firm when the long-run average total cost curve declines as the scale of the firm increases. Economies of scale may occur because of the specialization that the division of labor in larger firms permits.
- Although economies of scale probably exist over some regions of production, the evidence indicates that as firms grow very large, diseconomies of scale set in.
- The smallest scale of production at which long-run average total cost is at a minimum is called the minimum efficient scale of the firm.

- Instead of changing by increasing the capital stock, firms sometimes change via mergers. Mergers between firms that produce similar products can result in lower costs and a higher minimum efficient scale of production.
- Mergers are also a common way for firms with different types of skills and expertise to combine that knowledge and widen the scope of what they jointly produce. Firms that have the ability to do this type of merger are said to have economies of scope.

8.6 End-of-Chapter Materials

Conclusion

In this chapter, we have developed a model for studying why firms shut down, expand, or contract. This analysis of changes at firms over time is an extension of the analysis of a firm's short-run behavior in Chapter 6.

A centerpiece of the model is a graph (see Figure 8.8) that shows the firm's average total cost and average variable cost. Using this graph, we can determine whether a firm will shut down in the short run. Using additional average total cost curves corresponding to alternative levels of capital, we also can determine whether the firm will expand or contract.

We showed how this model can be used to find the firm's long-run total cost and average cost curves. By looking at a firm's long-run average total cost curve (see Figure 8.19), we can tell whether a firm has economies of scale. We will use the long-run average total cost curve extensively in the next several chapters of this book.

Key Points

1. Firms start up, expand, contract, or shut down when conditions in the economy change.
2. The short run and the long run are two broad categories into which economists categorize time periods. The short run is the period of time during which it is not possible for the firm to change all the inputs to production; only some inputs, such as labor, can be changed. The long run is the minimum period of time in which the firm can vary all inputs to production, including capital.
3. Total costs are all the costs incurred by the firm in producing goods or services. Fixed costs are the portion of total costs that do not vary with the amount produced in the short run. Variable costs are the remaining portion of total costs that do vary as production changes.
4. Average total cost, or cost per unit, is widely used by economists, accountants, and investors to assess a firm's cost behavior. The profit made by the firm in the short run depends on the difference between the price and average total cost at the quantity corresponding to that price.
5. When the market price equals the minimum of average total cost, the firm breaks even. At higher prices, profits are positive. At lower prices, profits are negative.
6. The firm will keep producing, in some circumstances, even if profits are negative in the short run. This is because the fixed costs would have to be incurred regardless of whether or not any production is done. So if the price is enough to cover variable costs, the firm should keep producing to minimize its losses.

7. When the market price equals the minimum of average variable cost, the firm is just at the point of shutting down. If the price is below average variable cost, the firm should shut down.

8. The long-run average total cost curve describes how a firm's costs behave when the firm expands its capital.

9. If long-run average total cost declines, then there are economies of scale. For many firms, there is a range over which the long-run average total cost curve is flat, and we say that there are constant returns to scale over that range. When firms get very large, diseconomies of scale set in.

10. Firms can expand by merging with other firms. Such mergers can be motivated by either economies of scale or economies of scope.

Questions for Review

1. What is the difference between total costs, fixed costs, and variable costs?
2. How is marginal cost related to total cost?
3. Why does the marginal cost curve cut through the average total cost curve exactly at the minimum of the average total cost curve?
4. Why does the marginal cost curve cut through the average variable cost curve exactly at the minimum of the average variable cost curve?
5. What rectangles in the cost curve diagram depict total revenue, total costs, and profits?
6. What is the difference between the breakeven point and the shutdown point?
7. How is the long-run average total cost curve derived?
8. What is the minimum efficient scale of a firm?
9. What is the relationship between the shape of the long-run total cost curve and economies of scale?
10. What are economies of scope? How are mergers related to economies of scale and scope?

Problems

1. Consider the relationship between your average grade (your grade point average [GPA]) and your marginal grade. Suppose you have taken 12 courses so far, and your average GPA is 3.25. Suppose the marginal grade is the grade you get in this course.

   a. If the grade you get in this class is an A (4.0), which is above your average, what will happen to your average GPA?

   b. If the grade you get in this class is a B (3.0), which is below your average, what will happen to your average GPA?

   c. What does this illustrate about the relationship between marginal and average curves in general?

2. Consider the age of the people working in the firm that you are doing an internship with this summer. Suppose the first person you meet is 40 years old, and the second and third are 33 and 27 years old, respectively. Graph the average and marginal age of the three people in the firm, placing age on the vertical axis and quantity of people on the horizontal axis in the order in which you met them. What do you notice about the relationship between marginal and average age?

3. Fill out the entries in the table below.

Q	TC	FC	VC	ATC	AVC	MC
0	8					
1	12					
2	14					
3	20					
4	30					
5	50					

4. Fill out the entries in the table below.

Quantity	Total Cost ($)	Fixed Cost ($)	Variable Cost ($)	Average Total Cost ($)	Average Variable Cost ($)	Marginal Cost ($)
0						
1				27.00		9.00
2				16.00		
3					5.00	
4					5.50	
5					8.40	

5. Draw the typical average total cost, average variable cost, and marginal cost curves for a profit maximizing, price-taking firm. For the case in which price equals average total cost, show the rectangles that represent

   a. total costs and total revenue.

   b. fixed costs and variable costs.

   c. profits.

   d. In your diagram, show what happens to the size of the areas as the market price increases.

6. Consider the firm whose cost function was provided in Problem 3. Suppose that the firm is a price-taker, and that the market price is $15 per unit.

   a. What quantity will the firm produce?

   b. Will this firm be earning economic profits? If so, how much?

   c. What is the breakeven price?

   d. What is the shutdown price?

7. Consider the firm whose cost function was provided in Problem 4. Suppose that the firm is a price-taker, and that the market price is $13 per unit.

   a. What quantity will this firm produce? Why?

   b. At that quantity level, what profits or losses will this firm make?

   c. In the short run, at what price would this firm break even? Explain briefly.

   d. At what price would the firm shut down? Explain briefly.

8. Suppose the average total cost curves for a firm for three different amounts of capital are as follows in the table. Plot the three average total cost curves in the same diagram. Then determine the long-run average total cost curve and show it in the same diagram.

Quantity	ATC_1	ATC_2	ATC_3
1	40	50	60
2	30	35	40
3	20	25	30
4	30	15	25
5	40	30	20
6	50	40	30

9. Plot the following data on quantity of production and long-run average total cost for a firm. Show the areas of economies and diseconomies of scale and constant returns to scale. What is the minimum efficient scale?

Quantity	Long-Run ATC
1	33
2	27
3	25
4	25
5	30
6	38
7	50

10. Are there economies of scale to teaching an introductory economics course? What economies of scale are realized if class sizes increase? Is there a maximum class size beyond which diseconomies of scale are experienced?

8.7 Appendix to Chapter 8: Producer Theory with Isoquants

In this chapter, we looked at how firms adjust their labor and capital inputs when the cost of these inputs changes over time. Here we give a graphic illustration of a firm's choice between labor and capital. The graphs are similar to the budget lines and indifference curves used to describe consumer choice in the appendix to Chapter 5. We use these graphs to show exactly how a firm's choice between labor and capital depends on the relative price of labor and capital.

Combining Capital and Labor

Consider an example of a firm with two inputs to production: capital and labor. Table 8.4 shows the possible combinations of inputs available to the firm. For example, if the firm has two units of capital and uses 24 hours of labor, it can produce three units of output. The hypothetical numbers in Table 8.4 could represent a wide variety of firms producing different types of products, but observe that we have chosen the units in the table to be the same as those for the firm shown in Table 8.1. (To make a comparison between Table 8.4 and Table 8.1, you can think of a "unit" of capital as corresponding to four trucks and two terminals with a cost of $300; two units of capital is eight trucks and four terminals at a cost of $600.) Table 8.4 could refer to a firm with any type of capital (computers, machine tools, telephones, or pizza ovens). To allow for all these possibilities, we refer to capital as a "unit" of capital.

TABLE 8.4 Production with Four Levels of Capital

Quantity Produced	Labor Input (hours)			
	With One Unit of Capital	With Two Units of Capital	With Three Units of Capital	With Four Units of Capital
0	0	0	0	0
1	15	9	6	5
2	27	17	12	10
3	37	24	17	13
4	48	32	22	18
5	60	41	29	23
6	74	51	36	29
7	90	62	43	35
8	109	74	52	41
9	134	87	61	49
10	166	101	71	57
11	216	128	90	72
12	290	170	119	95
13	400	270	189	151
14	—	400	300	220
15	—	—	425	300
16	—	—	—	430

Note: The column showing labor input with one unit of capital corresponds to the production function for Melodic Movements discussed in Chapter 8 (see Table 8.2). The omitted entries in the table (—) represent quantities of production that cannot be achieved without more capital.

The information in Table 8.4 can be represented graphically, as shown in Figure 8.20. Each column is plotted with labor input on the horizontal axis and the quantity produced on the vertical axis. Each column represents the production function for a given level of capital. Note that higher levels of capital increase the amount that can be produced with a given amount of labor. In other words, as we add more capital, the relationship between labor and output shifts up.

FIGURE 8.20 The Production Function with Four Levels of Capital
As the amount of labor input increases, so too does the amount of output. Each curve corresponds to a different level of capital. Higher curves represent higher levels of capital. The points on these four curves are obtained from the four columns of Table 8.4.

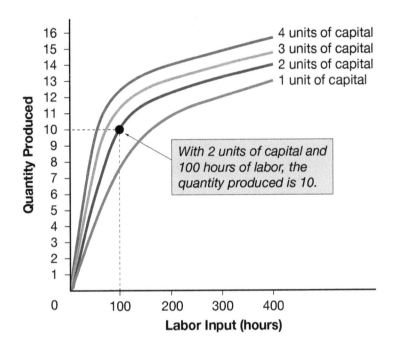

The information in Table 8.4 and Figure 8.20 can be displayed in another graph, Figure 8.21, which provides a visual picture of how labor and capital jointly help a firm produce its product. Figure 8.21 puts capital on the vertical axis and labor on the horizontal axis.We represent the quantity produced in Figure 8.21 by writing a number in a circle equal to the amount produced with each amount of labor and capital. For example, with one unit of capital and 60 hours of labor,the firm can produce five units of output, according to Table 8.4. Thus, we write the number 5 at the point in Figure 8.21 that represents labor input equal to 60 and capital input equal to one.

Isoquants

Observe in Figure 8.21 that the same amount of output can be produced using different combinations of capital and labor. We illustrate this in the figure by connecting the circles with the same quantity by a curved line. Each curve gives the combinations of labor and capital that produce the same quantity of output. The curves in Figure 8.21 are called isoquants, where iso means "the same" and quant stands for "quantity produced." Thus, an **isoquant** is a curve that shows all the possible combinations of labor and capital that result in the same quantity of production. Isoquants convey a lot of information visually. Higher isoquants—those up and to the right—represent higher levels of output. Each isoquant slopes down because ascapital input declines, labor input must increase if the quantity produced is to remain the same. The slope of the isoquants tells us how much labor must be substituted for capital (or vice versa) to leave production unchanged. Thus, the isoquants are good for studying how firms substitute one input for another when the prices of the inputs change. The slope of the isoquant is called the **rate of technical substitution**, because it tells us how much capital needs to be substituted for labor to give the same amount of production when labor is reduced by one unit.

isoquant

A curve that shows all the possible combinations of labor and capital that result in the same quantity of production.

rate of technical substitution

The rate at which one input must be substituted for another input to maintain the same production. The slope of the isoquant.

FIGURE 8.21 Isoquants

Each circled number gives the quantity produced for the amounts of labor and capital on the axes at that point. The lines connecting equal quantities are called isoquants.

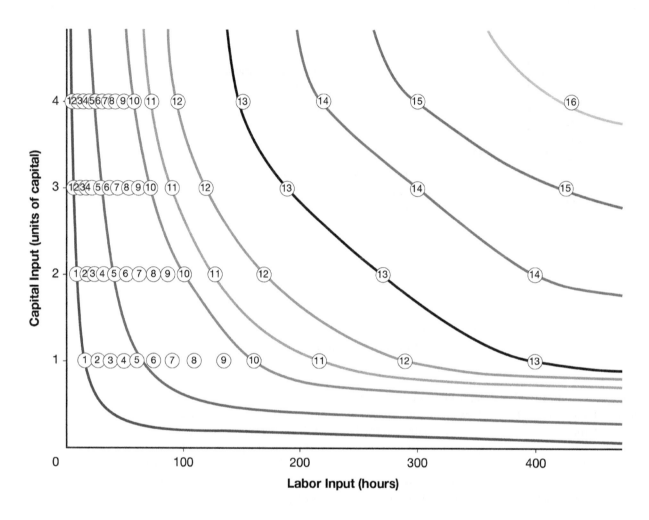

Remember that the points in Figure 8.21 do not display any information that is not in Table 8.4 or Figure 8.20. The same information appears in a different and convenient way.

Isocost Lines

A firm's total costs also can be shown on a diagram like Figure 8.21. In considering the choice between capital and labor, the firm needs to consider the price of both. Suppose that labor costs $10 per hour and capital costs $300 per unit. Then if the firm uses one unit of capital and 150 hours of labor, its total costs will be (1 × $300) + ($150 × $10) = $1,800. For the same total costs, the firm can pay for other combinations of labor and capital. For example, two units of capital and 120 hours of labor also cost $1,800. Other combinations are as follows:

TABLE 8.5 Different Combinations of Capital and Labor Resulting in the Same Cost

Hours of Labor	Units of Capital	Total Costs
180	0	(180 x $10) + (0 x $300) = $1,800
150	1	(150 x $10) + (1 x $300) = $1,800
120	2	(120 x $10) + (2 x $300) = $1,800
90	3	(90 x $10) + (3 x $300) = $1,800
60	4	(60 x $10) + (4 x $300) = $1,800
30	5	(30 x $10) + (5 x $300) = $1,800
0	6	(0 x $10) + (6 x $300) = $1,800

In other words, the $1,800 can be spent on any of these combinations of labor and capital. With $1,800, the firm can use six units of capital, but that would not enable the firm to hire any workers.

These different combinations of labor and capital that have total costs of $1,800 are plotted in Figure 8.22. Each combination of labor and capital in the table is plotted, and the points are connected by a line. The line is called an **isocost line**. An isocost line shows the combinations of capital and labor that have the same total costs.

isocost line

A line that shows the combinations of capital and labor that have the same total costs.

FIGURE 8.22 An Isocost Line

Each isocost line shows all the combinations of labor and capital that give the same total costs. In this case, the price of capital is $300 per unit and the price of labor is $10 per hour. Total costs are $1,800. For example, if one unit of capital and 150 hours of labor are employed, total costs are $1,800 = (1 x $300) + (150 x $10).

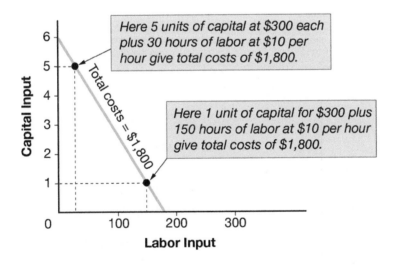

The position of the isocost line depends on the amount of total costs. Higher total costs are represented by higher isocost lines. This is shown in Figure 8.23. Observe that the isocost line for total costs of $2,100 is above the one for total costs of $1,800.

The slope of the isocost line depends on the ratio of the price of labor to the price of capital. In particular, the slope equals –1 times the ratio of the price of labor to the price of capital. This is illustrated in Figure 8.24 for the case in which total costs equal $1,800. If the price of labor falls from $10 to $6, then the isocost line gets flatter. Thus, if the hourly wage were $6 instead of $10, the firm would be able to pay for 250 hours of work and one unit of capital, compared with only 150 hours and one unit of capital, and still would have total costs of $1,800. Thus, as the price of labor (the wage) falls relative to the price of capital, the isocost line gets flatter.

FIGURE 8.23 Several Isocost Lines with Different Total Costs

Isocost lines with higher total costs are above and to the right of those with lower total costs. All the isocost lines in this diagram have a capital cost of $300 per unit and a labor cost of $10 per hour.

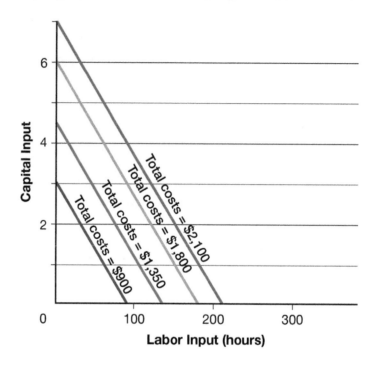

FIGURE 8.24 Effect of a Change in Relative Prices on the Isocost Line

When the price of labor falls relative to the price of capital, the isocost line gets flatter, as in this diagram. In this case, the price of labor falls from $10 per hour to $6 per hour while the price of capital remains at $300 per unit. Total costs remain equal to $1,800 in this case.

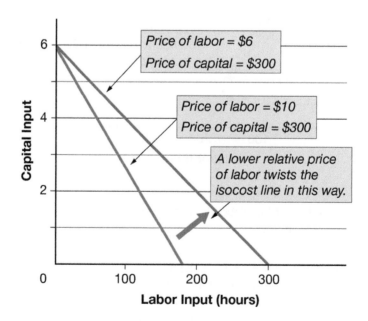

Minimizing Costs for a Given Quantity

The isoquant and isocost lines can be used to determine the least-cost combination of capital and labor for any given quantity of production. Figure 8.25 shows how. In Figure 8.25, we show three isocost lines, along with an isoquant representing 11 units of output. For the isocost lines, the price of labor is $10 and the price of capital is $300. The point at which the isocost line just touches the isoquant is a *tangency point*. It is labeled *A*.

FIGURE 8.25 Choosing Capital and Labor to Minimize Total Costs
This diagram illustrates how a firm chooses a mix of labor and capital to minimize total costs for a given level of output. Here the given level of output is 11 units, as shown by the single isoquant. Total costs are minimized by choosing the combination of labor and capital given by the tangency (point *A*) between the isocost line and the isoquant. For any other point on the isoquant, the quantity would be the same, but total costs would be higher.

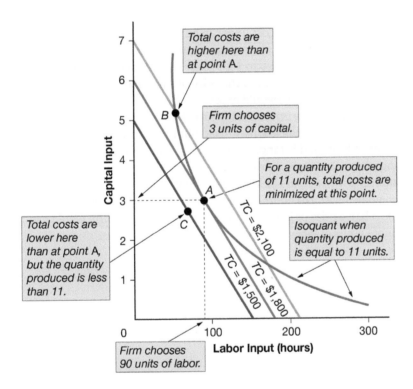

Point *A* is the point at which the firm minimizes the cost of producing 11 units of output. To see this, suppose you are at point *A* and you move to the left and up along the same isoquant to point *B*.

This means that the firm increases capital and decreases hours of labor, keeping the quantity produced constant at 11 units; that is, the firm substitutes capital for labor. But such a substitution increases the firm's costs, as shown in the figure. The payment for the extra capital will be greater than the saving from the reduced labor. Thus, moving along the isoquant from *A* to *B* would increase the total costs to the firm.

A similar reasoning applies to moving from point *A* to point *C*. The firm uses fewer labor hours and less capital at point *C*, so that total costs are lower than they are at point *A*. But at point *C*, the firm does not have enough inputs to produce 11 units of output. Thus, point *A* is the lowest-cost point at which the firm can produce 11 units of output. It is the point at which the lowest isocost line is touching the isoquant.

The Cost Minimization Rule

The rate of technical substitution of capital for labor and the ratio of the price of labor to the price of capital are equal at point A, because the slopes of the isoquant and of the isocost line are equal at point A. If the firm is minimizing its costs, then the rate of technical substitution must equal the input price ratio. The equality between the rate of technical substitution and the input price ratio is called the cost *minimization rule*.

Observe that isoquants are analogous to the indifference curves and the isocost lines are analogous to the budget line described in the appendix to Chapter 5. The cost minimization rule for a firm is much like the utility-maximizing rule for a consumer.

A Change in the Relative Price of Labor

Now we show how isoquants and isocost lines can be used to predict how a firm will adjust its mix of inputs when input prices change. For example, suppose that the hourly wage falls from $10 to $6 and the price of capital rises from $300 to $600. That is, labor becomes cheaper relative to capital. Originally, the ratio of the price of labor to the price of capital was 10/300 = 0.033; now it is 6/600 = 0.010. This is a big reduction, and we would expect the firm to adjust by changing capital and labor input. Figure 8.26 shows how the firm would adjust the mix of capital and labor for a given quantity of output. Figure 8.26 keeps the isoquant fixed but includes a new isocost line that reflects the lower relative price of labor and is tangent to the isoquant. Because the new isocost line is flatter, the point of tangency with the given isoquant no longer occurs at point A, at which three units of capital are combined with 90 hours of labor. Now tangency occurs at point D, at which two units of capital are combined with 130 hours of labor. In other words, the firm has substituted labor for capital when the relative price of labor fell. At the new point D, the firm would use one less unit of capital and 40 more hours of labor.

FIGURE 8.26 Effect of Lower Price of Labor Relative to Capital
The dark-orange isocost line has a lower price of labor relative to capital than the light-orange line. Hence, the amount of capital used by the firm decreases from three units to two units, and the amount of labor rises from 90 hours to 130 hours.

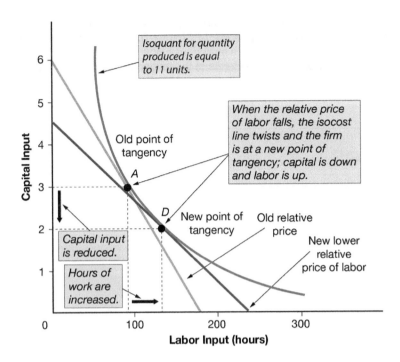

In summary, common sense tells us that the firm will hire more labor and use less capital when the price of labor falls relative to the price of capital. The isoquants and isocost lines confirm this and tell us by exactly how much.

Questions for Review

1. Why does the isoquant slope downward?
2. Why does the isocost line slope downward?
3. What determines the slope of the isocost line?
4. Why does the firm minimize cost for a given level of output by choosing capital and labor at the point at which the isocost line is tangent to the isoquant?

Problems

1. Graph the isocost line associated with a wage of $10 per hour and a price of capital of $50 for total costs of $200, $240, and $300. Suppose the wage rises to $15 and the price of capital stays at $50. Show how the isocost line moves for the case in which total costs are $300.

2. Sketch a typical isocost line and isoquant for which the firm has chosen a combination of capital and labor that minimizes total costs for a given quantity of output. Now suppose the price of capital rises and the wage does not change. What must the firm do to maintain the same level of output as before the increase in the price of capital and still minimize costs? Will it substitute away from capital?

3. Draw a diagram with an isocost line and an isoquant next to a diagram with a budget line and an indifference curve from the appendix to Chapter 5. List the similarities and differences. How are the isocost and budget lines analogous? How are the isoquant and the indifference curve analogous? What is the importance of the tangency point in each case?

Endnotes

---

1. Gabrielle Hamilton, "My Restaurant Was My Life for 20 Years. Does the World Need It Anymore?" *New York Times*, April 23, 2020. https://www.nytimes.com/2020/04/23/magazine/closing-prune-restaurant-covid.html.

CHAPTER 9
The Rise and Fall of Industries

Fred Smith's college term paper led to the birth of a new industry. In the paper, he described his idea for a new product: reliable overnight mail service. Although he got only a C on the paper, Fred Smith pursued his idea and became an entrepreneur. After graduating from college in 1973, he started a business firm that guaranteed next-day delivery of a letter or a package virtually anywhere in the United States. The firm, FedEx, was an extraordinary success; its sales reached $1 billion by 1982, $4 billion by 1988, $8 billion by 1992, $29 billion by 2005, and passed $50 billion for the first time in 2016.

Seeing the high profits earned by FedEx, many other firms entered the express delivery industry. In the late 1970s, United Parcel Service (UPS) and DHL entered; in the early 1980s, the U.S. Postal Service entered; many small local firms you probably have never heard of also got into the act. The entire industry expanded along with FedEx.

The express delivery industry is an example of an industry that grew rapidly over time. Many other examples of fast-growing industries exist in the annals of economic history. Estee Lauder founded a cosmetics firm years ago; it grew along with the cosmetics industry as a whole. Kemmons Wilson started the motel franchising industry when he saw the potential demand for clean, reliable rooms for travelers and opened his first Holiday Inn in Memphis in 1952; by 1968, there were 1,000 Holiday Inns, and now the industry includes other motel firms, such as Days Inn and Motel 6.

Of course, industries do not always grow. The mainframe computer industry declined as the personal computer industry grew. The long-distance telephone industry declined when the use of cellular phones increased. The video rental store industry shrank as the DVD rental by mail industry and satellite and cable television companies became more widespread, and taxi companies are struggling to deal with the entry of ride-sharing services like Uber and Lyft. FedEx and UPS themselves have been challenged by Amazon's increased use of gig-economy drivers to deliver packages in their own vans.

The causes of the rise and fall of industries can be traced to new ideas such as overnight delivery, to new cost-reducing technologies such as the Internet or DVDs, or to changes in consumer tastes. This latter shift, for example, is one reason behind the widespread popularity of low-carbohydrate diets, which favor reducing the intake of foods like bread and pasta in favor of high-protein foods like meat and cheese, providing an unexpected boost for meat producers. Some industries have recurring ups and downs. The oil tanker shipping industry, for example, regularly expands when oil demand increases and declines when oil demand falls.

In this chapter, we develop a model to explain the behavior of whole industries over time. We examine how economic forces cause industries to adjust to new technologies and to shifts in consumer tastes. Changes in the industry then occur as firms either enter or exit the industry. The initial forces causing an industry to rise or fall are described by shifts in a cost curve or a demand curve. Our analysis assumes that the firms are operating in competitive markets. The central task of this chapter is to show how an industry grows or contracts as firms enter or exit the industry. Do profits of individual firms fall or rise as a result? Do the prices consumers pay increase or decrease?

FIGURE 9.1 FedEx Serves Millions of Customers Every Day
FedEx trucks are a common sight on roads. Each day, they deliver millions of packages and documents to offices and residences across the country.

Source: Antonio Gravante/Shutterstock.com

9.1 Markets and Industries

industry

A group of firms producing a similar product.

We begin this analysis by providing a brief definition of what an industry is and by giving some examples of different industry types. An **industry** is a group of firms producing a similar product. The cosmetics industry, for example, refers to the firms producing cosmetics. The term *market* sometimes is used instead of industry. For example, the phrases "the firms in the cosmetics industry" and "the firms in the cosmetics market" typically mean the same thing. But the term *market* also can refer to the consumers who buy the goods and to the interaction of the producers and the consumers. Both firms and consumers are in the cosmetics market, but only firms are in the cosmetics industry.

Firms in an industry can produce *services* such as overnight delivery or overnight accommodations as well as manufactured goods. Many industries are global. Firms in the United States compete with firms in Japan, Europe, and elsewhere. Reduced transportation and communication costs in recent years have made many industries global. Until competition from Europe and Japan intensified in the 1980s, the automobile industry in the United States consisted mainly of three firms—General Motors, Ford, and Chrysler. Now the industry is truly global, with Honda, Toyota, Hyundai, and Nissan selling cars in the United States, and Ford and General Motors selling cars throughout the world.

Review

- An industry is a group of firms producing a similar product.
- A market refers to both the firms in the industry and the consumers who buy the goods produced by the firm.
- Firms can produce goods or services.

9.2 The Long-Run Competitive Equilibrium Model of an Industry

long-run competitive equilibrium model

A model of firms in an industry in which free entry and exit produce an equilibrium such that price equals the minimum of average total cost.

The model we develop to explain the behavior of industries assumes that firms in the industry maximize profits and that they are competitive. As in the competitive equilibrium model of Chapter 7, individual firms are price-takers; that is, they cannot affect the price. But to explain how the industry changes over time, in this chapter we add something new to the competitive equilibrium model. Over time, some firms will enter an industry and other firms will exit an industry. Because the entry and exit of firms takes time, we call this model the **long-run competitive equilibrium model**.

When we use the long-run competitive equilibrium model to explain the behavior of an actual industry, we do not necessarily expect that the industry conforms exactly to the assumptions of the model. A model is a means of explaining events in real-world industries; it is not the real world itself. In fact, some industries are competitive, and some are not competitive. But the model can work well as an approximation in many industries. In Chapter 10 and Chapter 11, we will develop alternative models of industry behavior that describe monopoly and the gray area between monopoly and competitive markets. For this chapter, however, we focus on the competitive model. This model was one of the first developed by economists to explain the dynamic behavior of an industry, and it has wide applicability and works well. Moreover, understanding the model will make it easier to understand the alternative models developed in later chapters.

Setting Up the Model with Graphs

Figure 9.2 illustrates the demand curve in a competitive market. The left graph views the market from the perspective of a single typical firm in an industry. The price is on the vertical axis, and the quantity produced by the single firm is on the horizontal axis. The assumption of a competitive firm implies that the firm faces a given price level, represented by a flat demand curve.

The market demand curve for the goods produced by the firms in the industry is shown in the right graph of Figure 9.2. The price is also on the vertical axis of the graph on the right, but the horizontal axis measures the *whole market or industry* production. Notice that even though the single firm takes the price as given, the market demand curve is downward sloping because it refers to the whole market. If the price in the market rises, then the quantity demanded of the product will fall. If the market price increases, then the quantity demanded will decline.

FIGURE 9.2 How a Competitive Firm Sees Demand in the Market
A competitive market is, by definition, one in which a single firm cannot affect the price. The firm takes the market price as given. Hence, the firm sees a flat demand curve, as shown in the graph on the left. Nevertheless, if all firms change production, the market price changes, as shown in the graph on the right. The two graphs are not alternatives. In a competitive market, they hold simultaneously. In the graph on the right, a given length along the horizontal axis represents a much greater quantity than the same length in the graph on the left.

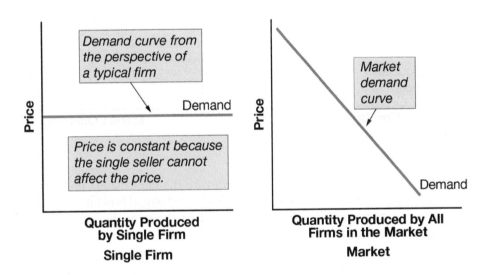

Entry and Exit

The new characteristic of competitive markets stressed in this chapter is the **free entry and exit** of firms in an industry. The question firms face is whether to *enter* an industry if they are not already in it or to *exit* from an industry they are in. The decisions are based on profits—total revenue less total costs. If profits are positive, firms have an incentive to enter the industry. If profits are negative, firms have an incentive to exit the industry. When profits are equal to zero, firms have no incentive for either entry or exit.

When firms enter or exit an industry, the entire market or industry supply curve is affected. Recall that the market or industry supply curve is the sum of all the individual firms' supply curves. With more firms supplying goods, the total quantity of goods supplied increases at every price.

free entry and exit

Movement of firms into and out of an industry that is not blocked by regulation, other firms, or any other barriers.

Thus, more firms in the industry means that the market supply curve shifts to the right; fewer firms in the industry means that the market supply curve shifts to the left.

Long-Run Equilibrium

Figure 9.3 is a two-part diagram that shows the profit maximizing behavior of a typical firm along with the market supply and demand curves. This diagram is generic; it could be drawn to correspond to the numeric specifications of the grape industry or any other industry. The left graph shows the cost curves of the typical firm in the industry with their typical positions: Marginal cost cuts through the average total cost curve at its lowest point. We did not draw in the average variable cost curve to keep the diagram from getting too cluttered.

FIGURE 9.3 Long-Run Equilibrium in a Competitive Market
The left graph shows the typical firm's cost curves and the market price. The right graph shows the market supply and demand curves. The price is the same in both graphs because the market has a single price. The price is at a level at which profits are zero because price equals average total cost.

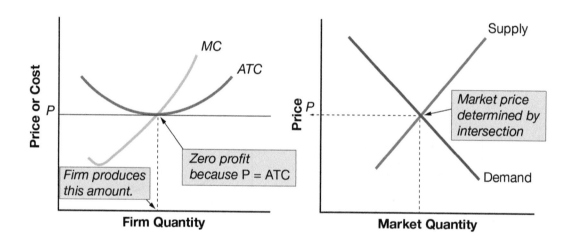

The left and right graphs of Figure 9.3 are drawn with the same market price, and this price links the two graphs together. This market price, which the individual firm takes as given, is determined by the market supply and demand curves, which are shown to the right of the cost curve diagram in Figure 9.3. As in Figure 9.2, even though the vertical axis on each graph shows the same price, the horizontal axes have different units, with an inch on the horizontal axis of the right-hand diagram representing much more production than an inch on the horizontal axis in the left-hand diagram.

long-run equilibrium

A situation in which entry into and exit from an industry are complete and economic profits are zero, with price (*P*) equal to average total cost (*ATC*).

The graphs are set up so that the price at the intersection of the market supply and demand curves is at a level that touches the bottom of the average total cost curve on the left graph. We know from Chapter 8 that profits are zero when *P* = *ATC*. Because profits are zero, firms have no incentive to either enter or exit the industry. This situation, in which profits are zero and there is no incentive to enter or exit, is called a **long-run equilibrium**.

An Increase in Demand

How does this long-run equilibrium come about? We can illustrate by examining what happens when demand shifts—for example, suppose the demand for grapes increases. We show this increase in demand in the top right graph of Figure 9.4; the market demand curve shifts out from D to D'.

FIGURE 9.4 The Rise of an Industry after a Shift in Demand
The diagrams at the top show the short run. A shift in the demand curve to the right causes the price to rise from P to P'; each firm produces more, and profits rise. Higher profits cause firms to enter the industry. The diagrams at the bottom show the long run. As firms enter, the market supply curve shifts to the right, and the price falls back to P. New entry does not stop until profits return to zero in the long run.

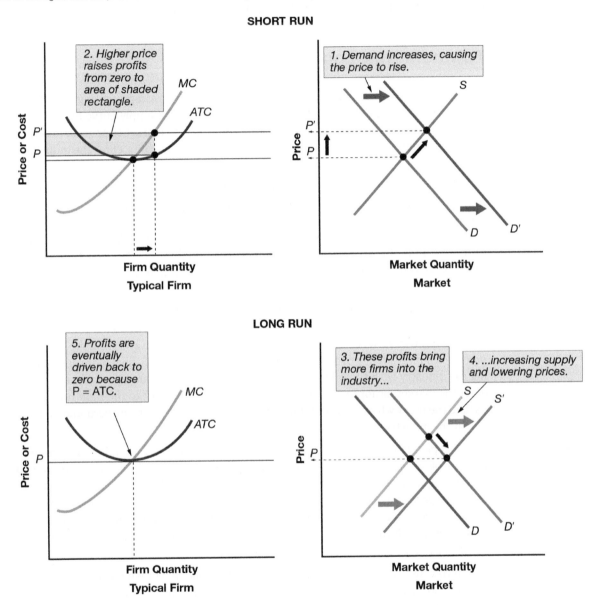

Short-Run Effects

Focus first on the top part of Figure 9.4, representing the short run. As the demand curve shifts out, we move up along the supply curve to a new intersection of the market supply curve and the market demand curve at a higher price, P'.

The implications of the rise in the market price for the individual firm are shown in the top left graph, where the price line is moved up from P to P'. A profit-maximizing firm already in the industry will produce more because the market price is higher. This result is seen in the top left graph of Figure 9.4; the higher price intersects the marginal cost curve at a higher quantity of production. Note also—and this is crucial—that at this higher price and higher level of production, the typical firm is now earning profits, as shown by the shaded rectangle in the top left graph. Price is above average total cost, and so profits have risen above zero.

We have gone from a situation in which profits were zero for firms in the industry to a situation in which profits are positive. This shift has created a profit opportunity in the market, encouraging new firms to enter the industry. Thus, we have moved away from a long-run equilibrium (which was defined as a situation in which profits are zero and firms have no incentive to enter or exit) because of the disturbance that shifted the market demand curve.

Toward a New Long-Run Equilibrium

Now focus on the two graphs in the bottom part of Figure 9.4, representing what happens in this industry in the long run. In the lower right-hand graph, the supply curve for the whole industry or market shifts to the right from S to S'. Why? Because the market supply curve is the sum of the individual supply curves; as more firms, attracted by higher profits, enter the industry, they add to supply.

The rightward shift in the supply curve causes a reduction in the price below P', where it was in the short run. The price will continue adjusting until the price line just touches the bottom of the average total cost curve, where average total cost equals marginal cost. At this point, profits will again be zero, no new firms have the incentive to enter, and the industry will be in long-run equilibrium. Of course, this adjustment to a new long-run equilibrium takes time. It takes time for firms to decide whether or not to go into business, and it takes time to set up a firm once a decision is made.

The new long-run equilibrium for the typical firm is shown in the lower left graph. It may take several years for an industry to move from the top of Figure 9.4 to the bottom. In fact, it would be more accurate to draw several rows of diagrams between the top and the bottom, showing how the process occurs gradually over time. These additional rows could show more and more firms entering the industry with the price falling until eventually profits are zero again and the incentive to enter the market disappears. The market supply curve will shift to the right until the price comes back to the point where average total cost is at a minimum, profits are zero, and no firms will enter or exit the industry.

This picture can capture the post-COVID 19 reality for certain industries where the demand increase observed during the crisis is likely to persist in the post-pandemic environment as well. A good example is the hand-sanitizer industry. Consumers will have developed a greater appreciation for the importance of personal hygiene in staving off the spread of infectious diseases. More companies, as well as more households, will be purchasing and using hand sanitizing products. At the same time, new firms that entered this industry during the pandemic will remain in the business of making hand-sanitizer products, even after the crisis has abated, to meet this increased demand.

In contrast, consider the market for residential toilet paper which also showed a spike during the first months of the COVID-19 pandemic. Even though that run up in demand may have brought some new entrants into the market—manufacturers of commercial-grade toilet paper and foreign producers selling their goods by mail through Amazon—once the dust settles, demand would likely return to pre-crisis levels. The new entrants would return back to their established markets—commercial-grade toilet paper and their home countries—and the situation would look more like the initial equilibrium rather than the new equilibrium depicted in Figure 9.4.

A Decrease in Demand

The long-run competitive equilibrium model also can be used to explain the decline of an industry. Suppose the demand curve shifts from D to D', as illustrated in the top right graph in Figure 9.5.

This change in demand causes the market price to fall. The lower market price (*P'*) causes existing firms to cut back on production in the short run: At the new lower price, the individual firm depicted in the top left panel of Figure 9.5 is now running losses.

FIGURE 9.5 The Decline of an Industry after a Shift in Demand
In the short run, a reduction in demand lowers the price from *P* to *P'* and causes losses. Firms leave the industry, causing prices to rise back to *P*. In the long run, profits have returned to zero, the number of firms in the industry has declined, and the total quantity produced in the industry has fallen.

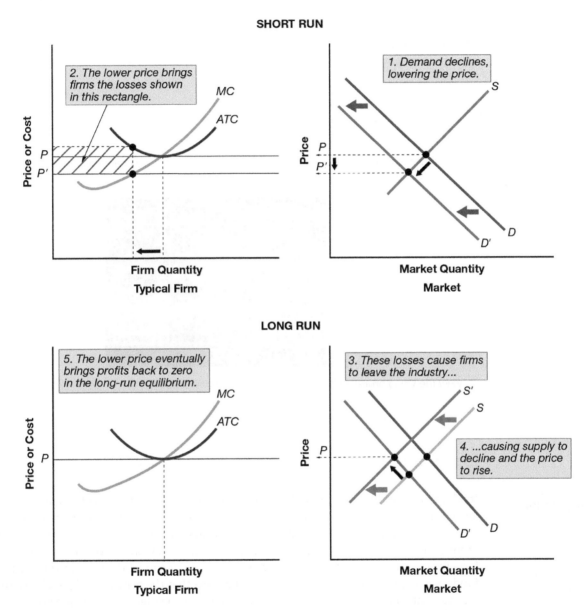

Over time, with profits less than zero, firms have an incentive to leave the industry. As they leave, the market supply curve shifts to the left from *S* to *S'*, as shown in the bottom right graph of Figure 9.5. This causes the price to rise again. The end of the process is a new long-run equilibrium, as shown in the bottom left graph of Figure 9.5. In the long run, fewer firms are in the industry, total production in the industry is lower, and profits are back to zero.

This picture can also capture the post-COVID reality for certain industries where the demand decrease observed during the crisis is likely to persist in the post-pandemic environment. Although one has to be cautious about confidently predicting future trends, two good examples may be self-service buffet restaurants and cruise ships. Consumers will have developed a greater wariness about eating food that has been touched by other customers. They are also likely to be concerned about the possibility of being trapped in a confined space with thousands of people among whom are scattered a few individuals carrying a virus. So even after the crisis has passed, some buffet restaurants and some cruise ship companies that existed and thrived prior to the crisis will not reopen. Furthermore, even the surviving cruise ship companies will be less likely to commission new ships or add new destinations even after the crisis has abated given the decreased demand.

As before, we can draw a contrast with other markets such as the demand for tickets for Major League Baseball or NFL Football. Most major league sports were shut down during the crisis but in the long run should return to normal activity. So once the dust settles (or more accurately once a vaccine or treatment has been discovered) demand for tickets to be at a baseball game or football game would also likely return to pre-crisis levels. The situation would then look more like the initial equilibrium rather than the new equilibrium depicted in Figure 9.5.

 The Retail Industry and COVID-19

Social distancing and stay-at-home orders during the COVID-19 pandemic hurt those who were already struggling.

View the video online at: http://www.youtube.com/embed/RakAiT5_Vv0?rel=0

Economic Profits versus Accounting Profits

accounting profits

Total revenue minus total costs, where total costs exclude the implicit opportunity costs; this is the definition of profits usually reported by firms.

economic profits

Total revenue minus total costs, where total costs include opportunity costs, whether implicit or explicit.

It is important at this point to emphasize that the economist's definition of profits is different from an accountant's definition. When you read about the profits of Apple in the newspaper, it is the accountant's definition that is being reported. Nothing is wrong with the accountant's definition of profits, but it is different from the economist's definition. When an accountant calculates profits for a firm, the total costs do not include the opportunity cost of the owner's time or the owner's funds. Such opportunity costs are *implicit*: The wage that the owner could get elsewhere and the interest that could be earned on the funds if they were invested elsewhere are not explicitly paid, and the accountant therefore ignores them. When computing **accounting profits**, such implicit opportunity costs are *not* included in total costs. When computing **economic profits**—the measure of profits economists use—implicit opportunity costs are included in total costs. Economic profits are equal to accounting profits less any opportunity costs that the accountants did not include when measuring total costs.

For example, suppose accounting profits for a convenience store are $40,000 a year. Suppose the owner of the store could earn $35,000 a year running a bakery. Suppose also that the owner could sell the business for $50,000 and invest the money in a bank, where it would earn interest at 6 percent per year, or $3,000. Then the opportunity cost—which the accountant would not have included in total costs—is $38,000 ($35,000 plus $3,000). To get economic profits, we have to subtract this opportunity cost from accounting profits. Thus, economic profits would be only $2,000.

Economic profits are used by economists because these profits measure the incentive that the owner of the firm has to stay in business rather than do something else. In this case, with $2,000 in economic profits, the owner has an incentive to stay in the business. But if the owner could earn $39,000 running a bakery, then economic profits for the convenience store would be –$2,000 ($40,000 − $39,000 − $3,000), and the owner would have an incentive to leave the convenience store business, even though accounting profits at the store were $40,000. Thus, economic profits are a better measure of incentives than accounting profits. Because we are interested in the incentives that firms have to either enter or exit an industry, when we refer to profits in this book, we mean economic profits.

Observe that if the store owner could earn exactly $37,000 at the bakery, then economic profits at the convenience store would be zero. Then the owner would be indifferent on economic considerations alone between staying in the convenience store business or running a bakery. The term **normal profits** refers to the amount of accounting profits that exist when economic profits are equal to zero. In this last case, normal profits would be $40,000.

normal profits

The amount of accounting profits when economic profits are equal to zero.

The Equilibrium Number of Firms

The long-run equilibrium model predicts that a certain number of firms will be in the industry. The equilibrium number of firms will be such that there is no incentive for more firms to enter the industry or for others to leave. But how many firms is this? If the minimum point on the average cost curve of the typical firm represents production at a small scale, then the industry will have many firms. That is, many firms will each produce a small amount. If the minimum point represents production at a large scale, then the industry will have fewer firms; that is, a few firms will each produce a large amount.

To see this, consider the hypothetical case in which all firms are identical. For example, if the minimum point on the average total cost curve for each firm in the grape industry occurs at 10,000 tons and the equilibrium quantity in the whole market is 100,000 tons, then the model predicts that 10 firms will be in the industry. If the quantity at which average total cost is at a minimum 1,000 tons, then 100 firms will be in the industry. If the demand for grapes increases and brings about a new long-run equilibrium of 130,000 tons, then the number of firms in the industry will rise from 100 to 130 (in the case in which the minimum efficient scale was 1,000 tons) or from 10 to 13 (in the case in which the minimum efficient scale was 10,000 tons).

Entry or Exit Combined with Individual Firm Expansion or Contraction

Thus far, we have described the growth or decline of an industry in terms of the increase or decrease in the number of firms. Recall from Chapter 8 that, in the long run, a firm can expand its size by investing in new capital or reduce its size by getting rid of some of its capital. So the industry can grow or shrink as a result of changes in the size of existing firms.

In reality, industries usually grow by a combination of the expansion of existing firms and the entry of new firms. Similarly, industries can shrink either because of the exit of firms or because of a contraction in the size of existing firms. For example, when the expedited package express industry began to grow, it grew both because UPS and other firms entered and because FedEx expanded.

The expansion of an existing firm can occur under one of two conditions. First, the original size of the firm may be smaller than the minimum efficient scale, so the firm maybe able to lower its average costs while producing more units. Second, a change in technology or in the prices of inputs may change the cost function of the firm, pushing the minimum efficient scale to a larger number of units. Note that if the firm is already producing at the minimum long-run average total cost, then an increase in demand will not affect the size of the firm, and you will observe only entry of new firms into the industry.

Shifts in Cost Curves

Our analysis of the rise and fall of an industry thus far has centered around shifts in demand. But new technologies and ideas for new products that reduce costs also can cause an industry to change. The long-run competitive equilibrium model can be used to explain these changes, as shown in Figure 9.6.

FIGURE 9.6 Effect of a Reduction in Costs
A new technology reduces costs and shifts the typical firm's *ATC* and *MC* curves down. The market supply curve shifts down by the same amount as the shift in marginal cost if other firms in the industry adopt the new technology right away. But because of the economic profits, new firms have incentives to enter the industry. As shown in the lower left graph, in the long run, profits return to zero.

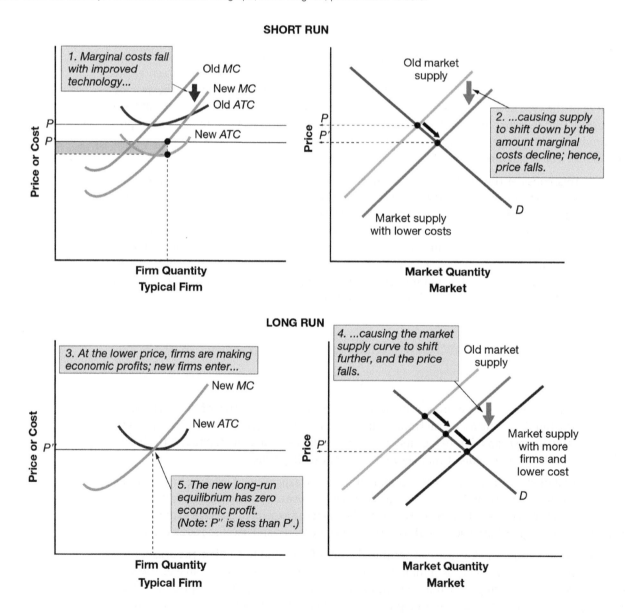

The case of cost-reducing technologies—as when Walmart introduced checkout counter scanners—can be handled by shifting down the average total cost curve and the marginal cost curve, as shown in Figure 9.6. This will lead to a situation of positive profits because average total cost falls below the original market price P. If other firms already in the industry adopt similar cost-cutting strategies, the market price will fall to P', but profits will still be positive, as shown in Figure 9.6. With positive profits, other firms will have incentives to enter the industry with similar technologies. As more firms enter the industry, the market supply curve shifts out. The price falls further to P'', and eventually competition brings economic profits back to zero.

If new entrants drive economic profits to zero in the long run, then what incentives do firms have to develop cost-cutting technologies? The answer is that the economic profits in the short run can be substantial. Walmart may have made hundreds of millions of dollars in economic profits before the competition eroded the profits away. Hence, Walmart benefited for a while from cost-cutting innovations. No idea will generate economic profits forever in a competitive market, but the short-run profits can provide plenty of incentive.

Average Total Cost Is Minimized

In the long-run equilibrium, average total cost is as low as technology will permit. You can see this in Figure 9.3, Figure 9.4, Figure 9.5, and Figure 9.6. In each case, the typical firm produces a quantity at which average total cost is at the minimum point of the firm's average total cost curve. This amount of production must occur in the long-run equilibrium because profits are zero. For profits to be zero, price must equal average total cost ($P = ATC$). The only place where $P = MC$ and $P = ATC$ is at the lowest point on the ATC curve. At this point, costs per unit are at a minimum.

That average total cost is at a minimum is an attractive feature of a competitive market in which firms are free to enter and exit. It means that goods are produced at the lowest cost, with the price consumers pay being equal to that lowest cost. If firms could not enter and exit, this attractive feature would be lost.

Efficient Allocation of Capital among Industries

An efficient allocation of capital among industries also is achieved by entry and exit in competitive markets. Entry of firms into a booming industry, for example, means that more capital has gone into that industry, where it can better satisfy consumer tastes. In the case of a declining industry, capital moves out of the industry to other industries, where it is used more efficiently. Thus, the long-run competitive equilibrium has another attractive property: Capital is allocated to its most efficient use. Again, this property is due to the free entry and exit of firms. If entry and exit were limited or if the market were not competitive for some other reason, this advantage would be lost.

The Rise of Some Industries in the COVID-19 Economy

Watch from minute 23:50 to 26:30 of this video for a discussion of how industries of new technologies can benefit from the COVID-19 outbreak.

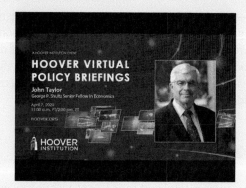

View the video online at: http://www.youtube.com/embed/zM3Rsp3FDnI?rel=0

Review

- Industries grow and shrink over time, with existing firms expanding or contracting in size, new firms entering the industry, and some existing firms going out of business. The long-run competitive equilibrium model explains how the entry and exit, expansion, and contraction patterns evolve.

- The decision to enter or exit an industry is determined by profit potential. Positive economic profits will attract new firms. Negative economic profits will cause firms to exit the industry. A long-run competitive equilibrium is a situation in which individual firms make zero profits ($P = ATC$) and no firms enter or exit an industry.

- If a demand increase causes market prices to rise, that increase in price will lead to positive profits for an individual firm in the short run because $P > ATC$. In response to the positive profit-making opportunity, new firms will enter, causing the market supply curve to shift to the right and causing price to come back down again until the profit-making opportunities have eroded, and the economy returns to long-run competitive equilibrium.

- If a demand decrease causes market prices to fall, that decrease in price will lead to negative profits for an individual firm in the short run because $P < ATC$. The negative profits increase the incentive for firms to leave the industry, causing the market supply curve to shift to the left. This raises price and reduces the losses incurred by individual firms until the economy returns to long-run competitive equilibrium.

- Similar adjustments take place if changes in technology bring about a shift of the cost curves of individual firms in the economy.

- How many firms are in an industry depends on the minimum efficient scale of the typical firm and the size of the industry. If firms are not operating at minimum efficient scale or if changes in technology make minimum efficient scale larger, then existing firms are likely to grow in size.

- When firms are allowed to freely enter and exit, another advantage is that average total cost is minimized. That goods are produced at the lowest possible cost is another advantage of competitive markets.

- Entry and exit also bring about an efficient allocation of capital. Booming industries will see entry of new firms and expansion of existing ones, which leads to more capital being allocated. Shrinking industries will see exit of firms and shrinking of firm size, which frees up capital for booming industries.
- Throughout this discussion, it is important to keep in mind that the profits being discussed are economic profits rather than accounting profits. Economic profits differ from accounting profits because they include the opportunity costs of the firm owners.

9.3 External Economies and Diseconomies of Scale

In Chapter 8, we introduced the concept of economies and diseconomies of scale for a firm. A firm whose long-run average total cost declines as the firm expands has economies of scale. If long-run average total cost rises as the firm expands, there are diseconomies of scale. Economies and diseconomies of scale may exist for whole industries as well as for firms.

The Standard Assumption: A Flat Long-Run Industry Supply Curve

Refer to the graphs in the lower right-hand panels of Figure 9.4 and Figure 9.5. You will see that the market price in the long-run equilibrium after the shift in demand is the same as that before the shift in demand. When demand increases, price rises, leading to higher profits for existing firms. The allure of positive profits brings new firms into the industry, pushing the supply curve out and lowering prices until profits are zero again. The intersections of the shifting demand and supply curves trace out the **long-run industry supply curve**, which, as you can see in Figure 9.7, is perfectly horizontal. The assumption of a flat long-run industry supply curve is the standard one economists use to study industries. Exceptions to this standard are examined below.

long-run industry supply curve

A curve traced out by the intersections of demand curves shifting to the right and the corresponding short-run supply curves.

FIGURE 9.7 The Standard Assumption

As demand increases and price rises, more firms enter the industry, attracted by the prospect of higher profits. The increase in the number of firms pushes the supply curve out, lowering prices and reducing incentives for further entry. In the long run, the industry supply curve will be horizontal, at the price at which profits for this typical firm are zero.

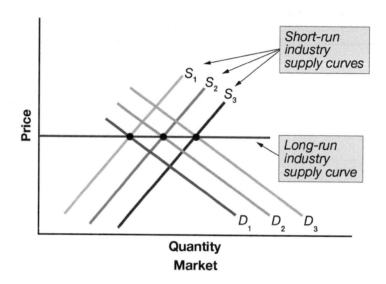

External Diseconomies of Scale

When the number of firms in the grape industry increases, the demand for water for irrigation in grape-growing regions also increases, and this may raise the price of water in these regions. Even though no single firm's decision affects the price of water for irrigation, the expansion of the industry does. If the price of water increases, then the cost of producing grapes increases for every firm. With the marginal cost of each grape producer increasing, the supply curve for each firm and for the industry or the market shifts up and to the left.

This is shown in the market supply and demand curves in Figure 9.8. Suppose the demand curve shifts from D_1 to D_2. As the industry expands, more firms enter the industry, and the supply curve shifts to the right from S_1 to S_2. Because the marginal cost at each firm rises as the industry expands, the supply curve does not shift to the right by as much as the demand curve shifts. Thus, the long-run equilibrium—the intersection of the demand curve D_2 and the supply curve S_2—occurs at a higher price than the intersection of S_1 and D_1.

external diseconomies of scale

A situation in which growth in an industry causes average total cost for the individual firm to rise because of some factor external to the firm; it corresponds to an upward-sloping long-run industry supply curve.

We could consider a further shift in demand to D_3, leading to a shift in supply to S_3. This change in demand would result in yet another long-run equilibrium at a higher price because average total cost is higher. Observe that as successive market demand curves intersect successive market supply curves, the price rises and quantity rises; an upward-sloping long-run industry supply curve is traced out. We call the phenomenon of an upward-sloping long-run industry supply curve **external diseconomies of scale**. The word *external* indicates that cost increases are external to the firm, for example, because of a higher price for inputs (such as water) to production. In contrast, the diseconomies of scale considered in Chapter 8 were internal to the firm, for example, because of increased costs of managing a larger firm; they can be called *internal diseconomies of scale* to distinguish them from the external case.

FIGURE 9.8 External Diseconomies of Scale

As demand increases and more firms enter the industry, each firm's costs increase, perhaps because the prices of inputs to production rise. The higher costs tend to limit the shift of the market supply curve to the right when new firms enter. The long-run industry supply curve slopes up, a phenomenon that is called external diseconomies of scale.

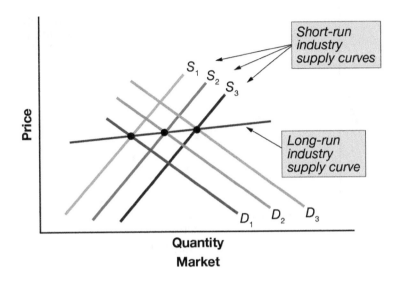

External Economies of Scale

External economies of scale also are possible. For example, an expansion of the domestic wine industry might make it worthwhile for students at agricultural schools to become specialists in wines made from domestic grapes. With a smaller industry, such specialization would not have been worthwhile. The expertise that comes from that specialization could reduce the cost of grape production by more than the cost of hiring the specialist. Then as the industry expands, both the average total cost and the marginal cost for individual firms may decline.

Another example is the expansion of the personal computer industry, which allowed many small specialized firms servicing personal computer manufacturers to emerge. With a smaller-scale industry, this would not have been possible.

The case of external economies of scale is shown in Figure 9.9. Again, suppose the demand curve shifts from D_1 to D_2. When the industry expands, the market supply curve shifts out from S_1 to S_2, or by *more* than the increase in demand, so that the price falls. The reason the market supply curve shifts more than the market demand curve is that marginal cost at each firm has declined as the number of firms in the industry has increased. This larger shift in supply compared with demand is shown in Figure 9.9. Thus, the price falls as the industry expands.

With additional shifts in demand from D_2 to D_3, the market demand curves intersect with successive market supply curves at lower prices, resulting in a long-run industry supply curve that is downward sloping. Again, the word *external* is used to distinguish these economies that occur outside the firm from those that are internal to the firm.

Note the difference between internal and external economies of scale. The expansion of a single firm can generate internal economies of scale with the number of firms in the industry fixed because individuals within the firm can specialize. The expansion of an industry can generate external economies of scale even if the size of each firm in the industry does not increase. As an industry expands, firms might even split up into several specialized firms, each concentrating on one part of the specialized work.

external economies of scale

A situation in which growth in an industry causes average total cost for the individual firm to fall because of some factor external to the firm; it corresponds to a downward-sloping long-run industry supply curve.

FIGURE 9.9 External Economies of Scale

As demand expands and more firms enter the industry, each firm's costs decline, which causes the supply curve to shift to the right by even more than it would as a result of the increase in the number of firms. The long-run industry supply curve thus is downward sloping, a phenomenon that is called external economies of scale.

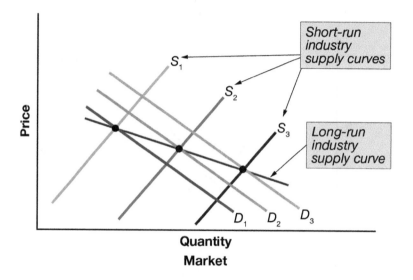

Reminder: *Internal economies or diseconomies of scale occur when a single firm expands (Chapter 8). External economies or diseconomies of scale occur when an industry expands (Chapter 9).*

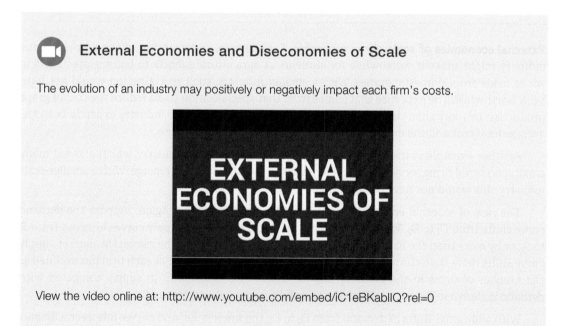

External and Internal Economies of Scale Together

In practice, it is possible for external and internal economies of scale to occur at the same time in one industry. When an industry grows in scale through the addition of new firms, it is common for the typical firm in the industry to expand its scale. FedEx has grown in size at the same time that more firms have entered the industry. Through its larger size, FedEx has achieved internal economies of scale (for example, by spreading the costs of its computer tracking system over more deliveries), and the larger industry as a whole has benefited from external economies of scale (as illustrated by the scanners shown in the photo).

FIGURE 9.10 External Economies of Scale

As an industry expands in size, firms in other industries have incentives to develop new products to service the industry. These new products reduce average total cost in the industry, thereby giving rise to economies of scale, as illustrated by the development of special electronic scanners for use by the expanding express delivery service industry (left). The new ideas in turn may be used to reduce costs in other industries, as illustrated by the use of electronic scanners for self-service checkout in the retail industry (right).

Source: photocritical/Shutterstock.com

Review

- The long-run industry supply curve is horizontal for the typical industry. When demand increases, raising prices and profits for existing firms, new firms enter into the industry. This results in an increase in supply, pushing prices back down to the original level in the long run so that profits are zero again. The shifting demand and supply curves trace out a horizontal long-run industry supply curve.

- External diseconomies of scale occur when the expansion of an industry raises costs at individual firms, perhaps because of a rise in input prices. An increase in demand in such an industry will see a smaller shift out in supply because the marginal cost for each firm rises as the industry expands. This implies that the long-run industry supply curve is upward sloping.

- External economies of scale arise when expansion of an industry lowers costs at individual firms in the industry. Opportunities for specialization for individuals and firms serving the industry are one reason for external economies of scale. An increase in demand in such an industry will see a larger shift out in supply because the marginal cost for each firm falls as the industry expands, bringing with it opportunities for specialization. This implies that the long-run industry supply curve is downward-sloping.

9.4 End-of-Chapter Materials

Conclusion

In this chapter, we have developed a model that explains why whole industries rise or fall over time. As consumer tastes change and new ideas are discovered, such changes are an ever-present phenomenon in modern economies around the world.

The model we developed in this chapter to explain such changes extends the competitive equilibrium model we developed in Chapter 5 through Chapter 8 to allow for the entry or exit of firms into or out of an industry. Because such entry or exit usually takes time, we emphasize that this modification applies to the long run. Profits draw firms into the industry over time, whereas losses cause firms to leave. As firms enter, the industry expands. As firms leave, the industry declines. In the long-run equilibrium, profit opportunities have disappeared, and entry or exit stops.

In Chapter 10 and Chapter 11, we begin to leave the realm of the competitive market. We will develop models of the behavior of monopolies and other firms for which the assumption of a competitive market is not accurate. In the process, we will see that many of the results we have obtained with competitive markets in this chapter are no longer true.

However, many of the ideas and concepts developed in this and the previous few chapters on the competitive model will be used in these chapters. The cost curve diagram will reappear in the model of monopoly in Chapter 10; the idea of entry and exit will reappear in Chapter 11.

As we consider these new models and new results, we will use the models of this chapter as a basis of comparison. A central question will be: "How different are the results from those of the long-run competitive equilibrium model?" Keep that question in mind as you study the coming chapters.

Key Points

1. Economic history is filled with stories about the rise and fall of industries. Industries grow rapidly when cost-reducing technologies are discovered or demand increases. They decline when demand decreases or when technological advances render an industry's product obsolete.

2. The long-run competitive equilibrium model assumes that firms will enter or exit an industry until economic profits are driven to zero. This model can be used to explain many facts about the rise and fall of industries over time.

3. When demand increases, the market price rises, leading to positive profits for individual firms in the short run. New firms will enter, causing the market supply curve to shift to the right and causing price to come back down again until the profit-making opportunities are eroded.

4. When demand decreases, the market price falls, leading to losses for individual firms in the short run. Firms will exit the industry, causing the market supply curve to shift to the left, and causing price to rise until losses are eliminated and there is no further exit.

5. In discussing the condition of zero profits in long-run competitive equilibrium, you should keep in mind that it is economic profits (not accounting profits) that are being driven to zero. Economic profits are accounting profits less opportunity costs.

6. Entry and exit can take place if changes in technology bring about a shift of the cost curves of individual firms in the economy.

7. An industry can expand either because more firms enter the industry or because existing firms become larger. An industry can shrink either because existing firms leave the industry or because they become smaller in size.

8. The number of firms in an industry depends on its size and the minimum efficient scale of the typical firm in the industry.

9. In the long run, the competitive equilibrium model implies that after entry and exit have taken place, average total costs are minimized and capital is allocated efficiently among industries.

10. The typical assumption is that the long-run industry supply curve is horizontal. However, industries may exhibit either external economies of scale, when the long-run industry supply curve slopes down, or external diseconomies of scale, when the long-run industry supply curve slopes up.

Questions for Review

1. What is the definition of an industry?

2. What are some possible sources of the rise of industries? Of the fall of industries?

3. What are the key characteristics of an economy that is in a long-run competitive equilibrium?

4. What happens to an industry in the long run when demand increases for the good produced by the industry?

5. What happens to an industry in the long run when demand decreases for the good produced by the industry?

6. What determines the number of firms in the economy?

7. When is it more likely for an increase in demand to lead to the entry of more firms in the economy rather than to existing firms becoming larger?

8. What is the difference between economic profits and accounting profits?

9. What are external economies of scale? How do they differ from internal economies of scale?

10. What are external diseconomies of scale? How do they differ from internal diseconomies of scale?

Problems

1. The data in the table are for a typical firm in a competitive industry (with identical firms). The firm can choose to have either one unit of capital or two units of capital in the long run. The two short-run average total cost curves (ATC_1 and ATC_2) and the two marginal cost curves (MC_1 and MC_2) are given in the table below.

	Costs with One Unit of Capital		Costs with Two Units of Capital	
Quantity	ATC_1	MC_1	ATC_2	MC_2
1	7.0	5	10.0	6
2	5.5	4	7.5	5
3	4.7	3	6.3	4
4	4.5	4	5.5	3
5	4.6	5	5.0	3
6	4.8	6	4.8	4
7	5.1	7	4.9	5

	Costs with One Unit of Capital		Costs with Two Units of Capital	
Quantity	ATC_1	MC_1	ATC_2	MC_2
8	5.5	8	5.0	6
9	5.9	9	5.2	7
10	6.3	10	5.5	8
11	6.7	11	5.8	9
12	7.2	12	6.2	10

a. Suppose the firm currently is producing with two units of capital. If the current price is $9 per unit, how much will the firm produce? How much are its profits?

b. Suppose the price falls to $7 per unit. How much will the firm produce now? How much are its profits?

c. What is the long-run ATC of the firm? Will the firm contract its output when it is able to change its capital?

d. What is the long-run industry equilibrium price and quantity for the typical firm? If there is a market demand of 4,000 units at that price, how many of these identical firms will the industry have?

2. Consider a typical office-cleaning firm that currently faces $24 in fixed costs and an $8 hourly wage for workers. The price the firm gets for each office cleaned in a large office building is $56 at the present equilibrium. The production function of the firm is shown in the following table.

Number of Offices Cleaned	Hours of Work
0	0
1	5
2	9
3	15
4	22

a. Find marginal costs and average total costs for the typical firm.

b. How many offices are cleaned by the typical firm at the present equilibrium price of $56? What are the firm's profits at this equilibrium?

c. What is the long-run equilibrium price level, assuming that the office-cleaning market is competitive?

d. How many offices are cleaned by the typical firm in long-run equilibrium?

3. Suppose corn farming in the United States can be represented by a competitive industry. Describe how this industry, currently in long-run equilibrium, would adjust to an increase in demand for corn. Explain your answer graphically, showing the cost curves for the typical farmer as well as the market supply and demand curves. Distinguish between the short run and the long run.

4. Consider developments in the airline industry. The old large airline firms relied on hubs to move passengers; passengers were flown to a hub airport, where they changed planes to continue their journeys. Southwest Airlines pioneered a new model of airline transportation that involved point-to-point transportation (with no stop at a hub), reliance on a single type of aircraft, and more flexible job descriptions that enabled planes to return to the air more rapidly after landing. These innovations reduced the costs per mile of transporting passengers. Describe the impact of this new model on the airline industry in the short run and in the long run.

5. Consider developments in the newspaper industry, which has been hit hard by the growth of the Internet. Many people have given up the habit of reading a newspaper daily and instead get their news from other online sources. Explain what the impact of this change in people's preferences will be on the newspaper industry in the short run and in the long run.

6. Suppose the government imposes a sales tax on a good sold by firms in a competitive industry. Describe what happens to the price of the good in the short run and in the long run when firms are free to enter and exit. What happens to the number of firms in the industry and to total production in the industry?

7. Because there are zero profits in the long run for any firm in a competitive industry, what incentive does a firm have in a competitive industry to pursue cost-cutting measures?

8. List some external economies of scale that might be realized by a computer-manufacturing firm that locates in a high-technology industrial park. List some diseconomies of scale that might be realized by a computer-programming firm that locates in an area of India that is attracting dozens of other such firms in search of software programmers. How do these economies or diseconomies of scale affect the shape of the long-run industry supply curve?

CHAPTER 10
Monopoly

In 2005, a lawsuit was filed against Apple charging that the company's iTunes software was creating a monopoly in the market for digital music. The plaintiffs argued that iTunes was preventing users from playing digital music purchased from other sites on Apple iPod devices. Shortly afterwards, in early 2007, France and several other European countries announced that they intended to take steps to ensure that songs purchased from the iTunes website could be used on music players other than the iPod. According to news reports, Norwegian consumer advocate Erik Thon described this action as being needed because "It cannot be good for the music industry for [Apple] to lock music into one system."

In response to these legal actions, Apple made the argument that the restrictions on digital music were mostly encryption technology needed to prevent hackers from controlling users' iPod content. Steve Jobs, the then chief executive officer of Apple, posted an item on Apple's website entitled "Thoughts on Music," in which he argued that most of the music that is played on iPods comes from CDs that users were free to put on any music player they wanted, meaning that consumers had plenty of choices in terms of music players. Furthermore, he argued that the restrictions that Apple had to impose on songs downloaded from iTunes were required by the companies that owned the rights to the music in the first place; these companies imposed such restrictions to prevent their songs from being copied and made available for free over the Internet.

What happened to these legal arguments? The European case was dropped in 2009 when Apple announced that it was lifting restrictions that limited songs purchased on Apple's iTunes store from being played on other devices. In 2015 Apple's arguments that it was justified in limiting the types of music that could be played on their own devices were vindicated in U.S. courts, when a federal jury ruled that these restrictions were not harmful to consumers. The crux of Apple's argument was that any company that was able to come up with its own system for preventing illegal copying would be able to license and sell songs over the Internet. Apple simply had designed a successful system in iTunes, a product that had given consumers access to more choices in how to listen to music instead of restricting their choices.

The iTunes case involves a situation in which governments bring, or threaten to bring, action against a company because they believe that the company has effectively become a monopolist, a sole producer of a good. Monopolies operate differently from firms in competitive markets. The biggest difference is that monopolies have the power to set the price in their markets. Consumers suffer because the monopolist restricts their choices, charges them higher prices, and supplies fewer goods than a competitive market would. Among the most notable cases in the past few decades were the breakup of AT&T in the 1980s and the decision in the early 2000s to split Microsoft in two (a decision that the Justice Department decided against carrying out). The most compelling current case to watch is with regard to Google. In September of 2019, attorneys-general of forty-eight U.S. states (all except Alabama and California) announced an investigation into "potential monopolistic behavior" by Google. The company was accused of using its monopoly power in search to unfairly restrict access and raise prices for online advertisers who were trying to reach customers online.

FIGURE 10.1 Does Apple Engage in Monopolistic Behavior?
Beginning in 2005, several lawsuits were filed against Apple, arguing that the company's iTunes software restricted users from playing music purchased from sources other than Apple on Apple devices.

Source: ms_pics_and_more/Shutterstock.com

The aim of this chapter is to develop a model of monopoly that can be used to understand how real world monopolies operate. The model explains how a monopoly decides what price to charge its customers and what quantity to sell. We also use the model to explain some puzzling pricing behavior, such as why some airlines charge a lower fare to travelers who stay over a Saturday night. Monopolies and the reasons for their existence raise important public policy questions about the role of government in the economy. The model we develop shows that monopolies cause a loss to society when compared with firms providing goods in competitive markets; the model also provides a way to measure that loss. This loss that monopolies cause to society creates a potential role for government to step in to try and reduce this loss.

Deciding when to, or whether to, intervene to break up a monopoly is an extremely complex task, however. As in the iTunes case or the Microsoft case, the Department of Justice often is faced with convincing arguments on both sides of the issue. Companies that are accused of being monopolists will argue that their products are simply superior to the competition and provide a service to consumers. Companies and governments will disagree on what the appropriate definition of the "market" is. For instance, Apple could argue that consumers buy music from a variety of sources and play it on a variety of different devices; hence, the iTunes–iPod combination, as popular as it is, hardly could be considered to be one that restricts consumer choice. In fact, even governments have a hard time agreeing with that notion. Shortly after the European action was announced, Thomas Barnett, a senior official in the Department of Justice's Antitrust Division, said in a speech that "consumers buy the expensive iPod device first, then have the option—not the obligation—to use the free iTunes software and buy the cheap iTunes songs."[1]

Finally, it is important to keep in mind that in the twenty-first-century economy, monopolies frequently do not last long. The increased use of the Internet and the decreased use of software that resides on one's own computer greatly reduced concerns about Microsoft's monopoly; the rise of cellular phones made us less concerned about local phone monopolies; satellite television and internet streaming services provided competition to your cable television company's local monopoly; the technological advances made by chip maker AMD eroded concerns about Intel's powerful role in the market for microprocessors. Similarly, as more music players and different music sales formats are introduced to the market, concerns about Apple may start to fade. Nevertheless, some monopolies do last a long time. De Beers is one of the most famous examples of a monopoly. It maintained its monopoly position from 1929 well into the 1980s, and even into the 2010s it controls about half of the diamond market (although the most recent surveys seem to suggest that millennials seem to have less of an attraction to the diamond as a symbol of lasting love and commitment).

10.1 A Model of Monopoly

A **monopoly** occurs when only one firm in an industry is selling a product for which there are no close substitutes. Thus, implicit in the definition of monopoly are **barriers to entry**—other firms are not free to enter the industry. For example, De Beers created barriers to entry by maintaining exclusive rights to the diamonds in most of the world's diamond mines. Microsoft was accused of creating a barrier to entry in software production by bundling together its software with the Windows operating system that came pre-installed on computers. Sometimes the barriers to entry are artificially created by the government through systems of copyrights and patents that prevent other firms from duplicating a company's products. These patents and copyrights allow a company to earn revenue by licensing the right to produce the particular good that resulted from the company's innovation and creativity.

The economist's model of a monopoly assumes that the monopoly will choose a level of output that maximizes profits. In this respect, the model of a monopoly is like that of a competitive firm. If increasing production will increase a monopoly's profits, then the monopoly will raise production, just as a competitive firm would. If cutting production will increase a monopoly's profits, then the monopoly will cut its production, just as a competitive firm would.

The difference between a monopoly and a competitive firm is not what motivates the firm but rather how its actions affect the market price. The most important difference is that a monopoly has **market power**. That is, a monopoly has the power to set the price in the market, whereas a competitor does not. This is why a monopoly is called a **price-maker** rather than a *price-taker*, the term used to refer to a competitive firm.

monopoly

One firm in an industry selling a product that does not have close substitutes.

barriers to entry

Anything that prevents firms from entering a market.

market power

A firm's power to set its price without losing its entire share of the market.

price-maker

A firm that has the power to set its price, rather than taking the price set by the market.

Getting an Intuitive Feel for the Market Power of a Monopoly

We can demonstrate the monopoly's power to affect the price in the market by looking at either what happens when the monopoly changes its price or what happens when the monopoly changes the quantity it produces. We consider the price decision first.

No One Can Undercut the Monopolist's Price

When several sellers are competing with one another in a competitive market, one seller can try to sell at a higher price, but no one will buy at that price because another seller is always nearby who will undercut that price. If a seller charges a higher price, everyone will ignore that seller; there is no effect on the market price.

The monopoly's situation is quite different. Instead of several sellers, the market has only one seller. If the single seller sets a high price, it has no need to worry about being undercut by other sellers. There are no other sellers. Thus, the single seller—the monopoly—has the power to set a high price. True, the buyers probably will buy less at the higher price—that is, as the price rises, the quantity demanded declines—but because no other sellers offer that product or service, they probably will buy something from the lone seller.

FIGURE 10.2 A Monopoly in Salt?
The monopoly power of the salt industry has been illustrated throughout history. Salt monopolies have contributed to the rise of several state powers—from governments in ancient China to medieval Europe, where Venice's control of the salt monopoly helped finance its navy and allowed it to dominate world trade.

Source: Marco Rubino/Shutterstock.com

The Impact of Quantity Decisions on the Price

Another way to see this important difference between a monopoly and a competitor is to examine what happens to the price when a firm changes the quantity it produces. Suppose that 100 firms are competing in the bagel-baking market in a large city, each producing about the same quantity of bagels each day. Suppose that one of the firms—Bageloaf—decides to cut its production in half. Although this is a huge cut for one firm, it is a small cut compared with the whole market—only 0.5 percent. *Thus, the market price will rise very little.* Moreover, if this little price increase affects the behavior of the other 99 firms at all, it will motivate them to increase their production slightly. As they increase the quantity they supply, they partially offset the cut in supply by Bageloaf, and so the change in market price will be even smaller. Thus, by any measure, the overall impact on the price from the change in Bageloaf's production is negligible. Bageloaf essentially has no power to affect the price of bagels in the city.

But now suppose that Bageloaf and the 99 other firms are taken over by Bagelopoly, which then becomes the only bagel bakery in the city. Now, if Bagelopoly cuts production in half, the total quantity of bagels supplied to the whole market is cut in half, and *this will have a big effect on the price in the market.*

If Bagelopoly cut its production even further, the price would rise further. If Bagelopoly increased the quantity it produced, however, the price of bagels would fall. Thus, Bagelopoly has immense power to affect the price. Even if Bagelopoly does not know exactly what the price elasticity of demand for bagels is, it can adjust the quantity it will produce either up or down to change the price.

Showing Market Power with a Graph

Figure 10.3 contrasts the market power of a monopoly with that of a competitive firm. The right-hand graph shows that the competitive firm views the market price as essentially out of its control. The market price is shown by the flat line and is thus the same regardless of how much the firm produces. If the competitive firm tried to charge a higher price, nobody would buy because many competitors would be charging a lower price; so, effectively, the competitive firm cannot charge a higher price.

FIGURE 10.3 How the Market Power of a Monopoly and a Competitive Firm Differ
A monopoly is the only firm in the market. Thus, the market demand curve and the demand curve of the monopoly are the same. By raising the price, the monopoly sells less. In contrast, the competitive firm has no impact on the market price. If the competitive firm charges a higher price, its sales will drop to zero because many other sellers offer identical products.

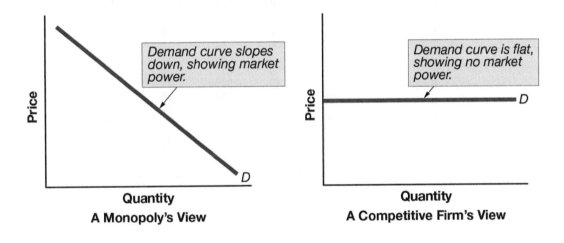

To a monopoly, on the other hand, things look quite different. Because the monopoly is the sole producer of the product, it represents the entire market. The monopoly—shown in the left-hand graph—sees a downward-sloping market demand curve for its product. *The downward-sloping demand curve seen by the monopoly is the same as the market demand curve.* If the monopoly charges a higher price, the quantity demanded declines along the demand curve. With a higher price, fewer people buy the item, but with no competitors to undercut that higher price, some demand still exists for the product. The difference in the market power of a monopoly and a competitive firm—illustrated by the slope of the demand curve each faces—causes the difference in the behavior of the two types of firms.

The Effects of a Monopoly's Decision on Revenues

Now that we have seen how the monopoly can affect the price in its market by changing the quantity it produces, let's see how its revenues are affected by the quantity it produces.

Figure 10.4 gives a specific numerical example of a monopoly. Depending on the units for measuring the quantity Q, the monopoly could be producing software, computer chips, or diamonds. The two columns on the left represent the market demand curve, showing a negative relationship between the price and the quantity sold: As the price falls from $130 to $120 per unit, for example, the quantity sold rises from three to four.

FIGURE 10.4 Revenue, Costs, and Profits for a Monopoly (price, revenue, and cost measured in dollars)
This figure shows how the firm's revenues, costs, and profits (the difference between revenues and costs) changes as output changes. Notice that profits increase as long as marginal revenue exceeds marginal cost (MR>MC).

Market Demand						
Quantity Produced and Sold (Q)	Price (P)	Total Revenue (TR)	Marginal Revenue (MR)	Total Costs (TC)	Marginal Cost (MC)	Profits
0	160	0	—	70	—	−70
1	150	150	150	79	9	71
2	140	280	130	84	5	196
3	130	390	110	94	10	296
4	120	480	90	114	20	366
5	110	550	70	148	34	402
6	100	600	50	196	48	404
7	90	630	30	261	65	369
8	80	640	10	351	90	289
9	70	630	−10	481	130	149
10	60	600	−30	656	175	−56

$TR = P \times Q$ $\dfrac{\text{Change in } TR}{\text{Change in } Q}$ $\dfrac{\text{Change in } TC}{\text{Change in } Q}$ $TR - TC$

Total Revenue and Marginal Revenue

The third column of Figure 10.4 shows what happens to the monopoly's *total revenue*, or price times quantity, as the quantity of output increases. Observe that at the beginning, when the monopoly increases the quantity produced, total revenue rises: When zero units are sold, total revenue is clearly zero; when one unit is sold, total revenue is 1 × $150, or $150; when two units are sold, total revenue is 2 x $140, or $280; and so on. As the quantity sold increases, however, total revenue rises by smaller and smaller amounts and eventually starts to fall. In Figure 10.4, total revenue reaches a peak of $640 at eight units sold and then starts to decline.

Marginal revenue, introduced in Chapter 6, is the change in total revenue from one more unit of that output sold. For example, if total revenue increases from $480 to $550 as output rises by one unit, marginal revenue is $70 ($550 - $480 = $70). Marginal revenue for the monopolist in Figure 10.4 is shown in the fourth column, next to total revenue. In addition, marginal revenue is plotted in the right-hand graph of Figure 10.5, where it is labeled *MR*.

The left-hand graph in Figure 10.5 shows how total revenue changes with the quantity of output for the example in Figure 10.4. It shows that total revenue increases by a smaller and smaller amount, reaches a maximum, and then begins to decline. In other words, *marginal revenue declines as the quantity of output rises and eventually becomes negative.* So, although a monopolist has the power to influence the price, this does not mean that it can get as high a level of total revenue as it wants.

FIGURE 10.5 Total Revenue, Marginal Revenue, and Demand
The graph on the left plots total revenue for each level of output in the table in Figure 10.4. Total revenue first rises and then declines as the quantity of output increases. Marginal revenue is the change in total revenue for each additional increase in the quantity of output and is shown by the bottom curve at the right. Observe that the marginal revenue curve lies below the demand curve at each level of output except Q = 1.

Why does total revenue increase by smaller and smaller amounts and then decline as production increases? To sell more output, the monopolist must lower the price to get people to buy the increased output. As it raises output, it must lower the price more and more, and this causes the increase in total revenue to get smaller. As the price falls to very low levels, revenue actually declines.

Marginal Revenue Is Less Than the Price

Another important relationship between marginal revenue and price is that for every level of output, *marginal revenue is less than the price* (except at the first unit of output, where it equals the price). To observe this, compare the price (P) and marginal revenue (MR) in Figure 10.4 or in the right-hand panel of Figure 10.5.

Note that the upper line in the right-hand graph in Figure 10.5 showing the price and the quantity of output demanded is simply the demand curve facing the monopolist. Thus, another way to say that marginal revenue is less than the price at a given level of output is to say that the *marginal revenue curve lies below the demand curve.*

Why is the marginal revenue curve below the demand curve? When the monopolist increases output by one unit, there are two effects on total revenue: (1) a positive effect, which equals the price P times the additional unit sold, and (2) a negative effect, which equals the reduction in the price on all items previously sold times the number of such items sold. For example, as the monopolist in Figure 10.4 increases production from four to five units and the price falls from $120 to $110, marginal revenue is $70. This $70 is equal to the increased revenue from the extra unit produced, or $110, less the decreased revenue from the reduction in the price, or $40 ($10 times the four units previously produced). Marginal revenue (MR = $70) is thus less than the price (P = $110). The two effects on marginal revenue are shown in the graph in Figure 10.6 when quantity increases from 3 to 4. Because the second effect—the reduction in revenue due to the lower price on the items previously produced—is subtracted from the first, the price is always greater than the marginal revenue.

FIGURE 10.6 Graph Showing the Two Effects on Marginal Revenue
When the monopoly raises output from three units to four units, revenue increases; that is, marginal revenue is greater than zero. There is a positive effect (vertical rectangle) because one more item is sold and a negative effect (horizontal rectangle) because prices on the first three units fall. Here the positive effect of the sale of an extra unit at $120 (vertical rectangle) is greater than the negative effect of selling each of the first three units at a price that is $10 less than before (horizontal rectangle), so marginal revenue is $120 - $30 = $90.

Marginal Revenue and Elasticity

Marginal revenue is negative when the price elasticity of demand is less than one. To see this, some algebra is helpful. Note from the examples in the table below that the following equation holds:

$$\text{marginal revenue} = (P \times \Delta Q) - (\Delta P \times Q)$$
$$\text{if MR} < 0 \text{ then}$$
$$(P \times \Delta Q) < (\Delta P \times Q)$$
$$\text{which implies that}$$
$$\frac{\left(\frac{\Delta Q}{Q}\right)}{\left(\frac{\Delta P}{P}\right)} < 1$$

or, in words, that the price elasticity of demand is less than one. Because it would be crazy for a monopolist to produce so much that its marginal revenue was negative, we conclude that a monopoly would never produce a level of output for which the price elasticity of demand would be less than one.

TABLE 10.1 Decomposing Marginal Revenue

Quantity Sold	Marginal Revenue (MR) ($)		Price x (Change in Quantity)	-	(Change in Price) x (Previous Quantity Sold)
			$P \times (\Delta Q)$		$(\Delta P) \times (Q)$
1	150	=	$150 x 1	-	$10 x 0
2	130	=	$140 x 1	-	$10 x 1
3	110	=	$130 x 1	-	$10 x 2
4	90	=	$120 x 1	-	$10 x 3
5	70	=	$110 x 1	-	$10 x 4
6	50	=	$100 x 1	-	$10 x 5
7	30	=	$90 x 1	-	$10 x 6
8	10	=	$80 x 1	-	$10 x 7
9	-10	=	$70 x 1	-	$10 x 8
10	-30	=	$60 x 1	-	$10 x 9

Average Revenue

We also can use average revenue to show that marginal revenue is less than the price. **Average revenue** is defined as total revenue divided by the quantity of output; that is, $AR = TR/Q$. Because total revenue (TR) equals price times quantity ($P \times Q$), we can write average revenue (AR) as ($P \times Q)/Q$ or, simply, the price P. In other words, the demand curve—which shows price at each level of output—also shows average revenue for each level of output.

Now recall from Chapter 8 that when the average of anything (costs, grades, heights, or revenues) declines, the marginal must be less than the average. Thus, because average revenues (prices) decline (that is, the demand curve slopes down), the marginal revenue curve must lie below the demand curve.

average revenue

Total revenue divided by quantity.

Finding Output to Maximize Profits at the Monopoly

Now that we have seen how a monopoly's revenues depend on the quantity it produces, let's see how its profits depend on the quantity it produces. Once we identify the relationship between profit and the quantity the monopoly will produce, we can determine the level of output that maximizes the monopoly's profits. Revenues alone cannot determine how much a firm produces. For instance, we know that a monopolist will never produce a quantity for which marginal revenue is negative. But that does not mean that it will produce until marginal revenue is zero. Even if each additional unit brings in extra revenue, the firm will have to look at the costs of producing that extra unit as well.

The last three columns of Figure 10.4 show the costs and profits for the example monopoly. There are no new concepts to introduce about costs for a monopoly, so we can continue to use the cost measures we developed in Chapter 7 to Chapter 9. The most important features to note are that total costs increase as more is produced and that marginal cost also increases, at least for high levels of output.

Comparing Total Revenue and Total Costs

The difference between total revenue and total costs is profits. Observe in Figure 10.4 that as the quantity produced increases, both the total revenue from selling the product and the total costs of producing the product increase. At some level of production, however, total costs start to increase more than revenue increases, so that eventually profits must reach a maximum.

A quick glance at the profits column in Figure 10.4 shows that this maximum level of profits is $404 and is reached when the monopoly produces six units of output. The price the monopoly must charge so that people will buy six units of output is $100, according to the second column of Figure 10.4. To help you visualize how profits change with quantity produced and to find the maximum level of profits, Figure 10.8 plots total costs, total revenue, and profits from Figure 10.4. Profits are shown as the gap between total costs and total revenue. The gap reaches a maximum when output Q equals six.

Equating Marginal Cost and Marginal Revenue

Economists use an alternative, more intuitive approach to finding the level of production that maximizes a monopolist's profits. This approach looks at marginal revenue and marginal cost and employs a rule that economists use extensively.

Consider producing different levels of output, starting with one unit and then rising unit by unit. Compare the marginal revenue from selling each additional unit of output with the marginal cost of producing it. If the marginal revenue is greater than the marginal cost of the additional unit, then profits will increase if the unit is produced. Thus, the unit should be produced, because total revenue rises by more than total costs. For example, in Figure 10.4, the marginal revenue from producing one unit of output is $150 and the marginal cost is $9, so producing that unit increases profits by $141. Thus, at least one unit should be produced. What about two units? Then marginal revenue equals $130 and marginal cost equals $5, so that second unit adds $125 to profits, meaning that it makes sense to produce two units.

Continuing this way, the monopolist should increase its output as long as marginal revenue is greater than marginal cost. But because marginal revenue is decreasing, at some level of output, marginal revenue will drop below marginal cost. The monopolist should not produce at that level. For example, in Figure 10.4, the marginal revenue from selling seven units of output is less than the marginal cost of producing it. Thus, the monopolist should not produce seven units; instead, six units of production, with $MR = 50$ and $MC = 48$, is the profit-maximization level. This is the highest level of output for which marginal revenue is greater than marginal cost. Note that this level of output is exactly what we obtain by looking at the gap between total revenue and total costs.

Thus, the monopolist should produce up to the level of production at which marginal cost equals marginal revenue (MC = MR). If the level of production cannot be adjusted so exactly that marginal revenue is precisely equal to marginal cost, then the firm should produce at the highest level of output for which marginal revenue exceeds marginal cost, as in Figure 10.4. In most cases, the monopoly will be able to adjust its output by smaller fractional amounts (for example, pounds of diamonds rather than tons of diamonds), and therefore marginal revenue will equal marginal cost.

A picture of how this marginal revenue equals marginal cost rule works is shown in Figure 10.7. The marginal revenue curve is plotted, along with the marginal cost curve. As the quantity produced increases above very low levels, the marginal cost curve slopes up and the marginal revenue curve slopes down. Marginal revenue equals marginal cost at the level of output at which the two curves intersect.

FIGURE 10.7 Marginal Revenue and Marginal Cost
The profit-maximizing monopoly will produce up to the point at which marginal revenue equals marginal cost, as shown in the diagram. If fractional units cannot be produced, then the monopoly will produce at the highest level of output for which marginal revenue is greater than marginal cost. These curves are drawn for the monopoly in the table in Figure 10.4.

$MC = MR$ at a Monopoly versus $MC = P$ at a Competitive Firm

It is useful to compare the $MC = MR$ rule for the monopolist with the $MC = P$ rule for the competitive firm that we derived in Chapter 6.

Marginal Revenue Equals the Price for a Price-Taker

For a competitive firm, total revenue is equal to the quantity sold (Q) multiplied by the market price (P), but the competitive firm cannot affect the price. Thus, when the quantity sold is increased by one unit, revenue is increased by the price. In other words, for a competitive firm, marginal revenue equals the price; to say that a competitive firm sets its marginal cost equal to marginal revenue is to say that it sets its marginal cost equal to the price. Thus, the $MC = MR$ rule applies to both monopolies and competitive firms that maximize profits.

A Visual Comparison

Figure 10.9 is a visual comparison of the two rules. A monopoly is shown on the right graph of Figure 10.9. We drew this kind of graph in Figure 10.8 except that it applies to any firm, so we do not show the units. A competitive firm is shown in the left graph of Figure 10.9. The scale on these two figures might be quite different; only the shapes are important for this comparison.

FIGURE 10.8 Finding a Quantity of Output to Maximize Profits

Profits are shown as the gap between total revenue and total costs in the graph on the left and are plotted on the graph on the right. Profits are at a maximum when the quantity of output is six.

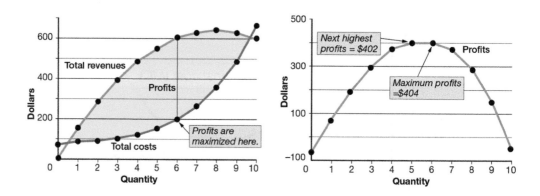

FIGURE 10.9 Profit Maximization for a Competitive Firm and a Monopoly

Total revenue for a competitive firm rises steadily with the amount sold; total revenue for a monopoly first rises and then falls. However, both the monopolist and the competitor maximize profits by making the gap between the total costs curve and the total revenue curve as large as possible or by setting the slope of the total revenue curve equal to the slope of the total costs curve. Thus, marginal revenue equals marginal cost. For the competitive firm, marginal revenue equals the price.

Look carefully at the shape of the total revenue curve for the monopoly and contrast it with the total revenue curve for the competitive firm. The total revenue curve for the monopoly starts to turn down at higher levels of output, whereas the total revenue curve for the competitive firm keeps rising in a straight line.

To illustrate the maximization of profits, we have put the same total costs curve on both graphs in Figure 10.9. Both types of firms maximize profits by setting production so that the gap between the total revenue curve and the total costs curve is as large as possible. That level of output, the profit-maximizing level, is shown for both firms. Higher or lower levels of output will reduce profits, as shown by the gaps between total revenue and total costs in the diagrams.

Observe that at the profit-maximizing level of output, the slope of the total costs curve is equal to the slope of the total revenue curve. Those of you who are mathematically inclined will notice that the slope of the total costs curve is how much total costs change when quantity is increased by one unit—that is, the marginal cost. Similarly, the slope of the total revenue curve is the marginal revenue—the increase in total revenue when output increases by one unit. Thus, we have another way of seeing that marginal revenue equals marginal cost for profit maximization.

For the competitive firm, marginal revenue is the price, which implies the condition of profit maximization at a competitive firm derived in Chapter 6: Marginal cost equals price. For the monopolist, however, marginal revenue and price are not the same thing.

Review

- When one firm is the sole producer of a product with no close substitutes, it is a monopoly. Most monopolies do not last forever. They come and go as technology changes. Barriers to the entry of new firms are needed to maintain a monopoly.
- Marginal revenue is the change in total revenue as output increases by one unit. Marginal revenue declines as quantity sold increases and may even become negative at some level of output.
- Marginal revenue is less than the price at each level of output (except the first). If we lower the price to increase the quantity sold by one unit, revenue increases by the amount of the sale price of the good, but revenue also decreases because the other units are now selling at a lower price.
- A monopolist will never produce at a quantity for which marginal revenue is negative. But it also will not produce until marginal revenue equals zero. Even if an additional unit brings in extra revenue, the firm's decision to produce depends on how much it costs to produce that extra unit.
- A monopoly is like a competitive firm in that it tries to maximize profits. But unlike a competitive firm, a monopoly has market power; it can affect the market price. The demand curve that the monopoly faces is the same as the market demand curve.
- The profit-maximizing quantity for a firm to produce is the quantity for which marginal revenue equals marginal cost ($MR = MC$). As long as $MR > MC$, the firm should keep producing, and if $MR < MC$, the firm should not produce that additional unit.
- For a competitive firm, marginal revenue equals price, because the firm cannot affect the price by increasing the quantity it sells. So marginal cost equals price, which in turn equals marginal revenue ($MR = MC = P$).
- For a monopoly, marginal revenue also equals marginal cost, but marginal revenue does not equal the price. Hence, for the monopolist, price is not necessarily equal to marginal cost.

10.2 The Generic Diagram of a Monopoly and Its Profits

Look at Figure 10.10, which combines the monopoly's demand and marginal revenue curves with its average total cost curve and marginal cost curve. This diagram is the workhorse of the model of a monopoly, just as Figure 8.9 in Chapter 8 is the workhorse of the model of a competitive firm. As with the diagram for a competitive firm, you should be able to draw it in your sleep. It is a generic diagram that applies to any monopolist, not just the one in Figure 10.5, so we do not put scales on the axes.

Observe that Figure 10.10 shows four curves: a downward-sloping demand curve (D), a marginal revenue curve (MR), an average total cost curve (ATC), and a marginal cost curve (MC). The position of these curves is important. First, the marginal cost curve cuts through the average total cost curve at the lowest point on the average total cost curve. Second, the marginal revenue curve is below the demand curve over the entire range of production (except at the vertical axis near one, where they are equal).

We already have given the reasons for these two relationships (in Chapter 8 and in the previous section of this chapter), but it would be a good idea for you to practice sketching your own diagram like Figure 10.10 to ensure that the positions of your curves meet these requirements.

FIGURE 10.10 The Generic Diagram for a Monopoly
The marginal revenue and demand curves are superimposed on the monopoly's cost curves. The monopoly's production, price, and profits can be seen on the same diagram. Quantity is given by the intersection of the marginal revenue curve and the marginal cost curve. Price is given by the demand curve at the point corresponding to the quantity produced, and average total cost is given by the ATC curve at that quantity. Monopoly profits are given by the rectangle that is the difference between total revenue and total costs.

Determining Monopoly Output and Price on the Diagram

In Figure 10.10 we show how to calculate the monopoly output and price. First, find the point of intersection of the marginal revenue curve and the marginal cost curve. Second, draw a dashed vertical line through this point and look down the dashed line at the horizontal axis to figure out the quantity produced. Producing a larger quantity would lower marginal revenue below marginal cost. Producing a smaller quantity would raise marginal revenue above marginal cost. The quantity shown is the profit-maximizing level. It is the amount the monopolist produces.

What price will the monopolist charge? We again use Figure 10.10, but be careful: Unlike the quantity, the monopolist's price is not determined by the intersection of the marginal revenue curve and the marginal cost curve. The price has to be such that the quantity demanded is equal to the quantity that the monopolist decides to produce. To find the price, we need to look at the demand curve in Figure 10.10. The demand curve gives the relationship between price and quantity demanded. It tells how much the monopolist will charge for its product to sell the amount produced.

To calculate the price, extend the dashed vertical line upward from the point of intersection of the marginal cost curve and the marginal revenue curve until it intersects the demand curve. At the intersection of the demand curve and the vertical line, we find the price that will generate a quantity demanded equal to the quantity produced. Now draw a horizontal line over to the left from the point of intersection to mark the price on the vertical axis. This is the monopoly's price, about which we will have more to say later.

Determining the Monopoly's Profits

Profits also can be shown on the diagram in Figure 10.10. Profits are given by the difference between the area of two rectangles, a total revenue rectangle and a total costs rectangle. Total revenue is price times quantity and thus is equal to the area of the rectangle with height equal to the monopoly price and length equal to the quantity produced. Total costs are average total cost times quantity and thus are equal to the area of the rectangle with height equal to ATC and length equal to the quantity produced. Profits are then equal to the shaded area that is the difference between these two rectangles.

It is possible for a monopoly to have negative profits, or losses, as shown in Figure 10.11. In this case, the price is below average total cost, and therefore total revenue is less than total costs. Like a competitive firm, a monopolist with negative profits will shut down if the price is less than average variable cost. It eventually will exit the market if negative profits persist.

FIGURE 10.11 A Monopoly with Negative Profits
If a monopoly finds that average total cost is greater than the price at which marginal revenue equals marginal cost, then it runs losses. If price is also less than average variable cost, then the monopoly should shut down, just like a competitive firm.

Review

- A monopolist's profit-maximizing output and price can be determined graphically. The diagram shows four curves: the marginal revenue curve, the demand curve, the marginal cost curve, and the average total cost curve.
- The monopoly's production is determined at the point at which marginal revenue equals marginal cost.

- The monopoly's price is determined from the demand curve at the point at which the quantity produced equals the quantity demanded.
- The monopoly's profits are determined by subtracting the total costs rectangle from the total revenue rectangle. The total revenue rectangle is given by the price times the quantity produced. The total costs rectangle is given by the average total cost times the quantity produced.

10.3 Competition, Monopoly, and Deadweight Loss

Are monopolies harmful to society? Do they reduce consumer surplus? Can we measure these effects? To answer these questions, economists compare the price and output of a monopoly with those of a competitive industry. First, observe in Figure 10.10 and Figure 10.11 that the monopoly does not operate at the minimum point on the average total cost curve even in the long run. Recall that firms in a competitive industry do operate at the lowest point on the average total cost curve in the long run. To go further in our comparison, we use Figure 10.12, which is a repeat of Figure 10.10, except that the average total cost curve is removed to reduce the clutter. All the other curves are the same.

Comparison with Competition

Suppose that instead of only one firm being in the market, it now includes many competitive firms. For example, suppose Bagelopoly—a single firm producing bagels in a large city—is broken down into 100 different bagel bakeries like Bageloaf. The production point for the monopolistic firm and its price before the breakup are marked as "monopoly quantity" and "monopoly price" in Figure 10.12. What are production and price after the breakup?

The market supply curve for the new competitive industry would be Bagelopoly's old marginal cost curve, because this is the sum of the marginal cost curves of all the newly created firms in the industry. Equilibrium in the competitive industry is the point at which this market supply curve crosses the market demand curve. The amount of production at that point is marked by "competitive quantity" in Figure 10.12. The price at that equilibrium is marked by "competitive price" on the vertical axis.

Compare the quantity and price for the monopolist and the competitive industry. It is clear that the quantity produced by the monopolist is less than the quantity produced by the competitive industry. It also is clear that the monopoly will charge a higher price than will emerge from a competitive industry. In sum, the monopoly produces less and charges a higher price than the competitive industry would.

This is an important result. The monopoly exploits its market power by holding back on the quantity produced and causing the price to rise compared with the competitive equilibrium. This is always the case. Convince yourself by drawing different diagrams. For example, when De Beers exercises its market power, it holds back production of diamonds, thereby raising the price and earning economic profits.

Even though the monopoly has the power to do so, it does not increase its price without limit. When the price is set very high, marginal cost rises above marginal revenue. That behavior is not profit maximizing.

FIGURE 10.12 Deadweight Loss from Monopoly
The monopolist's output and price are determined as in Figure 10.10. To get the competitive price, we imagine that competitive firms make up an industry supply curve that is the same as the monopolist's marginal cost curve. The competitive price and quantity are given by the intersection of the supply curve and the demand curve. The monopoly quantity is lower than the competitive quantity. The monopoly price is higher than the competitive price. The deadweight loss is the reduction in consumer plus producer surplus because of the lower level of production by the monopolist.

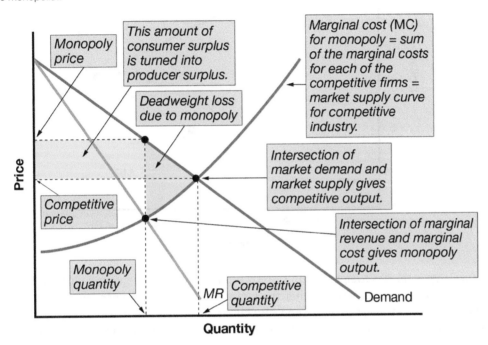

Deadweight Loss from Monopoly

The economic harm caused by a monopoly occurs because it produces less than a competitive industry would. How harmful, then, is a monopoly?

Consumer Surplus and Producer Surplus Again

Economists measure the harm caused by monopolies by the decline in the sum of consumer surplus plus producer surplus. Recall that *consumer surplus* is the area above the market price line and below the demand curve, the demand curve being a measure of consumers' marginal benefit from consuming the good. The *producer surplus* is the area above the marginal cost curve and below the market price line. Consumer surplus plus producer surplus is thus the area between the demand curve and the marginal cost curve. It measures the sum of the marginal benefits to consumers of the good less the sum of the marginal costs to the producers of the good. A competitive market will maximize the sum of consumer plus producer surplus.

With a lower quantity produced by a monopoly, however, the sum of consumer surplus and producer surplus is reduced, as shown in Figure 10.12. This reduction in consumer plus producer surplus is called the *deadweight loss due to monopoly*. It is a quantitative measure of the harm a monopoly causes the economy. A numerical example is given in Figure 10.13.

FIGURE 10.13 Numerical Example of Deadweight Loss Calculation

The monopoly shown in the diagram above produces only 12 items, but a competitive industry would produce 18 items. For the 13th through 17th items, which are not produced by the monopoly, the marginal benefit is greater than the marginal cost by the amounts $5, $4,$3, $2, and $1, respectively, as shown by the areas between the demand curve and the supply curve for the competitive industry. Hence, the deadweight loss caused by the monopoly is the sum $5 + $4 + $3 + $2 + $1 = $15.

How large is the deadweight loss in the U.S. economy? Using the method illustrated in Figure 10.12, empirical economists estimate that the loss is between 0.5 and 2 percent of gross domestic product (GDP), or between $60 billion and $240 billion, per year. Of course, the deadweight loss is a larger percentage of production in industries in which monopolies have a greater presence.

Figure 10.12 also shows that the monopoly takes, in the form of producer surplus, some of the consumer surplus that would have gone to the consumers in competitive markets. Consumer surplus is now the area below the demand curve and above the monopoly price, which is higher than the competitive price. This transfer of consumer surplus to the monopoly is not a deadweight loss, however, because what the consumers lose, the monopoly gains. This transfer affects the distribution of income, but it is not a net loss to society.

Meaningful Comparisons

In any given application, we need to be careful that the comparison of monopoly and competition makes sense. Some industries cannot be broken up into many competitive firms without changing the cost structure of the industry. For instance, having 100 sewer companies laying down pipes to serve one local area would be costly. Therefore, transforming a monopolistic sewer industry into a competitive sewer industry is unlikely to lead to greater societal benefits. Instead, we should try to affect the monopoly's decisions by government actions.

We also should be careful about concluding that a competitive industry of one type is preferable to a monopolistic industry of another type. History provides many such examples. Western settlers in the United States during the nineteenth century had a larger consumer surplus from railroads—in spite of the railroad monopolists' profits—than they did from competitive wagon trains. Modern-day users of the information highway—computers and telecommunications—reap a larger consumer surplus from Microsoft's software and Intel's computer chips, even if they are produced monopolistically, than they would from a competitive pocket calculator industry.

Deadweight Loss from a Monopoly

Learn more about production, pricing, and deadweight loss from a monopoly.

View the video online at: http://www.youtube.com/embed/YNcPxPz9fng?rel=0

The Monopoly Price Is Greater Than Marginal Cost

Another way to think about the loss to society from monopoly is to observe the difference between price and marginal cost. Figure 10.12, for example, shows that the monopoly price is well above the marginal cost at the quantity at which the monopoly produces.

Marginal Benefit Is More Than Marginal Cost

Because consumers will consume up to the point at which the marginal benefit of a good equals its price, the excessive price means that the marginal benefit of a good is greater than the marginal cost. This is inefficient because producing more of the good would increase benefits to consumers by more than the cost of producing it.

The size of the difference between price and marginal cost depends on the elasticity of the monopoly's demand curve. If the demand curve is highly elastic (close to a competitive firm's view as shown in Figure 10.3), then the difference between price and marginal cost is small.

The Price-Cost Margin

A common measure of the difference between price and marginal cost is the **price-cost margin**. It is defined as

$$\frac{\text{price} - \text{marginal cost}}{\text{price}}$$

For example, if the price is $4 and the marginal cost is $2, the price-cost margin is (4 - 2)/4 = 0.5. The price-cost margin for a competitive firm is zero because price equals marginal cost. Economists use a rule of thumb to show how the price-cost margin depends on the price elasticity of demand. The rule of thumb is shown in the equation below.

price-cost margin

The difference between price and marginal cost divided by the price. This index is an indicator of market power, where an index of zero indicates no market power and a higher price-cost margin indicates greater market power.

$$\text{price-cost margin} = \frac{1}{\text{price elasticity of demand}}$$

For example, when the elasticity of demand is two, the price-cost margin is 0.5. The flat demand curve has an infinite elasticity, in which case the price-cost margin is zero; in other words, price equals marginal cost.

Review

- A monopoly creates a deadweight loss because it restricts output below what the competitive market would produce. The cost is measured by the deadweight loss, which is the reduction in the sum of consumer plus producer surplus.
- Sometimes the comparison between monopoly and competition is only hypothetical because it would either be impossible or make no sense to break up the monopoly into competitive firms.
- Another way to measure the impact of a monopoly is by the difference between price and marginal cost. Monopolies always charge a price higher than marginal cost. The difference—summarized in the price-cost margin—depends inversely on the elasticity of demand.

10.4 Why Monopolies Exist

Given this demonstration that monopolies lead to high prices and a deadweight loss to society, you may be wondering why monopolies exist. In this section, we consider three reasons for the existence of monopolies.

Natural Monopolies

The nature of production is a key factor in determining the number of firms in the industry. If big firms are needed to produce at low cost, it may be natural for a few firms or only one firm to exist. In particular, *economies of scale*—a declining long-run average total cost curve over some range of production—can lead to a monopoly. Recall from Chapter 8 that the *minimum efficient scale* of a firm is the minimum size of the firm for which average total costs are lowest. If the minimum efficient scale is only a small fraction of the size of the market, then the market will have many firms.

For example, suppose the minimum efficient scale for beauty salons in a city is a size that serves 30 customers a day at each salon. Suppose the quantity of hair stylings demanded in the city is 300 per day. We can then expect the city to have ten beauty salons (300/30 = 10). But if the minimum efficient scale is larger (for example, 60 customers per day), then the number of firms in the industry will be smaller (for example, 300/60 = 5 salons). At the extreme case, where the minimum efficient scale of the firm is as large as or larger than the size of the market (for example, 300 per day), there probably will be only one firm (300/300 = 1), which will be a monopoly.

A sewer company in a small town, for example, has a minimum efficient scale larger than the number of houses and businesses in the town. The fixed costs to lay pipe down the street are huge, but each house connection has a relatively low cost, so average total cost declines as more houses are connected. Other industries that usually have a very large minimum efficient scale are electricity and water service. In each of these industries, average total cost is lowest if one firm delivers the service. **Natural monopolies** exist when average total cost is declining and the minimum efficient scale is larger than the size of the market.

The government regulates the prices charged by many natural monopolies. The purpose of the regulation is to keep the price below the monopoly price and closer to the competitive price. Such regulation thereby can reduce the deadweight loss from the monopoly. Alternative methods of regulating natural monopolies are discussed in Chapter 12. The government regulates water companies and electric companies.

A change in technology that changes the minimum efficient scale of firms can radically alter the number of firms in the industry. For example, AT&T used to be viewed as a natural monopoly in long-distance telephone service. Because laying copper wire across the United States required a huge cost, it made little sense to have more than one firm. The U.S. government regulated the prices that AT&T charged its customers, attempting to keep the price of calls below the monopoly price and closer to the competitive price. But when the technology for transmitting signals by microwave developed, it became easier for other firms also to provide services. Thus, MCI and Sprint, as well as AT&T, could provide services at least as cheaply as one firm. Because of this technological change, the government decided to end the AT&T monopoly by allowing MCI and Sprint to compete with AT&T. Nationwide telephone service is no longer a monopoly because the technology of providing telephone service has changed—almost all companies now provide landline phone service through digital voice technology that uses the same broadband connections that bring internet services to your home.

> ### 🎥 Natural Monopoly
>
> The costs and production of a natural monopoly explained when the natural monopoly is private or nationalized.
>
>
>
> View the video online at: http://www.youtube.com/embed/alelTql8Or4?rel=0

---

natural monopolies

A single firm in an industry in which average total cost is declining over the entire range of production and the minimum efficient scale is larger than the size of the market.

Patents and Copyrights

Another way monopolies arise is through the granting of patents and copyrights by the government. Intel's patent was the source of its monopoly on its computer chips. The U.S. Constitution and the laws of many other countries require that governments grant patents to inventors. If a firm registers an invention with the U.S. government, it can be granted a monopoly in the production of that item for 20 years. In other words, the government prohibits other firms from producing the good without the permission of the patent holder. Patents are given for many inventions, including the discovery of new drugs. Pharmaceutical companies hold patents on many of their products, giving them a monopoly to produce and sell these products. Copyrights on computer software, chips, movies, and books also give firms the sole right to market the products. Thus, patents and copyrights can create monopolies.

The award of monopoly rights through patents and copyrights serves a useful purpose. It can stimulate innovation by rewarding the inventor. In other words, the chance to get a patent or copyright gives the inventor more incentive to devote time and resources to invent new products or to take a risk and try out new ideas. Pharmaceutical companies, for example, argue that their patents on drugs are a reward for inventing the drugs. The higher prices and deadweight loss caused by the patent can be viewed as the cost of the new ideas and products. By passing laws to control drug prices, the government could lower the prices of drugs to help people who currently are sick. This action would be popular, but doing so would reduce the incentive for the firms to invent new drugs. Society—and, in particular, people who get sick in future years—could suffer a loss. When patents expire, we usually see a major shift toward competition. In general, when assessing the deadweight loss resulting from a monopoly, one must consider the benefits of the research and the new products that monopoly profits may create.

As technology has advanced, patents and copyrights have had to become increasingly complex to prevent firms from getting around them. Nevertheless, patent and copyright protection does not always work in maintaining the monopoly. Many times, potential competing firms get around copyrights on computer software and chips by "reverse engineering," in which specialists look carefully at how each part of a product works, starting with the final output. Elaborate mechanisms have been developed, such as "clean rooms," in which one group of scientists and programmers tells another group what each subfunction of the invention does but does not tell them how it is done. The other group then tries to invent an alternative way to perform the task. Because they cannot see how it is done, they avoid violating the copyright.

Licenses

Sometimes the government creates a monopoly by giving or selling to one firm a license to produce a product. The U.S. Postal Service is a government-sponsored monopoly. A law makes it illegal to use a firm other than the U.S. Postal Service for first-class mail. However, even this monopoly is diminishing with competition from overnight mail services and electronic transmission of documents.

National parks sometimes grant or sell to single firms licenses to provide food and lodging services. The Curry Company, for example, was granted a monopoly to provide services in Yosemite National Park. For a long time the Pennsylvania Turnpike—a toll road running the width of the state—licensed a monopoly to the Howard Johnson Company to provide food for travelers on the long stretches of the road. Seeing the advantage of competition, however, the turnpike authorities eventually allowed several different fast-food chains to get licenses.

Attempts to Monopolize and Erect Barriers to Entry

Adam Smith warned that firms would try to create monopolies to raise their prices. Smith favored free trade between countries because it would reduce the ability of firms in one country to form a monopoly. If a firm did form a monopoly and no restrictions on trade served as barriers to entry for firms in other countries, then foreign firms would break the monopoly.

History shows us many examples of firms attempting to monopolize an industry by merging with other firms and then erecting barriers to entry. De Beers is one example of such a strategy apparently being successful on a global level. In the last part of the nineteenth century, several large firms were viewed as monopolies. Standard Oil, started by John D. Rockefeller in the 1880s, is a well-known example. The firm had control of most of the oil-refining capacity in the United States. Thus, Standard Oil was close to having a monopoly in oil refining. However, the federal government forced Standard Oil to break up into smaller firms. We will consider other examples of the government's breaking up monopolies or preventing them from forming in Chapter 12.

Barriers to entry allow a monopoly to persist, so for a firm to maintain a monopoly, it needs barriers to entry. In addition to the ways mentioned earlier, barriers to entry also can be created by professional certification. For example, economists have argued that the medical and legal professions in the United States erect barriers to the entry of new doctors and lawyers by having tough standards for admittance to medical school or to the bar and by restricting the types of services that can be performed by nurses or paralegals. Doctors' and lawyers' fees might be lower if there were lower barriers to entry and, therefore, more competition.

Simply observing that a firm has no competitors is not enough to prove that barriers to entry exist. Sometimes the threat of potential entry into a market may be enough to get a monopolist to act like a competitive firm. For example, the possibility of a new bookstore's opening up off campus may put pressure on the campus bookstore to keep its prices low. When other firms, such as off-campus bookstores, can potentially and easily enter the market, they create what economists call a **contestable market**. In general, the threat of competition in contestable markets can induce monopolists to act like competitors.

contestable market

A market in which the threat of competition is enough to encourage firms to act like competitors.

 Is Amazon a Monopoly?

Experts argue whether Amazon is a monopoly.

View the video online at: http://www.youtube.com/embed/q1J3cnyGIUY?rel=0

10.5 Price Discrimination

price discrimination

A situation in which different groups of consumers are charged different prices for the same good.

In the model of monopoly we have studied in this chapter, the monopolists charge a single price for the good they sell. In some cases, however, firms charge different people different prices for the same item. This is called **price discrimination**. Price discrimination is common and is likely to become more common in the future as firms become more sophisticated in their price setting. Everyday examples include senior citizen discounts at movie theaters and discounts on airline tickets for Saturday-night stay overs.

Some price discrimination is less noticeable because it occurs in geographically separated markets. Charging different prices in foreign markets and domestic markets is common. For example, Japanese cameras are less expensive in the United States than in Japan. In contrast, the price of luxury German cars in the United States is frequently higher than in Germany. Volume or quantity discounts are another form of price discrimination. Higher prices are sometimes charged to customers who buy smaller amounts of an item. For example, electric utility firms sometimes charge more per kilowatt-hour to customers who use only a little electricity.

Consumers with Different Price Elasticities of Demand

What causes price discrimination? Figure 10.14 shows a diagram of a monopoly that gives one explanation. Suppose the good being sold is airline travel between two remote islands, and suppose only one airline operates between the two islands. The two graphs in Figure 10.14 represent demand curves with different elasticities. On the left is the demand for vacation air travel. Vacationers are frequently more price sensitive than business people. They can be more flexible with their time; they can take a boat rather than a plane; they can stay home and paint the house. Hence, for vacationers, the price elasticity of demand is high. Business travelers, however, do not have much choice. As shown in Figure 10.14, they are less sensitive to price. An important business meeting may require a flight to the other island with little advance notice. For business travel, the price elasticity of demand is low. Difference between price elasticities is a key reason for price discrimination.

In Figure 10.14, notice that both groups have downward-sloping demand curves and downward-sloping marginal revenue curves. For simplicity, marginal cost is constant and is shown with a straight line. Figure 10.14 predicts that business travelers will be charged a higher price than vacationers. Why? Marginal revenue equals marginal cost at a higher price for business travelers than for vacationers. The model of monopoly predicts that the firm will charge a higher price to those with a lower elasticity and a lower price to those with a higher elasticity.

FIGURE 10.14 Price Discrimination Targeted at Different Groups
The monopolist has two groups of potential buyers for its travel services. For convenience, we assume the marginal cost curve is flat. The group on the left has a high price elasticity of demand. The group on the right has a low price elasticity of demand. If the monopolist can discriminate between the buyers, then it is optimal to charge a lower price to the high-elasticity group and a higher price to the low-elasticity group.

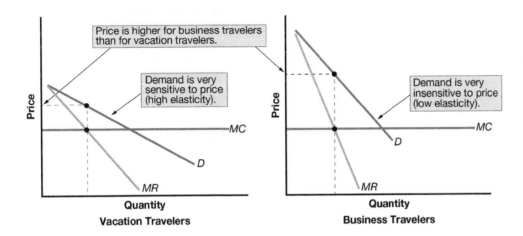

In fact, this is the type of price discrimination we see with airlines. But how can the airlines distinguish a business traveler from a vacation traveler? Clothing will not work: A business traveler easily could change from a suit to an aloha shirt and shorts to get the low fare. One device used by some airlines is the Saturday-night stay over. Business travelers prefer to work and travel during the week. They value being home with family or friends on a Saturday night. Vacationers frequently do not mind extending their travel by a day or two to include a Saturday night, and they may want to vacation over the weekend. Hence, a strong correlation exists between vacation travelers and those who do not mind staying over a Saturday night. A good way to price-discriminate, therefore, is to charge a lower price to people who stay at their destination on a Saturday night and to charge a higher price to those who are unwilling to do so.

Price discrimination based on different price elasticity of demand requires that the firm be able to prevent people who buy at a lower price from selling the item to other people. Thus, price discrimination is much more common in services than in manufactured goods.

Quantity Discounts

Another important form of price discrimination involves setting prices according to how much is purchased. If a business buys 1,000 units of a particular software package from a company, it probably has to pay a higher price per unit than if it purchases 10,000 units of that software. A software company can increase their profits by such a price scheme, as shown in Figure 10.15.

The single-price monopoly is shown in the bottom graph of Figure 10.15. Two ways in which the monopoly can make higher profits by charging different prices are shown in the top two panels. In both cases, there is no difference in the price elasticity of demand for different consumers. To make it easy, assume that all consumers are identical. The demand curve is the sum of the marginal benefits of all the consumers in the market.

FIGURE 10.15 Price Discrimination through Quantity Discounts or Premiums

The standard single-price monopoly is shown at the bottom. If the monopoly can charge a higher price to customers who buy only a little, profits can increase, as shown on the upper left. If the monopoly can give a discount to people who purchase a lot, it also can increase profits, as shown on the upper right. In this case, production increases.

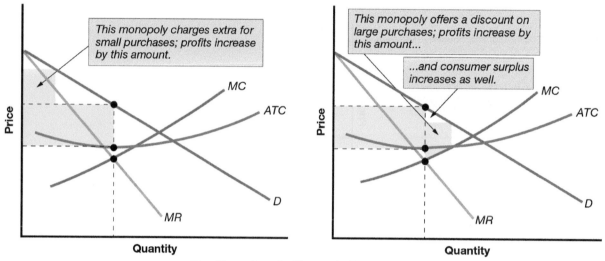

Two Examples of a Monopoly Charging Two Prices

Single-Price Monopoly

On the upper left, the firm sets a higher price for the first few items a consumer buys and a lower price for the remaining items. Frequent flier miles on airlines are an example of this kind of pricing. If you fly more than a certain number of miles, you get a free ticket. Thus, the per-mile fare for 50,000 miles is less than the per-mile fare for 25,000 miles. As the diagram shows, profits for the firm are higher in such a situation. In the example on the left, the higher price is the fare without the discount.

On the upper right, we see how profits can be increased if the firm gives even deeper discounts to high-volume purchasers. As long as the high-volume purchasers cannot sell the product to the low-volume purchasers, extra profits can be made. This type of volume discount is common in software sales to companies, for example.

The upper right graph in Figure 10.15 illustrates an important benefit of price discrimination: It can reduce deadweight loss. With price discrimination, a monopoly actually produces more. For example, those who get a lower price because of frequent flier discounts actually may end up buying more. The result is that the airline has more flights. As noted, the deadweight loss from a monopolist occurs because production is too low. If price discrimination allows more production, then it reduces deadweight loss.

Review

- Because a monopolist has market power, it can charge different prices to different consumers as long as it can prevent the consumers from reselling the good.
- Price discrimination explains telephone pricing as well as the complicated airfares on airlines.
- Deadweight loss is reduced by price discrimination.

10.6 End-of-Chapter Materials

Conclusion

The model of a monopoly that we developed in this chapter centers on a key diagram: Figure 10.10. Learning how to work with this diagram of a monopoly is important. In fact, economists use this same diagram to describe any firm that has some market power, not just monopolies, as we show in Chapter 11. Before proceeding, it is a good idea to practice sketching this generic diagram of a monopoly and finding output, price, and profits for different positions of the curve.

From the point of view of economic efficiency, the economic performance of monopolies is not nearly as good as that of competitive industries. Output is too low, marginal benefits are not equal to marginal costs, and consumer surplus plus producer surplus is diminished. But when assessing these losses, the fact that the expectation of monopoly profits—even if temporary—is the inducement for firms to do research and develop new products also must be considered.

Nevertheless, the deadweight loss caused by monopolies provides a potential opportunity for government to intervene in the economy. In fact, the U.S. government actively intervenes in the economy either to prevent monopolies from forming or to regulate monopolies when it is not appropriate to break them apart. We look further into government prevention or regulation of monopolies in Chapter 12.

Key Points

1. A monopoly occurs when only one firm sells a product that does not have a close substitute. Many local markets for water, sewage, electricity, and cable television are monopolies.
2. A monopolist possesses market power in the sense that it can lower the market price by producing more or raise the market price by producing less.
3. A monopoly's total revenue increases, but at a decreasing rate, as it increases production. This implies that its marginal revenue initially is positive but gradually becomes smaller.
4. Marginal revenue for a monopolist is always less than price. Even though the firm can increase its revenue by producing and selling an additional unit, it earns lower revenues on previously produced units because it had to lower its price to increase its sales.

5. The model of a monopoly assumes that the monopoly tries to maximize profits. To maximize profits, a monopolist chooses a quantity such that marginal revenue equals marginal cost.

6. A monopoly produces a smaller quantity and charges a higher price than a competitive industry; the lower production causes a deadweight loss.

7. Monopolies exist because of economies of scale that make the minimum efficient size of the firm larger than the market, or because of barriers to entry, including government patents and licenses.

8. Even though they create monopolies, patents and copyrights are useful to society because they provide incentives for creators of innovative products and works.

9. Many monopolies are short lived; technological change can rapidly change a firm from a monopoly to a competitive firm, as exemplified by the long-distance telephone market.

10. A price-discriminating monopoly charges different prices to different customers depending on how elastic their demand is. If price discrimination leads a monopolist to increase its production, then it can help reduce deadweight loss.

Questions for Review

1. What is a monopoly?
2. What market power does a monopoly have?
3. Why does marginal revenue decline as more is produced by a monopoly?
4. How does a monopoly choose its profit maximizing output and price?
5. Why is the marginal revenue curve below the demand curve for a monopoly but not for a competitive firm?
6. Why does a monopolist produce less than a competitive industry?
7. What forces tend to cause monopolies?
8. What is the deadweight loss from a monopoly?
9. What is price discrimination?
10. How does price discrimination reduce deadweight loss?

Problems

1. The following table gives the total cost and total revenue schedule for a monopolist.

Quantity	Total Cost (in dollars) ($)	Total Revenue (in dollars) ($)
0	144	0
1	160	90
2	170	160
3	194	210
4	222	240
5	260	250
6	315	240
7	375	210

a. Calculate the marginal revenue and marginal cost.

b. Determine the profit-maximizing price and quantity, and calculate the resulting profit.

c. Sketch the demand curve, the marginal revenue curve, and the marginal cost curve, and show how to derive the profit-maximizing quantity graphically.

2. Fill in the missing data on a monopolist, with fixed costs of $10, in the following table:

Quantity of Output	Price ($)	Total Revenue ($)	Marginal Revenue ($)	Marginal Cost ($)	Average Total Cost ($)
1	11				18.00
2	10				11.00
3	9				7.67
4	8				7.00
5	7				6.60
6	6				7.00
7	5				8.00

a. At what quantity will the monopolist produce to maximize profits? What will be the price at this level of output? What will be the profits?

b. What quantity maximizes total revenue? Why is this not the profit-maximizing quantity?

c. Sketch the demand curve, the marginal revenue curve, the marginal cost curve, and the average total cost curve. Show how to derive the profit-maximizing quantity and the profits earned by the monopolist graphically.

3. Suppose you are an economic adviser to the president, and the president asks you to prepare an economic analysis of MonoTV, Inc., a firm that sells a patented device used in high-definition television sets. You have the following information about MonoTV, Inc.

Quantity (millions)	Price ($)	Marginal Cost ($)
1	10	4
2	9	5
3	8	6
4	7	7
5	6	8
6	5	9
7	4	10
8	3	11
9	2	12
10	1	13

a. Given the data in the table, graphically show all the elements necessary to represent the monopolist's profit maximization. Note: You do not need to draw the average total cost curve.

b. What level of output does MonoTV, Inc., produce? What price does it sell this output at?

c. Does MonoTV, Inc., produce at the socially optimal level? Why or why not? Show any inefficiency on your graph.

4. Consider the monopoly described in the following table.

Quantity	Price ($)	Total Revenue ($)	Marginal Revenue ($)	Total Cost ($)	Marginal Cost ($)	Profit ($)
0	320	0	--	140	--	-140
2	305	610	305	158	9	452
4	290	1,160	275	168	5	992
6	275	1,650	245	188	10	1,462
8	260	2,080	215	228	20	1,852
10	245	2,450	185	296	34	2,154
12	230	2,760	155	392	48	2,368
14	215	3,010	125	522	65	2,488
16	200	3,200	95	712	95	2,488
18	185	3,330	65	962	125	2,368
20	170	3,400	35	1,302	170	2,088
22	155	3,410	5	1,762	225	1,648
24	140	3,360	-25	2,322	280	1,038

a. What are the profit-maximizing quantity and price?

b. How much is the monopolist making in profits?

c. What would the equilibrium price and quantity have been if the market were competitive?

d. Calculate the deadweight loss caused by the monopolist.

5. Sketch the diagram for a monopoly with an upward-sloping marginal cost curve that is earning economic profits. Suppose the government imposes a tax on each item the monopoly sells. Draw the diagram corresponding to this situation. How does this tax affect the monopoly's production and price? Show what happens to the area of deadweight loss.

6. Why might a local electric company be a monopoly? Would your answer be the same for a local cable television company? How about your long-distance telephone company?

7. Under the Copyright Act of 1976, in the United States, authors and creators like Walt Disney were granted copyrights over their creations that would last for the life of the author plus 50 years. What are the trade-offs involved in granting monopoly rights to an author? In 1998, the U.S. Congress decided to allow companies to extend copyrights that were reaching the end of their 50-year protected period and would be expiring by an additional twenty years. What do you think about the merits and demerits of that decision?

8. The following table gives the round-trip airfares from Los Angeles to New York offered by United Airlines.

Price ($)	Purchase Advance	Minimum Stay	Cancellation Policy
418	14 days	Overnight on Saturday	100%
683	3 days	Overnight on Saturday	100%
1,900	None required	None required	None

Explain why United might want to charge different prices for the same route. Why are there minimum-stay requirements and cancellation penalties?

9. Why do firms need market power to price-discriminate? What other circumstances are required for a firm to price-discriminate? Give an example of a firm or industry that price-discriminates and explain how it is possible in that case.

10. Children, students, and senior citizens frequently are eligible for discounted tickets to movies. Is this an example of price discrimination? Explain the conditions necessary for price discrimination to occur and draw the graphs to describe this situation.

Endnotes

1. U.S. Department of Justice. (2006). Interoperability Between Anititrust and Intellectual Property: Washington, D.C: Presentation to the George Mason University School of Law Symposium Managing Antitrust Issues in a Global Marketplace. Retrieved from: https://www.justice.gov/atr/speech/interoperability-between-antitrust-and-intellectual-property.

CHAPTER 11
Product Differentiation, Monopolistic Competition, and Oligopoly

When John Johnson launched his magazine business in 1942, he differentiated his products from existing products in a way that was valued by millions of African Americans. As a result, the new product lines, the magazines Ebony and Jet, were huge successes. Johnson became a multimillionaire, and his firm became the second-largest black-owned firm in the United States. Similarly, when Liz Claiborne started her new clothing firm in 1976, she differentiated her products from existing products in a way that was valued by millions of American women. She offered stylish yet affordable clothes for working women, and she too was successful: Thirty years later, Liz Claiborne, Inc., was one of the largest producers of women's clothing in the world. Such stories of people finding ways to differentiate their products from existing products are told thousands of times a year, although not everyone is as successful as John Johnson and Liz Claiborne.

John Johnson's magazines and Liz Claiborne's suits and dresses were different in a way that was valued by consumers. Because their products were different from the products made by the many other firms in their industries—magazine publishing and women's clothing, respectively—they each had market power in the sense that they could charge a higher price for their products and not lose all their customers. Thus, neither Johnson Publishing nor Liz Claiborne, Inc., was just another firm entering a competitive industry in which every firm sold the same product. But Johnson Publishing and Liz Claiborne, Inc., were not monopolies either; other firms were in their industries, and they could not prevent entry into the industries by even more firms. As is typical of many firms, they seemed to be hybrids between a competitive firm and a monopoly.

In this chapter, we develop a model that is widely used by economists to explain the behavior of such firms. It is called the *model of monopolistic competition*. **Monopolistic competition** occurs in an industry with many firms and free entry, where the product of each firm is slightly differentiated from the product of every other firm. We contrast the predictions of this model with those of the models of competition and monopoly developed in previous chapters.

FIGURE 11.1 Success from Differentiation

John Johnson's magazines *Ebony* and *Jet* were extremely successful because they targeted a segment of the population, African-American readers, that other magazines had not catered to up to that point.

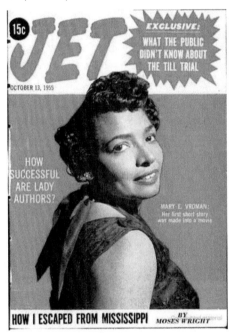

Source: Jet Magazine. (1955). JET Magazine cover of Mary Elizabeth Vroman, October 13, 1955. Retrieved from: https://commons.wikimedia.org/wiki/File:Jet_Vroman_October_13_1955_cover.jpg.

monopolistic competition

A market structure characterized by many firms selling differentiated products in an industry that has free entry and exit.

oligopoly

An industry characterized by few firms selling the same product with limited entry of other firms.

We also study another type of industry whose structure seems to fall between the models of monopoly and competition. In an **oligopoly**, very few firms are in the industry. Because the industry has very few firms, each firm has market power—the actions of any one firm can significantly affect the market price. In an oligopoly, each firm needs to anticipate what the others will do and develop a strategy to respond. Neither the model of a competitive industry, in which case no one firm can affect the price, nor the model of monopoly, in which case one firm completely dominates the market, adequately describes such a situation. To develop a model of oligopoly, therefore, we need to extend our tools of economic analysis to deal with strategic behavior: How firms think about, anticipate, and react to other firms' moves.

Figure 11.2 compares the models of monopolistic competition, oligopoly, monopoly, and competition. Over time, an industry can change from being a monopoly to monopolistic competition, to oligopoly, to competition, and back again, as a result of changes in the number of firms or the degree of product differentiation.

FIGURE 11.2 Four Types of Industries
Monopoly and competition are at the extreme ends. Monopolistic competition and oligopoly are in between.

Competition
- Many firms, free entry
- One product

Monopolistic Competition
- Many firms, free entry
- Differentiated product

Oligopoly
- Few firms, limited entry
- One or differentiated product

Monopoly
- One firm, no entry
- One product

To emphasize the distinction between the models of competition and monopolistic competition or between the models of monopoly and monopolistic competition, the terms *pure competition* and *pure monopoly* sometimes are used. In this book, we simply use the terms *competition* and *monopoly*.

11.1 Product Differentiation

product differentiation

The effort by firms to produce goods that are slightly different from other types of goods.

The effort by firms to fashion products that are different from other firms' products in ways that people value is called **product differentiation**. Product differentiation is pervasive in market economies. It leads to a great variety of consumer goods and capital goods. Goods that do not have product differentiation, such as aluminum ingots or gold bullion, are called *homogeneous products*, meaning that they are all exactly the same.

Variety of Goods in a Market Economy

Product differentiation is obvious from a casual examination of the wide variety of goods in a modern market economy. Table 11.1 gives an indication of this wide variety. If you like to run, you have a choice of 285 different types of running shoes. You can choose among 340 different types of cereals for breakfast and wear 70 different types of Levis' jeans.

TABLE 11.1 Variety: An Illustration of Product Differentiation

Item	Number of Different Types	Item	Number of Different Types
Automobile models	260	National soft drink brands	87
Automobile styles	1,212	Bottled water brands	50
SUV models	38	Milk types	19
SUV styles	192	Colgate toothpastes	17
Personal computer models	400	Mouthwashes	66
Movie releases	458	Dental flosses	64
Magazine titles	790	Over-the-counter pain relievers	141
New book titles	77,446	Levis' jeans styles	70
Amusement parks	1,174	Running shoe styles	285
TV screen sizes	15	Women's hosiery styles	90
Frito-Lay chip varieties	78	Contact lens types	36
Breakfast cereals	340		

Source: 1998 Annual Report, Federal Reserve Bank of Dallas.

The wide variety of products in a market economy contrasts starkly with the absence of such variety that existed in the centrally planned economies of Eastern Europe and the Soviet Union. Stores in Moscow or Warsaw typically would have only one type of each product—one type of wrench, for example—produced according to the specifications of the central planners. Even food and clothing had relatively little variety. One of the first results of market economic reform in these countries has been an increase in the variety of goods available.

Product differentiation is a major activity of both existing firms and potential firms. Business schools teach managers that product differentiation ranks with cost cutting as one of the two basic ways in which a firm can improve its performance. An entrepreneur can enter an existing industry either by finding a cheaper way to produce an existing product or by introducing a product that is differentiated from existing products in a way that will appeal to consumers.

Product differentiation usually means something less than inventing an entirely new product. Aspirin was an entirely new product when it was invented; wrapping aspirin in a special coating to make it easier to swallow is product differentiation. Coke, when it was invented in 1886, was a new product, whereas Pepsi, RC Cola, Jolt Cola, Yes Cola, and Mr. Cola, which followed over the years, are differentiated products.

Product differentiation also exists for capital goods—the machines and equipment used by firms to produce their products. The large earth moving equipment produced by Caterpillar is different from that produced by other firms, such as Komatsu of Japan. One difference is the extensive spare parts and repair service that go along with Caterpillar equipment. Bulldozers and road graders frequently break down and need quick repairs; by stationing parts distributorships and knowledgeable mechanics around the world, Caterpillar can offer quick repairs in the event of costly breakdowns. In other words, the products are differentiated on the basis of service and a worldwide network.

FIGURE 11.3 Product Differentiation versus Homogeneous Product
Even bottled water has become a highly differentiated product, more like breakfast cereal and soft drinks than like gold bullion, a homogeneous product that does not have product differentiation.

Source: Shutterstock.com

Puzzles Explained by Product Differentiation

Product differentiation explains certain facts about a market economy that could be puzzling if all goods were homogeneous.

Intra-industry Trade

intra-industry trade

Trade between countries in goods from the same or similar industries.

inter-industry trade

Trade between countries in goods from different industries.

Differentiated products lead to trade between countries of goods from the *same industry*, called **intra-industry trade**. Trade between countries of goods from *different industries*, called **inter-industry trade**, can be explained by comparative advantage. Bananas are traded for wheat because one of these goods is grown better in warm climates and the other is grown better in cooler climates. But why should intra-industry trade take place? Why should the United States both buy beer from Canada and sell beer to Canada? Beer is produced in many different countries, but a beer company in one country will differentiate its beer from that of a beer company in another country. For people to benefit from the variety of beer, we might see beer produced in the United States (for example, Budweiser) being exported to Canada and, at the same time, see beer produced in Canada (for example, Molson) being exported to the United States. If all beer were exactly the same (a homogeneous commodity), such trade within the beer industry would make little sense, but it is easily understood when products are differentiated.

Advertising

Product differentiation also explains why firms use so much advertising—that is, the attempt by firms to tell consumers what is good about their products. If all products were homogeneous, then advertising would make little sense: A bar of gold bullion is a bar of gold bullion, no matter who sells it. But if a firm has a newly differentiated product in which it has invested millions of dollars, then it needs to advertise that product to prospective customers. You can have the greatest product in the world, but it will not sell if no one knows about it. Advertising is a way to provide information to consumers about how products differ.

Economists have debated the role of advertising in the economy for many years. Many have worried about the waste associated with advertising. For instance, the parent companies of Pepsi-Cola and Coca-Cola spend large sums of money on advertising for Aquafina and Dasani, their bottled water brands. It is hard to see how catchy phrases like "make your mouth water" and large advertising campaigns are providing useful information to consumers about a product that essentially is filtered tap water. One explanation is that the purpose of the advertising in these cases is to get people to try the product. If they like it, they will buy more; if they do not like it, they will not—but without the ad they might not ever try it. Whatever the reason, advertising will not sell an inferior product—at least, not for long. For example, despite heavy advertising, Federal Express failed miserably with Zapmail—a product that guaranteed delivery of high-quality faxes of documents around the country within hours—because of the superiority of inexpensive fax machines that even small businesses could buy. The Iridium satellite phone service was forced into bankruptcy in late 1999 because of the rapid spread of cell phone technology and networks all over the world.

Others say that advertising is wasteful partly because it is used to create a perception of product differentiation rather than genuine differences between products. For example, suppose Coke and Pepsi are homogeneous products (to some people's tastes, they are identical). Then advertising simply has the purpose of creating a perception in people's minds that the products are different. If this is the case, product differentiation may be providing a false benefit, and the advertising used to promote it is a waste of people's time and effort.

Consumer Information Services

The existence of magazines such as *Consumer Reports* is explained by product differentiation. These magazines would be of little use to consumers if all products were alike.

Such services also may help consumers sort through exaggerated claims in advertising or help them get a better perception of what the real differences between products are. It is hard to sell an expensive product that ends up last on a consumer-rating list, even with the most creative advertising.

How Are Products Differentiated?

Altering a product's *physical characteristics*—the sharpness of the knife, the calorie content of the sports drink, the mix of cotton and polyester in the shirt, and so on—is the most common method of product differentiation. JetBlue differentiated itself from other airlines by offering leather seats and satellite television on every seat on its airplanes. As the example of Caterpillar shows, products also can be differentiated on features other than the physical characteristics. Related features such as low installation costs, fast delivery, large inventory, and money-back guarantees also differentiate products.

Location is another important way in which products are differentiated. A CVS Pharmacy or a McDonald's down the block is a very different product for you from a CVS Pharmacy or a McDonald's one hundred miles away. Yet only the location differentiates the product.

Time is yet another way to differentiate products. An airline service with only one daily departure from Chicago to Dallas is different from a service with twelve departures a day. Adding more flights of exactly the same type of air service is a way to differentiate the product. A 24-hour supermarket provides a different service from one that is open only during the day.

Convenience increasingly is being used by firms to differentiate products. How could peanut butter and jelly sandwiches, a standard for lunch, be more convenient? You can buy frozen peanut butter and jelly sandwiches on white bread. Prepackaged salads containing greens, dressing, and croutons; yogurt in a tube; single-serving microwaveable soup containers—these all are products that have become very popular in recent times as people's lives have become busier and more hectic. Similarly, a firm like Netflix has eliminated the need to make a trip to the video store by making it possible for consumers to get movie rentals delivered to their homes.

The Optimal Amount of Product Differentiation at a Firm

Product differentiation is costly. Developing a new variety of spot remover that will remove mustard from wool (no existing product is any good at this) would require chemical research, marketing research, and sales effort. Opening another Lenscrafters (the United States already has hundreds of stores) requires constructing a new store and equipping it with eyeglass equipment, trained personnel, and inventory.

But product differentiation can bring in additional revenue for a firm. The new spot remover will be valued by football fans who want to keep warm with woolen blankets or scarves but who also like mustard on their hot dogs. The people who live in the neighborhood where the new Lenscrafters opens will value it because they do not have to drive or walk as far.

The assumption of profit maximization implies that firms will undertake an activity if it increases profits. Thus, firms will attempt to differentiate their products if the additional revenue from product differentiation is greater than the additional costs. This is exactly the advice given to managers in business school courses. "Create the largest gap between buyer value ... and the cost of uniqueness" is the way Harvard Business School professor Michael Porter puts it in his book *Competitive Advantage*.[1] If the additional revenue is greater than the additional cost, then business firms will undertake a product-differentiation activity.

For a given firm, therefore, there is an *optimal* amount of product differentiation that balances out the additional revenue and the additional cost of the product differentiation. This is illustrated in Figure 11.4, which shows the amount of product differentiation chosen by a firm. For a company that owns and operates a haunted house, the horizontal axis is the amount of gore and scary features in the haunted house. The additional revenue from adding more gore and scary features to a haunted house is shown by the downward-sloping line. Although more gore and scary features attract additional customers, the additional revenue from increasing the amount of gore and scary features declines because only so many people would consider visiting a haunted house in a given area. It, therefore, is increasingly difficult to attract additional customers. The additional cost of adding more gore and scary features to a haunted house is shown by the upward sloping line. This additional cost increases because the cheapest effects that could be included for differentiation would be added first. The optimal amount of gore and scary features for a haunted-house operator is the point at which the additional revenue from more gore and scary features is just equal to the additional cost. Beyond that point, more gore and scary features would reduce profits, because the additional cost would exceed the additional revenue.

FIGURE 11.4 A Firm's Decision about Product Differentiation

Determining how much product differentiation a firm should undertake is a matter of equating the additional revenue from and additional cost of another differentiated product. (Note that these "additional cost" and "additional revenue" curves are analogous to marginal cost and marginal revenue curves except that they depend on the amount of product differentiation rather than the quantity of a particular product.)

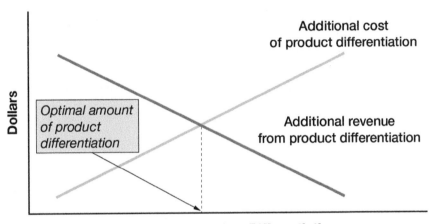

This analysis for haunted-house owners is far from trivial. Theme parks increasingly are interested in attracting Halloween traffic, and more gore and scary features attract more customers. In some theme parks, Halloween is the largest event all year.

Using this analysis in practice is difficult because the revenue gains from product differentiation depend on what other firms do. The amount of additional revenue generated by additional gore and scary features in a haunted house depends on how much gore and how many scary features are included in other nearby haunted houses. In the next section, we will look at more formal models of industries with differentiated products.

 The Role of Product Differentiation in the COVID-19 Economy

Watch from minute 37:01 to 38:39 of this video for a conversation on how some firms can differentiate their goods or services in the COVID-19 environment.

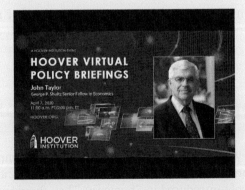

View the video online at: http://www.youtube.com/embed/zM3Rsp3FDnl?rel=0

11.2 Monopolistic Competition

The model of monopolistic competition, first developed by Edward Chamberlin of Harvard University in the 1930s, is designed to describe the behavior of firms operating in differentiated product markets. Monopolistic competition gets its name from the fact that it is a hybrid of monopoly and competition. Recall that monopoly has one seller facing a downward-sloping market demand curve with barriers to the entry of other firms.

Competition has many sellers, each facing a horizontal demand curve with no barriers to entry and exit. Monopolistic competition, like competition, has many firms with free entry and exit, but, as in monopoly, each firm faces a downward-sloping demand curve for its product.

The monopolistically competitive firm's demand curve slopes downward because of product differentiation. When a monopolistically competitive firm raises its price, the quantity demanded of its product goes down but does not plummet to zero, as in the case of a competitive firm. For example, if Nike raises the price of its running shoes, it will lose some sales to Adidas or New Balance, but it will still sell a considerable number of running shoes because some people prefer Nike shoes to other brands. Nike running shoes and New Balance running shoes are differentiated products to many consumers. On the other hand, a competitive firm selling a product like wheat, which is a much more homogeneous product, can expect to lose virtually all its customers to another firm if it raises its price above the market price.

As we will see, free entry and exit is an important property of monopolistic competition. Because of it, firms can come into the market if they can make a profit or leave the market if they are running losses.

A Typical Monopolistic Competitor

Figure 11.5 illustrates the key features of the model of monopolistic competition. Each graph in Figure 11.5 shows a typical monopolistically competitive firm. At first glance, the graphs look exactly like the graph for a monopoly, introduced in Chapter 10. They should, because both monopolistic and monopolistically competitive firms face downward-sloping demand curves. The demand curve facing a monopolistically competitive firm, however, has a different interpretation because other firms are in the industry. The demand curve is not the market demand curve; rather, it is the demand curve that is *specific* to a particular firm. When new firms enter the industry—for example, when Saucony enters with Nike and New Balance—the demand curves specific to both Nike and

New Balance shift to the left. When firms leave, the demand curves of the remaining firms shift to the right. The reason is that new firms take some of the quantity demanded away from existing firms, and when some firms exit, a greater quantity is demanded for the remaining firms.

FIGURE 11.5 Monopolistic Competition
Each graph shows a typical firm in a monopolistically competitive industry. Firms enter the industry if they can earn profits, as in graph (a). This will shift the demand and marginal revenue curves to the left for the typical firm because some buyers will switch to the new firms. Firms leave if they face losses, as in graph (b). This will shift the demand and marginal revenue curves to the right because the firms that stay in the industry get more buyers. In the long run, profits are driven to zero, as in graph (c).

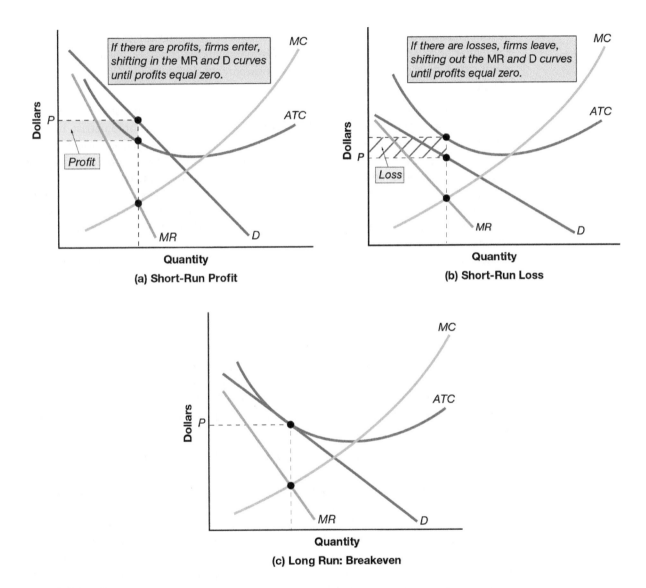

The difference between the graphs for a monopolist and a monopolistic competitor shows up when we move from the short run to the long run, that is, when firms enter and exit. This example is illustrated in Figure 11.5. Note that the three graphs in the figure have exactly the same average total cost curve. The graphs differ from one another in that the location of the demand and marginal revenue curves relative to the average total cost curve is different in each. Graphs (a) and (b) represent the short run. Graph (c) represents the long run, after the entry and exit of firms in the industry.

Observe that the demand curve in graph (c) is drawn so that it just touches the average total cost curve. At this point, the profit-maximizing price equals average total cost. Thus, total revenue is equal to total costs, and profits are zero. On the other hand, in graphs (a) and (b), the demand curve is drawn to show either a positive profit or a negative profit (loss) because price is either greater than or less than average total cost.

The Short Run: Just Like a Monopoly

Consider the short-run situation, before firms either enter or exit the industry. The monopolistic competitor's profit maximization decision is like that of the monopoly. To maximize profits, it sets its quantity to the point at which marginal revenue equals marginal cost. Because the monopolistically competitive firm faces a downward-sloping demand curve, its profit-maximizing price and quantity balance the increased revenue from a higher price with the lost customers brought on by the higher price. The marginal-revenue-equals-marginal-cost condition achieves this balance. The profit-maximizing quantity of production is shown by the dashed vertical lines in graphs (a) and (b) of Figure 11.5.

For example, For Eyes, Lenscrafters, and Pearle Vision are monopolistic competitors in many shopping areas in the United States. Each local eyeglass store has an optometrist, but each offers slightly different services. At a shopping area with several of these eyeglass stores, if one of them raises prices slightly, then fewer people will purchase glasses from that store. Some people will walk all the way to the other end of the mall to the store with the lower-priced glasses. Others, however, will be happy to stay with the store that raised its prices because they like the service and the location. These outlets are not monopolists, but the downward slope of their demand curves makes their pricing decision much like that of monopolists. The slope of the demand curve for a monopolistic competitor may be different from that for a monopolist, but the qualitative relationship between demand, revenue, and costs—and the firm's decisions in setting quantity and price—is the same.

Entry and Exit: Just Like Competition

Now consider entry and exit, which can take place over time. In the model of long-run competitive equilibrium in Chapter 9, we showed that if economic profits could be made, new firms would enter the industry. If firms were running losses, then firms would exit the industry. Only when economic profits were zero would the industry be in long-run equilibrium, with no tendency for firms either to enter or to exit.

In monopolistic competition, the entry and exit decisions are driven by the same considerations. If profits are positive, as in graph (a) of Figure 11.5, firms have an incentive to enter the industry. Consider the market for skin care products. Beginning in the 1980s, liquid soap products, especially soaps scented with natural oils, were introduced by a few manufacturers and quickly caught on with consumers. Soon, virtually every manufacturer of soap and shampoo products began to offer liquid soap products fortified with vitamins and flavored by aromatics. In contrast, if profits are negative, as shown in graph (b) of Figure 11.5, firms have an incentive to exit the industry. During the dotcom boom of the late 1990s, several companies entered the business of home delivery of groceries. Perhaps the best known of these firms, Webvan, tried to differentiate its product by offering to deliver groceries within a 30-minute delivery window requested by the consumer. Despite a promising start, most of these new entrants were unable to make profits and left the industry. Webvan, for example, foundered after the costs of building its own warehousing and distribution network turned out to be far greater than the revenue it could earn from grocery sales.

As we move from the short run to the long run, the entry and exit of competing firms will tend to shift the demand curve for each of the firms remaining in the industry to the point at which the demand curve and the average total cost curve are tangent—that is, the point at which the two curves just touch and have the same slope. Entry into the industry will shift the demand curve of each existing firm to the left because the existing firms will be sharing their sales with the new firms. If Suave sells a new brand of shampoo similar to Pantene shampoo, then some consumers who had been buying Pantene will instead buy Suave's similar new shampoo. The demand for Pantene and other shampoos therefore will decline because of the availability of Suave's new product. Thus, the existing firms will see their demand curves shift to the left—each one will find that it sells less at each price. The differences in the positions of the demand (and marginal revenue) curves in the short run and the long run illustrate this shift. The shift in the demand curve causes each firm's profits to decline, and profits eventually decline to zero. (Recall that these are economic profits, not accounting profits, and therefore are a good measure of the incentive for firms to enter the industry.)

The case of negative profits and exit is similar. If demand is such that firms are running a loss, then some firms will exit the industry, leaving their share of sales to the surviving firms. This action causes the demand curve facing the remaining firms to shift to the right until the losses (negative economic profits) are driven to zero. When Caribou Coffee closed in Ann Arbor, University of Michigan students bought coffee at other nearby coffee shops instead, increasing the demand for coffee at these nearby shops. This is illustrated by comparing graph (b) of Figure 11.5, which shows losses in the short run, with graph (c), which shows zero profits.

The Long-Run Monopolistically Competitive Equilibrium

Two differences are notable between monopolistically competitive firms and competitive firms in the long run. To see these differences, consider Figure 11.6, which replicates graph (c) of Figure 11.5, showing the position of the typical monopolistic competitor in long-run equilibrium, after entry and exit have taken place.

First, observe that the price is greater than marginal cost for a monopolistically competitive firm. This was also true for the monopoly; it means that the market is not as efficient as a competitive market. Production is too low because the marginal benefit of additional production is greater than the marginal cost. Because each firm has some market power, it restricts output slightly and gets a higher price. The sum of producer plus consumer surplus is reduced relative to that in a competitive market. In other words, the result is a loss of efficiency—a deadweight loss.

Second, as shown in Figure 11.6, the quantity produced is not at the minimum point on the average total cost curve, as it was for the competitive industry. That is, the quantity that the monopolistic competitor produces is at a higher-cost point than the quantity that the perfectly competitive firm would produce. Thus, monopolistically competitive firms operate in a situation of **excess costs**. If each firm expanded production and lowered its price, average total cost would decline. Each firm operates with some **excess capacity** in the sense that it could increase output and reduce average total cost. The firms choose not to do so because they have some market power to keep their prices a little higher and their output a little lower than that. Their market power comes from the downward-sloping demand curve that they face. For example, each coffee shop charges a little more and sells slightly fewer cups of coffee than it would in a perfectly competitive market.

excess costs

Costs of production that are higher than the minimum average total cost.

excess capacity

A situation in which a firm produces below the level that gives the minimum average total cost.

FIGURE 11.6 Excess Costs per Unit and Excess Capacity with Monopolistic Competition

In the long run, profits are zero for a monopolistically competitive firm, but the firm does not produce the quantity that minimizes average total cost. If the firm increases production, costs per unit will decline. In this sense, the firm operates at less than full capacity; it has excess capacity.

Comparing Monopoly, Competition, and Monopolistic Competition

Table 11.2 compares the different effects of competition, monopoly, and monopolistic competition.

TABLE 11.2 A Comparison of Monopolistic Competition with Monopoly and Competition

Type of Model	Price	Deadweight Loss?	Average Total Cost Minimized?	Profit in Long Run?
Competition	$P = MC$	No	Yes	No
Monopolistic competition	$P > MC$	Yes	No	No
Monopoly	$P > MC$	Yes	No	Yes

A competitive firm will produce the quantity that equates price and marginal cost. A competitive market is efficient in that consumer surplus plus producer surplus is maximized and no deadweight loss results. Average total cost is minimized.

In a monopoly, price is greater than marginal cost. A monopoly is inefficient because consumer surplus plus producer surplus is not maximized, so a deadweight loss results. Moreover, average total cost is not minimized. Economic profits remain positive because firms cannot enter the market.

In monopolistic competition, price is also greater than marginal cost. Thus, consumer surplus plus producer surplus is not maximized, and deadweight loss results; average total cost is not minimized. Profits are zero in the long-run equilibrium, however, because of entry and exit. Monopolistic competition does not result in as efficient an outcome as competition. Monopolistic competition, as well as monopoly, is inefficient.

Product Variety versus Deadweight Loss

When comparing monopolistic competition with competition, we must recognize—as with the comparison of monopoly and competition in the last chapter—that replacing monopolistic competition with competition may be an impossibility or require a loss to society. Remember that product differentiation is the key reason for monopolistic competition. We showed in the previous section that consumers usually value the variety of products that comes from product differentiation. Some people like having both Pepsi and Coke. Roads and airports are better because of the different capabilities of earth-moving equipment sold by Caterpillar and Komatsu. Thus, eliminating monopolistic competition by having a single competitive product, whether Coksi or Catematsu, even if it were possible, probably would reduce consumer surplus by more than the gain that would come from competition over monopolistic competition.

More generally, product differentiation may be of sufficient value to consumers that it makes sense to have monopolistically competitive firms despite the deadweight loss. Or, to state it somewhat differently, the deadweight loss from monopolistic competition is part of the price consumers pay for the variety or the diversity of products.

 Monopolistic Competition

Learn more about short and long run cost and revenue curves in monopolistic competitive markets.

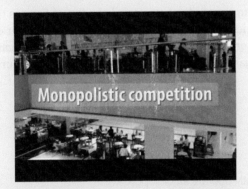

View the video online at: http://www.youtube.com/embed/aB7O0qgp3ns?rel=0

Review

- The model of monopolistic competition is a hybrid of competition and monopoly. Entry and exit are possible, as in competition, but firms see a downward-sloping demand curve, as in monopoly, although the market has many firms.
- The analysis of monopolistic competition in the short run is much like that of monopoly, but entry and exit lead to zero economic profits in the long run.
- Monopolistic competitors produce less than competitive firms and charge prices higher than marginal costs. Thus, a deadweight loss results from monopolistic competition. In the long run, monopolistic competition produces less than the quantity that would minimize average total cost.
- The deadweight loss and excess costs can be viewed as the price of product variety.

11.3 Oligopoly

Thus far, we have seen two situations in which firms have market power: monopoly and monopolistic competition. But those are not the only two. When an industry has *very few* producers—a situation termed *oligopoly*—each firm can have an influence on the market price even if the goods are homogeneous. For example, if Saudi Arabia—one of the major producers of crude oil in the world and a member of the Organization of Petroleum Exporting Countries (OPEC)—decides to cut its production of crude oil, a relatively homogeneous commodity, it can have a significant effect on the world price of oil. The effect on the price, however, will depend on what other producers do. If the other producing countries—Iran, Kuwait, and so on—increase their production to offset the Saudi cuts, then the price will not change by much. Thus, Saudi Arabia, either through formal discussion with other oil-producing countries in OPEC or by guessing, must take account of what the other producers will do.

Such situations are not unusual. The managers of a firm in an industry with only a few other firms know that their firm has market power. But they also know that the other firms in the industry have market power too. If the managers of a firm make the right assessment about how other firms will react to any course of action they take, then their firm will profit. This awareness and consideration of the market power and the reactions of other firms in the industry is called **strategic behavior**. Strategic behavior also may exist when product differentiation exists, as in monopolistically competitive industries, but to study and explain strategic behavior, it is simpler to focus on oligopolies producing homogeneous products.

A common approach to the study of strategic behavior of firms is the use of **game theory**, an area of applied mathematics that studies games of strategy like poker or chess. Game theory has many applications in economics and the other behavioral sciences. Because oligopoly behavior has many of the features of games of strategy, game theory provides a precise framework to better understand oligopolies.

strategic behavior

Firm behavior that takes into account the market power and reactions of other firms in the industry.

game theory

A branch of applied mathematics with many uses in economics, including the analysis of the interaction of firms that take each other's actions into account.

 Oligopolies

Several industries currently operate as oligopolies.

View the video online at: http://www.youtube.com/embed/gLeQbkaRst4?rel=0

An Overview of Game Theory

Game theory, like the basic economic theory of the firm and consumer (described in Chapter 5 and Chapter 6 of this book), makes the assumption that people make purposeful choices with limited resources. More precisely, game theory assumes that the players in a game try to maximize their payoffs—the amount they win or lose in the game. Depending on the application, a payoff might be measured by utility, if the player is a person, or by profits, if the player is a firm.

Game theory endeavors to go beyond basic economic theory in that each player takes explicit account of the actions of each and every other player. It asks questions like: "In a poker game, what should Mary do if Deborah sees her bet and raises her by $10?" The aims of game theory are to analyze the choices facing each player and to design utility-maximizing actions, or strategies, that respond to every action of the other players.

An important example in game theory is the game called the **prisoner's dilemma**, illustrated in Figure 11.7. The game is between Bonnie and Clyde, two prisoners who have been arrested for a crime that they committed. The **payoff matrix** shown in Figure 11.7 has two rows and two columns. The two columns for Bonnie show her options, which are labeled at the top "confess" and "remain silent." The two rows for Clyde show his options; these also are labeled "confess" and "remain silent." Inside the boxes, we see what happens to Bonnie and Clyde for each option, confess or remain silent. The top right of each box shows what happens to Bonnie. The bottom left of each box shows what happens to Clyde. Each year of prison sentence is considered to have a payoff equal to negative one. Both Bonnie and Clyde would like to maximize their payoff, which means they would prefer a shorter sentence of one year (with a payoff equal to negative one) to longer sentences of five years (with a payoff equal to negative five) or seven years (with a payoff equal to negative seven).

prisoner's dilemma

A game in which individual incentives lead to a nonoptimal (noncooperative) outcome. If the players credibly commit to cooperate, then they achieve the best (cooperative) outcome.

payoff matrix

A table containing strategies and payoffs for two players in a game.

FIGURE 11.7 Two Prisoners Facing a Prisoner's Dilemma
Clyde and Bonnie are in separate jail cells, held for a crime they did commit. The payoff for each—with each year of prison having a payoff of -1—is given in the appropriate box and depends on whether they both confess or they both remain silent or one confesses while the other remains silent. The top right of each box shows Bonnie's payoff; the bottom left of each box shows Clyde's payoff.

The police already have enough information to get a conviction for a lesser crime, for which Bonnie and Clyde would each get a three-year jail sentence. Thus, if both Bonnie and Clyde remain silent, they are sent to jail for three years each, as shown in the lower right-hand corner of the table.

But Bonnie and Clyde each have the option of confessing to the more serious crime that they committed. If Bonnie confesses and Clyde does not, she gets a reward. If Clyde confesses and Bonnie does not, he gets a reward. The reward is a reduced penalty: The jail sentence is only one year—not as severe as the three years it would be if the prosecutor had no confession. The penalty for being convicted of the more serious crime in the absence of a confession is seven years. Thus, if Bonnie confesses and Clyde does not, he gets a seven-year sentence. If both confess, they each get a five-year sentence.

What should Clyde and Bonnie do? The answer depends on their judgment about what the other person will do. And this is the point of the example. Bonnie can either confess or remain silent. The consequences of her action depend on what Clyde does. If Bonnie confesses and Clyde confesses, she gets five years. If Bonnie confesses and Clyde remains silent, Bonnie gets one year. If Bonnie remains silent and Clyde remains silent, she gets three years. Finally, if Bonnie remains silent and Clyde confesses, she gets seven years. Clyde is in the same situation as Bonnie.

Think about a strategy for Bonnie. Bonnie is better off confessing, regardless of what Clyde does. If Clyde confesses, then by confessing herself, Bonnie gets five years rather than the seven years she would get by remaining silent. If, on the other hand, Clyde remains silent, then Bonnie is still better off by confessing because she gets only one year rather than the three years she would get by remaining silent. Hence, Bonnie has a great incentive to confess because she gets a reduced sentence in either case.

Clyde is in the same situation. He can compare what his sentence would be whether Bonnie confesses or remains silent. In this case, Clyde also is better off confessing regardless of whether Bonnie confesses or remains silent.

What this reasoning suggests is that both Bonnie and Clyde will confess. If they both had remained silent, they would have gone to jail for only three years, but the apparently sensible strategy is to confess and go to jail for five years. This is the prisoner's dilemma. The case where both remain silent is called the **cooperative outcome** of the game because to achieve this, they would somehow have to agree in advance not to confess and then keep their word. The case in which both confess is called the **noncooperative outcome** of the game because Clyde and Bonnie follow an "everyone for himself or herself" strategy. Note that the cooperative outcome is preferred to the noncooperative outcome by both Clyde and Bonnie, yet both choose the option that results in the noncooperative outcome.

The mathematician and Nobel laureate in economics John Nash defined the noncooperative equilibrium—which economists call a **Nash equilibrium**—as a set of strategies from which no player would like to deviate unilaterally—that is, no player would see an increase in his or her payoff by changing his or her strategy while the other players keep their strategies constant.

 Game Theory and Oligopolies

Learn more about game theory and its application to firm decision making.

View the video online at: http://www.youtube.com/embed/JMq059SAQXM?rel=0

Applying Game Theory to Oligopolies

How do we apply game theory to determine the strategy of firms in an oligopoly? The easiest case is in an industry with only two firms. This is a particular type of oligopoly called *duopoly*. A prominent example of an industry characterized by a duopoly is the large commercial airplane manufacturing industry, where Boeing and Airbus have to plan their strategy taking the other's strategy into account. The competition between FedEx and UPS in the overnight package delivery business is another example. In a duopoly, market supply is determined by the output of the two firms, so in deciding how much more to produce of a good, the firm has to consider its own additional costs of production, the change in the market price when it increases production, and how the other firm's subsequent response in terms of increasing or decreasing its production will affect the market price. Economics and game theory predict that the outcome of the duopoly will be the Nash equilibrium of the game—that is, the quantity levels at which neither firm has an incentive to deviate.

Competition in Quantities versus Competition in Prices

The model of oligopoly in which firms compete by choosing what quantities to produce, given the other firm's production decision, is called *Cournot competition* in honor of the French economist Augustin Cournot, who created the original version of this model in 1838 (Cournot did not use game theory and the concept of Nash equilibrium, which was not invented until 1950). Instead of competing in quantities, oligopolists can also compete in prices; this is called *Bertrand competition* for the French mathematician who reworked Cournot's model in terms of prices in 1883. We do not analyze the Bertrand model in this book, but it predicts that with a homogeneous good, oligopolists will charge the same price and sell the same number of units as competitive firms would.

Comparison with Monopoly and Perfect Competition

How does the outcome for a duopoly compare with the outcomes for a perfectly competitive market and a monopoly? Suppose the market demand for giant pumpkins is Price = $241 - $2 \times$ Quantity, where the quantity is the sum of what Jack and Jill independently and simultaneously bring to the market, and with a cost of $1 for harvesting and transporting each pumpkin to market.

In a competitive market, price equals marginal cost. Since marginal cost equals a dollar, that means $P = \$1$ and we can solve for Quantity = 120. Profits will be zero.

Now suppose that Jack and Jill get together and behave like a monopolist. Further suppose that marginal revenue in this example can be found by the relationship Marginal revenue = $241 - \$4 \times$ Quantity. Setting marginal revenue equal to marginal cost (which is $1) gives us a total quantity of 60 pumpkins. So if Jack and Jill between them bring sixty pumpkins to market, the price will be $241 - 2 \times (60) = \$121$. Monopoly profits would equal $121 \times 60 - \$1 \times 60 = \$7,200$.

Now consider the duopoly case. To simplify our analysis, let's assume that Jack's and Jill's strategies are limited to three actions: They can bring either 30, 40, or 60 pumpkins to the market. The payoff matrix for Jack and Jill is shown in Figure 11.8. This is a three-by-three matrix with a total of nine blank boxes, one for each combination of Jack's and Jill's actions; the boxes are numbered for easy reference. Each of these boxes lists the profits that Jack and Jill obtain given their actions. For example, in box 1, both Jack and Jill choose to harvest and transport only 30 pumpkins to the market. In this case, Jack's payoff is $3,600, which we write on the bottom left corner of the first box. The payoff for Jill is also $3,600 (top right corner of the first box). The rest of the payoff matrix in Figure 11.8 can be interpreted in a similar way.

FIGURE 11.8 Payoff Matrix for Jack and Jill
The payoff matrix contains the profits for Jack and Jill for every possible combination of their actions. For example, in box 6, Jack sends 40 pumpkins to the market, while Jill delivers 60; Jack's payoff is $1,600. Jill has a payoff of $2,400.

Jack and Jill are aware of the nine possible outcomes, and the question is how each of them is going to choose a quantity to deliver to the farmer's market. How many pumpkins each of them should harvest and bring to the market depends on how many the other person chooses to bring. So Jack and Jill engage in a mental exercise, each trying to figure out what the other will do.

Put yourself in Jill's shoes. She can easily see that her maximum payoff of $4,000 happens when she sends 40 pumpkins to the market while Jack sends only 30. If Jill sells 40 pumpkins, however, then Jack can increase his payoff from $3,000 to $3,200 by selling 40 instead of 30 pumpkins. So box 2 cannot be a solution to Jill's and Jack's problem. Similarly, Jack's maximum payoff of $4,000 happens when he sends 40 pumpkins to the market while Jill sends only 30. But were he to do so, then Jill would be able to increase her payoff by selling 40 pumpkins instead of 30. So box 4 cannot be a solution.

At this point you can guess that we are looking for a combination of strategies from which neither player would like to deviate unilaterally—that is, a Nash equilibrium. By carefully exploring all the boxes and checking to see whether either player has an incentive to deviate from that particular combination, we find that the only Nash equilibrium in this example is in box 5, where Jack and Jill sell 40 pumpkins each, for a payoff of $3,200 each. At that level, neither Jack nor Jill wants to produce more or less pumpkins, given the production of their competitor. The duopoly solution will have a total of 80 pumpkins supplied to the market (40 by Jack and 40 by Jill). The market price will be $241 – $2 * 80 = $81 and profits for each producer will be $3,200.

Figure 11.9 shows the demand and marginal cost curves for pumpkins in the case study involving the pumpkin duopoly. The intersection of demand and marginal cost represents the competitive equilibrium, in which case Jack and Jill each supply sixty pumpkins at a price of $1 and obtain zero profits. The maximum combined payoff is the monopoly solution, which occurs when each farmer sells thirty pumpkins at a price of $121 per pumpkin. The duopoly solution lies between the monopoly and competitive equilibria in terms of price, quantity, and profit.

FIGURE 11.9 Comparison of Monopoly, Duopoly, and Competitive Equilibria
Prices and quantities for a Cournot duopoly lie between the equilibria for a monopoly and a competitive market.

Collusion

Firms in an oligopoly know that their combined profits can be maximized if they act together as a monopolist. Firms might act together in three ways. The first is by **explicit collusion**, in which the managers communicate with each other and agree to fix prices or cut back on production. Although explicit collusion is illegal, it still happens. In the 1980s and 1990s, several firms in Florida and Texas were found guilty of agreeing to fix prices for milk sold to schools. In 1990, the Justice Department charged that several Ivy League universities colluded to offer similar financial aid packages to admitted students, thus depriving these students of the more generous aid packages that would have resulted from the schools competing with one another for the best students. The governments of many countries that produce oil routinely collude to cut back production and raise prices. A group of producers that coordinates its pricing and production decisions is called a **cartel**.

Second, in **tacit collusion** no explicit communication occurs between firms, but firms keep prices high by regularly following the behavior of one firm in the industry. The dominant firm is sometimes called a **price leader**. Third, the firms could merge and form a single entity.

Incentives to Defect

In oligopoly, game theory predicts that unless there is a way to bind each firm to cooperation, there is a tendency to defect. Because the defection results in a lower than monopoly price, consumers gain from the defection, and deadweight loss is reduced.

explicit collusion

Open cooperation by firms to make mutually beneficial pricing or production decisions.

cartel

A group of producers in the same industry who coordinate pricing and production decisions.

tacit collusion

Implicit or unstated cooperation of firms to make mutually beneficial pricing or production decisions.

price leader

The price-setting firm in a collusive industry in which other firms follow the leader.

Incentives to Cooperate: Repeated Games

Although the prisoner's dilemma and the Cournot duopoly suggest a tendency toward the noncooperative outcome, a difference exists between the situation of the prisoners Bonnie and Clyde and the farmers Jack and Jill: Pumpkinville's farmer's market probably will be open for many years, allowing Jack and Jill to interact with each other in the future. Firms that interact with each other repeatedly may behave quite differently from firms that interact only once. If the same game is to be played year after year—a repeated game—then the firms might be able to build up a reputation for not defecting.

Experimental economists have conducted experiments in which two people play the same prisoner's dilemma game over and over again. (The people in the experiments are given small monetary rewards rather than jail penalties.) These experiments indicate that people frequently end up using strategies that lead to a cooperative outcome. A typical strategy that people use is called "tit-for-tat." Using a tit-for-tat strategy, one player regularly matches, *in the next game,* the actions of the other player *in the current game.* For example, Clyde's tit-for-tat strategy would be to confess the next time the game is played if Bonnie confesses in the current game, and not to confess the next time the game is played if Bonnie does not confess in the current game. A tit-for-tat strategy gives the other player an incentive to follow the cooperative action—not confess—and thereby leads to a cooperative outcome. Players can use several other strategies to support a specific outcome in a repeated game.

Secret Defections

Even though reputational consequences may help firms better sustain a cooperative outcome, firms still have incentives to defect. The incentives for a firm to defect from an agreement will be greater if it is difficult for other firms to detect the defection. In the pumpkin example, it is impossible for Jack to increase his production without Jill's knowing it. This makes defection less likely. If one firm can secretly increase production or cut prices, enforcing the agreement will be more difficult. But it may be possible for a member of OPEC to sell oil to China under a secret agreement, or for a member of the world coffee cartel to ship coffee without being detected, at least for a while. The impact of such secret defections is much like the situation in boxes 2 and 4 in Figure 11.8. Profits to the defector increase, and profits to the other producers decrease. Consumers are better off because the quantity supplied to the market increases, helping to lower the price.

For a long time, Japanese construction firms operated a now well-known collusion scheme called *dango.* Firms took turns offering a slightly lower bid, while all the other firms submitted high-priced bids to the government. This collusion ensured that each construction firm would get periodic contracts that were lucrative, without worrying about being undercut by its competitors. Ironically, and unfortunately for consumers, making the bids public made it harder for any firm to defect because firms in the agreement would know at once which firm had lowered its prices.

Review

- Game theory provides a framework to study strategic behavior in an oligopoly. A game theory setting typically describes how the outcomes that a player can achieve by pursuing a particular strategy vary depending on the strategies pursued by the other players.
- A game theory setting can have a cooperative outcome, in which the players agree to cooperate, or a noncooperative outcome, which results when players follow their individual incentives.

- The concept of a Nash equilibrium—a set of strategies from which no player wishes to unilaterally deviate—is used to identify the noncooperative solution.
- The prisoner's dilemma is a widely known example in which the two parties will not be able to achieve the superior cooperative equilibrium. Instead, they have to settle for the inferior noncooperative equilibrium.
- Firms can compete with one another on the basis of quantity (Cournot) or price (Bertrand). The examples we look at in this chapter are for Cournot competition.
- Game theoretic concepts can illustrate why firms in an oligopoly will be tempted to defect from any agreement and not act like a monopolist. Because a market has only a few producers, however, the outcome will not be the same as in the case of perfect competition. Prices and quantities for an oligopoly lie in between the solutions for a monopolist and for a competitive market.
- To the extent that a firm colludes, either explicitly or tacitly, it acts more like a monopolist and reduces economic efficiency by raising price above marginal cost.
- Repeated interactions among firms and the inability to defect secretly from an agreement make it more likely that collusive behavior among a group of firms is sustainable.

11.4 End-of-Chapter Materials

Conclusion

In this chapter, we have explored two different types of models—monopolistic competition and oligopoly—that lie in the complex terrain between competition and monopoly. The models were motivated by the need to explain how real-world firms—Johnson Publications, Liz Claiborne, Nike, and PepsiCo—and the members of OPEC operate in markets with differentiated products or with a small number of other firms or countries.

In the models introduced in this chapter, firms have market power in that they can affect the price of the good in their market. Market power enables a firm to charge a price higher than marginal cost. It is a source of deadweight loss. Observations of the behavior of actual firms show a wide variation in market power among firms.

Economists in government and businesses use the ideas about monopolistic competition and oligopoly discussed in this chapter. Economists working in the U.S. Department of Justice use them to determine whether the government should intervene in certain industries, as we will explore in Chapter 12. Consultants to business use them to help firms decide how to differentiate their products from those of other firms.

Having concluded our discussion of the four basic types of models of markets in this chapter, it is useful to remember the important distinction between models and the facts that the models endeavor to explain or predict. None of the assumptions of these models—such as homogeneous products or free entry—hold exactly in reality. For example, when contrasted with the monopolistic competition model of this chapter, the model of competition (with its assumption of homogeneous goods) might seem not to apply to many markets. Few goods are exactly homogeneous. But when economists apply their models, they realize that these models are approximations of reality. How close an approximation comes to reality heavily depends on the application. The model of competition can be helpful in explaining the behavior of firms in industries that are approximately competitive, just as the model of monopoly can be helpful in explaining the behavior of firms in industries that are approximately monopolistic. We now have a richer set of models that apply to situations far removed from competition or monopoly.

Key Points

1. Firms that can differentiate their product and act strategically are in industries that fall between competition and monopoly.
2. Product differentiation—the effort by firms to create different products of value to consumers—is pervasive in a modern market economy. It helps explain intra-industry trade, advertising, and information services.
3. Monopolistic competition arises because of product differentiation. With monopolistic competition, firms have market power, but exit from and entry into the industry lead to a situation of zero profits in the long run.
4. With monopolistic competition, the firm sets the quantity produced so that price exceeds marginal cost. A deadweight loss results, and average total cost is not minimized.
5. The deadweight loss and excess costs of monopolistic competition are part of the price paid for product variety.
6. Strategic behavior occurs in industries with a small number of firms because each firm has market power to affect the price, and each firm cannot ignore the response of other firms to its own actions.
7. The tools of game theory, such as the Nash equilibrium, help us identify the cooperative and noncooperative outcomes of strategic interaction by firms competing on the basis of quantity or price.
8. The price, quantity, and deadweight loss outcomes from an oligopoly fall in between the outcomes from a monopoly and a competitive market.
9. Game theory suggests that collusive behavior frequently will break down, making noncooperative outcomes more likely.
10. Collusion is more likely when firms interact repeatedly in a market and secret defections can be prevented.

Questions for Review

1. What is product differentiation?
2. What factors are relevant to the determination of optimal product differentiation?
3. Why is product differentiation an important reason for monopolistic competition?
4. What are two key differences between monopolistic competition and monopoly?
5. Why don't monopolistic competitors keep their average total cost at a minimum?
6. Why is the noncooperative outcome of a prisoner's dilemma game likely?
7. Why is duopoly like a prisoner's dilemma?
8. How does the market outcome for an oligopoly compare with the outcome for a monopoly? To the outcome for a competitive market?
9. What is the difference between explicit and tacit collusion?
10. Why are secret defections a problem for cartels?

Problems

1. Match the following characteristics with the appropriate models of firm behavior and explain the long-run efficiency (or inefficiency) of each.

   a. Many firms, differentiated product, free entry
   b. One firm, patents, licenses, or barriers to entry

   c. Many firms, homogeneous product, free entry

   d. Few firms, strategic behavior

2. You are traveling by taxi in a South American city. When the taxi stops at a stoplight, you observe several people walking among the stopped cars offering apples for sale. Your taxi driver rolls down the window and purchases an apple from one of the vendors. You ask the taxi driver, "Why did you buy the apple from that vendor?" The driver replies, "I often buy from that vendor because the apple is always of excellent quality." In what market structure are the vendors operating at that site? Why?

3. Consider Al's gasoline station, which sells Texaco at a busy intersection along with three other stations selling Shell, Conoco, and Chevron.

   a. Draw the marginal cost, average total cost, demand, and marginal revenue curves for Al's station, assuming that the profit-maximizing price is greater than average total cost.

   b. Show Al's profits on the diagram.

   c. Explain what would happen in this situation to bring about a long-run equilibrium. Would more stations open, or would some leave?

4. Compare the long-run equilibrium of a competitive firm with that of a monopolistically competitive firm with the same cost structure. Why is the long-run price different in these two models? Which type of firm operates at a minimum cost? Draw a diagram and explain.

5. Suppose 10 monopolistically competitive restaurants operate in your town with identical costs. Given the following information, calculate the short-run price and quantity produced by each of the firms.

Each Firm's Demand		Each Firm's Costs	
Quantity	Price ($)	Average Total Cost ($)	Marginal Cost ($)
1	10	12	—
2	8	9	6
3	6	8	6
4	4	9	12
5	2	10	14

   a. Would the price rise or fall at the typical firm in the long run? Explain.

   b. What would be the level of production if this industry were a competitive industry?

   c. If free entry and exit is an option in both monopolistic competition and competition, explain the difference in the quantity the typical firm produces.

6. Suppose the government places a sales tax on firms in a monopolistically competitive industry. Draw a diagram showing the short-run impact and the adjustment to the new long-run industry equilibrium. What happens to the equilibrium price and number of firms in the industry?

7. Which of the following conditions will tend to induce collusion among sellers in a market?

   a. The transactions are publicly announced.

   b. The market has few sellers.

   c. Some sellers have lower costs than other sellers.

   d. The market is open for only one year.

   e. The sellers cannot meet one another

8. How can firms in an oligopoly ensure that their industry earns the largest possible profit? Why is it likely that this outcome will not be reached? If this outcome is not reached, will the deadweight loss in the market be larger or smaller?

9. Two firms, Faster and Quicker, are the only two producers of sports cars on an island that has no contact with the outside world. The firms collude and agree to share the market equally. If neither firm cheats on the agreement, each firm makes $3 million in economic profits. If only one firm cheats, the cheater can increase its economic profit to $4.5 million, while the firm that abides by the agreement incurs an economic loss of $1 million. If both firms

cheat, they earn zero economic profit. Neither firm has any way of policing the actions of the other.

   a. What is the payoff matrix of the game if it is played just once?

   b. What is the equilibrium if the game is played only once? Explain.

   c. What do you think will happen if the game can be played many times? Why?

   d. What do you think will happen if a third firm comes into the market? Will it be harder or easier to achieve cooperation among the three firms? Why?

10. Store A and Store B are the only two flower shops in a small town. The demand for a dozen roses is $P = 25 = Q$. Neither Store A nor Store B has any fixed costs, whereas the marginal cost of Store A is constant at $3, and the marginal cost of Store B is constant at $5. Each seller can sell either five dozen or 10 dozen roses, and they meet only once in this market.

   a. Create the payoff matrix. Show your calculations and explain verbally as necessary.

   b. Find the Nash equilibrium or equilibria. Explain verbally.

   c. If multiple equilibria exist, which equilibrium do you think is most likely to occur and why?

Endnotes

1. Michael Porter, *Competitive Advantage* (New York: Free Press, 1985), p. 153.

CHAPTER 12
Antitrust Policy and Regulation

It was the biggest breakup that never happened. In April 2000, a federal judge issued a ruling that software giant Microsoft should be broken up into two entities—one that sold operating systems and the other that sold its web browser, Internet Explorer, and the company's flagship Microsoft Office software. In issuing this ruling, the court concluded that "Microsoft maintained its monopoly power by anticompetitive means and attempted to monopolize the Web browser market, both in violation of [Section] 2 [of the Sherman Antitrust Act]."[1] Subsequently, an appeals court overturned the ruling that Microsoft be broken up because certain actions of the judge who had issued the ruling had called his impartiality into question. The appeals court, however, did uphold the legal finding that Microsoft had a monopoly in the market for operating systems and was sustaining that monopoly by anticompetitive actions.

FIGURE 12.1 **The Federal Trade Commission**
The Federal Trade Commission (FTC) is one of the agencies in Washington that works to protect consumers by ensuring that companies comply with antitrust laws designed to prevent the exercise of monopoly power.

Source: Paul Brady Photography/Shutterstock.com

The U.S. government has been involved in many cases in which it intervened to prevent a restriction of competition in an industry. When two office superstores, Staples and Office Depot, wanted to merge in 1997, the U.S. Federal Trade Commission (FTC) objected and eventually succeeded in stopping the merger. Two decades later, the two firms tried to merge again but the FTC blocked the merger again in 2016. When DIRECTV and Echostar, two competing satellite television providers, wanted to unite to form a single company, the Federal Communications Commission (FCC)—the federal agency that regulates the telecommunications industry—rejected the merger on the grounds that this would create a monopoly that would raise prices for satellite television customers. In 2017, reports that the FTC might block a merger between two drugstore chains—RiteAid and Walgreens—sent the stocks of both companies down sharply, but after the deal was reworked to meet some of those antitrust concerns, the merger was approved. In 2019, news broke that the federal government was considering opening antitrust investigations into the four tech giants—Apple, Amazon, Facebook, and Google. Although formal governmental charges have not been unveiled, Apple has been accused by other companies of using market power over its App Store, which controls how companies can access the community of iPhone users. Google has been accused of using its dominance over search to limit how online advertisers can reach clients. Amazon has been accused of using its online sales platform to control how small businesses can sell products on the platform. And Facebook, like Google, has been accused of using its market power in online advertising to control how companies can target users online.

The intent of the government in these cases was to promote competition, which we know is an essential ingredient of market efficiency. The models of monopoly and monopolistic competition that you studied in Chapter 10 and Chapter 11 showed that when firms have market power, they raise prices above marginal cost, reduce the quantity produced, and create a deadweight loss to society. In such cases, the government may be able to reduce the deadweight loss and increase economic efficiency by taking actions that can lead to increased competition.

In this chapter, you will learn about some of the different ways the government can promote competition and regulate firms with market power. We consider two broad types of policy: (1) antitrust policy, which is concerned with preventing anticompetitive practices like price fixing and with limiting firms' market power by preventing mergers or breaking up existing firms; and (2) regulatory policy, in which the government requires firms that have a natural monopoly to set prices at prescribed levels. We also will talk about the limits and difficulties of government intervention. The government may step in and regulate markets even when a clear indication of anticompetitive behavior is lacking. In fact, because government agencies are susceptible to external influences, sometimes the regulators may end up limiting competition through their interventions. The ability to understand and appreciate the problems associated with both market failure and government failure is an important skill for an economist to possess.

12.1 Antitrust Policy

antitrust policy

Government actions designed to promote competition among firms in the economy; also called competition policy or antimonopoly policy.

Antitrust policy refers to the actions the government takes to promote competition among firms in the economy. Antitrust policy includes challenging and breaking up existing firms with significant market power, preventing mergers that would increase monopoly power significantly, prohibiting price fixing, and limiting anticompetitive arrangements between firms and their suppliers.

Attacking Existing Monopoly Power

Antitrust policy began in the United States more than one hundred years ago in response to a massive wave of mergers and consolidations. Similar merger movements occurred in Europe at about the same time. These mergers were made possible by rapid innovations in transportation, communication, and management techniques. Railroads and telegraph lines expanded across the country, allowing large firms to place manufacturing facilities and sales offices in many different population centers. It was during this period that the Standard Oil Company grew rapidly, acquiring about one hundred firms and gaining about 90 percent of U.S. oil refinery capacity. Similarly, the United States Steel Corporation was formed in 1901 by merging many smaller steel companies. It captured about 65 percent of the steel ingot market. These large firms were called *trusts*.

Sherman Antitrust Act

A law passed in 1890 in the United States to reduce anticompetitive behavior; Section 1 makes price fixing illegal, and Section 2 makes attempts to monopolize illegal.

The **Sherman Antitrust Act** of 1890 was passed in an effort to prevent these large companies from using their monopoly power. Section 2 of the act focused on the large existing firms. It stated, "Every person who shall monopolize, or attempt to monopolize...any part of the trade or commerce among the several states, or with foreign nations, shall be deemed guilty of a felony."

A Brief History: From Standard Oil to Microsoft

It was on the basis of the Sherman Antitrust Act that Theodore Roosevelt's administration took action to break apart Standard Oil. After 10 years of litigation, the Supreme Court ruled in 1911 that Standard Oil monopolized the oil-refining industry illegally. To remedy the problem, the courts ordered that Standard Oil be broken into a number of separate entities. Standard Oil of New York became Mobil; Standard Oil of California became Chevron; Standard Oil of Indiana became Amoco; Standard Oil of New Jersey became Exxon. Competition among these companies was slow to develop, because John D. Rockefeller still controlled their shares. But as the shares were distributed to heirs and then sold, the companies began to compete against each other. Now the oil-refining companies have much less monopoly power. In fact, with the greater degree of competition, the Clinton administration allowed some of these firms to merge, although not into one single oil refining firm. For example, on November 30, 1999, Exxon and Mobil merged to form a new firm called ExxonMobil.

Soon after its success in splitting apart Standard Oil, the U.S. government took successful action under the Sherman Act against the tobacco trust, splitting up the American Tobacco Company into sixteen different companies. It also broke up several monopolies in railroads, food processing, and chemicals. The government was not successful, however, in using the Sherman Act against United States Steel. As part of the Standard Oil decision, the Supreme Court developed a **rule of reason** that required not only that a firm have monopoly power but also that it intends to use that power against other firms in a way that would restrict competition. Monopoly per se, in and of itself, was not enough, according to the Supreme Court in 1911. Because most competitors and customers of United States Steel said that the company's actions did not restrain competition, the Supreme Court, applying its rule of reason, decided in 1920 that United States Steel was not guilty under the Sherman Act.

Twenty-five years later, a 1945 Supreme Court decision that found Alcoa Aluminum guilty of monopolization refined the rule of reason to make it easier to prove guilt. Although a monopoly per se still was not enough, the intent to willingly acquire and maintain a monopoly—easier to prove than an intent to restrict competition—was enough to establish guilt.

In 1969, the U.S. government brought antitrust action against IBM because of its dominance in the mainframe computer market. After a number of years of litigation, the government dropped the case, in part because of the rapid change in the computer market. Mainframes were facing competition from smaller computers. Firms such as Digital Equipment and Apple Computer were competing with IBM by 1982, when the government withdrew its case. Looking at the competition picture more broadly and recognizing that it already had spent millions, the government decided that antitrust action was no longer warranted.

The U.S. government took action against AT&T in the 1970s. It argued that AT&T, as the only significant supplier of telephone service in the nation, was restraining trade. As a result of that antitrust action, AT&T was broken apart and had to compete with MCI and Sprint to provide long-distance telephone service nationwide. This increase in competition lowered the cost of long-distance calls.

In the 1990s, attention switched to the computer industry. After several antitrust-related investigations, negotiations, and lawsuits in the 1990s, a federal judge found that Microsoft had monopoly power and used it to harm its competitors and consumers, and ordered the firm's breakup in June 2000. That order was reversed in 2001, however, and the federal government reached an agreement whereby the U.S. Department of Justice proposed that Microsoft should instead permit computer manufacturers to install software from Microsoft's competitors and that Microsoft should make enough information about its operating system available so that other companies could write software that worked well with Microsoft's operating systems.

One of the more important cases to be filed recently was the one filed in December 2010 against American Express, MasterCard, and Visa. This suit argued that these companies, the three largest issuers of credit cards in the United States, were preventing stores from "offering their customers a discount or benefit for using a network credit card that is less costly to the merchant. Merchants cannot reward their customers based on the customer's card choice. Merchants cannot even suggest that their customers use a less costly alternative card by posting a sign stating 'we prefer' another card or by disclosing a card's acceptance fee."[2] The U.S. Department of Justice estimated that more than $1.6 trillion in economic transactions were done using these three major credit cards and thus lowering transaction fees could save stores (and the customers to whom a portion of the charges get passed on to) tens of billions of dollars a year.

The Staples/Office Depot case is also interesting because in 1997 the FTC objected to the merger arguing that it would reduce competition and increase the cost of office supplies for consumers, individual-owned businesses and small businesses. By 2017, the rise of retailers like Amazon meant that the merger of brick and mortar office supply stores was not as much of a concern but the objection of the FTC was based on a complaint that the merger would adversely impact competition in the market supplying office supplies to large businesses.

rule of reason

An evolving standard by which antitrust cases are decided, requiring not only the existence of monopoly power but also the intent to restrict trade.

Predatory Pricing

predatory pricing

Action on the part of one firm to set a price below its shutdown point to drive its competitors out of business.

Attempts by firms to monopolize by predatory pricing also have been challenged by the government and by other firms, though breakup usually is not the intended remedy. **Predatory pricing** refers to an attempt by a firm to charge a price below its shutdown point to drive its competitors out of business, after which it then forms a monopoly.

A 1986 Supreme Court decision, *Matsushita v. Zenith*, made predatory pricing harder to prove. Matsushita and several other Japanese companies were accused by Zenith of predatory pricing of televisions in the U.S. market. After five years of litigation and appeals, the Court decided that evidence was insufficient to determine predatory pricing. The Court argued that the Japanese firms' share of the U.S. market was too small compared with Zenith's share to make monopolization plausible. Moreover, the low price of the Japanese televisions seemed to be based on low production costs. Thus, the Court's majority opinion stated that this predatory pricing case appeared to make "no economic sense."

Predatory pricing is difficult to distinguish from vigorous competition, which is essential to a well-functioning market economy. For example, Walmart has been accused of predatory pricing by smaller retailers, who find it hard to compete with Walmart's low prices. Yet, in many of these cases, it is likely that Walmart is more efficient. Its lower prices are due to lower costs. In 1993, Northwest Airlines sued American Airlines for predatory pricing in Texas but lost. Although American Airlines was charging prices below its shutdown point, the jury decided that it was not attempting to monopolize the market. In 2016, a cab firm in San Francisco filed a complaint in federal court charging that the ride-share firm Uber was engaged in predatory pricing—using the many millions of venture capital funds to bankroll a strategy of driving fares so low as to put local taxi companies out of business as Uber sought to expand and consolidate in many cities across the world.

Merger Policy

Clayton Antitrust Act

A law passed in 1914 in the United States aimed at preventing monopolies from forming through mergers.

Federal Trade Commission

The government agency established to help enforce antitrust legislation in the United States; it shares this responsibility with the Antitrust Division of the Justice Department.

The frequency of government-forced breakups has declined in recent years, perhaps due to greater international competition or due to the effectiveness of merger policy, which we now consider. For firms to occupy a huge share of the market, they must either grow internally or merge with other firms. If the government can implement a merger policy that manages to prevent the formation of firms with substantial market power, then the need to break up firms because they have gained too much market power will be lower.

The Sherman Antitrust Act dealt with monopolies that were already in existence. The **Clayton Antitrust Act** of 1914 aimed to prevent the creation of monopolies and now provides the legal basis for preventing mergers that would reduce competition significantly. The **Federal Trade Commission (FTC)** was set up in 1914 to help enforce these acts along with the Justice Department.

To this day, the **Antitrust Division of the Justice Department** and the FTC have dual responsibility for competition policy in the United States. The U.S. Department of Justice has more investigative power and can bring criminal charges, but for the most part, the agencies share a dual responsibility.

How does the government decide whether a merger by firms reduces competition in the market? The economists and lawyers in the U.S. Department of Justice and the FTC provide much of the analysis. They focus on the market power of the firm. The more concentrated the firms are in an industry, the more likely it is that the firms have significant market power.

The "Herf"

Concentration usually is measured by the **Herfindahl-Hirschman Index (HHI)**. This index is used so frequently to analyze the impact of mergers on the competitive structure of an industry that it has a nickname: the "Herf." The HHI is defined as the sum of the squares of the market shares of all the firms in the industry. The more concentrated the industry, the larger the shares and, therefore, the larger the HHI. For example, if one firm controls the entire market, the HHI is $(100)^2$ = 10,000, the maximum value it can attain. If two firms each have a 50 percent share, the HHI is $(50)^2 + (50)^2$ = 5,000. If 10 firms have equal shares, the HHI is 1,000. Values of the HHI for several hypothetical examples of firm shares in particular industries are listed in Table 12.1.

Observe that the HHI is not merely a measure of the number of firms that exist within an industry. The HHI tends to be lower when an industry has more firms, but it also tends to be lower when all the firms' shares are more equal. Even when the number of firms in the industry is very large, the HHI can be large if one or two firms have a large share. For example, an industry with 20 firms in which one firm has 81 percent of the market and the others each have 1 percent has a very large HHI of 6,580, even greater than that of a two-firm industry with equal shares.

According to the *merger guidelines* put forth by the U.S. Justice Department and the FTC, mergers in industries with a post-merger HHI *above 1,800* are likely to be challenged if the HHI rises by 50 points or more. When the HHI is *below 1,000*, a challenge is unlikely. *Between 1,000 and 1,800*, a challenge is likely to occur if the HHI rises by 100 points or more.

Some examples are found in Table 12.1. Suppose that the two smallest firms in industry C in Table 12.1 merge, and the industry thereby takes the form of industry B. Then the HHI rises by 32, from 3,376 to 3,408. It is unlikely that the government would challenge this merger. In contrast, suppose that the two smallest firms in industry B merge. Then the HHI increases by 192, from 3,408 to 3,600, and the government would be likely to challenge the merger.

TABLE 12.1 Examples of the HHI in Different Industries

Industry Example	Number of Firms	Shares (percent)	HHI
A	3	40, 40, 20	3,600
B	4	40, 40, 12, 8	3,408
C	5	40, 40, 12, 4, 4	3,376

The HHI is used because it indicates how likely it is that firms in the industry after the merger will have enough market power to raise prices well above marginal cost, reduce the quantity produced, and cause economic inefficiency. For example, when the FTC blocked the merger of Office Depot and Staples in 1997, it stated that the "post-merger HHIs average over 3000" and that "increases in HHIs are on average over 800 points."[3]

Antitrust Division of the Justice Department

The division of the U.S. Justice Department that enforces antitrust legislation, along with the Federal Trade Commission.

Herfindahl-Hirschman Index (HHI)

An index ranging in value from 0 to 10,000 indicating the concentration in an industry; it is calculated by summing the squares of the market shares of all the firms in the industry.

contestable market

A market in which the threat of competition is enough to encourage firms to act like competitors.

The FTC or the U.S. Justice Department looks at other things in addition to concentration measures. Ease of entry of new firms into the industry is an important factor, as is the potential contestability of the market by other firms. Recall the idea of **contestable markets** discussed in Chapter 10: Even if firms are highly concentrated in an industry, potential entry by other firms provides competitive pressure on the industry. Thus, an industry with a high degree of concentration, in fact, may be acting competitively because of the threat of new firms coming into the business.

Price-Cost Margins

price-cost margin

The difference between price and marginal cost divided by the price. This index is an indicator of market power, where an index of zero indicates no market power and a higher price-cost margin indicates greater market power.

Another way to measure market power is the **price-cost margin**. The greater the price (P) is above the marginal cost (MC), the more market power firms have. Table 12.2 gives some estimates of the price-cost margin [$(P - MC)/P$] for firms in several different industries. The higher the price-cost margin, the more market power firms in the industry have. Observe in Table 12.2 that the price-cost margin is very small for coffee roasting, rubber, textiles, retail gasoline, and standard automobiles. The firms in these markets apparently have little market power. In contrast, the price-cost margin is very high for food processing and tobacco.

TABLE 12.2 Price-Cost Margins in Several Industries

Industry	Price-Cost Margin
Food processing	0.50
Coffee roasting	0.04
Rubber	0.05
Textiles	0.07
Electrical machinery	0.20
Tobacco	0.65
Retail gasoline	0.10
Standard automobiles	0.10
Luxury automobiles	0.34

Source: T. F. Bresnahan, "Empirical Studies of Industries with Market Power," Handbook of Industrial Organization, Vol. II, ed. R. Schmalensee and R. D. Willig (Amsterdam: Elsevier Science Publishers, 1989).

An interesting example is Anheuser-Busch, the producer of Budweiser beer. Before the introduction of Lite Beer by Miller, Anheuser-Busch had considerable market power; the price-cost margin was 0.3. After Lite Beer was introduced, the firm lost market power. The price-cost margin dropped to 0.03. Evidently Lite Beer made Miller a more visible player in the beer market, thus increasing competition in the market, and Anheuser-Busch's market power declined.

Market Definition

market definition

Demarcation of a geographic region and a category of goods or services in which firms compete.

When measuring concentration in a market, the market definition is very important. A **market definition** is a demarcation of a geographic region and a category of goods and services in which firms compete. Table 12.3 shows the range of possibilities for market definitions when considering the merger of soft drink producers. Should the market definition be narrow (carbonated soft drinks) or broad (all nonalcoholic beverages)? The market definition makes a big difference for concentration measures. In 1986, the FTC blocked a merger between Coca-Cola and Dr. Pepper that would have increased the HHI by 341 in the carbonated soft drink market. The HHI would have increased by only 74, however, if bottled water, powdered soft drinks, tea, juices, and coffee also were included in the market, along with carbonated soft drinks.

TABLE 12.3 Different Market Definitions in the Beverage Industry

						Milk
					Tea	Tea
				Coffee	Coffee	Coffee
			Juice drinks	Juice drinks	Juice drinks	Juice drinks
		Bottled water	Bottled water	Bottled water	Bottled water	Bottled water
	Powdered soft drinks	Powdered soft drinks	Powdered soft drinks	Powdered soft drinks	Powdered soft drinks	Powdered soft drinks
Carbonated soft drinks	Carbonated soft drinks	Carbonated soft drinks	Carbonated soft drinks	Carbonated soft drinks	Carbonated soft drinks	Carbonated soft drinks
Narrow Market Definition			Medium Market Definition			Broad Market Definition

Defining the geographic area of a market is also a key aspect of defining the market for a good or service. In an integrated world economy, a significant amount of competition comes from firms in other countries. For example, the automobile industry in the United States has featured only three major producers. Although this industry is highly concentrated, intense competition coming from Japanese, Korean, German, and other automobile companies increases the amount of competition. The rationale for challenging a merger is mitigated substantially by international competition.

 ## Introduction to Antitrust Policy

Watch this video that includes examples of anticompetitive behavior targeted by the United States antitrust laws.

View the video online at: http://www.youtube.com/embed/8tQa92BWjvM?rel=0

Horizontal versus Vertical Mergers

horizontal mergers

A combining of two firms that sell the same good or the same type of good.

vertical mergers

A combining of two firms, one of which supplies goods to the other.

Merger policy also distinguishes between **horizontal mergers**, in which two firms selling the same good or the same type of good merge, and **vertical mergers**, in which a firm merges with its supplier—for example, when a clothing manufacturer merges with a retail clothing store chain. The merger guidelines refer to horizontal mergers. Virtually all economists agree that horizontal mergers have the potential to increase market power, all else being the same.

Economists disagree considerably about the effects of vertical mergers, however. A vertical merger seldom will reduce competition if firms are competing at each level of production. However, some feel that a vertical merger may aid in reducing competition at the retail store level.

 Types of Mergers

Listen to this discussion of conglomerate, horizontal, and vertical mergers, and the Herfindahl-Hirschman Index.

View the video online at: http://www.youtube.com/embed/wlLdX0fs6hE?rel=0

Price Fixing

price fixing

The situation in which firms conspire to set prices for goods sold in the same market.

treble damages

Penalties awarded to the injured party equal to three times the value of the injury.

In addition to breaking up firms and preventing firms with a great amount of market power from merging, antitrust policy prevents firms from conspiring to restrict competition. For example, when two or more firms conspire to fix prices, they engage in an illegal anticompetitive practice. **Price fixing** is a serious offense that is deemed to be illegal per se by Section 1 of the Sherman Antitrust Act.

Laws against price fixing are enforced by bringing lawsuits against the alleged price fixers. Suits can be brought both directly by the U.S. Department of Justice and by individual firms that are harmed by price fixing; typically, the number of private suits greatly exceeds the number of government suits. Individual firms can collect **treble damages** (a provision included in the Clayton Act)—three times the actual damages. The treble damage penalty aims to deter price fixing.

One of the most famous price-fixing cases in U.S. history occurred in the 1950s and involved Westinghouse and General Electric. Through an elaborate system of secret codes and secret meeting places, the executives of these two firms agreed to set the price of electrical generators and other equipment that they were selling in the same market. Through this agreement, they set the price well above competitive levels, but they were discovered and found guilty of price fixing. Treble damages amounting to about $500 million were awarded, and criminal sentences were handed down; some executives went to prison.

A more recent price-fixing case involved the production of computer memory chips. Several firms, including the leading chipmaker Samsung, were fined $300 million for fixing prices for computer memory chips. Newspapers reported at the time that the fine was the second largest in U.S. history. Other notable cases included the 1996 suit filed by the U.S. Department of Justice against the large agricultural firm Archer-Daniels-Midland (ADM) for fixing prices of animal feed and the 2001 settlement of a lawsuit brought against the legendary auction houses Sotheby's and Christie's by clients who had bought or sold items at auction. Both cases resulted in large fines: ADM paid more than $100 million in fines, while Sotheby's and Christie's each paid more than $250 million in fines.

Vertical Restraints

The price-fixing arrangements just described are an effort to restrict trade in one horizontal market, such as the electrical machinery market or the market for computer memory chips. Such restraints of trade clearly raise prices, reduce the quantity produced, and cause deadweight loss. But firms also attempt to restrain trade vertically by limiting the number of sellers of a particular product in a market. Trade in a product can be restrained vertically in several ways. For example, **exclusive territories** occur when a manufacturer of a product gives certain retailers or wholesalers exclusive rights to sell that product in a given area. This practice is common in soft drink and beer distribution. **Exclusive dealing** is the practice by which a manufacturer does not allow a retailer to sell goods made by a competitor. **Resale price maintenance** is the practice of a manufacturer's setting a list price for a good and then forbidding the retailer to offer a discount.

Do vertical restraints reduce economic efficiency? Economists agree that manufacturers cannot increase their own market power by placing restraints on the firms to which they supply goods. A manufacturer's requirement that a retailer take a certain action with respect to the manufacturer's product does not give the manufacturer a greater ability to raise prices over competitors without losing sales. In addition, in some circumstances, such restraints actually may increase economic efficiency.

Consider resale price maintenance, for example. Suppose that low-price, low-service discount stores compete with high-price retail stores that provide lots of useful services to customers. If a discount store could offer the same product with little or no service, then people could go to the high-price store, look the product over, get some useful advice from knowledgeable salespeople, and then buy at the discount store. In such a world, the high-service stores would disappear. Resale price maintenance thus can be viewed as a means to preserve stores that offer such service by preventing the discount store from charging a lower price.

Sometimes stores are able to maintain this high level of service by other means: High-end wedding dress stores often will remove the labels from wedding dresses so that prospective brides will not be able to try on dozens of dresses using the time and expertise of a knowledgeable store assistant, choose the perfect dress, and then go buy it for a much lower price from a discount store that provides no such service. But for most goods, resale price maintenance will ensure that more stores are selling the product, with some providing a high level of service for those who value that attribute over a lower price, and others offering a low level of service for those customers who value lower prices more than service. In 2007, the Supreme Court ruled that minimum resale price maintenance would no longer be illegal *per se* under the Sherman Antitrust Act. Instead such agreements would have to be examined on a case-by-case basis to determine whether they were being used to reduce competition.

Similar arguments can be made for exclusive territories and for exclusive dealing. If McDonald's wants to allow only two franchises to serve a particular town, nothing prevents Wendy's or

exclusive territories

The regions over which a manufacturer limits the distribution or selling of its products to one retailer or wholesaler.

exclusive dealing

A condition of a contract by which a manufacturer does not allow a retailer to sell goods made by a competing manufacturer.

resale price maintenance

The situation in which a producer sets a list price and does not allow the retailer to offer a discount to consumers.

Burger King from opening franchises in that town to cater to potential customers. If a producer wants to limit stores that carry its product from selling competitors' products, it would be no different from the case in which a producer and a retailer are vertically integrated into one firm. For example, the Gap sells only its own products in its retail outlets. Why should a producer like Levi Strauss be treated differently and not be permitted to dictate that stores sell only Levis, were it to want to impose such a limitation?

Some argue, however, that resale price maintenance is a way to reduce competition at the retail level. They see retailers having competitive pressure to keep prices low as more important than the possible loss of some retail customer services. In sum, controversy among economists is greater about the effect of vertical restraints than about horizontal restraints.

Review

- Breaking up monopolies, preventing mergers that would create too much market power, and enforcing laws against price fixing are the main government actions that constitute antitrust policy.
- These actions are backed by several important laws. Section 1 of the Sherman Antitrust Act outlaws price fixing, while Section 2 of the Sherman Antitrust Act allows the government to break up firms with monopoly power. The Clayton Antitrust Act provides the legal basis for merger policy.
- All these policies aim to increase competition and thus improve the efficiency of a market economy.
- The U.S. government has broken up several monopolies since the Sherman Act was passed, including Standard Oil, American Tobacco, and AT&T. In recent years the number of breakups of firms has decreased.
- The U.S. government also takes action to prevent mergers that can create too much market power. It uses tools like the HHI to gauge how competitive an industry is. The HHI tends to be lower, indicating more competition, when the market shares of firms are more equal and the market has more such equal firms.
- Both the U.S. government and private entities that have been harmed by higher prices can bring lawsuits against firms that conspire to fix prices. In recent years, several firms have been found guilty of price fixing and have been fined hundreds of millions of dollars.
- Mergers and price restraints are differentiated into two types: vertical (suppliers, producers, manufacturers, and retailers of a particular product) and horizontal (firms selling the same product). Vertical mergers and vertical restraints on making markets are considered less likely to make markets anticompetitive than are horizontal mergers and horizontal restraints.

12.2 Regulating Natural Monopolies

The goal of antitrust policy is to increase competition and improve the efficiency of markets. Under some circumstances, however, using antitrust policy to break up a monopoly into several competing firms is not necessarily in the interest of efficiency. For example, to provide its services, a water company must dig up the streets, lay the water pipes, and maintain them. It would be inefficient to have two companies supply water because that would require two sets of pipes and would be a duplication of resources. Another example is electricity. It makes no sense to have two electric utility firms supply the same neighborhood with two sets of wires. A single supplier of electricity is more efficient.

Water and electricity are examples of **natural monopolies**—industries in which one firm can supply the entire market at a lower cost than two firms can. Recall from the discussion in Chapter 10 that the key characteristic of a natural monopoly is that the minimum efficient scale is larger than the size of the market; the average total cost curve is declining over the entire range of production. Average total cost declines as more is produced because fixed costs are very large compared with variable costs. Once the main line is laid for the water supply, it is relatively easy to hook up another house. Similarly, with electricity, once the main lines are installed, it is relatively easy to run wires into a house. A large initial outlay is necessary to lay the main water pipes or main electrical lines, but thereafter the cost is relatively low. The greater the number of houses that are hooked up, the lower the average total cost.

Figure 12.2 shows graphically why one firm always can produce more cheaply than two or more firms when the average total cost curve is downward-sloping. The figure shows quantity produced on the horizontal axis and dollars on the vertical axis; a downward-sloping average total cost curve is plotted. If two firms divide up the market (for example, if two water companies supply water to the neighborhood), then the average total cost is higher than if one firm produces for the entire market. In the case of a declining average total cost curve, it is more costly for two or more firms to produce a given quantity than for one firm.

FIGURE 12.2 Natural Monopoly: Declining Average Total Cost
If two firms supply the market, dividing total production between them, costs are higher than if one firm supplies the market. The costs would be even greater if more than two firms split up the market.

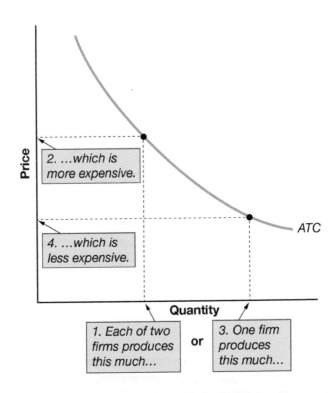

Methods of Regulating a Natural Monopoly

What is the best government policy toward a natural monopoly? On the one hand, having one firm in an industry will result in a lower average cost of production, but inefficiencies will be associated with a monopoly: Price will be higher than marginal cost, and there will be a deadweight loss. On the other hand, breaking up the monopoly into two firms will result in more competition, but each firm will be saddled with a higher average cost of production and it will be inefficient to have both firms incur the high fixed costs. To get both the advantages of one firm producing at a lower average cost *and* a lower price, the government can regulate the firm.

The monopoly price and quantity of a natural monopoly with declining average total cost are illustrated in Figure 12.3. The monopoly quantity occurs when marginal revenue equals marginal cost, the profit-maximizing point for the monopolist. The monopoly price is above marginal cost. If the firm's price is regulated, then the government can require the firm to set a lower price, thereby raising output and eliminating some of the deadweight loss associated with the monopoly. The government can regulate price in three ways: marginal cost pricing, average total cost pricing, and incentive regulation. We discuss each in turn.

FIGURE 12.3 Monopoly Price versus Alternative Regulatory Schemes
Two alternatives, marginal cost pricing and average total cost pricing, are compared with the monopoly price. Marginal cost pricing gives the greatest quantity supplied, but because price is less than average total cost, the firm earns negative profits. Average total cost pricing results in a larger quantity supplied, and the firm earns zero economic profits.

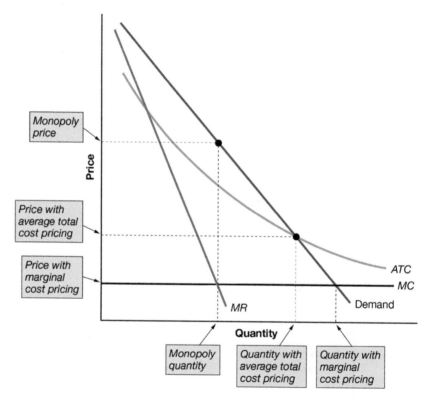

Marginal Cost Pricing

marginal cost pricing

A regulatory method that stipulates that the firm charge a price that equals marginal cost.

We know that there is no deadweight loss with competition because firms choose a quantity of output such that marginal cost is equal to price. One possibility to create competition is for the government to require the monopoly to set its price equal to marginal cost. This method is called **marginal cost pricing**. However, with declining average total cost, the marginal cost is lower than average total cost. This is shown in Figure 12.3 for the case in which marginal cost is constant. Thus, if price were equal to marginal cost, *the price would be less than average total cost*, and the monopoly's profits would be negative (a loss). Firms would not have an incentive to enter the market.

For example, if the regulators of an electrical utility use a pricing rule with price equal to marginal cost, the electrical utility would not have an incentive to build a plant or produce electricity. Although the idea of mimicking a competitive firm by setting price equal to marginal cost might sound reasonable, it fails to work in practice.

Average Total Cost Pricing

Another method of regulation requires the firm to set the price equal to average total cost. This method is called **average total cost pricing** or, sometimes, cost-of-service pricing. It also is illustrated in Figure 12.3. When price is equal to average total cost, we know that economic profits will be equal to zero. With the economic profits equal to zero, there will be enough to pay the managers and the investors in the firm their opportunity costs. Although price is still above marginal cost, it is less than the monopoly price. The deadweight loss will be smaller, and more electricity will be produced compared with the monopoly.

But average total cost pricing has serious problems. Suppose the firm knows that whatever its average total cost is, it will be allowed to charge a price equal to average total cost. In that situation, firms do not have an incentive to reduce costs. Sloppy work or less innovative management could increase costs. With the regulatory scheme in which the price equals average total cost, the price would rise to cover any increase in cost. Inefficiencies could occur with no penalty whatsoever. This approach provides neither an incentive to reduce costs nor a penalty for increasing costs at the regulated firm.

> **average total cost pricing**
>
> A regulatory method that stipulates that the firm charge a price that equals average total cost.

Incentive Regulation

The third regulation method endeavors to deal with the problem that average total cost pricing provides too little incentive to keep costs low. The method is called **incentive regulation**. It is a relatively new idea, but it is spreading quickly, and most economists predict that it is the way of the future. The method projects a regulated price out over a number of years. That price can be established on the basis of an estimate of average total cost. The regulated firm is told that the projected price will not be revised upward or downward for a number of years. If the regulated firm achieves an average total cost that is lower than the price, it will be able to keep the profits, or perhaps pass on some of the profits to a worker who came up with the idea for the innovation. Similarly, if sloppy management causes average total cost to rise, then profits will fall because the regulatory agency will not revise the price.

> **incentive regulation**
>
> A regulatory method that sets prices for several years ahead and then allows the firm to keep any additional profits or suffer any losses over that period of time.

Thus, under incentive regulation, the regulated price is only imperfectly related to average total cost. The firm has a profit incentive to reduce costs. If a firm does poorly, it pays the penalty in terms of lower profits or losses.

Under incentive regulation, the incentives can be adjusted. For example, the California Public Utility Commission (the regulator of utility firms in California) has incentive schemes by which electrical utility firms and their customers share equally in the benefits of reduced costs and in the penalties from increased costs. This reduces the firm's incentive to lower costs in comparison to the case in which the benefits and penalties are not shared.

Incentive regulation is sometimes made difficult by *asymmetric information*—that is, when one of the parties has access to more or better information. In this case, the regulated firm has more information than the regulator about its equipment, technology, and workers. Thus, the firm can mislead the regulator and say that its average total cost is higher than it actually is to get a higher price, as shown in Figure 12.4.

FIGURE 12.4 Asymmetric Information and Regulation

If a regulator uses average total cost pricing but does not have complete information about costs at the firm, the firm could give misleading information about its costs to get a higher price from the regulator. In an extreme case, shown in this figure, the firm could say its costs were so high that it could get the monopoly price.

Review

- A natural monopoly is said to exist when the minimum efficient scale is larger than the size of the market, implying that one firm can produce at a lower average total cost than two or more firms.

- A government may not want to allow a natural monopoly to exist unhindered, even though the single firm is producing at the lowest average total cost, because a monopoly creates deadweight loss. Conversely, breaking up the natural monopoly can reduce deadweight loss but also will lead to inefficiently high costs of production.

- The solution is to allow a single firm to produce the output to take advantage of the declining average total cost, but regulate the firm so that it charges a price less than the monopoly price. The government has several alternatives, including marginal cost pricing, average total cost pricing, and incentive regulation.

- If the government regulates the monopoly by setting a price equal to marginal cost, the firm will run losses because, for natural monopolies, average total cost tends to exceed marginal cost given the high level of fixed costs.

- If the government regulates the monopoly by setting a price equal to average total cost, it encourages firms to incur high costs because the price they are allowed to charge increases with costs.

- Incentive regulation is becoming the preferred method of regulation. By allowing firms to charge a price that is not revised up or down for a number of years, firms are encouraged to pursue strategies to lower costs and increase profits.

12.3 To Regulate or Not to Regulate

Our analysis thus far suggests that the government should regulate firms' prices in situations in which natural monopolies exist. In practice, this requires deciding when a natural monopoly exists, which is frequently difficult.

U.S. history includes many examples of government regulation of a firm's prices even when it is far-fetched to think of the firm as a natural monopoly. For example, for a long time, trucking was regulated by the federal government. Trucking regulation grew out of railroad regulation, which originally was justified when railroads were the only rapid form of transportation and thus were natural monopolies. Under trucking regulation, the federal government controlled which companies had permits to ship goods across state lines and also set uniform rates that the trucking firms could charge. Federal regulation of trucking was disbanded in the early 1980s. Studies have shown that trucking rates fell as a result.

Borderline Cases

Clearly, trucking is not a natural monopoly. The trucking industry is at the opposite end of the spectrum from water or electrical utility companies, which almost always are regulated.

But many borderline cases are more controversial. Many of these arise in high technology industries such as telecommunications and computing. An important example is cable television. In 1992, there was considerable debate about whether the federal government should regulate cable television. At first glance, it may have appeared that cable television is no different from electricity or water. Once a cable television company lays down the cable in a neighborhood, the cost is fairly small to connect each individual house to it. On the other hand, consumers have alternatives to cable television for many homes. For example, over-the-air television channels do provide some competition to cable television. If one lives in an area with few over-the-air channels, competition is low. If, however, an area has six, seven, or eight over-the-air channels, then competition is higher.

FIGURE 12.5 Competition for Cable
Satellites provide customers in remote areas with access to television broadcasts. In more densely populated areas, satellites provide competition to cable companies and help keep cable prices lower than they would be otherwise.

Source: yui/Shutterstock.com

Until 1992, the FCC measured competition by the number of over-the-air channels. At first, the commission decided that three over-the-air channels represented effective competition. It did not regulate cable television companies in areas that had more than three over-the-air channels. Later on, when it noticed that prices of cable television were rising and consumers were complaining, the FCC raised the limit to six over-the-air channels. In 1992, Congress passed a law saying that it did not matter how many channels there were; the law required the FCC to regulate cable television firms in any case.

Over-the-air channels are not the only competition for cable television. People can use satellite dishes, which provide access to numerous channels at a price competitive with cable. The rise of broadband internet and its use for providing telephone services has allowed companies like Verizon, which used to provide only landline telephone services, to now provide mobile phone service, home telephone service, and also compete with the cable television companies to provide cable television.

Because high-tech industries change quickly, it is difficult for government regulators to keep up with the changes. Inflexible regulatory rules could slow innovation, but inadequate regulation could stifle competition. In 2002, the FCC ruled that neither phone nor cable companies would be required to share their broadband connections with competitors like America Online. The FCC argued that such restrictions discouraged phone and cable companies from investing in high-speed Internet service. Critics of the FCC decision argued that this would reduce competition in the broadband market and limit high-speed Internet access. Both critics and supporters of the FCC decision argued that the action was needed to ensure that the United States did not fall behind in broadband access compared with countries like South Korea.

More recently, the FCC has had to make decisions involving technologies that were barely in existence a few years ago, and that will change and evolve rapidly in the years immediately ahead. Recent examples include Net Neutrality, a proposal to ensure that broadband providers would not be able to charge different rates to certain types of websites, especially ones that provide telephone services or video and audio content. In 2014, the FCC announced a policy decision on Net Neutrality that was built on former chairman Michael Powell's Four Freedoms: (1) that Internet users had the right to use the software they desired to access the internet, (2) that they could access their desired content, (3) that they could use whatever devices they wanted to access that content, and (4) that they could obtain accurate information about what they received from their online provider for the price they pay. This ruling did leave open the possibility that consumers could be charged different amounts for different tiers of Internet usage; however, providers were not allowed to favor their content through creating "high-speed lanes" for their own content and for the content of firms who were willing to pay a higher price to use those lanes while leaving a slower internet for other firms.

In 2017, the newly appointed chairman of the FCC, Ajit Pai, announced that the FCC was reversing the previous decision because the additional limits it placed on broadband companies reduced incentives for large companies to invest in their networks and made it more challenging for smaller companies to provide services to rural customers. In December of 2017, after a highly contentious campaign on both sides of the issue, the FCC voted to repeal the previous legislation. Companies could voluntarily adhere to the Net Neutrality principles but were not required to do so. The first eighteen months after net neutrality was repealed did not conform to the extreme concerns that opponents had voiced—internet service providers had not created a different-tiered internet where content providers with deep pockets were able to deliver content at lower prices or higher speeds than less well-resourced competitors. This situation could, however, change as the number of streaming services increases and more consumers seek greater bandwidth to download content seamlessly on mobile devices and smart televisions.

Regulators as Captives of Industry

Government and government agencies are run by people who have their own motivations, such as being reelected or increasing their power, wealth, and influence, which may differ from doing what's best for society. Thus, despite the economic advice about what government regulatory agencies should do, the agencies may end up doing something else.

The railroad industry is an example of how regulators sometimes have helped the industry at the expense of the consumer. Originally, railroads were considered to be a natural monopoly for moving goods across the country, and regulation was intended to reduce prices below the monopoly price. But as competition to the railroads from trucks and eventually airlines increased, the industry continued to be regulated. Eventually, the regulators were helping the industry; they kept prices from falling to prevent railroad firms from failing. Furthermore, to keep trucking firms from competing with the railroads, government authorities regulated trucking prices as well to keep them at a high level. The Teamsters Union, which represents truck drivers, was one of the strongest supporters of regulation because it knew that the regulations were keeping trucking prices high. In a sense, the regulators became captives of both the firms and the workers in the industry.

An economist, George Stigler, won the Nobel Prize for showing how regulatory agencies can become captive to an industry and thwart competition. The concern that regulators will become captives is one reason some economists worry about allowing the government to regulate a new industry, like broadband Internet. Eventually, the government may try to protect the broadband Internet operators to prevent them from failing. The government might limit competition in the future from DSL (digital subscriber line) service or from fiber-optic lines laid by the telephone company or from wireless Internet providers.

The Deregulation Movement

Starting in the late 1970s under Jimmy Carter and continuing in the 1980s under Ronald Reagan, the **deregulation movement**—the lifting of price regulations—radically changed several key industries. The list of initiatives that constitute this deregulation movement is impressive. For example, air cargo was deregulated in 1977, air travel was deregulated in 1978, satellite transmissions were deregulated in 1979, trucking was deregulated in 1980, cable television was deregulated in 1980 (although regulation was reimposed in 1992), crude oil prices and refined petroleum products were deregulated in 1981, and radio was deregulated in 1981. Price deregulation also occurred in the financial industry. Before the 1980s, the price—that is, the interest rate on deposits—was controlled by the financial regulators. Regulation of brokerage fees also was eliminated. This deregulation of prices reduced deadweight loss. Airline prices have declined for many travelers, it is now cheaper to ship goods by truck or by rail, and both satellite television and satellite radio options are available for consumers.

But deregulation has its critics. Deregulation of the airline industry led to widespread fears that large airlines would dominate the industry because of their market power at the hubs. However, the large airlines are now so cost heavy that smaller regional airlines have made significant headway in attracting even business travelers with their low-cost flights. Boston-based business travelers, for example, might be willing to suffer the inconvenience of traveling to Providence to take a cheaper Southwest Airlines flight rather than fly out of Boston on one of the large carriers. Also when price regulations are lifted, firms may figure out ways to price-discriminate. Price discrimination can be welfare-enhancing if it allows the firm to sell to a larger customer base, but clearly some groups will be unhappy. For instance, business travelers complain that they now have to pay more for air travel, although vacation travelers can pay less.

 Government Regulations versus Market Efficiency

Watch from minute 17:07 to 23:27 of this video for a discussion on the efficiency of government regulations versus the market system.

View the video online at: http://www.youtube.com/embed/Fo6Yiq9_nsQ?rel=0

deregulation movement

Begun in the late 1970s, the drive to reduce the government regulations controlling prices and entry in many industries.

Review

- In many cases, determining whether or not a natural monopoly exists (and thus that price regulation is needed) is a challenge.
- There frequently has been price regulation even when there is no natural monopoly, as in trucking. Continuing to regulate an industry long after it has ceased to be a natural monopoly will keep prices artificially high.
- With certain industries, such as cable television or broadband Internet access, it is much more difficult to definitively determine whether the industry is a natural monopoly. Fast-changing technology and the need to balance incentives for innovation with effective competition make the task of a regulator a challenging one.
- Regulators can become captives of the industries they are assigned to regulate. If individuals are motivated more by personal gain than by societal benefit, they may use their regulatory power to protect the interests of the firms they regulate by thwarting competition rather than to protect the interests of consumers by enhancing competition.
- In response to economic analysis that showed that it is harmful to regulate the prices of firms that are not natural monopolies, many industries were deregulated in the 1970s and the 1980s. Trucking, airline, and railroad transportation prices are lower as a result of this deregulation.
- As with most economic changes, not everyone benefited, and not everyone agreed that all industries saw enhanced competition. Some industries, like cable television, were reregulated in the 1990s.

12.4 End-of-Chapter Materials

Conclusion

This chapter analyzed a key role of government in a market economy: maintaining competitive markets through antitrust policy or the regulation of firms. By reducing the deadweight loss caused by monopoly, the government can reduce market failure and improve people's access to services and affordable goods.

This analysis must be placed in the context of what really motivates government policy makers. The example of regulators becoming captives of industry reminds us that analyzing what should be done is different from getting it done. Government failure is a problem that must be confronted just like market failure. Reducing government failure requires designing government institutions that give decision makers the proper incentives.

Key Points

1. The government has an important role to play in maintaining competition in a market economy.
2. Part of antitrust policy is breaking apart firms with significant market power, although this technique is now used infrequently. Section 2 of the Sherman Antitrust Act provides the legal authority for challenging existing monopolies.
3. A more frequently used part of antitrust policy is preventing mergers that would cause significant market power. In the United States, the government must approve mergers.

4. Concentration measures such as the HHI are used to decide whether a merger should take place.

5. Price fixing is a serious antitrust offense in the United States, and the laws against it are enforced by allowing private firms to sue, providing for treble damages, and allowing the government to ask for criminal penalties.

6. In the case of natural monopolies, the government can either run the firm or regulate a private firm. In the United States, the latter route usually is taken.

7. A natural monopoly can be regulated by using marginal cost pricing, average total cost pricing, or incentive regulation. Marginal cost pricing will discourage firms from making the investments needed to provide services, and average total cost pricing discourages firms from producing in a cost-efficient manner, so regulatory agencies have been using incentive regulation more frequently to give firms incentives to hold costs down.

8. Determining whether regulation is needed is a challenging task, especially in industries in which technology changes rapidly.

9. Even when regulation is needed, the regulator is vulnerable to regulatory capture—acting to protect the interests of the firms being regulated by thwarting competition instead of acting to protect the interests of consumers by enhancing competition.

10. In response to economic research showing that several industries were no longer natural monopolies and regulatory capture had taken place, many industries were deregulated in the 1970s and 1980s, including trucking and airlines.

Questions for Review

1. What historical development gave the impetus to the original antitrust legislation in the United States?

2. What are the key laws that govern antitrust policy in the United States?

3. What are the different ways in which the government intervenes to promote competition in the economy?

4. What does the HHI measure? Under what type of market structure would the HHI be highest? When would it be lowest?

5. Why does the government allow firms affected by price fixing to file lawsuits and collect treble damages if they win?

6. Why are vertical mergers and price restraints considered less likely to be anticompetitive than horizontal mergers and price restraints?

7. Why would a government prefer a regulated natural monopoly to an unregulated natural monopoly or to breaking up the natural monopoly firm into several competing firms?

8. What are the different ways in which the government can regulate the price of a natural monopoly? Which of these methods is an improvement on the others?

9. What is regulatory capture? Why is it damaging for the economy?

10. Why is controversy greater about regulating industries in which technology changes rapidly?

Problems

1. Which legislation—Section 1 of the Sherman Act, Section 2 of the Sherman Act, or the Clayton Act—gives the government the authority to take action in each of the following areas: prosecuting price fixing, preventing proposed mergers, breaking up existing monopolies, and suing for predatory pricing?

2. Consider an industry with 10 firms whose market shares are given in the frequency table here:

Market Share	Number of Firms
5 percent	2
10 percent	7
20 percent	1

   a. Calculate the HHI for this industry.

   b. Suppose one of the firms with a 5 percent market share announces a plan to buy the other firm with a 5 percent market share. Is the U.S. Department of Justice likely to challenge the merger? Why or why not?

   c. Suppose the firm with the 20 percent market share announces a plan to buy one of the firms with a 5 percent market share. Is the U.S. Department of Justice likely to challenge the merger? Why or why not?

   d. Suppose one of the firms with a 10 percent market share announces a plan to buy the firm with the 20 percent market share. Is the U.S. Department of Justice likely to challenge the merger? Why or why not?

3. The table here shows the market share of firms in three different industries.

Industry	Number of Firms	Shares	HHI
1	100	Each firm with 1 percent	
2	15	10 firms with 5 percent	
		5 firms with 10 percent	
3	3	1 firm with 60 percent	
		2 firms with 20 percent	

   a. Complete the above table by calculating the Herfindahl-Hirschman Index.

   b. Will the FTC try to prevent a significant merger in Industry 2? In Industry 3? Why?

4. Compare the following two hypothetical cases of price fixing. Which is more likely to raise prices and cause a deadweight loss? Explain.

   a. General Motors, Ford, and Chrysler are found to be coordinating their prices for Chevy Blazers, Ford Broncos, and Jeep Cherokees.

   b. General Motors is coordinating with Chevy dealers around the country to set the price for Chevy Blazers.

5. In 2007, the European Union sued Apple under its antitrust laws. Apple has established country-specific websites for European customers of iTunes. The music inventory and prices vary among the different country-specific sites, and customers are prohibited from purchasing music from an iTunes site outside their country of residence. The European Union claims that this is an unlawful territorial sales restriction. Do you think Apple should be permitted to engage in this practice?

6. Why is it better to break up monopolies that are not natural monopolies than to regulate them, even if it is possible to regulate them?

7. Sketch a graph of a natural monopoly with declining average total cost and constant marginal cost.

   a. Show how the monopoly causes a deadweight loss.

   b. Describe the pros and cons of three alternative ways to regulate the monopoly and reduce deadweight loss: marginal cost pricing, average total cost pricing, and incentive regulation.

8. The demand schedule and total costs for a natural monopoly are given in the following table.

Price ($)	Quantity	Total Costs ($)
16	6	82
15	7	87
14	8	92
13	9	97
12	10	102
11	11	107
10	12	112
9	13	117
8	14	122
7	15	127
6	16	132
5	17	137
4	18	142

a. Why is this firm a natural monopoly? What will the monopoly price be? Calculate profits.

b. Suppose the government sees that this is a natural monopoly and decides to regulate it. If the regulators use average total cost pricing, what will the price and quantity be? What should profits be when the regulators are using average total cost pricing?

c. If the regulators use marginal cost pricing, what will the price and quantity be? What are profits in this situation? Why is this policy difficult for regulators to pursue in practice?

d. Why might the government want to use incentive regulation?

9. Before 1982, AT&T had a monopoly on local telephone service throughout most of the United States. It also provided long-distance telephone service and did not give other companies access to its local telephone lines. As a result of the development of satellites, fiber-optic cable, and other technological advances, it became possible for other companies to provide long-distance service, but their lack of access to local lines seriously inhibited the development of this service. The U.S. Department of Justice sued AT&T under the antitrust laws, and a 1982 settlement required AT&T to sell its local operating companies. In the years after 1982, the local operating companies gradually merged, and by 2006, almost all the local operating companies had merged and rejoined with AT&T long distance. The U.S. Department of Justice did not challenge the re-creation of the 1982 AT&T structure. What changes occurred between 1982 and 2006 that led to this lack of action by the U.S. Department of Justice?

10. In reflecting on a recent term of service, a former head of the Antitrust Division of the U.S. Department of Justice said, "I was convinced that a little bit of efficiency outweighs a whole lot of market power." Evaluate this statement by considering two sources of efficiency: decreasing average total cost and research and development. Describe how these should be balanced against the deadweight loss from market power.

Endnotes

1. United States v. Microsoft Corporation, Civil Action No. 98-1232 (D.C. 1998). Retrieved from: https://www.justice.gov/atr/complaint-us-v-microsoft-corp.

2. U.S. and Plaintiff States v. American Express Co., et al., Civil Action No.1:10-cv-04496 (E.D.N.Y., 2010). Retrieved from: https://www.justice.gov/atr/case-document/complaint-equitable-relief-violation-section-1-sherman-act-15-usc-1.

3. Public Brief to D.C. District Court on FTC v. Staples and Office Depot, April 7, 1997.

CHAPTER 13
Labor Markets

The labor market touches more people than any other market, and it is by far the most important market in people's lives. Odds are that you will be asking questions about the labor market long after you finish this course. In your twenties, you may have to make a decision about moving to work in a new location or about leaving work temporarily to pursue graduate work or to raise a family. In your thirties, you may have to worry about hitting a ceiling in your career progress or about whether it is too late to make a career switch. In your forties, you may worry about earning enough money to pay for your kid's college or your own retirement. In your fifties, you may worry about your ability, at your age, to find a comparable job were you to lose your job, and about how you would cope without health insurance. In your sixties, you will try to figure out how long to keep working and how to coordinate retirement decisions with your spouse. Understanding how labor markets work is even more important than learning how the stock market works.

The importance of labor markets is not confined to one's own experiences. Many important economic policy issues relate to labor markets. What is the effect of the minimum wage? What impact do labor unions have on wages and unemployment? Why do certain vital occupations, such as nursing, firefighting, or teaching, pay less than other occupations that seem to have less of a beneficial social impact?

In this chapter, we show that the standard supply and demand model can be applied to the labor market. Many people are surprised to hear that the same model used to explain changes in the price and quantity of oil helps us understand wage and employment trends. Although we have to adapt the basic model to the labor market, it still is based on the central idea that people make purposeful choices with limited resources and interact with other people when they make these choices.

FIGURE 13.1 The Importance of the Labor Market
Labor markets impact people's lives more than any other market. For a group of nurses, like the ones shown in the picture, the health of the labor market will impact job locations, working conditions, salaries, and even the incentives to acquire a nursing degree.

Source: Monkey Business Images/Shutterstock.com

13.1 The Measurement of Wages

We begin our discussion of labor markets by defining what exactly is meant by "the wage" and showing how it is measured. We also will look at recent wage trends in the United States to see whether wages have been increasing, and if they have been increasing, whether they have been increasing more rapidly or more slowly than in the recent past.

Measuring Workers' Pay

When examining data on workers' pay, we must be specific about (1) what is included in the measure of pay, and (2) whether inflation may be distorting that measure.

Pay Includes Fringe Benefits

fringe benefits

Compensation that a worker receives excluding direct money payments for time worked: insurance, retirement benefits, vacation time, and maternity and sick leave.

Pay for work includes not only the direct payment to a worker—whether in the form of a payroll check, currency in a pay envelope, or a direct deposit into the worker's bank account—but also **fringe benefits**. Fringe benefits may include many of the following: health or life insurance, such as employer provided partial or full insurance; retirement benefits, such as employer-funded retirement plans; paid time off, such as vacations and sick or maternity leave; and discounts on company products.

Fringe benefits are a large share of total compensation in the United States and in many other countries. In recent years in the United States, fringe benefits have accounted for about a third of total pay. For example, in 2019, the average cost per hour to employ a worker was $37.10, of which $11.63 (31.318 percent) came in the form of fringe benefits.

wage

The price of labor defined over a period of time worked.

The term *wage* sometimes refers to the part of the payment for work that excludes fringe benefits. But in most economics textbooks, the term **wage** refers to the *total* amount a firm pays workers, *including* fringe benefits. This book uses the usual textbook terminology. Thus, the wage is the total price of labor.

Adjusting for Inflation: Real Wages versus Nominal Wages

real wage

The wage or price of labor adjusted for inflation; in contrast, the nominal wage has not been adjusted for inflation.

When comparing wages in different years, it is necessary to adjust for inflation, that is, the general increase in prices over time. The term *nominal wage* is used to emphasize that a wage has not been corrected for inflation. The **real wage** is a measure of the wage that has been adjusted for changes in inflation. The real wage is computed by dividing the stated wage by a measure of the price of the goods and services. The most commonly used measure of the price for this purpose is the consumer price index (CPI), which gives the price of a fixed collection, or market basket, of goods and services each year compared with some base year. For example, the CPI increased from 1 in the 1983 base year to 1.75 in 2000; it rose further to 2.58 in 2019. This increase means that the same goods and services that cost $100 in 1983 would cost $175 in 2000 and $258 in 2018.

Suppose the hourly wage for a truck driver increased from $20 to $32 between 2000 and 2019. The nominal wage increase would be 60 percent. The real wage is found by dividing this hourly wage by the CPI. Thus, the real wage would have changed from $11.43 (= $20/1.75) to $12.40 (= $32/2.58), which would only be an 8.5 percent increase. Because of the increase in prices, the real wage for the truck driver rose much less than the stated wage increase. The real wage is the best way to compare wages in different years.

Wage Trends

Having described how to measure wage trends, let's now look at wages in the United States. Figure 13.2 shows average real and nominal hourly wages in the United States over the past three decades. In 2019, the average real wage was about $36.27 per hour (in year 2018 dollars), including about $11.37 per hour in real fringe benefits.

FIGURE 13.2 Average Hourly Real and Nominal Wages Since 1991

In the last three decades, the average hourly wage, including fringe benefits, has more than doubled, increasing from about $16.50 per hour in 1991 to about $37.10 per hour in 2019, an increase of around 2.9 percent per year. Note, however, that in real terms, the average real wage has changed considerably less, rising from around $30.00 (in 2018 dollars) in 1991 to around $36.27 (in 2018 dollars) in 2019, an increase of 0.7 percent per year.

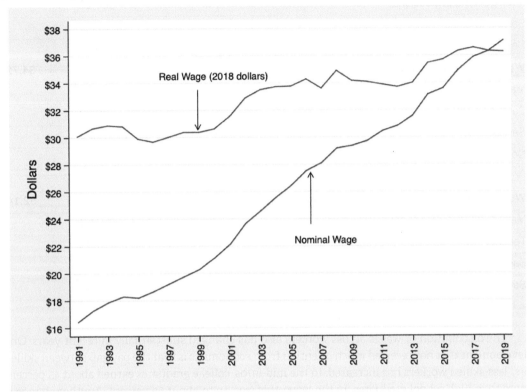

Source: "Employer costs for employee compensation per hour worked," U.S. Bureau of Labor Statistics.

What is most noticeable in Figure 13.2 is that the real wage (including fringe benefits) did not change very much over this period, rising from $29.00 in 1991 to $36.27 in 2019, an increase of less than 1 percent per year. When we look at the same figure in nominal terms, the increase looks more impressive, more than doubling from $16.45 per hour in 1991 to $37.10 per hour in 2019.

Figure 13.2 shows the change in the average wage over time for all workers. What about differences across workers? Table 13.1 shows the differences for major occupation categories of workers at private firms as well as at state and local governments. Jobs requiring higher skills, such as teaching or management, pay more than jobs with lower skills, such as service workers. A more detailed breakdown would show much larger differences between the wages of different people. Top athletes, entertainment celebrities, and corporate executives at large firms are paid many times the average wage in the United States.

TABLE 13.1 Average Hourly Wages of Workers in the United States in 2019 (nominal dollars)

All workers (excluding federal)		**$37.10**
Management, professional	$61.28	
Sales and office	27.09	
Service	19.82	
Workers at private firms		**34.72**
Management, professional	60.83	
Sales and office	26.32	
Service	17.29	
Construction	36.52	
Production, transportation	28.95	
Workers at state and local governments		**52.14**
Management, professional	62.63	
Teachers	68.94	
Sales and office	35.81	
Service	37.93	

Source: "Employer Costs of Employee Compensation" (Bureau of Labor Statistics).

The distribution of wages across workers also has changed substantially in recent years. One development that has received much attention from economists is that the pay gap between skilled and less-skilled workers has increased. In the mid-1970s, college graduates earned about 45 percent more than high school graduates. In the 1990s, this was up to about 65 percent. Another change is in the wage difference between women and men, which, although still wide, has been narrowing in recent years. In the mid-1970s, women on average earned less than $0.60 for each $1 men earned. By 2019, the gap had closed to around $0.80. Some of the remaining difference in earnings comes from the fact that women work fewer hours than men and from occupational differences between men and women.

What causes these changes? Can the economists' model of labor markets explain them? After developing the model in the next section, we will endeavor to answer these questions.

Review

- Workers' pay includes the direct payments plus fringe benefits, which are about 30 percent of workers' pay in the United States.
- When you talk about wages, you should be clear as to whether it is about wages including benefits or wages without benefits and whether it is about the real wage or the nominal wage.
- Real hourly wages have grown at a slow rate in the past 25 years.
- Discussions about the average real wage in the economy must be accompanied by an understanding of how wages are dispersed by skill, gender, industry, occupation, size of firm, part-time or full-time status, and geographic region.
- In recent times, the dispersion of wages between skilled and unskilled workers has increased, with college-educated workers gaining over those without a college education. The difference between the average wage of women and men is substantial, although it has narrowed in recent years.

13.2 The Labor Market

The **labor market** consists of firms that have a demand for labor and people who supply the labor. In analyzing labor markets, economists stress their similarity to other markets; this enables economists to use the standard supply and demand model. To see the analogy, consider Figure 13.3, which illustrates a typical *labor market*. It shows a typical labor supply curve and a typical labor demand curve. On the vertical axis is the price of labor, or the wage. On the horizontal axis is the quantity of labor, either the number of workers or the number of hours worked. People work at many different types of jobs—physical therapists, accountants, mechanics, teachers, Web developers, judges, and professional athletes—and each type has a labor market. The labor market diagram in Figure 13.3 could refer to any one of these particular types of labor.

labor market

The market in which individuals supply their labor time to firms in exchange for wages and salaries.

FIGURE 13.3 Labor Demand Curve and Labor Supply Curve
The basic economic approach to the labor market is to make an analogy with other markets. Labor is what is bought or sold on the labor market. The demand curve shows how much labor firms are willing to buy at a particular wage. The supply curve shows how much labor workers are willing to sell at a particular wage.

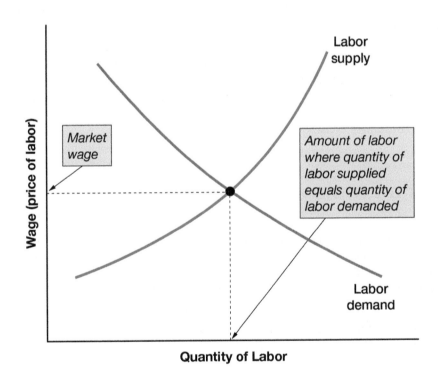

The first thing to remember about the labor demand curve and the labor supply curve is that firms demand labor and people supply it. Firms demand labor—like other factors of production—because it can be used to produce goods and services. The labor demand curve tells us the quantity of labor demanded by firms at each wage; the labor supply curve tells us the quantity of labor supplied by workers at each wage.

Note that the labor demand curve slopes downward and the labor supply curve slopes upward, just like other demand and supply curves. Thus, a higher wage reduces the quantity of labor demanded by firms, and a higher wage increases the quantity of labor supplied by people. Note also that the curves intersect at a particular wage and a particular quantity of labor. As with any other market, this intersection predicts the quantity of something (in this case, labor) and its price (in this case, the wage). Having defined the basics of the labor supply and demand model, we will more closely study how these curves are derived.

13.3 Labor Demand

labor demand

The relationship between the quantity of labor demanded by firms and the wage.

labor supply

The relationship between the quantity of labor supplied by individuals and the wage.

derived demand

Demand for an input derived from the demand for the product produced with that input.

In this section, we look at **labor demand**, the relationship between the quantity of labor demanded by firms and the wage. In the next section, we look at **labor supply**, the relationship between the quantity of labor supplied by people and the wage. We start with a single firm's demand for labor and then sum up all the firms that are in the labor market to get the market demand for labor.

In deriving a firm's labor demand, economists assume that the firm's decision about how many workers to employ, like its decision about how much of a good or service to produce, is based on profit maximization. The demand for labor is a **derived demand**; that is, it is derived from the firm's decision about how many goods or services it can produce with the labor. The firm sells these goods and services to consumers in product markets, which are distinct from the labor market. Labor and other factors of production are not directly demanded by consumers; the firm's demand for labor is derived from consumers' demand for the firm's goods and services.

A Firm's Employment Decision

Recall how the idea of profit maximization was applied to a firm's decision about the optimal quantity to produce: If producing another ton of steel will increase a steel firm's profits—that is, if the marginal revenue from producing a ton is greater than the marginal cost of producing that ton—then the firm will produce that ton of output. However, if producing another ton of steel reduces the firm's profits, then the firm will not produce that ton.

The idea of profit maximization is applied in a similar way to a firm's decision about how many workers to employ: If employing another worker increases the firm's profits, then the firm will employ that worker. If employing another worker reduces the firm's profits, then the firm will not employ the worker.

We have already seen that a firm produces a quantity that equates marginal revenue to marginal cost ($MR = MC$). The firm satisfies an analogous condition in deciding how much labor to employ, as we discuss next.

From Marginal Product to Marginal Revenue Product

To determine a firm's demand curve for labor, we must examine how the firm uses labor to produce its output of goods and services. We start by assuming that the firm sells its output in a *competitive market*; that is, the firm is a *price-taker*. We also assume that the firm takes the wage as given in the labor market; in other words, the firm is hiring such a small proportion of the workers in the labor market that it cannot affect the market wage for those workers. Figure 13.4 gives an example of such a competitive firm. It shows the weekly production and labor input of a firm called Getajob, which produces professional-looking job resumes in a college town. To produce a resume, workers at Getajob talk to each of their clients (usually college seniors), give advice on what should go into the resume, and then produce the resume.

FIGURE 13.4 Labor Input and Marginal Revenue Product at a Competitive Firm
This figure shows how production changes as more workers are employed by the firm. The increase in output produced by each additional worker is the marginal product of labor. We can use the price of each of the additional units of output to calculate the increase in revenue generated by each additional worker, holding other inputs fixed.

Workers Employed Each Week (L)	Quantity Produced (Q)	Marginal Product of Labor (MP)	Price of Output (dollars) (P)	Total Revenue (dollars) (TR)	Marginal Revenue Product of Labor (dollars) (MRP)
0	0	—	100	0	—
1	17	17	100	1,700	1,700
2	31	14	100	3,100	1,400
3	42	11	100	4,200	1,100
4	51	9	100	5,100	900
5	58	7	100	5,800	700
6	63	5	100	6,300	500
7	66	3	100	6,600	300
8	68	2	100	6,800	200
9	69	1	100	6,900	100

$\frac{\text{Change in } Q}{\text{Change in } L}$ | P does not depend on Q | $P \times Q$ | $\frac{\text{Change in } TR}{\text{Change in } L}$ or $P \times MP$

The first two columns of Figure 13.4 show how Getajob can increase its production of resumes each week by employing more workers. This is the *production function* for the firm; it assumes that the firm has a certain amount of capital—word-processing equipment, a small office near the campus, and so on. We assume that labor is the only variable input to production in the short run, so that the cost of increasing the production of resumes depends only on the additional cost of employing more workers. Observe that the **marginal product of labor (MP)**—which we defined in Chapter 6 as the change in the quantity produced when one additional unit of labor is employed, holding other inputs fixed—declines as more workers are employed. In other words, there is a diminishing marginal product of labor, or diminishing return to labor: As more workers are hired, with office space and equipment fixed, each additional worker adds less and less to production. For example, the first worker employed can produce 17 resumes a week, but if Getajob already employed eight workers, hiring a ninth worker will increase production by only one resume.

Suppose that the market price for producing this type of resume service is $100 per resume, as shown in the fourth column of Figure 13.4. Because Getajob is assumed to be a *competitive firm*, it cannot affect this price. Then, the total revenue of the firm for each amount of labor employed can be computed by multiplying the price (P) times the quantity produced (Q) with each amount of labor (L). This calculation is shown in the next-to-last column. For example, total revenue with L = 3 workers employed is P = $100 times Q = 42, or $4,200.

marginal product of labor

The change in production due to a one-unit increase in labor input, holding other inputs fixed.

marginal revenue product of labor

The change in total revenue due to a one-unit increase in labor input, holding other inputs fixed.

The last column of Figure 13.4 shows the **marginal revenue product of labor (MRP)**. *The marginal revenue product of labor is defined as the change in total revenue when one additional unit of labor is employed, holding all other inputs fixed.* For example, the marginal revenue product of labor from hiring a third worker is the total revenue with three workers ($4,200) minus the total revenue with two workers ($3,100), or $4,200 – $3,100 = $1,100. The marginal revenue product of labor is used to find the demand curve for labor, as we will soon see.

What is the difference between the marginal product (*MP*) and the marginal revenue product (*MRP*)? The marginal product is the increase in the quantity produced when labor is increased by one unit, holding other inputs fixed. The marginal revenue product is the increase in total revenue when labor is increased by one unit, holding other inputs fixed. For a competitive firm taking the market price as given, the marginal revenue product (*MRP*) can be calculated by multiplying the marginal product (*MP*) by the price of output (*P*). For example, the marginal product when the third worker is hired is 11 resumes; thus, the additional revenue that the third worker will generate for the firm is $100 per resume times 11, or $1,100.

Observe in Figure 13.4 that the marginal revenue product of labor declines as more workers are employed. This result occurs because the marginal product of labor declines.

Reminder: *Wait—before you read any further, make sure you can explain the difference between marginal product (MP) and marginal revenue product (MRP).*

The Marginal Revenue Product of Labor Equals the Wage (*MRP = W*)

Now we are almost ready to derive the firm's demand curve for labor. Suppose first that the wage for workers with the type of skills Getajob needs to produce resumes is $600 per week (for example, $15 per hour for 40 hours). Then, hiring one worker certainly makes sense because the marginal revenue product of labor is $1,700, or much greater than the $600 wage cost of hiring the worker. How about two workers? The marginal revenue product from employing a second worker is $1,400, still greater than $600, so it makes sense to hire a second worker. Continuing this way, we see that *the firm will hire a total of five workers when the wage is $600 per week*, because hiring a sixth worker would result in a marginal revenue product of only $500, less than the $600 per week wage.

Thus, if a firm maximizes profits, it will hire the largest number of workers for which the marginal revenue product of labor is greater than the wage; if fractional units of labor input (for example, hours rather than weeks of work) are possible, then the firm will keep hiring workers until the marginal revenue product of labor exactly equals the wage. Thus, we have derived a key rule of profit maximization: Firms will hire workers up to the point at which *the marginal revenue product of labor equals the wage*. The rule that the marginal revenue product of labor equals the wage can be written in symbols as *MRP = W.*

FIGURE 13.5

Looking for Work

Day workers who are job hunting for construction cleanup work will signal their availability by showing up at a specified location; labor contractors will come by and hire the number of workers they need that day.

Source: sirtravelalot/Shutterstock.com

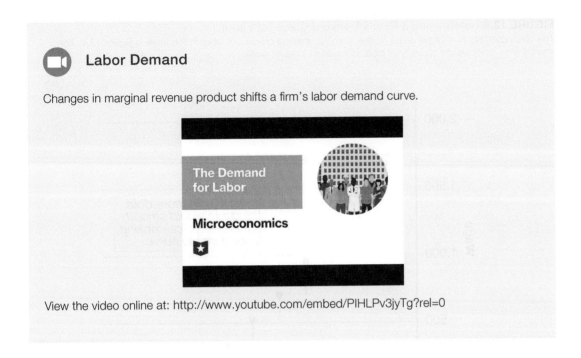

Labor Demand

Changes in marginal revenue product shifts a firm's labor demand curve.

View the video online at: http://www.youtube.com/embed/PIHLPv3jyTg?rel=0

The Firm's Derived Demand for Labor

Now, to find the demand curve for labor, we need to determine how many workers the firm will hire at *different* wages. We know that Getajob will hire five workers if the wage is $600 per week. What if the wage is $800 per week? Then the firm will hire only four workers; the marginal revenue product of the fifth worker ($700) is now less than the wage ($800), so the firm will not be maximizing its profits if it hires five workers. Thus, we have shown that a higher wage reduces the quantity of labor demanded by the firm. What if the wage is lower than $600? Suppose the wage is $250 a week, for example. Then the firm will hire seven workers. Thus, a lower wage increases the quantity of labor demanded by the firm.

Figure 13.6 shows how to determine the entire demand curve for labor. It shows the wage on the vertical axis and the quantity of labor on the horizontal axis. The plotted points are the marginal revenue products from Figure 13.4. To find the demand curve, we ask how much labor the firm would employ at each wage. Starting with a high wage, we reduce the wage gradually, asking at each wage how much labor the firm would employ. At a weekly wage of $2,000, the marginal revenue product is less than the wage, so it does not make sense to hire any workers. Therefore, the quantity demanded is zero at wages more than $2,000. At a weekly wage of $1,500, it makes sense to hire one worker, and so on. As the wage is lowered gradually, the quantity of labor demanded rises, as shown by the vertical lines in Figure 13.6. The step-like downward-sloping curve is the labor demand curve. There would be more black dots and the curve would be smooth if we measured work in fractions of a week rather than in whole weeks.

FIGURE 13.6 Determining a Firm's Demand Curve for Labor
The black dots are exactly the same as the marginal revenue product of labor in the table in Figure 13.4. The vertical lines indicates the quantity of labor demanded at each wage.

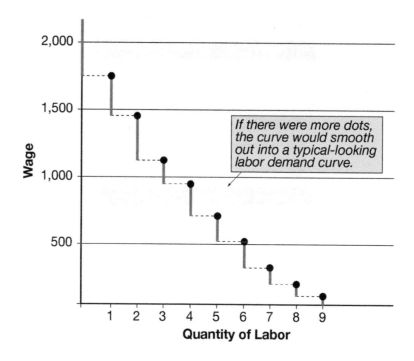

Observe in Figure 13.6 that a firm's demand curve for labor is completely determined by the firm's marginal revenue product of labor. We have shown that the demand curve for labor is downward sloping because the marginal revenue product of labor curve is downward sloping. A higher wage will reduce the quantity of labor demanded, and a lower wage will increase the quantity of labor demanded, because workers with a marginal revenue product that is lower than the wage will not be hired. Changes in the quantity of labor demanded that result from changes in the wage are *movements along* the downward-sloping labor demand curve.

We also can explain why a firm's labor demand curve would *shift*. For example, if the price (*P*) of the good (resumes) rises—perhaps because the demand curve for resumes shifts outward—then the marginal revenue product of labor (*MRP* = *P* x *MP*) will rise and the firm will be willing to employ more workers at any given wage level. This result implies that the demand curve for labor will shift outward. Similarly, a rise in the marginal product of labor (*MP*) also will lead the firm to increase the quantity demanded of labor at each wage level, shifting the labor demand curve outward. On the other hand, a decline in the price (*P*) or a decline in the marginal product (*MP*) will shift the labor demand curve to the left.

What If the Firm Has Market Power?

This approach to deriving the demand curve for labor works equally well for the case of a firm that is not a price-taker but instead is a monopoly or a monopolistic competitor. Figure 13.7 shows an example of such a firm. The key difference between the firm in Figure 13.4 and this firm is in the column for the price. Rather than facing a constant price for its output and thus a horizontal demand curve, this firm faces a downward-sloping demand curve: It can increase the quantity of resumes demanded by lowering its price. For example, if Getajob's resumes are differentiated slightly from those of other resume producers in town, then the demand curve that Getajob faces when selling resumes may be downward sloping.

Once we observe that the price and output are inversely related, we can continue just as we did with the competitive firm. Again, total revenue is equal to the price times the quantity, and marginal revenue product is the change in total revenue as one more worker is hired. Again, the marginal revenue product declines as more workers are hired, as shown in the last column of Figure 13.7. However, now the marginal revenue product declines more sharply as more workers are employed, and it even turns negative. It turns negative as more workers are hired and more output is produced and sold, because the price of output must fall. This cuts into revenue because all units, not just the last unit, are sold at the lower price. But the principle of labor demand is the same: Firms hire up to the point at which the marginal revenue product of labor equals the wage. The marginal revenue product determines the labor demand curve.

FIGURE 13.7 Labor Input and Marginal Revenue Product for a Firm with Power to Affect the Market Price

For a firm with market power, marginal revenue product is no longer equal to price x marginal product. This is because as the firm hires more workers, it produces more output, which in turn leads to a change in the price. Marginal revenue product can be calculated as shown below, and equals marginal revenue x marginal product.

Workers Employed Each Week (L)	Quantity Produced (Q)	Marginal Product of Labor (MP)	Price of Output (dollars) (P)	Total Revenue (dollars) (TR)	Marginal Revenue Product of Labor (dollars) (MRP)
0	0	—	100	0	—
1	17	17	92	1,564	1,564
2	31	14	85	2,635	1,071
3	42	11	79	3,318	683
4	51	9	75	3,825	507
5	58	7	71	4,118	293
6	63	5	69	4,347	229
7	66	3	67	4,422	75
8	68	2	66	4,488	66
9	69	1	65	4,485	–3

Change in Q / Change in L   P declines with Q   P x Q   Change in TR / Change in L

In the case of a firm with market power, the simple relationship $MRP = P \times MP$ no longer holds, however, because the firm does not take the market price as given. Instead, we replace the price (P) by the more general marginal revenue (MR) in that relationship. Marginal revenue product is now equal to the marginal revenue (MR) times the marginal product (MP). The relationship $MRP = MR \times MP$ holds for all firms, whether they have market power or not. Only for a competitive firm is $MR = P$.

Market Demand for Labor

To get the demand for labor in the market as a whole, we must add up the labor demand curves for all the firms demanding workers in the labor market. At each wage, we sum the total quantity of labor demanded by all firms in the market; this is illustrated in Figure 13.8 for the case of two firms producing resumes. The two curves on the left are the labor demand curves for two resume-producing firms, Getajob and Careerpro. (The curves are smoothed out compared with that in Figure

13.6 so that they are easier to see.) The process of summing individual firms' demands for labor to get the market demand is analogous to summing individual demand curves for goods to get the market demand curve for goods. At each wage, we sum the labor demand at all the firms to get the market demand.

FIGURE 13.8 Summing Firms' Demands to Get the Labor Market Demand Curve
The labor demand curve in the market is obtained by summing the quantities of labor demanded by all the firms at each wage.

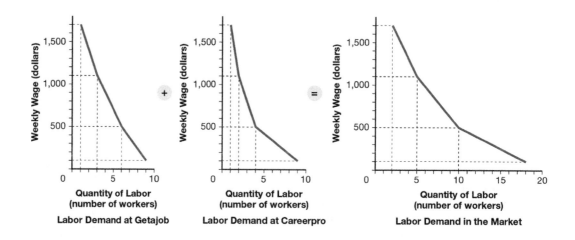

A Comparison of *MRP* = *W* with *MC* = *P*

A firm's decision to employ workers is closely tied to its decision about how much to produce. We have emphasized the former decision in this chapter and the latter decision in earlier chapters. To draw attention to this connection, Figure 13.9 shows the marginal cost when the wage is $600. Marginal cost is equal to the change in variable costs divided by the change in quantity produced. Variable costs are the wage times the amount of labor employed.

Now, consider the quantity of output the firm would produce if it compared price and marginal cost as discussed in earlier chapters. If the price of output is $100, the firm will produce 58 resumes, the highest level of output for which price is greater than marginal cost. This is exactly what we found using the *MRP* = *W* rule, because 58 units of output require five workers. Recall that employing five workers is the profit-maximizing labor choice when the wage is $600.

If the profit-maximizing firm could produce fractional units, then it would set marginal cost exactly equal to price (*MC* = *P*). The resulting production decision would be exactly the same as that implied by the rule that the marginal revenue product of labor equals the wage.

FIGURE 13.9 Marginal Cost and the Production Decision at Getajob

This table shows variable costs and marginal costs for various levels of production at Getajob. The firm will produce the highest level of output for which price is greater than marginal cost.

Workers Employed Each Week (L)	Quantity Produced (Q)	Variable Costs (dollars) (VC)	Marginal Cost (dollars) (MC)
0	0	0	0
1	17	600	35
2	31	1,200	43
3	42	1,800	55
4	51	2,400	67
5	58	3,000	86
6	63	3,600	120
7	66	4,200	200
8	68	4,800	300
9	69	5,400	600

$600 wage × L

Change in VC
Change in Q

Review

- The demand for labor is a relationship between the quantity of labor a firm will employ and the wage, which is the price of labor.
- The demand for labor is a derived demand because it is derived from the goods and services produced by labor.
- If the marginal revenue product of an additional worker exceeds the wage, the firm should employ that worker. If the marginal revenue product of an additional worker is less than the wage, the firm should not employ that worker.
- Accordingly, a profit-maximizing firm will hire workers until the marginal revenue product of labor equals the wage.
- When the wage rises, the quantity of labor demanded by firms declines. When the wage falls, the quantity of labor demanded increases. These are movements along the labor demand curve.
- When the marginal revenue product of labor rises, the demand curve for that type of labor shifts outward. The marginal revenue product of labor can increase if either the marginal product of labor rises or the price of the good produced using labor rises.
- The market demand for labor is obtained by adding up the labor demand curves of all firms looking for workers in the labor market.

13.4 Labor Supply

We now focus on *labor supply*. An individual's labor supply curve is derived from that person's decision about whether to work and how much to work, at different wage rates. The market labor supply curve is the sum of many people's individual labor supply curves. The decision about whether to work and how much to work depends very much on individual circumstances, so we begin by examining the individual's decision.

Work versus Two Alternatives: Home Work and Leisure

Consider a person deciding how much to work—either how many hours a week or how many weeks a year. As with any economic decision, we need to consider the alternative to work. Economists traditionally have called the alternative *leisure*, although many of the activities that make up the alternative to work are not normally thought of as leisure. These activities include "home work," like painting the house or caring for children at home, as well as pure leisure time, such as simply talking to friends on the telephone, going bowling, or hiking in the country. The price of leisure is the opportunity cost of not working, that is, the wage. If a person's marginal benefit from more leisure is greater than the wage, then the person will choose more leisure. The decision to consume more leisure is thus like the decision to consume more of any other good. This analogy may seem strange, but it works quite well in practice.

Effects of Wage Changes: Income and Substitution Effects

Like the decision to consume a commodity, the decision to work can be analyzed with the concepts of the *substitution effect* and the *income effect*.

Recall that the *substitution effect* says that a higher price for a good will make that good less attractive to purchase relative to alternatives. In the case of the labor market, because the wage is the price of leisure (or home work), the higher the wage, the less attractive leisure (or home work) will seem relative to work. In other words, a higher wage makes work more rewarding compared with the alternatives. So even if you really enjoy your nonwork activities, including sleeping, watching movies, playing video games, or even studying, if the wage paid for part-time student employment triples from $10 an hour to $30 an hour, you would be more likely to sacrifice these nonwork activities and work an extra hour each day. The sacrifice—less time to study, sleep, watch television, and so on—will be worth the higher wage. Therefore, the quantity of labor supplied tends to increase when the wage rises because of the substitution effect.

Recall also that the *income effect* reflects the fact that changes in the price of a good either reduce (if a price increase) or expand (if a price decrease) your ability to buy all goods, even ones whose prices have not changed, by changing your real income. In the case of the labor market, a higher wage will increase the real income of an individual and enable that individual to buy more of all goods, including leisure. For example, if you were working 10 hours a week at a wage of $10 an hour, you might decide that at a wage of $30 an hour, you would be happier working five hours a week and enjoying five more hours of leisure. In this case, even after working fewer hours, you have more money to buy other goods. The income effect works in the opposite direction from the substitution effect: The quantity of labor supplied tends to decrease, rather than increase, when the wage rises because of the income effect.

The Shape of Supply Curves

Because the substitution effect and the income effect work in opposite directions, the labor supply curve can slope either upward or downward. The supply curve slopes upward if the substitution effect dominates—that is, as the wage rises, individuals work more because the price of leisure (the opportunity cost of not working) rises. The labor supply curve slopes downward if the income effect dominates—as the wage rises, individuals choose to work less because they can earn as much if not more money by working fewer hours. Several possibilities for the shape of a labor supply curve are illustrated in Figure 13.10.

FIGURE 13.10 Three Labor Supply Curves
The three curves differ in the relative strength of the income and substitution effects. The labor supply curve on the left slopes upward because the substitution effect is stronger than the income effect. For the curve on the right, the income effect is stronger than the substitution effect. For the vertical curve in the middle, the two effects are the same.

Moreover, the same supply curve may slope upward for some range of wages and downward for another range. For example, at high wage levels—when people earn enough to take long vacations—the income effect may dominate. At lower wages, the substitution effect may be dominant, which then would result in a **backward-bending labor supply curve**, as shown in Figure 13.11.

FIGURE 13.11 Backward-Bending Labor Supply Curve
A person may have a labor supply curve that is positively sloped for a low wage, is steeper for a higher wage, and then bends backward for a still higher wage.

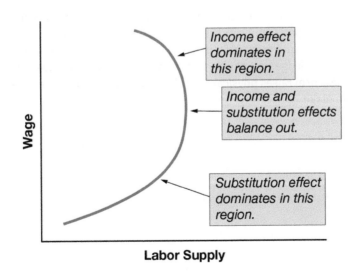

backward-bending labor supply curve

The situation in which the income effect outweighs the substitution effect of an increase in the wage at higher levels of income, causing the labor supply curve to bend back and take on a negative slope.

This derivation of the labor supply curve may seem unrealistic. After all, the work week is forty hours for many jobs; you may not have much choice about the number of hours you work per week. In fact, the sensitivity of the quantity of labor supplied to the wage is probably small for many workers. But economists have shown that the effect is large for some workers, and therefore it is useful to distinguish one worker's supply curve from another's.

In a family with two adults and children, for example, one of the adults already may have a job and the other may be choosing between working at home and working outside the home. This decision may be sensitive to the wage and perhaps the cost of childcare or of consuming more prepared meals. In fact, the increased number of women working outside the home may be the result of increased opportunities and wages for women. The increase in the wage induces workers to work more in the labor market. Economists have observed a fairly strong wage effect on the amount women work.

One also needs to distinguish between the effects of a temporary change in the wage and those of a more permanent change. Empirical studies show that the quantity of labor supplied rises more in response to a temporary increase in the wage than to a permanent increase. What's the explanation? Consider an example. If you have a special one-time opportunity tomorrow to earn $100 an hour rather than your usual $6 an hour, you are likely to put off some leisure for one day; the substitution effect dominates. But if you are lucky enough to land a lifetime job at $100 an hour rather than $6 an hour, you may decide to work fewer hours and have more leisure time; the income effect dominates.

This difference between temporary and permanent changes helps explain the dramatic decline in the average hours worked per week as wages have risen over the last century. These are more permanent changes, for which the income effect dominates.

Work versus Another Alternative: Getting Human Capital

The skills of a worker depend in part on how much schooling and training the worker has had. The decision to obtain these skills—to finish high school and attend a community college or obtain a four-year college degree—is much like the choice between work and leisure. In fact, an important decision for many young people is whether to go to work or to finish high school; if they have finished high school, the choice is whether to go to work or to go to college.

human capital

A person's accumulated knowledge and skills.

Economists view the education and training that raise skills and productivity as a form of *investment*, a decision to spend funds or time on something now because it pays off in the future. Continuing the analogy, an investment in a college education raises the amount of **human capital**—a person's knowledge and skills—in the same way that the investment in a factory or machine by a business firm raises physical capital. Figure 13.12 demonstrates the kind of difference this investment can make.

FIGURE 13.12 Higher Education and Economic Success

According to this chart, education pays off in terms of earnings, with doctorate degree holders earning the most, followed by workers with professional and master's degrees. The data shown are for 2019.

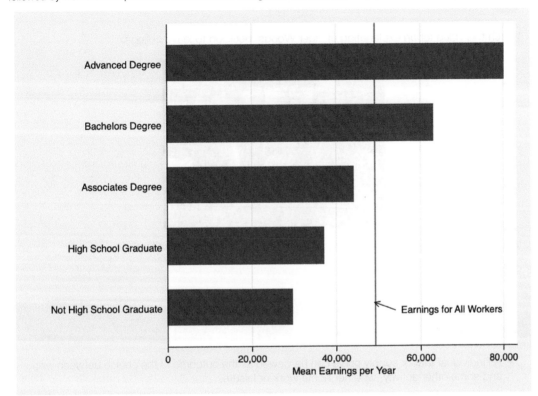

Source: "Current Population Survey (weekly earnings figure multiplied by 50)," Bureau of Labor Statistics.

The decision to invest in human capital can be approached like any other economic choice. Suppose the decision is whether Angela should go to college or get a job. If she does not go to college, she saves on tuition and can begin earning an income right away. If she goes to college, she pays tuition and forgoes the opportunity to earn income at a full-time job. However, if Angela is like most people, college will improve her skills and land her a better job at higher pay. The returns on college education are the extra pay. Angela ought to go to college—invest in human capital—if the returns are greater than the cost.

People can increase their skills at work as well as in school. In fact, **on-the-job training** is one of the most important ways in which workers' productivity increases. On-the-job training can be either *firm specific*, in which case the skills are useful only at one firm, or *general purpose*, in which case the skills are transferable to other jobs.

on-the-job training

The building of the skills of a firm's employees while they work for the firm.

The Opportunity Cost of Tiger Woods

Watch this video for an explanation of Tiger Woods' decision to leave college.

View the video online at: http://www.youtube.com/embed/tj4-tweDQuQ?rel=0

Review

- An individual's labor supply curve can be viewed as the outcome of the choice between work and some other activity, whether home work or leisure.

- Wages can be thought of as the price of that alternative activity, whether home work or leisure. This is because the opportunity cost of allocating an hour to that activity is the forgone wage that could have been earned from work.

- Changes in wages have both a substitution effect and an income effect on the labor supply. The substitution effect is that as wages rise, the cost of not working rises—the attractiveness of work increases relative to its alternatives. The income effect is that a rise in the wage increases the real income of an individual and enables that individual to enjoy more of all goods, including leisure.

- The income effect will tend to lower the incentive to work as the wage rises, while the substitution effect will increase the incentive to work. In some situations, the substitution effect dominates, leading to an increase in the quantity of labor supplied as the wage rises—an upward-sloping labor curve. In other situations, the income effect dominates, leading to a decrease in the quantity of labor supplied as the wage rises—a downward-sloping labor curve.

- Individuals also have to make decisions between working and acquiring human capital through education and training. Then the cost of acquiring human capital is the forgone wages, whereas the benefit of human capital is the extra wages one can earn using the knowledge and skills accumulated from going to school or receiving on-the-job training. If the returns are greater than the costs, then individuals should continue with their education.

13.5 Explaining Wage Trends and Differences

Labor Productivity

When we combine the labor demand and labor supply curves derived in the previous two sections, we get the model of the labor market summarized in Figure 13.3. The model predicts that the wage in the labor market will be at the intersection of the supply and demand curves. The point of intersection, where the quantity of labor supplied equals the quantity of labor demanded, is the **labor market equilibrium**.

The model also predicts that the equilibrium wage equals the marginal revenue product. If the marginal product of labor employed at a firm increases, then the model predicts that the firm's labor demand curve will shift to the right, as the firm will be willing to hire more workers at any given wage. Suppose the marginal product of labor rises for the economy as a whole; then the labor demand curve for the economy should shift to the right and both the equilibrium quantity of labor and the equilibrium wage should also rise. Is this what occurs in reality?

The Relationship between Real Wages and Labor Productivity

The lines in Figure 13.13 show the relationship between output per hour of work and the real wage. Output per hour of work is called **labor productivity** and is a good indication of trends in the marginal product of labor on average in the United States. Labor productivity growth in the United States was robust in the decade from the mid-1990s to the mid-2000s; it has slowed down somewhat since then. The labor market model predicts that wages in the United States should increase when labor productivity increases. Do they?

Figure 13.13 shows a strong correlation between labor productivity and the real wage. As labor productivity declined in the 1970s and 1980s, so did real wages and when labor productivity rebounded in the late 1990s, so did real wages. Note that the empirical association between wages and labor productivity was less pronounced in the period leading up to the 2008–09 recession. Nevertheless, the data series shown in this chart suggests that labor productivity is a key explanation of changes in real wages over time.

> **labor market equilibrium**
>
> The situation in which the quantity of labor supplied equals the quantity of labor demanded.

> **labor productivity**
>
> Output per hour of work.

FIGURE 13.13 Labor Productivity Growth and Real Wage Growth

As the figure shows, real wages and labor productivity are correlated. The relationship is not perfect though, in the 1980s and 1990s, real wage growth was consistently lower than labor productivity growth even though the two series seemed to move in concert to each other.

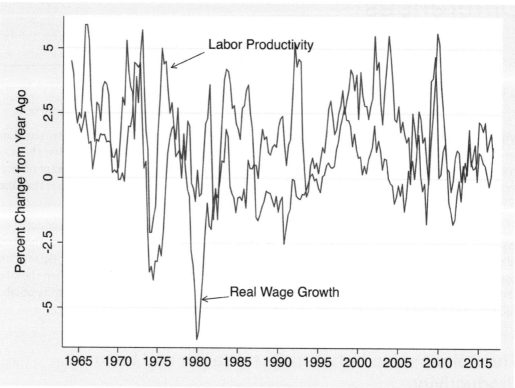

Source: Author's calculation following a data exercise suggested by the St. Louis Fed Economics blog of 8/29/2016, at https://fredblog.stlouisfed.org/2016/08/testing-theory-marginal-product-and-wages.

Wage Dispersion and Productivity

Can labor productivity also explain wage differences between groups of people? As we saw earlier in this chapter, real wages vary across workers depending on their occupation, the industry they work in, full- or part-time status, union status, and education, among other reasons. For instance, if the marginal product of labor increases with additional skills from investment in human capital, then, on average, wages for people with a college education should be higher than those for people without a college education. Hence, productivity differences are an explanation for the wage gap between workers who do not receive education beyond high school and those who are college educated.

Although human capital differences undoubtedly explain some of the dispersion of wages, some people have argued that the greater productivity of college-educated workers is due not to the skills learned in college, but to the fact that colleges screen applicants. For example, people who are not highly motivated or who have difficulty communicating have trouble getting into college. Hence, college graduates would earn higher wages even if they learned nothing in college. If this is so, a college degree signals to employers that the graduate is likely to be a productive worker.

Unfortunately, it is difficult to distinguish the skill-enhancing from the signaling effects of college. Certainly your grades and your major in college affect the kind of job you get and how much you earn, suggesting that more than signaling is important to employers. In reality, signaling and human capital both probably have a role to play in explaining the higher wages of college graduates.

Whether it is signaling or human capital that explains the higher wages of college graduates, labor productivity differences still are the underlying explanation for the wage differences. Labor productivity, however, does not explain everything about wages. Consider now some other factors.

Compensating Wage Differentials

Not all jobs that require workers with the same level of skill and productivity are alike. Some jobs are more pleasant, less stressful, or safer than other jobs. For example, the skills necessary to be a deep-sea salvage diver and a lifeguard are similar—good at swimming, good judgment, and good health. But the risks—such as decompression sickness—for a deep-sea diver are greater and the opportunity for social interaction is less. If the pay for both jobs were the same, say, $10 per hour, most people would prefer the lifeguard job.

But this situation could not last. With many lifeguard applicants, the beach authorities would be unlikely to raise the wage above $10 and might even try to cut the wage if they faced budget cuts. With few applicants, the deep-sea salvage companies would have to raise the wage. After a while, it would not be surprising to see the equilibrium wage for lifeguards at $9 per hour and the equilibrium wage for deep-sea divers at $18 per hour. Thus, we would be in a situation in which the skills of the workers were identical, but their wages were much different. The higher-risk job pays a higher wage than the lower-risk job.

FIGURE 13.14 High Wages for High Work
Compensating wage differentials are illustrated by the relatively high wages paid to someone for performing risky jobs such as window washing on a skyscraper.

Source: Matthew Xan/Shutterstock.com

Situations in which wages differ because of the characteristics of the job are widespread. Hazardous duty pay is common in the military. Wage data show that night-shift workers in manufacturing plants are paid wages that are about 3 percent higher on average than those of daytime workers, presumably to compensate for the inconvenience. Another example is gig economy workers for companies like InstaCart or DoorDash who are hired to bring pre-ordered groceries or restaurant meals to consumers' homes. During the COVID-19 pandemic, many people were reluctant to venture out from their homes and potentially expose themselves to the coronavirus. As a result, the demand for these services skyrocketed and, at least initially, it became very difficult to obtain a grocery delivery spot on InstaCart. But consumers then began to tip more for these services and the higher wage began to attract more workers laid off from other jobs in the service industry to these gig economy jobs.

However, hazard pay is not always the norm as workers at grocery stores, pharmacies, and meatpacking plants found out during the COVID-19 crisis. Even though these workers were expected to keep on working to keep these essential services going, examples of them receiving hazard pay as compensation for the increased exposure were few and far between. For example Smithfield Foods, the owner of several meatpacking plants where there were large outbreaks of COVID-19 among plant workers, drew unwelcome press attention for offering a $500 bonus for workers who did not miss work rather than offering them hazard pay: the attraction of the bonus could have led workers who were sick with the virus to keep coming to work.

Such differences in wages are called **compensating wage differentials**. They are an important source of differences in wages that are not based on marginal product. With compensating differentials, workers may seek out riskier jobs to be paid more.

compensating wage differentials

A difference in wages for people with similar skills based on some characteristic of the job, such as riskiness, discomfort, or inconvenience of the work schedule.

Hazard Pay and COVID-19

Some private employers pay essential workers more during the pandemic.

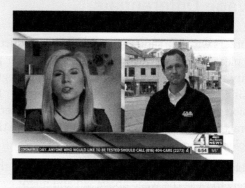

View the video online at: http://www.youtube.com/embed/o3YI-Y99Vkg?rel=0

Discrimination

As noted, a gap in earnings exists between women and men, even though that gap has been narrowing in recent years. Women now make close to 80 percent of the wages of men, whereas 50 years ago, women earned only about 50 percent of the wages of men. The gap between the wages of blacks and whites is also closing, although not quite as quickly. In the 1950s, the ratio of the wages of blacks to those of whites was about 60 percent; it has narrowed to about 70 percent since then. Wage differences between white and minority workers and between men and women are indications of discrimination if the wage differences cannot be explained by differences in marginal product or other factors unrelated to race or gender.

Some, but not all, of these differences may be attributed to differences in human capital. The wage gaps between blacks and whites and between men and women with comparable education and job experience are smaller than the ratios in the preceding paragraph. But a gap still exists.

Discrimination on the basis of race or gender prejudice can explain such differences. This is shown in Figure 13.15. *Discrimination* can be defined in the supply and demand model as not hiring women or minority workers even though their marginal product is just as high as that of other workers, or paying a lower wage to such workers even though their marginal product is equal to that of other workers. Either way, discrimination can be interpreted as a leftward shift of the labor demand curve for women or minority workers. As shown in Figure 13.15, this reduces the wages and employment for those discriminated against.

FIGURE 13.15 Discrimination in the Labor Market

Firms that discriminate against women pay them a wage that is less than their marginal product. But this gives other firms an opportunity to recruit workers from prejudiced firms by paying higher wages.

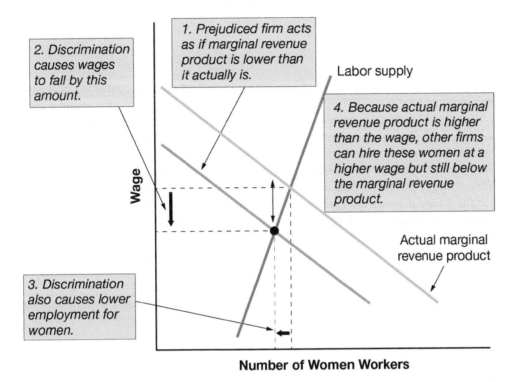

An important implication of this supply and demand interpretation of the effects of discrimination is that competition among firms may reduce it. Why might competition reduce discrimination? Remember that a firm will increase profits if the wage is less than the marginal revenue product. If markets are competitive, then firms that discriminate against women or minorities will pay them a wage lower than their marginal revenue product, as shown in Figure 13.15. In this situation, any profit-maximizing firm will see that it can raise its profits by paying these workers a little more—but still less than their marginal revenue product—and hiring them away from firms that discriminate. Thus, firms in competitive markets that discriminate will lose out to firms that do not. Much like firms that do not keep their costs as low as other firms, they eventually will be driven out of the industry. This advantage of competitive markets should be added to the advantages mentioned thus far. Furthermore, competition for workers will raise wages until the wages eventually are equal to the marginal products of labor.

This description of events relies on a market being competitive. If firms have monopoly power or entry is limited, so that economic profits are not driven to zero, then discrimination can continue to exist. That discrimination effects on wages do persist may be a sign of market power and barriers to entry. In this case, laws against discrimination give those who are discriminated against for race, gender, or other reasons the right to sue those who are discriminating.

Some laws have been proposed requiring that employers pay the same wage to workers with comparable skills. Such proposals are called *comparable worth proposals*. The intent of such proposals is to align the wages of different groups. However, such laws might force wages to be the same in situations in which wages are different for reasons other than discrimination, such as compensating wage differentials. This law would lead to shortages or surpluses, much as price ceilings or price floors in any market do. In the lifeguard/deep-sea diver example, a law requiring employers to pay lifeguards and deep-sea divers the same wage would cause a surplus of lifeguards and a shortage of deep-sea divers. For example, suppose that with comparable worth legislation, the wage for both lifeguards and deep-sea divers was $10 per hour. Because the labor market equilibrium wage for lifeguards, $9 per hour, is less than $10 per hour, there would be a surplus of lifeguards: More people would be willing to be lifeguards than employers would be willing to hire. And because the labor market equilibrium wage for deep-sea divers, $18 per hour, is greater than $10, there would be a shortage of deep-sea divers: Firms would be willing to hire more deep-sea divers than the number of deep-sea divers willing to dive for the $10 per hour wage.

Minimum Wage Laws

Another example in which the wages received by a worker may not be connected to the worker's marginal product is seen when the government stipulates a wage floor, or a *minimum wage*, which must be paid to workers. Because wages differ due to skills, the impact of the minimum wage depends on the skills of the workers. Figure 13.16 shows what the supply and demand model predicts about the impact of the minimum wage on skilled and unskilled workers. A labor market for unskilled workers is shown on the left; the minimum wage is shown to be above the labor market equilibrium wage. Thus, a surplus arises, or unemployment: The quantity of labor demanded by firms at the minimum wage is less than the quantity of labor that workers are willing to supply at that wage. A labor market for skilled workers is shown on the right: The minimum wage is shown to be below the market equilibrium wage for skilled workers. Thus, a minimum wage at the level shown in the graph would not cause unemployment among skilled workers.

FIGURE 13.16 Effects of a Minimum Wage

If government restrictions on wages hold them above the labor market equilibrium, then a surplus (unemployment) will arise. Unemployment is more likely for unskilled workers because the equilibrium wage is lower.

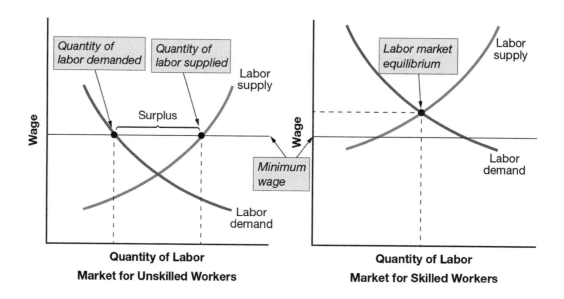

Therefore, the labor supply and demand model predicts that the minimum wage is a cause of unemployment among less skilled or less experienced workers, and thereby ends up hurting some of the least well off in society. This unintended result is why many economists are concerned about the impact of minimum wage legislation.

In interpreting this result, remember that the supply and demand model is a *model* of reality, not reality itself. Although the model explains much about wages, its predictions about minimum wage laws should be verified like the predictions of any other economic model. In fact, labor economists have been trying to check the predictions of the model for the minimum wage for many years. Some economists, such as David Card of the University of California at Berkeley and Alan Krueger of Princeton University, have examined the effects of different minimum wage laws in different states on low skilled fast-food workers and have not found evidence of the predicted impact on unemployment. Others, like David Neumark of Michigan State University and William Wascher of the Federal Reserve, have disputed Card's and Krueger's data and have found that the minimum wage enacted in those same states did have a negative effect on employment.

Fixed Wage Contracts

The agreement to buy or sell labor is frequently a long-term one. Job-specific training and the difficulty of changing jobs make quick turnover costly for both firms and workers. Most workers would prefer a certain wage to an uncertain one; such workers will prefer a fixed wage that does not change every time the marginal revenue product changes. Long-term arrangements of this kind are quite common. A worker—a person working at Getajob, for example—is hired at a given weekly wage. If marginal revenue product declines because of a week of stormy winter weather with frequent power outages, Getajob will not reduce the weekly wage. On the other hand, when college graduation season arrives in May, the Getajob workers will have to work harder—their marginal revenue product will rise—but they will not be paid a higher wage. Thus, the weekly wage does not change with the actual week-to-week changes in the marginal revenue product of the worker. The wage reflects marginal revenue product over a longer period. Most workers in the United States are paid in this way.

An alternative wage payment arrangement endeavors to match productivity with the wage much more closely. Such contracts are used when the weekly or hourly wage does not provide sufficient *incentive* or in cases in which the manager cannot observe the worker carefully. Under a **piece-rate system**, the specific amount that workers are paid depends on how much they produce. Thus, if their marginal product drops off, for whatever reason, they are paid less. Piece rates are common in the apparel and agriculture industries.

Consider California lettuce growers, for example. The growers hire crews of workers to cut and pack the lettuce. A typical crew consists of two cutters and one packer, who split their earnings equally. The crew is paid a piece rate, about $1.20 for a box of lettuce that might contain two dozen heads of lettuce. A three-person crew can pick and pack about 75 boxes an hour. Thus, each worker can earn about $30 an hour. But if they slack off, their wages decline rapidly.

On the same lettuce farms, the truck drivers, the workers who carry the boxes to the trucks, and the workers who wash the lettuce may be paid by the hour. Why the difference? Piece rates are used when it is difficult to monitor the quantity of a worker's effort. If you pay crews of lettuce workers in the field by the hour, then some of them will put in less effort and generate less output. Paying them according to the quantity of lettuce they pick ensures that those with the highest marginal revenue product earn the highest wages. This system would not work with the workers washing lettuce at the main building or the workers carrying the boxes to the trucks. The quality of their work (whether the lettuce was damaged by rough handling, whether all the dirt was properly washed out) cannot be measured as easily as with the lettuce pickers. These workers might sacrifice quality for speed under a piece-rate system.

piece-rate system

A system by which workers are paid a specific amount per unit they produce.

Deferred Wage Payments

deferred payment contracts

An agreement between a worker and an employer whereby the worker is paid less than the marginal revenue product when young, and subsequently paid more than the marginal revenue product when old.

Yet another payment arrangement occurs when a firm pays workers less than their marginal revenue product when they are young and more than their marginal revenue product at a later time as a reward for working hard. Lawyers and accountants frequently work hard at their firms when they are young; if they do well, they make partner and then are paid much more than their marginal revenue product when they are older. Such contracts are called **deferred payment contracts**. Generous retirement plans are another form of deferred payment contract. A reward for staying at the firm and working hard is a nice retirement package.

Review

- The labor supply and demand model predicts that economywide increases in marginal product should lead to an increase in the real wage.

- Using labor productivity as a measure of marginal product for an economy, we can see that the growth rate of labor productivity is positively correlated with the growth rate of real wages. The relationship was especially strong in the mid-1990s.

- Differences in labor productivity also provide an explanation for some of the differences in wages across groups, especially the differences between workers with different levels of education.

- Other factors bring about a disconnect between labor productivity and real wages. These include compensating wage differentials, discrimination, minimum wage laws, fixed wage contracts, and deferred wage payments.

- Compensating wage differentials occur because some jobs are more attractive than others. Workers with the same level of productivity will earn more in the sector that is less desirable to work in.

- Discrimination reduces the wages of those who are discriminated against below their marginal revenue product. Competition can be a force against the effects of discrimination because other firms can step in and hire the workers who are being discriminated against, offering to pay them a wage that is higher than what they currently are getting but still less than their marginal revenue product.

- Minimum wage laws also can lead to workers being paid a wage higher than their marginal revenue product. If the government imposes a minimum wage that is higher than the marginal revenue product of unskilled workers, it will cause some of these workers to lose their jobs, while the lucky ones earn a wage that is higher than what their marginal revenue product will indicate.

- Many labor market transactions are long term. Most employees receive a fixed hourly or weekly wage, even though their marginal revenue product fluctuates.

- In certain types of jobs, piece-rate contracts adjust the payment directly according to actual marginal product; they are a way to increase incentives to be more productive.

- Deferred compensation is another form of payment that aims at improving incentives and worker motivation.

13.6 Labor Unions

The model of labor supply and demand also can help us understand the impact of labor unions. **Labor unions** such as the United Auto Workers or the United Farm Workers are organizations with the stated aim of improving the wages and working conditions of their members. There are two types of unions: **industrial unions** represent most of the workers in an industry—such as the rubber workers, farm workers, or steelworkers—regardless of their occupation; **craft unions** represent workers in a single occupation or group of occupations, such as printers or dockworkers. In the 1930s and 1940s, disputes arose between those organizing craft unions and industrial unions. John L. Lewis, a labor union leader, argued that craft unions were not suitable for large numbers of unskilled workers. Hence, he and other union leaders split in 1936 from the American Federation of Labor (AFL), a group representing many labor unions, and formed the Congress of Industrial Organizations(CIO). It was not until 1955 that the AFL and the CIO resolved their disputes and merged; one reason behind their reconciliation was that union membership was beginning to decline.

But the decline continued. In 2005, a split occurred within the AFL-CIO. Three large unions representing service workers, truck drivers, and food and commercial workers withdrew from the AFL-CIO, expressing their unhappiness over the decline of union membership. About 12.5 percent of the U.S. labor force currently is unionized, down from about 25 percent in the mid-1950s. The fraction is much higher in other countries.

Unions negotiate with firms on behalf of their members in a collective bargaining process. Federal law, including the National Labor Relations Act (1935), gives workers the right to organize into unions and bargain with employers. The National Labor Relations Board has been set up to ensure that firms do not illegally prevent workers from organizing and to monitor union elections of leaders.

In studying unions, it is important to distinguish between the union leaders who speak for the union members and the union members themselves. Like politicians, union leaders must be elected, and as with politicians, we sometimes can better understand the actions of union leaders by assuming that they are motivated by the desire to be elected or reelected.

labor unions

A coalition of workers, organized to improve the wages and working conditions of the members.

industrial unions

A union organized within a given industry, whose members come from a variety of occupations.

craft unions

A union organized to represent a single occupation, whose members come from a variety of industries.

Union-Nonunion Wage Differentials

Studies of the wages of union workers and nonunion workers have shown that union wages are about 15 percent higher than nonunion wages, even when workers' skills are the same. Two different theories explain how unions raise wages.

The Restricted Supply Explanation

One theory is that unions raise wages by restricting supply. By restricting membership, for example, they shift the labor supply curve to the left, raising wages, just as a monopolist raises the price of the good it sells by restricting supply. But when a union restricts supply, workers outside the union in another industry get paid less.

This effect of unions is illustrated in Figure 13.17. The graph on the right is one industry; the graph on the left is another industry. Suppose both industries require workers of the same skill level. Imagine the situation before the union is formed. Then the wages for the workers on the left and on the right in Figure 13.17 would be the same.

FIGURE 13.17 The Effect of Unions on Wages
According to one view of labor unions, the union wage is increased relative to nonunion wages as a result of restricting the supply of workers. The supply in the union sector is reduced, but the supply in the nonunion sector is increased.

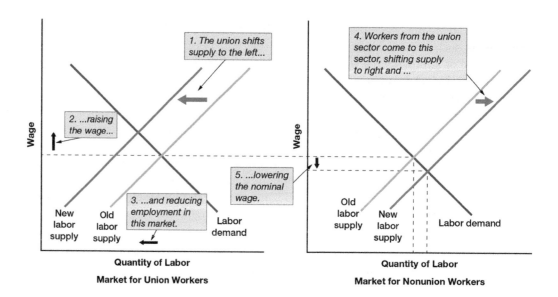

Now suppose a union organizes the industry on the left. Wages rise in the industry on the left, but the quantity of labor demanded in the industry falls. The workers in the industry on the left who become unemployed probably will move to the industry on the right. As they do so, the labor supply curve in the right-hand graph of Figure 13.17 shifts and the wage in that industry declines. Thus, a wage gap between the similarly skilled union and nonunion workers is created.

The Increased Productivity Explanation

Another theory, which was developed extensively in the book *What Do Unions Do?* by Richard Freeman and James Medoff of Harvard University, is that labor unions raise the wages of workers by increasing their marginal product. They do this by providing a channel of communication with management, motivating workers, and providing a democratic means of resolving disputes.

A worker who has a dispute with the management of a firm or who sees the opportunity to get a higher wage at another firm, in principle, could move. But such moves can have huge costs: The firm may have invested in job-specific training, and the worker might like the area where the firm is located. In situations in which exit from a firm is costly, people find other ways to improve their situation without exiting. The economist Albert Hirschman, in a famous book called *Exit, Voice, and Loyalty*, has called this alternative "voice." Rather than exit or quit, the worker may try to show the firm that a raise is deserved. Or the worker can discuss with the employer how conditions can be changed. The choice between exit and voice arises in many contexts: Should you transfer to a new college or tell the dean how the teaching might be improved? Should parents send their children to a private school or work to improve the local public school?

In many situations, exercising your voice requires collective action. If you alone complain to the dean, nothing much will happen, but if you organize a "students against lousy teaching" group, you may see some changes. Those who emphasize this collective-voice role of labor unions argue that unions provide a means through which workers improve their productivity. This collective-voice approach explains why the wages of union workers are higher than those of nonunion workers with the same skills and training.

Labor Unions

The following is a history of the rise (and fall) of labor unions.

View the video online at: http://www.youtube.com/embed/8isqqmqllFw?rel=0

Monopsony and Bilateral Monopoly

The analysis of labor unions in Figure 13.17 stresses the market power of unions as *sellers* of their members' labor in the labor market: By restricting supply, the union can raise the price of its members' wages, much as a monopolist or a group of oligopolists with market power can raise the price of the goods they sell.

However, the *buyers* in the labor market—that is, the firms that purchase the labor—also may have market power to affect the wage, contrary to the assumption we have made throughout this chapter that firms do not have such market power in the labor market. **Monopsony** is a situation in which only one buyer exists. By reducing its demand for the good (in this case, labor), a monopsony can reduce the price in the market (in this case, the wage). In fact, few examples of monopsony exist; most types of workers—such as sales clerks, accountants, or engineers—typically have many potential employers. Exceptions are found in small towns, for example, that have only one auto repair shop. Then, if auto mechanics do not want to move, the auto repair shop is effectively the only employer. Another exception is found in professional sports leagues, where team owners form agreements with one another restricting workers' (that is, the players') mobility between teams.

The situation in which a market has only one seller (a monopoly) and one buyer (a monopsony) is called a **bilateral monopoly**. A labor market with one labor union deciding the labor supply (the monopolist) and one firm deciding the labor demand (the monopsonist) is an example of a bilateral monopoly. Even though we typically associate a monopolist with the creation of deadweight loss, the outcome of a bilateral monopoly is difficult to predict. Compared with a situation in which a monopsony faces competitive sellers, however, the bilateral monopoly can lead to a more efficient outcome.

For instance, a firm with monopsony power over the labor market would choose to hire fewer workers, to drive down the wage, than would a group of competitive firms. By banding together in a labor union, the workers can confront this monopsony power with their own monopoly power. For example, they could refuse to work for less than the competitive wage. If their refusal is credible, they could take away the incentive for the monopsony to reduce labor demand because doing so would not reduce the wage. An example is in the arena of professional sports, in which powerful players' unions have helped reduce the effects of the teams' monopsony power and led to players' salaries rising dramatically in recent years. The players were aided in their cause by the erosion of

monopsony

A situation in which there is a single buyer of a particular good or service in a given market.

bilateral monopoly

The situation in which there is one buyer and one seller in a market.

teams' monopsony power through rulings that allowed for things like free agency in major league baseball.

Review

- In the twenty-first century, less than 15 percent of U.S. workers belong to labor unions, a significant decline from the mid-1950s, when about a quarter of workers belonged to unions.
- Workers who belong to unions are paid about 15 percent more on average than workers with the same skills who are not in unions.
- One explanation for this difference is that labor unions improve productivity by improving worker motivation and providing workers with a collective voice.
- Another view is that labor unions raise productivity by restricting supply, much as a monopolist would, rather than by increasing productivity.
- In certain situations in which a single firm, a monopsonist, has market power in hiring workers, the creation of a labor union as a monopoly provider of labor services actually can increase the efficiency of the resulting market outcome.

13.7 End-of-Chapter Materials

Conclusion

In this chapter, we have shown that the labor supply and demand model is a powerful tool with many applications. In fact, the model may apply to you, so consider carefully what it implies.

First, increasing your own labor productivity is a good way to increase your earnings. Many of the large differences in wages across individuals and across time are due to differences in productivity. Productivity is enhanced by increases in human capital, whether obtained in school or on the job. Such human capital also will prove useful if your firm shuts down and you need to find another job.

Second, if you are choosing between two occupations that you like equally well, choose the one that is less popular with other students of your generation and for which it looks like demand will be increasing. Both the supply and the demand for labor affect the wage, and if the supply is expected to grow more rapidly than the demand in the occupation for which you are training, wages will not be as high as in the occupation for which labor is in relatively short supply.

Third, be sure to think about the wage you receive or the raises you get in real terms, not nominal terms, and make sure you are aware of fringe benefits offered or not offered. Fourth, think about your job in a long-term perspective. Partly for incentive reasons, some jobs pay little at the start, with the promise of higher payments later.

Key Points

1. When measuring workers' pay, it is important to consider fringe benefits and to adjust for inflation before comparing wages at different points in time.

2. Wage growth in the United States, which is defined by the real hourly average pay (including fringe benefits), began increasing at a faster rate in the mid-1990s but has flattened out somewhat more recently. Wage dispersion also has increased.

3. The supply and demand framework can be applied to the labor market to gain insight into labor market trends. The demand for labor is a derived demand that comes from the profit-maximizing decisions of firms. Firms adjust their employment until the marginal revenue product of labor becomes equal to the wage.

4. The supply curve for labor can be explained by looking at the choices of individuals or households. A person will work more hours if the wage is greater than the marginal benefit of more leisure.

5. An increase in the wage will have both an income effect (real income rises, so the worker does not have to work as many hours as before to afford other goods and services) and a substitution effect (the opportunity cost of engaging in leisure or home work activities instead of working rises, increasing the incentive to work).

6. The substitution effect and the income effect work in opposite directions, so that the labor supply curve can be upward sloping, vertical, downward sloping, or backward bending.

7. Long-term trends in wages are correlated closely with changes in labor productivity.

8. Labor productivity differences also explain some of the differences in wages paid to different people. However, differences in marginal productivity do not explain everything. Compensating wage differentials, discrimination, minimum wages, long-term contracts, and deferred compensation are all examples of why workers may not be paid a wage equivalent to their marginal revenue product.

9. The number of union workers in the United States has been declining, but union workers still earn more than nonunion workers who have the same skills. This occurs either because unions increase labor productivity or because they restrict the supply of workers in an industry.

10. Even though unions act like monopolists or oligopolists in the labor market in terms of selling the services of their members, they are not always associated with inefficient economic outcomes. In cases of bilateral monopoly, a monopoly seller of labor (such as a union) can counter a monopsony buyer of labor services and bring about more efficient economic outcomes.

Questions for Review

1. What are fringe benefits? How significant a part of average pay are they in the United States?

2. Why is it important to distinguish between real wages and nominal wages? What about between hourly wages and weekly wages?

3. Why do we say that the demand for labor is a derived demand?

4. How does the relationship between marginal revenue product and the wage determine how many workers the firm should hire?

5. Why is the demand for labor downward sloping?

6. Provide an intuitive explanation of the income and substitution effects. Then explain why the substitution effect and the income effect of a wage increase work in opposite directions on labor supply.

7. What is the empirical relationship between labor productivity and the real wage in the United States since 1990?

8. What factors can lead to workers being paid a wage that differs from their marginal revenue product of labor?

9. What are the two main views of labor unions?

10. Explain when a labor union will reduce economic efficiency. When could it increase economic efficiency?

Problems

1. Marcelo farms corn on 500 acres in a competitive industry, receiving $3 per bushel. The relationship between the number of workers Marcelo hires and his production of corn is shown below.

Number of Workers	Production (bushels per year)
1	30,000
2	43,000
3	51,000
4	55,000
5	57,000
6	58,000

    a. Calculate the marginal product and marginal revenue product of labor for Marcelo's farm.

    b. If the wage for farm workers is $8,000 per year, how many workers will Marcelo hire? Explain.

    c. Suppose the yearly wage for farm workers is $8,000, the fixed rent is $600 per acre per year, and there are no other costs. Calculate Marcelo's profits or losses.

    d. Will there be entry into or exit from this industry?

2. Suppose a firm with some market power faces a downward-sloping demand curve for the product it produces. Using the information on demand given in the table below, complete the table and draw the resulting demand curve for labor. If the hourly wage is $30, how many workers will this firm hire?

Quantity of Labor	Quantity of Output	Marginal Product of Labor	Price of Output ($)	Total Revenue ($)	Marginal Revenue ($)	Marginal Revenue Product of Labor ($)
10	100		9			
20	180		8			
30	240		7			
40	280		6			
50	300		5			
60	310		4			

3. Recently, demand has increased for corn-based ethanol to substitute for gasoline in the United States. How will this affect the marginal product, marginal revenue product, and wages of farm workers on corn farms?

4. Use the definition of the demand for labor as the marginal revenue product to argue that the increasing wage dispersion between skilled and unskilled workers could come from (a) increases in the relative productivity of skilled workers and (b) increases in the demand for the products produced by skilled workers.

5. Since 1950, Americans have greatly reduced their home cooking in favor of eating at restaurants.

    a. What is the explanation for this?

    b. Do you expect it to continue in the next half century?

6. Analyze the labor supply schedules for Joshua and Scott below.

Wage	Hours Worked by Scott	Hours Worked by Joshua
$5	5	0
$8	10	8
$12	20	15
$15	30	25
$18	40	35
$20	45	33
$25	50	30

a. Draw the labor supply schedules for Joshua and Scott.

b. How does Scott's marginal benefit from more leisure compare with Joshua's?

c. At what point does the income effect begin to outweigh the substitution effect for Joshua? Explain.

7. College professors frequently are paid less than others with equivalent skills working outside academia. Use the idea of compensating differentials to explain why professors' wages are relatively low.

8. The government of Egalitariania wants to favor firms, and it is considering implementing a maximum wage. As an economic adviser to the government of Egalitariania, explain (verbally and graphically) the consequences of the maximum wage in the competitive labor market. Ensure that your explanation includes the gains or losses to firms, workers, and the people of Egalitariania as a whole.

9. Draw a typical supply and demand for labor diagram to represent a labor market. Now suppose you are asked to modify this diagram to depict the market for doctors. To practice medicine in the United States, your medical education has to be certified, and you have to obtain a state license after completing a residency program.

a. What impact does this restriction have on the wage rate for doctors in the economy?

b. Will there be a shortage or a surplus of doctors at that wage rate?

c. Should the government intervene and reduce these requirements to increase the supply of doctors?

d. Would your answer change if the market (and the licensing requirement) were for lawyers?

e. What about economists?

10. A toy manufacturing company is considering hiring sales representatives to market its new toys to retail stores. Under what circumstances should it pay a commission for every order of toys promoted by its sales representatives, and under what circumstances should it pay the sales representatives an hourly wage?

CHAPTER 14
Taxes, Transfers, and Income Distribution

In 1996 one of the most significant and controversial pieces of legislation affecting government transfers and taxes was enacted. Called "welfare reform," this legislation allowed state governments to limit the period of time during which people with low incomes could receive transfers—welfare payments—without working. As a result of the legislation, millions of people left the welfare rolls and the percentage of the federal budget going to this form of public assistance was reduced. The legislation was popular because it removed people from the welfare rolls and placed many in jobs. It also reduced the amount of taxes needed to pay for welfare. But it was severely criticized as being unfair and too harsh on families with low incomes.

In 2010, another significant and controversial piece of legislation was enacted—health care reform, which also affected taxes and transfers. This legislation expanded government assistance by increasing the income level below which people could qualify for Medicaid—the major health care program for the poor in the United States—and by providing subsidies to people at higher income levels to buy private health insurance. The act increased the number of people receiving public assistance for health care expenses and thus, in contrast to the 2006 legislation, it increased the amount of taxes needed to pay for public assistance.

FIGURE 14.1 Stark Inequalities
In cities like Rio de Janeiro, Mumbai, Manila, or Johannesburg, vast inequalities are readily apparent as sprawling shantytowns and high-rise penthouses often exist side-by-side.

Source: Donatas Dabravolskas/Shutterstock.com

As the reactions to these two major pieces of legislation illustrate, individual opinion ranges widely about income inequality and what the government should do about it. Many feel compassion and amoral obligation to help the poor. Others feel it is unfair that some people make more in one day than others do in an entire year. Some see nothing unfair about an unequal income distribution as long as opportunities are equal. Others worry that government programs will reduce incentives to work, increase dependency on government, and lower incomes further. Still others worry that a very unequal distribution of income can cause social unrest and deter a society from achieving other goals, including a growing economy.

The purpose of this chapter is to provide an economic analysis of these issues. We begin the chapter with an analysis of the tax system, which is used to pay not only for transfer payments to the poor but also for government spending of all types—military, police, road building, and schools. We then consider transfers, such as welfare and health care payments to the poor and social security payments to the elderly. After we examine how various features of the tax and transfer system affect incentives, we examine the actual distribution of income and discuss how it has been affected by the tax and transfer system in the United States.

14.1 The Tax System

We begin by considering the tax system. The first part of our analysis is descriptive, looking at the different types of taxes used in the United States. Then we move into a more analytical mode, and review the efficiency and distributional implications of the tax system. Finally, we draw on these analytical findings to look at some policy proposals for reforming the tax system and discuss their merits.

The major types of taxes that exist in the United States are the *personal income tax* on people's total income, the *payroll tax* on wage and salary income, the *corporate income tax* on corporate profit income, *excise/sales taxes* on goods and services purchased, estate and *gift taxes* on inheritances and gifts from one person to another, and *tariffs*, which are taxes on goods imported into the country. In addition, many local governments raise revenue through *property taxes*.

As shown in Figure 14.2, the personal income tax and the payroll tax are by far the largest sources of tax revenue for the federal government. Together they account for about 85 percent of federal tax revenue. Hence, we focus most of our attention on these two taxes in the following discussion.

FIGURE 14.2 Taxes Paid to the Federal Government in 2019
More than 85 percent of federal taxes comes from the personal income tax and the payroll tax.

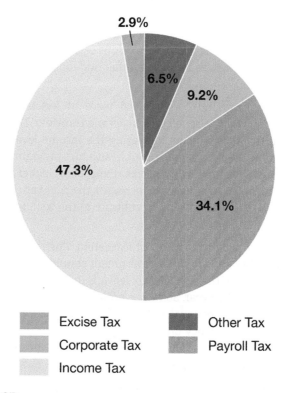

Source: Congressional Budget Office.

The Personal Income Tax

The **personal income tax** is a tax on all the income an individual or household receives, including wage and salary income, interest and dividend income, income from a small business, rents on property, royalties, and capital gains. (A *capital gain* is the increase in the value of an asset like a corporate stock. When the asset is sold, the capital gain—equal to the difference between the original purchase price and the selling price of the asset—is treated as income and is taxed.) The personal income tax was introduced in 1917 in the United States, soon after the ratification of the Sixteenth Amendment to the U.S. Constitution, which authorized income taxes. Most states have now followed the federal government and have enacted a personal income tax at the state level; we focus our attention on the personal income tax collected by the federal government.

Computing the Personal Income Tax

To explain the economic effects of the personal income tax, we must examine how the amount of tax a household owes is determined. The amount of tax owed by a household depends on the tax rate and the amount of taxable income. **Taxable income** is defined as a household's income minus certain exemptions and deductions. An *exemption* is a dollar amount that can be subtracted from income for each person in the household. *Deductions* are other expenditure items actually incurred—such as interest payments on a home mortgage, charitable contributions, and moving expenses—that can be subtracted from income before taxes are assessed. The 2017 tax reform eliminated personal exemptions and increased deductions, but both exemptions and deductions are used for state income tax calculations in certain states.

> **taxable income**
>
> A household's income minus exemptions and deductions.

Consider, for example, the Lee family, which has four members: a wife, a husband, and two children. Suppose the Lees can subtract $24,000 as a deduction from their income. Suppose that the husband and wife together earn a total income of $80,000. Then their taxable income is $56,000 ($80,000 - $24,000).

Now let us see how we combine taxable income with the tax rate to compute the tax. Figure 14.3 shows the tax brackets for 2019 (throughout this chapter, the examples use the tax law as of 2019). There are two tax rate schedules: one for a taxpayer who is single and one for married taxpayers who are paying their taxes together. The first two columns give a range for taxable income, while the next two columns tell how to compute the tax. The percentages in the tax rate schedule are the tax rates.

Look first at the schedule for *Married, filing jointly* tax filers: The 10 percent tax rate in the schedule applies to all taxable income up to $19,400, at which point any additional income up to $78,950 is taxed at 12 percent. Any additional income over $78,950 but less than $168,400 is taxed at 22 percent, and so on for tax rates of 24 percent, 32 percent, 35 percent, and 37 percent. Each of the rows in these schedules corresponds to a different tax rate; the range of taxable income in each row is called a **tax bracket**.

> **tax bracket**
>
> A range of taxable income that is taxed at the same rate.

As an example, let us compute the Lees' tax. Recall that their taxable income is $56,000. They are married and filing jointly, so we look at the corresponding schedule. We go to the second line because $56,000 is between $19,400 and $78,950. In other words, the Lees are in the 12 percent tax bracket. We find that they must pay $1,940 plus 12 percent of the amount their income is over $19,400—that is 0.12 x ($56,000 - $19,400) = $4,392. Thus, the amount of tax they must pay is $1,940 + $4,392 = $6,332.

FIGURE 14.3 Two Tax Rate Schedules for 2019

The tables show how to compute the tax for each amount of taxable income. Observe how the marginal rates rise from one tax bracket to the next.

Use if your filing status is **Single**

If your taxable income is:		The tax is	plus	of the amount
Over—	But not over—			over—
$0	$9,700	$0 +	10%	$0
$9,700	$39,475	$970 +	12%	$9,700
$39,475	$84,200	$4,543 +	22%	$39,475
$84,200	$160,725	$14,383 +	24%	$84,200
$160,725	$204,100	$32,749 +	32%	$160,725
$204,100	$510,300	$46,629 +	35%	$204,100
$510,300		$153,799 +	37%	$510,300

Taxable income

Marginal tax rates

If your filing status is **Married, Filing jointly**

If your taxable income is:		The tax is	plus	of the amount
Over—	But not over—			over—
$0	$19,400	$0 +	10%	$0
$19,400	$78,950	$1,940 +	12%	$19,400
$78,950	$168,400	$9,086 +	22%	$78,950
$168,400	$321,450	$28,765 +	24%	$168,400
$321,450	$408,200	$65,497 +	32%	$321,450
$408,200	$612,350	$93,257 +	35%	$408,200
$612,350		$164,710 +	37%	$612,350

The Marginal Tax Rate

Now consider what happens when the Lees' income changes. Suppose that one of the Lees decides to earn more income by working more hours and the Lees' income rises by $5,000. Thus, their taxable income rises from $56,000 to $61,000. Now what is their tax? From their tax schedule, we see that the tax is $1,940 + 0.12 × ($61,000 - $19,400) = $1,940 + $4,992 = $6,932. Thus, the Lees' tax has increased from $6,332 to $6,932, or by $600, as their income rose by $5,000. Observe that the tax rose by exactly 12 percent of the increase in income.

marginal tax rate

The change in total tax divided by the change in income.

The amount by which taxes change when an individual's income changes is the **marginal tax rate**. It is defined as the change in taxes divided by the change in income. In examining how the Lees compute their tax, we have discovered that their marginal tax rate is 12 percent. In other words, when their income increased, their taxes rose by 12 percent of the increase in income. As long as they stay within the 12 percent tax bracket, their marginal tax rate is 12 percent.

Observe that the marginal tax rate depends on one's income. The marginal rate varies from 10 percent for low incomes up to 37 percent for very high incomes. Suppose that one of the Lees did not work and that their taxable income was $15,000 rather than $56,000. Then they would be in the 10 percent bracket, and their marginal tax rate would be 10 percent.

In contrast to the marginal tax rate, the **average tax rate** is the total tax paid divided by the total taxable income. For example, the Lees' average tax rate before we considered changes in their income was (6,332/56,000) = 0.113, or 11.3 percent, which is lower than the 12 percent marginal tax rate. In other words, the Lees pay 11.3 percent of their total taxable income in taxes but must pay 12 percent of any additional income in taxes. The average tax rate is less than the marginal tax rate because the Lees pay only 10 percent on the first $19,400 of taxable income.

Economists feel that the marginal rate is important for assessing the effects of taxes on individual behavior. Their reasoning can be illustrated with the Lees again. Suppose that the Lees' marginal tax rate was 10 percent rather than 12 percent. Then, if one of the Lees decided to work an additional half day a week, the family would be able to keep $0.90 of each extra dollar earned, sending $0.10 to the government. But with a marginal tax rate of 12 percent, the Lees could keep only $0.88 on the dollar. If the marginal tax rate for the Lees was 35 percent, then they could keep only $0.65 of each dollar earned. To take the example to an even greater extreme, suppose the marginal rate was 91 percent, which was the highest marginal rate before President Kennedy proposed reducing tax rates. Then, for each extra dollar earned, one could keep only $0.09. Clearly, the marginal tax rate is going to influence people's choices about how much to work if they have a choice. The marginal tax rate has a significant effect on what people gain from working additional hours. This is why economists stress the marginal tax rate rather than the average tax rate when they look at the impact of the personal income tax on people's behavior.

Figure 14.4 provides a visual perspective on marginal tax rates. It plots the marginal tax rate for *Married Couples, Filing Jointly* given in Figure 14.3; the marginal tax rate is on the vertical axis, and the taxable income is on the horizontal axis. Observe how the marginal tax rate rises with income.

> **average tax rate**
>
> The total tax paid divided by the total taxable income.

FIGURE 14.4 Marginal Tax Rates

As an example, the marginal tax rates from the IRS tax rate for *Married Couples, Filing Jointly* are plotted. The marginal tax rate is the change in the amount of tax paid for an extra dollar earned. The marginal tax rate increases with income. Each step takes the taxpayer to a higher tax bracket. Thus, higher-income people have a higher marginal tax rate than lower-income people. Under a flat tax, the marginal tax rate would be constant for all taxable income levels.

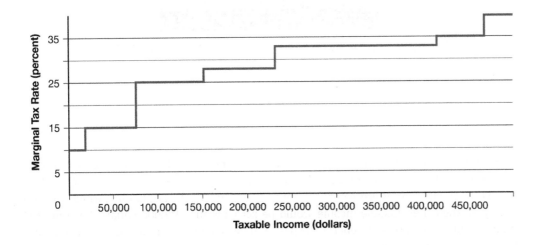

Source: Internal Revenue Service.

progressive

A tax for which the amount of an individual's taxes rises as a proportion of income as the person's income increases.

regressive

A tax for which the amount of an individual's taxes falls as a proportion of income as the person's income increases.

proportional

A tax for which the amount of an individual's taxes as a percentage of income is constant as the person's income rises.

A tax is **progressive** *if the amount of the tax as a percentage of income rises as income increases.* If the marginal tax rate rises with income—in which case people with higher incomes pay a larger percentage of their income in taxes—then the tax is progressive. *A tax is* **regressive** *if the amount of the tax as a percentage of income falls as income rises.* An income tax would be regressive if the marginal tax rate declined as income rose, or if people with high incomes could use deductions or other schemes to reduce the tax they paid to a smaller percentage of income than people with lower incomes paid. *A tax is* **proportional** *if the amount of the tax as a percentage of income is constant as income rises.*

 Marginal Tax Rates

Under a progressive system, marginal income tax rates increase as income increases.

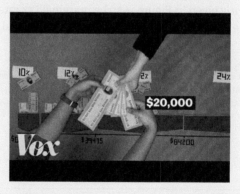

View the video online at: http://www.youtube.com/embed/VJhsjUPDulw?rel=0

Zero Tax on Low Incomes

In assessing how progressive the income tax is, remember that the taxes are based on taxable income, which is less than the income a household actually receives. Taxable income can be zero even if a household's income is greater than zero. For example, if the Lee family earned only $24,000 for the year, then their taxable income would be zero, because $24,000 equals the sum of their exemptions and deductions. In general, the personal income tax is zero for household incomes up to the sum of the exemptions and deductions.

flat tax

A tax system in which a marginal tax rate for all levels of taxable income is constant.

A **flat tax** occurs when the marginal tax rates are constant for all levels of taxable income, in which case the line in Figure 14.4 would become flat. Even a flat rate tax system would have a degree of progressivity: The tax paid would rise as a percentage of income from zero (for workers below the sum of exemptions and deductions) to a positive amount as income rises.

The Payroll Tax

The **payroll tax** is a tax on the wages and salaries of individuals; the payroll tax goes to finance Social Security benefits, Medicare, and unemployment insurance. Employers submit payroll taxes to the government. For example, the Lees' employers must submit 15.3 percent of the Lees' wage and salary income to the federal government. Thus, the payroll tax on the Lees' wage and salary income of $80,000 would be $12,240 (that is, 0.153 x $80,000), almost double the total that the Lees would pay in personal income taxes.

The tax law says that half of the 15.3 percent payroll tax is to be paid by the worker and half is to be paid by the employer. Thus, the Lees would be notified of only half of the payroll tax, or $6,120, even though their employer sent $12,240 to the government. If a person is self-employed—a business consultant, say, or a freelance editor—then the person pays the full 15.3 percent, because a self-employed person is both the employee and the employer. One of the most important things to understand about the payroll tax is that, as we will soon prove, its economic effects do not depend on who is legally required to pay what share of the tax; only the total 15.3 percent matters.

payroll tax

A tax on the wages and salaries of individuals.

Other Taxes

All other federal taxes together amount to a little over one-fifth of total revenue. **Corporate income taxes** are taxes on the accounting profits of corporations. The 2017 tax reform lowered the corporate tax rate to a rate of 21 percent, a substantial decrease from the previous rate, which was as high as 35 percent.

Excise taxes are taxes on goods that are paid when the goods are purchased. The federal government taxes several specific items, including gasoline, tobacco, beer, wine, and hard liquor. A **sales tax** is a type of excise tax that applies to total expenditures on a broad group of goods. For example, if your expenditures on many different goods at a retail store total $100 and the sales tax rate is 5 percent, then you pay $5 in sales tax. There is no national sales tax in the United States, but sales taxes are a major source of revenue for many state and local governments.

The federal government also raises revenue by imposing tariffs on goods as they enter the United States. Until the Sixteenth Amendment was ratified and the personal income tax was introduced, tariffs were the major source of revenue for the U.S. government. Now revenue from tariffs is a minor portion of total revenue.

Local governments rely heavily on **property taxes**—taxes on residential homes and business real estate—to raise revenue. Recall that income taxes—both personal and corporate—are used at the state level to raise revenue for state governments.

corporate income taxes

A tax on the accounting profits of corporations.

excise taxes

A tax paid on the value of goods at the time of purchase.

sales tax

A type of excise tax that applies to total expenditures on a broad group of goods.

property taxes

A tax on the value of property owned.

The Effect of Taxes

The purpose of most of these taxes is to raise revenue, but taxes can have significant effects on people's behavior. To examine these effects, let us start with a tax we looked at before in Chapter 7: a tax on a good or service.

The Effect of Tax on a Good

Recall that a tax on a good adds the amount of the tax to the marginal cost of the seller of the good. For example, a tax of $1 on a gallon of gasoline will shift the supply curve up by the amount of the tax, a result shown in Figure 7.11. Once the supply curve shifts as a result of the tax, equilibrium price and quantity also will change. The ultimate impact on price and quantity will depend on the price elasticities of supply and demand.

The four panels of Figure 14.5 are designed to enable us to show how the price elasticity of demand and the price elasticity of supply determine the impact of the tax. In each of the figure's four panels, the supply curve shifts up because of a tax of the same amount, shown by the arrow to the left of each vertical axis. As a result of the tax, in each of the four panels, the equilibrium price rises and the equilibrium quantity falls. The decline in the equilibrium quantity creates a loss of consumer surplus plus producer surplus, which we call the deadweight loss from the tax. The size of the deadweight loss and the relative size of the impact on the price and the quantity are different in each panel of Figure 14.5 because the supply curve and the demand curve have different price elasticities.

A key point illustrated in Figure 14.5 is that *when the price elasticity of demand or the price elasticity of supply is very low, the deadweight loss from the tax is small.* This deadweight loss is shown in the two graphs in the left part of Figure 14.5, which have either a low elasticity of demand (top left) or a low elasticity of supply (bottom left). In either case, the deadweight loss is small compared with that in the graphs at the right, which have higher elasticities.

The intuitive reason why low elasticities result in small deadweight losses is that the quantity of the good does not change very much when the price changes. Recall that a low price elasticity of demand means that quantity demanded is not very sensitive to a change in the price, as, for example, in the case of a good like salt, which has few substitutes. A low elasticity of supply means that only a small change occurs in the quantity supplied when the price changes. Thus, in the case of low elasticities, only a small difference exists between the efficient quantity of production and the quantity of production with the tax. There is little loss of efficiency. On the other hand, *when the price elasticity of demand or the price elasticity of supply is very high, the deadweight loss from the tax will be relatively large.* In this case, changes in price have big effects on either the quantity demanded or the quantity supplied, and the deadweight loss is large.

tax incidence

The allocation of the burden of the tax between buyer and seller.

The price elasticities of supply and demand also affect how much the price changes in response to a tax. If the price rises by a large amount, then the tax is passed on to buyers in the form of higher prices, and the burden of the tax falls more on buyers. If the price rises little or not at all, then the seller absorbs the burden of the tax, and most of the tax is not passed on to buyers. **Tax incidence** refers to who actually bears the burden of the tax, the buyers or the sellers.

The graphs in Figure 14.5 suggest the general principle that *the smaller the price elasticity of demand and the larger the price elasticity of supply, the greater the rise in the price.* The opposite will be true if the elasticity of demand is large and the elasticity of supply is small—that is, the impact of the tax will raise the price by only a little.

This tells us that taxing a good like cigarettes, with a low elasticity of demand, will result in the buyers of cigarettes bearing the tax. The seller will be able to pass the tax on to the buyers in the form of higher prices. In contrast, taxing a good like land, which has a low elasticity of supply, will not affect the price very much. The supplier of the land will not be able to pass on the tax to the consumers in the form of higher prices and will bear the burden of the tax.

FIGURE 14.5 How Elasticities Determine the Effects of Taxes

(1) Deadweight loss effects: When price elasticities are low, as in the left graphs, the deadweight loss is small and the change in equilibrium quantity is small. When price elasticities are high, as in the right graphs, the deadweight loss is large and the change in equilibrium quantity is large. (2) Tax incidence and price effects: When the price elasticity of demand is low or the price elasticity of supply is high, the tax is largely passed on to the consumer in the form of higher prices. In contrast, when the price elasticity of demand is high or the price elasticity of supply is low, the burden of the tax falls on the producer because the price changes little.

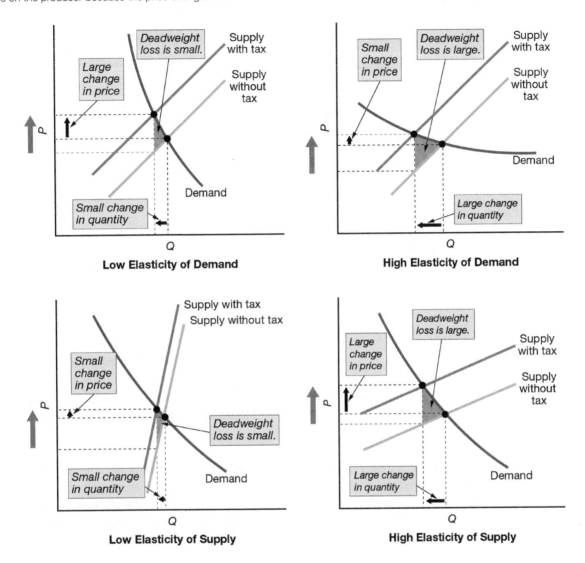

Effects of the Personal Income Tax

We can apply the results of this analysis to the personal income tax. The personal income tax is a tax on *labor* income (wages and salaries) as well as on *capital* income (interest, dividends, small business profits). Labor income, however, is by far the larger share of most people's income: For all 1040 forms filed, wages and salaries account for more than 75 percent of total income. Thus, we model the personal income tax as a tax on labor income.

The analysis of the personal income tax is illustrated in Figure 14.6. Because the personal income tax is a tax on labor income, we need a model of the labor market to examine the effects of the tax. Figure 14.6 shows a labor demand curve and a labor supply curve. The wage paid to the worker is on the vertical axis, and the quantity of labor is on the horizontal axis. Figure 14.6 shows that the personal income tax shifts the labor supply curve up. The size of the upward shift depends on the marginal tax rate because the income received from work would be reduced by the marginal tax. If the person was in the 15 percent bracket, the income received from working would be $0.85

for each extra dollar earned working. Thus, to supply exactly the same quantity as without the tax, people require a higher wage. Because the wage paid to the worker is on the vertical axis, the labor supply curve shifts up to show this.

FIGURE 14.6 Effects of a Higher Income Tax on Labor Supply
An income tax shifts the labor supply curve up by the amount of the tax on each extra hour of work because the worker must pay part of wage income to the government and thus receives less for each hour of work. Thus, the quantity of labor supplied declines. The decline in hours worked would be small if the supply curve had a low elasticity.

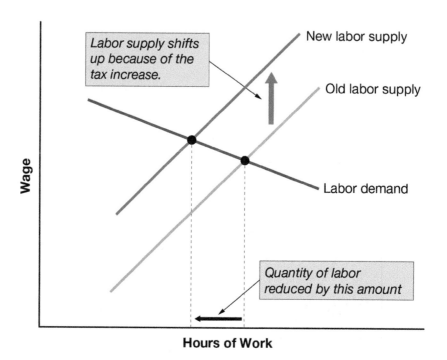

As the labor supply curve shifts up, the equilibrium quantity of labor declines. Thus, we predict that an income tax will reduce the amount of work. The reduced amount of work will cause a deadweight loss just like that caused by the tax on a commodity. The size of the decline in hours of work will depend on the labor supply and labor demand elasticities. The higher the labor supply elasticity, the greater the reduction in the quantity of labor supplied in response to the personal income tax.

Economists disagree about the size of the labor supply elasticity. One thing that is certain is that the elasticity is different for different people. For example, the labor supply elasticity appears to be quite high for second earners in a two-earner family such as the Lees. If elasticity is high, a high marginal tax rate can reduce hours of work and thereby income. But if the labor supply curve has a low elasticity, it has little effect on hours of work.

The Effect of a Payroll Tax

We can use the same type of labor market diagram to analyze a payroll tax, as shown in Figure 14.7. Clearly, the payroll tax is a tax on labor in that it applies to wages and salaries. In the case of the payroll tax, however, we need to consider that both the employer and the employee pay this tax, as required by law. Figure 14.7 handles the two cases.

Suppose that the wage before the tax is $10 per hour and that the payroll tax is 10 percent, or $1 per hour. The case in which the employee pays the tax is shown on the right of Figure 14.7. This picture looks much like Figure 14.6. The labor supply curve shifts up by the amount of the tax ($1) because the worker now has to pay a tax to the government for each hour worked. In other words, the worker will supply the same amount of work when the wage is $11 and the tax is $1 as when the wage is $10 and the tax is zero.

When the labor supply curve shifts up, the equilibrium quantity of labor employed declines (see the right-hand panel of Figure 14.7). Observe that, because of the lower supply of labor, the wage paid by the employer rises. The after-tax wage—that is, the wage less the tax—declines, however, because the increase in the wage is less than the tax increase.

The case in which the employer pays the tax is shown in the left graph of Figure 14.7. In this case, the labor demand curve shifts down by the amount of the tax ($1) because the firm has to pay an additional $1 for each hour of work. When the labor demand curve shifts down, the equilibrium quantity of labor employed declines and the wage falls. Observe that the impact of the payroll tax is the same in both cases: A new equilibrium emerges in the labor market with a lower wage and a lower quantity of labor.

FIGURE 14.7 The Effect of a Payroll Tax

If a payroll tax is paid by the employer, the labor demand curve shifts down by the amount of the tax because the firm's labor costs increase by the amount of the tax. Thus, the quantity of labor employed declines, as does the wage paid to the worker (shown on the left). A payroll tax paid by the employee (shown on the right) causes the labor supply curve to rise by the amount of the tax, but the effects on after-tax wages received by the worker and the quantity of work are the same as when the employer pays.

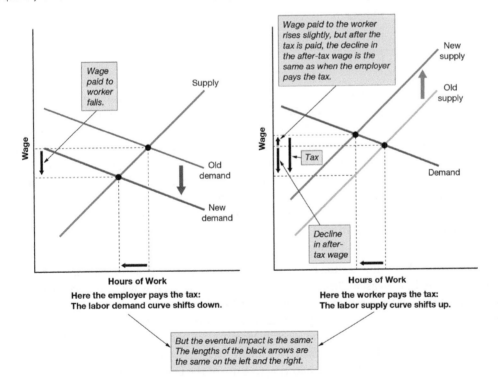

Thus, a payroll tax has both an employment-reduction effect and a wage-reduction effect. As with any tax, the size of the quantity change and the price (wage) change depends on the supply and demand elasticities. If we apply the results from Figure 14.5, we know that when the labor supply elasticity is low and the labor demand elasticity is high, the reduction in employment will be small, but the wage will fall by a large amount. If the labor supply elasticity is high and the labor demand elasticity is low, however, the employment effect will be large, but the wage effect will be small.

The Possibility of a Perverse Effect on Tax Revenue

tax revenue

The tax rate times the amount subject to tax.

Tax revenue received by the government is equal to the tax rate times the amount that is subject to the tax. For example, in the case of a gasoline tax, the tax revenue is the tax per gallon times the number of gallons sold. As the tax rate increases, the amount subject to the tax will fall because the higher price resulting from the tax reduces the quantity demanded. If the quantity demanded falls sharply enough, then tax revenue actually could fall when the tax rate is increased.

The same possibility arises in the case of taxes on labor, either the payroll tax or the personal income tax. In the case of the payroll tax or the personal income tax for a worker, tax revenue is equal to the tax rate times the wage and salary income. As the tax rate rises, the amount of income subject to tax may fall if labor supply declines. Thus, in principle, it is possible that a higher tax rate could result in reduced tax revenue. For example, consider the high marginal tax rates shown in Table 14.1: 50 percent, 75 percent, and 90 percent. If labor supply declines with a higher tax rate, as assumed in the table, then tax revenue first increases as the tax rate goes from 50 to 75 percent but then declines as the tax rate goes from 75 to 90 percent.

TABLE 14.1 Tax Rates and Tax Revenue: An Example

Tax Rate	Wage ($)	Hours Worked	Tax Revenues ($)
0.50	10/hour	2,000	10,000
0.75	10/hour	1,500	11,250
0.90	10/hour	500	4,500

The general relationship between tax rates and tax revenue is illustrated in Figure 14.8. As in the example of Table 14.1, tax revenue first rises and then falls as the tax rate increases. Figure 14.8 can apply to any tax on anything. At the two extremes of zero percent tax rate and 100 percent tax rate, tax revenue is zero. What happens between these two extremes depends on the elasticities. This relationship between the tax rate and tax revenue, frequently called the Laffer curve after the economist Arthur Laffer, who made it popular in the 1980s, has long been known to economists. It implies that if the tax rate is so high that we are on the downward-sloping part of the curve, then reducing the tax rate may increase tax revenue. Economists debate greatly, however, about the tax rate at which the curve bends around. Few economists believe that the curve bends at the current top marginal rate in the United States, which is 37 percent.

Other factors that influence tax revenue, especially when marginal tax rates get very high, are tax avoidance and tax evasion. *Tax avoidance* means finding legal ways to reduce taxes, such as buying a home rather than renting, to have a deduction for interest payments on a mortgage. Tax evasion is an illegal means of reducing one's tax. For example, at high tax rates, people have incentives to evade the tax by not reporting income. Workers are tempted not to report tips. Or people resort to barter, which is difficult for the government to track down. For example, an employer may "pay" a little extra to a truck driver by allowing free use of the truck on weekends for fishing trips.

FIGURE 14.8 The Tax Rate and Tax Revenue

As the tax rate increases from low levels, tax revenue rises. At some point, however, the high tax rate reduces the quantity of the item that is taxed and encourages so much tax avoidance that the amount of tax revenue declines. This curve is frequently called the Laffer curve. The particular tax rate at which the curve bends depends on the price elasticity of the item being taxed and is a subject of great debate among economists.

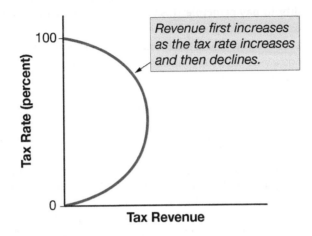

Tax Policy and the Trade-off between Efficiency and Equality

We have observed in our analysis of each tax that the equilibrium quantity of the item taxed declines when the tax rate rises. This is where the inefficiency of the tax comes from. If the tax rate is very high, or the elasticities are very high, the inefficiency can be so severe that it could thwart one of the purposes of raising the taxes: that is, to provide income support to increase the well-being of the least well-off in the society. This is because a reduction in the quantity of labor supplied or goods produced could be so great that society would have less total income, and thus less support would go to the poor even if they received a larger share of total income. In other words, a *trade-off exists between equality and efficiency.* If one raises taxes too high for the purpose of making the income distribution more equal, the total amount of income may decline. In that event, there will be less available to redistribute.

Given these considerations, how should the tax system—the combination of all the taxes in society—be designed or improved? First, to reduce deadweight loss to a minimum, the ideal tax system should tax items with small price elasticities of supply and demand rather than items with large elasticities. We know that the deadweight loss is small when elasticities are small. The optimal tax system would inversely relate tax rates to the elasticities.

Second, the ideal tax system would try to keep the marginal tax rates low and the amount that is subject to tax high. For example, we saw that deductions reduce the amount subject to personal income tax by lowering taxable income. Some deductions are put in the tax system to encourage certain activities: A deduction for research expenses may encourage firms to fund research, for example. The more deductions there are, however, the higher the tax rate has to be to get the same tax revenue. Economists use the term *broadening the tax base* to describe an increase in the amount of income subject to taxation by limiting or eliminating deductions and exemptions. With a broader tax base, a lower marginal tax rate can generate the same amount of revenue; the lower marginal tax rate has the additional advantage of reducing the inefficiency of the tax. Most tax reform efforts have involved trying to broaden the tax base while lowering marginal tax rates. This was the idea behind the tax reform efforts in the 1960s under President Kennedy and in the 1980s under President Reagan. In the early 2000s, the marginal tax rates on all taxpayers were reduced substantially. Because many new deductions, exemptions, and credits also were introduced, however, the tax base was not broadened.

Third, the ideal tax system should be as simple and as fair as possible. If a tax system is not simple, then valuable resources—people's time, computers, and so on—must be devoted to paying and processing taxes. A tax system is seen as unfair if it is regressive. Another view of fairness frequently used is the **ability-to-pay principle**; this view is that those with greater income should pay more in taxes than those with less income. The tax system also is viewed as unfair if people with the same incomes are taxed at different rates. For example, in the U.S. tax system, a married couple with each making $80,000 a year pays a higher tax than an unmarried couple with exactly the same income. Some view this system as unfair.

ability-to-pay principle

The view that those with greater income should pay more in taxes than those with less income.

Review

- Taxes are a vital source of revenue for the government. In the United States, the personal income tax and the payroll tax are the largest sources of tax revenue for the government. Other sources of tax revenue include corporate income taxes, excise taxes, and gift taxes.

- In analyzing how a tax system works, key variables to pay attention to include deductions and exemptions, tax brackets and the associated marginal tax rates, and how progressive the tax code is.

- Taxes cause inefficiencies in the form of reduced economic activity and deadweight loss. The deadweight loss associated with a tax is high when the price elasticities of supply and demand are high.

- Tax incidence identifies who bears the burden of paying the tax. When the elasticity of demand is low and the elasticity of supply is high, the burden of paying the tax falls largely on the consumer. Conversely, in situations in which the elasticity of demand is high and the elasticity of supply is low, the burden of paying the tax is largely borne by the seller.

- The impact of higher taxes on tax revenue depends on the impact of equilibrium quantity. If the equilibrium quantity falls by a sufficiently large amount, then tax revenue actually could decline.

- A trade-off exists between efficiency and equality in designing tax policy; raising taxes to reduce inequality may increase economic inefficiency and thereby reduce the amount of total income and tax revenue.

- To minimize the inefficiencies, items with low elasticities should be taxed more than items with high elasticities. Other methods of eliminating inefficiencies include policies that broaden the tax base while lowering the marginal tax rate, and keeping the tax system simple and fair to avoid creating incentives for tax evasion and tax avoidance.

- The criterion of "fairness" also is used to evaluate how ideal a tax system is. Principles of fairness include progressivity and treating people who have the same income identically—regardless of marital status, for example.

14.2 Transfer Payments

transfer payments

A grant or funds from the government to an individual.

Transfer payments, payments made by the government to an individual that are not in exchange for goods or services, have important implications for the alleviation of poverty and the distribution of income in the United States. Transfer payments can be either in cash or in kind, such as vouchers that can be used to buy food or housing.

The United States has two types of government transfer payments: **means-tested transfers**, which depend on the income (the means) of the recipient and focus on helping poor people, and **social insurance transfers**, which do not depend on the income of the recipient.

Means-Tested Transfer Programs

Means-tested transfer payments are made to millions of people in the United States each year. The major programs are listed in Table 14.2.

TABLE 14.2 Means-Tested Transfer Programs in the United States
Each of these federal programs requires that the recipient's income or assets be below a certain amount to receive payment.

Temporary Assistance to Needy Families (TANF)	Payments to poor families with children as determined by each state
Medicaid	Health insurance primarily for welfare recipients
Supplemental Security Income (SSI)	Payments to poor people who are old, disabled, or blind
Supplemental Nutritional Assistance Program (SNAP)	Also known as the food stamp program. Coupons allowing low-income people to buy food
Head Start	Preschool education for low-income children
Housing Assistance	Rental subsidies and aid for construction

The 1996 federal welfare law (called the Personal Responsibility and Work Opportunity Reconciliation Act, or PRWORA) created the **Temporary Assistance to Needy Families program (TANF)**, replacing the Aid to Families with Dependent Children (AFDC) program, which was what people typically referred to as "welfare" in the United States. TANF is a transfer program that provides cash payments to eligible poor families with children. The federal government provides grants to the states, which then decide which poor families are eligible. Unlike AFDC, TANF assistance is limited in duration (the program has a five-year lifetime limit) and requires that recipients work a certain number of hours per week.

Medicaid is a health insurance program that is designed primarily to pay for health care for people with low incomes. Once income increases to a certain level, Medicaid support stops, so that the family must find another means of obtaining health insurance. **Supplemental Security Income (SSI)** is designed to help the neediest elderly as well as poor people who are disabled or blind. About 6.6 million people receive SSI assistance, including 4.6 million disabled and 2 million elderly people.

The **Supplemental Nutritional Assistance Program (SNAP)**, also known as the food stamp program, is a major means-tested transfer program; it makes payments to about 17 million people each year. Like Medicaid, food stamps are an in-kind payment. People are not supposed to use the coupons to buy anything but food. This program is popular because the intent of the money is to provide nutrition and because the program is fairly inexpensive to run. The National School Lunch Program is similar to food stamps in that it aims to provide food to lower-income children. It provides school lunches for about 29 million children.

Head Start

A government transfer program that provides day care and nursery school training for poor children.

housing assistance programs

Government programs that provide subsidies either to low-income families to rent housing or to contractors to build low-income housing.

Earned Income Tax Credit

A part of the personal income tax through which people with low income who work receive a payment from the government or a rebate on their taxes.

Head Start, another in-kind program, provides for preschool assistance to poor children to help them get a good start in school. It also is a popular program because evidence indicates that it improves the performance, at least temporarily, of preschool children as they enter elementary school.

Housing assistance programs provide rental subsidies to people who cannot afford to buy a home. The programs sometimes provide aid to business firms that construct low-income housing. Those that oppose the programs complain about waste and poor incentives in the housing programs and argue that these programs are in need of reform.

The **Earned Income Tax Credit (EITC)** program is a means-tested transfer payment program received by about 20 million working poor families. The EITC actually is part of the personal income tax, and the form to obtain the transfer payment is sent to people by the IRS along with the 1040 form. Working people whose income is below a certain level, either because their wage is very low or because they work part time, get a refundable credit that raises their take-home pay. For example, consider the four-person Lee family again. We know that if the Lees earn less than $24,000 in taxable income, they pay no income tax. However, if the Lees earn between $0 and $14,300 in wages and salary and have no other income, then the EITC will pay $0.40 for each dollar they earn up to a maximum of $5,716 per year. To ensure that the EITC does not make payments to high-income people, the payments decline if the Lees make more than $24,350. For each dollar they earn above $24,350, they lose $0.21 of their $5,716 until the benefits run out, when their income reaches $51,450.

Observe that the EITC raises the incentive to work for incomes up to $14,300 and reduces the incentive to work for incomes greater than $24,350 and less than $51,450. With the EITC, the marginal tax rate is effectively *negative* 40 percent for income below $14,300; that is, you *get* $0.40 rather than *pay* $0.40 for each dollar you earn. But the EITC adds 21 percent to the marginal tax rate for incomes between $24,350 and $51,450.

Incentive Effects

The previous section describes a variety of government programs that aim to transfer funds to the poor. As we will see, evidence suggests that these programs do have an impact on reducing income inequality. Some people feel that the programs may create a disincentive to work, however, because welfare payments are reduced when income from work rises.

The top panel of Figure 14.9 illustrates the first disincentive problem. The total income of an individual is plotted against the number of hours worked. Total income consists of wage income from work plus a welfare payment. The more steeply sloped solid black line shows the individual's wage income from work: The more hours worked, the more wage income the individual receives. This line intercepts the horizontal axis at zero income, so if the person does not have work and does not receive welfare or charity, the person is in a state of extreme poverty.

FIGURE 14.9 Welfare Reform to Improve Work Incentives
The top graph shows how welfare reduces the marginal earnings from working more hours because welfare payments are phased out. The two basic approaches to reform are (1) phasing out the payments more slowly (as in the middle graph) or (2) lowering the welfare payment (as in the lower graph). Both approaches have advantages and disadvantages.

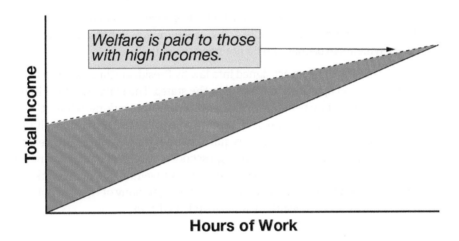

Reform by phasing out
payments more slowly

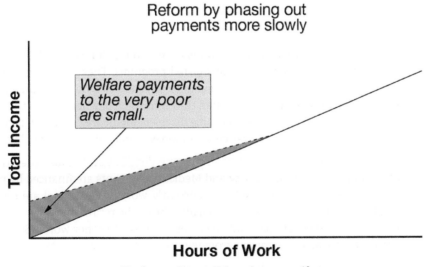

Reform by paying less welfare

The individual's total income is shown by the less steeply sloped dashed line in the top graph of Figure 14.9. This line intercepts the vertical axis at an amount equal to the welfare payment the individual gets when he or she is not working at all. As the individual begins to work, the need for welfare declines, and so the welfare payment declines. Observe that the amount of the welfare payment, which is represented by the shaded gap between the steep line and the less steep line, diminishes as the hours of work increase, and finally, after a certain number of hours worked, the welfare payment disappears.

Because the welfare payment is reduced when the individual's income from work rises, it creates a disincentive. The flatter the dashed line, the greater the disincentive. For example, if someone decides to work 10 hours a week for a total of $50 per week, but the welfare payment is reduced by $30 per week, then effectively the marginal tax rate is 60 percent, which is high enough to discourage work.

Welfare reform seeks to change the welfare system to reduce this disincentive. Looking at Figure 14.9, there are two ways to make the dashed line steeper and thereby provide more incentive to work. One way is to reduce the amount of welfare paid at the zero income amount. Graphically, this is shown in the lower graph of Figure 14.9. This reduction twists the dashed line because the intercept on the vertical axis is lower, but the intersection of the dashed line and the solid line appears at the same number of hours of work as in the top graph. This will increase the slope of the dashed line and therefore provide more incentive to work. But the problem with this approach is that poor people receive less welfare: The poverty rate could rise.

A second way to make the dashed line steeper is to raise the place at which it intersects the black solid line, as in the middle graph of Figure 14.9. But that change could result in making welfare payments to people who do not need them at all.

The welfare reform act signed into law by President Clinton in 1996 left the decision as to which welfare reform approach to take up to the states. The states went off in different directions; some chose to cut welfare benefits for those who were not working, while others raised the amount that can be earned before welfare is reduced. Some states require adult welfare recipients to go to work immediately. Twenty-four states require that people work after two years on welfare. Other states require that a single parent finish high school to receive the full welfare payment. These proposals are aimed at increasing the incentive to get off welfare and go to work. In fact, welfare rolls have been reduced dramatically, but critics contend that many of these people do not have adequate support services, such as health insurance and child care.

Social Insurance Programs

Social Security

The system through which individuals make payments to the government when they work and receive payments from the government when they retire or become disabled.

Medicare

A government health insurance program for the elderly.

unemployment insurance

A program that makes payments to people who lose their jobs.

The largest transfer payment programs in the United States, Social Security, Medicare, and unemployment insurance, are not means-tested programs. These programs are called *social insurance* programs because they make payments to anyone—rich or poor—under certain specific circumstances. **Social Security** is the system through which payments from the government are made to individuals when they retire or become disabled. **Medicare** is a health insurance program for older people. **Unemployment insurance** pays money to individuals who are laid off from work.

These programs have effects on income distribution because they transfer income between different groups. Social Security and Medicare payments are financed by payroll taxes from workers. But the payroll taxes paid by a currently working individual are related only loosely to the funds paid out to the same individual after he or she retires. In reality, each year, the funds paid in by current workers are paid out to current retirees. In other words, Social Security and Medicare are, in effect, transfer programs from young people to older people.

Because these social insurance programs are not means-tested, they can end up transferring income from the current working poor to middle-income and even wealthy retirees. In other words, these programs are not well targeted at the low-income groups. For this reason, many people have suggested that these programs be means-tested. The arguments for means-testing have become stronger as the aging of the U.S. population increases the strain on these programs, especially on

Medicare. In fact, recent legislation has effectively reduced Social Security benefits to high-income older people by requiring that a major part of the benefits be included in taxable income; Social Security benefits formerly were excluded from taxable income.

Another large non means-tested social insurance program is the unemployment insurance program. This program provides payments to individuals who are looking for work but unable to find work but specific details vary widely across countries and even within the United States. In the United States, not every unemployed worker is eligible, those who leave jobs voluntarily, the self-employed,

These programs are particularly valuable in times of economic crisis such as the global recession that followed the 2008 financial crisis and the economic turmoil and unprecedented spike in unemployment caused by the COVID-19 pandemic. Unemployment insurance provides workers with the temporary assistance needed to weather the initial turmoil and meet the needs of their families until work is available again. During these acute crisis periods, some states extended the time that workers can collect benefits with the assistance of the Federal government. In 2020, for example, the Coronavirus Aid, Relief, and Economic Security (CARES) Act provided funds for states to expand unemployment insurance to cover workers who were not ordinarily eligible for unemployment benefits. The program also provided funding to support additional payments of $600 per week during the months of April–July to support workers who lost their jobs. This was a substantial source of financial support for workers who would have only made around $300/week if they earned the Federal minimum wage for a 40-hour week.

 Stimulus Payments During the COVID-19 Pandemic

Many households and individuals received stimulus payments during the pandemic.

View the video online at: http://www.youtube.com/embed/Kg8y850lwwU?rel=0

Mandated Benefits

Mandated benefits occur when a firm is required by the government to provide a benefit for its workers. For example, a federal law requires firms to give unpaid leave to employees to care for a newborn baby or a sick relative. Such benefits are a cost to the firm (for example, the cost of finding and training replacements or providing health insurance to the workers on leave). But, of course, they are a benefit to the workers.

mandated benefits
Benefits that a firm is required by law to provide to its employees.

We can analyze the effects of mandated benefits using the supply and demand for labor diagram, much as we analyzed the effects of a payroll tax. As shown in Figure 14.10, the labor demand curve shifts down, as it did in Figure 14.7 for the employer-paid payroll tax—to hire a given quantity of labor, the wage that the firm will be willing to pay is lower because it also has to pay the mandated benefits. But the mandated benefits also shift the labor supply curve down—workers will be willing to work for a lower wage because they receive the mandated benefits by working. The labor supply curve probably will not shift down as much as the labor demand curve does because the workers probably will not value the benefit quite as much as the benefit costs the firm.

FIGURE 14.10 Effect of a Mandated Benefit
A mandated benefit is a cost to the firm; it shifts down the demand curve for labor just as a payroll tax does. But in the case of a mandated benefit, the labor supply curve shifts down too. Hence, the wage paid to the worker falls, as does employment.

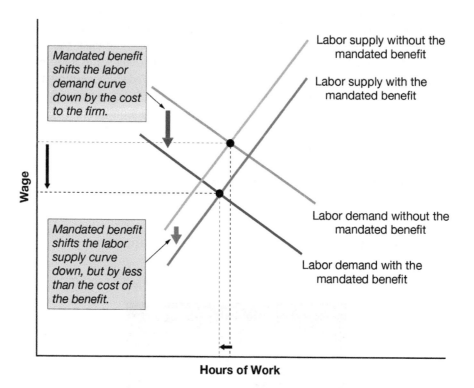

The new equilibrium in Figure 14.10 shows that the wage paid to the workers will fall as a result of the creation of the mandated benefit. In other words, despite the fact that the employer is the one supposedly "paying" for the mandated benefit, both the employer and the employee end up paying the benefit. Employment also will be reduced. If the workers value the benefit exactly as much as it costs the firm, then the wage will fall by the full amount of the benefit. In this case, employment will not fall at all.

Review

- The two major types of transfer payments are means-tested programs, which depend on the income of the recipient, and social insurance programs, which do not depend on the income of the recipient.

- The major means-tested transfer programs in the United States include the following: the TANF program, Medicaid, and the EITC program. These transfer programs all target their benefits to the poor and reduce benefits as the income levels of individuals rise.

- As a result, means-tested transfer payments create disincentives for work. The loss of assistance from means-tested programs as one's labor income rises implies that these programs act as a tax on labor income.

- The purpose of welfare reform is to reduce those disincentives for the TANF program by imposing work requirements and time limits on payment of benefits to welfare recipients. The

EITC program also is designed to create an incentive for the very poor to work because their benefits initially rise with labor income.

- Social insurance programs like Social Security and Medicare are the largest transfer programs in the United States. These programs are not means- tested, which means that they transfer income from current workers to current retirees regardless of how poor the current worker is and how wealthy the current retiree is.

- As the number of elderly Americans rises and the cost of these transfer programs increases, economists and policy makers have advocated turning social insurance programs into means-tested programs.

- Another way that the government can transfer money to individuals is through mandated benefits, such as family leave. If individuals do not value the benefit as much as it costs firms to provide the benefit, then the workers' wages will fall by an amount less than the increase in the benefit. If the workers value the benefit at exactly the level that it costs the firm to provide it, then the wage will fall by the full amount of the benefit. In either case, the costs of the benefit are borne by both the firm and the worker, even if the firm technically pays for the benefit.

14.3 The Distribution of Income in the United States

Now that we have understood some important details about the tax and transfer system in the United States, we can take a closer look at how these have affected the distribution of income in the United States. We begin by examining what the distribution of income in the United States actually looks like, and how that distribution compares to the distribution in other countries. We then ask what changes in income distribution have occurred over time, and how those changes are related to the tax and transfer policies adopted by the government.

The Personal Distribution of Income

To answer questions about income distribution in the United States, we first need to know what kinds of data are available and how we can construct a quantitative measure of income distribution using those data. Data about people's income in the United States are collected by the U.S. Census Bureau in a monthly survey of about 60,000 households called the **Current Population Survey**.

Economists and statisticians usually study the income distribution of families or households rather than individuals. A *family* is defined by the Census Bureau as a group of two or more people related by birth, marriage, or adoption who live in the same housing unit. A *household* consists of all related family members and unrelated individuals who live in the same housing unit. Because the members of a family or a household typically share their income, it usually is more sensible to consider families or households rather than individuals. One would not say that a young child who earns nothing is poor if the child's mother or father earns $100,000 a year. In a family in which one spouse works and the other remains at home, one would not say that the working spouse is rich and the nonworking spouse is poor.

Current Population Survey

A monthly survey of a sample of U.S. households done by the U.S. Census Bureau; it measures employment, unemployment, the labor force, and other characteristics of the U.S. population.

quintiles

Divisions or groupings of one-fifth of a population ordered by income, wealth, or some other statistic.

Because the population comprises so many people, it is necessary to have a simple way to summarize the income data. One way to do this is to arrange the population into a small number of groups ranging from the poorest to the richest. Most typically, the population is divided into fifths, called **quintiles**, with the same percentage of households in each quintile. For example, in Table 14.3, the 128.5 million households in the United States are divided into five quintiles, with approximately 26 million in each quintile. The first row shows the poorest 20 percent—the bottom quintile. The next several rows show the higher-income quintiles, with the last row showing the 20 percent with the highest incomes.

TABLE 14.3 Range of Annual Family Incomes (in 2018 dollars) for Five Quintiles

Quintile	Income Greater Than ($)	Income Less Than ($)
Bottom 20 percent	0	25,600
Second 20 percent	25,600	50,000
Third 20 percent	50,000	79,542
Fourth 20 percent	79,542	130,000
Top 20 percent	130,000	--

Source: Table A-4, "Current Population Survey, 2019 Annual Social and Economic Supplement," U.S. Census Bureau.

The second and third columns of Table 14.3 show the range of household incomes earned in each of the five groups. The bottom 20 percent of households have incomes below $25,600, the households in the next quintile have incomes greater than $25,600 but less than $50,000, and so on. Note that the lower limit for families in the top 20 percent is $130,000. The lower limits for the top 10 percent and top 5 percent (not shown in the table) are $184,292 and $248,728 respectively.

Inequality can be better measured by considering the total income in each quintile as a percentage of the total income in the country. Table 14.4 provides this information. The second column in Table 14.4 shows the income received by families in each quintile as a percentage of total income in the United States.

A quick look at Table 14.4 shows that the distribution of income is far from equal. Those in the lower 20 percent earn only 3.4 percent of total income. On the other hand, those in the top 20 percent earn 50.2 percent of total income. Thus, the amount of income earned by the richest quartile is over 15 times the amount of income earned by the poorest quartile.

TABLE 14.4 Distribution of Family Income by Quintile

Quintile	Percentage of Income	Cumulative Percentage of Income
Bottom 20 percent	3.8	3.8
Second 20 percent	8.9	12.7
Third 20 percent	13.6	26.3
Fourth 20 percent	20.5	46.8
Top 20 percent	54.4	100.0

Source: "Projected Changes in the Distribution of Household Income," Congressional Budget Office.

The Lorenz Curve and the Gini Coefficient

The third column of Table 14.4 shows the cumulative portion of income earned by the different segments of the distribution in the year 2009 (the last year for which coverage is available in the Statistical Abstract of the United States). The bottom 20 percent earned 3.4 percent of the income, the bottom 40 percent earned 12.7 percent of the income, the bottom 60 percent earned 26.3 percent of the income, and the bottom 80 percent earned just 46.8 percent of the income. The top 5 percent, not shown in Table 14.4, earned 29.1 percent of the aggregate income.

These data can be presented in a useful graphic form. Figure 14.11 shows the cumulative percentage of income from the third column of Table 14.4 on the vertical axis and the percentage representing each quintile from the first column on the horizontal axis. The five dots in the figure are the five pairs of observations from the table. For example, point *A* at the lower left corresponds to the 3.8 percent of income earned by the lowest 20 percent of people. Point *B* corresponds to the 12.7 percent of income earned by the lowest 40 percent of people. The other points are plotted the same way. The uppermost point occurs where 100 percent of the income is earned by 100 percent of the people.

FIGURE 14.11 The Lorenz Curve for the United States
Each point on the Lorenz curve gives the percentage of income received by a percentage of households. The plotted points are for the United States. Point *A* shows that 3.8 percent of income is received by the lowest 20 percent of families. Point *B* shows that 12.7 percent of income is received by the lowest 40 percent of families. These two points and the others in the figure come from Table 14.4. In addition, the 45-degree line shows perfect equality, and the solid lines along the horizontal and right-hand vertical axes show perfect inequality. The shaded area between the 45-degree line and the Lorenz curve is a measure of inequality. The ratio of this area to the area of the triangle below the 45-degree line is the Gini coefficient. The Gini coefficient for 2018 is 0.486.

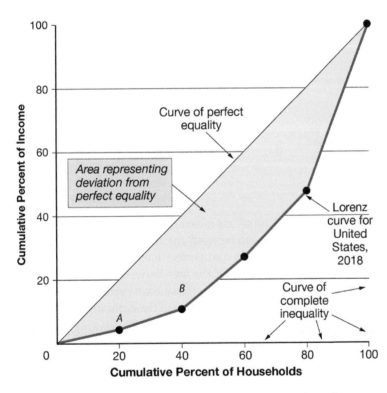

Source: "Selected Measures of Household Income Dispersion: 1967 to 2018," United States Census Bureau.

If we connect these five points, we get a curve that is bowed out. This curve is called the **Lorenz curve**. To measure how bowed out the curve is, we draw the solid black 45-degree line. The 45-degree line is a line of perfect equality. On that line, the lowest 20 percent earn exactly 20 percent of the income, the lowest 40 percent earn exactly 40 percent of the income, and so on. Every household earns exactly the same amount.

The degree to which the Lorenz curve is bowed out from the 45-degree line provides a visual gauge of the inequality of income. The more bowed out the line is, the more unequal the income distribution. The most unequal distribution possible would occur when only one person earns all the income. In that case, the curve could be so bowed out from the 45-degree line that it would consist of a straight line on the horizontal axis up to 100 and then a vertical line. For example, 99.9

Lorenz curve

A curve showing the relation between the cumulative percentage of the population and the proportion of total income earned by each cumulative percentage. It measures income inequality.

percent of the households would earn 0 percent of the income. Only when the richest person is included do we get 100 percent of the income.

FIGURE 14.12 Changes in Income Inequality: The U.S. Gini Coefficient

The Gini coefficient is large when inequality is greater, as measured by the Lorenz curve in Figure 14.11. Thus, by this measure, inequality in the United States has increased steadily over the past fifty years.

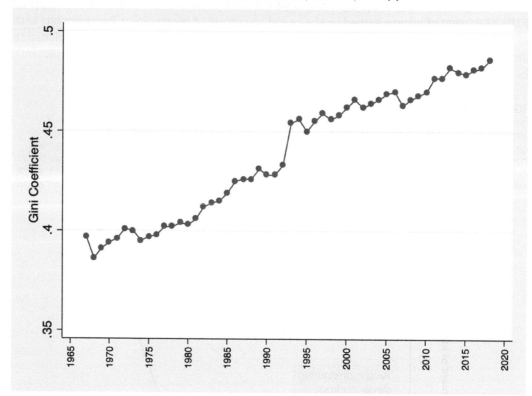

Source: *"Selected Measures of Household Income Dispersion: 1967 to 2018,"* United States Census Bureau.

Gini coefficient

An index of income inequality ranging between zero (for perfect equality) and one (for absolute inequality); it is defined as the ratio of the area between the Lorenz curve and the perfect equality line to the area between the lines of perfect equality and perfect inequality.

The **Gini coefficient** is a useful numerical measure of how bowed out the Lorenz curve is. It is defined as the ratio of the area of the gap between the 45-degree line and the Lorenz curve to the area between the lines of perfect equality and perfect inequality. The Gini coefficient can range between zero and one. It has a value of one if the area between the diagonal line and the Lorenz curve is one. Thus, when the Gini coefficient is zero, we have perfect equality. The Gini coefficient would be one if only one person earned all the income in the economy.

Figure 14.12 shows how the Gini coefficient has changed in the United States over the last fifty years. It is clear that income inequality has increased in recent years. Higher earnings of skilled and educated workers relative to the less skilled and less educated may partly explain this change in income distribution. But the reason for these changes in income inequality remains a major unsettled question for economists.

An increase in income inequality, as in Figure 14.12, does not necessarily mean that the rich got richer and the poor got poorer. For example, if one looks at average income in each quintile, one finds an increase for all groups from 1970 to 2004, even after adjusting for inflation. However, average income, in the top quintile increased by a larger percentage amount than average income in the bottom quintile.

Lorenz Curve

This video discusses shifts in the Lorenz curve.

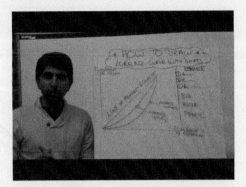

View the video online at: http://www.youtube.com/embed/TsmZskDLTCQ?rel=0

Comparison with Other Countries

Lorenz curves and Gini coefficients can be calculated for different countries or groups of countries. For most European countries, the Lorenz curve is closer to equality than it is for the United States. Canada, Australia, and the United Kingdom have Lorenz curves similar to that of the United States. Income distribution, however, varies much more when we look beyond the industrial countries. As Figure 14.13 shows, Bangladesh, an extremely poor country, has a more equal income distribution than the United States. Brazil, a middle-income country also much poorer than the United States, has a much less equal income distribution. Among individual countries, Bangladesh and Brazil are close to the extremes: 60 percent of the population receives 40 percent of the income in Bangladesh, 19 percent of the income in Brazil, and 29 percent in the United States.

Income distribution for the world as a whole is far more unequal than that for any one country because the very poor in some countries are combined with the very rich in other countries. For example, when West Germany united with East Germany to form one country, the income distribution became more unequal for the unified country as a whole than it had been for either country before unification. The Lorenz curve for the world as a whole would show far greater inequality than the curve for any one country: 60 percent of the world's population receives only 5 percent of the income.

FIGURE 14.13 Income Distribution around the World
Income distributions vary widely around the world. Bangladesh and Brazil are on either side of the United States.

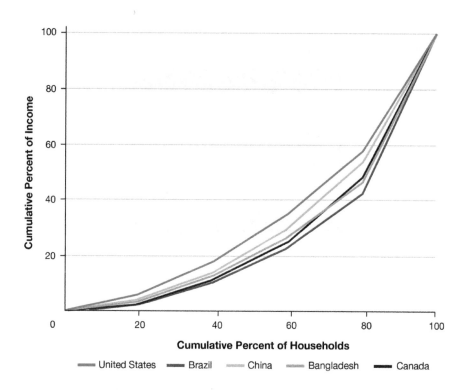

Source: World Income Inequality Database, United Nations University.

Income Mobility

In interpreting income distribution statistics, it is important to recognize that the quintiles do not refer to the same people as years pass. In its 2003 *Survey of Income and Program Participation*, the U.S. Census Bureau reported that 38 percent of those households in the lowest-income quintile in 1996 were in a higher-income quintile in 1999. People who are in the top quintile in one year may be in the bottom quintile the next year (perhaps because they retired, or because they temporarily left the labor force). And people who are in the bottom quintile one year may be in the top quintile the next year (because they completed their MBA degree or because they reentered the work force after a short absence).

How significant is income mobility? Economic research on the United States shows that about two-thirds of the people in any one quintile move to another over a 10-year period. About half of those in the top quintile move to a lower quintile, and about half of those in the bottom quintile move to a higher quintile. Some recent studies have shown, however, that the persistence of income inequality across generations is higher in the United States than in other OECD countries, like Germany.

Long-Term Income Inequality

Distinguishing between income in any one year and income over several years is also important. In a typical life span, people usually earn less when they are young than when they are middle aged. As they grow older and become more experienced, their wages and salaries increase. When people retire, their income usually declines again. Thus, even if everyone had the exact same lifetime income, one would see inequality in the income distribution every year. Middle-aged people would be relatively rich, whereas young and old people would be relatively poor.

Changing Composition of Households

The formation or splitting up of households also can affect the distribution of income. For example, if two individuals who were living separately form a household, the household income doubles. Households splitting apart can alter the income distribution drastically. If one adult leaves the family, perhaps because of divorce or desertion, and the other one stays home with the children, the income of the household declines substantially. It appears that the splitting apart of households has had an impact on income distribution in the United States. According to some estimates, if household composition had not changed in the United States in the last 20 years, the increase in inequality as measured by the Gini coefficient would have been only half as great.

Distribution of Income versus Distribution of Wealth

Another factor to keep in mind when interpreting data on the income distribution is the distinction between *income* and *wealth*. Your annual income is what you earn each year. Your wealth, or your net worth, is all you own minus what you owe others. Wealth changes over a person's lifetime even more than income does as people save for retirement. For example, a young person who has just graduated and gotten a high-paying job may have a high income but little wealth or, with a college loan still to pay off, may even have negative net worth. Conversely, a diligent saver who has just retired will have little income, but may have a sizable retirement fund, and thus be relatively wealthy.

According to most recent surveys, the top 10 percent of households have two-thirds of the wealth in the United States and the top 1 percent hold one-third of the wealth. Although such surveys are not as accurate as the regular monthly surveys of 60,000 households on which our information about income distribution is based, it is clear that the distribution of wealth is less equal than the distribution of income.

Poverty and Measurement

Poverty can be observed virtually everywhere. The poor are visible in the blighted sections of cities and in remote rural areas. Almost everyone has seen the serious problems of the homeless in cities of the United States. CNN has brought the agony of poverty from faraway countries like Somalia and from nearby cities like New Orleans closer to us through our television screens.

As with inequality, economists have developed quantitative measures of poverty. The **poverty rate** is the percentage of people who live in poverty. To calculate the poverty rate, one needs to define what it means to live in poverty. In the United States, poverty usually is defined quantitatively by a **poverty line**, an estimate of the minimal amount of annual income a family needs to avoid severe economic hardship. The poverty line in the United States is based on a survey showing that families spend, on average, one-third of their income on food. The poverty line is thus obtained by multiplying by three the U.S. Department of Agriculture's estimate of the amount of money needed to purchase a low-cost nutritionally adequate amount of food. In addition, adjustments are made for the size of the family. Table 14.5 shows the poverty line for several different family sizes. Since the 1960s, when it was first developed, the poverty line has been increased to adjust for inflation.

poverty rate

The percentage of people living below the poverty line.

poverty line

An estimate of the minimum amount of annual income required for a family to avoid severe economic hardship.

TABLE 14.5 The Poverty Line in the United States, 2019

Persons in Family or Household	Poverty Line ($)
1	12,490
2	16,910
3	21,330
4	25,750
5	30,170

Source: U.S. Census Bureau.

Using the poverty line and data on the income distribution, one can determine the number of people who live in poverty and the poverty rate. The overall poverty rates in the United States have varied over the last 50 years. The overall poverty rate declined sharply from 22 percent in 1960 to 11.1 percent in 1973, but it has not decreased much more. In 2018, the poverty rate was 11.8 percent, or 38.1 million people.

Important trends in poverty emerge among different groups in the U.S. population. For example, the percentage of children who live in poverty rose in the 1970s, 1980s, and early 1990s. During the same time period, the poverty rate for the elderly declined, and this held down the overall poverty rate. In 1993, when child poverty was at a peak, 22.7 percent of children were living in poverty; at the same time, the poverty rate for the elderly was 12.2 percent. In 2018, 16.2 percent of children and 9.7 percent of the elderly were living in poverty. The dramatic decline in the poverty rate for the elderly since the 1970s (from 24.6 percent in 1970) is largely attributed to the change in Social Security benefits and other retirement benefits.

The increase in poverty for children is troublesome, and it is difficult to explain. Some of it may have to do with the increase in single-headed households with children, which are usually poorer than two-adult households. Poverty rates in households with a single head and at least one child have ranged between 35 and 40 percent in the last twenty years—three times the overall poverty rate. Compared to poverty rates among the elderly, childhood poverty rates are much more dependent on the state of the economy (Social Security benefits do not vary with recessions or booms). Between 1993 and 2000, when the economy was doing well, the poverty rate for children declined from 22.7 percent to 16.2 percent. After the 2008–09 recession, it rose higher, reaching a rate of 19.7 percent in 2015 before declining as the economy improved.

Effects of Taxes and Transfers on Income Distribution and Poverty

Many believe that the main purpose of government redistribution of income through taxes and transfers is to help the poor. For this reason, the term *social safety net* sometimes is used for an income redistribution system. These programs try to prevent those who were born into poverty, or who have become poor, from falling too far down in income and therefore in nutrition, health, and general well-being.

How successful has this redistribution effort been? Estimates by the U.S. Census Bureau indicate that the tax and transfer system reduces the poverty rate by about 10 percentage points: These estimates ignore any of the incentive effects mentioned earlier, such as the reduced work incentives that might result from the tax and transfer system. And they ignore any possible response of private efforts to redistribute income—such as charities—that might occur as a result of changes in the government's role.

Review

- The distribution of income can be measured by the percentage of income earned by quintiles of households or families. In the United States in 2004, the bottom quintile earned about 4 percent of the income, whereas the top quintile earned about 48 percent.

- The Lorenz curve provides a graphic summary of the relationship between the cumulative quintiles (ordered from poorest to richest) and cumulative income. If income inequality is not pronounced, the Lorenz curve will lie closer to the 45-degree "line of perfect equality."

- The Gini coefficient is a numerical measure of inequality—it captures how bowed out the Lorenz curve is from the 45-degree line. The higher the Gini coefficient, the more unequal the distribution of income is.

- Income inequality has risen in the United States since 1970. Part of the explanation may be the materialization of higher returns to educated and skilled workers in recent times, but this by no means is the only explanation.

- Before we worry about the magnitude of the Gini coefficient, we should recognize the possibility that (1) people may be mobile across quintiles, (2) long-term income inequality may paint a different picture from that provided by a study done at one point in time, (3) aging populations and changing compositions of households can affect income inequality measures without any changes in the earning patterns of different groups in the economy, and (4) the distribution of wealth is also an important measure of inequality.

- Taxes and transfers are used widely to combat poverty and reduce income inequality in the United States. Evaluating the success of these programs requires an understanding of how poverty is defined and measured.

- The poverty rate is a quantitative measure of the amount of poverty in the United States; it is defined as the percentage of people living below a poverty line. The poverty line for the United States is an estimate of how much money a family needs to avoid severe economic hardship.

- Over the last three decades in the United States, the poverty rate among children has increased and the poverty rate for the elderly has declined. Estimates indicate that the tax and transfer system currently makes the poverty rate lower than it otherwise would be. Nevertheless, the increase in poverty among children has raised serious concerns about the tax and transfer system in the United States.

14.4 End-of-Chapter Materials

Conclusion

In a democracy, the people and their representatives determine the amount of government redistribution of income. A majority seems to want some redistribution of income, but debate continues about how much the government should do. Why doesn't a democracy lead to much more redistribution? After all, 60 percent of the people, according to Table 14.4, receive only 26.6 percent of the income. Because 60 percent of the voting population is enough to win an election, this 60 percent could vote to redistribute income much further. Why hasn't it?

This probably has not happened for a number of reasons. The first reason is the trade-off that exists between equality and efficiency. People realize that taking away incentives to work will reduce the size of the pie for everyone. Another reason is that most of us believe that people should be rewarded for their work. Just as we can think of a fair income distribution, we can think about a fair reward system. If some students want to work hard in high school so that they can attend college, why shouldn't they earn the additional income that comes from that hard work?

The second reason is the connection between personal freedom and economic freedom. Government involvement in income distribution means government involvement in people's lives. Those who cherish the idea of personal freedom worry about a system that takes a large amount of income from people who work.

The third reason is that much income redistribution occurs through the private sector—private charities and churches. The distribution of food and the provision of health care have long been supported by nongovernment organizations. In times of floods or earthquakes, it is common for people to volunteer to help those in distress. Private charity has certain advantages over government. Individuals become more personally involved if they perform a public service, whether volunteering at a soup kitchen or tutoring at an elementary school.

In recent years, the United States has experienced a rise in income inequality, which has raised concerns about the adequacy of the existing transfer and tax policies. Expanding the EITC program, means-testing social insurance programs, and changing the progressivity of the income tax system all have been proposed to deal with the fact that the incomes of the poor have been growing much more slowly than have the incomes of the rich. Similar concerns have been raised about poverty, including the increase in poverty among children and the rising number of people without adequate health insurance programs, who could suffer a serious hit to their net worth if they were to fall ill. If income inequality continues to rise, and more people begin to worry about its potential to have detrimental effects on the economy, the democratic system should bring about policies and policy makers who take a keen interest in the issues discussed in this chapter.

Key Points

1. In modern democracies, the government plays a major role in trying to help the poor and in providing a more equal income distribution through the use of taxes and transfers.

2. Taxes are needed to pay for transfers and other government spending. In the United States, the personal income tax and the payroll tax are by far the most significant sources of tax revenue at the federal level. Sales taxes and property taxes play a significant role at the local level.

3. Taxes cause inefficiencies, as measured by deadweight loss, because taxes reduce the amount of the economic activity being taxed—whether it is the production of a good or the labor of workers.

4. The incidence of a tax depends on the price elasticity of supply and demand. The deadweight loss from taxes on goods with low price elasticities is relatively small.

5. Transfer payments are classified into means-tested programs—such as welfare and food stamps—and social insurance programs—such as Social Security and unemployment insurance.

6. Transfer payments can cause inefficiency as a result of disincentives to work or the incentive for families to split up.

7. A trade-off exists between equality and efficiency. Tax reform and welfare reform try to improve incentives and reduce inefficiency.

8. The distribution of income has grown more unequal in recent years.

9. Poverty among children has increased, while poverty among the elderly has declined in recent years.

10. The tax and transfer system has reduced income inequality and lowered poverty rates, but much room exists for improvement and reform.

Questions for Review

1. Provide simple definitions of the following: tax bracket, marginal tax rate, average tax rate, deductions, and exemptions.

2. Why does a deadweight loss result from the personal income tax? What factors can lead to the deadweight loss being large or small?

3. What do economists mean when they talk about "tax incidence"? How is the incidence of taxes related to the elasticities of demand and supply?

4. What are the impacts of an increase in the income tax on the labor market?

5. Intuitively explain why the effects of a payroll tax are the same whether the employer or the worker pays it.

6. What is the relationship between the tax rate and tax revenue? Explain under what circumstances a Laffer curve would emerge.

7. What are the major types of transfer programs in the United States? Provide examples of specific programs that fall under each type.

8. How do these transfer programs affect the incentives to work? Describe both positive and negative effects.

9. How is the distribution of income measured by the Lorenz curve and the Gini coefficient?

10. Why are income mobility and lifetime income important to consider in interpreting Gini coefficients and other income distribution statistics?

Problems

1. Consider the following 2016 personal income tax schedule obtained from the IRS website. It applies to a taxpayer who is not married (single).

If Taxable Income Is Over	But Not Over	The Tax Is
$0	$9,275	10% of the amount over $0
$9,275	$37,650	$927.50 plus 15% of the amount over $9,275
$37,650	$91,150	$5,183.75 plus 25% of the amount over $37,650

a. What is the tax due on a taxable income of $25,000?

b. What is the tax due on a taxable income of $50,000?

c. Why does the tax more than double when the income doubles?

d. Is this tax system progressive?

2. Consider the following 2016 personal income tax schedule obtained from the IRS website. It applies to a married couple that is combining their incomes and filing jointly.

If Taxable Income Is Over	But Not Over	The Tax Is
$0	$18,550	10% of the amount over $0
$18,550	$75,300	$1,855 plus 15% of the amount over $18,550
$75,300	$151,900	$10,367.50 plus 25% of the amount over $75,300

a. What is the tax due for a couple if each spouse has a taxable income of $25,000?

b. Use the results from the preceding question to compare the tax the couple would have paid if they were not married (and filed as single persons) to the amount of tax they pay as a married couple (filing jointly).

c. What is the tax due for a couple if one spouse has a taxable income of $50,000 and the other spouse has no taxable income?

d. Does the tax system treat households making the same amount of income in an identical manner? Can it do so while remaining a progressive system?

3. Two popular programs for helping workers with very low incomes are to raise the minimum wage and to raise the EITC. Why do economists tend to favor the EITC?

4. California tried to impose a "snack" tax—one that applied only to what the legislators thought was junk food. Suppose snack food has a higher elasticity of demand than non-snack food. Draw a supply and demand diagram to explain which tax—on snack food or on non-snack food—will cause the price to rise more. Which will produce a greater deadweight loss?

5. Suppose the government decides to increase the payroll tax paid by employers. If the labor supply curve has a low elasticity, what will happen to the workers' wages? Who actually bears the burden of the tax, the workers or the firms? Would it be different if the labor supply had a high elasticity?

6. Suppose that the labor demand curve is perfectly flat. What is the impact on a typical worker's hourly wage if the government increases the payroll tax paid by employers by 10 percent of the wage? Show what happens in a labor supply and labor demand graph. Why does the slope of the labor supply curve not affect your answer?

7. The Family Leave Act is a federal law that requires employers to give employees unpaid leave to care for a newborn or a sick relative. Show how the Family Leave Act affects the supply and demand for labor. According to this model, what will happen to wages and employment compared with the situation before the law was passed?

8. The following table gives hours worked and the welfare payment received.

Hours Worked	Wage Payment ($)	Welfare Payment ($)	Total Income ($)
0		10,000	
500		8,000	
1,000		6,000	
1,500		4,000	
2,000		2,000	

a. Calculate the missing data in the table, given that the hourly wage is $5 and total income is the sum of the wage payment and the welfare payment.

b. Draw a graph that shows how much total income a worker earns with and without this welfare program. Put the number of hours worked on the horizontal axis and total income on the vertical axis.

c. What is the increase in total income for each additional hour worked without any welfare program? Compare it with the increase in total income for each additional hour worked under the welfare program.

d. How could the welfare program be changed to increase the incentive to work without reducing total income for a full-time worker (40 hours per week, 50 weeks per year, $5 per hour) below $12,000, which is already below the poverty line for a family of four?

9. The following table gives the income distribution in Brazil and in Australia. Draw the Lorenz curve for each. Which country has the larger Gini coefficient?

Quintile	Percent of Income in Brazil	Percent of Income in Australia
Bottom 20 percent	2.4	4.4
Second 20 percent	5.7	11.1
Third 20 percent	10.7	17.5
Fourth 20 percent	18.6	24.8
Top 20 percent	62.6	42.2

10. Analyze the distribution of income, using the household incomes in the following table. Rank the families by income. Compute the percentage of total income going to the poorest 20 percent of the families, the second 20 percent, and the richest 20 percent. Draw a Lorenz curve for the income distribution of these 10 families. Is their distribution more equal or less equal than that of the U.S. population as a whole?

Family	Income ($)
Jones	12,000
Pavlov	100,000
Cohen	24,000
Baker	87,000
Dixon	66,000
Sun	72,000
Tanaka	18,000
Bernardo	45,000
Smith	28,000
Lopez	33,000

CHAPTER 15
Public Goods, Externalities, and Government Behavior

When asked what it was like to work on the President's Council of Economic Advisers, Nobel Laureate Robert Solow answered:

> *On any given day in the executive branch, there are more meetings than Heinz has varieties. At a very large proportion of these meetings, the representative of some agency or some interest will be trying to sell a hare-brained economic proposal. I am exaggerating a little. Not every one of these ideas is crazy. Most of them are just bad: either impractical, inefficient, excessively costly, likely to be accompanied by undesirable side effects, or just misguided—unlikely to accomplish their stated purpose. Someone has to knock those proposals down.... That is where the Council's comparative advantage lies.... [But that] does not mean that we won all the battles; we lost at least as many as we won. The race is not always won by the best arguments, not in political life anyway. But we always felt we had a chance and we kept trying.*[1]

FIGURE 15.1 Parks as Public Goods

A large public park in a city is an example of a public good, defined later in this chapter as a good that satisfies two key criteria: it is non-rival and non-excludable.

Source: cdrin/Shutterstock.com

The purpose of this chapter is to examine two of the most basic economic principles—public goods and externalities—that economists on the President's Council of Economic Advisers and elsewhere use to determine whether proposals for government intervention are crazy, just bad, or actually good. We also show how cost-benefit analysis can help make decisions about particular government programs. Finally, we examine models of government behavior to understand why "in political life," as Solow puts it, the best economic arguments do not always win. We will see that politicians are influenced by incentives as much as anyone else.

15.1 Public Goods

Table 15.1 shows the range of goods and services produced by all levels of government in the United States: The federal government, the 50 state governments, and more than 85,000 local governments (counties, cities, towns, and school districts). According to data from the U.S. Census Bureau, in terms of employment, the largest sector of government production in the United States is education at all levels, from elementary school to graduate school. Education is followed by health and hospital services, police, national defense, the postal service, corrections (prisons), and highways. (The figures for national defense include only civilian workers; if Table 15.1 included those serving in the armed forces, national defense would be second on the list.) The other categories, ranging from the judicial and legal system (federal, state, and county courts) to parks and recreation, each are significant but small relative to the total.

TABLE 15.1 Types of Goods and Services Produced by Government in the United States

Type of Good or Service	Employment as a Percent of Total Government
Education	49.8
Health and hospitals	8.6
Police protection	5.4
National defense (civilian)	3.6
Corrections (prisons)	3.4
Postal Service	2.7
Highways	2.4
Judicial and legal	2.2
Parks and recreation	1.9
Fire protection	1.9
All other	18.1

Source: Bureau of Census, 2012 Census of Governments: Employment Summary Report

Observe also the types of goods and services that are not on the list because they are produced by the private sector. Manufacturing, mining, retail trade, wholesale trade, hotel services, and motion picture production are some of the items that are largely left to the private sector. Note also that for all the goods and services on the list in Table 15.1, the private sector provides at least some of the production. The private health care sector has 60 million workers, for example, compared with 2 million in government health care. The private sector also is involved in mail delivery, education, garbage collection, and even fire protection (volunteer fire departments).

Why is the government involved in the production of police services and education services but not in the production of automobiles? Why are education and health services provided by both the private sector and the government sector, whereas judicial services and national defense services are provided only by the government? In more general terms, why is it necessary for governments to produce *any* goods and services? The concept of a public good helps us answer the question.

Nonrivalry and Nonexcludability

A **public good** is a good or service that has two characteristics: *nonrivalry in consumption* and *nonexcludability*. **Nonrivalry** in consumption means that more consumption of a good by one person does not imply less consumption of it by another person. Clean air and national defense are examples of goods with nonrivalry. For example, if you were to take a walk outside and bask in the warm sunshine and breathe more clean air, you are not depriving another person of the opportunity to enjoy the sunshine or to breathe the clean air. Similarly, the sense of security that you get from a country's national defense—the military personnel, the strategic alliances, the missile defense system—is not reduced by the fact that your neighbor enjoys the same benefits of a national defense system.

In contrast, for most goods, there is rivalry in consumption. For example, if you purchase a ripe apple from the supermarket and eat it, then no one else can consume that apple. When you sit in the library and read this economics textbook, no one else can read this particular copy of the textbook. But for a good with nonrivalry in consumption, everybody can consume more if they want to. The good has a collective aspect, and the total benefit is the sum of the benefits to every person.

Nonexcludability means that one cannot exclude people from consuming the good. For example, the supermarket will not let you eat the apple unless you pay for it. The library will not let you check out the copy of the textbook unless you have a valid student ID card. These are excludable goods. On the other hand, no one can stop you from going outside, basking in the sunshine, and breathing clean air. The security provided by national defense is available to you, and no one can prevent you from benefiting from that security. A good or service that has nonrivalry in consumption and nonexcludability is a *public good*. In contrast, a *private good* has excludability and *rivalry*.

public good

A good or service that has two characteristics: nonrivalry in consumption and nonexcludability.

nonrivalry

The situation in which increased consumption of a good by one person does not decrease the amount available for consumption by others.

nonexcludability

The situation in which no one can be excluded from consuming a good.

Free Riders: A Difficulty for the Private Sector

People can enjoy the consumption of a nonexcludable good or service without having to pay for it. Furthermore, if that good is also a nonrival good, then its use by nonpaying consumers does not reduce the ability of paying consumers to enjoy that good. Hence, instead of people clamoring to deny the use of a good to nonpaying consumers, you would see previously paying consumers also turn into nonpaying consumers. Pretty soon, the only consumers of the nonrival, nonexcludable good will be nonpaying ones, and hence no one will have the incentive to provide that public good to the marketplace. We describe this situation as a **free-rider problem** associated with public goods: People who do not contribute to the costs of providing the good end up benefiting from the good because they cannot be excluded.

To better understand this concept, imagine that you bought a huge bus for the purpose of transporting students around the college town and collecting a little money for your service. But suppose the bus had a broken rear door that allowed people to get on and off without paying and without interfering with other people's travel. In that situation, you soon would find that all your riders would be nonpaying ones. If you could not fix the door or do something else to exclude the free riders, you would not be in the transportation business long, because without fares, you would have losses.

free-rider problem

A problem arising in the case of public goods because those who do not contribute to the costs of providing the public good cannot be excluded from the benefits of the good.

A Chinook helicopter drops sand bags to plug a canal levee break in the Gentilly neighborhood of New Orleans, Louisiana, on September 11, 2005. Levees are a public good, having characteristics of both nonrivalry and nonexcludability.

Source: Terry Poche/Shutterstock.com

National defense is like the huge bus with the broken rear door. You cannot exclude people from enjoying it, even if they do not pay—for instance, if an enemy aircraft is intent on dropping bombs on a city, then shooting down that plane protects everyone's house, not just those of the people who paid for the antiaircraft missile. It is clear, then, that a private firm will have difficulty producing and selling national defense to the people of a country, because everyone will be hoping that someone else will pay for the antiaircraft missile that protects his or her house. Given the free-rider problem, the public good, such as national defense, would have to be provided by the government. Similar actions are taken with other public goods such as police protection, fire protection, and the judicial system. The government can broadly fund its provision of these public goods by assessing taxes on households.

Certain types of information also have the features of a public good. Everyone can benefit from information that a hurricane is on the way; there is no rivalry in consuming this information. Excluding people from consuming that information also would be difficult, because the most effective ways of notifying people quickly would involve radio and television broadcasts that are accessible to all. The U.S. Weather Service therefore will collect and distribute information about hurricanes and other adverse weather events. But you should keep in mind that not all information is nonexcludable. For example, if you want to analyze broad trends in the U.S. economy, you will find that much of the information you need is freely available through the Department of Commerce. If you want to analyze detailed information about companies trading on the New York Stock Exchange, however, you will have to pay a fee to a company before you can gain access to that information. We focus on the type of information that has a public good feature associated with it.

Avoiding Free-Rider Problems

FIGURE 15.3

The Classic Lighthouse Example

How can the free-rider problem be avoided without government providing the service?

Source: Frank L Junior/
Shutterstock.com

Even though we define public goods as being goods and services that are nonrival and nonexcludable, few goods are completely nonexcludable. Sometimes the private sector is able to find ways of making a good excludable to a degree sufficient to overcome the free-rider problem. A classic example used by economists to explore the nature of public goods is the lighthouse that warns ships of nearby rocks and prevents them from running aground. A lighthouse has the feature of nonrivalry. If one ship enjoys the benefit of the light and goes safely by, this does not mean that another ship cannot go by. Similarly, it is impossible to exclude ships from using the lighthouse because any ship can benefit from the light it projects.

Lighthouse services, however, are not always provided by the government. Early lighthouses were built by associations of shippers, who charged fees to the ships in nearby ports. This system worked well because the fees could be collected from most shippers as they entered nearby ports. So even if not every ship that used the lighthouse's services could be charged individually for that service (for instance, a ship that did not come into port but sailed by, using the lighthouse to gauge where land was, would not be charged for lighthouse services), many of those who benefited from the good were charged fees, thus alleviating the free-rider problem without government involvement.

Another example is over-the-air radio or television broadcasts. Such broadcasts have both characteristics of a public good. They are nonexcludable because anyone can tune into the broadcast, regardless of whether they have paid to see or hear that particular show. They are nonrival because the use of an antenna or an aerial to capture a television or radio signal does not prevent anyone else from doing the same. Despite the public good characteristics of radio and television services, however, private firms always have provided the vast majority of such services in the United States. They are able to do so by using advertising to pay for the provision of the broadcast service, thus avoiding the free-rider problem.

Sometimes governments are able to charge people for the use of particular services that have a certain amount of excludability. This charge is called a **user fee**. In recent years, user fees have become more common in many government-provided services, including the national parks. The aim is to target the payments more closely to the users of the goods and services.

user fee

A fee charged for the use of a good normally provided by the government.

Some public goods and services have closely associated supplements that are provided privately. For instance, even though police services almost always are provided by a local government, businesses and wealthier families in a town may choose to avail themselves of security services provided by private firms to supplement the police services. In these cases, no free-rider problem arises because the private security service is excludable; it is targeted at a particular group, which will be charged for the use of that service.

Changes in Technology and Excludability

Modern technology is constantly changing the degree to which certain goods are nonexcludable. A good example is the changing public good features of television. Cable television and the ability to scramble signals for those who use satellites to obtain their television signals have reduced the problem of nonexcludability. If one does not pay a cable television bill, the service can be turned off. If one does not pay the satellite fee, the signals can be scrambled so that reception is impossible. Thus, it is now common to see cable television stations like HBO and Showtime delivering specialized programming to small audiences that pay extra for the special service. Such broadcasts may have the luxury of being free of advertising because users can be charged directly for the services.

The Production of Goods by the Government

If we look at the types of goods produced by government in Table 15.1, we see many public goods, such as national defense, police protection, and the judicial and legal system. Other goods in the list, however, do not have features of public goods. Postal delivery, for example, is a service that has rivalry both in consumption and excludability. If you do not put a stamp on your letter, it is not delivered, and a postal delivery worker's time certainly has rivalry. In principle, education also is characterized by rivalry in consumption and excludability. For a given-size school, an additional student may reduce the education of other students, and it is technologically feasible to exclude a student who does not pay school fees or meet certain admissions criteria.

The mere production of a good by the government does not make that good a public good. In centrally planned economies, the government produces virtually everything, private goods as well as public goods. The economist's definition of a public good is specific and is useful for determining when the government should produce something and when it is better left to the market. If a good or service being produced by the government is not a public good, then it is important to find out the other reasons why the government is involved in the production of that good or service.

Cost-Benefit Analysis

Suppose the government decides that a particular good or service is a public good and that because of free-rider problems, the private sector will not get involved in the production of that good. Should the good be produced by the government? If so, how much of the good should be produced? Such decisions ultimately are made by voters and elected officials after much political debate. Economic analysis of the costs and benefits of providing the goods and services is critical if the

cost-benefit analysis

An appraisal of a project based on the costs and benefits derived from it.

participants in this debate are to make informed decisions. Balancing the costs and benefits of providing a good or service before making a decision is called **cost-benefit analysis**.

Marginal Cost and Marginal Benefit

To determine the quantity of a government-provided service that should be produced, the marginal cost and marginal benefit of the service should be considered. In the case of police services, for example, a decision about whether to increase the size of the police force should consider both the marginal benefit to the people in the city—the reduction in the loss of life and property caused by crime, the increased enjoyment from a secure environment, and safer schools—and the marginal cost—the increased payroll for the police. If the marginal benefit of having more police is greater than the marginal cost of providing more police, then the police force should be increased. The optimal size of the police force should be such that the marginal cost of providing more police is equal to the marginal benefit of having more police.

contingent valuations

An estimation of the willingness to pay for a project on the part of consumers who may benefit from the project.

Measuring the costs of producing government-provided services is not difficult because government workers' wages and materials used in production have explicit dollar values. But measuring the benefits of government-provided services is much more difficult. How do we measure how much people value greater security in their community? How do we value a reduction in violence at schools or a reduced murder rate? Public opinion polls in which people are asked how much they would be willing to pay are a possibility. For example, people can be asked in surveys how much they would be willing to pay for more police in an area. Such estimates of willingness to pay are called **contingent valuations** because they give the value contingent on the public good's existing and the person's having to pay for it. Some economists think that contingent valuation is not reliable if people actually do not have to pay for the good or service. People may not give a good estimate of their true willingness to pay.

Review

- Public goods have two characteristics: nonrivalry, which means that more consumption of the good by one person does not mean that less of the good would be available for someone else, and nonexcludability, which means that it is not possible to exclude those who do not pay for the good from consuming the good.

- These two characteristics lead public goods to have a free-rider problem—people who do not pay for the good can use it without interfering with the ability of those who paid for the good to use it. Instead of objecting to nonpayers' use of the good, the paying customers will soon stop paying. This means that private producers have little incentive to produce this good; thus, government production is frequently necessary.

- If the goods are not completely nonexcludable, the private sector may be able to come up with ways to charge at least some users of the good, enabling it to deal with the free-rider problem and produce goods in the market. Changes in technology also can help make previously nonexcludable goods and services at least partially excludable. Sometimes, even the government may levy user fees on users of some public goods that the government provides.

- In deciding how much of a public good should be provided, cost-benefit analysis can be used. The optimal quantity of the public good or service is the quantity at which the marginal benefit of the good or service equals its marginal cost.

- Even though the marginal cost of providing a public good can be fairly easily calculated, the marginal benefit is harder to calculate. Estimates of willingness to pay, known as contingent valuations, are a somewhat controversial measure of the marginal benefit of a public good.

15.2 Externalities: From the Environment to Education

We have seen that the existence of public goods provides an economic rationale for government involvement in the production of certain goods and services. Another rationale for government involvement in production is a market failure known as an externality. An **externality** occurs when the costs of producing a good or the benefits from consuming a good spill over onto individuals who are not producing or consuming the good. The production of goods that cause pollution is the classic example of an externality. For example, when a coal-fired electric utility plant produces energy, it emits smoke that contains carbon dioxide, sulfur dioxide, and other pollutants into the air. These pollutants can make life miserable for people breathing the air and can cause serious health concerns. Similarly, people who smoke cigarettes pass on the health risks associated with secondhand smoke to those in their vicinity and reduce the quality of life for people who have negative reactions to the smell of cigarette smoke. These are examples of **negative externalities** because they have a negative effect—a cost—on the well-being of others. A **positive externality** occurs when a positive effect—a benefit—from producing or consuming a good spills over onto others. A particularly relevant example in the current context is the decision to get a vaccination. If a vaccine for coronavirus is discovered, your decision to get vaccinated provides not just a benefit to yourself in protecting you from the disease, it also provides substantial benefits to others who you are likely to encounter during the course of your daily activities, protecting them from infection as well. Current generations have experienced the widespread social benefits of vaccinations against seasonal flu, previously fatal diseases like smallpox and tuberculosis, as well as against childhood diseases like measles, chicken pox, and whooping cough. Another example particularly relevant to the current COVID-19 situation is wearing masks and practicing social distancing. These are both activities that bring benefits to the practitioner as well as to others who would have otherwise been exposed to the virus if you were infected with COVID-19. In fact, some of the research on cloth masks suggest that all the benefits of mask wearing may come in the form of an externality. We will first look at the effects of negative externalities and then consider positive externalities.

FIGURE 15.4 Oil Spill: A Negative Externality

The BP oil spill that lasted three months beginning in April 2010 is an example of a negative externality: The production of goods or services (oil for fuel) raises costs and/or reduces benefits to the livelihoods of people living in and around the Gulf of Mexico who work in the fishing and tourism industries.

Source: Cheryl Casey/Shutterstock.com

externality

The situation in which the costs of producing or the benefits of consuming a good spill over onto those who are not producing or consuming the good.

negative externality

The situation in which costs spill over onto someone who is not involved in producing or consuming the good.

positive externality

The situation in which benefits spill over onto someone who is not involved in producing or consuming the good.

Negative Externalities

In the case of negative externalities, a competitive market produces a quantity that exceeds the efficient amount of production. For example, companies may be too inclined to use air-polluting fossil fuels to generate energy instead of using a nonpolluting source of energy like solar power. The reason is that producers do not take into account the external costs when they calculate their costs of production. If they did take these costs into account, they would produce less.

marginal private cost

The marginal cost of production as viewed by the private firm or individual.

marginal social cost

The marginal cost of production as viewed by society as a whole.

   The reason why competitive markets are not efficient in the case of negative externalities can be illustrated using the supply and demand curves. For example, consider an example of a negative externality resulting from pollution caused by the production of electricity. This negative externality occurs because the production of electricity raises pollution costs to other firms and to individuals. The actual cost of producing electric power is greater than the costs perceived by the electrical utility. In other words, because of the externality, the marginal cost as perceived by the private firm, which we now call the **marginal private cost**, is less than the true marginal cost that is incurred by society, which we call the **marginal social cost**. Marginal social cost is the sum of the firm's marginal private cost and the marginal external cost, that is, the increase in external costs to society as more is produced.

$$Marginal\ social\ cost = marginal\ private\ cost + marginal\ external\ cost$$

We illustrate this equation in Figure 15.5 by drawing a marginal private cost curve below the marginal social cost curve. We use the term *marginal private cost* to refer to what we have thus far called marginal cost to distinguish it from marginal social cost. Recall that adding up all the marginal (private) cost curves for the firms in a market gives the market supply curve, as labeled in the diagram.

FIGURE 15.5 Illustration of a Typical Negative Externality
Because production of the good creates costs external to the firm, the marginal social cost is greater than the marginal private cost to the firm. Thus, the equilibrium quantity that emerges from a competitive market is too large: Marginal benefit is less than marginal social cost.

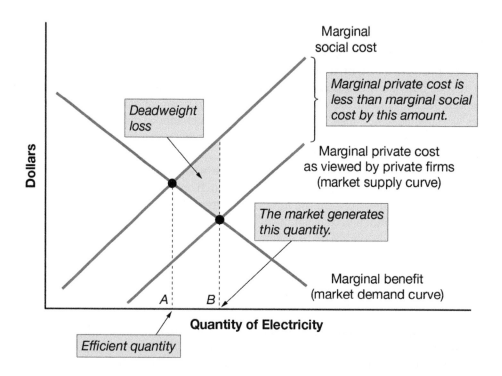

   Figure 15.5 also shows the marginal benefit to consumers from using the product, in this case, electrical energy. This is the market demand curve for electricity. According to the supply and demand model, the interaction of firms and consumers in the market will result in a situation in which the marginal cost of production—the marginal private cost—equals marginal benefit. This situation occurs at the market equilibrium, the point at which the quantity supplied equals the quantity demanded. The resulting quantity produced is indicated by point *B* in Figure 15.5.

   At this amount of production, however, the marginal benefit of production is less than the *marginal social cost* of production. Marginal benefit equals marginal private cost but is less than marginal social cost. Only at point *A* in the figure is marginal benefit equal to marginal social cost.

Thus, point *A* represents the efficient level of production. Because of the externality, too much is produced. Firms produce too much because they do not incur the external costs.

Recall that we calculated how well off an economy is as a result of a particular outcome by adding up the values of consumer surplus and producer surplus. The sum of consumer and producer surplus is the area between the market supply curve and the market demand curve over the range of output produced. Another way to think about it is as the difference between marginal benefit (demand) and marginal cost (supply) over the range of output produced.

In the presence of a negative externality, how well off an economy is really should be measured as the difference between marginal benefit and the *marginal social cost* of production. For each additional unit that is produced above point *A* and below point *B*, the marginal benefit is *less* than the marginal social cost. Hence, the production of each additional unit is a net loss to society, and the overall deadweight loss from producing at the market equilibrium quantity of *B* is indicated by the shaded triangle in Figure 15.5.

 ## Transmission of the Coronavirus as an Externality

Watch from minute 4:00 to 6:00 of this video for a conversation on the impacts of a virus contagion as an externality.

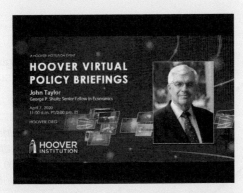

View the video online at: http://www.youtube.com/embed/zM3Rsp3FDnI?rel=0

Positive Externalities

A positive externality occurs when the activity of one person makes another person better off, either by reducing costs or by increasing benefits. For example, an individual who acquires additional education will obtain private benefits in the form of increased earnings. But the education also benefits society. Going to school and learning to read, write, and think makes people better citizens who will be able to teach their kids how to read and write, who will be able to pass on knowledge about discoveries they make to others, and who will be able to read about proper hygiene and health practices and thus reduce the burden on the public health system.

Another example of a good with a positive externality is research. Firms that engage in research get some of the benefits of that research through the products that they can sell—for instance, a new pharmaceutical to treat a particular disease. But the benefits from the research expenditures often go well beyond the individual or the company undertaking the research. The research spreads, and other people take advantage of it as well. An example is military research into global positioning systems (GPS), which spilled over into the private sector and found its way into devices such as navigation systems for automobiles.

marginal private benefit

The marginal benefit from consumption of a good as viewed by a private individual.

marginal social benefit

The marginal benefit from consumption of a good from the viewpoint of society as a whole.

Let us examine what happens when a positive externality raises social benefits above private benefits. To show how positive externalities affect the quantity produced in a competitive market, we need to look at the supply and demand curves. The externality makes the marginal benefit as perceived by the consumer, which we now call the **marginal private benefit**, less than the true benefit to society, which we call the **marginal social benefit**. With a positive externality, the marginal social benefit is greater than the marginal private benefit because a marginal external benefit results from more consumption. That is,

marginal social benefit = marginal private benefit + marginal external benefit

We illustrate this equation in Figure 15.6 by drawing a marginal private benefit curve that lies below the marginal social benefit curve. We use the term *marginal private benefit* curve to refer to what we have thus far called marginal benefit or the market demand curve to distinguish it from marginal social benefit. Suppose that Figure 15.6 refers to the market for education. The market equilibrium is the point at which the marginal private benefit curve (the market demand curve) intersects the marginal cost curve (the market supply curve). The resulting quantity produced is indicated by point C in Figure 15.6.

FIGURE 15.6 Illustration of a Typical Positive Externality

Because consumption of the good gives benefits to others, the marginal social benefit is greater than the marginal private benefit. Hence, the equilibrium quantity that emerges from a competitive market is too low.

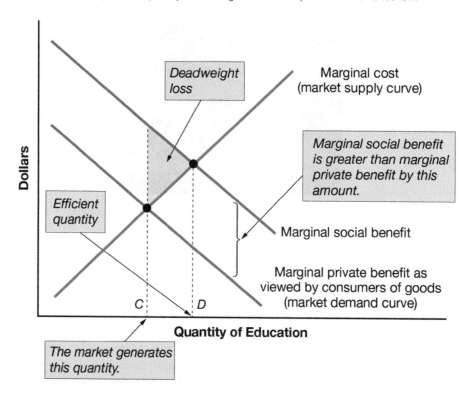

At this amount of production, however, the marginal social benefit of production exceeds the marginal cost of production. Only at point D in the figure is marginal social benefit equal to marginal cost. Thus, point D represents the efficient level of production. Because of the positive externality, too little is produced. Firms do not have the incentive to produce more because they do not gain directly from the benefits that are spilling over onto others.

In the presence of a positive externality, the sum of consumer and producer surplus really should be measured as the difference between the *marginal social benefit* and marginal cost. You can see that each additional unit that is not produced above point C and below point D results in forgone net benefit to society because the marginal social benefit exceeds the marginal cost of production. By not increasing production from point *C* to point *D*, we incur a deadweight loss that is indicated by the shaded triangle in Figure 15.6.

Externalities

This video discusses positive and negative externalities and government incentives.

View the video online at: http://www.youtube.com/embed/CuJ4E1UMk3c?rel=0

Externalities Spread across Borders

Externalities are by no means limited in their geographic impact. Sulfur dioxide emissions from electrical utility plants are an externality with international effects. The sulfur dioxide travels high into the air and then is dispersed by winds across long distances. Rainfall then brings the sulfur dioxide back to Earth in the form of acid rain, which lands on forests and lakes hundreds of miles away. In some cases, the acid rain occurs in countries different from the country in which the sulfur dioxide was first emitted. In North America, acid rain that results from burning fuel in the Midwest industrial centers may fall in Canada or upstate New York.

Global warming is another example of an externality with international dimensions. When too much carbon dioxide accumulates in the Earth's atmosphere, it prevents the sun's warmth from escaping out of the atmosphere, causing a greenhouse effect. Global warming is caused by the emission of carbon dioxide by firms and individuals but has effects around the world.

The ease and prevalence of modern air travel also leads to negative spillover effects on other countries from a poor health care system in one country. For instance, if patients in one country fall victim to an infection like the avian flu but go untreated, they very easily can spread that disease to many other countries as the people they come into contact with travel the world.

Review

- Externalities occur when the benefits or costs of producing and consuming spill over onto others. The spillovers can be negative, as in the case of air pollution, or positive, as in the case of vaccinations.
- Externalities are a cause of market failure. For goods with negative externalities, more than the efficient amount is produced because the marginal social cost exceeds the marginal private cost. Private firms produce until the marginal benefit equals the marginal private cost, even though the optimal level is lower—the point at which the marginal benefit equals the marginal social cost.

- For goods with positive externalities, less than the efficient amount is produced because the marginal social benefit exceeds the marginal private benefit. Private firms will produce only until the marginal private benefit equals the marginal cost, even though the optimal level is higher—the point at which the marginal social benefit equals the marginal cost.

- Both positive and negative externalities result in deadweight loss. In the case of negative externalities, this loss occurs because too many goods are being produced; these additional goods have a marginal social cost that exceeds the marginal benefit. In the case of positive externalities, this loss occurs because too few goods are being produced; the forgone goods have a marginal social benefit that exceeds the marginal cost.

- Externalities are not necessarily local in their impact. Air pollution and global warming are examples of externalities whose effects are not hemmed in by borders. Changes in technology also are increasingly making the impact of one country's policy on, say, public health issues have a spillover effect on other countries.

15.3 Remedies for Externalities

As the previous section shows, competitive markets do not generate an efficient level of production when externalities exist. What are some of the ways in which a society can alleviate problems caused by these externalities? In some cases involving positive externalities, the solution has been for the government to produce the good or service because the private sector will produce less than the socially efficient level of output. For instance, elementary education is provided by governments around the world with requirements that children attend school through a certain age. But in most cases in which externalities are present, production is left to the private sector, and the government endeavors to influence the quantity produced.

internalize

The process of providing incentives so that externalities are taken into account internally by firms or consumers.

How can production in the private sector be influenced by government to lead to a more efficient level of production of goods and services in the economy? We will see that the answer involves changing behavior so that the externalities are taken into account internally by firms and consumers. In other words, the challenge is to **internalize** the externalities.

Four alternative ways can bring about a more efficient level of production in the case of externalities. The first method we discuss, private remedies, does not require direct government intervention. The other three—command and control, taxes or subsidies, and tradable permits—do.

Private Remedies: Agreements between the Affected Parties

private remedies

A procedure that eliminates or internalizes externalities without government action other than defining property rights.

In some cases, through **private remedies**, people can eliminate externalities without government assistance. A Nobel Prize winner in economics, Ronald Coase of the University of Chicago, pointed out this possibility in a famous paper published in 1960.

Consider the following simple example. Suppose that the externality relates to the production of two products: health care and candy. Suppose that a hospital is built next door to a large candy factory. Making candy requires noisy pounding and vibrating machinery. Unfortunately, the walls of the new hospital are thin. The loud candy machinery can be heard in the hospital. Thus, we might call this noise pollution an externality. It has a cost. It makes the hospital less effective; for example, it is difficult for the doctors to hear their patients' hearts through the stethoscopes.

What can be done? The city mayor could adopt a rule prohibiting loud noise near the hospital, but that would severely impinge on candy production in the city. Or, because the hospital was built after the candy factory, the mayor could say, "Too bad, doctors; candy is important too" and tell the hospital to relocate somewhere where the noise is not too great. Alternatively, it might be better for the candy workers and doctors to work this externality out on their own. The supervisor of the candy workers could negotiate with the doctors. Perhaps the candy workers could agree to use the loud machines only at designated hours during the afternoon, during which time the doctors would avoid scheduling procedures that are sensitive to noise. Or perhaps the hospital would be willing to pay for a more insulated wall between the candy company and the hospital so that the noise is dampened, especially because that option would be cheaper than relocation. Or perhaps the candy company will be willing to pay for newer, less noisy machinery because it is preferable to the risk of having to shut down because of the noise pollution.

Thus, it is possible to resolve the externality by negotiation between the two parties affected. The privately negotiated alternatives seem more efficient than the mayor's rulings because the production of both candy and health care continues. Note that, in these alternatives, both parties alter their behavior. For example, the doctors change their scheduling of noise-sensitive procedures, and the candy factory limits loud noise to the afternoon. Thus, the parties find a solution in which the polluter does not make all the adjustments, as would be the case if the mayor adopted a "no loud noise" rule.

Another example of private Coase-like remedies you are likely to experience in a post COVID-19 world are social distancing arrangements put into place by grocery stores, restaurants, and cafes. Grocery stores will limit the number of customers in a store, provide sanitized carts, and use restrictions on direction of travel in grocery aisles. In exchange, they will ask customers to obey these restrictions to deliver a safe service to everyone. If you do not agree with a particular store's requirements—say an insistence that every customer wear a face mask—then you are free to shop elsewhere at a store that is not as stringent about the use of face masks.

The Importance of Assigning Property Rights

For a negotiation like this to work, however, it is essential that property rights be well defined. **Property rights** determine who has the right to pollute or infringe on whom. Who, for example, is being infringed on in the case of the noise pollution? Does the candy factory have the right to use loud machinery, or does the hospital have the right to peace and quiet? The mayor's ruling could establish who has the property right, but it is more likely that the case would be taken to a court and the court would decide. After many such cases, precedent would establish who has the property rights in future cases.

The property rights will determine who actually pays for the adjustment that remedies the externality. If the candy factory has the right, then the workers can demand some compensation (perhaps free health care services) from the hospital for limiting their noise in the afternoon, or the candy company can demand that the hospital bear some of the cost of the new machinery. If the hospital has the right, then perhaps the hospital staff and patients can get compensated with free candy, or the hospital can ask the candy company to pay for some of the cost of building a thicker wall. The **Coase theorem** states that no matter who is assigned the property rights, the negotiations will lead to an efficient outcome as described in the candy–health care example. The assignment of the property rights determines who pays the compensation.

property rights

Rights over the use, sale, and proceeds from a good or resource.

Coase theorem

The idea that private negotiations between people will lead to an efficient resolution of externalities regardless of who has the property rights as long as the property rights are defined.

Transaction Costs

transaction costs

The costs of buying or selling in a market, including search, bargaining, and writing contracts.

Even if property rights are well defined, for a private agreement like this to occur, transaction costs associated with the agreement must be small compared with the costs of the externality itself. **Transaction costs** are the time and effort needed to reach an agreement. As Coase put it,

> In order to carry out a market transaction, it is necessary to discover who it is that one wishes to deal with, to inform people that one wishes to deal and on what terms, to conduct negotiations leading up to a bargain, to draw up the contract, to undertake the inspection needed to make sure that the terms of the contract are being observed, and so on. These operations are often extremely costly.[2]

Real-world negotiations are clearly time-consuming, requiring skilled and expensive lawyers in many cases. If these negotiation costs are large, then the private parties may not be able to reach an agreement. If the negotiation in the health care–candy example took many years and had to be repeated many times, then it might be better to adopt a simple "no loud noise" rule or an "existing firms get precedence over new arrivals" rule.

The Free-Rider Problem Again

Free-rider problems also can prevent a private agreement from taking place. For example, a free-rider problem might occur if the hospital was very large, say, 400 doctors. Suppose that the candy workers have the right to noise pollute, so that they require a payment in the form of health care. The hospital would need contributions from the doctors to provide the care. Thus, if each doctor worked in the hospital an extra day a year, this might be sufficient.

Any one of those 400 doctors, however, could refuse to work the extra day. Some of the doctors could say that they have other job opportunities that do not require them to work an extra day. In other words, doctors who did not pay could free-ride: They could work at the hospital and still benefit from the agreement. Because of this free-rider problem, the hospital might find it hard to provide health care to the candy workers, and a private settlement might be impossible.

Thus, in the case in which the transaction costs are high or free-rider problems exist, a private remedy may not be feasible. Then the role of government comes into play, much as it did in the case of public goods, in which case the free-rider problem was significant. Again, as Coase put it, "Instead of instituting a legal system of rights which can be modified by transactions on the market, the government may impose regulations which state what people must or must not do and which have to be obeyed."[3]

Command and Control Remedies

When private remedies for externalities are not feasible, either because transaction costs are too high or because of free-rider problems, the government has a role for intervention. One form of government intervention to solve the problem of externalities is the placement of restrictions or regulations on individuals or firms, often referred to as **command and control**. Firms that do not heed these restrictions and regulations are fined for their violations. Command and control methods are used widely by agencies such as the U.S. Environmental Protection Agency (EPA), which is responsible for federal environmental policy in the United States. For example, in the United States, the corporate average fleet efficiency (CAFE) standards require that the fleet of cars produced by an automobile manufacturer each year achieve a stated number of miles per gallon on the average. Another example is a government requirement that electrical utilities put "scrubbers" in their smokestacks to remove certain pollutants from the smoke they emit. Through *commands*, the government *controls* what the private sector does. The government's actions, in principle, make the externalities internal to the firm by requiring that the firm act as if it was taking the external costs into account.

The use of command and control to reduce externalities has many disadvantages, especially in the environmental area. The most significant disadvantage is that command and control does not allow firms to find other, cheaper ways to reduce pollution. For example, under command and control, electrical utilities have to install a scrubber to remove pollutants; they do not have the incentive to discover a cheaper alternative technology that might be more effective at reducing pollution. Similarly, CAFE standards can lead to inefficient production decisions—because firms have to produce smaller, more fuel-efficient cars that they did not want to produce simply to offset the production of the less fuel-efficient SUVs—or to more gasoline consumption because people find that the per-mile cost of driving has fallen because of the higher fuel efficiency, and hence they drive more.

Taxes and Subsidies

Because of the disadvantages associated with command and control, economists recommend alternative techniques to reduce the inefficiencies that result from externalities. The use of taxes and subsidies often is recommended by economists, with goods and services that have negative externalities being taxed while goods and services that have positive externalities are subsidized.

For example, consider the negative externalities that are imposed by drivers. When a city has many drivers, roads become congested, leading to traffic backups and delays. Each driver contributes to the congestion, imposing external costs on the other drivers. In 2003, a new tax, called a congestion charge, was imposed on vehicles that drive in central London during the day. Drivers can pay £8 before they travel or £10 the day after they travel; cameras mounted above the roads check vehicle registration numbers to ensure that the taxes are paid. The idea was to internalize the externality of congestion in central London during rush hour by making drivers pay for the external congestion costs through the tax. If the demand for days of driving in central London is downward sloping, the tax will bring about a cutback in driving in central London, lower the external costs imposed on drivers by reducing congestion, and create government revenue. In fact, the evidence suggests that traffic in central London fell by one-third.

The way that taxes can be used to reduce negative externalities is illustrated graphically in Figure 15.8, which uses the same curves as Figure 15.5. Recall that the marginal social cost of production is greater than the marginal private cost, as viewed from the private firm, because of the negative externality, resulting in the equilibrium quantity produced by the market exceeding the efficient quantity. We know that taxes raise the marginal cost to the individual firm. They thereby

FIGURE 15.7
Big Brother Is Watching Your Car!
Closed circuit television cameras loom above traffic in central London to monitor the license plates of the estimated 250,000 cars entering the city each day. Drivers pay a "congestion charge" to drive in central London, making it more expensive to drive in that area of the city, with the ultimate goal of reducing traffic backups.

Source: Michael Felix Photography/Shutterstock.com

command and control

The regulations and restrictions that the government uses to correct market imperfections.

shift up the market supply curve. If the tax is chosen to exactly equal the difference between the marginal social cost and the marginal private cost, then the quantity produced by the market will decline from the inefficient quantity shown at point *B* to the efficient quantity shown at point *A* in Figure 15.8.

FIGURE 15.8 Using Taxes in the Case of a Negative Externality
A tax equal to the difference between the marginal private cost and the marginal social cost in Figure 15.5 shifts the supply curve up. This reduces the equilibrium quantity produced to the lower, more efficient level.

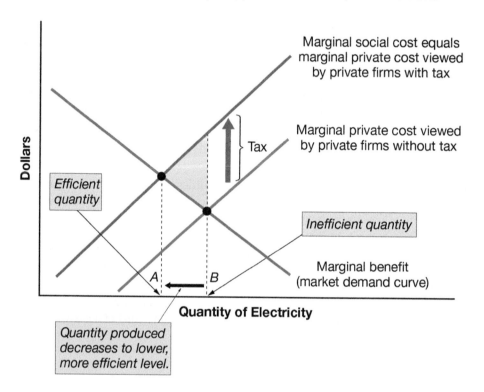

Many examples illustrate the use of taxes in part to reduce pollution. Gasoline taxes reduce gasoline consumption and thus pollution. In the United States, a federal tax is levied of $0.184 per gallon and a variety of state taxes are assessed averaging an additional $0.236 per gallon. The big advantage of taxes or subsidies compared with command and control is that the market is used. Instead of restricting the ratio of SUVs to small, fuel-efficient cars that a producer can manufacture, the government simply raises the relative cost of driving an SUV versus driving a subcompact car by increasing the gasoline tax. If users of SUVs respond by switching over to smaller cars, then the car manufacturer has an incentive to produce smaller cars that consumers actually want to buy, or to research more fuel-efficient SUV engines.

Next, we consider the use of subsidies for goods that have positive externalities. Recall that when a good has a positive externality, too little of it is produced in a competitive economy; a subsidy can be used to increase production and consumption of the good. The Vaccines for Children (VFC) program provides free vaccines for children who are poor and do not have access to health insurance. This program was implemented following an outbreak of measles that killed hundreds of children in the late 1980s. Vaccinations not only protect the child directly, but also produce a positive externality for others who will no longer risk being infected by that child. Government intervention to effectively drive the price of vaccinations to zero through the use of a subsidy will enable more children to be vaccinated and allow parents to internalize the positive externality of having their children vaccinated.

In Figure 15.9, which uses the same curves as Figure 15.6, we demonstrate how a subsidy can be used to encourage the production and consumption of a good with a positive externality. In this case, a subsidy to the user will raise the demand for the good. If the subsidy is chosen to be exactly the difference between the marginal private benefit and the marginal social benefit, then the quantity of the good that is produced and consumed will rise from the inefficient level (*C*) to the efficient level (*D*), as illustrated in Figure 15.9.

FIGURE 15.9 Using Subsidies in the Case of a Positive Externality
A subsidy equal to the difference between the marginal social benefit and the marginal private benefit of education or research shifts the demand curve up. This increases the equilibrium quantity produced to the higher, more efficient level and eliminates the deadweight loss resulting from the externality.

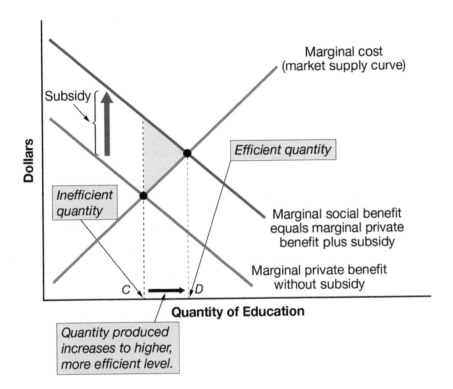

A 2020 research paper by Yale University academics[4] used cross-country data to demonstrate that face mask use slowed the spread of the virus and thus resulted in thousands of dollars of economic value to the country from reduced morbidity and mortality. They also concluded that high quality masks for medical professionals and health care workers would generate millions of dollars in additional benefits. This research, if conclusive, would provide strong arguments for the provision of subsidies to encourage the production and wearing of masks to mitigate the damage caused by the spread of the coronavirus.

Another example of subsidizing positive externalities is the government's funding of research by providing grants to private firms and individuals. The National Science Foundation supports basic research, and the National Institutes of Health support medical research. In supporting research with a limited budget, it is important for the government to place more emphasis on research that has large positive externalities. Many view basic research as having larger positive externalities than applied research. The ideas in basic research, such as that on the structure of the atom, affect many parts of the economy. Applied research, such as that on a new lightweight metal for a bike, has more limited spillover effects, and the products developed through applied research usually can be sold by the creator for profit. In fact, the U.S. federal government does spend more to subsidize basic research than applied research.

Emission Taxes

emission taxes

A charge made to firms that pollute the environment based on the quantity of pollution that they emit.

A more direct way to use taxes to deal with pollution externalities is to tax the firm based on the amount of pollution emitted rather than on the quantity of the potentially polluting good that is produced or consumed. For example, an electrical utility could be charged fees depending on how many particles of sulfur dioxide it emits, rather than on how much electricity it produces. Such charges are called **emission taxes**. These taxes are much like those levied on the amount of the product sold, but they focus directly on the amount of pollution.

Emission taxes have an advantage over taxes on production in that the firm can use technology to change the amount of pollution associated with its production. Thus, rather than producing less electricity, the firm can reduce the amount of pollution associated with a given amount of electricity, if it can find a cheaper way to do so. Emission taxes have an even greater advantage over command and control than a tax on the product has.

Why Is Command and Control Used More Than Taxes?

Many people like one feature of command and control: The total amount of pollution can be better controlled than with a tax. This perceived advantage may explain why command and control is used more than taxes. Suppose, for example, that a tax is used to equate marginal social cost with marginal benefit, as in Figure 15.8. Now suppose that the private cost of producing electricity suddenly reduces. The private marginal cost curve will shift down, and, with the tax unchanged, production (and pollution) will increase. A regulation that stipulates a certain quantity to produce would not have this problem. The total amount of pollution would be fixed. Fortunately, in recent years, a new idea in pollution control has emerged that has both this advantage of command and control and the flexibility of the market. This new idea is tradable permits.

Tradable Permits

tradable permits

A governmentally granted license to pollute that can be bought and sold.

Tradable permits use the market to help achieve the standards set by the government. The way these permits work is as follows. The government decides what limit it wants to impose on the overall level of a particular pollutant. The government then issues a number of permits specifying permissible amounts of pollution. The total amount of pollution in the economy is equal to the total amount specified in the permits issued. If a firm plans to emit more pollutants than it has permits for, it will have to acquire additional permits from other firms. On the other hand, if a firm has more permits than the pollutants it plans to emit, it can sell its permits to another firm that wants them.

Firms now have an incentive to lower their emissions because they can sell the permits if they do not use them. Firms that can lower their emissions cheaply will choose to do so and benefit by selling their permits to other firms for which reducing the pollution is more costly. Tradable permits not only allow the market system to work, but also give firms an incentive to find the least costly form of pollution control. Rather than forcing individual firms to limit the quantity of the pollutant that they can release, tradable permits enable those firms that can reduce the emissions in the most cost-efficient manner to do the bulk of the emissions reduction. Firms that face a high cost of reducing pollution will cut back less on their pollution, but they will have to internalize their pollution costs because of the need to buy permits. Those firms also will have an incentive to adopt technologies that eventually will emit fewer pollutants.

Tradable permits illustrate how important property rights are for resolving externalities. The role of government in this case is to create a market by defining certain rights to pollute and then allowing firms to buy and sell these rights. Once rights are assigned, the market can work and achieve efficiency.

Perhaps the best-known use of tradable permits in the United States has been to reduce emissions of sulfur dioxide. Tradable permits also can work in combating global warming. The amount of global warming depends on the total amount of carbon dioxide emissions in the world's atmosphere. It does not matter whether a firm in Los Angeles or in Shanghai emits the carbon dioxide. Tradable permits could control the total amount of pollution. The permits would let firms or individuals decide on the most cost-effective way to reduce their total amount of pollution.

Balancing the Costs and Benefits of Reducing Externalities

As with public goods, it is important to use cost-benefit analysis when considering how best to intervene in the economy to fix problems caused by externalities. Clear benefits can accrue from reducing pollution, but associated costs can result in the form of lower production, lost jobs, administrative expenses, and so on. These costs should be compared with the associated benefits on a case-by-case basis before deciding on the appropriate intervention method.

For example, the EPA introduced a new rule for stricter standards on the amount of sulfur allowed in diesel fuel in 2000. Environmentalists saw a clear benefit from these new standards because they were concerned that diesel exhaust was causing accelerated cancer rates. On the other hand, trucking companies that use diesel fuel saw a clear cost because the effect of the stricter standards was to raise the price of the fuel needed to run their trucks. The EPA estimated that the new, stricter standards would prevent 8,300 deaths and 360,000 asthma attacks, while increasing the price of diesel fuel by $0.04 to $0.05 per gallon. The oil industry reported that implementation of the stricter standards would cost $8 billion. Policy makers would have to do a cost-benefit analysis to determine whether the additional benefits coming from a stricter standard on sulfur justified the additional costs.

As the following two examples illustrate, policy makers sometimes rule that the benefits justify the costs, whereas at other times they conclude that the costs outweigh the benefits. The first example was the regulation of carbon dioxide emissions, a policy that President George W. Bush had advocated during his 2000 campaign for the presidency. In 2001, President Bush changed his mind about regulating carbon dioxide emissions. A study by the Energy Department showed that this regulation would result in nearly a quadrupling of the cost of producing electricity from coal, causing large price increases for both electricity and natural gas. President Bush stated that the impact on utility prices made the cost of regulating carbon dioxide emissions too high.

The second example relates to stricter standards on the level of arsenic allowed in drinking water that President Clinton imposed shortly before leaving office. In March 2001, the EPA rescinded the new, stricter standard and debated its merits. Scientific studies showed that higher levels of arsenic in drinking water lead to higher risks of fatal cancer, heart disease, and diabetes. The cost of the stricter standard for arsenic in drinking water was estimated at billions of dollars because arsenic is a by-product in mining, is used as a wood preservative for lumber, and occurs naturally in water in some areas. After examining the evidence, the Bush administration decided to impose the stricter standard, convinced that the health benefits were worth the cost.

Some people object to the use of cost-benefit analysis for deciding whether environmental regulations should be implemented. They argue that environmental regulations can benefit rather than cost the economy, because requiring individuals to reduce pollution creates a demand for pollution-reducing devices and creates jobs in the pollution reducing industry. But unless the pollution-reducing equipment is creating a benefit to society greater than the benefits of other goods, shifting more resources to pollution abatement will not be an efficient allocation of society's resources.

In recent years, there has been significant concern about rising pollution levels in other parts of the world, especially in very fast-growing economies like China, India, and Brazil. As more factories start producing goods and services, more forests are cleared to meet the space needs of expanding cities, more power generation is needed to meet the demands of newly electrified homes, more vehicles enter the streets as people spend their rising incomes, and air- and water-pollution problems in these countries become magnified. This poses a dilemma for policy makers because asking these countries to cut back on their rates of economic growth to reduce pollution clearly does not seem like a feasible plan. In fact, many people argue that the surest way to reduce pollution around the world is to ensure that the less-developed economies of the world increase their level of income. This will give them more resources to spend on pollution control.

Environmental economists and policy makers will continue to study these vexing cost-benefit analyses of how to reduce pollution at both local and global levels. What you have learned in this chapter about externalities, public goods, taxes, regulations, tradable permits, and private remedies will play an important role in their deliberations.

Review

- There are four basic ways to improve the efficiency of markets in the presence of externalities: private remedies, command and control, taxes and subsidies, and tradable permits. In each of these approaches, the goal is to get firms to internalize the externality—to change their behavior to take into account the impact their actions have on others.

- Private remedies do not require direct government intervention. The affected parties can negotiate among themselves and efficiently resolve the externalities. The Coase theorem states that as long as property rights are defined clearly, parties will come to an agreement. This approach also requires that transaction costs not be too high and that free-rider problems associated with the settlement be minimized.

- Command and control refers to direct rules and regulations imposed by the government to limit market imperfections. Examples include the imposition of fuel-efficiency standards on auto manufacturers and requirements that coal-burning utilities install scrubbers.

- Taxes and subsidies are considered by economists to be superior to command and control techniques because they use the market to internalize the externality. Taxes of an appropriate magnitude can help reduce the output of goods with negative externalities to the socially efficient level. Similarly, subsidies at an appropriate level can help increase the consumption and production of goods with positive externalities to the socially efficient level.

- Tradable permits are a method of internalizing externalities that economists typically favor. The government can set strict limits on the production of a negative externality, such as a pollutant, by issuing a limited number of permits. By allowing the permits to be traded, however, the reduction in the pollutant can be done efficiently by allowing firms that are able to reduce it at the lowest cost to do the bulk of the reductions. Firms also have incentives to come up with new ways to reduce the externality because they can sell their permits to less efficient producers.

- Regardless of which method is used to eliminate the impact of an externality, policy makers still have to do a cost-benefit analysis of the proposed intervention.

15.4 Models of Government Behavior

The previous two sections outlined what government should do to correct market failure caused by public goods and externalities. Regardless of the reason that market failure occurs, the outcome is similar: Production may be too little or too much, and producer surplus plus consumer surplus is not maximized, resulting in deadweight loss. The role of government is to intervene in the economy to reduce this deadweight loss.

Using economics to explain the role of government in this way is considered a *normative* analysis of government policy. Normative economics is the study of what *should be* done. But another way to look at government policy falls into the area of *positive* economics and looks at what governments *actually do* rather than what they should do.

One of the reasons for studying what governments actually do is that governments sometimes fail because the normative recommendations are ignored or poorly implemented. **Government failure** occurs when the government intervention fails to improve on the market or even makes things worse. One objective of positive analysis of government is to understand why success occurs in some situations and failure results in others.

> **government failure**
>
> The situation in which the government fails to improve on the market or even makes things worse.

Public Choice Models

People run the government. Government behavior depends on the actions of voters, members of political parties, elected politicians, civil servants, and political appointees from judges to cabinet officials. The work of government also depends on the large number of people who lobby and who participate in grassroots campaigns, from letter writing to e-mail messages to political protests. What motivates the behavior of all these people?

The motivations of politicians and government workers are complex and varied. Many people enter politics for genuine patriotic reasons and are motivated by a desire to improve the well-being of people in their city, state, or country, or even the world. Their motivations may be deeper than watching out for their own best interests, narrowly defined.

For example, Alexander Hamilton, the first secretary of the U.S. Department of Treasury, worked hard to put the newly formed country on a firm economic foundation by having the federal government assume the debts of the states after the Revolutionary War. But to get the votes of the Virginia and Maryland representatives for the federal government to assume the debts of the states, Hamilton had to agree to vote to place the capital of the new country along the banks of the Potomac River between the two states, instead of selecting New York City, which was his home base.

At the same time, many other politicians are motivated by their own self-interest. The central idea of economics that people make purposeful choices with limited resources should apply to politics and government, as well as to consumers and firms. Economic models of government behavior are called **public choice models**. They start from the premise that politicians are motivated by increasing their chances of getting themselves or the members of their party elected or reelected. And without explicit incentives to the contrary, government workers are presumed to be motivated by increasing their power or prestige by increasing the size of their department or by getting promoted. By understanding this self-interest, we can learn much about government, including the reasons for government failure and the reasons for government success.

> **public choice models**
>
> Models of government behavior that assume that those in government take actions to maximize their own well-being, such as getting reelected.

The Voting Paradox

Let us first examine how voting is used to make economic policy decisions in a political environment. We will use the assumption of public choice models: that getting elected is the primary motivation of politicians.

Unanimity

Let us start with the easiest case: Only one economic policy decision can be made, and all the voters agree on what that decision should be. For example, suppose that the issue is spending on national defense, a public good for which the government has a key role to play according to the normative economic analysis. Suppose the specific issue is how much to spend on national defense. Some alternatives are shown in Table 15.2.

TABLE 15.2 Alternative Levels of National Defense Spending

National Defense as a Share of Gross Domestic Product	
1 percent	Japan's maximum
2 percent	U.S. in 1940
4 percent	U.S. in 2000
6 percent	U.S. in 2010
10 percent	U.S. in 1960
39 percent	U.S. in 1944

Suppose that everyone agrees that a level of national defense spending of around 4 percent of gross domestic product (GDP) in the United States is appropriate, in the absence of major world political changes such as the events of September 11, 2001. In reality, of course, opinions differ greatly about the appropriate level of spending. But suppose that after looking at history or making international comparisons or listening to experts on defense and world politics, everyone agrees that 4 percent of GDP is the right amount to spend.

Under these circumstances, when all voters agree on only one issue, voting will lead to the action that everyone prefers, that is, 4 percent, even if politicians are motivated by nothing other than getting elected. Suppose that one politician or political party runs for election on a plank of 39 percent defense spending and that the other argues in favor of 2 percent. Clearly, the party with 2 percent will win because it is much closer to the people's views. But then the other politician or party will see the need to move toward the consensus and will run on a 5 percent spending platform. Thus, if the other party stays at 2 percent, then the higher-spending party will win. But clearly the other party then will try to get closer to 4 percent, and eventually 4 percent will be the winner.

This example shows that the political system yields the preferred outcome. Of course, after being elected, the politician might break the promise made during the campaign. But if such a change cannot be justified on the basis of a change in circumstances, that politician may have difficulty getting reelected.

The Median Voter Theorem

What if people have different views? Suppose there is no unanimity about a 4 percent share of GDP for defense. Instead, the country consists of people with many different opinions. Some want more than 4 percent; some want less than 4 percent. Suppose that about half of the people want more than 4 percent and half want less than 4 percent; in other words, 4 percent is the desire of the *median* voter.

If only one issue is on the ballot, the positions of the politicians or the parties will converge toward the median voter's belief. For example, if one party or politician calls for 7 percent spending and the other party calls for 4 percent, then the party calling for 4 percent will attract more voters. The **median voter theorem** predicts that the politicians who run on what the median voter wants will be elected. The views of the people at the extremes will not matter at all.

Convergence of Positions in a Two-Party System

An interesting corollary to the median voter theorem is that political parties or politicians will gravitate toward the center of opinion—toward the median voter. For example, in the case of national defense, it makes no sense for any politician to run on a 39 percent recommendation. The parties will gravitate toward the median voter. This **convergence of positions** may explain the tendency for Democrats and Republicans to take similar positions on some issues. On the other hand, if the political process is changed by gerrymandering to collect scattered groups of partisan voters into a single constituency, then the preferences of median voters in one Congressional district may be starkly different from the preferences of median voters in the adjoining district. This leads to a stark divide between representatives of the two parties, even from the same state.

Voting Paradoxes

When many different issues are on the ballot—defense, taxes, welfare, health care reform—and people have different opinions and views about each of those issues, the outcome of voting becomes more complicated. Certain decision-making problems arise. The example of the **voting paradox** illustrates some of these problems.

Suppose three voters have different preferences on three different economic policy options—A, B, and C. Ali likes A best, B second best, and C the least; Betty likes B best, C second best, and A the least; and Camilla likes C best, A second best, and B the least. The three policy options could be three different levels of defense spending (high, medium, and low) or three different pollution control plans (emission taxes, tradable permits, and command and control). Table 15.3 shows the three voters and their different preferences on each option.

TABLE 15.3 Preferences That Generate a Voting Paradox
Note the paradox: A wins over B and B wins over C, yet C wins over A.

Ranking	Ali	Betty	Camilla
First	A	B	C
Second	B	C	A
Third	C	A	B
In voting on one option versus another, we get:			
On A versus B: A wins 2 to 1			
On B versus C: B wins 2 to 1			
On A versus C: C wins 2 to 1			

Consider three different elections held at different points in time, each with one issue paired up against another. First, an election is held on A versus B, then on B versus C, and then on C versus A. The voting is by simple majority: The issue with the most votes wins. When the vote is on the alternatives A versus B, we see that A wins two to one. That is, both Ali and Camilla like A better than B and vote for it, whereas only Betty likes B better than A and votes for B. When the vote is on B versus C, we see that B wins two to one. Finally (this vote might be called for by a frustrated Camilla, who sees an opportunity), a vote is taken on C versus A, and we see that now C wins two

median voter theorem

This theorem predicts that the politicians who run on what the median voter wants will be elected. The views of the people at the extremes will not matter at all.

convergence of positions

The concentration of the stances of political parties around the center of citizens' opinions.

voting paradox

A situation in which voting patterns will not consistently reflect citizens' preferences because of multiple issues on which people vote.

to one. Although it looked like A was a winner over C—because A was preferred to B and B was preferred to C—we see that in the third vote, C is preferred to A: This is the paradox.

The voting paradox suggests the possibility of instability in economic policies. Depending on how the votes were put together, the policy could shift from high defense to medium defense to low defense, or from one pollution control system to another, then to another, and then back again. Or taxes could be cut, then raised, and then raised again. All these changes could happen with nothing else in the world having changed. We even could imagine shifting between different economic systems involving different amounts of government intervention—from Communism to Capitalism to Socialism to Communism and back again.

This particular voting paradox has been known for 200 years, but only relatively recently have we come to know that the problem is not unique to this example. Kenneth Arrow showed that this type of paradox is common to any voting scheme. That no democratic voting scheme can avoid inefficiencies of the type described in the voting paradox is called the **Arrow impossibility theorem**.

The voting paradox suggests a certain inherent degree of instability in decisions made by government. Clearly, shifting frequently between different tax systems is a source of uncertainty and inefficiency. The voting paradox may be a reason for government failure in cases in which the government takes on some activity such as correcting a market failure.

Arrow impossibility theorem

A theorem that says that no democratic voting scheme can avoid a voting paradox.

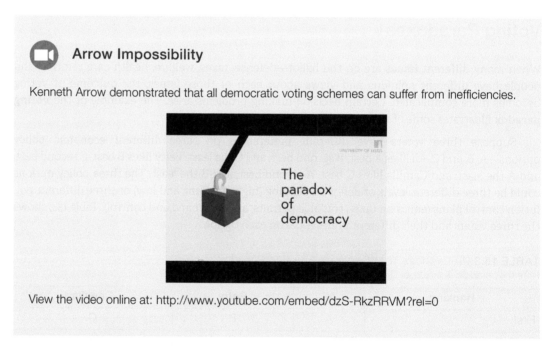

Arrow Impossibility

Kenneth Arrow demonstrated that all democratic voting schemes can suffer from inefficiencies.

View the video online at: http://www.youtube.com/embed/dzS-RkzRRVM?rel=0

Special Interest Groups

The voting paradox is one reason for government failure. Special interest groups are another. It is not unusual for special interest groups to spend time and financial resources to influence legislation. They want policies that are good for them, even if those policies are not necessarily good for the country as a whole. For example, the farming industry has a history of being able to successfully lobby for government intervention in the form of subsidies. If you look back at the reasons for government intervention—income distribution, public goods, and externalities—you will see that they do not apply to the farm sector. Food does not fit the definition of a public good, farming does not have positive externalities, and many farmers who benefit from the intervention have higher incomes than other people in the society who do not benefit from such intervention. One can thus view the government regulation of agricultural markets as a form of government failure.

Concentrated Benefits and Diffuse Costs

One explanation for government failure in such situations is that special interest groups can have powerful effects on legislation that harms or benefits a small group of people a great deal but affects almost everyone else only a little. For example, the federal subsidy to the sugar growers in the United States costs taxpayers and consumers somewhere between $800 million and $2.5 billion per year, or about $3.20 to $10 per consumer per year. The gain from the subsidy, however, amounts to about $136,000 per sugar grower. When a proposal to repeal the subsidy comes before Congress, almost no consumers are going to expend the resources to travel to Washington and support the legislation or even to call up their representatives to encourage them to vote for the repeal; the $3 to $10 benefit is just not worth the time. However, the prospect of losing $136,000 is certainly worth the sugar growers' time and effort. These growers will travel to Washington, lobby representatives vigorously, and contribute to some political campaigns. Because the process of obtaining funds for election or getting support from the powerful interest groups is critical for politicians' reelection chances, these elected officials will be much more likely to listen to those interest groups that have the incentive to lobby and work hard for the policy even if the majority of voters oppose it.

Wasteful Lobbying

Another economic harm results from special interest lobbying. It is the waste of time and resources that the lobbying entails. Lobbyists are usually highly talented and skilled people, and millions of dollars in resources are spent on lobbying for legislation or other government actions. In many less-developed countries—where special interest lobbying is more prevalent than in the United States—such activity consumes a significant amount of scarce resources.

Incentive Problems in Government

In any large government, many of the services are provided by civil servants rather than by politicians and political appointees. In fact, it was to avoid the scandals of the spoils system—in which politicians would reward those who helped in a political campaign with jobs—that the civil service system set rules to protect workers against firing and established examinations and other criteria to qualify workers for jobs.

But what motivates government managers and workers? Profit maximization as in the case of business firms is not a factor. Perhaps increasing the size of the agency or the department of government, rather than an efficient delivery of services, is the goal of managers. Profit motives and competition with other firms also give private firms an incentive to keep costs down and look for innovative production techniques and new products. These incentives do not automatically arise in government; thus, it is likely that a government service, whether a public good or a regulation, will not be provided as efficiently as a good provided by the private sector.

In recent years, economists have suggested incentives to improve the efficiency of government by using market-like incentives, such as more competition. Vouchers—including food stamps, housing vouchers, school vouchers, college tuition grants, and elementary school grants—have been suggested by economists as a way to add competition and improve government efficiency. The successes of these policies often are hotly debated, with both opponents and proponents being able to point to specific cases that bolster their side's arguments.

Review

- Public choice models of government behavior assume that politicians and government workers endeavor to improve their own well-being, much as models of firms and consumer behavior assume that firms and consumers do.

- In cases in which voters have consensus, voting will bring about the consensus government policy. When voters do not have consensus, the median voter theorem shows that the center of opinion is what matters for decisions. In more complex decisions with many options, however, the voting paradox points out that the decisions can be unstable, leading to government failure.

- Other causes for government failure include special interest groups, especially in cases in which policies whose costs are greater but widely distributed while benefits are smaller but more narrowly concentrated are involved. By the use of campaign contributions and lobbying, special interest groups are able to influence politicians to implement policies that are inefficient and run contrary to the wishes of a majority of voters.

- Poor incentives in government also lead to government failure. Government employees may be more interested in enhancing their own power and influence than in carrying out policies that increase societal well-being.

- Economic models of government behavior suggest ways to reduce the likelihood of government failure and increase government efficiency through the use of incentives and competition. The success of these policies remains a hotly debated topic.

15.5 End-of-Chapter Materials

Conclusion

In this chapter, we have explored market failure resulting from public goods and externalities. A competitive market provides too little in the way of public goods, such as national defense, and too little in the way of goods for which positive externalities result, such as education and research. A competitive market results in too much production of goods for which negative externalities arise, such as goods that pollute the environment.

Most of the remedies for market failure involve the action of government. The provision of public goods by the government should require a careful cost-benefit analysis to ensure that the benefits are greater than the cost of producing a public good. Even though private parties can work out externalities by themselves, their ability to do so may be limited by transaction costs and free-rider problems. In that case, the government can intervene by using command and control policies, taxes and subsidies, or tradable permits. In these cases, the main role of the government is to ensure that firms internalize the externalities.

In addition to reaching normative conclusions about government intervention, it is important to consider a positive analysis of government intervention. Doing so requires developing models of government behavior and recognizing the possibility of government failure. In reality, political considerations enter into the production of public goods. To be reelected, a member of Congress from one part of the country might push for a public works project in his or her local district. Moreover, the externality argument emphasized in this chapter is frequently abused as a political device, providing justification for wasteful expenditures. Thus, finding ways to improve decision making in government, such as through market-based incentives, is needed if government is to play its role in providing remedies for market failures.

Key Points

1. Public goods are defined by two key characteristics: nonrivalry and nonexcludability. Nonrival goods are goods for which increased use of the good by one person does not result in decreased use by another. Nonexcludable goods are goods whose use cannot be restricted to only those who have paid for them.

2. The nonexcludable and nonrival aspects of public goods result in the existence of free riders, people who use the good without paying for it. Free riding can explain why the private sector typically will not provide, or will underprovide, public goods. This creates a role for government intervention in the form of government supply of public goods like defense services.

3. Cost-benefit analysis is a technique for deciding how much of a public good should be produced. Measuring benefits is often difficult in the case of public goods. Furthermore, not all goods produced by the government are public goods. Examples in the United States include the postal service and education.

4. Externalities occur when the costs or benefits of a good spill over onto other parts of the economy. They create another potential role for government intervention because the private sector will supply less than the socially efficient quantity of goods with positive externalities, and more than the socially efficient quantity of goods with negative externalities.

5. To move the economy to the socially efficient outcome, producers and consumers of goods with externalities have to be made to internalize those externalities. This can be accomplished in certain cases by private agreements between the affected parties. In other cases, it will require government intervention in the form of regulations and restrictions, taxes and subsidies, or tradable permits.

6. Command and control, or regulations and restrictions imposed by the government on the economy, is the least flexible method of reducing externalities.

7. Taxes on goods with negative externalities and subsidies for goods with positive externalities can either restrict or expand output from the level provided by the market to the socially efficient level.

8. Tradable permits are favored by economists for reducing negative externalities because they allow the government to maintain a tight control on the quantity of the externality-causing good, while allowing the market to play a major role. Firms that can reduce pollution most effectively will do so, and they will be rewarded for their actions by being able to sell permits to firms with a high cost of reducing pollution.

9. Even though public goods and externalities provide a normative theory for government intervention, you also should consider the positive theory of government intervention. Models of government behavior are based on the economic assumption that people try to improve their well-being. They can be used to explain why government failure occurs.

10. The voting paradox, the prominent role of special interest groups, and poor incentives for government employees are some of the other reasons for government failure. Market-like incentives and competition are ways suggested by economists to reduce government failure.

Questions for Review

1. What types of goods are produced or supplied by the government at the federal, state, and local levels?

2. Define the concepts of nonexcludability and nonrivalry, and provide examples of goods that are nonexcludable, nonrival, neither, and both.

3. Define the concept of free riding. How is it related to public goods?

4. What is the use of cost-benefit analysis for governments in deciding whether to supply public goods?

5. What is an externality? What is the difference between a positive externality and a negative externality?

6. What is the Coase theorem? How is it related to externalities?

7. What is the advantage of a system of taxes over command and control as a method of reducing the production of a good with a negative externality?

8. What are the advantages of using a system of tradable permits to reduce pollution?

9. What is government failure? How similar is it to market failure?

10. What are some explanations for why government failure occurs?

Problems

1. Suppose there is a neighborhood crime watch in which people volunteer to patrol the street where you live. If you do not participate in the patrol, but your neighborhood is safer because of the crime watch, are you a free rider? Why? What can your neighbors do to eliminate the free-rider problem?

2. The following table shows the marginal benefit per year (in dollars) to all the households in a small community from the hiring of additional firefighters. The table also shows the marginal cost per year (in dollars) of hiring additional firefighters.

Number of Firefighters	Marginal Benefit for the Community	Marginal Cost ($)
1	1,000,000	34,000
2	500,000	35,000
3	300,000	36,000
4	100,000	37,000
5	70,000	38,000
6	50,000	39,000
7	40,000	40,000
8	30,000	41,000
9	20,000	42,000
10	10,000	44,000

a. Is the service provided by the additional firefighters a public good?

b. Plot the marginal benefit and the marginal cost in a graph, placing the number of firefighters on the horizontal axis.

c. What is the optimal amount of this public good (in terms of the number of firefighters)? Illustrate your answer on the graph in part (b).

d. Is this marginal benefit schedule the same as the town's demand curve for firefighters?

3. Suppose that there are only three households in the town in Problem 2. Each household's marginal benefit (in dollars) from additional firefighters is described in the following table:

Number of Firefighters	Household A ($)	Household B ($)	Household C ($)
1	500,000	300,000	200,000
2	300,000	100,000	100,000
3	200,000	50,000	50,000
4	50,000	30,000	20,000
5	36,000	20,000	14,000

Number of Firefighters	Household A ($)	Household B ($)	Household C ($)
6	25,000	15,000	10,000
7	20,000	14,000	6,000
8	15,000	13,000	2,000
9	10,000	9,000	1,000
10	5,000	4,500	500

a. Plot each of the three marginal benefit schedules and the marginal benefit schedule for the whole town on the same graph, with the number of firefighters on the horizontal axis. (You will need a big vertical scale.) What is the relationship between the three household curves and the curve for the whole town?

b. Consider a system in which the town chooses the optimal amount of the public good and decides to pay for it by taxing each household the identical dollar amount. Which of the households would rather free-ride than pay the taxes, if it were possible to evade paying taxes?

4. Suppose that people value the continued existence of dolphins in the Pacific Ocean, but that tuna-fishing fleets kill large numbers of these mammals. Draw a graph showing the externality. Describe two alternative approaches to remedy the externality.

5. Is public education a public good? Does it have positive externalities? Explain what the implications are for whether public education should be provided by the government. Could the same outcomes be achieved if private education were subsidized by the government?

6. Consider two college roommates, one who smokes and one who does not. The smoker wishes to smoke in the room, and the nonsmoker dislikes smoking in the room. Suppose the smoker would be willing to pay $500 to be allowed to smoke in the room during the semester, and the nonsmoker would be willing to pay $600 to keep the room smoke-free.

a. What would be the socially optimal outcome? Why is it optimal?

b. How might this outcome be achieved by an agreement between the two roommates? What theorem does this illustrate?

c. Suppose that the most the nonsmoker would be willing to pay was $200. Would this change the socially optimal outcome? Why or why not?

7. After the September 11 terrorist attacks, the media paid closer attention to the potential use of shipped cargo containers to smuggle weapons and terrorists into the United States.

a. Discuss why a negative externality may be associated with the use of shipping containers.

b. Graphically show the market for ship transportation of cargo. Make sure you include all the relevant aspects of this market, given your answer to part (a). Explain verbally as necessary.

c. Graphically show any deadweight loss that occurs in this market.

d. Discuss potential ways of reducing or eliminating deadweight loss in this market and the advantages and disadvantages of these remedies, including their impact on other markets.

8. The world's oceans are in trouble. Recently, experts have noted that stocks of fish are declining as the seas' resources are overused. Governments increasingly are becoming interested in ways of preserving fish stocks by limiting the catch. Consider the following four ways of doing so:

- Assign property rights so that each shipping vessel is assigned a specific patch of ocean to catch fish in.
- Tax fishing vessels heavily to reduce the number of such vessels that go out into the ocean.
- Impose strict quotas on the amount of each species that a fishing vessel can catch.
- Issue tradable permits to all fishing vessels such that the sum of the catch allowed by the permits is the desired catch limit.

   a. Which of these do you think is the best way to accomplish the conservation of the resource (fish in the ocean) efficiently? Explain.

9. Use the set of preferences for Ali, Betty, and Camilla shown in the following table to show that the paradox of voting does not always occur.

	Ali	Betty	Camilla
First	A	B	C
Second	B	A	A
Third	C	C	B

10. In recent years, we have heard much about the rise of extremely ideologically rigid attachment of segments of the population to particular political parties. Suppose that 25 percent of the population remains attached to Republicans, no matter what the party does, and a similar fraction stays attached to Democrats, no matter what the party does.

   a. Should this be a cause for concern in that the preferences of these voters will start driving public policy in the United States toward the fringes? Explain.

   b. Would your answer change if you were told that less than half of the U.S. population regularly votes in national elections and that the more ideologically attached voters have a higher likelihood of voting?

Endnotes

1. Robert M. Solow, "It Ain't the Things You Don't Know That Hurt You, It's the Things You Know That Ain't So," *The American Economic Review*, Vol. 87, No. 2, Papers and Proceedings of the Hundred and Fourth Annual Meeting of the American Economic Association (May, 1997), pp. 107-108.

2. Ronald Coase, "The Problem of Social Cost," *Journal of Law and Economics* 3 (October 1960): 15.

3. Ronald Coase, "The Problem of Social Cost," *Journal of Law and Economics* 3 (October 1960): 17.

4. *Abaluck, Jason and Chevalier, Judith A. and Christakis, Nicholas A. and Forman, Howard Paul and Kaplan, Edward H. and Ko, Albert and Vermund, Sten H.,* "The Case for Universal Cloth Mask Adoption and Policies to Increase Supply of Medical Masks for Health Workers" (April 1, 2020). Available at SSRN: https://ssrn.com/abstract=3567438.

CHAPTER 16
Capital and Financial Markets

In this chapter we extend our analysis of markets to *financial markets*, such as the stock market and the bond market, as well as to markets in physical capital, such as housing, office buildings, and factories. These markets have a profound impact on people's lives, especially during times of economic and financial crisis when prices fluctuate wildly.

FIGURE 16.1 The Ups and Downs of Financial Markets
The prices of many financial assets rise and fall substantially over the course of a year, and sometimes even over the course of a day or an hour. These fluctuations result in vast sums of money being gained or lost by the people investing in these markets.

Source: Andrey Burmakin/Shutterstock.com

Figure 16.2 shows why. Each bar in the figure shows how much $1 invested in the stock market back at the beginning of 1987 would have given back to the buyer if sold at the beginning of subsequent years. For example, $1 invested in the stock market in 1987 would have given back $5.35 at the beginning of 2009. That sounds good, but if you had sold the stocks one year before, prior to the huge drop in the stock market in 2008, you would have gotten much more, $8.25. And if you held on after the 2008 crash, you would have gotten back to where you were before the crash by the end of 2012 and reached almost $25 by the end of 2019.

As Figure 16.2 makes clear, although the long-term trend in stock market investments is positive, the market experienced short-term setbacks in 2008 and in other years such as 2001–2003. This volatility is what makes investing in the stock market risky, especially over shorter periods of time. A recent vivid example occurred in March of 2020 when stock prices fell by so much in a single month that they erased all gains accrued from January 2018. However, if an investor did not panic at the end of March and held on for the next two months, the subsequent gains would have brought them back to the level they had reached in December 2019. Whether holding on through and after May or selling off in March was the better decision will only be revealed in hindsight.

FIGURE 16.2 Returns from Investing in the Stock Market
Although the trend is up over several decades, the volatility over shorter periods of time can be dramatic and risky.

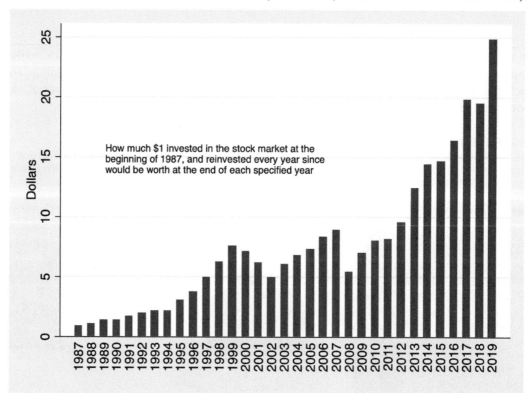

Source: Computed from S&P 500 data available to the public on the website of Prof. Robert Shiller (http://www.econ.yale.edu/~shiller/data.htm).

The returns on individual stocks can be even more volatile. For example, the price of the stock of the financial firm JP Morgan Chase & Co. fell from $53 in April 2007 to a low of $16 in March 2008 and then bounced back to $92 in March of 2017. The price of a share of Marathon Oil fell by almost 50 percent in the early part of 2020 as global oil prices cratered following the COVID-19 pandemic spread. In contrast, the price of a share of stock in the pharmaceutical company Moderna, which is at the forefront of efforts to create a COVID-19 vaccine, tripled over the first few months of 2020 as investors were excited by snippets of news about the success of early vaccine trials. Once again, whether those rumors materialized into an actual vaccine would go a long way in determining in which direction Moderna's stock price would go in the future.

Markets in physical capital also can be volatile, as illustrated in Figure 16.3, which shows the median price of a house in the United States during the same period of time as Figure 16.2. Note that housing prices were stable through most of the 1990s, but they rose rapidly from 2000 to 2006 before coming back down rapidly. By the end of 2008, housing prices had returned to the levels of early 2004. As with the individual stock price, the prices of different houses rise or fall at rates different from the averages, depending on individual and local demand and supply factors. Prices in Michigan did not rise much during the national housing boom, whereas prices rose more rapidly than average in California and Florida. The bust in housing prices in California and Florida was also sharp.

FIGURE 16.3 Housing Boom and Bust

House prices rose rapidly—a boom—until 2006, then fell rapidly—a bust—illustrating how prices in physical capital markets can be as volatile as in financial markets. The recovery in the housing market did not happen until 2013, and prices remain below their pre-crash peak as of 2019.

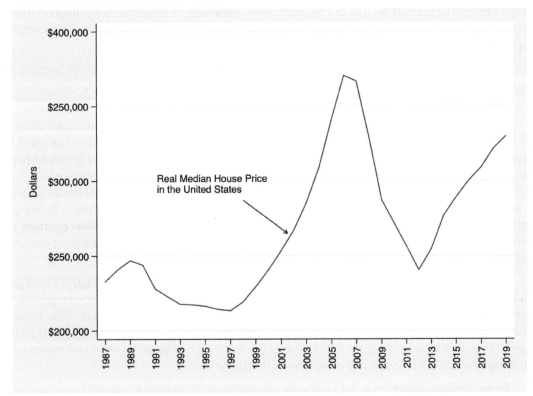

Source: Computed from the Case-Shiller Price Index using the median price of a U.S. house in the year 2018.

We begin by defining physical and financial capital and describing how firms use them. We then consider the specific markets for financial capital, stocks, and bonds, while developing new tools to handle risk and uncertainty.

16.1 The Distinction between Physical Capital and Financial Capital

Some basic terminology about physical and financial capital is useful in studying capital markets. *Physical capital* refers to all the machines, factories, oil tankers, office buildings, and other physical resources used in the production of goods or services. In previous chapters on the behavior of firms, we simply used the term *capital* when referring to "physical capital" because we were not contrasting it with financial capital. Firms combine physical capital with labor inputs to produce goods and services. They obtain physical capital by either building it, buying it, or renting it. For example, McDonald's might hire a construction firm to build a new facility near a highway, a local school district might purchase several hundred computers for use in classrooms, and a real estate developer might rent a construction crane for a year to help move building materials onto the site of a large apartment building project.

An important characteristic of physical capital is that it provides productive services for a number of years. Residential housing—single-family homes, apartments, and trailers—also is a form of physical capital. It provides productive services in the form of living space that people can enjoy year after year. Government-owned roads, schools, and military equipment also are physical capital. It is useful to think of government capital as helping to produce services, whether transportation services, education services, or national security.

Another important characteristic of physical capital is that it does not remain in new condition permanently. The gradual decline in the productive usefulness of capital is called **depreciation**. Trucks, trailers, roads, machines, and even buildings wear out and eventually must be either replaced or refurbished.

To purchase, rent, or build capital, a firm needs to obtain funds. These funds are an example of financial capital. Firms can obtain *financial capital* in two different ways: by issuing debt (borrowing) and by issuing equity (selling an ownership stake in the firm).

When a firm takes out a loan, it agrees to pay back the amount it borrowed plus interest at a future date. The amount of interest is determined by the *interest rate*. If the amount borrowed is $10,000 and is due in one year and the interest rate is 10 percent per year, then the borrower pays the lender $11,000 at the end of the year. The $11,000 includes the *principal* on the loan ($10,000) plus the *interest payment* ($1,000 = 0.1 times $10,000). Larger firms also can issue *corporate bonds*. A bond is an agreement by the issuer to make a specified number of payments in the future in exchange for a sum of money today. Both loans and bonds are a type of contract called a **debt contract** in which the lender agrees to provide funds today in exchange for a promise that the borrower will pay back the funds at a future date with interest.

Firms are not the only entities that take out debt contracts. Most people who buy a house get a **mortgage**, which is a loan of funds to purchase real estate. In addition, many people get loans from banks to buy cars and consumer appliances. The biggest single issuer of bonds in the United States is the federal government. The federal government borrows funds by selling *government bonds*. State and local governments also issue bonds to finance physical capital investments like building a new public school, fixing a highway, or building a tunnel.

Firms also can obtain financial capital by issuing *stock*, or shares of ownership in the firm. Shares of ownership are a type of contract called an **equity contract**. The purchaser of an equity contract acquires an ownership share in the firm that typically is proportional to the size of the equity contract. In contrast to a debt contract, in which case the payment by the firm (the interest payment) does not depend on the profits of the firm, in an equity contract the payment by the firm does depend on the firm's profits. Firms that make lots of profits will pay out more in *dividends* to their shareholders. Shareholders also can benefit if the firm increases in value because their shares will be worth more when they are sold.

Once bonds or stocks have been issued, they can be exchanged or traded. Highly organized financial markets trade stocks and bonds. The government and corporate bond markets are located in New York City, London, Tokyo, and other large financial centers. The stock markets include the New York Stock Exchange, the Nasdaq, several regional stock exchanges in the United States, and many stock exchanges in other countries.

Having defined some key terms, we now proceed to discuss the different types of capital markets. We begin with markets for physical capital.

depreciation

The decrease in an asset's value over time; for capital, it is the amount by which physical capital wears out over a given period of time.

debt contract

A contract in which a lender agrees to provide funds today in exchange for a promise from the borrower, who will repay that amount plus interest at some point in the future.

mortgage

A loan to purchase a house.

equity contract

Shares of ownership in a firm; payments to the owners of the shares depend on the firm's profits.

Review

- Physical capital and financial capital are distinct but closely related. Physical capital refers to the machines, buildings, and physical resources needed to produce output. To expand their physical capital, firms need to raise funds in some way. These funds are known as financial capital.
- Firms can buy, build, or rent physical capital. They can acquire financial capital by means of debt contracts or equity contracts.
- Debt contracts, such as bonds or loans, allow borrowers access to a sum of money today in exchange for a promise to repay that sum of money plus interest in the future. Equity con-

tracts allow firms to obtain money today in exchange for handing over an ownership stake in the firm.

- The bonds or stocks that firms issue can be traded. Organized markets for trading bonds and stocks are found in all the world's financial centers.

16.2 Markets for Physical Capital

The demand for physical capital is a relationship between the quantity of capital demanded by firms and the price of this capital. The demand for capital is a *derived demand* in the same sense that the demand for labor is a derived demand; that is, the demand for capital derives from the goods and services that firms produce with capital. In this section we show that just as the quantity of labor that the firm employs depends on the marginal revenue product of labor, the quantity of capital that the firm employs depends on the marginal revenue product of capital.

Rental Markets

The firm's capital decision is best understood if we first assume that the firm rents capital in a competitive rental market. In fact, it is common for firms to rent capital; many types of equipment have a rental market in which many rental firms specialize in renting the equipment to other firms. For example, a construction firm can rent a dump truck; a clothing store can rent a storefront at a mall; an airline can lease an airplane. The price in the rental market is called the **rental price of capital**. It is the amount that a rental firm charges for the use of capital equipment for a specified period of time, such as a month.

Consider a hypothetical construction company, called Lofts-R-Us, deciding whether to rent a dump truck from a rental company called Acme Truck Rental. To show how much capital a firm like Lofts-R-Us would rent, we need to consider the effect of this capital on the firm's profits. The marginal revenue product of capital can be used to assess this effect on profits. The **marginal revenue product of capital** is defined as the change in total revenue as the firm increases its capital by one unit. We assume that the marginal revenue product of capital declines as more capital is employed at the firm. For example, suppose the marginal revenue product of capital is $3,000 as capital rises from zero trucks to one truck, $1,500 as capital rises from one truck to two trucks, and $500 as capital rises from two trucks to three trucks.

Suppose the rental price of a dump truck is $1,000 a month. This price is what Acme Truck Rental charges, and all other rental firms in the area charge essentially the same price. Because the rental market is competitive, neither Acme Truck Rental nor Lofts-R-Us has enough market power to affect the rental price. How many dump trucks would Lofts-R-Us use? With the marginal revenue product of capital from one dump truck equal to $3,000 a month, the firm will employ at least one dump truck. In other words, if the firm's total revenue increases by $3,000 and the rental price for the truck is $1,000, then it makes sense to rent the dump truck. With the marginal revenue product of capital from a second dump truck equal to $1,500, the firm will employ a second dump truck; by doing so, it can increase its profits by $500. With the marginal revenue product of capital from a third dump truck equal to only $500, however, the firm will lower its profits if it rents a third dump truck. Thus, if the rental price of the dump truck is $1,000, the firm will employ exactly two dump trucks. The firm rents the largest amount of capital for which the marginal revenue product of capital is greater than the rental price; if fractional units of capital were possible, then the firm would

rental price of capital

The amount that a rental company charges for the use of capital equipment for a specified period of time.

marginal revenue product of capital

The change in total revenue because of a one-unit increase in capital.

keep renting more capital until *the marginal revenue product of capital was exactly equal to the rental price.*

The Demand Curve for Capital

To derive the demand curve for capital, we must determine the quantity of capital demanded by the firm as the rental price of capital changes. For example, if the rental price of dump trucks declines to $400, then the quantity of dump trucks demanded by the firm will increase; a third dump truck will be rented because the price is now below the marginal revenue product of capital. In other words, as the rental price of capital falls, the quantity of capital demanded increases. Similarly, as the rental price of capital rises, the quantity of capital demanded decreases.

Figure 16.4 illustrates this general principle. It shows the marginal revenue product of capital for any firm. As more capital is employed, the marginal revenue product declines. For profit maximization, the firm will rent capital to the point at which the marginal revenue product of capital equals the rental price. Thus, as we lower the rental price, the quantity of capital demanded increases. In other words, the demand curve for capital is downward sloping.

FIGURE 16.4 Demand for Physical Capital by One Firm
A profit-maximizing firm chooses a quantity of capital that gives a marginal revenue product of capital equal to the rental price. Because the marginal revenue product of capital declines as more capital is used, a lower rental price of capital results in a larger quantity of capital demanded.

The demand curve for capital is determined by the marginal revenue product of capital. If the marginal revenue product changes, the demand curve for capital will shift. For example, if the marginal product of dump trucks rises, the demand for dump trucks by Lofts-R-Us will shift outward.

Demand for Factors of Production in General

Observe that the marginal revenue product of capital equals the rental price. This same principle applies to any factor of production for which the market in that factor is competitive. *For any input to production, a profit-maximizing firm will choose a quantity of that input such that the marginal revenue product equals the price of that input.*

The Market Demand and Supply

The market demand for physical capital is found by adding up the demand for physical capital by many firms. Figure 16.5 shows such a market demand curve.

FIGURE 16.5 Market Supply and Demand for Physical Capital
The market demand for capital is the sum of the demands of the individual firms that use the equipment. The market supply is the sum of the supplies at the individual firms that provide the equipment. Market equilibrium occurs in cases in which the quantity of capital demanded equals the quantity of capital supplied.

On the same diagram, we show the market supply curve. It is the sum of the supply curves for all the firms in the industry providing capital for rent, such as Acme Truck Rental. The higher the rental price of capital, the more likely Acme Truck Rental is to buy new dump trucks and offer them as rentals to firms like Lofts-R-Us. If other rental firms behave the way that Acme Truck Rental does, then the market supply of rental capital will be increasing with rental prices.

The equilibrium rental price and the equilibrium quantity of capital rented are shown in the diagram. The supply and demand model for capital illustrated in Figure 16.5 then can be used to predict the effects of tax changes or other changes in the capital market in much the same way as any other supply and demand model. For example, if the government places a tax on construction firms like Lofts-R-Us proportional to the quantity of trucks they rent, perhaps because the heavy trucks damage city roads more than cars do, then the marginal revenue product of capital will decline and the demand curve for capital will shift down, or to the left. This shift in demand will lower the equilibrium rental price received by Acme and reduce the quantity of capital rented. Alternatively, if the city government is eager to have new apartment buildings in the city, it may offer a subsidy on the rental of capital by construction firms. This would shift the demand curve for capital up, or to the right, and increase the quantity of capital rented.

The Case of Fixed Supply: Economic Rents

An important special case of a market for physical capital occurs when the supply of physical capital is completely fixed. Alfred Marshall gave the following famous example of physical capital with a completely fixed supply: "Let us suppose that a meteoric shower of a few thousand largest ones harder than diamonds fell all in one place, so that they were all picked up at once, and no amount of search could find any more. These stones, able to cut every material, would revolutionize many branches of industry."[1]

The important thing about Marshall's stones is that their supply cannot be increased or decreased regardless of the price of the stones. In other words, the supply curve for Marshall's stones is perfectly vertical, or perfectly inelastic, as shown in Figure 16.6.

FIGURE 16.6 The Case of a Fixed Supply of Capital
When the supply of capital is perfectly inelastic, a shift in demand changes the rental price but not the quantity supplied. Marshall's stones are a hypothetical example of capital with a perfectly inelastic supply.

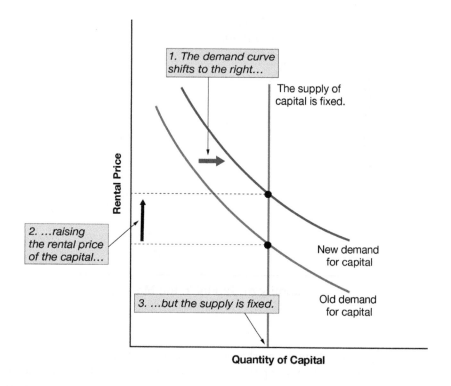

Figure 16.6 shows what happens when the demand for capital that is in fixed supply shifts, such as Marshall's stones. A change in demand will change the price, but it will not change the quantity. Demand completely determines the price in this case because the quantity supplied cannot change.

economic rent

The price of something that has a fixed supply.

Economists have a special terminology for the price in this circumstance: **economic rent** is the price of anything that has a fixed supply. Economic rent is also sometimes called *pure rent*. Economic rent is a significant concept in economics precisely because the quantity supplied does not depend on the price. Thus, a tax on economic rents would not change the amount supplied; it would not affect economic efficiency or cause a dead weight loss. For example, if the government passed a tax (even a 99.9 percent tax) on the rental payments charged by the lucky owners of Marshall's stones, the quantity of stones supplied would not change.

Marshall's stones are of course a hypothetical example. In practice, certain types of land may come close to being an item in fixed supply, but it is always possible to improve land or clear land and thereby change its supply to some degree. The perfectly inelastic supply of Marshall's stones or the near perfectly inelastic supply of certain types of land is in sharp contrast to the higher elasticity of supply of most capital goods. The supply of dump trucks, apartment buildings, and other types of capital is sensitive to changes in the price. Increases in the price provide an incentive to increase the quantity supplied, and decreases in the price provide an incentive to decrease the quantity supplied. In reality, therefore, taxes on capital would be expected to change the quantity of capital supplied.

📹 Economic Rents

Economic rent will occur when an asset or good has a fixed supply.

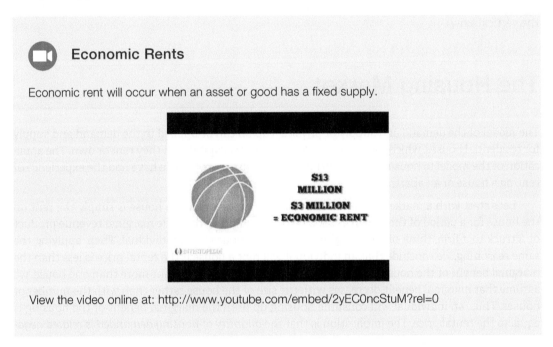

View the video online at: http://www.youtube.com/embed/2yEC0ncStuM?rel=0

The Ownership of Physical Capital

Rental markets for capital are common, but they are not the only way in which firms obtain capital. The same construction firm that rents dump trucks might choose to purchase and own a dump truck rather than rent one, especially if it expects to continually be engaged in projects for which a truck is required. The firm also may own the warehouse where it stores its building materials and the office where it keeps its books and meets prospective customers. Although legal and tax differences exist between renting and ownership, the economic principles are similar. In fact, even though owners of physical capital do not pay a rental price, economic considerations indicate that they pay an *implicit* rental price.

When a firm buys equipment, it must either borrow funds to pay for the equipment or use its own funds, funds that it could have put in an interest-earning account at a bank. If it borrows the funds, the monthly interest payment on the loan is like a rental payment. If it uses its own funds, the interest it would have received at the bank is an opportunity cost and is considered to be similar to a rental payment. In addition to these payments, the firm that owns the equipment must factor in the wear and tear, or depreciation, on the equipment. The amount by which the firm's equipment deteriorates is also a cost.

implicit rental price

The cost of the funds used to buy the capital plus the depreciation of the capital over a given period of time.

In sum, for a firm that chooses to purchase and own capital, the **implicit rental price** of capital for a year equals the interest payments for the year plus the amount of depreciation during the year. For example, suppose the interest rate is 10 percent, the purchase price of a dump truck is $40,000, and the dump truck depreciates $8,000 per year. Then the implicit rental price is $12,000 per year (0.10 times $40,000, plus $8,000), or $1,000 a month, the same as the rental price in our dump truck example. The implicit rental price depends on the interest rate. The higher the interest rate, the higher the interest payments during the year, and thus the higher the implicit rental price. When the interest rate rises, the implicit rental price rises. When the interest rate falls, the implicit rental price falls.

The concept of the implicit rental price makes the firm's decision to buy a dump truck, or any other piece of capital, analogous to the decision to rent. The demand curve looks the same as that in Figure 16.4, except that it is the implicit rental price rather than the actual rental price that is on the vertical axis.

The Housing Market

The model of the demand and supply of physical capital can be applied to the demand and supply for residential houses, which for many people is the largest capital item they rent or own. The application of the model to housing is straightforward because many people have had the experience of renting a house or an apartment.

Let's start with a market for rental housing. The rental price of a house is simply the rent on the house for a period of time, such as $500 per month. Rather than the marginal revenue product of a truck to a firm, think of the marginal benefit of a house to an individual. Then, applying the same reasoning, we conclude that an individual will rent a house if the rental price is less than the marginal benefit of the house to the individual. Because few people rent more than one house, we assume that marginal benefit decreases with the size of the house rather than with the number of houses. Thus, an individual will consume housing up until the marginal benefit of the housing is equal to the rental price. The implication is that the *quantity of housing demanded is related negatively to the rental price of housing.*

Finally, by adding up all the individual demand curves, we get a market demand for housing. In the housing market as a whole, the higher the rental price on houses, the lower the quantity of houses demanded. Hence, *the demand curve for housing is sloped negatively.* The supply curve of housing is analogous to the supply curve for other kinds of capital. Rather than the Acme Truck Rental company, we might have the Acme Student Apartment Rental company. The concepts are similar.

To move from markets in which people rent their homes to markets in which people own their homes, we can use the implicit rental price concept. For a house owned by an individual or a family, the *implicit rental price* will equal the interest rate on the mortgage (the loan on the house) plus the amount of depreciation on the house during the year. The quantity of housing demanded depends negatively on the implicit rental price. Hence, we have a demand for housing that looks just like the demand curve in Figure 16.5.

Observe that because the quantity of housing demanded depends negatively on the implicit rental price, it also depends negatively on the mortgage interest rate. Hence, if mortgage interest rates decline, we would predict an increase in the demand for housing. Indeed, many experts think a major reason for the housing boom during the years leading up to the housing bust in 2006 was that mortgage interest rates were low. The theory thus explains important trends in housing markets.

Review

- The demand for physical capital at a firm is a derived demand. What firms are willing to pay for capital depends on the value of the goods and services they can produce with that capital.
- Firms that rent capital will choose to rent capital up to the point at which the marginal revenue product of capital equals the rental price of capital.
- The marginal revenue product of capital decreases as the quantity of capital used by the firm increases. So when the rental price goes down, the firm will want to add extra machines until the marginal revenue product of capital equals the rental price.
- If capital is purchased rather than rented, the firm still faces an implicit rental price.
- The demand curve for purchased capital, then, looks similar to the demand curve for rental capital; the demand curve is downward sloping in the (implicit) rental price.
- The theory also implies a demand curve for housing and offers an explanation for the housing boom in 2002–2006.

16.3 Markets for Financial Capital

Having seen how markets for physical capital work, let us turn to the examination of markets for financial capital. As we discussed, firms that want to acquire physical capital need to obtain financial capital. They can obtain financial capital by issuing stocks and bonds. Stocks and bonds are traded on financial markets. Their prices are determined by the actions of buyers and sellers, like prices in any other market. Understanding what drives the prices of stocks and bonds is important for determining firms' ability to acquire financial capital. It is also important for investors who buy stocks and bonds as a way to save for their future retirement or simply as a way to make money.

Stock Prices and Rates of Return

return

The income received from the ownership of an asset; for a stock, the return is the dividend plus the capital gain.

capital gain

The increase in the value of an asset through an increase in its price.

capital loss

The decrease in the value of an asset through a decrease in its price.

dividend yield

The dividend stated as a percentage of the price of the stock.

rate of return

The return on an asset stated as a percentage of the price of the asset.

earnings

The accounting profits of a firm.

price-earnings ratio

The price of a stock divided by its annual earnings per share.

Prices of the stocks of most large firms can be found in daily newspapers. Investors are interested in buying those stocks whose prices are likely to rise and that are more likely to pay back their profits to shareholders in the form of dividends. We can define the annual **return** from holding a stock as the *dividend* plus the *capital gain* during the year. The **capital gain** during the year is the increase in the price of the stock during the year. A **capital loss** is a negative capital gain: a decrease in the price. When comparing dividends across companies, we typically look at the **dividend yield**, that is, the dividend stated as a percentage of the price. Similarly, in comparing returns across companies, we typically look at the **rate of return**, that is, the return stated as a percentage of the price of the stock.

A simple example can illustrate these terms. For example, suppose you had purchased a share of stock in the giant communications technology company Verizon at the end of 2018 and held the stock for one year. The cost of a share of Verizon stock at the end of 2018 was $56.22. The dividend for Verizon in 2019 was $2.42 per year. At the purchase price of $56.22, the dividend yield was 4.30 percent. During 2019, the price of Verizon stock rose from $56.22 to $61.40, a capital gain of $5.18. Combined with the dividend, the total return was $7.60, a rate of return of 13.5 percent on the original $56.22 purchase price. In this example, the capital gain is a much bigger portion of the rate of return than the dividend.

Check the result. *The dividend was $2.42. The closing price was $56.22. Dividing 2.42 by 56.22 gives 0.043, or 4.3 percent.*

But stock market returns are not always as good as in this example. Consider what happened to Verizon's stock price in 2008, when it fell from $43.69 to $33.90 per share, a *negative* capital gain or a capital loss of $9.79. Including the $1.67 in dividends it paid during the year, Verizon's total return was negative $8.12, which would represent a rate of return of negative 18.5 percent for someone who purchased the share at the end of 2007. 2008 was not a good year for stocks. The stock price of Caterpillar, the famous maker of large-scale construction equipment, fell from $72.56 to $44.67 during the year. Including a $1.56 dividend payout, its return was negative 36.3 percent. Indeed, the average stock price of all the 500 major U.S. companies—as measured by the Standard and Poor's (S&P) 500 Index—fell by 38.5 percent during 2008, which substantially cut into gains made in the previous two decades, as shown in Figure 16.2.

You can figure out which firms are the most profitable, and hence more likely to generate a high rate of return for their shareholders, by looking at firms' accounting profits, also known as **earnings**. Firms pay out some of their profits as dividends; the rest of the profits are retained and invested in physical capital or research. Stock tables list the **price-earnings ratio**: the price of the stock divided by the annual earnings per share. The price-earnings ratio for Verizon in 2019 was 13.20. With the year-end price of the stock at $61.40, this means that earnings for the year were $4.65 per share ($61.40/$4.65 = 13.20). A firm's earnings ultimately influence the return on the firm's stock, so the price-earnings ratio is watched closely.

Stock Markets React to Government Policy Changes

Watch this video for an explanation of why financial markets react to government policy changes.

View the video online at: http://www.youtube.com/embed/WjGa8DzVTno?rel=0

Bond Prices and Rates of Return

Bond prices for both corporate and government bonds also can be found in the financial pages of the newspaper. A bond has four key characteristics: *coupon, maturity date, face value,* and *yield*. The **coupon** is the fixed amount that the borrower agrees to pay the bondholder each year. The **maturity date** is the time when the coupon payments end and the principal is paid back. The **face value** is the amount of principal that will be paid back when the bond matures. Consider a $1,000 face value bond issued in 2019 that has a maturity date of February 2049 and a coupon equal to 1.75 percent of the face value of the bond. That is, the bond will pay 1.75 percent of the $1,000 face value, or $17.50, a year, until 2049, and in February 2049, the $1,000 face value will be paid back.

Once the government has issued bonds, they can be sold or bought in the bond market. In the bond market, bond traders make a living buying and selling bonds. The bond traders will *bid* a certain price at which they will buy, and they will *ask* a certain price at which they will sell. The bid price is slightly lower than the ask price, which enables the bond traders to earn a profit by buying at a price that is slightly lower than the price at which they sell.

The **yield to maturity**, sometimes shortened to yield, is defined as the annual rate of return on the bond if the bond were bought at the current price and held to maturity. Are bond yields the same as the coupon rate? An inverse, or negative, relationship exists between the yield to maturity and the price. They have an inverse relationship because the payments of the bond are fixed—the borrower (bond issuer) agrees to pay back the lender (bondholder) the principal on the maturity date and make coupon payments in the interim—regardless of what the buyer paid for the bond. The higher the price you pay today to get this fixed stream of interest and principal payments in the future, the lower the rate of return (yield to maturity) you earn. So unlike the coupon rate, which stays fixed, the yield to maturity will fluctuate with price. Furthermore, as the price rises, the yield to maturity will fall, and vice versa.

Here is a typical quote on bond yields: *"The price of the 30-year Treasury bond rose less than 1/8 point, or less than $1.25 for a bond with $1,000 face value, to 84 4/32. Its yield, which moves in the opposite direction of its price, dropped to 7.60 percent from 7.61 percent on Thursday."*

Why do bond yields fluctuate? Consider a simple example. Suppose you just bought a one-year bond for $100 that says that the government will pay 5 percent of the face value, or $5, plus $100 at

coupon

The fixed amount that a borrower agrees to pay to the bondholder each year.

maturity date

The date when the principal on a loan is to be paid back.

face value

The principal that will be paid back when a bond matures.

yield to maturity

The annual rate of return on a bond if the bond were held to maturity.

the end of the one-year period. Now suppose that just after you bought the bond, interest rates on bank deposits suddenly jumped to 10 percent. Your bond says that you earn 5 percent per year, so if you hold it for the entire year, your rate of return is less than you could get on a bank deposit. Suddenly the bond looks much less attractive. You probably would want to sell it, but everyone else knows the bond is less attractive, also. You would not be able to get $100 for the bond. The price would decline until the rate of return on the bond was close to the interest rate at the bank. For example, if the price fell to $95.45, then the payment of $105 at the end of the year would result in a 10 percent rate of return [that is, $0.10 = (105 - 95.45)/95.45$]. In other words, the yield to maturity on the bond would rise until it reached a value closer to 10 percent than to 5 percent.

If you look at a table listing the yields of government bonds, you will notice bonds maturing in 2020 with very high coupon rates: an example is a 30-year U.S. government bond maturing in February 2020 that had a coupon rate of 8.5 percent. This bond was issued at a time (1990) when market interest rates were higher. As interest rates in the United States fell, people found that holding the bond was a more attractive proposition than keeping money in the bank, so they bid up the price of the bond, driving down the yield to maturity until it approached the new market interest rates in the United States. This implies that periods of falling interest rates are good for bond holders and bond issuers because the prices of their bonds rise, while periods of rising interest rates are bad for both bond holders and bond issuers.

On the basis of these considerations, we can use a formula to calculate the relationship between the price and the yield to maturity for bonds of any maturity. Let P be the price of the bond. Let R be the coupon. Let F be the face value. Let i be the yield. The formula relating to the price and the yield in the case of a one-year bond is indicated in the first row of Table 16.1.

TABLE 16.1 Bond Price Formula

One-year maturity:	$P = \dfrac{R}{(1+i)} + \dfrac{F}{(1+i)}$
Two-year maturity:	$P = \dfrac{R}{(1+i)} + \dfrac{R}{(1+i)^2} + \dfrac{F}{(1+i)^2}$
Three-year maturity:	$P = \dfrac{R}{(1+i)} + \dfrac{R}{(1+i)^2} + \dfrac{R}{(1+i)^3} + \dfrac{F}{(1+i)^3}$
For very long term:	$P = \dfrac{R}{i}$

P = price of bond; R = coupon; F = face value; i = yield

For a one-year bond, a coupon payment of R is paid at the end of one year together with the face value of the bond. The price P is what you would be willing to pay *now, in the present*, for these future payments. It is the *present discounted value* of the coupon payment plus the face value at the end of the year. By looking at the formula in the first row of Table 16.1, you can see the negative relationship between the price (P) of the bond and the yield to maturity (i) on the bond. The higher the yield to maturity, the lower the price; and conversely, the lower the yield to maturity, the higher the price.

A two-year-maturity bond is similar. You get R at the end of the first year and R plus the face value at the end of the second year. Now you want to divide the first-year payment by $1 + i$ and the second-year payment by $(1 + i)^2$. The formula still shows the inverse relationship between the yield to maturity and the price. A bond with a three-year or longer maturity is similar. Computers do the calculation for the news reports, so even 30-year bond yields can easily be found from their price.

We can use a convenient and simple approximation method to determine the price or yield on bonds with very long maturity dates. It says that the price is equal to the coupon divided by the yield to maturity: $P = R/i$. This formula is the easiest way to remember the inverse relationship between the price and the yield to maturity. It is a close approximation for long term bonds like the 30-year bond.

Review

- Firms that want to purchase physical capital need financial capital to do so. They obtain financial capital by issuing stocks and bonds. Stocks and bonds are traded on financial markets.
- The return from holding stock is the dividend plus the change in the price. The rate of return is equal to the return measured as a percentage of the price of the stock.
- The return from holding bonds to maturity is the yield to maturity of the bond. Bond yields and bond prices move in opposite directions.
- Periods of falling interest rates are good for bond holders and bond issuers because the prices of bonds rise, while periods of rising interest rates are bad for both bond holders and bond issuers.

16.4 The Trade-off between Risk and Returns

One of the hallmarks of financial markets is volatility. The prices of individual stocks and bonds rise and fall over time. Over the long run, stock prices show a positive trend, but there are periods of significant decline from time to time, and the prices of individual stocks traded in the financial markets are volatile. Similarly, even though you always can earn a rate of return equivalent to the yield by holding a bond issued by the U.S. government to maturity, in the interim, the price of the bond will vary.

If you had bought stock in United Airlines in the summer of 2007 you would have paid around $45 a share. By the following summer, however, shares in United Airlines were trading around $4 a share, so you would have lost almost 90 percent of your investment. On the other hand, if you had held on to the stock for another decade, the price would have been almost $88 a share, a 22-fold increase from the depths it had sunk to in 2007. Because of such variability, buying stocks is a risky activity. Even the broad S&P 500 Index fell by 38.5 percent in 2008. The price of bonds can also change by a large amount. For example, from mid-1996 to mid-1997, the price of government bonds rose by nearly 20 percent, but from mid-1993 to mid-1994, the price of government bonds *fell* by nearly 20 percent. Thus, government bonds are also a risky investment.

In this section, we show that the riskiness of stocks and bonds affects the decision of people to trade in financial markets. To do so, we first examine how individuals behave when they face risk.

Behavior under Uncertainty

Most people do not like uncertainty. They are *risk averse* in most of their activities. Given a choice between two jobs that pay the same wage, most people will be averse to choosing the riskier job where there is a good chance of being laid off. Similarly, given a choice between two investments that pay the same return, people will choose the less risky one.

Let us examine this idea of risk aversion further. To be more precise, suppose that Melissa has a choice between the two alternatives shown in Table 16.2. She must decide what to do with her life savings of $10,000 for the next year. At the end of the year, she plans to buy a house, and she will need some money for a down payment. She can put her $10,000 in a bank account, where the interest rate is 5 percent, or she can buy $10,000 worth of a stock that pays a dividend of 5 percent and will incur either a capital gain or a capital loss. In the bank, the value of her savings is safe, but if she buys the stock, she has a 50 percent chance that the price of the stock will fall by 30 percent and a 50 percent chance that the price of the stock will rise by 30 percent. In other words, the risky stock will leave Melissa with the possibility of a return of negative $2,500 (a loss) or a return of $3,500 (a gain). The bank account leaves her with a guaranteed $500 return.

TABLE 16.2 Two Options: Different Risks, Same Expected Return

Low-Risk Option	High-Risk Option
A bank deposit with	*A corporate stock with either*
5 percent interest (return = $500)	a. A 5 percent dividend and a 30 percent price decline ($500 - $3,000 = -$2,500)
	b. A 5 percent dividend and a 30 percent price increase ($500 + $3,000 = $3,500)

expected return

The return on an uncertain investment calculated by weighting the gains or losses by the probability that they will occur.

Both of the options in Table 16.2 have the same **expected return**. The expected return on an investment weights the different gains or losses according to how probable they are. In the case of the safe bank account, there is a 100 percent chance that the return is $500, so the expected return is $500. In the case of the stock, the expected return would be negative $2,500 times the probability of this loss (1/2) plus $3,500 times the probability of this gain (also 1/2). Thus, the expected return is $500 (-2,500/2 + 3,500/2 = -1,250 + 1,750 = 500), the same as the return on the bank account.

The expected return is one way to measure how attractive an investment is. The word *expected* may appear misleading, because in the risky option $500 is not "expected" in the everyday use of the word. You do not expect $500; you expect either a loss of $2,500 or a gain of $3,500. If the term is confusing, think of the expected return as the average return that Melissa would get if she could take the second option year after year for many years. The losses of $2,500 and gains of $3,500 would average out to $500 per year after many years. (The term *expected return* has been carried over by economists and investment analysts from probability and statistics, in which case the term *expected value* is used to describe the mean, or the average, of a random variable.)

Given that the expected returns are the same, if Melissa is a risk-averse person (that is, if she would dread a capital loss more than she would cherish a capital gain of a similar magnitude), she will choose the less risky of these two options. Although it is clear that Melissa would choose the less risky of the two options in Table 16.2, perhaps Melissa would accept some compensation to offset her risk aversion. Although most people are averse to risk, they are willing to take on some risk if they are compensated for it. In the case of a risky financial investment, the compensation for higher risk could take the form of a higher expected return.

How could we make Melissa's expected return higher in the risky investment? Suppose Melissa had the choice between the same safe option as in Table 16.2 and a high risk stock that paid a dividend of 20 percent. This new choice is shown in Table 16.3; the difference is that the risky stock now offers a dividend of 20 percent, much greater than the 5 percent in the first example and much greater than the 5 percent on the bank account. With the greater chance of a higher return on the stock, Melissa might be willing to buy the stock. Even in the worst situation, she loses just $1,000, which may still leave her with enough for the down payment on her new house. The expected return for the high-risk option is now $2,000, much greater than the $500 for the bank account (-1,000/2 + 5,000/2 = -500 + 2,500 = 2,000).

TABLE 16.3 Two Options: Different Risks, Different Expected Returns

Low-Risk Option	High-Risk Option
A bank deposit with	*A corporate stock with either*
5 percent interest (return = $500)	a. A 20 percent dividend and a 30 percent price decline ($2,000 - $3,000 = -$1,000)
	b. A 20 percent dividend and a 30 percent price increase ($2,000 + $3,000 = $5,000)

In other words, Melissa probably would be willing to take on the risky investment. And if the 20 percent dividend in the example is not enough for her, some higher dividend (25 percent? 30 percent?) would be. This example illustrates the general point that risk-averse people are willing to take risks if they are paid for it.

Before we develop the implication of our analysis of individual behavior under uncertainty, we should pause to ask about the possibility that some people might be risk lovers rather than risk avoiders. The billions of dollars that are bet in state lotteries in the United States and in private gambling casinos in Las Vegas, Atlantic City, and Monte Carlo indicate that some people enjoy risk. With few exceptions, however, most of the gambling on lotteries, slot machines, and even roulette wheels represents a small portion of the income or wealth of the gambler. Thus, you might be willing to spend $0.50 or even $5 on lottery tickets or a slot machine for the chance of winning big, even if the odds are against you. Many people get enjoyment out of such wagers; but if the stakes are large compared with one's income or wealth, then few people want to play. For small sums, some people are risk lovers, but for large sums, virtually everybody becomes a risk avoider to some degree or another.

FIGURE 16.7 Playing It Safe?
Most people are risk-averse when it comes to large sums, but many are risk lovers when the stakes are low or when they can limit their potential losses—such as at casinos where people can choose to gamble a set amount or combine gambling with entertainment.

Source: IVASHstudio/Shutterstock.com

Risk and Rates of Return in Reality

What are the implications of our conclusion that investors will be willing to take risks if they are compensated with a higher return on the stock or bond? In the stock market, the prices of individual stocks are determined by the bidding of buyers and sellers. Suppose a stock, AOK, had a price that gave it the same expected rate of return as a bank account. Now AOK, being a common stock, clearly has more risk than a bank account because its price can change. Hence, no risk averse investor will want to buy AOK. Just as Melissa will prefer to put her funds in a bank account in the example in Table 16.2, rather than into the risky option, investors will put their funds in a bank rather than buy AOK. People who own shares of AOK will sell and put their funds into a bank. With everybody wanting to sell AOK and no one wanting to buy it, the price of AOK will start to fall.

Now, the price and the expected rate of return are inversely related—recall that for a stock, the rate of return is the return divided by the price. Thus, if the price falls and the dividend does not change, the rate of return will rise. This fall in the price will drive up the expected rate of return on AOK. As the expected rate of return increases, it eventually will reach a point at which it is high enough to compensate risk-averse investors. In other words, when the expected rate of return rises far enough above the bank account rate to compensate people for the risk, the price fall will stop. We will have an equilibrium, at which point the expected rate of return on the stock is higher than the interest rate on the safe bank account. The higher rate of return will be associated with the higher risk.

Now some stocks are more risky than others. For example, the risk on the stocks of small firms tends to be higher than the risk on the stocks of larger firms, because small firms tend to be those that are just starting up. Not having yet proved themselves, small firms have a higher risk. People like Melissa will sell the more risky stocks of smaller companies until the expected rate of return on those stocks is high enough compared with the less risky stocks of larger companies.

In equilibrium, we therefore expect to see a positive relationship between risk and the expected rate of return on securities. Securities with higher risks will have higher returns than securities with lower risks. Figure 16.8 shows the resulting **equilibrium risk-return relationship**.

equilibrium risk-return relationship

The positive relationship between the risk and the expected rate of return on an asset, derived from the fact that, on average, risk-averse investors who take on more risk must be compensated with a higher return.

FIGURE 16.8 The Equilibrium Relationship between Return and Risk
More risky securities tend to have higher returns on average over the long term. For example, bank deposits are low risk and have a low expected return. Corporate stocks are higher risk—their price fluctuates—but on average over the long term have a higher return. The higher return is like a compensating wage differential in the labor market. It compensates those who take on more risk.

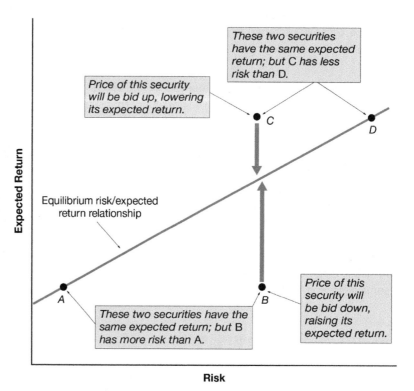

There is probably no more important lesson about capital markets than this relationship. Individual investors should know it well. It says that to get a higher rate of return *on average over the long run*, you have to accept a higher risk. Again, the market forces at work are the same as the ones that led to the compensating wage differentials in the labor market. In the labor market, the higher wage in some jobs is the price that workers accept to take on the greater risk, or, more generally, the less pleasant aspects of the job.

Risk and Rates of Return in Theory

In reality, this theoretical relationship works very well. A tremendous amount of data over long periods of time on the financial markets support this relationship. The most widely cited evidence was compiled by Roger Ibbotson of Yale University who tabulated data, shown in Table 16.4, on the average return over many years for the four important types of securities we have mentioned in the theoretical discussion. The most risky of the four—the stocks of small firms—has the highest rate of return. The next highest in risk are the common stocks of large firms. The least risky—short-term U.S. Treasury bills that are as safe as bank deposits—has the smallest rate of return. Long-term bonds, for which price changes can be large, have a rate of return greater than that of U.S. Treasury bills. Although the relative risks of these four types of securities may seem obvious, a measure of the differences in the sizes of their price volatility is shown in the second column and confirms the intuitive risk rankings. In general, Table 16.4 is a striking confirmation of this fundamental result of financial markets that higher expected rates of return are associated with higher risk.

TABLE 16.4 Average Rates of Return for Different Risks

	Average Rate of Return per Year (percent)	Risk (average size of price fluctuations)
U.S. Treasury bills	3.7	3.1
Long-term government bonds	5.9	9.5
Large-company stocks	11.9	20.4
Small-company stocks	16.7	32.6

Source: © 2011 Morningstar, Inc. All Rights Reserved. Reproduced with permission. The information contained herein: (1) is proprietary to Morningstar and/or its content providers; (2) may not be copied or distributed; (3) does not constitute investment advice offered by Morningstar; and (4) is not warranted to be accurate, complete or timely. Neither Morningstar nor its content providers are responsible for any damages or losses arising from any use of this information. Past performance is no guarantee of future results. Use of information from Morningstar does not necessarily constitute agreement by Morningstar, Inc. of any investment philosophy or strategy presented in this publication. *Note:* These rates of return are for 1926-2010 and are not adjusted for inflation. The average rate of inflation was 3.1 percent, which can be subtracted from each of the average returns to get the real return. The risk is the "standard deviation," a measure of volatility commonly used in probability and statistics.

Diversification Reduces Risk

The familiar saying "Don't put all your eggs in one basket" is particularly relevant to stock markets. Rather than a basket of eggs, you have a portfolio of stocks. A portfolio is a collection of stocks. Putting your funds into a portfolio of two or more stocks, whose prices do not always move in the same direction, rather than one stock is called **portfolio diversification**. The risks from holding a single stock can be reduced significantly by putting half your funds in one stock and half in another. If one stock falls in price, the other stock may fall less, may not fall at all, or may even rise.

Holding two stocks in equal amounts is the most elementary form of diversification. With thousands of stocks to choose from, however, diversification is not limited to two. Figure 16.9 shows how sharply risk declines with diversification. By holding ten different stocks rather than one, you can reduce your risk to about 30 percent of what it would be with one stock. If you hold some international stocks, whose behavior will be even more different from that of any one U.S. stock, you can reduce the risk even further. Mutual fund companies provide a way for an investor with only limited funds to diversify by holding 500 or even 5,000 stocks along with other investors. Some mutual funds—called *index funds*—consist of all the stocks in an index like the S&P 500 Index.

portfolio diversification

Spreading the collection of assets owned to limit exposure to risk.

FIGURE 16.9 Risk Declines Sharply with Diversification
By holding more than one stock, risk can be reduced. By holding 10 U.S. securities, the risk is reduced to 30 percent of the risk of holding one security. Diversifying internationally permits one to reduce risk further. (The risk is measured by the standard deviation.)

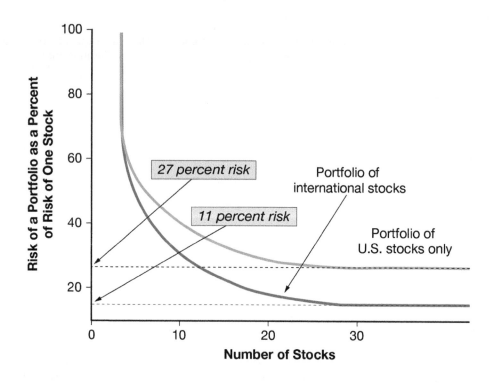

Portfolio Diversification

A portfolio of assets with low correlation reduces the risk of the portfolio.

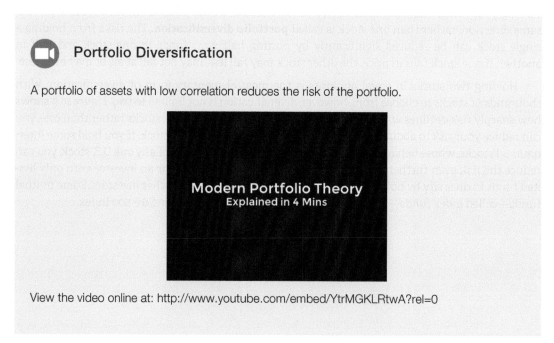

View the video online at: http://www.youtube.com/embed/YtrMGKLRtwA?rel=0

Efficient Market Theory

The shares of firms' stock on the market can be traded quickly at any time of day. For most large and medium-size companies, some people are always willing to buy and sell. If people hear that Intel has made a discovery that is expected to raise its profits, they rush to buy Intel stock. If people suddenly learn about a decline in a company's profits or about losses, then people rush to sell that company's stock. This rush to buy and sell changes prices instantaneously, so that the price adjusts rapidly to good news or bad news. The rapid adjustment means that unexploited profit opportunities are rare for regular investors without inside information or a special ability to anticipate news, whether good or bad. The **efficient market hypothesis** states that profit opportunities are eliminated in financial markets as stock prices adjust quickly to new information. Rates of return greater than those resulting from the price of risk disappear soon after any good news about a stock appears.

Many tests over the years have found the efficient market hypothesis to be a close approximation of security price determination. It has led to the growth in popularity of index funds, for which investors do not pay advisers to tell them when to buy and sell stock. They simply invest in a fund that includes a large number of stocks.

> **efficient market hypothesis**
>
> The idea that markets adjust rapidly enough to eliminate profit opportunities immediately.

Review

- Financial markets are volatile; both stock prices and bond prices tend to rise and fall over time. The riskiness of bonds and stocks affects the willingness of people to buy and sell these financial assets, and hence, affects their return.
- We can calculate the expected return of a risky asset by weighting the possible gains and losses by the probability that these gains or losses will occur. Given the choice between a risky asset and a safe asset that have the same expected return, an individual who is risk averse always will choose the safe asset.
- Risk-averse investors will hold risky assets only if they are compensated in the form of a higher expected return. Thus, when buyers and sellers trade stocks or bonds in the market, a relationship between return and risk emerges: Higher risk is associated with higher returns.
- Investors can reduce risk by diversifying their portfolio, that is, by holding many different stocks. Mutual funds and index funds offer diversification opportunities even to investors who have little money to put into the stock market.
- Earning stock returns in excess of those justified by the greater level of associated risk is difficult. The efficient market hypothesis predicts that stock prices adjust quickly to eliminate such lucrative return opportunities.

16.5 Corporate Governance Problems

When corporations issue stock to buy physical capital or to start up operations, a separation between the owners of the corporation—the stockholders—and the managers of the corporation is created. This separation leads to incentive problems—the manager might not act in the interest of the shareholder. Here we show how these problems can be analyzed with a theory called *asymmetric information theory*.

Asymmetric Information: Moral Hazard and Adverse Selection

asymetric information

Different levels of information available to different people in an economic interaction or exchange.

moral hazard

In insurance markets, a situation in which a person buys insurance against some risk and subsequently takes actions that increase the risk; analogous situations arise when other markets have asymetric information.

adverse selection

In insurance markets, a situation in which the people who choose to buy insurance will be the riskiest group in the population; analogous situations apply in other markets.

Consider a start-up firm. When an entrepreneur at a start-up firm obtains financial capital by issuing stock, a special relationship is formed. Those who supplied the financial capital by buying the stock become owners or at least part owners of the company. If the entrepreneur does well and the company is successful, they reap large returns. But shareholders of a firm have less information than the managers about the firm. This difference in information, called **asymetric information**, can cause several problems. First, the manager might not act in the interest of the owners. Taking unnecessary business trips on the company's aircraft to exotic places or not working hard to find the right employees is harmful to the shareholders' interests. This is sometimes called **moral hazard**, a term borrowed from research on the insurance industry, for which asymmetric information is also a problem. Moral hazard in insurance occurs when people are less careful about trying to prevent fires after they get fire insurance. In the case of the firm, the manager may be less careful about the firm after the shareholders' or investors' funds have been obtained.

Another problem is that those entrepreneurs who have more risky projects would seek equity financing—for which dividend payments to shareholders would be optional—rather than debt financing, for which interest payments are required. This is called **adverse selection**, yet another term borrowed from insurance. In insurance, adverse selection occurs, for example, when people who are unhealthy select health insurance while healthy people do not. In this case, managers who have more risky projects elect equity financing more often than those who have less risky projects. This makes potential shareholders or investors less willing to supply funds to equity markets.

Incentives to Overcome Adverse Selection and Moral Hazard Problems

profit-sharing

Programs in which managers and employees receive a share of profits earned by the firm.

One way in which problems of moral hazard and adverse selection can be limited is through the use of **profit-sharing** agreements, whereby managers are given a share of the profits earned by the firm. That way, the managers of the firms have a financial stake in the firm's success, and hence, their interests are aligned with the shareholders' interests—agents gain when the principal gains and agents lose when the principal loses.

Another way to overcome the problems caused by moral hazard and adverse selection is for shareholders to get together and take over the company so that the problematic management team can be replaced. The mere threat of such a takeover can be an incentive for management to act in shareholders' interest rather than their own. *Private equity* firms like the Blackstone Group specialize in buying shares of a public company and taking it private, so that they can replace the existing management with managers who presumably can improve the firm's performance.

Such takeovers also have been criticized. Some say that the threat of being bought out by a hostile takeover firm or a private equity firm leads management to adopt a more shortsighted attitude toward the operation of the company's affairs than is ideal. Companies also expend considerable resources constructing "takeover defenses," which attempt to make it more difficult for outsiders to use a hostile takeover to take control of the firm.

FIGURE 16.10 A Shareholder Meeting: Principals, Agents, and Asymmetric Information

Theories of corporate governance view a firm's shareholders (shown in the crowd) as the principals and the managers (shown on the stage) as the agents. Management incentive plans such as profit sharing are seen as ways to foster good management performance when the principals have little information about what the *agents* actually do—a situation called *asymmetric information*.

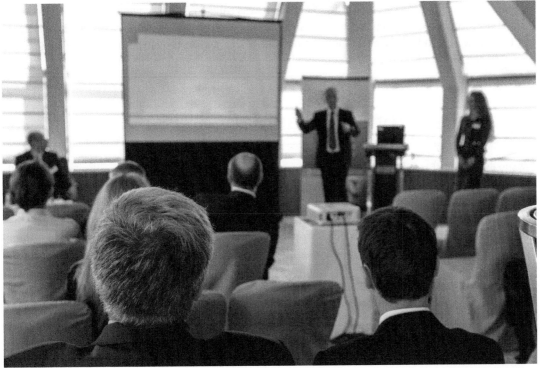

Source: Elena11/Shutterstock.com

Review

- Managers of a firm usually know more about the firm than the shareholders. This asymmetric information causes moral hazard—in which the firm's managers may run the firm less efficiently than the shareholders would want.

- Profit sharing—in which the managers share in the profits of the firm or in the returns to holding the stock—is a way to prevent moral hazard.

16.6 The Role of Government in Financial Markets

Government policy has a role to play in financial markets. Poor governance which takes the extreme form of outright fraud is illegal under U.S. law. Indeed, managers who commit fraud against their shareholders are prosecuted and sent to jail if they are caught; the Federal Bureau of Investigation has a whole division on the lookout for such crimes.

One common type of fraud in financial markets—securities fraud—occurs when managers lie or misreport facts about the firm's financial statements or the firm's profitability to entice investors to buy or hold their stock. The Securities and Exchange Commission (SEC) has responsibilities for such securities violations. It also regulates certain investment management firms, such as mutual funds, under the Investment Act of 1940 to promote accurate financial reporting.

One glaring example of fraud arose in the case of Bernard Madoff, who ran an investment company with responsibility for managing billions of dollars of his clients' money. His fraudulent scheme cost his investors a reported $50 billion. It was called a *Ponzi scheme*, in which his existing investors' returns were paid using his new investors' funds rather than from legitimate investments in the stock or bond markets. Madoff was sentenced to prison for 150 years in June 2009. Some accused the SEC for failing in its responsibility to detect this fraud long before it became so big.

Examples from a Financial Crisis

Many examples of mismanagement and fraudulent action can be found during the financial crisis in 2007 and 2008. Indeed, some analysts think that such actions were in part responsible for the crisis. For example, mortgage loans were offered to high-risk individual homeowners who were unlikely to make the interest payments. The resulting high risk mortgages were then sold to other financial institutions, whose managers apparently were unaware of the risks. When the homeowners with these mortgages stopped making their payments, the financial institutions found the mortgages were nearly worthless. In the meantime, the originators were far from the scene and no longer accountable. As a result, the risk at these financial institutions rose; they were reluctant to make more loans or they charged much higher interest rates on the loans, which added to the crisis.

Another possible role for government is to intervene to prevent the failure of large financial institutions and thereby prevent instability in the financial markets. Indeed, during 2008, the federal government intervened in several ways by loaning or investing funds to help some of these financial institutions. The expectation of such intervention can cause its own form of moral hazard, however, if investors expect the government always to rescue them. This expectation will reduce the incentives they have to manage risks themselves. Moreover, government intervention can cause uncertainty and perhaps make matters worse, an example of government failure.

Consider the financial panic of 2008. Although the financial crisis had been going on for more than a year, it suddenly worsened into a full-fledged sell-off in the fall of 2008. The S&P 500 Index fell from 1,255 on September 19 to 899 on October 10, a decline of 28 percent in three weeks, a staggering loss for many people.

Many argued that the panic was caused by the U.S. government's decision not to intervene to prevent the bankruptcy of a financial institution, Lehman Brothers, which then led to expectations of more failures and instability. An examination of the timing of stock price movements, however, shows that the answer is more complicated. Figure 16.11 focuses on a few key dates and events, including the panic itself, which is marked with the brackets.

FIGURE 16.11 Stock Prices during the Panic

The S&P 500 Index fell by nearly 30 percent, but was it the result of the Lehman bankruptcy or the government actions?

Source: Computed from daily S&P 500 data available to the public on many sites such as Yahoo Finance.

Monday, September 15, is the day that Lehman declared bankruptcy after learning over the previous weekend that the government would not provide funds to pay its creditors and keep it open. You can see that the stock market moved down a bit, but it then bounced back up on September 16. By the end of the week, the S&P 500 was virtually the same as it was one week earlier, so the decision to let Lehman Brothers go bankrupt apparently was not what caused the panic. But if not, then what was the cause?

On Friday of that same week, the U.S. Treasury announced that it was going to propose a large rescue package for the entire U.S. banking system, although the size and details were not determined. During the weekend, the package was put together; on Tuesday, September 23, Federal Reserve Board Chairman Ben Bernanke and Treasury Secretary Henry Paulson testified in the Senate about the package, which they called the Troubled Assets Relief Program(TARP). They said it would be enormous, $700 billion, yet provided few details and made no mention of oversight or restrictions on the use. They were questioned intensely and the reaction was quite negative. Members of Congress received a large volume of critical mail.

As shown in Figure 16.11, following this poorly received testimony, the crisis seriously deepened, as measured by the sharp fall in the stock market for the next three weeks. It is plausible that events around September 23 increased risks and drove the markets down, including the realization by the public that the intervention plan had not been fully thought through and that conditions were much worse than many had been led to believe. A great deal of uncertainty about what the government would do to aid financial institutions, and under what circumstances, was revealed. Such uncertainty would have driven up risk and thereby driven down the market. Clarity about the TARP improved on October 13 when the government announced it would buy shares in banks with the TARP money. The panic ended at that time.

Government Regulation of Financial Institutions

Financial institutions—especially banks—are the most heavily regulated firms in the United States. The main rationale for the federal government to regulate banks is that the federal government guarantees the deposits that people hold at the banks. If the bank takes on too much risk and fails as a result, then the deposit holders will be paid off, subject to certain limits, by the government. Because taxpayer money is at risk, the government has responsibility for ensuring that the banks do not put too much risk on the taxpayers.

The government does this by issuing regulations that require that the banks' capital, including the dollar amount of shares held by shareholders, to be above a certain fraction of the bank's loans and other investments. This ensures that the shareholders will pay before the government in the case of large loan losses. The government also supervises the banks to ensure that the loans they hold do not exceed certain risk levels.

In the United States, the banks are regulated by the Office of the Comptroller of the Currency, the Federal Reserve System, and in some cases the state governments. It is now clear that many banks—including the large Citicorp, headquartered in New York City—took on too much risk in the years leading up to the financial crisis, and this has raised questions about the effectiveness of the regulation and supervision. People ask why hundreds of government regulators on the premises of banks like Citicorp did not see or report such risks or take actions to limit the risks. Because of these concerns, many of the regulations were changed in legislation passed in 2010 after the financial crisis. But economists and others debate whether the new legislation actually will improve the effectiveness of the regulation and supervision.

One concern is that the operations of the financial institutions are too complex for government regulators to monitor. Another concern is that government supervisors are too close to the management of the banks, a form of regulatory capture in which the regulators are "captured" by the banks and tend to overlook certain risky activities.

Indeed, a book published in 2011 by Gretchen Morgenson and Joshua Rosner, *Reckless Endangerment: How Outsized Ambition, Greed, and Corruption Led to Economic Armageddon*, argues that such cozy relationships were responsible for the risks taken leading up to the financial crisis. The authors give many examples of cases in which government officials took actions that benefited banks and other financial institutions and showed that these individuals in turn helped the government officials. This mutual support system thwarted good economic policies and encouraged reckless ones. It thereby brought on the crisis, sending the economy into a deep recession.

Moral Hazard and the Financial Crisis

During the financial crisis, corporations which contributed to the financial crisis were rescued through government bailouts.

View the video online at: http://www.youtube.com/embed/0mq4-fNCbhY?rel=0

Review

- The government has a role to play in the financial markets, including enforcing the law against securities fraud.
- The government also has a role to play in regulating and supervising financial firms that can cause a risk to taxpayers or the economy.
- In considering the role of government in financial markets, however, the possibility of government failure also must be considered.

16.7 End-of-Chapter Material

Conclusion

This chapter has used some basic economic tools to analyze capital and financial markets. In reviewing the chapter, it is helpful to see how the key results apply to you personally.

First, by diversifying a portfolio of stocks, you can reduce risk substantially. Conversely, by holding an undiversified portfolio, you are needlessly incurring risk.

Second, remember the efficient market hypothesis that profit opportunity disappears quickly in financial markets. Instead of buying and selling securities frequently, you may be better off investing in a mutual fund.

Third, if you do try to pick your own portfolio rather than use a mutual fund, concentrate on areas with which you are familiar. If you go into a medical career, you may know more than even the best investors about the promise of a new medical device or drug.

Fourth, over the short run, holding corporate stocks is more risky than putting your funds in a bank account, but over the long term, the higher rate of return on stocks outweighs the risks for most people. If you need money in the short term—to pay next year's tuition, for example—stocks may not be worth the risk. Years like 2008 during which stocks fall by as much as 38 percent are a reminder of these risks.

Key Points

1. Physical capital refers to the physical resources used to produce goods and services.
2. Financial capital, which includes stocks and bonds, is used by firms to obtain funds to invest in physical capital.
3. A firm's demand for physical capital is a derived demand. A firm will use capital up to the point at which the marginal revenue product of capital equals the rental price.
4. The supply and demand for capital determines the rental price or the implicit rental price. Tax and subsidy policies that affect the demand for capital goods will affect both the equilibrium rental price of capital and the equilibrium quantity of capital used by firms.
5. Firms raise money for investing in physical capital by issuing stocks and bonds. Once issued, the stocks and bonds trade on financial markets.
6. The rate of return on stocks is equal to the dividend plus the change in the price as a percentage of the price. The rate of return on bonds held to maturity is the yield of the bond.
7. The rate of return on stocks tends to rise when firms have higher earnings, which are either paid out in the form of dividends or reinvested in the company. The rate of return on bonds tends to rise in periods during which market interest rates are falling.
8. Stock markets and bond markets tend to be extremely volatile. To understand how the riskiness of these assets affects their return, we need to understand how investors behave. Risk-averse investors will buy more risky stocks or bonds only if the expected rate of return is higher.
9. In market equilibrium, a positive relationship exists between risk and rate of return. If you want to get a higher rate of return, you have to accept higher risk.
10. Diversification helps reduce risk. Even individuals with limited resources can diversify their portfolios by investing in mutual funds.

Questions for Review

1. What is the difference between physical capital and financial capital?
2. How is the relationship between the marginal revenue product of capital and the rental price related to the firm's decision to rent additional units of physical capital?
3. Why is the quantity of physical capital demanded negatively related to the rental price of capital?
4. How does the implicit rental price of capital depend on the interest rate and depreciation?
5. What is the difference between a stock and a bond?
6. What determines the rate of return on stocks? On bonds?
7. What does it mean for an individual to be risk averse?
8. How do the actions of risk-averse individuals influence the relationship between risk and return in financial markets?
9. What is diversification? How does it affect risk?
10. What do economists mean when they say that financial markets are efficient?

Problems

1. Which of the following are physical capital, and which are financial capital?

   a. A Toyota Camry at Avis Car Rental.

   b. A loan you take out to start a newspaper business.

   c. New desktop publishing equipment.

   d. A bond issued by the U.S. government.

   e. A pizza oven at Pizza Hut.

2. Suppose that Marshall's stones were dropped all over the earth and finding them was difficult.

   a. Would the supply curve for capital still be perfectly inelastic?

   b. Would there be economic rent?

3. Suppose a company owns a computer that costs $5,000 and depreciates $1,000 per year.

   a. If the interest rate is 5 percent, what is the implicit rental price of the computer?

   b. Explain why the implicit rental price depends on the interest rate.

4. The U.S. government issues a one-year bond with a face value of $1,000 and a zero coupon.

   a. If the yield is 10 percent, what will the market price of the bond be?

   b. Now suppose you observe that the bond price falls by 5 percent What happens to its yield?

5. Suppose a two-year bond has a 5 percent coupon and a $1,000 face value, and the current market interest rate is 5 percent.

   a. What is the price of the bond?

   b. Now suppose that you believe that the interest rate will remain 5 percent this year, but next year will fall to 3 percent. How much are you willing to pay for the two-year bond today? Why?

6. Consider the following possibilities for your stock market investment portfolio.

	Good Market	Bad Market	Disastrous Market
Probability	0.50	0.30	0.20
Rate of return	0.25	0.10	-025

   a. What is the expected return of this stock market investment portfolio?

   b. Would you choose this expected return or take a safe return of 7 percent from a savings deposit in your bank? Why?

   c. Suppose your teacher chooses the safe return from the bank. Is your teacher risk averse? How can you tell?

7. You are considering the purchase of stocks of two firms: a biotechnology corporation and a supermarket chain. Because of the uncertainty in the biotechnology industry, you estimate that there is a 50–50 chance of your either earning an 80 percent return on your investment or losing 80 percent of your investment within a year. The food industry is more stable, so you estimate that you have a 50–50 chance of either earning 10 percent or losing 10 percent.

   a. Which stock would you buy if you were a risk-averse individual? Why?

   b. What do you think other investors (most of whom are risk averse) would do?

   c. What would be the effect of these actions on the relative prices of the two stocks?

8. Graph the data on risk and expected return (in percent) for the following securities.

Asset	Expected Rate of Return	Risk
Bank deposit	3	0
U.S. Treasury bills	4	3
Goodcorp bonds	9	10
ABC stock	11	24
XYZ	13	24
Riskyco stock	16	39

Draw an equilibrium risk-return line through the points.

   a. Which two assets should have changes in their prices in the near future?

   b. In which direction will their prices change?

9. Suppose a study indicated that stock prices usually were lower during the holiday season than during the rest of the year. What would be the likely reaction of the market?

10. Suppose you have $10,000 and must choose between investing in your own human capital or investing in physical or financial capital.

   a. What factors will enter into your decision-making process?

   b. How much risk will be involved with each investment?

   c. What would you do? Why?

16.8 Appendix: Present Discounted Value

A dollar in the future is worth less than a dollar today. This principle underlies all economic decisions involving actions over time. Whether you put some dollars under the mattress to be spent next summer, borrow money from a friend or family member to be paid back next year, or are a sophisticated investor in stocks, bonds, or real estate, that same principle is essential to making good decisions. Here we explain why the principle is essential and derive a formula for determining exactly *how much* less a dollar in the future is worth than a dollar today. The formula is called the *present discounted value formula.*

Discounting the Future

First let's answer the question, why is the value of a dollar in the future less than the value of a dollar today? The simplest answer is that a dollar can earn interest over time. Suppose a person you trust completely to pay off a debt gives you an IOU promising to pay you $100 in one year: How much is that IOU worth to you today? How much would you be willing to pay for the IOU today? It would be less than $100, because you could put an amount less than $100 in a bank and get $100 at the end of a year. The exact amount depends on the interest rate. If the interest rate is 10 percent, the $100 should be worth $90.91. If you put $90.91 in a bank earning 10 percent per year, at the end of the year you will have exactly $100. That is, $90.91 plus interest payments of $9.09 ($90.91 times 0.1 rounded to the nearest penny) equals $100.

The process of translating a future payment into a value in the present is called **discounting**. The value in the present of a future payment is called the **present discounted value**. The interest rate used to do the discounting is called the **discount rate**. In the preceding example, a future payment of $100 has a present discounted value of $90.91, and the discount rate is 10 percent. If the discount rate were 20 percent, the present discounted value would be $83.33 (because if you put $83.33 in a bank for a year at a 20 percent interest rate, you would have, rounding to the nearest penny, $100 at the end of the year). The term *discount* is used because the value in the present is less than the future payment; in other words, the payment is "discounted," much as a $100 bicycle on sale might be "discounted" to $83.33.

discounting

The process of translating a future payment into a value in the present.

present discounted value

The value in the present of future payments.

discount rate

An interest rate used to discount a future payment when computing present discounted value.

Finding the Present Discounted Value

The previous examples suggest that a formula can calculate present value, and indeed it can. Let the present discounted value be PDV, the discount rate be i and the future payment be F. The symbol i is measured as a decimal, but we speak of the discount rate in percentage terms; thus, we would say, "the discount rate is 10 percent" and write, i = 0.1.

Now, the present discounted value *PDV* is the amount for which, if you put it in a bank today at an interest rate *i*, you would get an amount in the future equal to the future payment *F*. For example, if the future date is one year from now, then if you put the amount *PDV* in a bank for one year, you would get *PDV* times $(1 + i)$ at the end of the year. Thus, the *PDV* should be such that

$$(PDV)\,(1+i) = F$$

Now divide both sides by $(1 + i)$; you get

$$PDV = \frac{F}{1+i}$$

which is the formula for the present discounted value in the case of a payment made one year in the future. That is,

$$\text{present discounted value} = \frac{\text{payment in one year}}{1 + \text{discount rate}}$$

For example, if the payment in one year is $100 and the discount rate i = 0.1, then the present discounted value is $90.91 [$100/(1 + 0.1)], just as we reasoned previously.

To obtain the formula for the case for which the payment is made more than one year in the future, we must recognize that the amount in the present can be put in a bank and earn interest at the discount rate for more than one year. For example, if the interest rate is 10 percent, we could get $100 at the end of two years by investing $82.64 today. That is, putting $82.64 in the bank would give $82.64 times (1.1) at the end of one year; keeping all this in the bank for another year would give $82.64 times (1.1) times (1.1), or $82.64 times 1.21, or $100, again rounding off. Thus, in the case of a future payment in two years, we would have

$$PDV = \frac{F}{(1+i)^2}$$

Analogous reasoning implies that the present discounted value of a payment made N years in the future would be

$$PDV = \frac{F}{(1+i)^n}$$

For example, the present discounted value of a $100 payment to be made 20 years in the future is $14.86 if the discount rate is 10 percent. In other words, if you put $14.86 in the bank today at an interest rate of 10 percent, you would have about $100 at the end of 20 years. What is the present discounted value of a $100 payment to be made 100 years in the future? The above formula tells us that the PDV is only $0.00726, less than a penny. All of these examples indicate that the higher the discount rate or the further in the future the payment is to be received, the lower the present discounted value of a future payment.

In many cases, we need to find the present discounted value of a *series* of payments made in several different years. We can do this by combining the previous formulas. The present discounted value of payments F_1 made in one year and F_2 made in two years would be

$$PDV = \frac{F_1}{(1+i)} + \frac{F_2}{(1+i)^2}$$

For example, the present discounted value of $100 paid in one year and $100 paid in two years would be $90.91 plus $82.64, or $173.55. In general, the present discounted value of a series of future payments $F_1, F_2, ..., F_N$ over N years is

$$PDV = \frac{F_1}{(1+i)} + \frac{F_2}{(1+i)^2} + \cdots + \frac{F_N}{(1+i)^N}$$

Key Points

1. A dollar to be paid in the future is worth less than a dollar today.
2. The present discounted value of a future payment is the amount you would have to put in a bank today to get that same payment in the future.
3. The higher the discount rate, the lower the present discounted value of a future payment.

Questions for Review

1. Why is the present discounted value of a future payment of $1 less than $1?
2. What is the relationship between the discount rate and the interest rate?
3. What happens to the present discounted value of a future payment as the payment date stretches into the future?
4. Why is discounting important for decisions involving actions at different dates?

Problems

1. Find the present discounted value of
   a. $100 to be paid at the end of three years.
   b. $1,000 to be paid at the end of one year plus $1,000 to be paid at the end of two years.
   c. $10 to be paid at the end of one year, $10 at the end of two years, and $100 at the end of three years.

2. Suppose you win $1 million in a lottery and your winnings are scheduled to be paid as follows: $300,000 at the end of one year, $300,000 at the end of two years, and $400,000 at the end of three years. If the interest rate is 10 percent, what is the present discounted value of your winnings?

3. You are considering two job offers. You expect to work for the employer for five years. For simplicity, we assume that you will be paid at the end of each year. The two offers are summarized in the following table.

Year	Offer 1 ($)	Offer 2 ($)
1	30,000	40,000
2	33,000	30,000
3	36,000	33,000
4	39,000	36,000
5	42,000	39,000

The primary difference between the two offers is a signing bonus of $10,000 paid under Offer 2. The annual salary paid in years two through five is higher under Offer 1 than under Offer 2. If the interest rate is 5 percent, which is the better offer? If the interest rate is 10 percent, which is better?

Endnotes

1. Alfred Marshall, *Principles of Economics*, 8th ed. (New York: Macmillan, 1920), 415.

Index

yield to maturity
477-479